FORENSIC ANTHROPOLOGY

2000 TO 2010

FORENSIC ANTHROPOLOGY

2000 TO 2010

EDITED BY
SUE BLACK AND EILIDH FERGUSON

CRC Press
Taylor & Francis Group
Boca Raton   London   New York

CRC Press is an imprint of the
Taylor & Francis Group, an **informa** business

Taylor & Francis
6000 Broken Sound Parkway NW, Suite 300
Boca Raton, FL 33487-2742

© 2011 by Taylor and Francis Group, LLC
Taylor & Francis is an Informa business

No claim to original U.S. Government works

Printed in the United States of America on acid-free paper
10 9 8 7 6 5 4 3 2 1

International Standard Book Number: 978-1-4398-4588-2 (Paperback)

Library of Congress Cataloging-in-Publication Data

Forensic anthropology : 2000 to 2010 / editors, Sue Black and Eilidh Ferguson.
    p. cm.
  Includes bibliographical references and index.
  ISBN 978-1-4398-4588-2
  1. Forensic anthropology. I. Black, Sue M. II. Ferguson, Eilidh. III. Title.

GN69.8.F645 2011
614'.17--dc22
                                                       2010034505

Visit the Taylor & Francis Web site at
http://www.taylorandfrancis.com

and the CRC Press Web site at
http://www.crcpress.com

Contents

Foreword

A summit of world leaders meeting at Lyon in 1996, when Bill Clinton was U.S. president, decided to establish an International Commission on Missing Persons (ICMP). The heads of government had agreed that if there was ever to be reconciliation in the former Yugoslavia, it would be necessary to investigate the fate of those who had disappeared during the conflict and to identify the remains of as many as possible of those who lost their lives. Senator Robert Dole, whom Clinton had defeated for the U.S. presidency, took the chair, and after an interval I was appointed a commissioner, having been U.K. secretary of state for defense during the last phase of the wars. The ICMP embraced a task unprecedented in its scale, seeking to identify up to 40,000 bodies using blood samples taken from 100,000 relatives, many of whom were refugees living abroad.

A little later, I became aware of the important work being undertaken by Professor Sue Black at the University of Dundee and was honored to launch her BSc honors course in forensic anthropology in 2003.

The usefulness of identifying victims had by then been underlined in Kosovo, where Sue had served. The ICMP had also offered its services to New York City after September 11, 2001, and to Iraq after the Allied invasion. Identification became an issue in Chile, Argentina, and even Spain, as it dealt with the secrets of its civil war and postwar repression. This interested me because my father was a refugee from that war, being on the losing side. Not that identification always seems to me to be the right course of action: as they exhumed the remains presumed to belong to Federico García Lorca, I yearned for the poet to be allowed to rest in peace. At least we now know where his bones do not lie.

On the Dundee campus, Sue Black was wrestling with a paradoxical and unsatisfactory phenomenon. Television programs about forensic work in criminal cases were producing a flood of applicants for undergraduate courses, but the students' preparation and academic quality were often poor. She was determined to change that by establishing the BSc course on rigorous academic lines, and as a result her department, current students, and former students have earned a reputation for excellence.

Even so, it is an admirable achievement that a cohort of undergraduates can produce a textbook for their peer group: a collection of topic reviews that prove how much they have learned and that passes that knowledge to contemporaries

in their field and to future cohorts. The students are to be congratulated heart-
ily, but they will know well that their work is a tribute to Sue Black and her
colleagues in the Centre for Anatomy and Human Identification.

Advances in our ability to capture DNA from skeletal remains and the
development of forensic anthropology make it possible to identify more of
the victims of homicide, mass-fatality disasters, and genocide. Establishing
an identity helps to define a crime, and that makes it possible for a criminal investigation to be launched. I believe that this scientific progress makes
detection, prosecution, and conviction more likely, and it is essential that we
remain current with the scientific literature. That, I hope, makes warlords
and tyrants ponder, for now the most abominable crimes are not beyond the
reach of justice.

Rt. Hon. Michael Portillo

Foreword

I am so pleased to be able to provide a Foreword to this book. In thinking about what to say, I remembered my first accepted writings in the early 1980s and what a supreme pleasure it gave me to complete a manuscript, to receive correspondence of its acceptance, and then to see proofs of how it would look in print. It was for me an exciting accomplishment, and I imagine it will be so for the student authors who have worked so hard on this book.

This volume is based on selected themes that are fundamental to contemporary forensic anthropology. Each chapter gives an overview of the theme under discussion, identifies present trends in research, and suggests areas in which future research could be developed. Chapters conclude with bibliographies focused on the past decade of publications dealing with advances in chapter themes, as well as key readings prior to 2000. The bibliographies in some ways are the heart of the book, assembled with students in mind to provide them a foundation for a reference library. And, the book will no doubt be helpful to professionals as well.

What better gift to students on the part of their professors than to encourage and support them in developing their first publication, as undergraduates no less, and what better learning experience than to actually complete the project? This opportunity is a sign of trust in their students and their future contributions. It is hoped that this publication will be an inspiration and sign for students around the globe: They also have much to contribute.

William D. Haglund, PhD

Preface

In 2002, when I was in my fourth year of duty as a forensic anthropologist in Kosovo, the Foreign and Commonwealth Office funded some studentships for individuals to gain practical experience in a mass fatality mortuary. Watching, listening, and working with those students made me realize a number of things, and when the University of Dundee offered me the opportunity to develop a degree program in forensic anthropology in 2003, I decided that it would be an undergraduate and not a postgraduate program that would include a full year of gross anatomy dissection. I had realized in Kosovo that although the students' understanding of the osteology side of our subject was admirable, their depth of knowledge in relation to soft tissue anatomy was largely poor, and I felt that anatomically trained forensic anthropologists would provide a skills base for our students that would prove highly beneficial—as it had to me in my training. Even though there may not be many jobs out there for forensic anthropologists, there is a world shortage of gross anatomists, and this not only would offer the best opportunity for future employment for our students but also would serve well to enhance the skills of our future practitioners in forensic anthropology.

In 2003, the Right Honourable Michael Portillo launched the bachelor of science (honours) program in forensic anthropology at the University of Dundee. His understanding of the importance of identification was a driving force behind his commitment to the exhumations and identifications associated with the Spanish Civil war in particular and entrenched his association with the International Commission on Missing Persons (ICMP). He has proved to be a great supporter of the Dundee program.

The undergraduate degree in forensic anthropology was the first of its kind in the United Kingdom, and its aim was not to graduate hundreds of students every year but rather to train a small and selective number of students who would exit with a solid understanding of science, biology, anatomy, and osteology and its application to matters of forensic relevance. We restrict our intake to only 25 students every year, and we have over 300 applications a year to gain entry to the program. While studying, the student must maintain a high pass rate to remain in the program. This results in a highly motivated student group that is academically capable and committed to the subject.

Each year, I have watched as our undergraduate students submit essays and literature reviews that rival the quality seen in many master's programs, and it was felt that so much more could be achieved if the students did not have to cover the same ground every year in searching out the basic literature. The idea for this project was born during a lecture given to our students by the inspirational Bill Haglund, who has been a firm supporter of the project; I am inordinately grateful to him. Persuading a publishing company to take on an undergraduate text written by undergraduates was actually easier than I could have imagined. Becky Masterman at Taylor and Francis is an ambitious, accomplished, and inspirational editor who is not afraid to take a risk on new challenges, so a tight deadline was set to ensure that publication was within the 2010 academic year to fulfill the requirements for the decade-long literature review.

A member of staff was assigned to each chapter to ensure that the quality was suitable for publication and that the full spectrum of the subject, if possible, was addressed. However, the basis for each section was student initiated, and they decided the headings to be addressed and the partnerships for each chapter that would be submitted as a part of their in-course assessment. As a result, there is some variation in the way in which the students (and staff) have chosen to present their part of this review. Some have included all the references in the text, some have produced an additional reading list, and some have chosen to provide a full review list but omit individual references from the text simply because it broke the text up into an almost unreadable, fragmented format. Therefore, we ask that you, the student reader, accept that this text was produced by students to assist your literature search, and it is not intended to be an erudite and academic discourse on forensic anthropology. Of course, there are areas that are not covered, and certainly there are some parts that are better written than others, but with patience, please realize that these chapters represent coursework from an undergraduate program, and the aim is purely to provide a literature review from the decade 2000 to 2010. Its true value lies in the accumulation of references.

I have been fortunate to lead the Centre for Anatomy and Human Identification (CAHID; http://www.lifesci.dundee.ac.uk/CAHId/) for the past seven years, and I am inordinately proud of the achievements of all of our students and none more so than the class of 2010, who have been responsible for this text.

Professor Sue Black, OBE, BSc, PhD, DSc, FRSE, FRAI, HFRCPSG
Director, CAHID

Acknowledgments

I would like to acknowledge the good grace with which each member of the Centre for Anatomy and Human Identification (CAHID) undertook this task at a time in their academic year that was already fraught with pressures. In particular, my thanks go to Eilidh Ferguson, who willingly accepted the role of coeditor, and to Caroline Needham, who designed the cover of this text. Warm thanks are extended to Becky Masterman at Taylor and Francis, who was prepared to take the brave step of publishing a text produced by undergraduate students (a first, we think), and to Jill Jurgensen and Jay Margolis, also at Taylor and Francis, who made the transition as pain free as they possibly could.

Contributors

All participants in this text either worked or studied in the Centre for Anatomy and Human Identification (CAHID) at the University of Dundee.

At the time of writing, the following students were studying for their undergraduate honours bachelor of science degree in forensic anthropology:

Neal Archibald BSc	Iain Armstrong BSc
Joanne Bristow BSc	Sally Carr BSc
Louise Cullen BSc	Kylie Davidson BSc
Catriona Davies BSc	Charlotte Dawson BSc
Susan Edmond BSc	Eilidh Ferguson BSc
Rachel Gilchrist BSc	Natalie Kerr BSc
Nicholas Lockyer BSc	Aymie Maxwell
Stacey Purves BSc	Duncan Ross BSc
Zoe Simms BSc	Sarah Voogt BSc
Kayleigh Wood BSc	Lianne Woodley BSc
Katie Nicoll Baines BSc	

All other participants are members of staff within CAHID:

Sue Black is the professor of anatomy and forensic anthropology and director of the centre. She is a founder and director of the Centre for International Forensic Assistance (CIFA), founder and past president of the British Association for Human Identification, and advisor to the Home Office on issues pertaining to disaster victim identification (DVI). She is a Fellow of the Royal Society of Edinburgh, a Fellow of the Royal Anthropological Institute, and an honorary Fellow of the Royal College of Physicians and Surgeons of Glasgow. She was awarded an Order of the British Empire (OBE) in 2001 for her services to forensic anthropology in Kosovo, the Lucy Mair medal for humanitarian services in anthropology, and a police commendation in 2008 for DVI training.

Jan Bikker is a postdoctoral researcher working on an FP7 research grant partnered with Interpol. He holds a doctoral degree from the University of Sheffield on the subject of disaster victim identification, with the research carried out in the Department of Forensic Pathology and the School of Medicine. He has gained experience in the recovery, examination, and identification of fresh, decomposed, fragmented, burned, and skeletal remains in international disasters, including those in Thailand, Peru, and more recently the 2010 earthquake in Haiti. He has also been working for Her Majesty's Coroner and local police forces in the United Kingdom. Jan is currently a council member for the British Association for Human Identification (BAHID). Research interests include disaster and mass grave victim identification, soft tissue identification of human remains, biological human variation, and taxonomical models.

Craig Cunningham is a lecturer in anatomy and forensic anthropology. He holds a joint honors bachelor of science degree in anatomical and physiological sciences and a doctorate in anatomy and forensic anthropology. He is module leader for the juvenile human osteology course undertaken by all forensic anthropology undergraduates at the University of Dundee and has responsibility for the curation of the unique Scheuer collection of juvenile skeletal remains housed at the center. His research involves investigating the microarchitecture of the developing skeleton through the use of noninvasive imaging techniques.

Roos Eisma is currently a postdoctoral researcher, having achieved a first-class degree in forensic anthropology at the centre. Her work focuses on establishing Thiel soft-fix embalming at CAHID and exploring the use of Thiel-embalmed cadavers in training and research. Due to her previous background in physics and computing, her further research interests include virtual forensic anthropology based on computed tomography (CT).

Eilidh Ferguson was nominated to be coeditor for this text by her student peers. She graduated with a first-class honours bachelor of science degree in forensic anthropology from the Centre for Anatomy and Human Identification at the University of Dundee. Eilidh served as class representative during her period of study at the university, and this is her first venture into publications.

Lucina Hackman is the National U.K. DVI program coordinator for the advanced mortuary training program. She teaches undergraduate and postgraduate students and supervises research projects. She is studying parttime for a doctoral degree under the supervision of Professor Black, and her area of specialty is in the assessment of age in the living for the purposes of assisting investigations in asylum seekers and refugees. She has coauthored a chapter in a recent text on this subject and is coeditor of two texts related to DVI. She holds a master of science degree in biological and forensic anthropology and is a consultant on the Virtual Anthropology Service run by the University of Dundee. She has worked a significant number of forensic cases both within the United Kingdom and overseas and is a registered expert on the National Police Improvements Agency register.

Won-Joon Lee is a graduate of Chonnam National University in the Republic of Korea. Following graduate work in human identification at the University of Dundee, he is now undertaking doctoral research on the accuracy of forensic facial reconstruction and recognition of the human face.

Stenton MacKenzie graduated with a master of science in human identification from the centre. He completed a postgraduate certificate in human anatomy and is currently a Greenhouse-funded doctoral student at the centre studying craniofacial changes in transsexuals.

Xanthé Mallett is a lecturer in forensic anthropology. She holds a first-class bachelor of sciences (honours) degree, a master of philosophy (Cantab), and a doctorate in forensic facial recognition. She has considerable experience as a forensic anthropologist, undertakes casework and research, and teaches both undergraduate and postgraduate students in techniques of human identification. Her research largely relates to human biometrics, looking at quantifiable analysis of both the face and the hands; currently, her main direction is the development of a research stream relating to hand comparison analysis. She has also worked on a major collaborative biometrics project in association with the U.S. Federal Bureau of Investigation (FBI).

Stella McClure is a lecturer in anatomy and lead in undergraduate clinical anatomy with a special interest in medical and dental education.

Caroline Needham is a lecturer in medical art for the master of science programs in medical and forensic art. As well as teaching, she is responsible for much of the course planning and coordination. She completed a two-year master of philosophy in medical art in 2002. Since this time, she has been working as an artist in the fields of medical, forensic, and archaeological sciences. Her previous research included the reconstruction of individuals whose archaeological skeletal remains showed evidence of disease or trauma. These were presented as two-dimensional reconstruction illustrations. Her research interests are currently focused around a parttime doctoral degree in medical visualization, looking at the use of virtual reality technologies and haptic feedback in anatomy teaching.

Patrick Randolph-Quinney is lecturer and course leader for the undergraduate program in forensic anthropology. He holds a bachelor of science degree in archaeological sciences and a doctoral degree in biological anthropology. He originally started his academic life as an archaeologist specializing in the recovery and analysis of human skeletal remains and has directed long-running excavations in southern Africa, investigating human evolution during the Middle Pleistocene. His research interests include the forensic quantification of modern human variation through the use of geometric morphometrics and statistical analysis of shape, the analysis of skeletal trauma using three-dimensional (3D) imaging and experimental biomechanical analyses, and the effects of burning on the human body. He is actively involved in forensic casework and acts as a consultant to U.K. police forces in the areas of forensic anthropology, forensic archaeology, and body recovery.

Christopher Rynn has a background in anatomy and medicoforensic art and a doctoral degree in forensic facial reconstruction, specifically dealing with the prediction of the nose from the skull. Since 2007, he has worked in CAHID on the U.K. DVI police training courses, the master of science forensic and medical art course, and a number of facial reconstruction and forensic image enhancement and comparison cases. He is currently researching the facial imaging component of the FASTid project at Interpol.

Roger Soames is the principal anatomist for the University of Dundee and currently holds the Cox Chair of anatomy. His main interest is in the maintenance and promotion of anatomy as a discipline in terms of teaching, research, and training. During his career, he has been involved in the development of several new programs of study, as well as a large number of anatomy-related individual modules, the most recent new program being the master of science degree in human anatomy at Dundee. His main research interests focus on the musculoskeletal system, although he remains interested in all aspects of clinical and surgical anatomy.

Caroline Wilkinson is a senior lecturer in forensic anthropology. She is an expert in facial anthropology and author of *Forensic Facial Reconstruction*. Her main research focuses on the relationship between the soft and hard tissues of the face, juvenile facial reconstruction, facial recognition, anthropometry, and facial image analysis. Previous research has included the analysis of juvenile facial tissues using ultrasound measurements, facial reconstruction standards, facial reconstruction accuracy studies, skull reassembly, the use of facial reconstruction in Egyptology and archaeology, and juvenile facial reconstruction. She developed and assessed a computerized facial reconstruction system employing "virtual" sculpture, which is now in use within the United Kingdom for forensic identification and internationally for archaeological investigation.

Age Determination in the Juvenile

1

KAYLEIGH WOOD
DR. CRAIG A. CUNNINGHAM

Contents

Introduction

Age determination is a principal element in both anthropological and archaeological investigations (Cattaneo 2009a). It is generally assessed through the analysis of maturational milestones that manifest in the skeleton and dentition. Indicators of skeletal maturity can be used in both clinical and forensic examinations to assess developmental status; from this, chronological age may be inferred (Lewis and Rutty 2003). In a forensic context, the estimated age at death of the deceased constitutes a fundamental component of the biological profile, which is used by anthropologists to narrow the range of potential matches during the process of identification (Scheuer and Black 2007). Indeed, when presented with juvenile remains, the age at death is often the only biological parameter that can be determined with any degree of accuracy (Scheuer and Black 2000). However, age determination is not limited to situations involving individuals who are deceased and can also be utilized to assess age in the living (Cattaneo 2009b). This can be important in certain judicial circumstances, when authorities require age to be established

1

to determine an appropriate course of action (Lewis and Rutty 2003). Such circumstances can be civil or criminal and can include cases involving pedo-pornography; sex with a minor; lack of legitimate identification; and criminal culpability (Lewis and Rutty 2003; Cunha et al. 2009). Age determination can also be important in clinical cases for the diagnosis of pathological versus normal growth and development (Scheuer and Black 2000). This chapter provides a review of the literature that has addressed age determination in the juvenile skeleton for the purposes of the objectives mentioned. This includes a discussion of the increasingly sophisticated investigative methods employed in juvenile age assessment combined with an evaluation of the accuracy and limitations inherent in the utility of these techniques.

Prior to discussion of the recent juvenile age assessment literature, it is appropriate to define the developmental boundaries addressed. The term *juvenile* refers to a minor and, for the purposes of this chapter, encompasses all subadult stages of maturation. In the literature, the juvenile life span is commonly divided into the following developmental phases: prenatal (prior to birth); infancy (birth to 1 year); childhood (1 year to adolescence or puberty); and adolescence (Ritz-Timme et al. 2000; Scheuer and Black 2004). In the United Kingdom, the age of 18 years is the threshold that legally defines adult status; therefore, this chapter only considers the age assessment literature dealing with individuals below this age. Details regarding postado-lescent events are described in Chapter 2.

Trends in the Literature

The common methods available for juvenile age assessment are perfuncto-rily discussed in textbooks on the general subject of forensic anthropology (Scheuer and Black 2007; Lewis 2007; Cattaneo 2009a) and in numerous reviews (Ritz-Timme et al. 2000; Schmeling, Olze, et al. 2004; Schmeling, Reisinger, et al. 2006; Schmeling et al. 2007; Konigsberg et al. 2008; Cunha et al. 2009; Franklin 2010). Such texts, particularly the concise contributions by Saunders (2000), Scheuer and Black (2007), Cattaneo (2009a; 2009b), Cunha et al. (2009), and Franklin (2010), provide general overviews of the area and are useful as summaries for both students and practicing anthropologists. However, the remaining majority are repetitive and simply reiterate information previously available. For example, certain articles combine the discussion of techniques available for adult and juvenile material without providing an adequate coverage of the range of techniques specific to juveniles (Ritz-Timme et al. 2000; Schmeling, Reisinger, et al. 2006; Schmeling et al. 2007). Fortunately, core texts have been produced that go some way to alleviate this inadequacy in the anthropological literature (Scheuer and Black 2000, 2004; Baker et al. 2005; Schaefer et al. 2009).

The majority of work that has been performed in relation to the chronology of skeletal development is outwith the present text's 10-year scope. Therefore, for a comprehensive overview of the work before 2000, readers are directed to the seminal text by Scheuer and Black (2000), which provides a detailed account of skeletal development and includes an extensive compilation of the juvenile ageing literature encompassing work carried out over the 300 years preceding its publication.

In recent years, as a result of escalating trends in global mobility, immigration, and asylum, it has become increasingly pertinent to assess whether individuals have reached the threshold age that signifies legal adulthood (Schmeling et al. 2007). This can be important because some countries do not have central systems documenting dates of birth or individuals may attempt to falsify their age to receive beneficial treatment in criminal or civil cases. Consequently, radiological assessment directed toward the adolescent and young adult age range has become a prominent area of investigation (Schulze et al. 2006; Meijerman et al. 2007; Ríos et al. 2008; Schmidt, Baumann, et al. 2008; Baumann et al. 2009; Cardoso and Severino 2009; Ríos and Cardoso 2009). The majority of the literature in relation to this has been produced by the Arbeitsgruppe Forensische Altersdiagnostik (AGFAD), a multidisciplinary international research group founded in Germany in 2000 (Schmeling, Olze, et al. 2004; Schmeling, Schulz, et al. 2004; Schmeling et al. 2005, 2007; Schmeling, Baumann, et al. 2006; Schmeling, Reisinger, et al. 2006; Schulz et al. 2005; Muhler et al. 2006; Meijerman et al. 2007; Schmidt et al. 2007; Schmidt, Baumann, et al. 2008; Schmidt, Koch, et al. 2008; Schmidt, Nitz, et al. 2008; Baumann et al. 2009). The goal of AGFAD is to establish standard practices for applying forensic ageing techniques (Schmeling et al. 2007); however, this may be difficult to achieve considering that legal age thresholds vary between countries. Other prominent researchers working in the area of juvenile age assessment are involved in improving the current methods of age assessment by applying discriminant statistical treatments (Cameriere et al. 2006; Cameriere and Ferrante et al. 2008) or by investigating skeletal timings in specific populations (Schaefer and Black 2005, 2007; Rissech et al. 2008; Schaefer 2008; Cardoso 2008a, 2008b; Cardoso and Severino 2009; Coqueugniot and Weaver 2007).

Skeletal Maturation

Skeletal maturation is a relatively reliable indicator of growth and development that has resulted in well-documented patterns of skeletal development in relation to chronological age. Age assessment from the skeleton relies on specific changes that occur as an individual matures and progresses through a distinctive series of maturational milestones. These changes are relatively stable and predictable and involve the appearance of primary and secondary ossification centers, morphological changes in size and shape of these centers, and finally fusion of these centers, resulting in the attainment of adult form (Scheuer and Black 2000; 2004; Schaefer et al. 2009).

Skeletal Age Assessment in Fetal and Neonatal Specimens

Age evaluation of the fetus and neonate places heavy emphasis on the number of primary ossification centers present and their location (Degani 2001). The majority of primary centers of ossification appear during the embryonic and fetal periods (Scheuer and Black 2000); however, there are inherent difficulties associated with assessing age in the prenatal period because the timing of conception can be difficult to determine. Therefore, the date of the last menstrual period (LMP) is usually selected as the preferred indicator to predict the date of birth and therefore the potential *in utero* age of the fetus (Taipale and Hiilesmaa 2001). Knowledge of the sequence of appearance of ossification centers permits the investigator to assign a "most likely" age based on those centers present compared to those not yet developed (Scheuer and Black 2000, 2004; Schaefer et al. 2009).

A number of methods that can be utilized to determine the appearance of ossification centers in fetal remains and the accuracies and subsequent reported timings of appearance vary depending on the technique applied (Scheuer and Black 2000). The most precise method is reported to be histological sectioning, which although little reported in the modern literature, has provided fundamental knowledge regarding the appearance times of ossification centers. A contemporary study applying histomorphomentry evaluated the proximal femoral metaphysis and considered its implications on providing information regarding fetal bone development (Salle et al. 2002). Alizarin staining is a further technique that was heavily used in the seminal juvenile ageing literature and involved destroying the soft tissues with potassium hydroxide and then applying the stain to visualize the skeletal material (Scheuer and Black 2000). Use of this technique is not reported in the recent literature, most likely due to advances in nondestructive imaging modalities, which allow for a comprehensive assessment of skeletal development without the requirement to remove the soft tissues. Radiographic techniques have proved to be particularly useful for the purposes of ageing the juvenile skeleton and continue to be used along with other more modern nondestructive imaging techniques (Sherwood et al. 2000; Taipale and Hiilesmaa 2001; Salpou et al. 2008). The suite of imaging modalities available for the assessment of ossification status includes radiography, computed tomography (CT), magnetic resonance imaging, and ultrasonography (Bilgili et al. 2003; Laor and Jaramillo 2009). Radiographic imaging has often been used for age assessment in fetal and neonatal individuals; however, this modality has significant limitations as the appearance of ossification centers tends to precede radiographic visualization. This is due to the degree of mineralization of a particular bone being insufficient for appropriate visualization during the initial stages of ossification (Scheuer and Black 2000). For age estimation in the living, ultrasound is now the preferred mode of imaging to capture the developmental stage of individual bones as it does not risk exposing the fetus to harmful radiation (Taipale and Hiilesmaa 2001; Salpou et al. 2008).

Traditionally, skeletal age estimation has been concerned with dry bone analyses of human remains, and it would be remiss to review juvenile age assessment without including the significant early contributions to the area by Stevenson (1924), Todd (1937), and Stewart (1934). However, the forensic utility of juvenile age estimation from dry bone is variable, depending on the age of the individual and the particular skeletal element examined (Scheuer and Black 2007). Because ossification centers initially develop as small, nonspecific nodules, these are unlikely to be recovered or be of particular significance until they have reached a distinguishable morphology (Lewis and Rutty 2003).

The most significant study of fetal dry bone material was performed by Fazekas and Kosa (1978), who studied 136 fetuses and correlated gestational age to ossification stage using metric measurements. There are problematic issues with the sample utilized in this study because a number of the specimens were naturally aborted and may therefore have had developmental defects (Scheuer and Black 2000). Specimens were also of undocumented gestational age, which was estimated based on crown-rump length. Despite these issues, the data collected regarding osseous development are still of significant value in modern forensic practice (Scheuer and Black 2000). Recent methods applying CT and plain plate radiography have been initiated in an attempt to validate the seminal metric data produced by Fazekas and Kosa (Nemzek et al. 2000; Adaline et al. 2001; Piercecchi-Marti et al. 2002). Additional, dry bone studies have also assessed the dimensions of certain skeletal elements, such as the atlas and axis for the determination of age with encouraging results (Castellana and Kosa 2001).

Skeletal Age Estimation of Infants, Children, and Adolescents

Prior to discussion of the age assessment literature for infants, children, and adolescents, it must be acknowledged that different skeletal maturation rates are exhibited between the sexes, with females having an accelerated maturation rate over males throughout the entire juvenile period (Molinari et al. 2004).

A major focus of recent research has been directed toward the assessment of age from radiographic atlases. This work has built on the longitudinal radiographic studies of the mid-20th century, which documented growth in living individuals by assessing the developmental status of the bones in the hand and wrist (Greulich and Pyle 1959; Tanner et al. 1962, 1975). These can be broadly divided into two categories: those that require direct visual matching of an x-ray to a representative standard (Greulich and Pyle 1959) and those that involve the use of a cumulative scoring system (Tanner et al. 2001). Direct comparison methods are relatively straightforward to use and rely on skeletal atlases illustrating the most representative radiograph for a particular age. Radiographic scoring methods involve assigning each skeletal element a numeric score based on the assessment of size and morphology. The sum of these is then used to calculate a total maturity score, which further corresponds to a particular age. Radiological techniques have inherent methodological issues, such as noted by Scheuer and Black (2000) that atlases inherently include the order of fusion, which can be variable, and an examiner may incorrectly categorize an age as a result of this. Scoring methods eliminate this problem but are more onerous to use (Scheuer and Black 2000) and have limitations due to the degree of subjectivity involved in assigning a categorical value to the continuous process of growth. The most recent revision to the Tanner and Whitehouse method, termed "TW3," was published by Tanner et al. in 2001. This version used more recent information from European children to allow secular changes that occurred in the time that had passed since the first editions to be addressed. It is argued that TW3 is more reliable than the previous Tanner Whitehouse versions for use in forensic identification as it is based on a more contemporary population (Bertaina et al. 2007).

The development of these radiographic atlases was originally intended for the clinical purpose of establishing normal skeletal development in relation to age for detecting growth disturbances. However, they have also proved to be invaluable within the forensic field (Cattaneo 2009b). Recent research has shown that the Greulich and Pyle atlas approach is poor at recognizing racial differences in growth patterns (Zhang et al. 2009), thus suggesting that alternative data should be developed for different populations. Indeed, this has been acknowledged, and in the past decade numerous studies have produced population-specific data (Koc et al. 2001; Mora et al. 2001; Van Rijn et al. 2001; Krailassiri et al. 2002; Lewis et al. 2002; Garamendi et al. 2005; Lynnerup et al. 2008). An ultrasonographic version of the Greulich and Pyle atlas has also been produced that has been shown to be highly correlated and a valid alternative to plain radiography for bone age estimation (Bilgili et al. 2003).

Population-specific studies have also been performed for the Tanner Whitehouse methods (Dvorak et al. 2007; Ortega et al. 2006; Nig et al. 2007; Ashizawa et al. 2005; Freitas et al. 2004; Ranjitkar et al. 2006). In addition, further atlases of hand-wrist skeletal development have been developed (Gilsanz and Ratib 2005; Cameriere et al. 2006); however, the suitability of some of these methods for forensic age estimation has been suggested to be limited

(Schmidt et al. 2009). There is continued research aimed at developing a more accurate and simplistic system that also reflects the growth and maturation parameters as evidenced on a modern population (Schmidt, Baumann, et al. 2008; Zhang et al. 2009). This has involved the attempted automation of the Tanner Whitehouse system (Bocchi et al. 2003; Aja-Fernandez et al. 2004).

Other skeletal areas have also been investigated recently in terms of their utility for age assessment from a radiographic scoring system or atlas; these include the foot (Whitaker et al. 2002) and knee (O'Connor et al. 2008). In addition, further studies have also attempted to compare methods of age assessment using different areas of the skeleton (Aicardi et al. 2000). Radiographic assessment has also been applied to investigate the correlation between chronological age and cervical vertebral maturation (CVM) by the CVM method, which assesses change in the shape of the cervical vertebral bodies with increasing age (Baccetti et al. 2005, 2006). Many of these studies have correlated CVM with hand-wrist skeletal maturity indicators. Such studies have demonstrated that CVM is a valid indicator of skeletal growth during the circumpubertal period and has a high correlation with hand-wrist maturity (Chang et al. 2001; Mito et al. 2002; Grave and Townsend 2003; Flores-Mir et al. 2006; Gandini et al. 2006; Kamal and Goyal 2006; Alkhal et al. 2008; Lai et al. 2008; Soegiharto et al. 2008; Stiehl et al. 2009; Wong et al. 2009).

Much work has also concentrated on the assessment of epiphyseal fusion times on dry bone populations. It has been acknowledged that different epiphyses have different fusion and formation rates, with those that develop and fuse within a short time frame being of higher forensic utility (Scheuer and Black 2007). Caution has been advised when ageing using epiphyseal fusion times as epiphyses may not survive inhumation, and taphonomic damage can mean that stages of epiphyseal fusion may not be distinguishable (Lewis and Rutty 2003). Patterns of epiphyseal fusion have been extensively studied for various populations, including a Bosnian male population (Schaefer and Black 2005, 2007; Schaefer 2007, 2008); Portuguese populations (Coqueugniot and Weaver 2007; Cardoso 2008a, 2008b; Cardoso and Severino 2009; Rios and Cardoso 2009); and European American, African American, and Mexican American populations (Crowder and Austin 2005).

Further studies have examined the closure times of the sutures, fontanelles, and other growth areas within the skull to determine their use in age estimation. Such studies are beginning to produce data that contradicts previous knowledge in the ageing literature. Examples include the finding that normal or physiologic closure of the metopic suture occurs much earlier than had been described previously (Vu et al. 2001). A further study has examined the closure times of the foramen of Huschke, concluding that the previously reported chronology of closure times in the literature are erroneous (Humphrey and Scheuer 2002). In addition, the state of fusion of the basilar synchondrosis as an indicator of age has demonstrated that the stage of fusion is not a good indicator of age in males, while in females the feature could be useful when estimating age of unknown human remains (Kahana et al. 2003).

A further developing area within the arena of juvenile age assessment involves the application of morphometrics and procrustes-based geometric morphometrics. Morphometric studies examining the growth of ilium, ischium, and pubis using simple metric measurements have demonstrated age-related patterns that can be applied to subadult age determination (Rissech et al. 2003; Rissech and Malgosa 2005, 2007). Additionally, morphometrics have been used to document the development of the femur and scapula from the neonatal period through to skeletal maturity, which proves useful in the prediction of age at death (Rissech et al. 2008; Rissech and Black 2007). Furthermore, diaphyseal lengths from long-bone measurements have been reviewed for the purposes of age assessment and build on the large pre-2000 literature base of long-bone metrics (Smith and Buschang 2004, 2005).

Further sophisticated, procrustes-based geometric morphometric techniques are beginning to enable the quantification of size and shape variation within juvenile skeletal remains and have been useful for age estimation (Braga and Treil 2007; Franklin and Cardini 2007; Franklin et al. 2008). These studies have produced age-related data for three-dimensional cranial size changes (Braga and Treil 2007), mandibular morphology (Franklin and Cardini 2007; Franklin et al. 2007, 2008), and cervical vertebrae shape (Chatzigianni and Halazonetis 2009). As data produced using these modern methods are considered to be less subjective than those based on visual scoring systems, related studies investigating other areas of the developing skeleton are becoming increasingly popular for application to forensic anthropology (Franklin 2010).

Common Issues in Juvenile Skeletal Age Estimation

A major problem associated with both dry bone and radiographic methods of estimating juvenile age is the reference material utilized for comparative purposes (Usher 2002). There are only a limited number of collections of juvenile remains, and some of these are of undocumented age; many are of specific, noncontemporary populations (Usher 2002; Lewis and Rutty 2003). Only a limited number of population-specific studies have been performed (Schaefer 2008). Similarly, standard radiographic atlases have been created using data retrieved from growth studies on subjects from the middle of the 20th century (Greulich and Pyle 1959; Tanner et al. 1975). The applicability of such data to modern populations is arguable as secular changes in nutrition and health status can influence growth and development (Scheuer and Black 2007). Standard atlases rely on data gathered from predominantly white, middle-class individuals from a specific population, so again these will not be directly comparable with other populations. Radiographic and dry bone methods are also not directly comparable, with radiography of living individuals giving different timings for both appearance and fusion of centers than those reported on dry bone. As a result, there may be discrepancies between these times and the two modalities (Coqueugniot and Weaver 2007; Schaefer 2008). In addition, many of the radiographic and prenatal studies are nonreproducible in the modern era due to ethical considerations.

The difficulties with some modern approaches to ageing juvenile individuals can be demonstrated through the critical evaluation of such a study. Schmeling et al. (2003) described the age assessment of 247 immigrants who lacked valid identification to determine whether the individuals required legal treatment as an adult or as a minor. On the basis that 41 cases allowed verification to within ±12 months, the authors concluded that age estimation was sufficiently reliable for legal purposes. However, when dealing with a narrow legal time frame, this error margin is not sufficiently narrow to distinguish accurately between minors and adult individuals. This article has been criticized in other respects as it not only lacks detail other than a brief overview of the procedures utilized, but also, importantly, it was impossible to evaluate the accuracy of results for the majority of cases (Clarot et al. 2004). Therefore, the reliability of estimations performed can be contested. The authors acknowledged that, for many migrant subjects, there is a lack of population-specific standards available for comparative purposes but dismissed ethnicity as a factor that could lead to over- or underestimations of age (Schmeling et al. 2003; Schmeling, Olze, et al. 2004). Schmeling and colleagues (2003) recognized that differences in socioeconomic circumstances can influence the rates of skeletal maturation but justified that, because the individuals originated from less-developed populations, the estimated ages would be underestimated and therefore not disadvantageous. The fallacy in such an approach is that there are legal instances, such as criminal cases involving pedopornography or sex with a minor, in which underestimations of age could have potentially devastating effects.

Skeletal versus Dental Age Assessment

The relationship between skeletal and dental age assessment has been well recognized; in general, it is accepted that although the skeleton is more likely to display retardation as a result of disadvantageous circumstances, the dentition seems to be better protected and is less affected. This has resulted in greater emphasis being placed on the reliability of dental ageing compared to skeletal ageing, especially when the ethnographic profile of the individual is unknown. Age evaluation in the living has unquestionably dominated the ageing literature of the last decade, and the proposed method for an age assessment utilizes a combination of both dental and skeletal age. It has been accepted that if the socioeconomic gradient is sufficiently unbalanced, then dental development can also be impaired. This topic is discussed at some length and has been summarized in a recent text (Black et al. 2010; Cameriere and Ferrante 2008; Cardoso 2007; Flores-Mir et al. 2005; Franklin 2010; Kanbur et al. 2006; Kimmerle, Jantx, et al. 2008; Kimmerle, Prince, and Berg 2008; Krailassiri et al. 2002; Matrille et al. 2007; Sahin Saglam and Gazilerli 2002; Sciulli 2007; Uysal et al. 2004).

The assessment of age in the living has been dominated by the aforementioned AGFAD research group (see all references related to Baumann, Schmeling, Schmidt, Schulz, and Olze), but there are an increasing number of studies that examine this specific area of legal age evaluation (Cameriere and Brcic et al. 2008; Cattaneo et al. 2009; Cunha et al. 2009; Nuzzolese and Di Vella 2008; Solheim and Vonen 2006; Stathopulu et al. 2003).

This subject is also discussed in some length in Chapter 2 as the important legal boundary between childhood and adulthood is 18 years of age, and this is a time of little demarcation in both skeletal and dental age.

Dental Age Assessment in the Juvenile

Age estimation from the juvenile dentition is based on a number of premises: (a) that all the teeth will erupt and grow, (b) that the teeth will erupt and grow in a prescribed sequence, and (c) that sequence can be correlated with the chronological age of the individual. Age techniques need not rely on imaging technology, for example, when counting the number of teeth present in the mouth. However, there is little doubt that the utilization of radiographic imaging (flat plate and CT) is particularly important in assessing the calcification of the tooth, its eruption process, and its maturation. That there are so many stages in the development of a tooth and that there are up to 20 deciduous and 32 adult teeth in the lifetime of the individual lends itself particularly well to rigorous statistical evaluation with regard to age estimation. With the additional benefit that dental growth seems to be protected from insults compared to skeletal development, there is no doubt that this is a viable and powerful tool for age estimation.

Much of the earlier work is well established, and a considerable proportion of the literature over the last 10 years has concentrated on two particular aspects: testing the reliability of the core techniques compared to other approaches and testing them on different ethnic populations. The consensus seems to be that the core techniques perform well on different populations, indicating their robusticity, but that the small variations may be sufficient to warrant ensuring that a wide age range is offered when age assessment is undertaken on individuals of unknown ethnic origin. The literature on this subject is extensive, so we have chosen to list it in a bibliography rather than intersperse the references in the text.

Identification of age in the early neonatal period has important implications for analysis of the survival period of the child after birth. The identification of a neonatal line in over 90% of all primary teeth and the first permanent molars has proved to be of significant value in assessing the age and time of postbirth survival of the baby. Recent work has concentrated on the morphological structure of the line and the relationship between time and the periodicity of dental microstructure deposition. Although a significant amount of research has been undertaken in the clinical environment, the importance of this topic to human evolution and primate comparative anatomy has also been examined in the current decade.

The Third Molars

Calcification, eruption, and growth of the third molars is one area of dental development that crosses the boundary between juvenile and adult ageing; as a result, it is considered only briefly in this chapter, and further discussion can be found in Chapter 2. A considerable amount of attention has been paid to the eruption and maturation of these molars in the past decade and again specifically to address the issue of age evaluation in the living. Within the dentition, the third molar is the only tooth that has not completed growth by the age of 18 years (an important legal milestone in most countries). There have been many warnings issued in relation to the unreliability or indeed unpredictability of the maturation of this tooth, but it remains one of the mainstays of age estimation in the living because it is one of the few areas readily available for inspection and analysis. Again, for ease in reading, a bibliographic list containing some of the references associated with this topic is included, but Chapter 2 contains further information.

Summary

The majority of research in relation to skeletal maturation was performed in the early and middle portions of the 20th century (Stevenson 1924; Stewart 1934; Todd 1937; Greulich and Pyle 1959; Tanner et al. 1975; Fazekas and Kosa 1978). However, the last decade has seen the production of core texts, including seminal work by Scheuer and Black (2000, 2004) and Schaefer et al. (2009), which provide a useful reference summary of skeletal development and the morphological determination of age. This has been supplemented by research aimed at establishing the growth and development of specific skeletal elements across a series of maturational milestones. It is also clear that a trend of research aimed toward distinguishing the skeletal maturity of legally relevant ages has begun to dominate the juvenile age assessment literature. Furthermore, age determination from the dentition in the past decade has concentrated heavily on evaluation from the living and testing of existing approaches on different populations. It is likely that the research in the area of juvenile age determination will expand markedly over the next decade as researchers strive to apply ever-advancing technologies to gain a better understanding of skeletal and dental development in different populations and relate this to the accurate determination of age in both the deceased and the living.

References

Adaline, P., Piercecchi-Marti, M. D., Bourliere-Najean, B., Panuel, M., Fredouille, C., Dutour, O., and Leonetti, G. (2001). Postmortem assessment of fetal diaphyseal femoral length: validation of a radiographic methodology. *Journal of Forensic Sciences*. 46: 215–219.

Aicardi, G., Vignolo, M., Milani, S., Naselli, A., Magliano, P., and Garzia, P. (2000). Assessment of skeletal maturity of the hand-wrist and knee: A comparison among methods. *American Journal of Human Biology*. 12(5): 610–615.

Aja-Fernandez, S., De Luis-Garcia, R., Martin-Fernandez, M. A., and Alberola-Lopez, C. (2004). A computational TW3 classifier for skeletal maturity assessment. A Computing with Words approach. *Journal of Biomedical Informatics*. 37(2): 99–107.

Alkhal, H. A., Wong, R. W., and Rabie, A. B. (2008). Correlation between chronological age, cervical vertebral maturation and Fishman's skeletal maturity indicators in southern Chinese. *Angle Orthodontist*. 78(4): 591–596.

Ashizawa, K., Kumakura, C., Zhou, X., Jin, F., and Cao, J. (2005). RUS skeletal maturity of children in Beijing. *Annals of Human Biology*. 32(3): 316–325.

Baccetti, T., Franchi, L., and McNamara, J. (2005). The cervical vertebral maturation (CMV) method for the assessment of optimal treatment timing in dentofacial orthopedica. *Seminars in Orthodontics*. 11(3): 119–129.

Baccetti, T., Franchi, L., De Toffol, L., Ghiozzi, B., and Cozza, P. (2006). The diagnostic performance of chronologic age in the assessment of skeletal maturity. *Progress in Orthodontics*. 7(2): 176–188.

Baker, B. J., Dupras, T. L., and Tocheri, M. W. (2005). *Osteology of infants and children*. College Station, TX: TAMU Press.

Baumann, U., Schulz, R., Reisinger, W., Heinecke, A., Schmeling, A., and Schmidt, S. (2009). Reference study on the time frame for ossification of the distal radius and ulnar epiphyses on the hand radiograph. *Forensic Science International*. 191: 15–18.

Bertaina, C., Staslowska, B., Benso, A., and Vannelli. (2007). Is TW3 height prediction more accurate than TW2? *Hormone Research*. 67: 220–223.

Bilgili, Y., Hizel, S., Kara, S. A., Sanli, C., Erdal, H. H., and Altinok, D. (2003). Accuracy of skeletal age assessment on children from birth to 6 years of age with the ultrasonographic version of the Greulich-Pyle Atlas. *Journal of Ultrasound Medicine.* 22: 683–690.

Black, S., Aggrawal, A., and Payne-James, J. (2010). *Age estimation in the living.* Wiley, London.

Bocchi, L., Ferrara, F., Nicoletti, I., and Valli, G. (2003). An artificial neural network architecture for skeletal age assessment. *International Conference on Image Processing.* 1: 1077–1080.

Braga, J., and Treil, J. (2007). Estimation of pediatric skeletal age using geometric morphometrics and three-dimensional cranial size changes. *International Journal of Legal Medicine.* 121: 439–443.

Cameriere, R., and Ferrante, L. (2008). Age estimation in children by measurement of carpals and epiphyses of radius and ulna and open apices in teeth: A pilot study. *Forensic Science International.* 174: 59–62.

Cameriere, R., Brkic, H., Ermenc, B., Ferrante, L., Ovsenik, M., and Cingolani, M. (2008). The measurement of open apices of teeth to test chronological age of over 14-year olds in living subjects. *Forensic Science International.* 174: 217–221.

Cameriere, R., Ferrante, L., Ermenc, B., Mirtella, D., and Strus, K. (2008). Age estimation using carpals: study of a Slovenian sample to test Cameriere's method. *Forensic Science International.* 174: 178–181.

Cameriere, R., Ferrante, L., Mirtella, D., and Cingolani, M. (2006). Carpals and epiphyses of radius and ulna as age indicators. *International Journal of Legal Medicine.* 120: 143–146.

Cardoso, H. F. V. (2007). Environmental effects on skeletal versus dental development: Using a documented sub adult skeletal sample to test a basic assumption in human osteological research. *American Journal of Physical Anthropology.* 132: 223–233.

Cardoso, H. F. V. (2008a). Age estimation in adolescent and young adult male and female skeletons II: Epiphyseal union at the upper limb and scapular girdle in a modern Portuguese skeletal sample. *American Journal of Physical Anthropology.* 137: 97–105.

Cardoso, H. F. V. (2008b). Epiphyseal union at the innominate and lower limb in a modern Portuguese skeletal sample, and age estimation in adolescent and young adult male and female skeletons. *American Journal of Physical Anthropology.* 135: 161–170.

Cardoso, H. F. V., and Severino, R. S. S. (2009). The chronology of epiphyseal union in the hand and foot from dry bone observations. *International Journal of Osteoarchaeology.* doi: 10.1002/oa.

Castellana, C., and Kosa, F. (2001). Estimation of fetal age from dimensions of atlas and axis ossification centers. *Forensic Science International.* 117: 31–43.

Cattaneo, C. (2009a). Anthropology: Age determination of remains. In *Wiley encyclopedia of forensic science.* Jamieson, A., and Moenssens, A. (Eds.). New York: Wiley.

Cattaneo, C. (2009b). Anthropology: Aging the living. In *Wiley encyclopedia of forensic science.* Jamieson, A., and Moenssens, A. (Eds.). New York: Wiley.

Cattaneo, C., Ritz-Timme, S., Gabriel, P., Gibelli, D., Giudici, E., Poppa, P., Nohrden, D., Assmann, S., Schmitt, R., and Grandi, M. (2009). The difficult issue of age assessment on pedo-pornographic material. *Forensic Science International.* 183: e21–e24.

Chang, H. P., Liao, C. H., Yang, Y. H., Chang, H. F., and Chen, K. C. (2001). Correlation of cervical vertebra maturation with hand-wrist maturation in children. *Kaohsiung Journal of Medical Science.* 17: 29–35.

Chatzigianni, A., and Halazonetis, D. J. (2009). Geometric morphometric evaluation of cervical vertebrae shape and its relationship to skeletal maturation. *American Journal of Orthodontics and Dentofacial Orthopedics.* 136(4): 481.e1–481.e9.

Clarot, F., Le Dosseur, P., Vaz, E., and Proust, B. (2004). Skeletal maturation and ethnicity. *Legal Medicine.* 6: 141–142.

Coqueugniot, H., and Weaver, T. D. (2007). Infracranial maturation in the skeletal collection from Coimbra, Portugal: New aging standards for epiphyseal union. *American Journal of Physical Anthropology.* 134: 424–437.

Crowder, C., and Austin, D. (2005). Age ranges of epiphyseal fusion in the distal tibia and fibula of contemporary males and females. *Journal of Forensic Sciences.* 50(5): 1001–1007.

Cunha, E., Baccino, E., Martrille, L., Ramsthaler, F., Prieto, J., Schuliar, Y., Lynnerup, N., and Cattaneo, C. (2009). The problem of aging human remains and living individuals: A review. *Forensic Science International.* 193: 1–13.

Degani, S. (2001). Fetal biometry: Clinical, pathological and technical considerations. *Obstetrics and Gynecological Survey.* 56: 159–167.

Dvorak, J., George, J., Junge, A., and Hodler, J. (2007). Age determination by magnetic resonance imaging of the wrist in adolescent male football players, *British Journal of Sports Medicine.* 41(1): 45–52.

Fazekas, I. G., and Kosa, F. (1978). *Forensic fetal osteology.* Budapest, Hungary: Akademiai Kiado.

Flores-Mir, C., Burgess, C. A., Champney, M., Jensen, R. J., Pitcher, M. R., and Major, P. W. (2006). Correlation of skeletal maturation stages determined by cervical vertebrae and hand-wrist evaluations. *Angle Orthodontist.* 76: 1–5.

Flores-Mir, C., Mauricio, F. R., Orellana, M. F., and Major, P. W. (2005). Association between growth stunting with dental development and skeletal maturation stage. *Angle Orthodontist.* 75: 935–940.

Franklin, D. (2010). Forensic age estimation in human skeletal remains: Current concepts and future directions. *Legal Medicine.* 12: 1–7.

Franklin, D., and Cardini, A. (2007). Mandibular morphology as an indicator of human subadult age: interlandmark approaches. *Journal of Forensic Science.* 52: 1015–1019.

Franklin, D., Cardini, A., O'Higgins, P., Oxnard, C. E., and Dadour, I. (2007). Sexual dimorphism in the subadult mandible: quantification using geometric morphometrics. *Journal of Forensic Science.* 52: 6–10.

Franklin, D., Cardini, A., O'Higgins, P., Oxnard, C. E., and Dadour, I. (2008). Mandibular morphology as an indicator of human subadult age: Geometric morphometric approaches. *Forensic Science Medicine and Pathology.* 4: 91–99.

Freitas, D., Maia, J., Beunen, G., Lefevre, J., Claessens, A., Marques, A., Rodrigues, A., Silva, C., Crespo, M., Thomis, M., Sousa, A., and Malina, R. (2004). Skeletal maturity and socioeconomic status in Portuguese children and youths: The Madeira growth study. *Annals of Human Biology*. 31(4): 408–420.

Gandini, P., Mancini, M., and Andreani, F. (2006). A comparison of hand-wrist bone and cervical vertebral analyses in measuring skeletal maturation. *Angle Orthodontist*. 76(6): 984–989.

Garamendi, P. M., Landa, M. I., Ballesteros, J., and Solano MA. (2005). Reliability of the methods applied to assess age minority in living subjects around 18 years old. A survey on a Moroccan origin population. *Forensic Science International*. 154(1): 3–12.

Gilsanz, V., and Ratib, O. (2005). *Hand bone age: A digital atlas of skeletal maturity*. Berlin: Springer-Verlag.

Grave, K., and Townsend, G. (2003). Hand-wrist and cervical vertebral maturation indicators: How can these events be used to time Class II treatments? *Australian Orthodontic Journal*. 19(2): 33–45.

Greulich, W. W., and Pyle, S. I. (1959). *Radiographic atlas of skeletal development of the hand and wrist*. Stanford, CA: Stanford University Press.

Humphrey, L. T., and Scheuer, L. (2002). Age of closure of the foramen of Huschke: An osteological study. *International Journal of Osteoarchaeology*. 16: 47–60.

Kahana, T., Birkby, W. H., Goldin, L., and Hiss, J. (2003). Estimation of age in adolescents—The basilar synchondrosis. *Journal of Forensic Sciences*. 48(3): 504–508.

Kamal, M., and Goyal, S. (2006). Comparative evaluation of hand wrist radiographs with cervical vertebrae for skeletal maturation in 10–12 year old children. *Journal of the Indian Society of Pedodontics and Preventive Dentistry*. 24(3): 127–135.

Kanbur, N. O., Kanli, A., Derman, O., Eifan, A., and Atac, A. (2006). The relationships between dental age, chronological age and bone age in Turkish adolescents with constitutional delay of growth. *Journal of Pediatric Endocrinology and Metabolism* 19: 979–985.

Kimmerle, E. H., Jantx, R. L., Konigsber, L. W., and Baraybar, J. P. (2008). Skeletal age estimation and identification in American and East European populations. *Journal of Forensic Sciences* 53: 524–532.

Kimmerle, E. H., Prince, D. A., and Berg, G. E. (2008). Inter-observer variation in methodologies involving the pubic symphysis, sternal ribs and teeth. *Journal of Forensic Sciences* 53: 594–600.

Koc, A., Karaoglanoglu, M., Erdogan, M., Kosecik, M., and Cesur, Y. (2001). Assessment of bone ages: Is the Greulich-Pyle method sufficient for Turkish boys? *Pediatrics International*. 43(6): 662–665.

Konigsberg, L. W., Herrmann, N. P., Wescott, D. J., and Kimmerle, E. H. (2008). Estimation and evidence in forensic anthropology: Age-at-death. *Journal of Forensic Sciences*. 53: 541–557.

Krailassiri, S., Anuwongnukroh, N., and Dechkunakorn, S. (2002). Relationships between dental calcification stages and skeletal maturity indicators in Thai individuals. *Angle Orthodontist*. 72(2): 155–166.

Lai, E. H. H., Liu, J. P., Chang, J. Z. C., Tsai, S. J., Yao, C. C. J., Chen, M. H., Chen, Y. J., and Lin, C. P. (2008). Radiographic assessment of skeletal maturation stages for orthodontic patients: Hand-wrist bones or cervical vertebrae? *Journal of the Formosan Medical Association.* 107(4): 316–325.

Laor, T., and Jaramillo, D. (2009). MR imaging insights into skeletal maturation: What is normal? *Radiology.* 250: 29–38.

Lewis, C. P., Lavy, C. B., and Harrison, W. J. (2002). Delay in skeletal maturity in Malawian children. *Journal of Bone and Joint Surgery.* 84(5): 732–734.

Lewis, M. E. (2007). *The bioarchaeology of children: Perspectives from biological and forensic anthropology.* Cambridge, UK: Cambridge University Press.

Lewis, M. E., and Rutty, G. N. (2003). The endangered child: The personal identification of children in forensic anthropology. *Science and Justice.* 43: 201–209.

Lynnerup, N., Belard, E., Buch-Olsen, K., Sejrsen, B., and Damgaard-Pedersen, K. (2008). Intra and interobserver error of the Greulich-Pyle method as used on a Danish forensic sample. *Forensic Science International.* 179(2–3): 242.e1–242.e6.

Matrille, L., Ubelaker, D. H., Cattaneo, C., Seguret, F., Tremblay, M., and Baccino, E. (2007). Comparison of four skeletal methods for the estimation of age at death on white and black adults. *Journal of Forensic Sciences.* 53: 302–307.

Meijerman, L., Maat, G. J. R., Schulz, R., and Schmeling, A. (2007). Variables affecting the probability of complete fusion of the medial clavicular epiphysis. *International Journal of Legal Medicine.* 121: 463–468.

Mito, T., Sato, K., and Mitani, H. (2002). Cervical vertebral bone age in girls. *American Journal of Orthodontic Dentofacial Orthopedics.* 122(4): 380–385.

Molinari, L., Gasser, T., and Largo, R. H. (2004). TW3 bone age: RUS/CB and gender differences of percentiles for score and score increments. *Annals of Human Biology.* 31: 421–435.

Mora, S., Boechat, M. I., Pietka, E., Huang, H. K., and Gilsanz, V. (2001). Skeletal age determinations in children of European and African descent: Applicability of the Greulich and Pyle standards. *Pediatric Research.* 50(5): 624–628.

Muhler, M., Schulz, R., Schmidt, S., Schmeling, A., and Reisinger, W. (2006). The influence of slice thickness on assessment of clavicle ossification in forensic age diagnostics. *International Journal of Legal Medicine.* 120: 15–17.

Nemzek, W. R., Brodie, H. A., Hecht, S. T., Chong, B. W., Babcook, C. J., and Seibert, J. A. (2000). MR, CT, and plain film imaging of the developing skull base in fetal specimens. *American Journal of Neuroradiology.* 21(9): 1699–1706.

Nig, G., Qu, H. B., Liu, G. J., Wu, K. M., Xie, S. X., and Chen, X. J. (2007). TW systems in estimation of carpal bone age and their potential applications in diagnosis of idiopathic precocious puberty in Chinese girls. *Fa Yi Xue Za Zhi.* 23(2): 97–100.

Nuzzolese, E., and Di Vella, G. (2008). Forensic dental investigations and age assessment of asylum seekers. *International Dental Journal* 58: 122–126.

O'Connor, J. E., Bogue, C., Spence, L. D., and Last, J. (2008). A method to establish the relationship between chronological age and stage of union from radiographic assessment of epiphyseal fusion at the knee: An Irish population study. *Journal of Anatomy.* 212: 198–209.

Ortega, A. I., Haiter-Neto, F., Ambrosano, G. M., Bo' Scolo, F. N., Almeida, S. M., and Casanova, M. S. (2006). Comparison of TW2 and TW3 skeletal age differences in a Brazilian population. *Journal of Applied Oral Science.* 14(2): 142–146.

Piercecchi-Marti, M. D., Adalian, P., Bourliere-Najean, B., Gouvernet, J., Maczel, M., Dutour, O., and Leonetti, G. (2002). Validation of a radiographic method to establish new fetal growth standards: Radio-anatomical correlation. *Journal of Forensic Sciences.* 47: 328–331.

Ranjitkar, S., Lin, N. H., Macdonald, R., Taylor, J. A., and Townsend, G. C. (2006). Stature and skeletal maturation of two cohorts of Australian children and young adults over the past two decades. *Australian Orthodontic Journal.* 22(1): 47–58.

Ríos, L., and Cardoso, H. F. V. (2009). Age estimation from stages of union of the vertebral epiphyses of the ribs. *American Journal of Physical Anthropology.* 140(2): 265–274.

Ríos, L., Weisensee, K., and Rissech, C. (2008). Sacral fusion as an aid in age estimation. *Forensic Science International.* 180: 111.e1–111.e7.

Rissech, C., and Black, S. (2007). Scapular development from the neonatal period to skeletal maturity: A preliminary study. *International Journal of Osteoarchaeology.* 17: 451–464.

Rissech, C., Garcia, M., and Malgosa, A. (2003). Sex and age diagnosis by ischium morphometric analysis. *Forensic Science International.* 135: 188–196.

Rissech, C., and Malgosa, A. (2005). Ilium growth study: applicability in sex and age diagnosis. *Forensic Science International.* 147: 165–174.

Rissech C., and Malgosa, A. (2007). Pubis growth study: Applicability in sexual and age diagnostic. *Forensic Science International.* 173: 137–145.

Rissech, C., Schaefer, M., and Malgosa, A. (2008). Development of the femur—implications for age and sex determination. *Forensic Science International.* 180: 1–9.

Ritz-Timme, S., Cattaneo, C., Collins, M. J., Waite, E. R., Schutz, H. W., Kaatsch, H.-J., and Borrman, H. I. M. (2000). Age estimation: The state of the art in relation to the specific demands of forensic practice. *International Journal of Legal Medicine.* 113: 129–136.

Sahin Saglam, A. M., and Gazilerli, U. (2002). The relationship between dental and skeletal maturity. *Journal of Orofacial Orthopedics.* 63: 454–462.

Salle, B. L., Rauch, F., Travers, R., Bouvier, R., and Glorieux, F. H. (2002). Human fetal bone development: Histomorphometric evaluation of the proximal femoral metaphysis. *Bone.* 30(6): 823–828.

Salpou, D., Kiserud, T., Rasmussen, S., and Johnsen, S. L. (2008). Fetal age assessment based in 2nd trimester ultrasound in Africa and the effect of ethnicity. *BMC Pregnancy and Childbirth.* 8: 48.

Saunders S. R. (2000). Subadult skeletons and growth related studies. In: *Biological anthropology of the human skeleton.* Katzenberg, M. A., and Saunders, S. R. (Eds.). New York: Wiley-Liss. 117–148.

Schaefer, M. (2007). Epiphyseal union timings in Bosnian males: An investigation of their applicability in the identification process. Ph.D. thesis, University of Dundee, UK.

Schaefer, M. C. (2008). A summary of epiphyseal union timings in Bosnian males. *International Journal of Osteoarchaeology.* 18: 536–545.

Schaefer, M., and Black, S. (2005). Comparison of ages of epiphyseal union in North American and Bosnian skeletal material. *Journal of Forensic Sciences*. 50: 777–784.

Schaefer, M., and Black, S. (2007). Epiphyseal union sequencing: Aiding in the recognition and sorting of comingled remains. *Journal of Forensic Sciences*. 52: 277–285.

Schaefer, M., Black, S., and Scheuer, L. (2009). *Juvenile osteology: A laboratory and field manual*. London: Academic Press.

Scheuer, L., and Black, S. (2000). *Developmental juvenile osteology*. London: Academic Press.

Scheuer, L., and Black, S. (2004). *The juvenile skeleton*. London: Elsevier Academic Press.

Scheuer, L., and Black, S. (2007). Osteology. In *Forensic human identification: An introduction*. Thompson, T., and Black, S. (Eds.). Boca Raton, FL: CRC Press.

Schmeling, A., Olze, A., Reisinger, W., König, M., and Geserick, G. (2003). Statistical analysis and verification of forensic age estimation of living persons in the Institute of Legal Medicine of the Berlin University Hospital Charité. *Legal Medicine*. 5: S367–S371.

Schmeling, A., Olze, A., Reisinger, W., and Geserick, G. (2004). Forensic age diagnostics of living people undergoing criminal proceedings. *Forensic Science International*. 144: 243–245.

Schmeling, A., Olze, A., Reisinger, W., and Geserick, G. (2005). Forensic age estimation and ethnicity. *Legal Medicine*. 7(2): 134–137.

Schmeling, A., Baumann, U., Schmidt, S., Wernecke, K. D., and Reisinger, W. (2006). Reference data for the Thiemann-Nitze method of assessing skeletal age for the purpose of forensic age estimation. *International Journal of Legal Medicine*. 120: 1–4.

Schmeling, A., Reisinger, W., Geserick, G., and Olze, A. (2006). Age estimation of unaccompanied minors. Part I. General considerations. *Forensic Science International*. 159S: S61–S64.

Schmeling, A., Geserick, G., Reisinger, W., and Olze, A. (2007). Age estimation. *Forensic Science International*. 165: 178–181.

Schmidt, S., Baumann, U., Schulz, R., Reisinger, W., and Schmeling, A. (2008). Study of age dependence of epiphyseal ossification of the hand skeleton. *International Journal of Legal Medicine*. 122: 51–54.

Schmidt, S., Koch, B., Schulz, R., Reisinger, W., and Schmeling, A. (2008). Studies in use of the Greulich-Pyle skeletal age method to assess criminal liability. *Legal Medicine*. 10(4): 190–195.

Schmidt, S., Nitz, I., Schulz, R., and Schmeling, A. (2008). Applicability of the skeletal age determination method of Tanner and Whitehouse for forensic age diagnostics. *International Journal of Legal Medicine*. 122: 309–314.

Schmidt, S., Nitz, I,. Schulz, R,. Tsokos, M., and Schmeling, A. (2009). The digital atlas of skeletal maturity by Gilsanz and Ratib: A suitable alternative for age estimation of living individuals in criminal proceedings. *International Journal of Legal Medicine*. 123: 489–494.

Schulz, R., Muhler, M., Mutze, S., Schmidt, S., Reisinger, W., and Schmeling, A. (2005). Studies on the time frame for ossification of the medial epiphysis of the clavicle as revealed by CT scans. *International Journal of Legal Medicine*. 119: 142–145.

Schulze, D., Rother, U., Fuhrmann, A., Richel, S., Faulmann, G., and Heiland, M. (2006). Correlation of age and ossification of the medial clavicular epiphysis using computed tomography. *Forensic Science International.* 158: 184–189.

Sciulli, P. W. (2007). Relative dental maturity and associated skeletal maturity in prehistoric native Americans of the Ohio Valley area. *American Journal of Physical Anthropology* 132: 545–557.

Sherwood, R. J., Meindl, R. S., Robinson, H. B., and May, R. L. (2000). Fetal age: Methods of estimation and effects of pathology. *American Journal of Physical Anthropology.* 113: 305–315.

Smith, S. L., and Buschang, P. H. (2004). Variation in longitudinal diaphyseal long bone growth in children three to ten years of age. *American Journal of Human Biology.* 16: 648–657.

Smith, S. L., and Buschang, P. H. (2005). Longitudinal models of long bone growth during adolescence. *American Journal of Human Biology.* 17: 731–745.

Soegiharto, B. M., Cunningham, S. J., and Moles, D. R. (2008). Skeletal maturation in Indonesian and white children assessed with hand-wrist and cervical vertebrae methods. *American Journal of Orthodontic Dentofacial Orthopedics.* 134(2): 217–226.

Solheim, T., and Vonen, A. (2006). Dental age estimation, quality assurance and age estimation of asylum seekers in Norway. *Forensic Science International.* 159: s56–s60.

Stathopulu, E., Hulse, J. A., and Canning, D. (2003). Difficulties with age estimation of internet images of south-east Asian girls. *Child Abuse Review.* 12: 46–57.

Stevenson, P. H. (1924). Age order of epiphyseal union in man. *American Journal of Physical Anthropology.* 7: 53–93.

Stewart, T. D. (1934). Sequence of epiphyseal union, third molar eruption and suture closure in Eskimos and American Indians. *American Journal of Physical Anthropology.* 19: 433–452.

Stiehl, J., Muller, B., and Dibbets, J. (2009). The development of the cervical vertebrae as an indicator of skeletal maturity: Comparison with the classic method of hand-wrist radiograph. *Journal of Orofacial Orthopedics-Fortschritte Der Kieferorthopadie.* 70(4): 327–335.

Taipale, P., and Hiilesmaa, V. (2001). Predicting delivery date by ultrasound and last menstrual period in early gestation. *Obstetrics and Gynecology.* 97: 189–194.

Tanner, J. M., Whitehouse, R. H., and Healy, M. J. R. (1962). *A new system for estimating skeletal maturity from the hand and wrist with standards derived from a study of 2600 healthy British children. Part II. The scoring system.* Paris: International Child Centre.

Tanner, J. M., Whitehouse, R. H., Marshall, W. A., Healy, M. J. R., and Goldstein, H. (1975). *Assessment of skeletal maturity and prediction of adult height (TW2 method).* London: Academic Press.

Tanner, J. M., Healy, M. J. R., Goldstein, H., and Cameron, N. (2001). *Assessment of skeletal maturity and prediction of adult height (TW3 method).* London: Saunders.

Todd, T. W. (1937). *Atlas of skeletal maturation.* St. Louis, MO: Mosby.

Usher, B. M. (2002). Reference samples: The first step in linking biology and age in the skeleton. In *Paleodemography: Age distribution from skeletal samples.* Hoppa, R. D., and Vaupel, I. W. (Eds.). Cambridge, UK: Cambridge University Press. 29–47.

Uysal, T., Sari, Z., Ramoglu, S. I., and Basciftci, F. A. (2004). Relationships between dental and skeletal maturity in Turkish subjects. *Angle Orthodontist.* 74: 657–664.

Van Rijn, R. R., Lequin, M. H., Robben, S. G., Hop, W. C., and Van Kuijk, C. (2001). Is the Greulich and Pyle atlas still valid for Dutch Caucasian children today? *Pediatric Radiology.* 31(10): 748–752.

Vu, H. L., Panchal, J., Parker, E. E., Levine, N. S., and Francel, P. (2001). The timing of physiologic closure of the metopic suture: A review of 159 patients using reconstructed 3D CT scans of the craniofacial region. *Journal of Craniofacial Surgery.* 12(6): 527–532.

Whitaker, J. M., Rousseau, L., Williams, T., Rowan, R. A., and Hartwig, W. C. (2002). Scoring system for estimating age in the foot skeleton. *American Journal of Physical Anthropology.* 118: 385–392.

Wong, R., Alkhal, H., and Rabie, B. (2009). Use of cervical vertebral maturation to determine skeletal age. *American Journal of Orthodontic Dentofacial Orthopedics.* 136: 484e1–484e6.

Zhang, A., Sayre, J. W., Vachon. L., Liu, B. J., and Huang, H. K. (2009). Racial differences in growth patterns of children assessed on the basis of bone age. *Radiology.* 250(1): 228–235.

Dental Bibliography

Al-Emran, S. (2008). Dental age assessment of 8.5–17 year old Saudi children using Demirjian's method. *Journal of Contemporary Dental Practice.* 9: 64–71.

Al-Qattan, S. I., and Elfawal, M. A. (2010). Significance of teeth lead accumulation in age estimation. *Journal of Forensic and Legal Medicine.* doi: 10.1016/j.jflm.2010.05.001.

Arnold, W. H., and Gaengler, P. (2007). Quantitative analysis of the calcium and phosphorus content of developing and permanent human teeth. *Annals of Anatomy.* 189: 183–190.

Bagherpour, A., Imanimoghaddam, M., Bagherour, M. R., and Einolghozati, M. (2010). Dental age assessment among Iranian children aged 6–13 years using the Demirjian method. *Forensic Science International.* 197: 121.e1–121.e4.

Bernabe, E., and Flores-Mir, C. (2005). Are the lower incisors the best predictors for the unerupted canine and premolars sums? An analysis of a Peruvian sample. *Angle Orthodontist.* 75: 198–203.

Bolanos, M. V., Manrique, M. C., Bolanos, M. J., and Briones, M. T. (2000). Approaches to chronological age assessment based on dental calcification. *Forensic Science International.* 110: 97–106.

Braga, J., Heuze, Y., Chabadel, O., Sonan, M. K., and Gueramy, A. (2005). Non-adult dental age assessment: correspondence analysis and linear regression versus Bayesian predictions. *International Journal of Legal Medicine.* 119: 260–274.

Butti, A. C., Clivio, A., Ferraroni, M., Spada, E., Testa, A., and Salvato, A. (2009). Haavikko's method to assess dental age in Italian children. *European Journal of Orthodontics.* 31: 150–155.

Cameriere, R., De Angelis, D., Ferrante, L., Scarpino, F., and Cingolani, M. (2007). Age estimation in children by measurement of open apices in teeth: A European formula. *International Journal of Legal Medicine.* 121: 449–453.

Cameriere, R., Ferrante, L., and Cingolani, M. (2006). Age estimation in children by measurement of open apices in teeth. *International Journal of Legal Medicine.* 120: 49–52.

Cameriere, R., Ferrante, L., Liversidge, H. M., Prieto, J. L., and Brkic, H. (2008). Accuracy of age estimation in children using radiographs of developing teeth. *Forensic Science International.* 176: 173–177.

Cameriere, R., Flores-Mir, C., Mauricio, F., and Ferrante, L. (2007). Effects of nutrition on timing of mineralization in teeth in a Peruvian sample by the Cameriere and Demirjian methods. *Annals of Human Biology.* 34: 547–556.

Cardoso, H. F. V. (2007a). Accuracy of developing tooth length as an estimate of age in human skeletal remains: The deciduous dentition. *Forensic Science International.* 172: 17–22.

Cardoso, H. F. V. (2007b). A test of the differential accuracy of the maxillary versus the mandibular dentition in age estimation of immature skeletal remains based on developing tooth length. *Journal of Forensic Sciences.* 52: 434–437.

Chaillet, N., and Demirjian, A. (2004). Dental maturity in South France: A comparison between Demirjian's method and polynomial functions. *Journal of Forensic Sciences.* 49: 1059–1066.

Chaillet, N., Nystrom, M., and Demirjian, A. (2005). Comparison of dental maturity in children of different ethnic origins: International maturity curves for clinicians. *Journal of Forensic Sciences.* 50: 1164–1174.

Chaillet, N., Nystrom, M., Kataja, M., and Demirjian, A. (2004). Dental maturity curves in Finnish children: Demirjian's method revisited and polynomial functions for age estimation. *Journal of Forensic Sciences.* 49: 1324–1331.

Chaillet, N., Willems, G., and Demirjian, A. (2004). Dental maturity in Belgian children using Demirjian's method and polynomial functions: New standard curves for forensic and clinical use. *The Journal of Forensic Odonto-Stomatology.* 22: 18–27.

Chen, J. W., Guo, J., Zhou, J., Liu, R. K., Chen, T. T., and Zou, S. J. (2010). Assessment of dental maturity of western Chinese children using Demirjian's method. *Forensic Science International.* 197: 119.e1–119.e4.

Cruz-Landeira, A., Linares-Argote, J., Martinez-Rodriguez, M., Rogriguez-Calvo, M., Otero, X. L., and Concheiro, L. (2010). Dental age estimation in Spanish and Venezuelan children. Comparison of Demirjian and Chaillet's scores. *International Journal of Legal Medicine.* 124: 105–112.

Davidson, L. E., and Rodd, H. D. (2001). Interrelationship between dental age and chronological age in Somali children. *Community Dental Health.* 18: 27–30.

Dean, M. C., Leakey, M. G., Reid, D. J., Schrenk, F., Schwartz, G. T., Stringer, C., and Walker, A. (2001). Growth processes in teeth distinguish modern humans from *Homo erectus* and earlier hominins. *Nature.* 414: 628–631.

Dean, M. C., and Reid, D. J. (2001). Perikymata spacing and distribution on hominid anterior teeth. *American Journal of Physical Anthropology.* 116: 209–215.

Deebaei, A., Moghaddam, H. F., and Delkhosh, P. (2008). The statistical analysis of application of teeth in forensic odontology centre, Tehran, Iran, 1980–2000. *Pakistan Journal of Medical Sciences.* 24: 48–51.

Diagne, F., Diop-Ba, K., Ngom, P. I., and Mbow, K. (2003). Mixed dentition analysis in a Sengalese population: elaboration of prediction tables. *American Journal of Orthodontics and Dentofacial Orthopedics.* 124: 178–183.

Diaz, G., Maccioni, P., Zedda, P., Cabitza, F., and Cortis, I. M. (2003). Dental development in Sardinian children. *Journal of Craniofacial Genetics and Developmental
Biology.* 13: 109–116.

Dirks, W., Reid, D. J., Jolly, C., Phillips-Conroy, J., and Brett, F. (2002). Out of the
mouths of baboons: Stress, life history and dental development in the Awash
National Park hybrid zone, Ethiopia. *American Journal of Physical Anthropology.*
118: 239–252.

Eid, R. M. R., Simi, R., Friggi, M. N. P., and Fisberg, M. (2002). Assessment of dental maturity of Brazilian children aged 6–14 years using Demirjian's method.
International Journal of Paediatric Dentistry. 12: 423–428.

FitzGerald, C. M., and Saunders, S. R. (2005). Test of histological methods of determining chronology of accentuated striae in deciduous teeth. *American Journal
of Physical Anthropology.* 127: 277–290.

Foti, B., Lalys, L., Adalian, P., Giustiniani, J., Maczel, M., Signoli, M., Dutour, O., and
Leonetti, G. (2003). New forensic approach to age determination in children
based on tooth eruption. *Forensic Science International.* 132: 49–56.

Frucht, S., Schnegelsberg, C., Schulte-Monting, J., Rose, E., and Jonas, I. (2000).
Dental age in southwest Germany. A radiographic study. *Journal of Orofacial
Orthopaedics.* 61: 318–329.

Garamendi, P. M., Landa, M. I., Ballesteros, J., and Solano, M. A. (2005). Reliability
of the methods applied to assess age minority in living subjects around 18 years
old: A survey on a Moroccan origin population. *Forensic Science International.*
154: 3–12.

Graham, J. P., O'Donnell, C. J., Craig, P. J. G., Walker, G. L., Hill, A. J., Cirillo, G. N.,
Clark, R. M., Gledhill, S. R., and Schneider-Kolsky, M. E. (2010). The application of computerised tomography (CT) to the dental ageing of children and
adolescents. *Forensic Science International.* 195: 58–62.

Habelitz, S., Denbesten, P. K., Marshall, S. J., Marshall, G. W., and Li, W. (2005).
Amelogenin conrol over apatite crystal growth is affected by the pH and degree
of ionic saturation. *Orthodontic and Craniofacial Research.* 8: 232–238.

Harris, E. F., and Buck, A. L. (2002). Tooth mineralization: A technical note on the
Moorrees-Fanning-Hunt standards. *Dental Anthropology.* 16: 15–20.

Hauk, M. J., Moss, M. E., Weinberg, G. A., and Berkowitz, R. J. (2001). Delayed tooth
eruption: Association with severity of HIV infection. *Pediatric Dentistry* 23:
260–262.

Hernandez, M., Espasa, E., and Boj, J. R. (2008). Eruption chronology of the permanent dentition in Spanish children. *Journal of Clinical Pediatric Dentistry.* 32:
347–350.

Heuze, Y., and Braga, J. (2008). Application of non-adult Bayesian dental age assessment methods to skeletal remains: The Spitalfields collection. *Journal of
Archaeological Science.* 35: 368–375.

Heuze, Y., and Cardoso, H. F. V. (2008). Testing the quality of non-adult Bayesian dental age assessment methods to juvenile skeletal remains: The Lisbon collection
children and secular trend effects. *American Journal of Physical Anthropology.*
135: 275–283.

Holman, D. J., and Yamaguchi, K. (2005). Longitudinal analysis of deciduous tooth
emergence: IV covariate effects in Japanese children. *American Journal of
Physical Anthropology.* 126: 352–358.

Jaroontham, J., and Godfrey, K. (2000). Mixed dentition space analysis in a Thai population. *European Journal of Orthodontics.* 22: 127–134.

Klingberg, G., Dietz, W., Oskarsdottir, S., Odelius, H., Gelander, L., and Noren, J. G. (2005). Morphological appearance and chemical composition of enamel in primary teeth from patients with 22q11 deletion syndrome. *European Journal of Oral Science.* 113: 303–311.

Lease, L. R., and Sciulli, P. W. (2005). Brief communication: discrimination between European-American and African-American children based on deciduous dental metrics and morphology. *American Journal of Physical Anthropology.* 126: 56–60.

Lee, S. E., Lee, S. H., Lee, J. Y., Park, H. K., and Kim, Y. K. (2008). Age estimation of Korean children based on dental maturity. *Forensic Science International.* 178: 125–131.

Legovic, M., Novosel, A., and Legovic, A. (2003). Regression equations for determining mesiodistal crown diameters of canines and premolars. *Angle Orthodontist.* 73: 314–318.

Lehtinen, A., Oksa, T., Helenius, H., and Ronning, O. (2000). Advanced dental maturity in children with juvenile rheumatoid arthritis. *European Journal of Oral Sciences.* 108: 184–188.

Leurs, I. H., Wattel, E., Aartman, I. H. A., Etty, E., and Prahl-Andersen, B. (2005). Dental age in Dutch children. *European Journal of Orthodontics.* 27: 309–314.

Liversidge, H. M., Chaillet, N., Mornstadt, H., Nystrom, M., Rowlings, K., Taylor, J., and Willems, G. (2006). Timing of Demirjian's tooth formation stages. *Annals of Human Biology.* 33: 454–470.

Liversidge, H. M., Lyons, F., and Hector, M. P. (2003). The accuracy of three methods of age estimation using radiographic measurements of developing teeth. *Forensic Science International.* 131: 22–29.

Liversidge, H. M., and Molleson, T. (2004). Variation in crown and root formation and eruption of human deciduous teeth. *American Journal of Physical Anthropology.* 123: 172–180.

Liversidge, H. M., and Speechly, T. (2001). Growth of permanent mandibular teeth of British children aged 4–9 years. *Annals of Human Biology.* 28: 262–265.

Maber, M., Liversidge, H. M., and Hector, M. P. (2006). Accuracy of age estimation of radiographic methods using developing teeth. *Forensic Science International.* 159s: s68–s73.

Macho, G. (2001). Primate molar crown formation times and life history evolution revisited. *American Journal of Primatology.* 55: 189–201.

Maia, M. C. G., Martins, M. G. A., Germano, F. A., Neto, J. B., and da Silva, C. A. B. (2010). Demirjian's system for estimating the dental age of northeastern Brazilian children. doi: 10.1016/j.forsciint.2010.03.030.

Mani, S. A., Naing, L., John, J., and Samsudin, R. (2008). Comparison of two methods of dental age estimation in 7–15 year old Malays. *International Journal of Paediatric Dentistry.* 18: 380–388.

McKenna, C. J., James, H., Taylor, J. A., and Townsend, G. C. (2002). Tooth development standards for South Australia. *Australian Dental Journal.* 47: 223–227.

Melgaco, C. A., Araujo, M. T., and Ruellas, A. C. O. (2006). Applicability of three tooth size prediction methods for white Brazilians. *Angle Orthodontist.* 76: 644–649.

Mitchell, J. C., Roberts, G. J., Donaldson, A. N. A., and Lucas, V. S. (2009). Dental age assessment (DAA): Reference data for British caucasians at the 16 year threshold. *Forensic Science International.* 189: 19–23.

Muller-Bolla, M., Lupi-Peurier, L., Quatrehomme, G., Velly, A. M., and Bolla, M. (2003). Age estimation from teeth in children and adolescents. *Journal of Forensic Sciences.* 48: 140–148.

Nourallah, A. W., Gesch, D., Khordaji, M. N., and Splieth, C. (2002). New regression equations for predicting the size of unerupted canines and premolars in a contemporary population. *Angle Orthodontist.* 72: 216–221.

Nystrom, M., Aine, L., Peck, L., Haavikko, K., and Kataja, M. (2000). Dental maturity in Finns and the problem of missing teeth. *Acta Odontologica Scandinavica.* 58: 49–56.

Nystrom, M., Peck, L., Kleemola-Kujala, E., Evalahti, M., and Kataja, M. (2000). Age estimation in small children: Reference values based on counts of deciduous teeth in Finns. *Forensic Science International.* 110: 179–188.

Nystrom, M., and Ranta, H. (2003). Tooth formation and the mandibular symphysis during the first five postnatal months. *Journal of Forensic Sciences.* 48: 1–6.

Nystrom, M., Ranta, H. M., Peltola, J. S., and Kataja, J. M. (2007). Timing of developmental stages in permanent mandibular teeth of Finns from birth to age 25. *Acta Odontologica Scandinavica.* 65: 36–43.

Olze, A., Reisinger, W., Geserick, G., and Schmeling, A. (2006). Age estimation of unaccompanied minors. Part II. Dental aspects. *Forensic Science International.* 159s: s65–s67.

Prabhakar, A. R., Panda, A. K., and Raju, O. S. (2002). Applicability of Demirjian's method of age assessment in children of Davangere. *Journal of the Indian Society of Pedodontics and Preventative Dentistry.* 20: 54–62.

Pretty, I. A. (2003). The use of dental aging techniques in forensic odontological practice. *Journal of Forensic Sciences.* 48: 1127–1132.

Quideimat, M. A., and Behbehani, F. (2009). Dental age assessment for Kuwaiti children using Demirjian's method. *Annals of Human Biology.* 23: 1–10.

Radlanski, R. J., and Renz, H. (2006). Developmental movements of the inner enamel epithelium as derived from micromorphological features. *European Journal of Oral Science.* 114: 343–348.

Rai, B., and Anand, S. C. (2006). Tooth developments: An accuracy of age estimation of radiographic methods. *World Journal of Medical Sciences* 1: 130–132.

Reid, D. J., and Dean, M. C. (2006). Variations in modern human enamel formation times. *Journal of Human Evolution.* 50: 329–346.

Reid, D. J., and Ferrell, R. J. (2006). The relationship between number of striae of Retzius and their periodicity in imbricational enamel formation. *Journal of Human Evolution.* 50: 195–202.

Reid, D. J., Ferrell, R. J., and Walton, P. (2002). Histologically derived canine crown formation times from a medieval Danish sample. *American Journal of Physical Anthropology.* 34: 129.

Roberts, G. J., Parekh, S., Petrie, A., and Lucas, V. S. (2008). Dental age assessment (DAA): A simple method for children and emerging adults. *British Dental Journal.* 204: 192–193.

Rozylo-Kalinowska, I., Kiworkowa-Raczkowska, E., and Kalinowski, P. (2008). Dental age in central Poland. *Forensic Science International.* 174: 207–216.

Sabel, N., Johansson, C., Kuhnisch, J., Robertson, A., Steiniger, F., Noren, J. G., Klingberg, G., and Nietzsche, S. (2008). Neonatal lines in the enamel of primary teeth—A morphological and scanning electron microscopic investigation. *Archives of Oral Biology.* 53: 954–963.

Sayin, M. O., and Turkkahraman, H. (2004). Factors contributing to mandibular crowding in the early mixed dentition. *Angle Orthodontist.* 74: 754–758.

Sciulli, P. W. (2001). Dental evolution in prehistoric Native Americans of Ohio Valley area. III. Morphology of the deciduous dentition. *American Journal of Physical Anthropology.* 116: 140–153.

Sema, A. P., Nergis, C., Rukiye, D., and Murat, Y. (2009). Age determination from central incisors of fetuses and infants. *Forensic Science International.* 184: 15–20.

Skobe, Z. (2006). SEM evidence that one ameloblast secretes one keyhole-shaped enamel rod in monkey teeth. *European Journal of Oral Science.* 114: 338–342.

Smith, P., and Avishai, G. (2005). The use of dental criteria for estimating postnatal survival in skeletal remains of infants. *Journal of Archaeological Science.* 32: 83–89.

Teivens, A., and Mornstad, H. A. (2001a). A comparison between dental maturity rate in the Swedish and Korean populations using a modified Demirjian method. *Journal of Forensic Odontostomatology.* 19: 31–35.

Teivens, A., and Mornstad, H. A. (2001b). A modification of the Demirjian method for age estimation in children. *Journal of Forensic Odontostomatology* 19: 26–30.

TeMoanuanui, R., Kieser, J. A., Herbison, G. P., and Liversidge, H. M. (2008). Estimating age in Maori, Pacific Island and European children from New Zealand. *Journal of Forensic Sciences.* 53: 401–404.

Tunc, E. S., and Koyuturk, A. E. (2008). Dental age assessment using Demirjian's method on northern Turkish children. *Forensic Science International.* 175: 23–26.

Uysal, T., Basciftci, F. A., and Goyenc, Y. (2009). New regression equations for mixed-dentition arch analysis in a Turkish sample with no Bolton tooth-size discrepancy. *American Journal of Orthodontics and Dentofacial Orthopedics.* 135: 343–348.

Uyasl, T., and Sari, Z. (2005). Intermaxillary tooth size discrepancy and mesiodistal crown dimensions for a Turkish population. *American Journal of Orthodontics and Dentofacial Orthopedics.* 128: 226–230.

Uysal, T., Sari, Z., Basciftci, F. A., and Memili, B. (2005). Intermaxillary tooth size discrepancy and malocclusion: Is there a relation? *Angle Orthodontist.* 75: 208–213.

Warren, J. J., Yonezu, T., and Bishara, S. E. (2002). Tooth wear patterns in the deciduous dentition. *American Journal of Orthodontics and Dentofacial Orthopedics.* 122: 614–618.

Willems, G. (2001). A review of the most commonly used dental age estimation techniques. *Journal of Forensic Odontostomatology.* 19: 9–17.

Willems, G., Thevissen, P. W., Belmans, A., and Liversidge, H. M. (2010). Willems II. Non-gender-specific dental maturity scores. *Forensic Science International.* doi: 10.1016/j.forsciint.2010.04.033.

Willems, G., Van Olmen, A., Spiessens, B., and Carels, C. (2001). Dental age estimation in Belgian children: Demirjian's technique revisited. *Journal of Forensic Sciences.* 46: 893–895.

Third Molar Bibliography

Arany, S., Iino, M., and Yoshioka, N. (2004). Radiographic survey of third molar development in relation to chronological age among Japanese juveniles. *Journal of Forensic Sciences.* 49: 534–538.

Bhat, V. J., and Kamath, G. P. (2007). Age estimation from root development of mandibular third molars in comparison with skeletal age of wrist joint. *The American Journal of Forensic Medicine and Pathology.* 28: 238–241.

Blakenship, J. A., Mincer, H. H., Anderson, K. M., Woods, M. A., and Burton, E. I. (2007). Third molar development in the estimation of chronologic age in American Blacks as compared with Whites. *Journal of Forensic Sciences.* 52: 428–433.

Bolanos, M. V., Moussa, H., Manrique, M. C., and Bolanos, M. J. (2003). Radiographic evaluation of third molar development in Spanish children and young people. *Forensic Science International.* 133: 212–219.

De-Salvia, A., Calzetta, C., Orrico, M., and De-Leo, D. (2004). Third mandibular molar radiological development as an indicator of chronological age in a European population. *Forensic Science International.* 146: s9–s12.

Dhanjal, K. S., Bhardwah, M. K., and Liversidge, H. M. (2006). Reproducibility of radiographic stage assessment of third molars. *Forensic Science International.* 159: s74–s77.

Friedrich, R. E., Ulbricht, C., and von Maydell, L. A. (2003). The influence of wisdom tooth impaction on root formation. *Annals of Anatomy* 185: 481–492.

Gunst, K., Mesotten, K., Carbonez, A., and Willems, G. (2003). Third molar root development in relation to chronological age: A large sample sized retrospective study. *Forensic Science International.* 136: 52–57.

Harris, E. F. (2007). Mineralization of the mandibular third molar: A study of American blacks and whites. *American Journal of Physical Anthropology.* 132: 98–109.

Knell, B., Ruhstaller, P., Prieels, F., and Schmeling, A. (2009). Dental age diagnostics by means of radiographical evaluation of the growth stages of lower wisdom teeth. *International Journal of Legal Medicine.* 123: 465–469.

Lewis, J. M., and Senn, D. R. (2010). Dental age estimation utilizing third molar development: A review of principles, methods and population studies used in the United States. *Forensic Science International.* doi: 10.1016/j.forsciint.2010.04.042.

Martin-de las Heras, S., Garcia-Fortea, P., Ortega, A., Zodocovich, S., and Valenzuela, A. (2008). Third molar development according to chronological age in populations from Spanish and Magrebian origin. *Forensic Science International.* 174: 47–53.

Meinl, A., Tangl, S., Huber, C. Maurer, B., and Watzek, G. (2007). The chronology of third molar mineralization in Austrian population—A contribution to forensic age estimation. *Forensic Science International.* 169: 161–167.

Mesotten, K., Gunst, K., Carbonez, A., and Willems, G. (2002). Dental age estimation and third molars: A preliminary study. *Forensic Science International.* 129: 110–115.

Olze, A., Bilang, D., Schmidt, S., Wernecke, K. D., Geserick, G., and Schmeling, A. (2005). Validation of common classification systems for assessing the mineralization of third molars. *International Journal of Legal Medicine.* 119: 22–26.

Olze, A., Schmeling, A., Taniguchi, M., Maeda, H., van Niekerk, P., Wernecke, K. D., and Geserick, G. (2004). Forensic age estimation in living subjects: the ethnic factor in wisdom tooth mineralization. *International Journal of Legal Medicine.* 118: 170–173.

Olze, A., Taniguchi, M., Schmeling, A., Zhu, B. I., Yamada, Y., Maeda, H., and Geserick, G. (2003). Comparative study on the chronology of third molar mineralization in a Japanese and a German population. *Legal Medicine.* 5: 256–260.

Olze, A., van Niekerk, P., Ishikawa, T., Zhu, B. L., Schulz, R., Maeda, H., and Schmeling, A. (2007). Comparative study on the effect of ethnicity on wisdom tooth eruption. *International Journal of Legal Medicine.* 121: 445–448.

Olze, A., van Niekerk, P., Schmidt, S., Wernecke, K. D., Rosing, F. W., Geserick, G., and Schmeling, A. (2006). Studies on the progress of third-molar mineralization in a Black African population. *Homo.* 57: 209–217.

Olze, A., van Niekerk, P., Schulz, R., and Schmeling, A. (2007). Studies of the chronological course of wisdom tooth eruption in black African population. *Journal of Forensic Sciences.* 52: 1161–1163.

Orhan, K., Ozer, L., Orhan, A. I., Dogan, S., and Paksoy, C. S. (2007). Radiographic evaluation of third molar development in relation to chronological age among Turkish children and youth. *Forensic Science International.* 165: 46–51.

Prieto, J. I., Barberia, E., Ortega, R., and Magana, C. (2005). Evaluation of chronological age based on third molar development in the Spanish population. *Journal of Legal Medicine.* 119: 349–354.

Sisman, Y., Uysal, T., Yagmur, F., and Ramoglu, S. I. (2007). Third molar development in relation to chronologic age in Turkish children and young adults. *Angle Orthodontist.* 77: 1040–1045.

Solari, A., and Abramovitch, K. (2002). The accuracy and precision of third molar development as an indicator of chronological age in Hispanics. *Journal of Forensic Sciences.* 47: 531–535.

Thevissen, P. W., Fieuws, S., and Willems, G. (2010). Human dental age estimation using third molar developmental stages: Does a Bayesian approach outperform regression models to discriminate between juveniles and adults? *International Journal of Legal Medicine.* 124: 35–42.

Thevissen, P. W., Pittayapat, P., Fieuws, S., and Willems, G. (2009). Estimating age of majority on third molars developmental stages in young adults from Thailand using a modified scoring technique. *Journal of Forensic Sciences.* 54: 428–432.

Uzamig, M., Kansu, O., Taner, T. U., and Alpar, R. (2000). Radiographic evaluation of third molar development in a group of Turkish children. *Journal of Dentistry for Children.* 136: 136–141.

Willershuasen, B., Loffler, N., and Schulze, R. (2001). Analysis of 1202 orthopantomograms to evaluate the potential of forensic age determination based on third molar developmental stages. *European Journal of Medical Research* 6: 377–384.

Age Determination in the Adult

2

STACEY PURVES
LIANNE WOODLEY
Ms. LUCINA HACKMAN

Contents

Introduction

For the purposes of this chapter, adult age is considered to be 18 years of age and older. The methods employed in adult age determination are largely dependent on the skeletal elements available for analysis and, unlike age assessment methods in the juvenile and adolescent, which rely on growth and developmental processes, are largely concerned with degenerative events, both within the dentition and the skeleton. In the past decade, the majority of research conducted in relation to ageing of the adult skeleton has concentrated on testing and refining methods developed in the 20th century;

this chapter examines this literature. Due to the large number of references produced over the last decade, rather than place these in the text, they are presented at the end of this chapter as a bibliography, which provides a guide to this subject area. The References section includes only citations mentioned specifically in the text discussion. Key texts on the subject from before 2000 are also included.

Adult Age Determination

All age estimation methods based on assessments of skeletal or dental changes are a measurement of skeletal or dental maturity. This is then converted into a chronological age that is subsequently communicated for judicial needs. Age assessment methods therefore have to utilise areas within the skeleton that change in a sequential and recordable manner. The problem for practitioners is that individual variation means that no two people will evidence age-related changes in exactly the same manner. Differential rates of physical change are observed both between individuals and between skeletal elements within an individual and are influenced by a complex interaction of genetic, cultural, and environmental factors, and any age estimation method has to be able to take this into account. Taking into consideration the differences that exist between individuals and the influences of environment, diet, etc., all age estimations have to be given as an age range rather than presented as a specific age. In a forensic situation, the age range must not only be narrow enough to be meaningful, that is, to reduce the possibilities of who that individual might be in relation to a missing persons' list, but also must be wide enough to include the actual age of the victim. To be too inclusive in a forensic age estimation would be as problematic for a forensic investigation as would be being too exclusive.

Forensic practitioners undertake age estimations for judicial reasons, and it is argued that techniques and methods should fulfill a number of criteria before they are utilised. The application of the age estimation process should be both ethical and legal, and all methodologies should be transparent, reproducible and have proven accuracy rates. Finally, any technique that is used in a forensic situation should have been presented to the scientific community in a recognized manner, usually through publication in peer-reviewed journals. At all times, the admissibility of the evidence must be foremost in the choice of a technique for age evaluation.

In the development of all skeletal and dental estimation techniques, all practitioners should be aware of the population on which the method has been developed; many osteological collections are historical, population specific and may be of assessed, rather than known, age and sex. Even those collections that earlier in the 20th century were contemporaneous are now no longer so. Socioeconomic changes have resulted in secular change both within and between populations. This must all be taken into account when applying any methodology to a modern-day individual. The differences that exist between present-day populations have come to the fore with the modern requirements of forensic anthropology in relation to work undertaken both for humanitarian purposes and on behalf of various tribunals. This has resulted in questions being asked at a judicial level about the accuracy of anthropological methodologies when applied to modern populations.

There are a number of articles and book chapters that give general guidelines and literature reviews on the subject of age assessment in the adult. These are a viable starting point for any student who is beginning to research the subject. Many of these texts are a reflection of the ongoing need for forensic age assessment, both in the living and in the deceased, and of the many methods that exist to age the adult utilizing the skeleton and dentition. Due to space constraints, we are able simply to give a brief overview of each approach and its validity, rather than discuss a single technique in detail. It is also important for anyone with an interest in this subject to be aware of the effects of ethnicity, socioeconomic background, and biological sex, among other influences, on each of the techniques mentioned.

Age assessment in adults, as stated, relies on skeletal and dental changes that occur throughout the life of the individual. These techniques, when used in the skeleton, include ossification patterns, cranial suture closure, arachnoid foveae presentation, rib morphology, pelvic morphology, and bone histology. For the dentition, methods include root translucency, tooth wear, dental cementum layering, and the racemization of aspartic acid. In addition, the maturation of the third molar also extends into the realm of age evaluation in the adult.

Ossification

While the majority of skeletal development occurs during the juvenile growth phase, a number of fusion events continue into adult life, effectively creating a link between juvenile and adult skeletal changes. These can assist in establishing the age of the individual during the period from 18 years of age to between 25 and 30 years of age. Most literature documenting skeletal fusion pre-dates the 21st century and is beyond the remit of this chapter; however, a collation of relevant data relating to ossification patterning was by Scheuer and Black in their 2000 and 2004 publications, which they have also condensed into a format that is more suited to laboratory use in collaboration with the work of Schaefer et al. (2009).

Skeletal transition from the juvenile to adult phase has been defined by the closure of the spheno-occipital synchondrosis, which is reported to occur between 11 to 16 years in females and between 13 to 18 years in males. Although this can skeletally define the move from juvenile to adult, further investigation has concluded that the age of fusion of the synchondrosis is too variable to be of forensic use, especially among males. Also in the skull, fusion of the vomer to the perpendicular plate of the ethmoid occurs between 20 and 30 years of age, and closure of the jugular growth plate is generally observed between 22 and 34 years. Ossification of the hyoid is predominantly complete by puberty but will continue throughout adult life, when fusion between the body and greater horns is often observed, although it should be noted that fusion rates are too irregular to be used in a forensic context.

Toward the end of the second decade, ossification of the thyroid and cricoid laryngeal cartilages may also be observed. The ossification process of the thyroid, cricoid, and laryngeal cartilages in relation to age assessment has been investigated by a number of authors. The original method of Cerný developed in 1983 has not withstood further examination. Timing of ossification of the cricoid, laryngeal, or thyroid cartilage has not been shown to bear a close enough relationship with chronological age for forensic use. Even those authors who argued that ossification proceeds in a regular fashion found individual differences created too great a spread of ossification patterns for use.

By the mid-20s, ventral fusion of the first and second sacral bodies is complete, as is fusion of all vertebral epiphyses. Generally, fusion of the annular rings of the vertebrae adds to the information collected about the age of the individual; however, these rings are fragile and do not always survive inhumation or weathering. For the living, there is as yet no work undertaken to see if they can be imaged using computed tomography (CT) or other methods. The sacrum is more robust, and a phase system that incorporates morphological changes, including the fusion process within the sacrum, has been developed. This is based on sacra from individuals of different ethnic and socioeconomic backgrounds from the Hamann-Todd collection and the W. M. Bass collection. The methodology includes both developmental and degenerative traits, and the author argues that it has forensic applicability, although he added the caveat that due to the large spread of some of the age ranges, this should be done in combination with other techniques whenever possible (Passalacqua 2009).

The fusion of the sternebrae spans a number of years, culminating in fusion between the first and second sections in the third decade of life. The xiphoid process of the sternum may commence fusion to the mesosternum over the age of 40 years. Of greater use to forensic specialists are the epiphyses of the clavicle. The lateral epiphyses of the clavicle may form and fuse at 19 to 20 years of age, with the medial epiphyses generally completing fusion by 30 years of age. Due to fusion extending into the third decade of life, and the development of imaging techniques such as CT, the epiphyses at the medial clavicle have become important in forensic age estimates of the living. The fact that a large number of studies addressed the use of different imaging techniques (e.g., radiography, ultrasound, magnetic resonance imaging, and CT) is a reflection of the importance of this skeletal area for age assessments in the living rather than for the deceased individual. As a final note, there is a suggestion that the presence of a large rhomboid fossa on the clavicle is highly indicative of a male in his 20s to 30s, although again this is not reliable enough for forensic ageing.

In the scapula, both coracoid epiphyses and the acromial epiphysis fuse by 20 years of age, with complete fusion of the inferior angle and medial border occurring by the age of 23 years. A number of ossification events occur in the pelvis beyond the age of 18 years: By the age of 20 years, the anterior inferior iliac spine has fused, and the ischial epiphysis extends halfway along the ischial ramus; from approximately 20 years of age onward, a number of changes occur at the pubic symphyseal surface, and by 23 years the ischial epiphysis and the iliac crest have completed fusion. This fusion of the iliac crest epiphysis has been studied by a number of authors because of its utility in the assessment of skeletal rather than chronological age in medical practice.

Recent studies have compared interpopulation ossification patterns. Studies on a contemporary Bosnian sample, Portuguese collections from Coimbra and Lisbon, as well as a study comparing samples from Sassari, Coimbra and India have revealed variations in fusion timings between populations. Recent work has suggested that these variations are due to socio-economic factors rather than ethnicity. The differences between populations add weight to the need for all practitioners to have an understanding of the population from which methodologies are developed and of how lifestyle may affect the age-related changes on which they are dependent for their assessment.

The Skull

The estimation of adult age based on cranial suture closure was one of the earliest methods of ageing the skeleton to be developed. Much of the work in the beginning was conducted by Todd and Lyon in the mid-1920s (Todd and Lyon 1924–1925). Since this time, several authors have macroscopically analyzed the ecto- and endocranial morphology of the sutures. While researchers describe sutural ossification as an age-related physiological process, in relation to age estimation for forensic purposes many find that it is highly variable and therefore unreliable as a method of age determination. Despite this, the closure of cranial sutures is frequently used to determine adult skeletal age in both forensic and archaeological contexts, although it is argued that perhaps it should be limited to the archaeological arena, in which errors in age estimation are not of judicial significance. The ongoing utilization of the skull may be related to the tendency for substantial preservation and retrieval of the neurocranium in addition to the relative simplicity of a number of the analysis methods employed.

Most studies of the last decade have concentrated on ways of improving accuracy by both testing and revising existing methods and exploring and comparing different sutures of the cranium for accuracy. Marking the move from macro- to microinvestigation, others have concentrated on differing imaging and measurement modalities, including wavelength analysis and fractal dimensioning on the squamous and petromastoid sutures, CT examination, and histological analysis of tissue changes. This has led some authors to conclude that estimates for adults over the age of 40 years were imprecise as suture closure may be influenced by nonbiological factors. More traditional analysis of 16 suture segments from 665 Indian cadavers, for which the degree of suture closure was scored on a scale of zero to four for both the ecto- and endocranial surfaces, found that there was no significant difference in closure time between the two surfaces, and that closure timings between the various segments were irregular and, as such, provided little assistance in age estimation. In conclusion, care must always be taken when using cranial sutures as an age estimation method.

Morphological changes to the skull have also been investigated as an age assessment method. Age-related increase in both the size and number of arachnoid foveae has been reported. Early work was conducted by Basmajian in 1952 with few analyses published since that time. However, work undertaken in 2006 involved a quantitative analysis of the change in frequency and total volume of arachnoid foveae in 63 males from the Hamann-Todd skeletal collection. Linear regression analysis revealed no significant correlation among frequency, total volume, and age, and the authors concluded that the presentation of arachnoid foveae may be under the influence of health factors rather than an age-related change (Duray and Martel 2006).

Dentition

Morphological and radiological estimations of dental age in juveniles are based on the development and eruption patterns of the dentition. This process slows toward the end of the second decade of life and is completed by the eruption and closure of the root apices of the third molars (wisdom teeth) in the late teens or early 20s. Although often thought of as the most inconsistent of all of the teeth in its developmental pattern, the wisdom tooth has become one of the methods of age assessment utilized in the living, and as a result many studies have spent time assessing its accuracy and reliability as an indicator of chronological age. Once the wisdom teeth have completed development, age estimation is limited to morphological changes that are observed to occur within the teeth.

The dentition commonly survives taphonomic influences more successfully than other less-robust areas of the skeleton; as a result, researchers have focused their efforts on investigating their use in the estimation of age at death. Dental ageing techniques include both destructive and nondestructive methods, limiting the utility of certain techniques in relation to forensic age estimation, especially cases involving age estimations of the living.

Changes in root translucency have been the focus for a number of methods of adult dental age assessment. Practitioners argued that both the simplicity and accuracy of the Bang and Ramm (1970) method of age estimation using root translucency make it an ideal forensic dental ageing method. As with many ageing methodologies, adjustments have to be made when applying it to alternative populations. As an alternative to the Bang and Ramm method, the Lamendin method (Lamendin et al. 1992) was originally designed as a simpler, if still destructive, age assessment method than the more complicated systems that had been utilized until that time. The application of this technique to alternative populations has again resulted in the development of revised formulae that have been proven to maintain their accuracy rates when applied to further population groups. Research has agreed that, of the two criteria utilized in the Lamendin method, it is only root translucency that is correlated with age. The need to be able to apply it nondestructively has led to tests to undertake the accurate quantification of root translucency using digital aids.

Dental wear, or attrition, has been utilized more often in archaeological than forensic age assessments, although recent work has found that one of the techniques developed on an archaeological population is relevant to a modern population in the Balkans. More recent work that has centered on developing a population-specific scoring system in other countries has also met with success, although the developed methodology is limited to those populations whose diet produces significant wear on the teeth.

Methods of adult age estimation based on the age-dependent racemization of aspartic acid are among the most reliable and accurate techniques available; however, their drawback again is that they are destructive. Proteins of the body are formed from amino acids, which exist in two nonsuperimposable mirror image forms; these are known as the L-form and the D-form. Initially, all amino acids exist in the L-form, gradually converting to the D-form with age. This change of L-form amino acids to D-form amino acids is known as *racemization*. The change occurs gradually over time and is heat dependent, so it theoretically continues throughout the lifetime of an individual and should cease once an individual is deceased. A measurement of the relative amounts of L-form and D-form of the amino acids therefore will give an estimation of the age at death of the individual. In 1976, Helfman and

Bada used gas chromatography (GC) to compare the proportions of L- and D-form aspartic acid in dentin; this method has since been updated, providing the analyst with a number of different choices in experimental processing. More recently, its use has not been limited to the study of dentine and has been expanded to include tooth enamel and other bodily tissues, including muscle, again using the same principles of ratios of L- and D-type amino acids.

The correlation between D-aspartic acid in dentin and age in a number of teeth from the same individual found levels of the D-form of the amino acid to be highest in the first molar, followed in turn by relatively lower levels in the second molar, second premolar, first premolar, canine, central incisor, and lateral incisor. These differences have been attributed to higher ambient temperatures deeper in the oral cavity, which result in faster rates of racemization, although this theory has not been supported by the work of other researchers. Accuracy rates in estimating chronological age from racemization have been acceptable enough to be used in a forensic situation, however, care should be taken when viewing teeth as a closed system as even here age assessments can be affected by the environment after death.

Pulp/tooth area ratios in multirooted and single-rooted teeth have been investigated as an age estimation method. Original methods utilized to measure the pulp/tooth ratio were destructive, and the possibility of using a modern imaging technique to get the same results has interested many researchers. The new technique has also been applied to different populations, with resultant claims that accuracy rates are within acceptable levels for forensic assessment of age.

Dental enamel is extremely hard and durable, so changes that occur within it during the life of an individual are limited. Areas of the tooth such as the roots do see some changes, however, and the accumulation of dental cementum is one that has been examined to see if it is related to the age of the individual. Researchers do not agree on the accuracy of this method. Some feel that the use of cementum incremental lines has an equivalent accuracy to the age estimators based within the skeleton, such as the pubic symphysis; others argue that these are of more use in dating life experiences such as illnesses and pregnancy.

Rib Morphology

Morphological changes to the sternal end of the rib in relation to age were first described by İşcan and Loth, who examined the sternal rib ends of an American population in the 1980s (İşcan et al. 1984a, 1984b, 1985, 1987; Loth 1995). A nine-phase classification system was developed in relation to morphological changes that occur in the right fourth rib. Much of the subsequent work was conducted throughout the 1980s and 1990s, with studies by İşcan, Loth, and Wright (1984a, 1984b, 1985) predominating. More recent work has shown that phase changes in the sternal end of the right fourth rib vary with population and sex. This has resulted in the formation of a new nine-phase classification system for males and a new eight-phase continuum for females; these systems are dependent on the form, shape, texture, and quality of the rib end.

The İşcan method has been tested by a number of authors, some of whom felt that the methodology was not without its difficulties, including poor reproducibility and repeatability due to differences in preservation and the presence of a significant intraobserver error. Despite these problems, researchers have still found a better correlation with chronological age when utilizing the sternal end of the rib when compared to the use of the pubic symphysis.

In 2001, the transferability of the İşcan method to right ribs 2, 3, and 5–9 and left ribs 2–9 was examined using an American data set. Transferability was beneficial when the right fourth rib is not available or seriation proves difficult. Right and left ribs 5–9 exhibited similar age-related changes and correlated with the phase scores obtained for the right fourth rib; results such as this increase the usefulness of this method in a forensic context. It should be noted that differences in phase scores have been shown to exist between ribs 2 and 3 from the left and right sides, which have been attributed to preferential arm utilization. Anatomically, there does not appear to be a reason why rib morphology would differ with arm preference as there are no muscles with an action on the upper limb that have a point of origin on ribs 2 and 3 only. In an attempt to improve the accuracy of the phase analysis approach, a number of authors recommended the use of a composite score method when working with ribs other than rib 4. The composite scores can then be compared to a table, giving the chronological age; it remains to be seen whether this will improve the accuracy of the use of this area of the skeleton for ageing. In a modern twist, the use of CT imaging has been shown to allow the analysis of all three morphological features required to apply the İşcan method (Dedouit et al. 2008).

While the utility of ribs 4–9 was being investigated, some argued that the more robust and easily identifiable first rib might be of assistance in age assessment. An age estimation method was developed that used the costal face, rib head, and tubercle facet; however, further studies have cast doubt on the reliability of this method, which is reported to be difficult to apply in practice and does not result in particularly accurate age estimations. A more updated method was developed in which firstly the costal end was assigned a score from one to five based on its geometric shape, and secondly the surface texture of the tubercle facet was assigned a score from one to four. The resulting score combination was compared to a table that was constructed using 470 Balkan male specimens. Subsequent analysis is required to test the accuracy of this method and its applicability to female samples.

Pelvis

The auricular surface, pubic symphysis, and acetabulum represent the three principal areas of the pelvis that have utility in adult age determination.

In 1985, Lovejoy et al. devised a method for ageing individuals from the auricular surface. This method was based on 250 specimens from the Libben population and 500 specimens from the Hamman-Todd skeletal collection. They identified morphological changes that occur at the auricular surface and classified them into eight phases, each covering a 5-year age range. The Lovejoy method was argued to be unaffected by both sex and ancestry, although testing had shown that there was a requirement to expand the potential age brackets to increase accuracy rates for age assignment. A revised method was developed by Buckberry and Chamberlain (2002) in which surface texture, apical change, transverse organization, and the degree of both macro- and microporosity were quantitatively scored. Totaling the scores produced a composite value that was then related to an ageing table containing relatively wide potential age ranges with some degree of overlap, allowing for the independent and variable nature of each of the features analyzed. This method was developed on the Spitalfields collection, which is an archaeological collection, and the authors argued that further analysis was required to determine the applicability of their method to other than this arguably limited population. In 2005, such a test was conducted utilizing 309 samples from the Terry and Huntington collection, again an archaeological collection. Results revealed that the newer technique is equally applicable to males and females as well as individuals of differing ethnicities (Mulhern and Jones 2005). While the revised method estimated age accurately for individuals between 50 and 69 years of age, it was deemed less accurate for individuals between 20 and 49 years. This conclusion has been echoed by others who undertook a test of accuracy on a historical Japanese collection (Igarashi et al. 2005). Despite being developed and tested successfully on archaeological remains, the new method did not perform well when applied to a fourth archaeological collection from St. Bride's, London (Falys et al. 2006). Difficulty detecting all of the morphological parameters involved in the assessment has been put forward as one of the limiting factors of this methodology in a forensic scenario. This has resulted in attempts to remove the need to subjectively estimate the degree of development of a feature. The new method involves a binary classification of presence or absence for up to 13 morphological features of relief, texture, and hypertrophied bone structure.

Ageing from the pubic symphysis was first described by Todd in 1920 using a 10-phase system. Numerous revisions have since been published; the most commonly used of these is the six-phase method by Brooks and Suchey

(1990). The research emphasis this decade has been on accuracy rates of the Brooks and Suchey method in relation to different populations. This research slant reflects the increased need to apply ageing methodologies to alternative populations, such as that found in the Balkans. It has been argued that relief of the symphyseal face, the ventral rim, definition of the symphyseal rim, and lipping of the margins are the four features that have the best relationship with chronological age. Asymmetry between the sympyseal faces was observed on the pubic symphyses of 130 individuals from the Hamann-Todd skeletal collection. The asymmetry observed between the left and right os pubis resulted in conflicting Suchey-Brook (1990) phase scores. The authors suggested that both the left and right innominate should be studied if possible, and when differing phase classifications result, the age estimate corresponding to the higher stage should be used. Studies of ancient Egyptian remains remind the practitioner that all ageing techniques should take into account the changes in morphology that have been wrought by the lifestyle of the individual.

Work on the use of the acetabulum has identified between four and seven characteristics that are of significance in age estimation methods. For the four-phase method, the appearance of the acetabular rim and acetabular fossa was found to have the highest correlation with age. The extended, seven-characteristic method includes the acetabular groove, acetabular rim shape, acetabular rim porosity, apex activity, activity on the outer edge of the acetabular fossa, activity of the acetabular fossa, and porosity of the acetabular fossa. The work that has been undertaken in relation to the use of the acetabulum has shown that, as with many of the other ageing methods, accuracy rates are population specific.

The applicability of imaging methods as an aid to age estimation from the pelvis has been investigated. Research showed that digital imaging may be used with caution when direct access to remains is not possible. Areas that are difficult to access, such as the pubic symphysis, have been subject to CT scans. Some argued that they have produced images of the articular surface that are accurate enough to apply developed ageing techniques. Other researchers did not agree and felt that features of the auricular surface, pubic symphysis, and acetabulum are not clear enough for accurate age estimation. With the ability to develop increasingly detailed CT scans, this research can only continue.

Bone Histology

Histological examination of Haversian systems in remodeled lamellar bone is argued to be one of the most accurate techniques available for age estimation from the adult skeleton, although it is affected by health, nutrition, population, and sex of the individual. It is a destructive ageing technique, limiting its usefulness when applied to forensic situations. The original method was developed by Kerley in 1965, using histological specimens from the femur, tibia, and fibula. The method has undergone small revisions and has been extended to include the mandible, clavicle, humerus, ulna, and ribs, having a particular utility in instances of bone fragment presentation. As with many age assessment methods, further improvements and changes have continued to be developed that augment the original technique.

Although accurate, age estimations that use osteon counting are of reduced usefulness for individuals over the age of 60 years, at which point new Haversian systems have removed traces of preexisting osteons, resulting in an underestimation of age. It has been shown that neither Haversian canal area nor relative cortical area is significantly related to age. As a further caveat, work on osteon counting from the anterior cortex of the femur of those of Korean origin has suggested that care should be taken when using this age estimation technique for individuals over the age of 50 years.

Conclusion

Age at death is a significant factor aiding human identification efforts in forensic anthropology. It represents one of the four key parameters involved in the construction of a biological profile. The majority of methods applicable in adults involve degenerative skeletal changes that exhibit both natural and environmentally induced variability. Although taphonomical factors affect the preservation of material and may limit the methodology utilized in any given situation, analyses of as many areas of the body as is practicable should be undertaken to allow for variation that might exist within the body of any given individual.

Care has to be taken when applying any technique since research has shown that there is poor transferability of methodologies between age ranges, sexes, and populations. It is significant that even in the last decade a majority of age estimation techniques have been developed and tested on archaeological collections. The applicability of methodologies that have been developed on archaeological populations to individuals from a modern population that has undergone secular change due to improvements in diet, medical care, and changes in lifestyle must always be questioned. It should be remembered that the accuracy required for age estimation in an archaeological scenario is different from that required in a forensic situation. For a number of techniques, the prevalence of inter- and intraobserver error has been noted in the literature; again, this is an ongoing problem in anthropology. The use of criteria that are subjective and descriptive will always introduce limitations due to interobserver interpretation.

With adult age estimation techniques, accuracy rates are limited for reasons that we are unable to control; especially in relation to the analysis of unidentified remains. It is true to say not only that the optimal analysis technique should be determined on a case-led basis to enable age to be determined as accurately as possible but also that ageing techniques should be performed in a transparent manner that allows them to be applied in a way that is helpful to the judicial system.

References

Bang, G., and Ramm, E. (1970). Determination of age in humans from root dentin transparency. *Acta Odontologica Scandinavica,* 28: 3–35.

Basmajian, J. V. (1952). The depressions for the arachnoid granulations as a criterion of age. *The Anatomical Record,* 112: 843–846.

Brooks, S., and Suchey, J. (1990). Skeletal age determination based on the os pubis: A comparison of the Acsádi-Nemeskéri and Suchey-Brooks methods. *Human Evolution,* 5: 227–238.

Buckberry, J. L., and Chamberlain, A. T. (2002). Age estimation from the auricular surface of the ilium: A revised method. *American Journal of Physical Anthropology,* 119: 231–239.

Cerný, M. (1983). Our experience with estimation of an individual's age from skeletal remains of the degree of thyroid cartilage ossification. *Acta Universitatis Plackianae Olomucensisi,* 3: 121–144.

Dedouit, F., Bindel, S., Gainza, D., Blanc, A., Joffre, F., Rouge, D., and Telmon, N. (2008). Application of the İşcan method to two- and three-dimensional imaging of the sternal end of the right fourth rib. *Journal of Forensic Sciences,* 53: 288–295.

Duray, S. M., and Martel, S. S. (2006). A quantitative method for estimation of volume changes in arachnoid foveae with age. *Journal of Forensic Sciences,* 51: 238–243.

Falys, C. G., Schutkowski, H., and Weston, D. (2006). Auricular surface aging: Worse than expected? A test of the revised method on a documented historic skeletal assemblage. *American Journal of Physical Anthropology,* 130: 508–513.

Helfman, P. M., and Bada, J. L. (1976). Aspartic acid racemization in dentine as a measure of ageing. *Nature,* 262: 279–281.

Igarashi, Y., Uesu, K., Wakebe, T., and Kanazawa, E. (2005). New method for estimation of adult skeletal age at death from the morphology of the auricular surface of the ilium. *American Journal of Physical Anthropology,* 128: 324–339.

İşcan, M. Y., Loth, S. R., and Wright, R. K. (1984a). Age estimation from the rib by phase analysis: white males. *Journal of Forensic Sciences,* 29: 1094–1104.

İşcan, M. Y., Loth, S. R., and Wright, R. K. (1984b). Metamorphosis at the sternal rib end: A new method to estimate age at death in White Males. *American Journal of Physical Anthropology,* 65: 147–156.

İşcan, M. Y., Loth, S. R., and Wright, R. K. (1985). Age estimation from the rib by phase analysis: White females. *American Journal of Physical Anthropology,* 30: 853–863.

İşcan, M. Y., Loth, S. R., and Wright, R. K. (1987). Racial variation in the sternal extremity of the rib and its effect on age determination. *Journal of Forensic Sciences,* 32: 452–466.

Kerley, E. R. (1965). The microscopic determination of age in human bone. *American Journal of Physical Anthropology,* 23: 149–163.

Lamendin, H., Baccino, E., Humbert, J. F., Tavernier, J. C., Nossintchouk, R. M., and Zerilli, A. (1992). A simple technique for age estimation in adult corpses: The two criteria dental method. *Journal of Forensic Sciences,* 37: 608–611.

Loth, S. R. (1995). Age assessment of the Spitalfields cemetery population by rib phase analysis. *American Journal of Human Biology,* 7: 465–471.

Lovejoy, C. O., Meindl, R. S., Pryzbech, T. R., and Mensforth, R. P. (1985). Chronological metamorphosis of the auricular surface of the ilium: A new method for the determination of adult skeletal age at death. *American Journal of Physical Anthropology,* 68: 15–28.

Mulhern, D. M., and Jones, E. B. (2005). Test of revised method of age estimation from the auricular surface of the ilium. *American Journal of Physical Anthropology,* 126: 61–65.

Passalacqua, N. V. (2009). Forensic age-at-death estimation from the human sacrum. *Journal of Forensic Sciences,* 54: 255–262.

Schaefer, M., Black, S.M., and Scheuer, L. (2009) *Juvenile Osteology: A Laboratory and Field Manual.* London: Academic Press.

Scheuer, L., and Black, S. (2000). *Developmental juvenile osteology.* London, Academic Press.

Scheuer, L., and Black, S. M. (2004). *The juvenile skeleton.* Amsterdam, the Netherlands: Elsevier.

Todd, T. W. (1920). Age changes in the pubic bone: The male white pubis. *American Journal of Physical Anthropology,* 3: 285–334.

Todd, T. W., and Lyon, D. (1924–1925). Cranial suture closure: Its progress and age relationship. *American Journal of Physical Anthropology,* 7: 325–384.

Bibliography

General

Ajaml, M., Mody, B., and Kumar, G. (2001). Age estimation using three established methods: A study on Indian population. *Forensic Science International,* 122: 150–154.

Anderson, M. F., Anderson, D. T., and Wescott, D. J. (2010). Estimation of adult skeletal age-at-death using the Sugeno fuzzy integral. *American Journal of Physical Anthropology,* 142: 30–41.

Baccetti, T., Franchi, L., De Toffol, L., Ghiozzi, B., and Cozza, P. (2006). The diagnostic performance of chronologic age in the assessment of skeletal maturity. *Progress in Orthodontics,* 7: 176–188.

Baccino, E., and Schmitt, A. (2006). Determination of adult age at death in the forensic context. In: Schmitt, A., Cunha, E., and Pinheiro, J. (Eds.), *Forensic anthropology and medicine.* Totowa, NJ: Humana Press, 259–280.

Bogin, B., and Rios, L. (2003). Rapid morphological change in living humans: Implications for modern human origins. *Comparative Biochemistry and Physiology—Part A: Molecular and Integrative Physiology,* 136: 71–84.

Byers, S. N. (2005). *Introduction to forensic anthropology.* New York: Pearson.

Cattaneo, C. (2007). Forensic anthropology: Developments of a classical discipline in the new millennium. *Forensic Science International,* 165: 185–193.

Christensen, A. M., and Crowder, C. M. (2009). Evidentiary standards for forensic anthropology. *Journal of Forensic Sciences,* 54: 1211–1216.

Clarot, F., Le Dosseur, P., Vaz, E., and Proust, B. (2004). Skeletal maturation and ethnicity. *Legal Medicine,* 6: 141–142.

Corsini, M.-M., Schmitt, A., and Bruzek, J. (2005). Aging process variability on the human skeleton: Artificial network as an appropriate tool for age at death assessment. *Forensic Science International,* 148: 163–167.

Cox, M. (2000). Ageing adults from the skeleton. In: Cox, M., and Mays, S. (Eds.), *Human osteology in archaeology and forensic science.* London: Greenwich Medical Media, 61–82.

Cunha, E., Baccino, E., Martrille, L., Ramsthaler, F., Prieto, J., Schuliar, Y., Lynnerup, N., and Cattaneo, C. (2009). The problem of aging human remains and living individuals: A review. *Forensic Science International,* 193: 1–13.

Ferrante, L., and Cameriere, R. (2009). Statistical methods to assess the reliability of measurements in the procedures for forensic age estimation. *International Journal of Legal Medicine,* 123: 277–283.

Franklin, D. (2010). Forensic age estimation in human skeletal remains: Current concepts and future directions. *Legal Medicine,* 12: 1–7.

Grabherr, S., Cooper, C., Ulrich-Bochsler, S., Uldin, T., Ross, S., Oesterhelweg, L., Bolliger, S., Christe, A., Schnyder, P., Mangin, P., and Thali, M. (2009). Estimation of sex and age of "virtual skeletons"—a feasibility study. *European Radiology,* 19: 419–429.

Jackes, M. K. (2000). Building the bases for paleodemographic analysis: Adult age determination. In: Katzenberg, M. A., and Saunders, S. R. (Eds.), *Biological anthropology of the human skeleton.* New York: Wiley-Liss, 417–466.

Kemkes-Grottenthaler, A. (2002). Aging through the ages: Historical perspectives on age indicator methods. In: Hoppa, R. D., and Vaupel, J. W. (Eds.), *Paleodemography: Age distributions from skeletal samples.* Cambridge, UK: Cambridge University Press, 48–72.

Kimmerle, E. H., Jantz, R. L., Konigsberg, L. W., and Baraybar, J. P. (2008). Skeletal estimation and identification in American and East European populations. *Journal of Forensic Sciences,* 53: 524–532.

Kimmerle, E. H., Prince, D. A., and Berg, G. E. (2008). Inter-observer variation in methodologies involving the pubic symphysis, sternal ribs, and teeth. *Journal of Forensic Sciences,* 53: 594–600.

Konigsberg, L. W., Herrmann, N. P., Wescott, D. J., and Kimmerle, E. H. (2008). Estimation and evidence in forensic anthropology: Age-at-death. *Journal of Forensic Sciences,* 53: 541–557.

Martrille, L., Baccino, E., and Payne-James, J. (2005). Age estimation in the living. In: Payne-James, J. (Ed.), *Encyclopedia of forensic and legal medicine.* Oxford, UK: Elsevier, 17–21.

Martrille, L., Ubelaker, D. H., Cattaneo, O., C., Seguret, F., Tremblay, M., and Baccino, E. (2007). Comparison of four skeletal methods for the estimation of age at death on White and Black adults. *Journal of Forensic Sciences*, 52: 302–307.

Milner, G. R., Buikstra, J., Murray, E., and Boldsen, J. L. (2008). Transition analysis: A new approach to skeletal age estimation for anthropologists. *Proceedings of the Annual American Academy of Forensic Sciences*, 14: 28.

Nagar, Y., and Hershkovitz, I. (2004). Interrelationships between various ageing methods, and their relevance to paleodemography. *Human Evolution*, 19: 145–156.

Passalacqua, N. V. (2010). The utility of the Samworth and Gowland age-at-death "lookup" tables in forensic anthropology. *Journal of Forensic Sciences*, 55: 482–487.

Ritz-Timme, S., Cattaneo, C., Collins, M. J., Waite, E. R., Schutz, H. W., Kaatsch, H. J., and Borrman, H. I. M. (2000). Age estimation: The state of the art in relation to the specific demands of forensic practise. *International Journal of Legal Medicine*, 113: 129–136.

Rogers, T. (2009). Skeletal age estimation. In: Blau, S., and Ubelaker, D. H. (Eds.), *Handbook of forensic anthropology and archaeology*. Walnut Creek, CA: West Coast Press, 208–221.

Rosing, F. W., Graw, M., Marre, B., Ritz-Timme, S., Rothschild, M. A., Rotzscher, K., Schmeling, A., Schroder, I., and Geserick, G. (2007). Recommendations for the forensic diagnosis of sex and age from skeletons. *HOMO—Journal of Comparative Human Biology*, 58: 75–89.

Samworth, R., and Gowland, R. (2007). Estimation of adult skeletal age-at-death: Statistical assumptions and applications. *International Journal of Osteoarchaeology*, 17: 174–188.

Scheuer, J. L. (2002). Application of osteology to forensic medicine. *Clinical Anatomy*, 15: 297–312.

Schmeling, A., Geserick, G., Reisinger, W., and Olze, A. (2007). Age estimation. *Forensic Science International*, 165: 178–181.

Schmeling, A., Grundmann, C., Fuhrmann, A., Kaatsch, H. J., Knell, B., Ramsthaler, F., Reisinger, W., Riepert, T., Ritz-Timme, S., Rosing, F., Rotzscher, K., and Geserick, G. (2008). Criteria for age estimation in living individuals. *International Journal of Legal Medicine*, 122: 457–460.

Schmeling, A., Olze, A., Reisinger, W., and Geserick, G. (2001). Age estimation of living people undergoing criminal proceedings. *The Lancet*, 358: 89–90.

Schmeling, A., Olze, A., Reisinger, W., and Geserick, G. (2005). Forensic age estimation and ethnicity. *Legal Medicine*, 7: 134–137.

Schmeling, A., Olze, A., Reisinger, W., Konig, M., and Geserick, G. (2003). Statistical analysis and verification of forensic age estimation of living persons in the Institute of Legal Medicine of the Berlin University Hospital Charité. *Legal Medicine*, 5: S367-S371.

Schmeling, A., Olze, A., Reisinger, W., Rosing, F. W., and Geserick, G. (2003). Forensic age diagnostics of living individuals in criminal proceedings. *Homo*, 54: 162–169.

Schmeling, A., Reisinger, W., Geserick, G., and Olze, A. (2005). The current state of forensic age estimation of live subjects for the purpose of criminal prosecution. *Forensic Science, Medicine and Pathology*, 1: 239–246.

Schmeling, A., Reisinger, W., Loreck, D., Vendura, K., Markus, W., and Geserick, G. (2000). Effects of ethnicity on skeletal maturation: consequences for forensic age estimations. *International Journal of Legal Medicine*, 113: 253–258.

Schmitt, A., Murail, P., Cunha, E., and Rouge, D. (2002). Variability of the pattern of aging on the human skeleton: Evidence from bone indicators and implications on age at death estimation. *Journal of Forensic Sciences*, 47: 1203–1209.

Schmitt, A., Wapler, U., Couallier, V., and Cunha, E. (2007). Are bone losers distinguishable from bone formers in a skeletal series? Implications for adult age at death assessment methods. *HOMO—Journal of Comparative Human Biology*, 58: 53–66.

Stavrianos, C., Mastagas, D., Stavrianou, I., and Karaiskou, O. (2008). Dental age estimation of adults: A review of methods and principals. *Research Journal of Medical Sciences*, 2: 258–268.

Steadman, D. W., Adams, B. J., and Konigsberg, L. W. (2006). Statistical basis for positive identification in forensic anthropology. *American Journal of Physical Anthropology*, 131: 15–26.

Ubelaker, D. H. (2008). Issues in the global applications of methodology in forensic anthropology. *Journal of Forensic Sciences*, 53: 606–607.

White, T. D. (2000). *Human osteology.* New York: Academic Press.

Willems, G. (2001). A review of the most commonly used dental age estimation techniques. *Journal of Forensic Odontostomatology*, 19: 9–17.

Wittwer-Backofen, U., Buckberry, J., Czarnetzki, A., Doppler, S., Grupe, G., Hotz, G., Kemkes, A., and Weise, S. (2008). Basics in paleodemography: A comparison of age indicators applied to the early medieval skeletal sample of Lauchheim. *American Journal of Physical Anthropology*, 137: 384–396.

Wright, L. E., and Yoder, C. J. (2003). Recent progress in bioarchaeology: Approaches to the osteological paradox. *Journal of Archaeological Research*, 11: 43–70.

Ossification Patterns

Albert, A. M. (1998). The use of vertebral ring epiphyseal union for age estimation in two cases of unknown identity. *Forensic Science International*, 97: 11–20.

Albert, M., Mulhern, D., Torpey, M. A., and Boone, E. (2010). Age estimation using thoracic and first two lumbar vertebral ring epiphyseal union. *Journal of Forensic Sciences*, 55: 287–294.

Bilkey, S. W., Marak, F. K., and Singh, S. (2007). Age determination in girls of northeastern region of India. *Journal of Indian Academy of Forensic Medicine*, 29: 971–973.

Cardoso, H.F. (2008). Age estimation of adolescent and young adult male and female skeletons. II—Epiphyseal union at the upper limb and scapular girdle in a modern Portuguese skeletal sample. *American Journal of Physical Anthropology*, 137: 97–105.

Cardoso, H. F. (2008). Epiphyseal union at the innominate and lower limb in a modern Portuguese skeletal sample, and age estimation in adolescent and young adult male and female skeletons. *American Journal of Physical Anthropology*, 135: 161–170.

Cerný, M. (1983). Our experience with estimation of an individual's age from skeletal remains of the degree of thyroid cartilage ossification. *Acta Universitatis Plackianae Olomucensisi,* 3: 121–144.

Charles, Y. P., Dimeglio, A., Canavese, F., and Daures, J. P. (2007). Skeletal age assessment from the olecranon for idiopathic scoliosis at Risser grade 0. *Journal of Bone and Joint Surgery,* 89: 2737–2744.

Dang-Tran, K.-D., Dedouit, F., Joffre, F., Rouge, D., Rousseau, H., and Telmon, N. (2010). Thyroid cartilage ossification and multislice computed tomography examination: A useful tool for age assessment? *Journal of Forensic Sciences,* 55: 677–683.

De La Grandmaison, G. L., Banasr, A., and Durigon, M. (2003). Age estimation using radiographic analysis of laryngeal cartilage. *American Journal of Forensic Medicine and Pathology,* 24: 96–99.

Gautum, R. S., Shah, G. V., Jadav, H. R., and Gohil, B. J. (2003). The human sternum—as an index of age and sex. *Journal of the Anatomical Society of India,* 52: 1–12.

Gupta, A., Kohi, A., Aggarwal, N. K., and Banerjee, K. K. (2008). Study of age of fusion of hyoid bone. *Legal Medicine,* 10: 253–256.

Kahana, T., Birkby, W. H., Goldin, L., and Hiss, J. (2003). Estimation of age in adolescents—The basilar synchondrosis. *Journal of Forensic Sciences,* 48: 504–508.

Kellinghaus, M., Schulz, R., Vieth, V., Schmidt, S., and Schmeling, A. (2010). Forensic age estimation in living subjects based on the ossification status of the medial clavicular epiphysis as revealed by thin-slice multidetector computed tomography. *International Journal of Legal Medicine,* 124: 149–154.

Kotwicki, T. (2008). Improved accuracy in Risser sign grading with lateral spinal radiography. *European Spine Journal,* 18: 1676–1685.

Langley-Shirley, N., and Jantz, R. L. (2010). A Bayesian approach to age estimation in modern Americans from the clavicle. *Journal of Forensic Sciences,* 55: 571–583.

Modi, H. N., Modi, C., Suh, S. W., Yang, J.-H., and Hong, J.-Y. (2009). Correlation and comparison of Risser sign versus bone age determination (TW3) between children with and without scoliosis in a Korean population. *Journal of Orthopaedic Surgery,* 4: 1–8.

Muhler, M., Schulz, R., Schmidt, S., Schmeling, A., and Reisinger, W. (2006). The influence of slice thickness on assessment of clavicle ossification in forensic age diagnostics. *International Journal of Legal Medicine,* 120: 15–17.

Quirmbach, F., Ramsthaler, F., and Verhoff, M. A. (2009). Evaluation of the ossification of the medial clavicular epiphysis with a digital ultrasonic system to determine the age threshold of 21 years. *International Journal of Legal Medicine,* 123: 241–245.

Reem, J., Carney, J., Stanley, M., and Cassidy, J. (2009). Risser sign inter-rater and intra-rater agreement: Is the Risser sign reliable? *Skeletal Radiology,* 38: 371–378.

Rios, L., and Cardoso, H. F. V. (2009). Age estimation from stages of union of the vertebral epiphyses of the ribs. *American Journal of Physical Anthropology,* 140: 265–274.

Schaefer, M. C. (2008). A summary of epiphyseal union timings in Bosnian males. *International Journal of Osteoarchaeology,* 18: 536–545.

Schaefer, M. C., and Black, S. M. (2005). Comparison of ages of epiphyseal union in North American and Bosnian skeletal material. *Journal of Forensic Sciences,* 50: 777–784.

Scheuer, L., and Black, S. (2000). *Developmental juvenile osteology*. London: Academic Press.

Scheuer, L., and Black, S. M. (2004). *The juvenile skeleton*. Amsterdam, the Netherlands: Elsevier.

Schidt, S., Muhler, M., Schmeling, A., Reisinger, W., and Schulz, R. (2007). Magnetic resonance imaging of the clavicular ossification. *International Journal of Legal Medicine*, 121: 321-324.

Schmeling, A., Schulz, R., Reisinger, W., Muhler, M., Wernecke, K. D., and Geserick, G. (2004). Studies on the time frame for ossification of the medial clavicular epiphyseal cartilage in conventional radiography. *International Journal of Legal Medicine*, 118: 5–8.

Schulz, D., Rother, U., Fuhrmann, A., Richel, S., Faulmann, G., and Heiland, M. (2006). Correlation of age and ossification of the medial clavicular epiphysis using computed tomography. *Forensic Science International*, 158: 184–189.

Schulz, R., Muhler, M., Mutze, S., Schmidt, S., Reisinger, W., and Schmeling, A. (2005). Studies on the time frame for ossification of the medial epiphysis of the clavicle as revealed by CT scans. *International Journal of Legal Medicine*, 119: 142–145.

Schulz, R., Muhler, K. D., Reisinger, M., Schmidt, S., and Schmeling, A. (2008). Radiographic staging of ossification of the medial clavicular epiphysis. *International Journal of Legal Medicine*, 122: 55–58.

Schulz, R., Zwiesigk, P., Schiborr, M., Schmidt, S., and Schmeling, A. (2008). Ultrasound studies on the time course of clavicular ossification. *International Journal of Legal Medicine*, 122: 163–167.

Shirley, N. R. (2009). Age and sex estimation from the human clavicle: An investigation of traditional and novel methods. *Unpublished Thesis, University of Tennessee, Knoxville*.

The Skull

Akhlaghi, M., Taghaddosinejad, F., Sheikhazadi, A., Vallzadeh, B., and Rezazadeh Shojaei, S. M. (2010). Age-at-death estimation based on the macroscopic examination of Spheno-occipital sutures. *Journal of Forensic and Legal Medicine*, doi: 10.1016/j.jflm.2010.04.009.

Basmajian, J. V. (1952). The depressions for the arachnoid granulations as a criterion of age. *The Anatomical Record*, 112: 843–846.

Beauthier, J.-P., Lefevre, P., Meunier, M., Orban, R., Polet, C., Werquin, J.-P., and Quatrehomme, G. (2010). Palatine sutures as age indicator: A controlled study in the elderly. *Journal of Forensic Sciences*, 55, 153–158.

Dorandeu, A., Coulibaly, B., Piercecchi-Marti, M.-D., Bartoli, C., Gaudart, J., Baccino, E., and Leonetti, G. (2008). Age-at-death estimation based on the study of frontosphenoidal sutures. *Forensic Science International*, 177: 47–51.

Dorandeu, A., De La Grandmaison, G., Coulibaly, B., Durigon, M., Piercecchi-Marti, M.-D., Baccino, E., and Leonetti, G. (2009). Value of histological study in the fronto-sphenoidal suture for the age estimation at the time of death. *Forensic Science International*, 191: 64–69.

Garvin, H. M. (2008). Ossification of laryngeal structures as indicators of age. *Journal of Forensic Sciences*, 53: 1023–1027.

Ginter, J. K. (2005). A test of the effectiveness of the revised maxillary suture oblitera-tion method in estimating adult age at death. *Journal of Forensic Sciences*, 50: 1303–1309.

Gupta, A., Kohli, A., Aggarwal, N. K., and Bannerjee, K. K. (2008). Study of age of fusion of hyoid bone. *Legal Medicine*, 10: 253–256.

Harth, S., Obert, M., Ramsthaler, F., Reub, C., Traupe, H., and Verhoff, M. A. (2010). Ossification degrees of cranial sutures determined with flat-panel computed tomography: Narrowing the age estimate with extrema. *Journal of Forensic Sciences*, 55: 690–694.

Harth, S., Obert, M., Ramsthaler, F., Reuss, C., Traupe, H., and Verhoff, M. A. (2009). Estimating age by assessing the ossification degree of cranial sutures with the aid of flat-panel-CT. *Legal Medicine (Tokyo)*, 11(Suppl. 1), S186–S189.

Key, C. A., Aiello, L. C., and Molleson, T. (1994). Cranial suture closure and its implica-tions for age estimation. *International Journal of Osteoarchaeology*, 4: 193–207.

Lynnerup, N., and Jacobsen, J. C. B. (2003). Brief communication: Age and fractal dimensions of human sagittal and coronal sutures. *American Journal of Physical Anthropology*, 121: 332–336.

Mann, R. W., Jantz, R. L., Bass, W. M., and Willey, P. S. 1991. Maxillary suture oblit-eration: A visual method for estimating skeletal age. *Journal of Forensic Sciences*, 36: 781–791.

Mann, R. W., Symes, A. A., and Bass, W. M. (1987). Maxillary suture obliteration: Ageing the human skeleton based on intact or fragmentary maxilla. *Journal of Forensic Sciences*, 32: 148–157.

Meindl, R. S., and Lovejoy, C. O. (1985). Ectocranial suture closure: A revised method for the determination of skeletal age at death based on the lateral-anterior sutures. *American Journal of Physical Anthropology*, 68: 57–66.

Sabini, R. C., and Elkowitz, D. E. (2006). Significance of differences in patency among cranial sutures. *Journal of American Osteopathic Association*, 106: 600–604.

Sahni, D., Jit, I., and Sanjeev, N. (2005). Time of closure of cranial sutures in north-west Indian adults. *Forensic Science International*, 148: 199–205.

Saito, K., Shimizu, Y., and Ooya, K. (2002). Age-related morphological changes in squamous and parietomastoid sutures of human cranium. *Cells Tissues Organs*, 170: 266–273.

Todd, T. W., and Lyon, D. (1924–1925). Cranial suture closure: Its progress and age relationship. *American Journal of Physical Anthropology*, 7: 325–384.

Dentition

Acharya, A. B. (2010). A new digital approach for measuring dentin translucency in forensic age estimation. *American Journal of Forensic Medicine and Pathology*, 31: 133–137.

Acharya, A., and Vimi, S. (2009). Effectiveness of Bang and Ramm's formulae in age assessment of Indians from dentin translucency length. *International Journal of Legal Medicine*, 123:483–488.

Aggarawal, P., Saxena, S., and Bansal, P. (2008). Incremental lines in root cementum of human teeth: an approach to their role in age assessment using polarizing microscopy. *Indian Journal of Dental Research,* 19: 326–330.

Arany, S., Ohtani, S., Yoshioka, N., and Gonmori, K. (2004). Age estimation from aspartic acid racemization of root dentin by internal standard method. *Forensic Science International,* 141: 127–130.

Babshet, M., Acharya, A. B., and Naikmasur, V. G. (2010). Age estimation in Indians from pulp/tooth area ratio of mandibular canines. *Forensic Science International,* 197: 125.e1–125.e4.

Ball, J. (2002). A critique of age estimation using attrition as the sole indicator. *Journal of Forensic Odontostomatology,* 20: 38–42.

Bang, G., and Ramm, E. (1970). Determination of age in humans from root dentin transparency. *Acta Odontologica Scandinavica,* 28: 3–35.

Blankenship, J. A., Mincer, H. H., Anderson, K. M., Woods, M. A., and Burton, E. L. (2007). Third molar development in the estimation of chronologic age in American Blacks as compared with Whites. *Journal of Forensic Sciences,* 52: 428–433.

Bolanos, M. V., Moussa, H., Manrique, M. C., and Bolanos, M. J. (2003). Radiographic evaluation of third molar development in Spanish children and young people. *Forensic Science International,* 133: 212–219.

Bosmans, N., Ann, P., Aly, M., and Willems, G. (2005). The application of Kvaal's dental age calculation technique on panoramic dental radiographs. *Forensic Science International,* 153: 208–212.

Brkic, H., Milicevic, M., and Petrovecki, M. (2006). Age estimation methods using anthropological parameters on human teeth. *Forensic Science International,* 162: 13–16.

Brkic, H., Strinovic, D., Kubat, M., and Petrovecki, V. (2000). Odontological identification of human remains from mass graves in Croatia. *International Journal of Legal Medicine,* 114: 19–22.

Cameriere, R., Brogi, G., Ferrante, L., Mirtella, D., Vutaggio, C., Cingolani, M., and Fornaciari, G. (2006). Reliability in age determination by pulp/tooth ratio in upper canines in skeletal remains. *Journal of Forensic Sciences,* 51: 861–863.

Cameriere, R., Cunha, E., Sassaroli, E., Nuzzolese, E., and Ferrante, L. (2009). Age estimation by pulp/tooth area ratio in canines: Study of a Portuguese sample to test Cameriere's method. *Forensic Science International,* 193: 128.e1–128.e6.

Cameriere, R., Ferrante, L., Belcastro, M. G., Bonfiglioli, B., Rastelli, E., and Cingolani, M. (2007a). Age estimation by pulp/tooth ratio in canines by mesial and vestibular peri-apical x-rays. *Journal of Forensic Sciences,* 52: 1151–1155.

Cameriere, R., Ferrante, L., Belcastro, M. G., Bonfiglioli, B., Rastelli, E., and Cingolani, M. (2007b). Age estimation by pulp/tooth ratio in canines by peri-apical x-rays. *Journal of Forensic Sciences,* 52: 166–170.

Cameriere, R., Ferrante, L., and Cingolani, M. (2004a). Precision and reliability of pulp/tooth area ratio (RA) of second molar as indicator of adult age. *Journal of Forensic Sciences,* 49: 1–5.

Cameriere, R., Ferrante, L., and Cingolani, M. (2004b). Variations in pulp/tooth area ratio as an indicator of age: A preliminary study. *Journal of Forensic Sciences,* 49: 1–3.

Cardoso, H.F.V. (2009). Accuracy of developing tooth length as an estimate of age in human skeletal remains. The permanent dentition. *American Journal of Medicine and Pathology,* 30: 127–133.

Czermak, A., Czermak, A., Ernst, H., and Grupe, G. (2006). A new method for the automated age-at-death evaluation by tooth-cementum annulation (TCA). *Anthropologischer Anzeiger,* 64: 25–40.

De Salvia, A., Calzetta, C., Orrico, M., and De Leo, D. (2004). Third mandibular molar radiological development as an indicator of chronological age in a European population. *Forensic Science International,* 146: S9–S12.

Dhanjal, K. S., Bhardwaj, M. K., and Liversidge, H. M. (2006). Reproducibility of radiographic stage assessment of third molars. *Forensic Science International,* 159: S74–S77.

Dobberstein, R. C., Huppertz, J., Von Wurmb-Schwark, N., and Ritz-Timme, S. (2008). Degradation of biomolecules in artificially and naturally aged teeth: Implications for age estimation based on aspartic acid racemization and DNA analysis. *Forensic Science International,* 179: 181–191.

Drusini, A. G. (1991). Age-related changes in root transparency of teeth in males and females. *American Journal of Human Biology,* 3: 629–637.

Foti, B., Adalian, P., Signoli, M., Ardagna, Y., Dutour, O., and Leonetti, G. (2001). Limits of the Lamendin method in age determination. *Forensic Science International,* 122: 101–106.

Frucht, S., Schneglelsberg, C., Sculte-Monting, J., Rose, E., and Jonas, I. (2000). Dental age in Southwest Germany. *Journal of Orofacial Orthopedics,* 61: 318–329.

Gonzalez-Colmenares, G., Botella-Lopez, M. C., Moreno-Rueda, G., and Fernandez-Cardenete, J. R. (2007). Age estimation by a dental method: A comparison of Lamendin's and Prince and Ubelaker's technique. *Journal of Forensic Sciences,* 52: 1156–1160.

Griffin, R. C., Chamberlain, A. T., Hotz, G., Penkman, K. E. H., and Collins, M. J. (2009). Age estimation of archaeological remains using amino acid racemization in dental enamel: A comparison of morphological, biochemical, and known ages-at-death. *American Journal of Physical Anthropology,* 140: 244–252.

Griffin, R. C., Moody, H., Penkman, K. E., and Collins, M. J. (2008). The application of amino acid racemization in the acid soluble fraction of enamel to the estimation of the age of human teeth. *Forensic Science International,* 175: 11–16.

Griffin, R. C., Penkman, K. E. H., Moody, H., and Collins, M. J. (2010). The impact of random natural variability on aspartic acid racemization ratios in enamel from different types of human teeth. *Forensic Science International,* 200: 148–152.

Gunst, K., Mesotten, K., Carbonez, A., and Willems, G. (2003). Third molar root development in relation to chronological age: a large sample sized retrospective study. *Forensic Science International,* 136: 52–57.

Helfman, P. M., and Bada, J. L. (1976). Aspartic acid racemization in dentine as a measure of ageing. *Nature,* 262: 279–281.

Heuze, Y., and Braga, J. (2008). Application of non-adult Bayesian dental age assessment methods to skeletal remains: The Spitalfields collection. *Journal of Archaeological Science,* 35: 368–375.

Jankauskas, R., Barakauskas, S., and Bojarun, R. (2001). Incremental lines of dental cementum in biological age estimation. *HOMO—Journal of Comparative Human Biology*, 52: 59–71.

Kagerer, P., and Grupe, G. (2001). Age-at-death diagnosis and determination of life-history parameters by incremental lines in human dental cementum as an identification aid. *Forensic Science International*, 118: 75–82.

Kasetty, S., Rammanohar, M., and Ragavendra, T. R. (2010). Dental cementum in age estimation: A polarized light and stereomicroscopic study. *Journal of Forensic Sciences*, 55: 779–783.

Kasper, K. A., Austin, D., Kvanli, A. H., Rios, T. R., and Senn, D. R. (2009). Reliability of third molar development for age estimation in a Texas Hispanic population: A comparison study. *Journal of Forensic Sciences*, 54: 651–657.

Kim, Y.-K., Kho, H.-S., and Lee, K.-H. (2000). Age estimation by occlusal tooth wear. *Journal of Forensic Sciences*, 45: 303–309.

Kimmerle, E. H., Prince, D. A., and Berg, G. E. (2008). Inter-observer variation in methodologies involving the pubic symphysis, sternal ribs and teeth. *Journal of Forensic Sciences*, 53: 594–600.

Konigsberg, L. W., Herrmann, N. P., Wescott, D. J., and Kimmerle, E. H. (2008). Estimation and evidence in forensic anthropology: Age-at-death. *Journal of Forensic Sciences*, 53: 541–557.

Lamendin, H., Baccino, E., Humbert, J. F., Tavernier, J. C., Nossintchouk, R. M., and Zerilli, A. (1992). A simple technique for age estimation in adult corpses: The two criteria dental method. *Journal of Forensic Sciences*, 37: 608–611.

Landa, M.I., Garamendi, P.M., Botella, M. C., and Aleman, I. (2009). Application of the method of Kvall et al. To digital orthopantomograms. *International Journal of Legal Medicine*, 123: 123–128.

Laskarin, M., Brkic, H., Pichler, G., and Bukovic, D. (2006). The influence of age on tooth root colour changes. *Collegium Antropologicum*, 30: 807–810.

Lee, S.-H., Lee, J.-Y., Park, H.-K., and Kim, Y.-K. (2009). Development of third molars in Korean juveniles and adolescents. *Forensic Science International*, 188: 107–111.

Legovi, M., Sasso, A., Legovi, I., Brumini, G., Abov, T., Laj, M., Vanoiodura, I., and Lapter, M. (2010). The reliability of chronological age determination by means of mandibular third molar development in subjects in Croatia. *Journal of Forensic Sciences*, 55: 14–18.

Lewis, J. M., and Senn, D. R. (2010). Dental age estimation utilizing third molar development: A review of principles, methods, and population studies used in the United States. *Forensic Science International*, doi: 10.1016/j.forsciint.2010.04.042.

Liversidge, H. M., Lyons, F., and Hector, M. P. (2003). The accuracy of three methods of age estimation using radiographic measurements of developing teeth. *Forensic Science International*, 131: 22–29.

Lynnerup, N., Kjeldsen, H., Zweihoff, R., Heegaard, S., Jacobsen, C., and Heinemeier, J. (2010). Ascertaining year of birth/age at death in forensic cases: review of conventional methods and methods allowing for absolute chronology. *Forensic Science International*, doi: 10.1016/j.forsciint.2010.03.026.

Martin-De Las Heras, S., Garcia-Fortea, P., Ortega, A., Zodocovich, S., and Valenzuela, A. (2008). Third molar development according to chronological age in populations from Spanish and Magrebian origin. *Forensic Science International,* 174: 47–53.

Martin-De Las Heras, S., Valenzuela, A., Bellinni, R., Salas, C., Rubino, M., and Garcia, J. A. (2003). Objective measurement of dental color for age estimation by spectroradiometry. *Forensic Science International,* 132: 57–62.

Mays, S. (2002). The relationship between molar wear and age in an early 19th century AD archaeological human skeletal series of documented age at death. *Journal of Archaeological Science,* 29: 861–871.

Megyesi, M.S., Ubelaker, D. H., and Sauer, N.J. (2006). Test of the Lamendin aging method on two historic skeletal samples. *American Journal of Physical Anthropology,* 131: 363–367.

Meinl, A., Huber, C.D., Tangl, S., Gruber, G. M., Teschler-Nicola, M., and Watzek, G. (2008). Comparison of the validity of three dental methods for the estimation of age at death. *Forensic Science International,* 178: 96–105.

Meinl, A., Tangl, S., Huber, C., Maurer, B., and Watzek, G. (2007). The chronology of third molar mineralization in the Austrian population—A contribution to forensic age estimation. *Forensic Science International,* 169: 161–167.

Meinl, A., Tangl, S., Pernicka, E., Fenes, C., and Watzek, G. (2007). On the applicability of secondary dentin formation to radiological age estimation in young adults. *Journal of Forensic Sciences,* 52: 438–441.

Miles, A. E. W. (2001). The Miles method of assessing age from tooth wear revisited. *Journal of Archaeological Science,* 28: 973–982.

Monzavi, B. F., Bhodoose, A., Savabi, O., and Hasanzadeh, A. (2003). Model of age estimation based on dental factors of unknown cadavers among Iranians. *Journal of Forensic Sciences,* 48: 379–381.

Nystrom, M., Aine, L., Peck, L., Haaviko, K., and Kataja, M. (2000). Dental maturity in Finns and the problem of missing teeth. *Acta Odontologica Scandinavica,* 58: 49–56.

Ohtani, S., Abe, I., and Yamamoto, T. (2005). An application of D- and L-aspartic acid mixture as standard specimens for the chronological age estimation. *Journal of Forensic Sciences,* 50: 1298–1302.

Ohtani, S., Ito, R., and Yamamoto, T. (2003). Differences in the D/L aspartic acid ratios in dentin among different types of teeth from the same individual and estimated age. *International Journal of Legal Medicine,* 117: 149–152.

Ohtani, S., Matsushima, Y., Kobayashi, Y., and Yamamoto, T. (2002). Age estimation by measuring the racemization of aspartic acid from total amino acid content of several types of bone and rib cartilage: A preliminary account. *Journal of Forensic Sciences,* 47: 32–36.

Ohtani, S., and Yamamoto, T. (2005). Strategy for the estimation of chronological age using the aspartic acid racemization method with special reference to coefficient of correlation between D/L ratios and ages. *Journal of Forensic Sciences,* 50: 1020–1027.

Olze, A., Ishikawa, T., Zhu, B. L., Schulz, R., Heinecke, A., Maeda, H., and Schmeling, A. (2008). Studies of the chronological course of wisdom tooth eruption in a Japanese population. *Forensic Science International,* 174: 203–206.

Olze, A., Schmeling, A., Taniguchi, M., Maeda, H., Niekerk, P., Wernecke, K.-D., and Geserick, G. (2004). Forensic age estimation in living subjects: the ethnic factor in wisdom tooth mineralization. *International Journal of Legal Medicine,* 118: 170–173.

Olze, A., Van Niekerk, P., Ishikawa, T., Zhu, B., Schulz, R., Maeda, H., and Schmeling, A. (2007). Comparative study on the effect of ethnicity on wisdom tooth eruption. *International Journal of Legal Medicine,* 121: 445–448.

Orhan, K., Ozer, L., Orhan, A. I., Dogan, S., and Paksoy, C. S. (2007). Radiographic evaluation of third molar development in relation to chronological age among Turkish children and youth. *Forensic Science International,* 165: 46–51.

Paewinsky, E., Pfeiffer, H., and Brinkmann, B. (2005). Quantification of secondary dentine formation from orthopantomograms—A contribution to forensic age estimation methods in adults. *Journal of Legal Medicine,* 119: 27–30.

Pilin, A., Cabala, R., Pudil, F., and Bencko, V. (2001). The use of the D-, L- aspartic ratio in decalcified collagen from human dentin as an estimator of human age. *Journal of Forensic Sciences,* 46: 1228–1231.

Pretty, I. A. (2003). The use of dental aging techniques in forensic odontological practice. *Journal of Forensic Sciences,* 48: 1127–1132.

Prieto, J. L., Barberia, E., Ortega, R., and Magana, C. (2005). Evaluation of chronological age based on third molar development in the Spanish population. *International Journal of Legal Medicine,* 119: 349–354.

Prince, D. A., Kimmerle, E. H., and Konigsberg, L. W. (2008). A Bayesian approach to estimate skeletal age-at-death utilizing dental wear. *Journal of Forensic Sciences,* 53: 588–593.

Prince, D. A., and Konigsberg, L. W. (2008). New formulae for estimating age-at-death in the Balkans utilizing Lamendin's dental technique and Bayesian analysis. *Journal of Forensic Sciences,* 53: 578–587.

Prince, D. A., and Ubelaker, D. H. (2002). Application of Lamendin's adult dental aging technique to a diverse skeletal sample. *Journal of Forensic Sciences,* 47: 107–116.

Renz, H., and Radlanski, R.J. (2006). Incremental lines in root cementum of human teeth—A reliable age marker? *Homo,* 57: 29–50.

Reppien, K., Sejrsen, B., and Lynnerup, N. (2006). Evaluation of post-mortem estimated dental age versus real age: a retrospective 21-year study. *Forensic Science International,* 159s: s84–s88.

Rozylo-Kalinowska, I., Kiworkowa-Raczkowska, E., and Kalinowski, P. (2008). Dental age in central Poland. *Forensic Science International,* 174: 207–216.

Sajdok, J., Pilin, A., Pudil, F., Zidkova, J., and Kas, J. (2006). A new method of age estimation based on the changes in human non-collagenous proteins from dentin. *Forensic Science International,* 156: 245–249.

Sandhu, S., and Kaur, T. (2005). Radiographic evaluation of the status of third molars in Asian-Indian students. *Journal of Oral and Maxillofacial Surgery,* 63: 640–645.

Santoro, V., Lozito, P., Mastrorocco, N., and Introna, F. (2008). Morphometric analysis of third molar root development by an experimental method using digital Oothopantomographs. *Journal of Forensic Sciences,* 53: 904–909.

Schmitt, A., Saliba-Serre, B., Tremblay, M., and Martrille, L. (2010). An evaluation of statistical methods for the determination of age of death using dental root translucency and periodontosis. *Journal of Forensic Sciences,* 55: 590–596.

Solari, A. C., and Abramovitch, K. (2002). The accuracy and precision of third molar development as an indicator of chronological age in Hispanics. *Journal of Forensic Sciences,* 47: 531–535.

Solheim, T., and Vonen, A. (2006). Dental age estimation, quality assurance and age estimation of asylum seekers in Norway. *Forensic Science International,* 159: S56–S60.

Soomer, H., Ranta, H., Lincoln, M. J., Pentilla, A., and Leibur, E. (2003). Reliability and validity of eight dental age estimation methods for adults. *Journal of Forensic Sciences,* 48: 149–152.

Stavrianos, C., Mastagas, D., Stavrianou, I., and Karaiskou, O. (2008). Dental age estimation of adults: A review of methods and principals. *Research Journal of Medical Sciences,* 2: 258–268.

Takasaki, T., Tsuji, A., Ikeda, N., and Ohishi, M. (2003). Age estimation in dental pulp DNA based on human telomere shortening. *International Journal of Legal Medicine,* 117: 232–234.

Thevissen, P., Fieuws, S., and Willems, G. (2010a). Human dental age estimation using third molar developmental stages: Does a Bayesian approach outperform regression models to discriminate between juveniles and adults? *International Journal of Legal Medicine,* 124: 35–42.

Thevissen, P. W., Fieuws, S., and Willems, G. (2010b). Human third molars development: Comparison of nine country specific populations. *Forensic Science International,* doi: 10.1016/j.forsciint.2010.04.054.

Thevissen, P. W., Pittayapat, P., Fieuws, S., and Willems, G. (2009). Estimating age of majority on third molars developmental stages in young adults from Thailand using a modified scoring technique. *Journal of Forensic Sciences,* 54: 428–432.

Tranasi, M., Sberna, M. T., Zizzari, V., D'Apolito, G., Mastrangelo, F., Salini, L., Stuppia, L., and Tete, S. (2009). Microarray evaluation of age-related changes in human dental pulp. *Journal of Endodontics,* 35: 1211–1217.

Ubelaker, D. H., and Parra, R. C. (2008). Application of three dental methods of adult age estimation from intact single rooted teeth to a Peruvian sample. *Journal of Forensic Sciences,* 53: 608–611.

Valenzuela, A., Marques, T., Exposito, N., Martin-De Las Heras, S., and Garcia, G. (2002). Comparative study of efficiency of dental methods for identification of burn victims in two bus accidents in Spain. *The American Journal of Forensic Medicine and Pathology,* 23: 390–393.

Vandevoort, F. M., Bergmans, L., Van Cleynebreugel, J., Bielen, D. J., Lambrechts, P., Wevers, M., Peirs, A., and Willems, G. (2004). Age calculation using x-ray microfocus computed tomographical scanning of teeth: A pilot study. *Journal of Forensic Sciences,* 49:787–790.

Van Vlierberghe, M., Boltacz-Rzepkowska, E., Van Langenhove, L., Laszkiewicz, J., Wyns, B., Devlaminck, D., Boullart, L., Thevissen, P., and Willems, G. (2010). A comparative study of two different regression methods for radiographs in Polish youngsters estimating chronological age on third molars. *Forensic Science International,* doi: 10.1016/j.forsciint.2010.04.019.

Whittaker, D. (2000). Ageing from the dentition. In: Cox, M., and Mays, S. (Eds.), *Human osteology in archaeological and forensic science*. London: Greenwich Medical Media, 83–100.

Willems, G. (2001). A review of the most commonly used dental age estimation techniques. *Journal of Forensic Odontostomatology*, 19: 9–17.

Willems, G., Moulin-Romsee, C., and Solheim, T. (2002). Non-destructive dental-age calculation methods in adults: Intra- and inter-observer effects. *Forensic Science International*, 126: 221–226.

Wittwer-Backofen, U., Gampe, J., and Vaupel, J. W. (2004). Tooth cementum annulation for age estimation: Results from a large known-age validation study. *American Journal of Physical Anthropology*, 123: 119–129.

Yang, F., Jacobs, R., and Willems, G. (2006). Dental age estimation through volume matching of teeth imaged by cone-beam CT. *Forensic Science International*, 159: S78–S83.

Yekkala, R., Meers, C., Van Schepdael, A., Hoogmartens, J., Lambrichts, I., and Willems, G. (2006). Racemization of aspartic acid from human dentin in the estimation of chronological age. *Forensic Science International*, 159: S89–S94.

Yun, J.-I., Lee, J.-Y., Chung, J.-W., Kho, H.-S., and Kim, Y.-K. (2007). Age estimation of Korean adults by occlusal tooth wear. *Journal of Forensic Sciences*, 52: 678–683.

Zeng, D., Wu, Z., and Cui, M. (2010). Chronological age estimation of third molar mineralization of Han in southern China. *International Journal of Legal Medicine*, 124: 119–123.

Ribs

Aktas, E. O., Kocak, A., Aktas, S., and Yemiscigil, A. (2004). Intercostal variation for age estimation—are the standards for the right 4th rib applicable for other ribs? *Collegium Anthropologicum*, 28(Suppl. 2), 267–272.

Digangi, E. A., Bethard, J. D., Kimmerle, E. H., and Konigsberg, L. W. (2009). A new method for estimating age-at-death from the first rib. *American Journal of Physical Anthropology*, 138: 164–176.

Fanton, L., Gustin, M.-P., Paultre, U., Schrag, B., and Malicier, D. (2010). Critical study of observation of the sternal end of the right fourth rib. *Journal of Forensic Sciences*, 55: 467–472.

Hartnett, K. M. (2010). Analysis of age-at-death estimation using data from a new, modern autopsy sample—Part II: Sternal end of the fourth rib. *Journal of Forensic Sciences*, doi: 10.1111/j.1556-4029.2010.01415.x.

Kunos, C. A., Simpson, S. W., Russell, K. F., and Hershkovitz, I. (1999). First rib metamorphosis: Its possible utility for human age-at-death estimation. *American Journal of Physical Anthropology*, 110: 303–323.

Kurki, H. (2005). Use of the first rib for adult age estimation: A test of one method. *International Journal of Osteoarchaeology*, 15: 342–350.

Oettle, A. C., and Steyn, M. (2000). Age estimation from sternal ends of ribs by phase analysis in South African Blacks. *Journal of Forensic Sciences*, 45: 1071–1079.

Rejtarova, O., Hejna, P., Soukup, T., and Kuchar, M. (2009). Age and sexually dimorphic changes in costal cartilages. A preliminary microscopic study. *Forensic Science International*, 193: 72–78.

Schmitt, A., and Murail, P. (2004). Is the first rib a reliable indicator of age at death assessment? Test of the method developed by Kunos et al. (1999). *HOMO— Journal of Comparative Human Biology,* 54: 207–214.

Verzeletti, A., Cassina, M., Micheli, L., Conti, A., and De Ferrari, F. (2010). Age estimation from the rib by components method analysis in white males. *American Journal of Forensic Medicine and Pathology,* 31: 27–33.

Yoder, C., Ubelaker, D. H., and Powell, J. F. (2001). Examination of variation in sternal rib end morphology relevant to age assessment. *Journal of Forensic Sciences,* 46: 223–227.

Pelvic Morphology

Barrier, P., Dedouit, F., Braga, J., Joffre, F., Rouge, D., Rousseau, H., and Telmon, N. (2009). Age at death estimation using multislice computed tomography reconstructions of the posterior pelvis. *Journal of Forensic Sciences,* 54: 773–778.

Belcastro, M. G., Rastelli, E., and Marriotti, V. (2008). Variation of the degree of sacral body fusion in adulthood in two European modern skeletal collections. *American Journal of Physical Anthropology,* 135: 149–160.

Berg, G. E. (2008). Pubic bone age estimation in adult women. *Journal of Forensic Sciences,* 53: 569–577.

Brooks, S., and Suchey, J. (1990). Skeletal age determination based on the os pubis: A comparison of the Acsádi-Nemeskéri and Suchey-Brooks methods. *Human Evolution,* 5: 227–238.

Djuric, M., Djonic, D., Nikolic, S., Popovic, D., and Marinkovic, J. (2007). Evaluation of the Suchey-Brooks method for aging skeletons in the Balkans. *Journal of Forensic Sciences,* 52: 21–23.

Ferrant, O., Rouge-Maillart, C., Guittet, L., Papin, F., Clin, B., Fau, G., and Telmon, N. (2009). Age at death estimation of adult males using coxal bone and CT scan: A preliminary study. *Forensic Science International,* 186: 14–21.

Hens, S. M., Rastelli, E., and Belcastro, G. (2008). Age estimation from the human os coxa: A test on a documented Italian collection. *Journal of Forensic Sciences,* 53: 1040–1043.

Hoppa, R. D. (2000). Population variation in osteological aging criteria: An example from the pubic symphysis. *American Journal of Physical Anthropology,* 111: 185–191.

Judd, M. A. (2010). Pubic symphyseal face eburnation: an Egyptian sport story? *International Journal of Osteoarchaeology,* 20: 280–290.

Kimmerle, E. H., Konigsberg, L. W., Jantz, R. L., and Baraybar, J. P. (2008). Analysis of age-at-death estimation through the use of pubic symphyseal data. *Journal of Forensic Sciences,* 53: 558–568.

Kimmerle, E. H., Prince, D. A., and Berg, G. E. (2008). Inter-observer variation in methodologies involving the pubic symphysis, sternal ribs and teeth. *Journal of Forensic Sciences,* 53: 594–600.

Nagaoka, T., and Hirata, K. (2008). Demographic structure of skeletal populations in historic Japan: a new estimation of adult age-at-death distributions based on the auricular surface of the ilium. *Journal of Archaeological Science*, 35: 1370–1377.

Osborne, D. L., Simmons, T. L., and Nawrocki, S. P. (2004). Reconsidering the auricular surface as an indicator of age at death. *Journal of Forensic Sciences*, 49: 905–911.

Overbury, R. S., Cabo, L. L., Dirkmaat, D. C., and Symes, S. A. (2009). Asymmetry of the os pubis: Implications for the Suchey-Brooks method. *American Journal of Physical Anthropology*, 139: 261–268.

Rios, L., Weisensee, K., and Rissech, C. (2008). Sacral fusion as an aid in age estimation. *Forensic Science International*, 180: 111.e1–111.e7.

Rissech, C., Estabrook, G. F., Cunha, E., and Malgosa, A. (2006). Using the acetabulum to estimate age at death of adult males. *Journal of Forensic Sciences*, 51: 213–229.

Rissech, C., Estabrook, G. F., Cunha, E., and Malgosa, A. (2007). Estimation of age-at-death for adult males using the acetabulum, applied to four western European populations. *Journal of Forensic Sciences*, 52: 774–778.

Rissech, C., and Malgosa, A. (2005). Ilium growth study: applicability in sex and age diagnosis. *Forensic Science International*, 147: 165–174.

Rouge-Maillart, C., Jousset, N., Vielle, B., Gaudin, A., and Telmon, N. (2007). Contribution of the study of acetabulum for the estimation of adult subjects. *Forensic Science International*, 171: 103–110.

Rouge-Maillart, C., Telmon, N., Rissech, C., Malgosa, A., and Rouge, D. (2004). The determination of male adult age at death by central and posterior coxal analysis—a preliminary study. *Journal of Forensic Sciences*, 49: 208–214.

Rouge-Maillart, C., Vielle, B., Jousset, N., Chappard, D., Telmon, N., and Cunha, E. (2009). Development of a method to estimate skeletal age at death in adults using the acetabulum and the auricular surface on a Portuguese population. *Forensic Science International*, 188: 91–95.

Schmitt, A. (2004). Age-at-death assessment using the os pubis and the auricular surface of the ilium: A test on an identified Asian sample. *International Journal of Osteoarchaeology*, 14: 1–6.

Sharma, G., Gargi, J., Kalsey, G., Singh, D., Rai, H., and Sandhu, R. (2008). Determination of age from pubic symphysis: An autopsy study. *Medicine, Science, and the Law*, 48: 163–169.

Sholts, S. (2008). Age-related changes in the pubic symphysis: A topographical approach. *American Journal of Physical Anthropology*, 135: 193.

Sinha, A., and Gupta, V. (1995). A study on estimation of age from pubic symphysis. *Forensic Science International*, 75: 73–78.

Sitchon, M. L., and Hoppa, R. D. (2005). Assessing age-related morphology of the pubic symphysis from digital images versus direct observation. *Journal of Forensic Sciences*, 50: 791–795.

Sugiyama, S., Tatsumi, S., Noda, H., Yamaguchi, M., Furutani, A., and Yoshimura, M. (1995). Estimation of age from soft x-ray findings of Japanese pubic symphysis based on image processing. *The Japanese Journal of Legal Medicine*, 49: 294–298.

Telmon, N., Gaston, A., Chemla, P., Blanc, A., Joffre, F., and Rouge, D. (2005). Application of the Suchey-Brooks method to three-dimensional imaging of the pubic symphysis. *Journal of Forensic Sciences,* 50: 507–512.

Todd, T. W. (1920). Age changes in the pubic bone: The male white pubis. *American Journal of Physical Anthropology,* 3: 285–334.

Histology

Boel, L. W., Boldsen, J. L., and Melsen, F. (2007). Double lamellae in trabecular osteons: Towards a new method for age estimation by bone microscopy. *HOMO—Journal of Comparative Human Biology,* 58: 269–277.

Britz, H. M., Thomas, C. D. L., Clement, J. G., and Cooper, D. M. L. (2009). The relation of femoral osteon geometry to age, sex, height and weight. *Bone,* 45: 77–83.

Cho, H., Stout, S. D., Madsen, R. W., and Streeter, M. A. (2002). Population-specific histological age-estimating method: A model for known African-American and European-American skeletal remains. 47: 12–18.

Crowder, C. (2009). Histological age estimation. In: Blau, S., and Ubelaker, D. H. (Eds.), *Handbook of forensic anthropology and archaeology.* Walnut Creek, CA: Left Coast Press, 222–235.

Crowder, C., and Rosella, L. (2007). Assessment of intra- and intercostal variation in rib histomorphometry: Its impact on evidentiary examination. *Journal of Forensic Sciences,* 52: 271–276.

Han, S.-H., Kim, S.-H., Ahn, Y.-W., Huh, G.-Y., Kwak, D.-S., Park, D.-K., Lee, U.-Y., and Kim, Y.-S. (2009). Microscopic age estimation from the anterior cortex of the femur in Korean adults. *Journal of Forensic Sciences,* 54: 519–522.

Keough, N., L'Abbe, E. N., and Steyn, M. (2009). The evaluation of age-related histomorphometric variables in a cadaver sample of lower socioeconomic status: Implications for estimating age at death. *Forensic Science International,* 191: 114.e1–114.e6.

Kerley, E. R. (1965). The microscopic determination of age in human bone. *American Journal of Physical Anthropology,* 23: 149–163.

Kerley, E. R., and Ubelaker, D. H. (1978). Revisions in the microscopic method of estimating age at death in human cortical bone. *American Journal of Physical Anthropology,* 49: 545–546.

Kim, Y.-S., KIim, D.-I., Park, D.-K., Lee, J.-H., Chung, N.-E., Lee, W.-T., and Han, S.-H. (2007). Assessment of histomorphological features of the sternal end of the fourth rib for age estimation in Koreans. *Journal of Forensic Sciences,* 52: 1237–1242.

Lynnerup, N., Frohlich, B., and Thomsen, J. L. (2006). Assessment of age at death by microscopy: Unbiased quantification of secondary osteons in femoral cross sections. *Forensic Science International,* 159: S100–S103.

Maat, G. J., Maes, A., Aarents, M. J., and Nagelkerke, N. J. (2006). Histological age prediction from the femur in a contemporary Dutch sample. The decrease of nonremodeled bone in the anterior cortex. *Journal of Forensic Sciences,* 51: 230–237.

Matrille, L., Irinopoulou, T., Bruneval, P., Baccino, E., and Fornes, P. (2009). Age at death estimation in adults by computer-assisted histomorphometry of decalcified femur cortex. *Journal of Forensic Sciences,* 54: 1231–1237.

Paine, R. R., and Brenton, B. P. (2006). Dietary health does affect histological age assessment: An evaluation of the Stout and Paine (1992) age estimation equation using secondary osteons from the rib. *Journal of Forensic Sciences,* 51: 489–492.

Pavon, M. V., Cucina, A., and Tiesler, V. (2010). New formulae to estimate age at death in Maya populations using histomorphological changes in the fourth human rib. *Journal of Forensic Sciences,* 55: 473–477.

Robling, A. G., and Stout, S. D. (2000). Histomorphometry of human cortical bone: Applications to age estimation. In: Katzenberg, M. A., and Saunders, S. R. (Eds.), *Biological anthropology of the human skeleton.* New York: Wiley-Liss, 187–214.

Thomas, C. D. L., Stein, M. S., Feik, S. A., Wark, J. D., and Clement, J. G. (2000). Determination of age at death using combined morphology and histology of the femur. *Journal of Anatomy,* 196: 463–471.

Yi-Suk, K., Deog-Im, K., Dae-Kyoon, P., Je-Hoon, L., Nak-Eun, C., Won-Tae L., and Seung-Ho, H. (2007). Assessment of histomorphological features of the sternal end of the fourth rib for age estimation in Koreans. *Journal of Forensic Sciences,* 52: 1237–1242.

Other

Snodgrass, J. J. (2004). Sex differences and aging of the vertebral column. *Journal of Forensic Sciences,* 49: 1–6.

Watanabe, S., and Terazawa, K. (2006). Age estimation from the degree of osteophyte formation of vertebral columns in Japanese. *Legal Medicine,* 8: 156–160.

Sex Determination

3

CHARLOTTE DAWSON
DUNCAN ROSS
DR. XANTHE MALLETT

Contents

Introduction

Sex determination is the classification of an individual as either male or female. This evaluation is an integral part of a biological profile, which also includes the assessment of age, living stature, and ancestral origin. To achieve an assignation of sex, the anthropologist uses biological traits of the skeletal system that vary between the sexes for functional reasons. This variation is exhibited in soft and hard tissue (Plavcan 2001). This analysis is based on the maxim that function dictates form, so the purpose an element undertakes will dictate what that element looks like and how it responds to biomechanical loading and stress. Largely, forensic anthropology focuses on sexing skeletal remains, with little or no associated soft tissue.

Within each sex, a number of elements undertake different functions; consequently, the form of those elements varies and presents differences in both size and shape. Many of the features that are described as indicative of sex include both factors. Size disparity between males and females of the same species is known as *sexual dimorphism*, which is calculated as the natural logarithm of the ratio of the male mean value divided by the female mean value. Humans (*Homo sapiens*) have an overall body size dimorphism that varies by approximately 20% between the largest males and the smallest females, along with a dimorphism of individual skeletal traits, which is less exaggerated than in other species (e.g. gorillas).

A problem in determining the probable sex of an individual is that elements used to assess sex, which utilize dimorphism, are not uniformly expressed between populations and within male and female groups. Instead, the expression of traits exists on a continuum, from typically male to typically female. Thus, one person's skeletal presentation may include what would be considered male and female indicators, or may be of indeterminate sex from the evidence available. All variables are assessed through morphological and metric analysis to determine sex based on a set of standards from known populations.

The reliability of correctly determining an individual's sex varies with the age at death of the subject. In adults, depending on the ancestral origin, assigning sex is often more straightforward than when assessing a prepubertal juvenile because an important element is the assessment of the secondary sexual characteristics that arise as a result of hormonal changes in preparation for adulthood. The differences that occur within the skeletal system, which are used to define remains as male or female, largely occur as a result of distinction between the sexes of biomechanical function of joints for efficiency in locomotion and partition.

A number of problems arise when attempting to accurately and reliably evaluate an individual's sex, including inter- and intrapopulation variation, which occurs in trait expression within all features commonly used to determine sex. As a result, ancestry must be assessed prior to sex classification. Furthermore, in recent years new issues have arisen because the terms *sex* and *gender* are often applied synonymously, but they are in fact separate concepts. Biological sex is determined by genetics: XX is a female, and XY is male. Although sex can be estimated, this does not consider how the individual presented him- or herself to society. Instead, *gender* refers to the socially constructed role of an individual in the way they act, dress, and behave. This can be thought of as the equivalent of genotype and phenotype; consequently, your biological sex (XX or XY) is your genotype, and your gender is your phenotype.

Due to the importance of this biological characteristic, a number of features have been investigated to assess the viability as a method of differentiating males and females, both juvenile and adult. However, there are really only two areas of the human body that have been found to be reliable when determining the likely sex of skeletal remains: The pelvis and the skull. The reason behind this relates to the fact that these two areas vary between males and females for functional reasons and are consequently subject to different developmental loadings and mechanical forces—resulting in variation in both size and shape. These are discussed in detail, followed by a short summary of other human elements that have been assessed for their use in sex estimation.

Sexing the Juvenile

The methods for determining the sex of adult skeletal remains utilize the morphological features that present through secondary sexual dimorphic changes. However, juvenile remains have not undergone this secondary sexual change; therefore, prepubertal individuals have a relatively featureless morphology from which to distinguish differences between males and females. Nevertheless, a small number of studies utilizing geometric and statistical shape analysis techniques have been employed to determine sexual dimorphism. These studies have concentrated on areas of the skeleton that show most sexual dimorphism in the adult, such as the pelvis, mandible and cranium.

The Juvenile Pelvis

The adult pelvis is known as one of the most sexually dimorphic regions of the skeleton because the female has the potential for childbirth. Due to these differences in functionality, the pelvis develops a different morphology under the influence of increased sex hormone levels released at puberty. These result in multiple sex-determining features, such as the shape of the greater sciatic notch, auricular surface, pelvic inlet, subpubic angle, obturator foramen shape, acetabulum size and orientation, and muscle markings. However, the sexing of the juvenile has focused on the greater sciatic notch and auricular surface of the ilium because these features are recognizable and can be measured; consequently, variation can be quantified.

Morphological and metric methods were the main techniques employed to try to determine sex of juveniles via the ilium (Boucher 1957; Schutkowski 1993; Weaver 1980). These studies did not take into consideration the implications of age on the morphological features found and the subjective nature of defining suitable landmarks on the juvenile ilium (Vlak et al. 2008). Wilson et al. (2008) also researched the variation found in the juvenile ilium; they used eigenshape analysis and found that 96% of the individuals included were correctly classified by sex using the shape of the greater sciatic notch. However, the sample size (*n* = 25) was small, thus limiting the reliability of the results, particularly as the population included a disproportionately large number of males (8 females, 17 males). In addition, the oldest female included in the study was 3.21 years. As with the study by Vlak and colleagues (2008), the results are not reliable as the variable "age" appears to be the determining factor for sex; that is, more mature, robust skeletal ilia were deemed "masculine," while more gracile and less-mature specimens were considered "feminine."

The Juvenile Mandible

The mandible is believed to be a suitable bone for sexing juveniles because it is thought to undergo endocrine, functional, and anatomical influences during juvenile development, leading to differences between the sexes. Consequently, as with the pelvis, techniques similar to those used to determine the sex of adults are employed to determine the biological sex of juveniles.

A morphological technique was proposed by Loth and Henneberg (2001) in which the shape differences in the symphyseal region and anterior body of the mandible were capable of determining sex with 81% accuracy. However, a blind test of this technique performed by Scheuer (2002) achieved an accuracy of only 64%, showing a large disparity between the original and subsequent study results. Geometric morphometric analysis of the mandible has also supported the notion that sex determination of the juvenile mandible is not feasible within a forensic context. The multivariate regressions of Franklin (2008) found no significant sexual dimorphism in the sample, with a cross-validated classification accuracy of only 59%.

Sexing of the Juvenile Cranium

The dimensions of the foramen magnum and occipital condyles of adults have been shown to be sexually dimorphic. Due to the foramen magnum reaching its adult size early in childhood (~6 years), it is unlikely to be responsive to significant secondary sexual changes, making it a suitable area for showing sexual dimorphism at an early age. Consequently, with the aim of determining if these could be used to sex individuals, a study by Veroni et al. (2010) analyzed the foramen magnum and the occipital condyle dimensions of 36 juveniles aged 8–18.9 years from the Lisbon skeletal collection. The results of their discriminant function analysis indicated that foramen magnum length and breadth and the left occipital condyle breadth were of use in discriminating sex in their sample set (17 females, 19 males), with a correct classification of 75.8%. Given the sample size, this percentage is rather low to be applicable within a forensic environment, and this method should be applied with caution.

Conclusion

As with previous decades, the accurate and reliable attribution of sex to juvenile remains is one of the four basic biological parameters. However, despite the advancement of techniques and associated software available and the application of statistical shape analyses, this parameter can still only offer unreliable results at best. This is not surprising considering the number of issues associated with estimating sex in prepubertal individuals. For example, there is still limited juvenile skeletal material of known age on which to conduct tests; as a result, statistically significant results are difficult to obtain, as is conducting unbiased tests due to the uneven distribution of the sexes (high male-to-female ratio). Another problem is the lack of easily identifiable bony characteristics that can be landmarked and measured with a reasonable degree of accuracy and repeatability, a fact which decreases the potential to differentiate between the sexes in a statistically robust manner.

Consequently, the most pertinent question remains unanswered: Why would the juvenile skeleton be different between males and females? As the skeletons of male and female prepubertal individuals perform the same functions, no differences would be expected as the onset of sex-related hormonal change has not yet taken place.

Sexing the Adult

The most reliable aspects of the human skeleton for sex determination are the pelvis and cranium due to their sexual dimorphism, which is expressed across all populations. However, when assigning sex to an individual, accuracy and reliability depend on the skeletal assemblage present for analysis. Without knowing the likely sex of an individual, assessing age and ancestry can be problematic. In a forensic setting, the reliability of a method implemented to determine sex should have a minimum threshold of 95%, although this is an optimum level and will depend very much on the condition of the remains for analysis.

Pelvis

The human pelvis is recognized as one of the most accurate skeletal elements for determining sex in the adult. This is because the pelvis has multiple morphological features that indicate its functions, including bipedalism, protection and containment of pelvic viscera, and parturition. Therefore, multiple methods were created prior to 2000 to determine sex, including the methods of İşcan and Derrick (1984) and Phenice (1969) as two of the principal approaches. Research between 2000 and 2010 has focused on many different

Table 3.1 Overview of Research on the Pelvis

Pelvic Region	References Referring to that Region
Acetabulum	Benazzi et al. 2008; Nagesh et al. 2007; Papaloucas et al. 2008
Greater sciatic notch	Biwasaka et al. 2009; Steyn et al. 2004; Takahashi 2006; Walker 2005
Subpubic angle	Igbigbi and Nanono-Igbigbi 2003
Pubis	Nagesh et al. 2007; Rissech and Malgosa 2007
Ishium	Rissech et al. 2003
Multiple regions	Brüžek 2002; Dixit et al. 2007; Durić et al. 2005; González et al. 2007, 2009; Listi and Bassett 2006; McBride et al. 2001; Patriquin et al. 2003; Steyn and Işcan 2008
Pubic symphysis to ischiopubic ramus (Phenice method)	Ubelaker and Volk 2002
Ilium	Rissech and Malgosa 2005
Pelvic inlet	Correia et al. 2005
Sacrum	Benazzi et al. 2009; Dar and Hershkovitz 2006; Tague 2007

regions of the pelvis, including those indicated in Table 3.1. These concentrate on population specific variation and have been investigated using geometric morphometrics and imaging technologies.

The human skeleton is plastic and will vary on both individual and population levels due to various external environmental factors. Population-specific standards for sexing skeletal remains have arisen in recent times as a result of skeletal characteristics that are known to vary among populations due to different nutritional status, health care, environmental conditions, activity level, and so on. Techniques utilizing the pelvis have been tested on numerous populations, including groups from the following countries: southern India (Nagesh et al. 2007), Greece (Papaloucas et al. 2008; Steyn and Işcan 2008), Uganda (Igbigbi and Nanono-Igbigbi 2003), America (Listi and Bassett 2006), India (Dixit et al. 2007), South Africa (Patriquin et al. 2003; Steyn et al. 2004), and Japan (Biwasaka et al. 2009). However, the applicability of determining population-specific standards has been questioned. Steyn and Patriquin (2009) identified that formulae cannot be created for every possible population from widely differing regions across the world, possibly due to a lack of skeletal collections from which to obtain standard data. Another issue recognized was the ability to identify the population affinity or ancestry of a skeleton to conduct population-specific formulae. Therefore, Steyn and Patriquin's (2009) proposal that a universal formula could be determined that could be applied to any-sex skeletal remains is potentially of value.

Biwasaka et al. (2009) undertook an analysis of sexual dimorphism of the greater sciatic notch in a contemporary Japanese population by analyzing the three-dimensional images reconstructed by multislice computed tomography (MSCT). Using this technique, the authors were able to determine sex correctly in 89.4% (161) of the 180 individuals. The authors found that because sexing was possible even in the deeper regions of the greater sciatic notch, which are more resistant to postmortem damage, the method could be useful in a forensic setting.

The use of digital image processing has been put forward by Benazzi et al. (2008). The method used digital photographs of the acetabular area, which were then analyzed using technical drawing software to trace the acetabular rim and to measure the related dimensions (area, perimeter, longitudinal and transverse maximum width). Based on these measurements, it was found that there were significant differences between the sexes, such that 96.4% (80) of the 83 specimens were correctly classified. However, the authors noted that interpopulation variability must be considered if this method is employed on a different population.

Skull

Sexual dimorphism of the skull is closely associated with ancestry; therefore, ancestral origin must be considered when assessing sex. Using the skull to assess sex has a lower accuracy than sexing from the pelvis as many features are a by-product of larger skeletal size, sexual selection, and larger muscle mass, although both the skull and pelvis allow for potential correct classification of over 90% of individuals examined. The skull, unlike the pelvis, is less liable to damage and survives inhumation better. As the skull can survive the decomposition process, many robust elements of the skull have been researched for sex determination.

Walker (2008) used morphological criteria, compiled by Buikstra and Ubelaker (1994) for a discriminant functional analysis based on visually assessed traits which had a rating scale of 1–5. The scores for the five classifiers provided a 90% correct sex accuracy and included the mastoid process, supraorbital margin, supraorbital ridge and glabella, mental eminence, and nuchal crest. The features were also evaluated independently using univariate analysis and as a group for multivariate analysis, with increasing degrees of accuracy. The univariate analysis provided correct sex identification with 70% accuracy from one variable, and multivariate analysis increased the correct classification, with two variables providing 84% accuracy, three providing 87% accuracy, and all five variables providing a correct classification in 88% of the sample.

The temporal bone, due to its robustness and capability of surviving trauma and inhumation, has been studied to determine sex as the mastoid process has been proven to be sexually dimorphic. The area of the mastoid process has been measured through three landmarks: the porion, asterion, and tip of the mastoid process (De Paiva and Segre 2003). These regions were then assessed through calculation of the area using a photocopy of the regions, with the sum of both sides used to counteract asymmetry. This provided sexed male and female skulls with 95% confidence with sectioning points of greater than 1,505.32 mm^2 male and less than 1,221.24 mm^2 female. This was tested by Suazo et al. (2008) from direct measurements taken on 81 skulls (50 male, 31 female). Correct male assignment was 93% accurate; however, only 17.7% of female skulls were correctly classified in this sample.

Metric analysis was also carried out by Wahl and Graw (2001) in a study that assessed 410 petrous temporal bones. In total, 15 landmarks were selected on the basis that each could be identified on fragmented and nonfragmented remains (for details of the landmarks, see Wahl and Graw 2001). The age of 50 years was set as a division, and those above this age were assessed separately from those under 50 years at the time of death. For individuals over 50 years, a correct classification by sex was achieved in 74.19% of cases, and for those under 50, this value was 68.15%. The internal auditory meatus was also investigated for dimorphism by Lynnerup et al. (2006), through assessment of the internal opening of the acoustic canal in the petrous portion of the temporal bone. Their sample consisted of 173 adults (>18 years of age) petrous bones, of which 120 were left and right pairs from 60 individuals, and the remaining 53 were all single, left-side only. They were measured using standard metal drill bits (Lynnerup et al. 2006), with a mean difference of 0.3 mm between males and females, with a diameter of 2.5 mm indicating female and 4.0 mm male sex. Males were correctly classified in 91% of cases; however, females were only correctly classified in 38% of cases. The use of drill bits may have limited the usefulness of the method; the auditory meatus is not round but oval in shape, and the method of measuring provided highly inaccurate results as the drill did not completely fill the space. Consequently, the use of a different medium for measuring may result in increased accuracy in recording the diameter and possibly improve the levels of correct sex classification.

The mandible is a robust bone that can be identified easily from fragments or as a whole unit. The mandible has been shown to be dimorphic between males and females through the difference in muscle mass as a result of strength and force applied by the masticatory muscles (Franklin, O'Higgins, Oxnard, et al. 2008). In this study, 225 individuals from five tribes in South Africa were studied to assess sex as an entire group and individually to investigate interpopulation variation. The nine measurements taken were compared by analysis of variance (ANOVA) to assess male and female variations from group means. This indicated male means were larger in all dimensions than female means, and sex was correctly classified in 84% of cases. The four most dimorphic traits (coronoid, ramus height, maximum length, and bicondylar breadth) when assessed with cross validation within the entire sample had an accuracy of 81.8%. When the populations were tested independently, the sex determination accuracy ranged from 63.6% to 84%, thus showing that population differences in dimorphism can affect sex determination.

For the skull, analysis has been focused more recently on individual robust elements that will allow sex to be determined accurately in fragmented and trauma-damaged skulls from mass disasters, human rights abuses, and comingled remains. Studies over the past 10 years that have investigated the cranium for sex determination are shown in Table 3.2.

The skull and pelvis each exhibit sexually dimorphic features, as indicated by many authors who confirmed the accuracy and precision available from sexing these skeletal elements. However, poor preservation can affect the reliability of the sex determination, and although accurate sexing can be achieved with an incomplete skull or pelvis, this will depend on the proportion and regions that are available for assessment, as well as the experience of the anthropologist. The pelvis has traits that are easily damaged, rendering the quality of the bone inadequate for assessment of sex. In forensic cases, the skull may be actively being targeted for damage or complete removal in an attempt to prevent identification of the deceased individual (Gapert et al. 2009a). In some skeletal assemblages, the pelvis and skull are not always present; therefore, determination of sex from other bones must be investigated to increase the accuracy of sex determination from incomplete remains as nearly all bones have some degree of sexual dimorphism (Deshmukh and Devershi 2006).

Pectoral Girdle

The ability to determine sex from different skeletal elements is important to give a more conclusive determination of sex. The scapula has been recently studied in this regard. While research relating to the clavicle has concentrated on the use of the rhomboid fossa to correctly sex individuals.

Dabbs (2009) tested Dwight's (1894) method for estimating sex on a sample of 803 individuals (308 females, 495 males) from the Hamann-Todd collection. Dwight's method involved measuring the maximum height of the scapula; if the height was greater than 170 mm, this was determined as male, and the determination was female if the height was less than 140 mm. The results of Dabbs's study showed that sex could be determined with high accuracy (96.81%) when the scapular height was above or below the sex specification demarcation points. However, the majority of the sample (68.74%) fell in between the two demarcation points. Therefore, the overall accuracy of the method was only 29.27%.

Table 3.2   Cranial Traits that Have Been Studied to Define Sex Differences Metrically and Morphologically

Cranial Trait	Characteristics	References
Nuchal crest	The nuchal crest is more prominent in males than females because of the attachment of the neck muscles, and the occipital protuberance is more pronounced in males.	Kjellström 2004; Walker 2008; Wilkinson 2004
Foramen magnum and occipital condyles	There were 146 crania analyzed of 18th and 19th century remains, St. Bride's collection. Six measurements were taken, and the best discriminant variable accuracies from the occipital condyle were minimum bicondylar breadth followed by maximum width of the left and right condyle, with provided accuracies of 53.4% and 67.3%, respectively; multivariate analysis produced higher accuracy with maximum length of left condyle, maximum width of right condyle, and minimum distance between condyles. There were 158 adult skeletons with an almost 1:1 male-to-female ratio used from the St. Bride's collection; the maximum length and width were measured along with the circumference of the foramen magnum. Descriptive statistics were applied, as were multi- and univariate analyses, which were subjected to leave-one-out and cross-validation discriminant functions. Accuracies ranged from 59% to 70%.	Gapert et al. 2009a, 2009b
Mastoid process	Larger, robust, and straight in males, whereas in females they are medially oriented and smaller. The sternocleidomastoid muscle has strong attachment marks and pronounced grooves in some males.	De Paiva and Segre 2003; Kjellström 2004; Suazo et al. 2008; Walker 2008; Wilkinson 2004
Supraorbital margin	In females, this is sharp, compared to males, and the orbits are positioned higher in the skull and are more rounded in appearance; they are more rectangular in males.	Kjellström 2004; Walker 2008; Wilkinson 2004
Supraorbital ridge and glabella	The supraorbital ridge is more pronounced in males than females, and the glabella is also larger in males than females.	Kjellström 2004; Walker 2005; Wilkinson 2004
Mental eminence	The mandible is more square in appearance in males and has larger condyles with gonial flaring.	Kjellström 2004; Walker 2005; Wilkinson 2004

(continued)

Table 3.2 Cranial Traits that Have Been Studied to Define Sex Differences Metrically and Morphologically (Continued)

Cranial Trait	Characteristics	References
Angle of the frontal bone	The frontal bone is smoother and more vertical in females in the Frankfurt plane than males; females also exhibit more rounding of the frontal bone.	Wilkinson 2004
Palate	The palates in males are U-shaped, whereas the females have a V-shaped palate, as males have a wider and broader arch.	Wilkinson 2004
Temporal bone	Internal acoustic meatus diameter was measured with a sectioning point of < 3.0 mm for females and > 3.5mm for males; accuracy was 70%. Based on a discriminant analysis, the petrous temporal measurements of 15 landmarks resulted in 68.15% accuracy in young individuals and 74.19% in older individuals. The lateral angle of the internal acoustic canal meatus was measured with the use of CT to determine if there was a dimorphism; females' mean angle was 45.5 ± 7.1 degrees and males' was 41 ± 6.7 degrees; although there was a large overlap, the significance was < .01, but males tended to have smaller angles than women. There was significant difference found between males and females under 18 years of age.	Akansel et al. 2008; Lynnerup et al. 2006; Wahl and Graw 2001
Frontal and parietal bossing	Males' frontal and parietal bones, compared to those of females, have reduced bossing.	Wilkinson 2004
Overall appearance or measurements	Female skulls are more gracile and rounded than those of males, with male skulls generally larger than female skulls. This size difference allows for metric assessment of sex from cranial measurements	Deshmukh and Devershi 2006; Kimmerle et al. 2008; Rooppakhun et al. 2009; Wilkinson 2004

As a follow-up to Dabbs's (2009) work, Dabbs and Moore-Jansen (2010) developed a new five-variable discriminant function for sex estimation from the scapula. A calibration sample of 724 individuals of different ancestral groups (447 males, 277 females) from the Hamann-Todd collection was utilized. The size and shape of the scapula were assessed through the use of 23 individual measurements. The five variables that represented the greatest sexual dimorphism were used to create a five-variable discriminant function for sex estimation. The accuracy of this method was 95.7% on the cross-validated calibration sample, 92.5% as tested on 80 individuals taken from the Hamann-Todd collection, and 84.4% on a sample of 32 individuals from the skeletal collection of Wichita State University. The reason for the difference in accuracy between the Hamann-Todd tests and the Wichita tests was that the Wichita sample contained only White individuals, and unpublished data indicated that there could be significant differences between White and Black scapulae. This stresses the importance of creating a population-specific model.

Assessment of the clavicle has concentrated on the rhomboid fossa, a potential pit or depression on the clavicle that may be present due to the connection of the costoclavicular ligament. It was therefore hypothesized as a possible sex indicator by Rogers et al. (2000). Using a contemporary sample of 344 clavicle pairs (113 females, 231 males; age range 10–92 years) from the William F. McCormick collection, the presence and type of skeletal trait at the costoclavicular ligament attachment site were noted. From this examination, it was determined that 93% of the fossae in the original sample were present in male clavicles. Using posterior probabilities, a fossa on the right clavicle was indicative of a male with 81.7% probability, and a fossa on the left was indicative of a male with a correct classification ratio of 92.2%. However, the lack of a fossa is not indicative of a female as males also presented without fossa, as a result of which this technique may only be of use if fossae can be detected. The sample in this experiment also had a bias toward male individuals, a factor that may have affected the results. It would be beneficial to apply such a test to different population groups, with a more even distribution of male and female samples.

A study that employed Rogers et al.'s (2000) method on a different population group assessed the incidence of the rhomboid fossa in paired clavicles of 209 Brazilian individuals (107 males, 102 females) (Prado et al. 2009). Their observations of rhomboid fossae were noted, and the qualitative statistical analysis undertaken showed a statistically significant difference between the sexes related to the frequency of rhomboid fossa. They found that the fossa was absent in 97.1% of female clavicles, and the incidence of bilateral fossa was present in only 2.9% of females, whereas the incidence of fossa was 63.6% for male clavicles, and bilateral fossa appeared in 29% of male clavicles. These results reflect those found by Rogers et al. (2000) and suggest that the presence of a rhomboid fossa could be a useful tool to indicate that a specimen may be male.

Long Bones of the Upper Limb

The long bones of the skeleton can be used to determine sex as the biomechanical forces affect bone growth and remodeling, and the forces that pass through the joints are different between males and females; this also can be related to differing sizes between ancestral groups. This difference in circumference between males and females extends to differing deposition of cortical bone in adolescence as males have greater deposition, which increases width and circumference of bone and activity patterns. This is often applied to fragmented bones, especially in archaeological specimens as they have a greater density at their distal end. These are also dependent on dimensions of bone within and between populations as the sexual dimorphism expressed varies. These differences within the long bones between males and females are subtle, and discriminant function analyses are formed to increase the variance to separate males and females.

It is believed that the different body shapes expressed by males and females (i.e., males generally have wide shoulders and narrow hips, and females have narrow shoulders and wide hips) equate to the different carrying angles required to enable the arms to swing successfully past the hip. This difference in carrying angles equates to the morphology of the elbow as sexually dimorphic. As such, the humerus has been realized as a potentially useful skeletal element for determining sex. Recent research concerning the humerus has focused on testing of the Rogers (1999) method (Falys et al. 2005) to assess the applicability for sex determination in a contemporary Cretan population (Kranioti and Michalodimitrakis 2009). In addition, sex determination utilizing the long bones has been tested on a recent Japanese population (Sakaue 2004), and the long bones of the arm have been used to estimate sex and stature from recent German specimens (Mall et al. 2001). Therefore, research seems to have concentrated on the ability to determine the sex of specific populations.

Falys et al. (2005) set out to reevaluate Rogers's technique (1999) to test its applicability to individuals from an archaeological sample of 351 humeri originating between the 17th and 19th centuries. For this study, the authors assessed the possibility of accurately sexing the sample using humeri in isolation. The results found that combination of all four of Rogers's proposed sexually dimorphic traits (trochlear constriction, trochlear symmetry, olecranon fossa shape, and angle of medial epicondyle) provided an overall accuracy of 79.1%, whereas the olecranon fossa shape was the most consistently accurate individual characteristic, resulting in 84.6% accuracy. It is specified that such accuracy renders the technique useful in forensic investigations; however, it must be noted that these results are based on an archaeological sample, and the best accuracy achieved was 84.6% with a slightly biased sample (184 males, 167 females). Therefore, use of such a method should be cautioned.

The other articles concerning sex determination from the humerus concentrated on specific modern population groups. This is due to the variety among populations regarding sexually dimorphic characteristics, and secular trends mean that applying standards developed on archaeological populations is not ideal. Kranioti and Michalodimitrakis (2009) aimed to create a sex identification technique based on the osteometric standards derived from a modern Cretan population because no data had been created for sexing of long bones. The sample consisted of left humeri from 84 males and 84 females who died between 1968 and 1998. Osteometric analysis and discriminant function were employed to select the variables that best discriminate males from females. Their results found that the highest accuracy (92.9%) of sexing the specimens was achieved by the stepwise discriminant function analysis and included maximum length of the humerus, vertical head diameter, midshaft minimum diameter, and epicondylar breadth. By employing discriminant function analysis, the effectiveness of individual dimensions could be determined; therefore, their method could be applicable for fragmented humeral material, although application beyond a Cretan population may be unreliable.

Sakaue (2004) also employed stepwise discriminant function analysis to the long bones (including the humerus) applied to a contemporary Japanese population. Based on their *t* values and the results of their discriminant function analysis, it was found that the width of the distal articular surface of the humerus was considered the best characteristic for determining sex from the humerus (correctly assigning sex with 95% accuracy).

Mall et al. (2001) applied discriminant function analysis to the long bones of a contemporary, elderly (mean age of sample 79 years), German population (64 males, 74 females). They found that the humerus was the second most discriminating long bone, resulting in 93.15% accuracy, with the humeral head diameter the best individual characteristic for determining sex (90.41%). However, these results were compiled using a population containing more males than females; therefore, the wider applicability of the results is limited as the population on which it was based is too limited demographically.

As with the humerus, research on the radius and ulna has focused on discriminant function analysis such that the results can be applied to fragmented remains. Barrier and L'Abbé (2008) applied discriminant function analysis to the radius and ulna of a contemporary South African sample to determine sex; Purkait (2001) analyzed measurements of the ulna from an Indian population; Cowal and Pastor (2008) applied discriminant function analysis to measurements of the proximal ulna from an archaeological sample (Spitalfields Coffin-Plate sample and the Raunds Furnells collection) to determine sexual dimorphism of the ulna; and Celbis and Agritmis (2006) employed discriminant function analysis to the measurements of both the ulna and the radius of a modern Turkish sample to determine sex.

Barrier and L'Abbé (2008) conducted their research because no population-specific osteometric standards had been developed for the bones of the forearm. This is problematic in South Africa as a large number of unidentified skeletal remains are found, and availability of population-specific osteometric standards is imperative for successful identification. Their sample consisted of 200 male and 200 female forearms from the Pretoria Bone Collection and Raymond Dart Collection (dating from 1870 to 1979). From stepwise and direct discriminant function analysis, it was determined that the distal breadth, minimum midshaft diameter, and maximum head diameter were the most discriminating determinants of sex for the radius, and the minimum midshaft diameter and the olecranon breadth were the best sex discriminators for the ulna. The classification accuracy ranged from 76% to 86%; therefore, it was concluded that sex should not be assigned solely based on the formulae presented, and that other methods should be incorporated.

Purkait (2001) aimed to obtain osteometric standards that could be applied to fragmentary remains to determine sex with accuracy. The study was based on 160 adult ulnae (100 males, 60 females) from a middle-class Indian population. Discriminant function analysis was used to analyze three measurements (olecranon-coronoid angle, length, and width of inferior medial trochlear notch). The results of analyses concluded that the olecranon-coronoid angle was the most important individual characteristic for determining sex and had an accuracy of 85%. However, the most discriminating variables were obtained when the olecranon-coronoid angle and length of the inferior medial trochlear notch were used together (correctly classifying 90.6% of the sample). This study was of course limited to middle-class individuals from India. The experiment also had a higher number of males compared to females, adding some bias to the results.

Cowal and Pastor (2008) applied discriminant function analysis to measurements (notch length, width of olecranon process, height of olecranon process, and radial notch height) from the proximal ulna of 223 (114 males, 109 females) ulnae from the Spitalfields Coffin-Plate Collection (AD 1729–1852) and the Raunds Furnells Collection (10th to 12th century AD). Stepwise and direct discriminant function analysis of the Spitalfields sample found that an accuracy of 85.4% (males 82.4%, females 88.4%) could be realized when the four measurements were used simultaneously. The authors concluded that the ulna was sexually dimorphic; however, its development is population specific. The article also highlighted that their method may not be accurate for analyzing modern populations due to secular trends and improvements in health care.

Celbis and Agritmis (2006) applied discriminant function analysis to the length measurements obtained from the radii and ulnae of a modern Turkish sample (80 males, 47 females). Sex could be determined for 91.3% of the sample using the ulna length and for 90.6% using the radius and ulna together or radius on its own. However, the sample was biased toward males, and such a bias may have affected the reliability and wider applicability of the results.

Vertebral Column, Sternum, and Ribs

The second cervical vertebra has been assessed as a sex indicator; this was carried out on the Hamann Todd and Terry skeletal collections using 100 White and 100 Black individuals (Wescott 2000). Eight dimensions were measured with sliding calipers to the nearest 0.1 mm, and the results were evaluated with stepwise and cross-validation procedures. The accuracy obtained within this study was high; however, one analysis with good results cannot dictate accepted usage. This element of the vertebral column needs more research to determine whether C2 is a useful determinant for sex. The reference list in Wescott's (2000) study only consisted of nine authors from 1995 and before, which is limited. It also based the higher weighting of the second cervical vertebra over the femur as an indicator of sex, for which only one study has been conducted (in Black 1978) on mid-shaft femoral fragments.

The ribs can be used to assess age and sex; the fourth rib was utilized in a study by Koçak et al. (2003). The sternal end of the fourth rib along with 5 cm of costochondral junction were removed from 78 females and 173 males of known age and sex. The sternal ends were measured with calipers in three dimensions (superior-inferior height, anterior-posterior breadth, and medial pit depth); SPSS was used for stepwise function analysis of these measurements. To assess sex without age affecting the analysis as the rib becomes broader with age, three groups were compiled: young (15–32 years), old (33–89 years), and the entire sample (15–89 years). The results were similar for the young and old groups, with a correct classification of sex in 88.6% for the younger group and 86.55% for the older group.

In another study, the sternum was x-rayed, and six measurements were taken, five from the sternum and one from the fourth rib (Torwalt and Hoppa 2005a; Torwalt and Hoppa 2005b). The results were used for an independent sample t test, and univariate and multivariate analyses were performed. Using two variables (fourth rib and sternal length) in multivariate analysis, accuracies of 90.3% and 95.8% were achieved for females and males, respectively. As technology improves, newer analyses can be undertaken on contemporary populations in a clinical setting as MSCT can be used to assess the sternum and ribs for sex identifiable markers. Ramadan et al. (2010) divided 340 patients (143 females and 197 males) into four age groups: 21–40 years, 41–60 years, 61–80 years, and 81 years and over. Six measurements and three indices were studied on the images produced from the MSCT. These indices have been presented in other studies to separate sex (e.g., Hyrtl's law, which states that the manubrium of the female sternum exceeds half the total length of the body, as compared to the male sternum which is at least twice as long as the manubrium; Hyrtl 1857 as cited in Dwight 1881) using sternal index and sternal area. All measurements were shown to have a significant effect on sex determination by multivariate ANOVA, with a $p < 0.001$. Sternal measurements produced 84.7% and 81.8% correct sex identification of males and females, respectively. The best model for determining sex was the sternal area and width of the fourth rib. Previous studies have noted, when assessing sex from the thorax, that accuracy increases the more variables are included in the analysis (ossification deposition pattern, fourth rib measurements, and sternal length).

Long Bones of Lower Limbs

The bones subjected to mechanical loading and stresses are felt to reliably separate sex more accurately in certain dimensions, such as bicondylar breadth for the femur and breadth of the proximal epiphysis of the tibia. It is noted that it is difficult to apply sex discriminant techniques to some populations as their parameters are different from other modern human groups, such as the Japanese populations (Sakaue 2004). Accuracies of sex determination from long bones can reach 80%, and with multivariate analysis, close to 90% accuracy was achievable from the circumference of the upper and lower limb bones of a Japanese population (Nagaoka and Hirata 2009). Techniques to determine sex have also been utilized in fossil skeletal assemblages and to determine the sexual dimorphism present by applying modern data analysis to the skeletal material (Fernández and Monchot 2007).

Males tend to have longer, thicker, and more prominent muscle attachment sites than females due to the differing times of pubertal onset and duration. Sex determination from Malawian femoral heads was studied by Igbigbi and Msamati (2000). In this study, 260 radiographs of male femora and 236 radiographs of female femora were utilized; both vertical and transverse diameters of the femoral head were measured, and a magnification correction factor was applied. The results were evaluated in SPSS, and a t test was undertaken to differentiate between males and females and to calculate a demarcation point. Male dimensions were larger than the female counterpart, and Malawian females had vertical diameters of 37.00 and 42.00 mm for right and left femoral heads, respectively, versus 53.00 and 56.00 mm, respectively, for males. These differences between males and females vary between populations (Asala 2001); therefore, ancestral origin must be predetermined to avoid misclassification. The femoral heads in Black and White South Africans were also researched by Igbigbi and Msamati (2000) to determine sex. Femora were selected from the Raymond Dart Collection, consisting of a sample that included 160 males and 100 females of European ancestry and 160 males and 100 females of African ancestry, totaling 520 femora for study. The femoral heads from the White male population were larger than those of the females, with a statistically significant result of $p < 0.005$; for the Black population, group mean vertical and transverse diameters were also greater for males than for females, with a significance of $p < 0.005$.

For an archaeological population, the tibiae of 59 individuals (45 males, 14 females) were measured by González-Reimers and colleagues (2000), with sex estimated using pelvis morphology. Seven measurements were taken and analyzed with SPSS with discriminant function analysis; the subsequent accuracies were 94.9–98.3% for males, depending on the number of variables selected, and 100% for females. Caution must be used when applying these methods, however, as the power of the analysis was reduced by the low number of females included in the analysis. Furthermore, the sample was of unknown sex; consequently, sex was estimated by the authors, which could have led to misclassification.

Hand

Few articles have been published between 2000 and 2010 regarding sex determination from bones of the hands or feet. Those published focused on the validity of metacarpal use in sex determination, the potential of using carpals for sex assessment, and the utility of length measurements of the feet to estimate sex.

Burrows et al. (2003) tested the available methods for determining sex from the metacarpals as all previous studies conflicted in terms of range of accuracy in predicting sex and which metacarpal yielded the most accurate results. Metacarpals from 23 cadavers (11 females, 12 males), with age at death ranging between 64 and 93 years, were measured according to the methods of previous authors, and the data obtained were subjected to regression equations and linear discriminant analysis. The results found that the accuracy in sex determination from the methods of Scheuer and Elkington (1993) (from 63.04% – 91.1% correctly classified) and Falsetti (1995) (ranging from 83.3% – 87%) were lower than originally published; however, the accuracy from the methods of Stojanowski (1999) were higher than previously reported (ranging from 65.2% – 95.7%). It was therefore concluded that the metacarpals may provide limited use in determining sex accurately as such large ranges in correct classification were found. The study by Burrows et al. (2003) did have a low sample size and an elderly population; therefore, it may be of benefit to conduct a study utilizing a larger sample size with a greater distribution of age.

An experiment by Case and Ross (2007) investigated the utility of metacarpals and phalanges of the hand and length measurements of the feet to estimate sex. A sample of 259 (123 females, 136 males; age range 18–60 years) White individuals from the Terry Collection was utilized. Maximum axial length measurements were taken from the metacarpals and all phalanges of the hand. Various discriminant function analyses were performed to classify individuals by sex. The results of these analyses were that the left hand was more useful (exceeding 80%) than the right hand and foot in correctly classifying sex. It is believed that by using the length measurements to define sex, activity-related variation is less of an impact compared to diaphyseal breadth measurements. Therefore, length measurements from the hands can be utilized to estimate sex. However, tests on a more modern population would be beneficial to determine if secular trends have affected the dimorphism of the hands and their ability to be used to determine sex.

The most recent paper by Sulzmann et al. (2008) investigated the potential for using the carpals to determine sex. A sample of 100 individuals (50 males, 50 females) from Christ Church, Spitalfields, was used; however, the number of each individual carpal recovered bone per individual varied. Multiple measurements were taken of each individual carpal bone. Independent *t* tests confirmed that all carpal bones were sexually dimorphic. Univariate measurements produced accuracy levels that ranged from 64.6% – 84.7%, and stepwise discriminant function analysis provided reasonably reliable methods for assessing sex from individual or multiple carpals, with an accuracy range of 71.7–88.6%. The authors also emphasized the importance of applying their method to further populations and larger sample sizes to establish population-specific discriminant functions. It would also be favorable if a modern population were tested to determine if secular trends have affected the ability of determining sex from the carpals.

Foot and Patella

The calcaneus and talus of the foot and the patella are robust, dense bones that are affected differentially in males and females as a result of varying biomechanical stresses and forces through the joints. These robust bones were measured to assess their sexual dimorphism, and the discriminant functions were assessed on length and breadth of the bones. Bidmos and Dayal (2003) assessed the talus by discriminant function analysis with univariate and multivariate analyses of variables. Sixty tali were evaluated using nine measurements; the results of the univariate test indicated that talar length and breadth of the posterior articular surface for the calcaneus provided the highest sex determination accuracy (82% and 85%, respectively). An average of 85% correct sex classification was provided by multivariate discriminant function analysis of four measurements: Talar length, breadth of the trochlea, and height of the head and length of the posterior articular surface for the calcaneus. This study indicated that length measurements provided higher accuracy for sex determination, leading to this as a useful determination of sex in White South African individuals.

Bidmos et al. (2005) assessed 120 patellae using six measurements based on a White South African population. The lengths of the patellae were analyzed with discriminant analysis and cross validated using the leave-one-out function. A significant difference was found in all variables, and a combination of all variables provided an accuracy of 85%. Kemkes-Grottenthaler (2005) evaluated patellae of archaeological populations of unknown age and sex taking seven measurements on a sample of 82 individuals. The results of the measurements were subjected to multivariate and univariate analyses, and the results demonstrated that the dimensions of males exceeded those of females. These results are in accordance with the findings of Bidmos and Dayal (2003) for the talus. Sex was accurately predicted in 81% of the specimens through the stepwise classification methods (Kemkes-Grottenthaler 2005). Dayal and Bidmos (2005) undertook a study of the dimensions of 120 patellae from a Black South African population, with a 1:1 male-to-female ratio. The measurements were based on those used by Bidmos et al. (2005), although two measurements were altered. The results showed that although male and female mean values did demonstrate that sexual dimorphism was a factor in the measured variables, the average accuracies in sex classification from independent samples ranged between 60% – 80%.

Mahfouz et al. (2007) analyzed the patellae through three-dimensional images on a nonlinear neural network to determine differences between males and females. In this study, 228 patellae (95 female and 133 male) were assessed through extraction using noninvasive computed tomography. All elements were similarly oriented, through midsagittal mirroring, and the height, breadth, and thickness of the patella were measured. The dimensionalities recorded were used to train a neural network to partition the sexes, which achieved an accuracy of 93.15%. This accuracy is the highest published in the literature for sex determination from the patella.

The talus and calcaneus were studied by Gualdi-Russo (2007); stepwise analysis of the results provided correct identification that was between 87.9% and 95.7% accurate. This was tested on a modern Italian population consisting of 118 adult individuals of known age and sex (62 male, 56 female) who died at the beginning of the 20th century. Concurrent with previous research, all mean male values were larger than female mean values, although no significant asymmetry was found. The talar variables provided a greater contribution of information that was more discriminating between the sexes than the calcaneus variables, with the lowest accuracies achieved (87.9%) using the right calcaneus in isolation.

In 2008, radiographs were analyzed to measure sex from the patella and the third metatarsal. Abdel Moneim et al. (2008) studied 160 people from an Egyptian population. Maximum breadth and height of the patellae were taken, and the length of a number of metatarsals from highest to lowest point was recorded. Univariate analysis was performed to test the individual power of each measurement for sex determination; accuracies ranged from 100% for the second and third metatarsal to 72.5% for length and 73.8% for breadth of the patella. Multivariate analysis was also performed, achieving an accuracy of 87.5% on a random sample. These accuracies fell within the range of the other studies that used the patella, although accuracies for metatarsal length are a promising avenue of research.

Other research into the sex classification accuracies from the foot has been undertaken (Case and Ross 2007; Zeybek et al. 2008), although to date only metric analysis has been undertaken on these robust bones. Key authors such as Bidmos and Dayal are at the forefront in this area of evaluation as they are consistently studying these robust bones and comparing their utility between populations.

The Use of Geometric Morphometrics in Sex Assessment

As mentioned, sex determination is assessed by morphological and metric interpretation of skeletal elements. Morphological features that have been used are subject to interpretation and interpreter error, culminating in variation in the results (Pretorius et al. 2006), and are also subjected to population variation (Walker 2008). The estimation of sex using osteological remains has lacked consistency between investigators (González et al. 2009a). This inconsistency of morphological feature assessment is highlighted when seriating large sample groups as the extremes are easily separated; however, problems arise when intermediate morphology is expressed, and only subtle differences are present. This technique does allow for accuracy and precision of sex estimation when applied by an experienced observer (Walker 2008). Metric analysis techniques have an advantage over morphological methods as they are more objective, with measurements set on a standard set of landmarks (González et al. 2009a). In essence, subjectivity can occur if the landmarks from which measurements are taken do not have clear definitions. Metric analysis results in lower inter- and intraobserver errors, and the continuous data produced can be subjected to statistical analysis, unlike morphological assessment. Linear measurements taken by metric evaluation can be investigated in univariate and multivariate statistical tests. Geometric morphometric techniques analyze the landmark coordinates in generalized procrustes analysis, which enables the data to be scaled, translated, and rotated to largely eliminate size as a variable (Kimmerle et al. 2008) and identify subtle differences between the points that can be analyzed, enabling the sexes to be separated with a high degree of accuracy (González et al. 2009a). The limitation with linear measurement analyses is that shape variations between the landmarks measured are not evaluated (Kimmerle et al. 2008), a problem largely eliminated by geometric morphometric techniques, which can be used to analyze shape quantitatively from morphological characteristics without size influencing the variance (Oettlé et al. 2005; Pretorius et al. 2006; Steyn et al. 2004). Geometric morphometrics allow for study of variation between populations, which morphological assessment cannot do efficiently (Pretorius et al. 2006), as these methods are objective because they are based on landmarks present on each object measured.

Although geometric morphometrics are proving a valid method of research, other already established methods to determine sex should not be disregarded (Pretorius et al. 2006). Many analyses use discriminant function analysis to test their results, a method that uses a set of axes that provides the maximum amount of variation to increase its ability to separate two or more groups, enabling a predictive classification of an individual (González et al. 2009a). This is then often tested by cross-validation methods, which assess one case at a time as an unknown by removing it from the analysis and retesting it anonymously to assess sex, based on all the cases in the analysis but its own to provide an unbiased estimation of accuracy of sex determination (González et al. 2007, 2009b; Patriquin et al. 2003; Steyn et al. 2004). Geometric morphometrics are becoming a widely used technique in forensic anthropology; however, it is time consuming to apply, therefore, quicker methods will probably be utilized preferentially in the analysis of remains for which there is a large skeletal assemblage.

The following are issues to take into account when applying sex determination techniques:

- Temporal and spatial variation within and between populations makes reevaluation of sexually dimorphic traits to determine sex necessary for application to modern skeletal remains.
- Modern populations need to be studied because populations of the past were affected by different nutritional, environmental, and living conditions. This means that studies of past populations are not directly comparable to populations of today due to secular and temporal trends that affect dimorphic expression.
- Age is an important factor as some features on the skull do not develop until late adolescence, providing ambiguous results from the crania as juvenile males may not express robust traits, leading to a female diagnosis (Kjellström 2004).
- Elderly females tend to adopt masculine characteristics that affect the morphology once menstruation has ceased, resulting in misclassifications of females as males (Kjellström 2004).
- Different parts of the skeleton have more value in determining sex; sex determination may be of increased importance in medicolegal situations, where the identity of an individual is sought (Kjellström 2004).
- There may be importance in a medicolegal sense (Gapert et al. 2009a, 2009b) in providing an identity for an individual.
- Sex bias is important as it affects the accuracy of evaluation of sex. A 1:1 sex ratio is hypothesised to account for the total variation a population may express.
- Discriminant function analysis is derived from one population and therefore cannot be applied interchangeably to any other sample.

- Dismemberment of remains occurs; therefore, even fragmented bones need to be utilized to determine sex from the skeleton (Asala 2001).

References

Abdel, Moneim, W. M., Abdel Hady, R. H., Abdel Maaboud, R. M., Fathy, H. M., and Hamed, A. M. 2008. Identification of sex depending on radiological examination of foot and patella. *American Journal of Forensic Medicine and Pathology*, 29, 136–140.

Akansel, G., Inan, N., Kurtas, O., Sarisoy, H. T., Arslan, A., and Demirci, A. 2008. Gender and the lateral angle of the internal acoustic canal meatus as measured on computerized tomography of the temporal bone. *Forensic Science International*, 178, 93–95.

Asala, S. A. 2001. Sex determination from the head of the femur of South African Whites and Blacks. *Forensic Science International*, 117, 15–22.

Barrier, I. L. O., and L'Abbe, E. N. 2008. Sex determination from the radius and ulna in a modern South African sample. *Forensic Science International*, 179, 85.e1–85.e7.

Benazzi, S., Maestri, C., Parisini, S., Vecchi, F., and Gruppioni, G. 2008. Sex assessment from the acetabular rim by means of image analysis. *Forensic Science International*, 180, 58.e1–58.e3.

Benazzi, S., Maestri, C., Parisini, S., Vecchi, F., and Gruppioni, G. 2009. Sex assessment from the sacral base by means of image processing. *Journal of Forensic Sciences*, 54, 249–254.

Bidmos, M. A., and Dayal, M. R. 2003. Sex determination from the talus of South African Whites by discriminant function analysis. *The American Journal of Forensic Medicine and Pathology*, 24, 322–328.

Bidmos, M. A., Steinberg, N., and Kuykendall, K. L. 2005. Patella measurements of South African whites as sex assessors. *HOMO—Journal of Comparative Human Biology*, 56, 69–74.

Biwasaka, H., Aoki, Y., Tanijiri, T., Sato, K., Fujita, S., Yoshioka, K., and Tomabechi, M. 2009. Analyses of sexual dimorphism of contemporary Japanese using reconstructed three-dimensional CT images—Curvature of the best-fit circle of the greater sciatic notch. *Legal Medicine*, 11, S260–S262.

Black, T. K. R. 1978. A new method for assessing the sex of fragmentary skeletal remains: Femoral shaft circumference. *Americal Journal of Physical Anthropology*, 48, 227–231.

Boucher, B. J. 1957. Sex differences in the foetal pelvis. *American Journal of Physical Anthropology*, 15, 581–600.

Brüžek, J. 2002. A method for visual determination of sex, using the human hip bone. *American Journal of Physical Anthropology*, 117, 157–168.

Buikstra, J. E., and Ubelaker, D. H. 1994. *Standards for data collection from human skeletal remains*. Fayetteville, AR: Arkansas Archaeological Society.

Burrows, A. M., Zanella, V. P., and Brown, T. M. 2003. Testing the validity of metacarpal use in sex assessment of human skeletal remains. *Journal of Forensic Sciences*, 48, 17–20.

Case, D. T., and Ross, A. H. 2007. Sex determination from hand and foot bone lengths. *Journal of Forensic Sciences*, 52, 264–270.

Celbis, O., and Agritmis, H. 2006. Estimation of stature and determination of sex from radial and ulnar bone lengths in a Turkish corpse sample. *Forensic Science International,* 158, 135–139.

Correia, H., Balseiro, S., and De Areia, M. 2005. Sexual dimorphism in the human pelvis: Testing a new hypothesis. *Homo,* 56, 153–160.

Cowal, L. S., and Pastor, R. F. 2008. Dimensional variation in the proximal ulna: Evaluation of a metric method for sex assessment. *American Journal of Physical Anthropology,* 135, 469–478.

Dabbs, G. R. 2009. Is Dwight right? Can maximum height of the scapular be used for accurate sex estimation? *Journal of Forensic Sciences,* 54, 529–530.

Dabbs, G. R., and Moore-Jansen, P. H. 2010. A method for estimating sex using metric analysis of the scapular. *Journal of Forensic Sciences,* 55, 149–152.

Dar, G., and Hershkovitz, I. 2006. Sacroiliac joint bridging: Simple and reliable criteria for sexing the skeleton. *Journal of Forensic Sciences,* 51, 480–483.

Dayal, M. R., and Bidmos, A. B. 2005. Discriminating sex in South African blacks using patella dimensions. *Journal of Forensic Sciences,* 50, 1294–1297.

De Paiva, L. A., and Segre, M. 2003. Sexing the human skull through the mastoid process. *Revista do Hospital das Clínicas,* 58, 15–20.

Deshmukh, A. G., and Devershi, D. B. 2006. Comparison of cranial sex determination by univariate and multivariate analysis. *Journal of the Anatomical Society of India,* 55, 48–51.

Dixit, S. G., Kakar, S., Agarwal, S., and Choudhry, R. 2007. Sexing of human hip bone of Indian origin by discriminant function analysis. *Journal of Forensic and Legal Medicine,* 14, 429–435.

Durić, M., Rakocević, Z., and Donić, D. 2005. The reliability of sex determination of skeletons from forensic context in the Balkans. *Forensic Science International,* 147, 159–164.

Dwight, T. 1881. The sternum as an index of sex, height and age. *Journal of Anatomical Physiology,* 15, 327–330.

Dwight, T. 1894. The range and significance of variation in the human skeleton. *Boston Medical Surgery Journal,* 131, 73–76.

Falsetti, A. B. 1995. Sex assessment from metacarpals of the human hand. *Journal of Forensic Sciences,* 40, 774–776.

Falys, C. G., Weston, D. A., and Schutkowski, H. 2005. The distal humerus—A blind test of Rogers' sexing technique using a documented skeletal collection. *Journal of Forensic Sciences,* 50, 1289–1293.

Fernández, H., and Monchot, H. 2007. Sexual dimorphism in limb bones of ibex (*Capra ibex* L.): Mixture analysis applied to modern and fossil data. *International Journal of Osteoarchaeology,* 17, 479–491.

Franklin, D., O'Higgins, P., Oxnard, C. E., and Dadour, I. 2008. Discriminant function sexing of the mandible of indigenous South Africans. *Forensic Science International,* 179, 84.e1–84.e5.

Gapert, G., Black, S., and Last, J. 2009a. Sex determination from the foramen magnum: Discriminant function analysis in an eighteenth and nineteenth century British sample. *International Journal of Legal Medicine,* 123, 25–33.

Gapert, R., Black, S., and Last, J. 2009b. Sex determination from the occipital condyle: Discriminant functional analysis in an eighteenth and nineteenth century British sample. *American Journal of Physical Anthropology,* 138, 384–394.

González, P. N., Bernal, V., and Perez, I. S. 2009a. Analysis of sexual dimorphism of craniofacial traits using geometric morphometric techniques. *International Journal of Osteoarchaeology*.

González, P. N., Bernal, V., and Perez, S. I. 2009b. Geometric morphometric approach to sex estimation of human pelvis. *Forensic Science International*, 189, 68–74.

González, P. N., Bernal, V., Perez, I. S., and Barrientos, G. 2007. Analysis of dimorphic structures of the human pelvis: Its implications for sex estimation in samples without reference collections. *Journal of Archaeological Science*, 34, 1720–1730.

González-Reimers, E., Velasco-Vázquez, J., Arnay-De-La-Rosa, M., and Santolaria-Fernández, F. 2000. Sex determination by discriminant function analysis of the right tibia in the prehispanic population of the Canary Islands. *Forensic Science International*, 108, 165–172.

Gualdi-Russo, E. 2007. Sex determination from the talus and calcaneus measurements. *Forensic Science International*, 171, 151–156.

Hyrtl, J. 1857. *Topographischen Anatomie*. Vienna: Wilhelm Braumuller.

Igbigbi, P. S., and Msamati, B. C. 2000. Sex determination from femoral head diameters in Black Malawians. *East African Medical Journal*, 77, 147–151.

Igbigbi, P. S., and Nanono-Igbigbi, A. M. 2003. Determination of sex and race from the subpubic angle in Ugandan subjects. *American Journal of Medical Pathology*, 24, 168–172.

İşcan, M. Y., and Derrick, K. 1984. Determination of sex from the sacroiliac joint: A visual assessment technique. *Florida Science*, 47, 94–98.

Kemkes-Grottenthaler, A. 2005. Sex determination by discriminant analysis: An evaluation of the reliability of patella measurements. *Forensic Science International*, 147, 129–133.

Kimmerle, E. H., Ross, A., and Slice, D. E. 2008. Sexual dimorphism in America: Geometric morphometric analysis of the craniofacial region. *Journal of Forensic Sciences*, 53, 54–57.

Kjellström, A. 2004. Evaluations of sex assessment using weighted traits on incomplete skeletal remains. *International Journal of Osteoarchaeology*, 14, 360–373.

Koçak, A., Aktas, E. Ö., Ertürk, S., Aktas, S., and Yemişçigil, A. 2003. Sex determination from the sternal end of the rib by osteometric analysis. *Legal Medicine*, 5, 100–104.

Kranioti, E. F., and Michalodimitrakis, M. 2009. Sexual dimorphism of the humerus in contemporary Cretans—A population-specific study and review of the literature. *Journal of Forensic Sciences*, 54, 996–1000.

Listi, G. A., and Bassett, H. E. 2006. Test of an alternative method for determining sex from the os coxae: Applications for modern Americans. *Journal of Forensic Sciences*, 51, 248–252.

Loth, S. R., and Henneberg, M. 2001. Sexually dimorphic mandibular morphology in the first few years of life. *American Journal of Physical Anthropology*, 115, 179–186.

Lynnerup, N., Schulz, M., Madelung, A., and Graw, M. 2006. Diameter of the human internal acoustic meatus and sex determination. *International Journal of Osteoarchaeology*, 16, 118–123.

Mahfouz, M., Badawi, A., Merkl, B., Abdel Fatah, E. E., Pritchard, E., Kesler, K., Moore, M., Jantz, R., and Jantz, L. 2007. Patella sex determination by 3D statistical shape models and nonlinear classifiers. *Forensic Science International*, 173, 161–170.

Mall, G., Hubig, M., Buttner, A., Kuznik, J., Penning, R., and Graw, M. 2001. Sex determination and estimation of stature from the long bones of the arm. *Forensic Science International*, 117, 23–30.

McBride, D. G., Dietz, M. J., Vennemeyer, M. T., Meadors, S. A., Benfer, R. A., and Furbee, N. L. 2001. Bootstrap methods for sex determination from the OS coxae using the ID3 algorithm. *Journal of Forensic Sciences*, 46, 427–431.

Nagaoka, T., and Hirata, K. 2009. Reliability of metric determination of sex based on long-bone circumferences: Perspectives from Yuigahama-minami, Japan. *Anatomy Science International*, 84, 7–16.

Nagesh, K. R., Kanchan, T., and Bastia, B. K. 2007. Sexual dimorphism of acetabulum-pubis index in South-Indian population. *Legal Medicine*, 9, 305–308.

Oettlé, A. C., Pretorius, E., and Steyn, M. 2005. Geometric morphometric analysis of mandibular ramus flexure. *Americal Journal of Physical Anthropology*, 128, 623–629.

Papaloucas, C., Fiska, A., and Demetriou, T. 2008. Sexual dimorphism of the hip joint in Greeks. *Forensic Science International*, 179, 83.e1–83.e3.

Patriquin, M. L., Loth, S. R., and Steyn, M. 2003. Sexually dimorphic pelvis morphology in South African Whites and Blacks. HOMO—*Journal of Comparative Human Biology*, 53, 255–262.

Phenice, T. W. (1969) A newly developed visual method of sexing the Os Pubis. *American Journal of Physical Anthropology*, 30(2), 297–301.

Plavcan, J. M. 2001. Sexual dimorphism in primate evolution. *Yearbook of Physical Anthropology*, 44, 25–53.

Prado, F. B., De Mello Santos, L. S., Caria, P. H. F., Kawaguchi, J. T., Preza, A. D. O. G., Daruge, E., De Silva, R. F., and Daruge, E. 2009. Incidence of clavicular rhomboid fossa (Impression for costoclavicular ligament) in the Brazilain population: Forensic application. *Journal of Forensic Odonto-Stomatology*, 27, 12–16.

Pretorius, E., Steyn, M., and Scholtz, Y. 2006. Investigation into the usability of geometric morphometric analysis in assessment of sexual dimorphism. *American Journal of Physical Anthropology*, 129, 64–70.

Purkait, R. 2001. Measurements of the ulna: A new method for determination of sex. *Journal of Forensic Sciences*, 46, 924–927.

Ramadan, S. U., Türkmen, N., Dolgun, N. A., Gökharman, D., Menezes, R. G., Kacar, M., and Kosar, U. 2010. Sex determination from measurements of the sternum and fourth rib using multislice computed tomography of the chest. *Forensic Science International*, 197, 120.e1–120.e5.

Rissech, C., Garcia, M., and Malgosa, A. 2003. Sex and age diagnosis by ishium morphometric analysis. *Forensic Science International*, 135, 188–196.

Rissech, C., and Malgosa, A. 2005. Ilium growth study: Applicability in sex and age diagnostic. *Forensic Science International*, 147, 165–174.

Rissech, C., and Malgosa, A. 2007. Pubis growth study: Applicability in sexual and age diagnostic. *Forensic Science International*, 173, 137–145.

Rogers, N. L., Flournoy, L. E., and McCormick, W. F. 2000. The rhomboid fossa of the clavicle as a sex and age estimator. *Journal of Forensic Sciences*, 45, 61–67.

Rogers, T. L. 1999. A visual method of determining the sex of the skeletal remains using the distal humerus. *Journal of Forensic Sciences*, 44, 57–60.

Rooppakhun, S., Piyasin, S. and Sitthiseripratip, K. 2009. 3D CT craniometric study of Thai skulls revelance to sex determination using logistic regression analysis. *IFMBE Proceedings*, 23, 761–764.

Sakaue, K. 2004. Sexual determination of long bones in recent Japanese. *Anthropological Science*, 112, 75–81.

Scheuer, J. L., and Elkington, N. M. 1993. Sex determination from the metacarpals and first proximal phalanx. *Journal of Forensic Sciences*, 38, 769–778.

Scheuer, L. 2002. Application of osteology to forensic medicine. *Clinical Anatomy*, 15, 297–312.

Schutkowski, H. 1993. Sex determination of infant and juvenile skeletons: I. morphognostic features. *American Journal of Physical Anthropology*, 90, 199–205.

Steyn, M., and İşcan, M. Y. 2008. Metric sex determination from the pelvis in modern Greeks. *Forensic Science International*, 179, 86.e1–86.e6.

Steyn, M., and Patriquin, M. L. 2009. Osteometric sex determination from the pelvis—Does population specificity matter? *Forensic Science International*, 191, 113.e–113.e5.

Steyn, M., Pretorius, E., and Hutten, L. 2004. Geometric morphometric analysis of the greater sciatic notch in South Africans. HOMO—*Journal of Comparative Human Biology*, 54, 197–206.

Stojanowski, C. M. 1999. Sexing potential of fragmentary and pathological metacarpals. *American Journal of Physical Anthropology*, 109, 245–252.

Suazo, G. I. C., Zavando, M. D. A., and Smith, R. L. 2008. Sex determination using mastoid process measurements in Brazilian skulls. *International Journal of Morphology*, 26, 941–944.

Sulzmann, C. E., Buckburry, J. L., and Pastor, R. F. 2008. The utility of carpals for sex assessment: A preliminary study. *American Journal of Physical Anthropology*, 135, 252–262.

Tague, R. G. 2007. Costal process of the first sacral vertebra: Sexual dimorphism and obstetrical adapation. *American Journal of Physical Anthropology*, 132, 395–405.

Takahashi, H. 2006. Curvature of the greater sciatic notch in sexing the human pelvis. *Anthropological Science*, 114, 187–191.

Torwalt, C. R., and Hoppa, R. D. 2005. A test of sexual determination from measurements of chest radiographs. *Journal of Forensic Sciences*, 50, 785–790.

Ubelaker, D. H., and Volk, C. G. 2002. A test of the phenice method for estimation of sex. *Journal of Forensic Sciences*, 47, 19–24.

Veroni, A., Nikitovic, D., and Schillaci, M. A. 2010. Brief communication: Sexual dimorphism of the juvenile basicranium. *American Journal of Physical Anthropology*, 141, 147–151.

Vlak, D., Roksandic, M., and Schillaci, M. A. 2008. Greater sciatic notch as a sex indicator in juveniles. *American Journal of Physical Anthropology*, 137, 309–315.

Wahl, J., and Graw, M. 2001. Metric sex differentiation of the pars petrosa ossis temporalis. *International Journal of Legal Medicine*, 114, 215–223.

Walker, P. L. 2005. Greater sciatic notch morphology: Sex, age, and population differences. *American Journal of Physical Anthropology*, 127, 385–391.

Walker, P.L. 2008. Sexing skulls using discriminant function analysis of visually assessed traits. *American Journal of Physical Anthropology*, 136:39–50.

Weaver, D. S. (1980). Sex differences in the ilia of a known sex and age sample of fetal and infant skeletons. *American Journal of Physical Anthropology*, 52, 191–195.

Wescott, D. J. 2000. Sex variation in the second cervical vertebra. *Journal of Forensic Sciences*, 45, 462–466.

Wilkinson, C. 2004. *Forensic Facial Reconstruction*, University Press, Cambridge.

Wilson, L. A., Macleod, N., and Humphrey, L. T. 2008. Morphometric criteria for sexing juvenile human skeletons using the ilium. *Journal of Forensic Sciences*, 53, 269–278.

Zeybek, G., Ergur, I., and Demiroglu, Z. 2008. Stature and gender estimation using foot measurements. *Forensic Science International*, 181, 54.e1–54.e5.

Bibliography

Albanese, J. 2003. A metric method for sex determination using the hipbone and the femur. *Journal of Forensic Sciences*, 48, 263–273.

Albanese, J., Cardoso, H. F. V., and Saunders, S. R. 2005. Universal methodology for developing univariate sample-specific sex determination methods: An example using the epicondylar breadth of the humerus. *Journal of Archaeological Science*, 32, 143–152.

Albanese, J., Eklics, G., and Tuck, A. 2008. A metric method for sex determination using the proximal femur and fragmentary hipbone. *Journal of Forensic Sciences*, 53, 1283–1288.

Alunni-Perret, V., Staccini, P., and Quatrehomme, G. 2003. Reexamination of a measurement for sexual determination using the supero-inferior femoral neck diameter in a modern European population. *Journal of Forensic Sciences*, 48, 517–520.

Asala, S. A. 2002. The efficiency of the demarking point of the femoral head as a sex determining parameter. *Forensic Science International*, 127, 114–118.

Asala, S. A., Bidmos, M. A., and Dayal, M. R. 2004. Discriminant function sexing of fragmentary femur of South African Blacks. *Forensic Science International*, 145, 25–29.

Badawi-Frayad, J., and Cabanis, E.-A. 2007. Three-dimensional Procrustes analysis of modern human craniofacial form. *Anatomical Record*, 290, 268–276.

Barrio, P. A., Trancho, G. J., and Sánchez, J. A. 2006. Metacarpal sexual determination in a Spanish population. *Journal of Forensic Sciences*, 51, 990–995.

Bastir, M., Rosas, A., and O'Higgins, P. 2006. Craniofacial levels and the morphological maturation of the human skull. *Journal of Anatomy*, 209, 637–654.

Bernal, V., Perez, S. I., and Gonzalez, P. N. 2006. Variation and causal factors of craniofacial robusticity in Patagonian hunter-gatherers from the Late Holocene. *American Journal of Human Biology*, 18, 748–765.

Bidmos, M. 2006. Metrical and non-metrical assessment of population affinity from the calcaneus. *Forensic Science International*, 159, 6–13.

Bidmos, M. A., and Asala, S. A. 2003. Discriminant function sexing of the calcaneus of the South African Whites. *Journal of Forensic Sciences*, 48, 1213–1218.

Bidmos, M. A., and Asala, S. A. 2004. Sexual dimorphism of the calcaneus of South African Blacks. *Journal of Forensic Sciences,* 49, 446–450.

Bidmos, M. A., and Dayal, M. R. 2004. Further evidence to show population specificity of discriminant function equations for sex determination using the talus of South African Blacks. *Journal of Forensic Sciences,* 49, 1165–1170.

Birkby, W. H. 1966. An evaluation of race and sex identification from cranial measurements. *American Journal of Physical Anthropology,* 24, 21–28.

Bogin, B., Smith, P., Orden, A. B., Varela Silva, M. I., and Loucky, J. 2002. Rapid change in height and body proportions of Maya children. *American Journal of Human Biology,* 14, 753–761.

Braga, J., and Treil, J. 2007. Estimation of pediatric skeletal age using geometric morphometrics and three-dimensional cranial size changes. *International Journal of Legal Medicine,* 121, 439–443.

Bruner, E., and Manzi, G. 2004. Variability in facial size and shape among north and east African human populations. *Italian Journal of Zoology,* 71, 51–56.

Bruner, E., and Ripani, M. 2008. A quantitative and descriptive approach to morphological variation of the endocranial base in modern humans. *American Journal of Physical Anthropology,* 137, 30–40.

Brüžek, J., and Murail, P. 2006. Methodology and reliability of sex determination from the skeleton. In: Schmitt, A., Cunha, E., and Pinheiro, J. (Eds.), *Forensic anthropology and medicine: Complementary sciences from recovery to cause of death.* Totowa, NJ: Humana Press, pp. 225–242.

Buck, T. J., and Vidarsdottir, U. S. 2004. A proposed method for the identification of race in sub-adult skeletons: A geometric morphometric analysis of mandibular morphology. *Journal of Forensic Sciences,* 49, 1159–1164.

Buretić-Tomljanović, A., Ostojić, S., and Kapović, M. 2006. Secular change of craniofacial measures in Croatian younger adults. *American Journal of Human Biology,* 18, 668–675.

Carlson, K. J., Grine, F. E., and Pearson, O. M. 2007. Robusticity and sexual dimorphism in the postcranium of mordern hunter-gatherers from Australia. *American Journal of Physical Anthropology,* 134, 9–23.

Coqueugniot, H., Tillier, A.-M., and Bruzek, J. 2000. Mandibular ramus posterior flexure: A sex indicator in *Homo Sapiens* fossil hominids? *International Journal of Osteoarchaeology,* 10, 426–431.

Coussens, A. K., Anson, T. J., Norris, R. M., and Henneberg, M. 2002. Sexual dimorphism in the robusticity of long bones of infants and young children. *Przegląd Anthropologiczng œ Anthropological Review,* 65, 3–16.

Dibernnardo, R., and Taylor, J. 1979. Sex assessment of the femur: A test of a new method. *American Journal of Physical Anthropology,* 50, 635–638.

Ferembach, D., Schwidetzky, I., and Stloukal, M. 1980. Recommendations for age and sex diagnoses of skeletons. *Journal of Human Evolution,* 9, 517–549.

Franklin, D., Freedman, L., and Milne, N. 2005a. Sexual dimorphism and discriminant function sexing in indigenous South African crania. *HOMO—Journal of Comparative Human Biology,* 55, 213–228.

Franklin, D., Freedman, L., and Milne, N. 2005b. Three-dimensional technology for linear morphological studies: A re-examination of cranial variation in four southern African indigenous populations. *HOMO—Journal of Comparative Human Biology,* 56, 17–34.

Franklin, D., Freedman, L., Milne, N., and Oxnard, C. E. 2006. A geometric morphometric study of sexual dimorphism in the crania of indigenous Southern Africans. *South African Journal of Science,* 102, 229–238.

Franklin, D., Freedman, L., Milne, N., and Oxnard, C. E. 2007. Geometric morphometric study of population variation in indigenous Southern African crania. *American Journal of Human Biology,* 19, 20–33.

Franklin, D., Freedman, L., O'Higgins, P., and Oxnard, C. E. 2009. A comment on assessment of sex using the skull. *HOMO—Journal of Comparative Human Biology,* 60, 139–142.

Franklin, D., O'Higgins, P., and Oxnard, C. E. 2008. Sexual dimorphism in the mandible of indigenous South Africans: A geometric morphometric approach. *South African Journal of Science,* 104, 101–106.

Franklin, D., O'Higgins, P., Oxnard, C. E., and Dadour, I. 2006. Determination of sex in South African Blacks by discriminant function analysis of mandibular linear dimensions: A preliminary investigation using the Zulu local population. *Forensic Science, Medicine, and Pathology,* 2, 263–268.

Franklin, D., O'Higgins, P., Oxnard, C. E., and Dadour, I. 2007. Sexual dimorphism and population variation in the adult mandible. Forensic applications of geometric morphometrics. *Forensic Science, Medicine, and Pathology,* 3, 15–22.

Frutos, L. R. 2005. Metric determination of sex from the humerus in a Guatemalan forensic sample. *Forensic Science International,* 147, 153–157.

Giles, E. 1964. Sex determination by discriminant function analysis of the mandible. *American Journal of Physical Anthropology,* 22, 129–135.

Graham, E. A. M. 2006. Sex determination. *Forensic Science, Medicine, and Pathology,* 2, 283–286.

Graw, M., Schulz, M., and Wahl, J. 2003. A simple morphological method for gender determination at the petrous portion of the os temporalis. *Forensic Science International,* 136, S165–166.

Graw, M., Wahl, J., and Ahlbrecht, M. 2005. Course of the meatus acusticus internus as criterion for sex differentiation. *Forensic Science International,* 147, 113–117.

Gülekon, I. N., and Turgut, H. B. 2003. The external occipital protuberance: Can it be used as a criterion in the determination of sex? *Journal of Forensic Sciences,* 48, 513–516.

Gustafsson, A., and Lindenfors, P. 2004. Human size evolution: No evolution allometric relationship between male and female stature. *Journal of Human Evolution,* 47, 253–266.

Hennessy, R. J., Kinsella, A., and Waddington, J. L. 2002. 3D laser surface scanning and geometric morphometric analysis of craniofacial shape as an index of cerebro-craniofacial morphogenesis: Initial application to sexual dimorphism. *Biological Psychiatry,* 51, 507–514.

Hennessy, R. J., and Stringer, C. B. 2002. Geometric morphometric study of the regional variation of modern human craniofacial form. *American Journal of Physical Anthropology,* 117, 37–48.

Hill, C. A. 2000. Evaluating mandibular ramus flexure as a morphological indicator of sex. *American Journal of Physical Anthropology,* 111, 573–577.

Holcomb, S. M. C., and Konigsberg, L. W. 1995. Statistical study of sexual dimorphism in the human fetal sciatic notch. *American Journal of Physical Anthropology,* 97, 113–125.

Hunter, W. S., and Garn, S. M. 1972. Disproportionate sexual dimorphism in the human face. *American Journal of Physical Anthropology, 36,* 133–138.

Introna, J., Di Vella, G., and Campobasso, C. 1998. Sex determination by discriminant function analysis of patella measurements. *Forensic Science International, 95,* 39–45.

İşcan, M. Y. 1985. Osteometric analysis of sexual dimorphism in the sternal end of the ribs. *Journal of Forensic Sciences, 30,* 1090–1099.

İşcan, M. Y. 2005. Forensic anthropology of sex and body size. *Forensic Science International, 147,* 107–112.

İşcan, M. Y., and Kedici, P. S. 2003. Sexual variation in bucco-lingual dimensions in Turkish dentition. *Forensic Science International, 137,* 160–164.

İşcan, M. Y., Loth, S., King, C., Shihai, D., and Yoshino, M. 1998. Sexual dimorphism in the humerus: A comparative analysis of Chinese, Japanese and Thais. *Forensic Science International, 98,* 17–29.

İşcan, M. Y., and Miller-Shaivitz, P. 1984. Determination of sex from the femur in Blacks and Whites. *College Anthropology, 8,* 169–175.

İşcan, M. Y., Yoshino, M., and Kato, S. 1994. Sex determination from the tibia: Standards for contemporary Japan. *Journal of Forensic Sciences, 39,* 785–792.

Jonke, E., Prossinger, H., Bookstein, F. L., Schaefer, K., Bernhard, M., and Freudenthaler, J. W. 2007. Secular trends in the facial skull from the 19th century to the present, analyzed with geometric morphometrics. *American Journal of Orthodontics and Dentofacial Orthopedics, 132,* 63–70.

Kemkes, A., and Göbel, T. 2006. Metric assessment of the "mastoid triangle" for sex determination: A validation study. *Journal of Forensic Sciences, 51,* 985–989.

King, C., Işcan, M., and Loth, S. 1998. Metric and comparative analysis of sexual dimorphism in the Thai femur. *Journal of Forensic Sciences, 43,* 954–958.

Lazenby, R. 2001. Sex dimorphism and bilateral asymmetry: Modeling developmental instability and functional adaptation. *American Journal of Physical Anthropology, 96,* S32.

Lazenby, R. A. 2002. Population variation in second metacarpal sexual size dimorphism. *American Journal of Physical Anthropology, 118,* 378–384.

Loth, S. R., and Henneberg, M. 1996. Mandibular ramus flexure: A new morphologic indicator of sexual dimorphism in the human skeleton. *American Journal of Physical Anthropology, 99,* 473–485.

Lynnerup, N. 2001. Cranial thickness in relation to age, sex, and general body build in a Danish forensic sample. *Forensic Science International, 117,* 45–51.

Mall, G., Graw, M., Gehring, K.-D., and Hubig, M. 2000. Determination of sex from femora. *Forensic Science International, 113,* 315–321.

Mays, S., and Cox, M. 2000. Sex determination in skeletal remains. In: Cox, M., and Mays, S. (Eds.), *Human osteology in archaeology and forensic science.* London: Greenwich Medical Media, pp. 117–130.

Monticelli, F., and Graw, M. 2008. Investigation on the reliability of determining sex from the human os zygomaticum. *Forensic Science, Medicine, and Pathology, 4,* 181–186.

Murphy, A. 2000. The acetabulum: Sex assessment of prehistoric New Zealand Polynesian innominates. *Forensic Science International, 108,* 39–43.

Oettlé, A. C., Pretorius, E., and Steyn, M. 2009. Geometric morphometric analysis of the use of mandibular gonial eversion in sex determination. *HOMO—Journal of Comparative Human Biology,* 60, 29–43.

Oettlé, A. C., and Steyn, M. 2000. Age estimation from sternal ends of ribs by phase analysis in South African Blacks. *Journal of Forensic Sciences,* 45, 1071–1079.

Patil, K. R., and Mody, R. N. 2005. Determination of sex by discriminant function analysis and stature by regression analysis: A lateral cephalometric study. *Forensic Science International,* 147, 175–180.

Patriquin, M. L., Loth, S. R., and Steyn, M. 2002. Sexually dimorphic pelvis morphology in South African Whites and Blacks. *Homo,* 53, 255–262.

Patriquin, M. L., Steyn, M., and Loth, S. R. 2005. Metric analysis of sex differences in South African Black and White pelves. *Forensic Science International,* 147, 119–127.

Perez, S. I., Bernal, V., and Gonzalez, P. N. 2006. Differences between sliding semi-landmark methods in geometric morphometrics, with an application to human craniofacial and dental variation. *Journal of Anatomy,* 208, 769–784.

Plavcan, M. J. 2001. Sexual dimorphism in primate evolution. *American Journal of Physical Anthropology,* 116, 25–53.

Pomeroy, E., and Zakrzewski, S. R. 2009. Sexual dimorphism in diaphyseal cross-sectional shape in the medieval Muslim population of Écija, Spain, and Anglo-Saxon Great Chesterford, UK. *International Journal of Osteoarchaeology,* 19, 50–65.

Purkait, R. 2002. Sexual dimorphism in the femoral head: A new approach. *Canadian Society of Forensic Science,* 35, 209–221.

Purkait, R. 2003. Sex determination from femoral head measurements: A new approach. *Legal Medicine,* 5, S347–350.

Purkait, R. 2005. Triangle identified at the proximal end of femur: A new sex determinant. *Forensic Science International,* 147, 135–139.

Purkait, R., and Chandra, H. 2004. A study of sexual variation in Indian femur. *Forensic Science International,* 146, 25–33.

Randolph-Quinney, P. S., Mallett, X., and Black, S. 2009. Forensic anthropology. In: Jamieson, A. (Ed.), *Wiley encyclopaedia of forensic sciences.* Chichester, UK: Wiley, 1, 152–178.

Ríos, L. 2002. Determination of sex from the clavicle and scapula in a Guatemalan contemporary rural indigenous population. *American Journal of Forensic Medicine and Pathology,* 23, 284–28.

Ríos, L. 2003. Brief communication: Sex determination accuracy of the minimum supero-inferior femoral neck diameter in a contemporary rural Guatemalan population. *American Journal of Physical Anthropology,* 122, 123–126.

Rogers, T. L., and Allard, T. T. 2004. Expert testimony and positive identification of human remains through cranial suture patterns. *Journal of Forensic Sciences,* 49, 203–207.

Rosas, A., and Bastir, M. 2002. Thin-plate spline analysis of allometry and sexual dimorphism in human craniofacial complex. *American Journal of Physical Anthropology,* 117, 236–245.

Rösing, F. W., Graw, M., Marré, B., Ritz-Timme, S., Rothschild, M. A., Rötzscher, K., Schmeling, A., Schröder, I., and Geserick, G. 2007. Recommendations for the forensic diagnosis of sex and age from skeletons. *HOMO—Journal of Comparative Human Biology, 58,* 75–89.

Safont, S., Malgosa, A., and Subirá, M. E. 2000. Sex assessment on the basis of long bone circumference. *American Journal of Physical Anthropology, 113,* 317–328.

Scheuer, L. 2002b. A blind test of mandibular morphology for sexing mandibles in the first few years of life. *American Journal of Physical Anthropology, 119,* 189–191.

Schmittbuhl, M., Le Minor, J. M., Taroni, F., and Mangin, P. 2001. Sexual dimorphism of the human mandible: Demonstration by elliptical Fourier analysis. *International Journal of Legal Medicine, 115,* 100–101.

Slaus, M., Strinović, D., Skavić, J., and Petrovecki, V. 2003. Discriminant function sexing of fragmentary and complete femora: Standards for contemporary Croatia. *Journal of Forensic Sciences, 48,* 509–512.

Steyn, M., and Işcan, M. 1997. Sex determination from the femur and tibia in South African Whites. *Forensic Science International, 90,* 111–119.

Steyn, M., and Işcan, M. Y. 1998. Sexual dimorphism in the crania and mandibles of South African Whites. *Forensic Science International, 98,* 9–16.

Steyn, M., and Işcan, M. Y. 1999. Osteometric variation in the humerus: Sexual dimorphism in South Africans. *Forensic Science International, 106,* 77–85.

Tague, R. G. 2005. Big-bodied males help us recognize that females have big pelves. *American Journal of Physical Anthropology, 127,* 392–405.

Uysal, S., Gokharman, D., Kacar, M., Tuncbilek, I., and Kosar, U. 2005. Estimation of sex by 3D CT measurements of the foramen magnum. *Journal of Forensic Sciences, 50,* 1310–1314.

Veldhuis, J. D., Metzger, D. L., Martha, P. M., Mauras, N., Kerrigan, J. R., Keenan, B., Rogol, A. D., and Pincus, S. M. 1997. Estrogen and testosterone, but not a nonaromatizable androgen, direct network integration of the hypothalamo-somatotrope (growth hormone)–insulin-like growth factor I axis in the human: Evidence from pubertal pathophysiology and sex-steroid hormone replacement. *The Journal of Clinical Endocrinology and Metabolism, 82,* 3414–3420.

Walrath, D. E., Turner, P., and Bruzek, J. 2004. Reliability test of the visual assessment of cranial traits for sex determination. *American Journal of Physical Anthropology, 125,* 132–137.

Wheatley, B. P. 2005. An evaluation of sex and body weight determination from the proximal femur using DXA technology and its potential for forensic anthropology. *Forensic Science International, 147,* 141–145.

Williams, B. A., and Rogers, T. L. 2006. Evaluating the accuracy and precision of cranial morphological traits for sex determination. *Journal of Forensic Sciences, 51,* 729–735.

Zanelle, V. P., and Brown, T. M. 2003. Testing the validity of metacarpal use in sex assessment of human skeletal remains. *Journal of Forensic Sciences, 48,* 17–20.

Further Reading

Ferembach, D., Schwidetzky, I., and Stloukal, M. (1980) Recommendations for age and sex diagnoses of skeletons. *Journal of Human Evolution, 9,* 517–549.

Giles, E. (1964). Sex determination by discriminant function analysis of the mandible. *American Journal of Physical Anthropology,* 22, 2, 129–135.

Holcomb, S. M. C., and Konigsberg, L. W. (1995). Statistical study of sexual dimorphism in the human fetal sciatic notch. *American Journal of Physical Anthropology,* 97, 113–125.

Hunter, W. S., and Garn, S. M. (1972). Disproportionate sexual dimorphism in the human face. *American Journal of Physical Anthropology,* 36, 1, 133–138.

İşcan, M. Y. (1985) Osteometric analysis of sexual dimorphism in the sternal end of the ribs. *Journal of Forensic Sciences,* 30(4), 1090–1099.

İşcan, M. Y., and Derrick, K. (1984) Determination of sex from the sacroiliac joint: A visual assessment technique. *Florida Science,* 47, 94–98.

Stature

4

KATIE NICOLL BAINES
SUSAN EDMOND
DR. ROOS EISMA

Contents

Introduction and Overview

The term *stature* originated from the Latin *statura*, meaning "height" or "size of body," and from the Latin verb *stare*, meaning "to stand": Stature relates to the natural standing height of a living individual. In the context of forensic anthropology, it forms part of the biological profile of an individual in the identification process. Stature, or more colloquially "height," is a generally accepted descriptor of an individual that the public, forensic experts, and criminal justice system recognize and understand.

Of the four principal components of this profile, stature can be considered the fourth in terms of importance. While stature does not affect the determination of sex, age, and ancestry, the other parameters play a role in the determination of stature and must be identified first.

A range of methods has been developed over time to determine stature from human remains of different degrees of completeness and preservation. The Fully method (Fully 1956), also known as the anatomical method, requires the presence of all skeletal elements that contribute to height to reconstruct the standing body. Mathematical methods, on the other hand, extrapolate stature from the size of a single bone or body part using regression formulae. This is most reliable using undamaged long bones of the limbs (Trotter and Gleser 1952), but methods are available for many other bones, for fragmented remains, and for body parts such as feet. While both the anatomical and the mathematical methods originated long before the time period covered in this review, work is ongoing to refine and revise them. More recently, methods have been added to determine stature from image-based material, such as closed-circuit television (CCTV) footage and computed tomographic (CT) scans of both dead and living individuals. Current research into each of these methods is discussed.

Methods to determine stature make assumptions about proportions of the human body. This is particularly the case for regression methods, which impose a simple relationship between the size of a specific bone and stature. However, people come in a variety of body shapes (Holliday and Ruff 2001; Sylvester et al. 2008); to account for this, separate formulae are needed for different groups and populations. The main grouping is sex; populations can be further defined by historical period, geography, and ancestry, and some methods take into account how body proportions depend on age or height. This is an area of ongoing activity, with standards developed for new populations as the need arises (İşcan 2005) and development of alternative statistical approaches. This is discussed further in a separate section before the regression methods themselves are considered.

The determination of stature produces a range within which it is expected to fall with 95% certainty. The width of this interval reflects measurement imprecision and individual variation in body proportions within a population but does not account for differences between the reference population used and the actual population. Such systematic errors related to population are difficult to estimate when applying a method.

Identification relies on a comparison between antemortem data and the estimated postmortem range. However, unlike age and sex, reliable data on antemortem height are not always available. Height in records is often self-reported (Giles and Hutchinson 1991), and errors can be made when using unfamiliar units. Estimates by other people, especially from memory, are not necessarily accurate. Instead, it may be more relevant to describe individuals as tall, average or short relative to their population (Komar 2003; Steyn and Smith 2007; Baraybar 2008).

Stature is also not a constant. After birth, there is an initial increase until adulthood, followed by a gradual decrease in later life. People are taller in the morning and become shorter during the day. Cadaver stature (measured lying down) is generally greater than living stature, and some authors (Ousley 1995) distinguished between biological stature (the actual standing height) and official stature (the documented height, e.g., on a driving license). The different approaches to defining and obtaining antemortem stature in population studies mean that care must be taken when applying methods or comparing studies, and this is an ongoing topic of discussion. An example of using stature information from different sources was given in a study of stature trends in the Dutch population (Maat 2005).

The lack of both appropriate reference populations and reliable antemortem data means that the contribution of stature to the identification process is limited in many mass grave investigations (Baraybar and Kimmerle 2002; Komar 2003; Djuric 2004; Baraybar 2008; Jantz et al. 2008; Kimmerle et al. 2008; Rios et al. 2010).

Steadman et al. (2006) discussed the statistical likelihood ratios for positive identification and the role of different components and demonstrated that stature contributes little to the identification in the case of individuals who fall within the average range of stature for their respective population, as a large proportion of this population will fall within the calculated interval.

The Fully Method

The Fully anatomical method of stature estimation (Fully 1956) involves the measurement of individual skeletal elements that contribute to the stature of an individual, using calipers and osteometric boards. There is a level of imprecision associated with the descriptions of how to measure the bones that could lead to problems using the technique. For example, there is potential confusion about how to measure the maximum height of the vertebrae, how to correctly position the articulated calcaneus and talus when measuring their maximum height, and how to measure the tibia correctly with current equipment. A revision of the method (Raxter et al. 2006) addressed these issues and provided explanations and descriptions of how to measure the individual elements. They also provided new soft tissue correction factors as the factors proposed by Fully were found to consistently underestimate stature (Bidmos 2005). Further research (Raxter et al. 2007) added age dependency to the soft tissue correction factors. Eight variations of the anatomical method, with some differences in measurement techniques and correction factors, have been compared on the Bass skeletal collection (Maijanen 2009).

The Fully method relies on relatively few assumptions about body proportions as most variation is accounted for directly. Remaining sources of variation are contained within the soft tissue correction factors. While some work has been done on how those depend on sex, height, and age, little is known about adjustments that should be made for juveniles or for groups with different spinal curvatures or extreme body weight. Some work has been done on how the method can be adjusted for individuals with nonstandard anatomy, such as variation in the number of vertebrae (Raxter and Ruff 2010), or how to make an estimate when a number of skeletal elements has not been recovered (Auerbach et al. 2005).

An alternative approach related to the anatomical method using the position of a skeleton in the grave has been proposed (Petersen 2005). It was reported to produce results similar to the Fully method.

Body Proportions, Populations, and Statistics

The linked issues of body proportions and populations and the statistical methods to describe them play a role in all methods discussed in the rest of this chapter. They should be kept in mind when assessing research, comparing methods, or implementing techniques, and developments in these areas are relevant to future and ongoing research into stature determination.

In stature determination, a known component (the size of the bone or body part) is combined with estimates for the missing information (the rest of the skeleton, missing soft tissue, exact body configuration such as spinal curvature, etc.) to produce an estimate for body height. This unknown component is the main cause of uncertainty in the result, and estimates are based on an average body shape in a reference population. Some of the variation in body shape can be linked to sex, ethnicity, historical period, geography, and socioeconomic class, and this necessitates the need for appropriate reference populations, an area of ongoing research.

It is thought that body proportions have a genetic as well as an environmental component, and changes have been shown to occur on both evolutionary and individual time scales. A full review of this area of research is outside the scope of this work, and only a selection of recent publications is mentioned here.

Evolutionary studies compare brachial, cormic, and crural indices (describing the proportions of upper vs. lower limbs, lower limbs vs. torso, and thigh vs. leg respectively) and other shape parameters of various hominid, (pre)historic, or contemporary populations and relate those to parameters such as climate, latitude, lifestyle, and socioeconomic status (Holliday and Ruff 2001; Ruff 2002; Holliday and Hilton 2010; Temple and Matsumura 2010). While many authors believe in a relationship between stature, body shape, and latitude, two linked studies (Gustafsson and Lindenfors 2004; Gustafsson and Lindenfors 2009) found that both stature and sexual dimorphism are most strongly associated with phylogeny.

Other studies showed that individuals exhibit variation in body proportions depending on conditions during their childhood. It has been proposed that high altitude differentially affects leg segment growth in modern populations (Bailey et al. 2007); studies of second-generation Mayan American children have shown them to be taller and longer legged than nonmigrant Mayans (Bogin et al. 2002; Bogin and Rios 2003), and adverse early life events have been related to shorter adult relative leg length (Li et al. 2007). Several authors addressed the complicated relationship among genetics, nutrition, environment, and development in an individual (Bogin and Rios 2003; Cole 2003; Bailey et al. 2007; Stinson 2009).

Secular changes in body proportions coupled with secular changes in stature have been observed in populations (Meadows Jantz and Jantz 1999; Jantz and Meadows Jantz 2000; Kromeyer-Hauschild and Jaeger 2000; Giannecchini and Moggi-Cecchi 2008; Kalichman et al. 2008; Malina et al. 2009). Jantz and Jantz (2000) found that lower-limb bone secular change is more pronounced than upper-limb bone change, and distal bones change more than proximal bones, particularly in the lower limb, while overall stature increased.

Within a population, further groupings can account for additional variation in body proportions. Age can play a role in two ways: First, age-related changes can shorten the trunk; second, the older generations of a population can reflect secular changes in living conditions. Allometry has been found between shorter and taller individuals, and groupings based on height within a population have been proposed (Duyar and Pelin 2003; Pelin and Duyar 2003; Duyar et al. 2006). A practical implication of this is that standards developed for a reference population with a certain range in stature and age are most valid for individuals within that range and cannot be extrapolated to different sizes or ages without incurring additional errors.

These studies illustrated that average proportions within a population can undergo rapid changes, and that a reference population can thus become unrepresentative for contemporary individuals after only a relatively short period of time. As current methods have generally been developed based on historical collections, this has been a topic of ongoing discussion since stature estimation methods were first published (Klepinger 2001). Klepinger, however, argued that secular trends in proportions and maturation rate are relatively small compared to the variation within a population and still fall within the confidence intervals of methods developed on older reference samples, and that other nonsecular sources of variability play a larger role when dealing with individual cases.

People are also not symmetrical (Auerbach and Ruff 2006; Kanchan, Kumar, et al. 2008; Krishan et al. 2010), and this means that methods developed using material from one side of the body may be less reliable when utilized on the opposite side.

To develop a new standard, a population with known stature is needed. The revised version of the Fully method has been used to develop or evaluate regression formulae in studies in which the living stature of the remains was not documented, usually in an archaeological context (Bidmos 2006; Chibba and Bidmos 2007; Bidmos 2008c; Dayal et al. 2008; Raxter et al. 2008; Maijanen and Niskanen 2009; Vercellotti et al. 2009; Auerbach and Ruff 2010; Kurki et al. 2010). While this provides only an approximation of living stature, it is generally considered to be adequate and not necessarily worse than documented stature as there is some evidence that this is not always recorded correctly (Bidmos 2005).

A number of studies have used an approach based on body proportions to select the most appropriate reference population. If anthropometric data are available for a population, the suitability of a reference population (and the corresponding regression formulae) has been assessed by comparing standing and sitting heights for both populations (Spradley et al. 2008). Using archaeological collections from different sites for North American indigenous populations, it has been shown, using crural indices, that this region can be divided into three populations for stature determination purposes (Auerbach and Ruff 2010). It has been suggested (Béguelin 2009) that latitude (climate) could help direct the choice toward a reference population with similar body proportions. The humero-femoral and femur-stature ratios have been used to select an appropriate reference for fossil hominids (Hens et al. 2000). The delta of Gini method, as applied to a study on historic Italians (Giannecchini and Moggi-Cecchi 2008), chooses the regression equation that gives the least variability of stature estimates derived from different limb segments in each individual.

Fordisc software uses a dynamic approach to a reference population (Wilson et al. 2010); the Forensic Anthropology Data Bank is a gradually expanding data set for individuals in the United States, and appropriate reference groups are selected from this to generate regression equations. Compared to many skeletal collections, this provides a more contemporary population. A number of authors have described and discussed other available skeletal collections (Komar and Grivas 2008; Dayal et al. 2009; Roberts and Mays 2010).

Most studies into the relationship between stature and skeletal elements use basic univariate linear regression, especially when dealing with long bones. Multivariate regression is sometimes undertaken on the lengths of multiple long bones or on a number of measurements from a fragment of a long bone or a nonlong bone. Few studies utilise nonlinear models such as curvilinear models (Agnihotri et al. 2007).

An extensive review of statistical issues and different approaches in stature determination was given by Konigsberg et al. (1998). They discussed such regression methods as classical calibration, inverse calibration (Bayesian), major axis, reduced major axis, and the zero-intercept ratio model and involving univariate and multivariate parameters. An important consideration in choosing a statistical technique is whether the unknown individual is expected to fall within the stature range of the reference population. This approach was illustrated in a study of choosing an appropriate statistical estimator and reference population in the context of fossil hominids (Hens et al. 2000). A Bayesian approach was used to develop stature prediction equations for Balkan populations (Ross and Konigsberg 2002). Maijanen and Niskanen (2009) showed that the reduced major axis method produced better results for their population than least squares equations. Use of stature calculated with the Fully method instead of actual living stature in the reference sample needs additional statistical consideration (Auerbach and Ruff 2010).

Estimating the precision of the result (i.e., the confidence interval in which the value is expected to fall) is as important as determining stature itself to ensure correct identification that will stand up to legal scrutiny. One source of error is the precision of the skeletal measurements, which depend on the type of measurement as well as the experience of the practitioner (Adams and Byrd 2002). A larger contribution to the size of the confidence interval is the result of the regression methods and reflects individual variation within the population. It has been argued that often the wrong method is used to calculate the confidence interval (Giles and Klepinger 1988), and that the interval should increase if an individual is further away from the average of the reference population.

Long-Bone Regression Methods

In many cases, skeletal remains do not contain all the elements needed for the anatomical method, or the anatomical method is considered too time consuming (especially if remains have to be macerated first), and stature is determined using the length of one or more bones and a regression formula. This is commonly referred to as a *mathematical method*.

Regression formulae using individual bones were developed by Trotter and Gleser (1952, 1958) utilizing the six major long bones of the limbs, measuring the maximum lengths of each and correlating that with known stature in their large collection. They also demonstrated that the long bones in the lower limb are more reliable in this regard than those in the upper limb and addressed the issue of ageing (Trotter and Gleser 1951). Their work mostly replaced earlier, simpler approaches using a static ratio between femur length and height.

Perhaps the most significant issue associated with this work was the way in which Trotter measured the tibia. Her description indicated that she did include the medial malleolus in her measurement, but a later study of the same collection indicated that this was not the case (Jantz et al. 1995).

A lot of the work in the past decade has focused on the evaluation of existing methods on different populations and the development of similar regression formulae if needed. Populations that have been studied in the past decade include those of Mesoamericans (Del Angel and Cisneros 2004) based on a much earlier study similar to Trotter and Gleser's work (Genoves 1967); indigenous North Americans (Auerbach and Ruff 2010); prehispanic Patagonians

(Béguelin 2009); Turks (Pelin and Duyar 2003; Celbis and Agritmis 2006); South African Whites (Dayal et al. 2008); Nigerians (Didia et al. 2009); Polish (Hauser et al. 2005); various Balkan populations (Ross and Konigsberg 2002; Petrovecki et al. 2007; Jantz et al. 2008; Kimmerle et al. 2008); medieval Scandinavians (Maijanen and Niskanen 2009); Germans (Mall et al. 2001); Portuguese (De Mendonca 2000); Spanish (Muñoz et al. 2001); Bulgarians (Radoinova et al. 2002); ancient Egyptians (Raxter et al. 2008); contemporary Egyptians (El-Meligy et al. 2006); medieval Polish (Vercellotti et al. 2009); Iron Age, Roman, and medieval Italians (Giannecchini and Moggi-Cecchi 2008); Indo-Mauritians (Agnihotri et al. 2009); Japanese (Hasegawa et al. 2009); and modern Americans (Wilson et al. 2010).

The methodologies of these various studies can be quite different from each other in some aspects, including how antemortem stature was obtained (measured on a cadaver, the use of a documented collection, whether stature was estimated with the Fully method, whether the measurements were from living individuals, etc.); which long bones were included in the study; population parameters such as the number of individuals studied; the ranges in age and height; and the male-female ratio. The material used for these studies ranged from dry bones in an archaeological collection, recent material from a mass grave, and bones dissected from fresh cadavers, to radiographs and percutaneous anthropometric measurements of living people. Usually, articular cartilage is not removed from bones extracted from cadavers (Hauser et al. 2005), or bone lengths are measured without disarticulating joints or removing soft tissue (Radoinova et al. 2002). Unfortunately, not all authors documented their method and materials with enough detail to allow comparison.

Current research agrees that the lower limb demonstrates a more reliable area for stature estimation than the upper limb (Muñoz et al. 2001; Dayal et al. 2008; Wilson et al. 2010). High degrees of correlation were found with the femur in a study of a modern population (Hauser et al. 2005). This suggests that while body proportions may have changed over time, Trotter and Gleser's original findings are still valid. This correlation is further reinforced by the poor correlations to living stature estimations found when using upper-limb bones (Mall et al. 2001; Celbis and Agritmis 2006). However, the results of the study by Mall et al. may have been compromised by the inclusion of osteoporotic individuals in the sample.

Non-Long-Bone and Body Part Regression Methods

While it is generally accepted that long bones provide the most reliable prediction of stature, these are not always available. Frequently, modern forensic anthropology also deals with nonskeletonized body parts. Bodies can be fragmented, for example, by the impact of a plane crash or an explosion or be deliberately dismembered to hinder identification. Limbs, especially their distal parts, are commonly found in isolation and have thus received most attention in research.

A range of methods has been developed to try to extract stature information from individual nonlong bones or from body parts consisting of articulated skeletal elements and soft tissue. Several regions of the body were studied before 2000 (Musgrave and Harneja 1978; Byers et al. 1989; Meadows and Jantz 1992; Holland 1995; Jason and Taylor 1995); however, research in this area is not very interconnected.

Correlation has been found between stature and size of the calcaneus (Bidmos and Asala 2005; Bidmos 2006) and metatarsals (Bidmos 2008b; Cordeiro et al. 2009).

Studies have been carried out to determine the relationship between stature and the shape and size of the foot and parts of the foot (Ozaslan et al. 2003; Ozden et al. 2005; Sanli et al. 2005; Krishan and Sharma 2007; Atamturk and Duyar 2008; Grivas et al. 2008; Kanchan, Menezes, Moudgil et al. 2008; Krishan 2008a; Sen and Ghosh 2008; Zeybek et al. 2008; Agnihotri et al. 2007); hands and parts of hands (Jasuja and Singh 2004; Sanli et al. 2005; Krishan and Sharma 2007; Agnihotri et al. 2008; Rastogi et al. 2008, 2009; Habib and Kamal 2010); and parts of limbs (Ozaslan et al. 2003; Agnihotri et al. 2009).

Related to this are studies into how stature relates to the shape and size of shoes and footprints (Ozden et al. 2005; Krishan 2008c; Fawzy and Kamal 2010); to the size of palm and fingerprints (Jasuja and Singh 2004); or even to the height of an ear print above the floor (Van Der Lugt et al. 2005). Correlation between hand and foot size and left and right sides of the body has also been studied (Kanchan, Krishan, et al. 2010).

Parts of the vertebral column (either as skeletal elements or as an articulated segment) have been found to provide acceptable estimates for stature (Pelin et al. 2005; Nagesh and Kumar 2006; Dayal et al. 2008; Karakas et al. 2010). Dayal also developed multivariate regression formulae for the lumbar spine combined with the femur or tibia. A study of the bony pelvis and proximal femur (Giroux and Wescott 2008) showed significant correlation with stature but insufficient accuracy for forensic use. A small study into the use of the (male) sternum (Menezes et al. 2009) showed some correlation with stature.

A skull or head is often the only item available, and a number of studies have, with varying success, explored different skull, teeth, and suture dimensions for use in stature determination (Ryan and Bidmos 2007; Kalia et al. 2008; Rao et al. 2009). Using radiographs, this has been extended to include a number of internal dimensions (Patil and Mody 2005). Other studies (Krishan and Kumar 2007; Krishan 2008b; Pelin et al. 2010; Sahni et al. 2010) related a number of facial dimensions of heads of living individuals to stature. Cranial thickness was found not to be related to height (Lynnerup 2001).

These methods, especially their sex and population dependency, are usually less-extensively researched than those for long bones. Many of the studies mentioned were based on relatively small and young populations and specific ethnic groups, and application to different populations has not been assessed. The measured parameters differ between studies, so results cannot be compared directly to each other. Authors find variable results for issues such as bilateral symmetry, dependency on age and sex, and the identification of the parameters that show the greatest correlation with stature. Some of the issues with foot-based methodologies were pointed out by Kanchan (Kanchan, Menezes, and Kotian 2008; Kanchan, Menezes, et al. 2010). Rastogi et al. (2008) found that a method based on bony landmarks in the wrist was more accurate than a method based on skin creases. One sacral study (Giroux and Wescott 2008) identified a large number of potential sources of differences between their study and another (Pelin et al. 2005).

The decreased correlation between stature and certain parts of the body increases the size of the confidence interval of the result, which further limits the usefulness of these methods in forensic practice. Reed and Algee-Hewitt (2010) commented on the work on sutures by Rao et al. (2009), pointing out that there is no anatomical basis for correlation and criticizing their methods and conclusions.

Further methods and data sets that are being developed in other disciplines can cross over into forensic anthropology. These deal, for example, with determining stature of elderly or disabled individuals using knee height (Li et al. 2000) or different body segments and sitting height (Canda 2009). A description of a number of anthropometric databases and their application to forensic anthropology was compiled by Adams and Herrmann (2009). They pointed out that anthropometric studies can be found in widely different fields, such as population health, the clothing industry, and equipment manufacturing. Detailed models of an "average" body and its segments have, for example, been developed for biomechanical studies (Shan and Bohn 2003; Nikolova and Toshev 2007).

Special Cases: Damaged or Juvenile Remains

The methods described were developed for intact adult material and do not apply directly when dealing with fragmented, damaged, or juvenile remains.

A number of studies have developed regression formulae for fragments of long bones. This has been done using various landmarks and dimensions, mainly near the articular ends of the bones (De Mendonca 2000; Wright and

Vasquez 2003; Akman et al. 2006; Chibba and Bidmos 2007; Bidmos 2008a, 2008c, 2009), continuing the approach initiated in older studies (Steele and Mckern 1969; Simmons et al. 1990). A similar study has been done for the talus and calcaneus (Koshy et al. 2002). Wright and Vasquez (2003) evaluated a large number of landmarks on long bones to assess which positions are allometric (i.e., scale with bone length) and which are more linked to functional stresses.

A number of authors (De Mendonca 2000; Koshy et al. 2002; Wright and Vasquez 2003) adopted a two-step approach, using regression to determine the size of the complete bone, which was then used as input for the regression formulae to determine stature. Others (Chibba and Bidmos 2007; Bidmos 2008a, 2008c, 2009) correlated the length of a fragment directly to stature as well as to the complete bone length. Some authors (De Mendonca 2000) acknowledged that the reliability of the results was not good enough for forensic practice.

These studies used univariate and multivariate linear regression models; different statistical approaches, such as geometric morphometrics using all available landmarks, could potentially lead to more robust (but more computing intensive and more time-consuming) methods.

A different type of damage relevant to stature determination is caused by burning, which has been shown (Thompson 2004; Thompson 2005) to cause both shrinkage and expansion of bone, depending on temperature and duration of the exposure.

Juvenile remains pose a number of problems in stature determination (Lewis and Rutty 2003). Body proportions change during growth (Kromeyer-Hauschild and Jaeger 2000; Ruff 2003; Smith and Buschang 2004; Smith and Buschang 2005), depend on nutritional status, metaphyseal plates are not preserved, and the availability of reference populations is limited. While size is more commonly used to asses age, a number of studies have developed (Ruff 2007; Smith 2007) and evaluated (Sciulli and Blatt 2008; Cardoso 2009) regression formulae for diaphyseal lengths of long bones. Both Ruff and Smith developed their regression formulae on the Denver Growth Study; Ruff developed separate formulae for each age, while Smith used sex as a parameter. In a small evaluation study (Cardoso 2009), it was found that, in contrast with adults, the lower-limb bones gave less-accurate results than the upper limbs. This was attributed to the sensitivity of lower-limb growth to environmental conditions and confirmed Smith's warning that results from the Denver Growth Study do not necessarily apply to different groups and populations.

One study has looked at correlation between stature and foot length for juveniles (Grivas et al. 2008). The best correlation was obtained when age and sex were known and a multivariate regression model was used, reflecting the changes in body proportions throughout childhood and differences between boys and girls in growth patterns. However, sex is often unknown for juvenile remains.

Image-Based Methods

Improvements in imaging technologies over the past decade have led to an increased interest in image-based methods. A common issue in image-based methods is the calibration between the size of an object in the image and the size of the object itself.

Radiographs have been used for a long time to study stature and bone lengths of living and recently deceased people, and this is ongoing (Muñoz et al. 2001; Patil and Mody 2005; Petrovecki et al. 2007; Kieffer 2010). While this enables the study of contemporary populations, there are some limitations to this approach; apart from the ethical issue of exposing people to radiation, there is potential distortion of the bone during imaging, either shortening by projection or magnification due to distance to the film. A new approach is to use DXA (dual-energy X-ray absorptiometry) (Hasegawa et al. 2009), which minimizes these problems.

Multislice CT has become more readily available, and image resolution has improved greatly. Combined with developments in computing, this opens new possibilities in the analysis of human remains, including determination of stature. Remains can be assessed without maceration and without damaging any soft tissue present; there is no size distortion in the resulting image. Most of the published work so far is via case studies and exploration of the potential of this approach (Dedouit et al. 2007, 2010; Sidler et al. 2007; Verhoff et al. 2008). One study has used CT scans to determine regression formulae between stature and sacrum height (Karakas et al. 2010).

To determine stature, authors used the osteological methods described, replacing the physical size measurement with an image-based measurement. Little work has been done to verify that the measurements are valid (Robinson et al. 2008), to identify potential sources of error, or to develop alternative methodologies based on, for example, geometric morphometric approaches.

A number of authors raised the question about which practitioner is best placed to do this work: a forensic anthropologist, a radiographer, or a collaboration of both (Robinson et al. 2008; O'Brien et al. 2009).

Magnetic resonance (MR) imaging has been used in few studies so far (Pelin et al. 2005); this approach will face similar issues as CT imaging.

The increased use of CCTV cameras has spurred new research into identification of individuals in photos or video. Stature (and its relationship with gait and body proportions) is one of the areas of interest (Lynnerup and Vedel 2005; De Angelis et al. 2007; Larsen, Hansen, et al. 2008; Larsen, Simonsen, et al. 2008; Krishan 2010).

Conclusions

The challenge of stature estimation is to find methods that are accurate enough (i.e., there is little systematic under- or overestimation of stature) and precise enough (i.e., producing a result with a small confidence interval) to make a useful difference in the identification of unknown remains, using the skeletal elements or body parts available and meeting the practical limitations of field- and casework.

The anatomical method is generally the most accurate and reliable but in many cases is the least practical.

Accuracy of mathematical methods can often only be achieved by developing new formulae for the population under study, as illustrated by the work done for Balkan populations. A better understanding of body proportions can facilitate the choice of a reference population.

For precision, a body part is needed that has a good correlation with stature (i.e., little variation within the population in body shape relevant to that body part) and a large enough population with known stature to develop the method. This has only been achieved for long bones, in particular the femur; methods using other parts of the body or damaged remains are normally a last resort when intact long bones are not available.

Stature estimation can gain from interdisciplinary studies in fields such as anthropometry and growth studies, geometric morphometrics, medical imaging, and computing.

References

Adams, B. J., and J. E. Byrd (2002). Interobserver variation of selected postcranial skeletal measurements. *Journal of Forensic Sciences* 47(6): 1193–1202.

Adams, B. J., and N. P. Herrmann (2009). Estimation of living stature from selected anthropometric (soft tissue) measurements: Applications for forensic anthropology. *Journal of Forensic Sciences* 54(4): 753–760.

Agnihotri, A. K., S. Agnihotri, N. Jeebun, and K. Googoolye (2008). Prediction of stature using hand dimensions. *Journal of Forensic and Legal Medicine* 15: 479–482.

Agnihotri, A. K., S. Kachhwaha, J. Vanda, and A. P. Singh (2009). Estimating stature from percutaneous length of tibia and ulna in Indo-Mauritian population. *Forensic Science International* 187: 109.e1–109.e3.

Agnihotri, A. K., B. Purwar, K. Googoolye, S. Agnihotri, and N. Jeebun (2007). Estimation of stature by foot length. *Journal of Forensic and Legal Medicine* 14: 279–283.

Akman, S. D., P. Karakas, and M. G. Bozkir (2006). The morphometric measurements of humerus segments. *Turkish Journal of Medical Sciences.* 36: 81–85.

Atamturk, D., and I. Duyar (2008). Age-related factors in the relationship between foot measurements and living stature and body weight. *Journal of Forensic Sciences* 53(6): 1296–1300.

Auerbach, B. M., M. H. Raxter, and C. B. Ruff (2005). If I only had A.: Missing element estimation accuracy using the Fully technique for estimating statures. *American Journal of Physical Anthropology* S40: 67.

Auerbach, B. M., and C. B. Ruff (2006). Limb bone bilateral asymmetry: Variability and commonality among modern humans. *Journal of Human Evolution* 50(2): 203–218.

Auerbach, B. M., and C. B. Ruff (2010). Stature estimation formulae for indigenous North American populations. *American Journal of Physical Anthropology* 141(2): 190–207.

Bailey, S. M., J. Xu, J. H. Feng, X. Hu, C. Zhang, and S. Qui (2007). Tradeoffs between oxygen and energy in tibial growth at high altitude. *American Journal of Human Biology* 19(5): 662–668.

Baraybar, J. P. (2008). When DNA is not available, can we still identify people? Recommendations for best practice. *Journal of Forensic Sciences* 53(3): 533–540.

Baraybar, J. P., and E. H. Kimmerle (2002). Thousands dead: The limited use of stature in individual identification. Paper presented at American Academy of Forensic Sciences 54th annual meeting, Atlanta, GA.

Béguelin, M. (2009). Stature estimation in a central Patagonian prehispanic population: Development of new models considering specific body proportions. *International Journal of Osteoarchaeology* doi: 10.1002/oa.1117.

Bidmos, M. A. (2005). On the non-equivalence of documented cadaver lengths to living stature estimates based on Fully's Method on bones in the Raymond A. Dart Collection. *Journal of Forensic Sciences* 50(3): 501–506.

Bidmos, M. (2006). Adult Stature reconstruction from the calcaneus of South Africans of European descent. *Journal of Clinical Forensic Medicine* 13(5): 247–252.

Bidmos, M. A. (2008a). Estimation of stature using fragmentary femora in indigenous South Africans. *International Journal of Legal Medicine* 122(4): 293–299.

Bidmos, M. A. (2008b). Metatarsals in the estimation of stature in South Africans. *Journal of Forensic Legal Medicine* 15(8): 505–509.

Bidmos, M. A. (2008c). Stature reconstruction using fragmentary femora in South Africans of European descent. *Journal of Forensic Sciences* 53(5): 1044–1048.

Bidmos, M. A. (2009). Fragmentary femora: Evaluation of the accuracy of the direct and indirect methods in stature reconstruction. *Forensic Science International* 192(1–3): 131.e1–131.e5.

Bidmos, M., and S. Asala (2005). Calcaneal measurement in estimation of stature of South African Blacks. *American Journal of Physical Anthropology* 126(3): 335–342.

Bogin, B., and L. Rios (2003). Rapid morphological change in living humans: Implications for modern human origins. *Comparative Biochemistry and Physiology. A, Molecular Integrative Physiology* 136(1): 71–84.

Bogin, B., P. Smith, A. B. Orden, M. I. Varela Silva, and J. Loucky (2002). Rapid change in height and body proportions of Maya American Children. *American Journal of Human Biology* 14(6): 753–761.

Byers, S., K. Akoshima, and B. Curran (1989). Determination of adult stature from metatarsal length. *American Journal of Physical Anthropology* 79: 275–279.

Canda, A. (2009). Stature estimation from body segment lengths in young adults—Application to people with physical disabilities. *Journal of Physiological Anthropology* 28(2): 71–82.

Cardoso, H. F. V. (2009). A test of three methods for estimating stature from immature skeletal remains using long bone lengths. *Journal of Forensic Sciences* 54(1): 13–19.

Celbis, O., and H. Agritmis (2006). Estimation of stature and determination of sex from radial and ulnar bone lengths in a Turkish corpse sample. *Forensic Science International* 158: 135–139.

Chibba, K., and M. A. Bidmos (2007). Using tibia fragments from South Africans of European descent to estimate maximum tibia length and stature. *Forensic Science International* 169(2–3): 145–151.

Cole, T. J. (2003). The secular trend in human physical growth: A biological view. *Economics and Human Biology* 1(2): 161–168.

Cordeiro, C., J. I. Munoz-Barus, S. Wasterlain, E. Cunha, and D. N. Vieira (2009). Predicting adult stature from metatarsal length in a Portuguese population. *Forensic Science International* 193: 131.e1–131.e4.

Dayal, M. R., A. D. Kegley, G. Strkalj, M. A. Bidmos, and K. L. Kuykendall (2009). The history and composition of the Raymond A. Dart Collection of human skeletons at the University of the Witwatersrand, Johannesburg, South Africa. *American Journal of Physical Anthropology* 140(2): 324–335.

Dayal, M. R., M. Steyn, and K. L. Kuykendall (2008). Stature estimation from bones of South African Whites. *South African Journal of Science* 104: 124–128.

De Angelis, D., R. Sala, A. Cantatore, P. Poppa, M. Dufour, M. Grandi, and C. Cattaneo (2007). New method for height estimation of subjects represented in photograms taken from video surveillance systems. *International Journal of Legal Medicine* 121(6): 489–492.

Dedouit, F., A. Geraut, V. Baranov, B. Ludes, D. Rouge, N. Telmon, and E. Crubezy (2010). Virtual and macroscopical studies of mummies—differences or complementarity? Report of a natural frozen Siberian mummy. *Forensic Science International.* 200 (1–3): e7–e13.

Dedouit, F., N. Telmon, R. Costagliola, P. Otal, F. Joffre, and D. Rouge (2007). Virtual anthropology and forensic identification: Report of one case. *Forensic Science International* 173(2–3): 182–187.

Del Angel, A., and H. B. Cisneros (2004). Technical note: Modification of regression equations used to estimate stature in Mesoamerican skeletal remains. *American Journal of Physical Anthropology* 125: 264–265.

De Mendonca, M. C. (2000). Estimation of height from the length of long bones in a Portuguese adult population. *American Journal of Physical Anthropology* 112(1): 39–48.

Didia, B. C., E. C. Nduka, and O. Adele (2009). Stature estimation formulae for Nigerians. *Journal of Forensic Sciences* 54(1): 20–21.

Djuric, M. P. (2004). Anthropological data in individualisation of skeletal remains from a forensic context in Kosovo—A case history. *Journal of Forensic Sciences* 49(3): 1–5.

Duyar, I., and C. Pelin (2003). Body height estimation based on tibia length in differ-
    ent stature groups. *American Journal of Physical Anthropology* 122(1): 23–27.
Duyar, I., C. Pelin, and R. Zagyapan (2006). A new method of stature estimation for
    forensic anthroplogical application. *Anthropological Science* 114: 23–27.
El-Meligy, M. M., R. H. Abdel-Hady, R. M. Abdel-Maaboud, and Z. T. Mohamed
    (2006). Estimation of human body build in Egyptians. *Forensic Science
    International* 159(1): 27–31.
Fawzy, I. A., and N. N. Kamal (2010). Stature and body weight estimation from vari-
    ous footprint measurements among Egyptian Population. *Journal of Forensic
    Sciences* doi: 10.1111/j.1556–4029.2010.01372.x.
Fully, G. (1956). Une nouvelle methode de determination de la taille. *Annales de
    Medecine Legale* 35: 266–273.
Genoves, S. (1967). Proportionality of the long bones and their relation to stature
    among Mesoamericans. *American Journal of Physical Anthropology* 26(1):
    67–77.
Giannecchini, M., and J. Moggi-Cecchi (2008). Stature in archeological samples from
    central Italy: Methodological issues and diachronic changes. *American Journal
    of Physical Anthropology* 135(3): 284–292.
Giles, E., and D. L. Hutchinson (1991). Stature- and age-related bias in self-reported
    stature. *Journal of Forensic Sciences* 36(3): 765–780.
Giles, E., and L. L. Klepinger (1988). Confidence intervals for estimates based on
    linear regression in forensic anthropology. *Journal of Forensic Sciences* 33(5):
    1218–1222.
Giroux, C. L., and D. J. Wescott (2008). Stature estimation based on dimensions of the
    bony pelvis and proximal femur. *Journal of Forensic Sciences* 53(1): 65–68.
Grivas, T. B., C. Mihas, A. Arapaki, and E. Vasiliadis (2008). Correlation of foot
    length with height and weight in school age children. *Journal of Forensic Legal
    Medicine* 15(2): 89–95.
Gustafsson, A., and P. Lindenfors (2004). Human size evolution: No evolutionary
    allometric relationship between male and female stature. *Journal of Human
    Evolution* 47(4): 253–266.
Gustafsson, A., and P. Lindenfors (2009). Latitudinal patterns in human stature and
    sexual stature dimorphism. *Annals of Human Biology* 36(1): 74–87.
Habib, S. R., and N. N. Kamal (2010). Stature estimation from hand and phalanges
    lengths of Egyptians. *Journal of Forensic Legal Medicine* 17(3): 156–160.
Hasegawa, I., K. Uenishi, T. Fukunaga, R. Kimura, and M. Osawa (2009). Stature
    estimation formulae from radiographically determined limb bone length in a
    modern Japanese population. *Legal Medicine (Tokyo)* 11(6): 260–266.
Hauser, R., J. Smolinski, and T. Gos (2005). Estimation of stature on the basis of mea-
    surements of the femur. *Forensic Science International* 147: 185–190.
Hens, S. M., L. W. Konigsberg, and W. L. Jungers (2000). Estimating stature in fos-
    sil hominids: Which regression model and reference sample to use? *Journal of
    Human Evolution* 38(6): 767–784.
Holland, T. D. (1995). Brief communication: Estimation of adult stature from the cal-
    caneus and talus. *American Journal of Physical Anthropology* 96: 315–320.
Holliday, T. W., and C. E. Hilton (2010). Body proportions of circumpolar peoples as
    evidenced from skeletal data: Ipiutak and Tigara (Point Hope) versus Kodiak
    Island Inuit. *American Journal of Physical Anthropology* 142(2): 287–302.

Holliday, T. W., and C. B. Ruff (2001). Relative variation in human proximal and distal limb segment lengths. *American Journal of Physical Anthropology* 116(1): 26–33.

İşcan, M. Y. (2005). Forensic anthropology of sex and body size. *Forensic Science International* 147: 107–112.

Jantz, R. L., D. R. Hunt, and L. Meadows (1995). The measure and mismeasure of the tibia: Implications for stature estimation. *Journal of Forensic Sciences* 40(5): 758–761.

Jantz, R. L., E. H. Kimmerle, and J. P. Baraybar (2008). Sexing and stature estimation criteria for Balkan populations. *Journal of Forensic Sciences* 53(3): 601–605.

Jantz, R. L., and L. Meadows Jantz (2000). Secular change in craniofacial morphology. *American Journal of Human Biology* 12(3): 327–338.

Jason, D. R., and K. Taylor (1995). Estimation of stature from the length of the cervical, thoracic, and lumbar segments of the spine in American Whites and Blacks. *Journal of Forensic Sciences* 40(1): 59–62.

Jasuja, O. P., and G. Singh (2004). Estimation of stature from hand and phalange length. *Journal of Indian Academy of Forensic Medicine* 26(3): 100–106.

Kalia, S., S. K. Shetty, K. Patil, and V. G. Mahima (2008). Stature estimation using odontometry and skull anthropometry. *Indian Journal of Dental Research* 19(2): 150–154.

Kalichman, L., I. Malkin, M. J. Seibel, E. Kobyliansky, and G. Livshits (2008). Age-related changes and secular trends in hand bone size. *Homo* 59(4): 301–315.

Kanchan, T., R. G. Menezes, and M. S. Kotian (2008). Stature estimation: Valuable precautions. *Journal of Forensic and Legal Medicine* 15(6): 413.

Kanchan, T., R. G. Menezes, R. Moudgil, R. Kaur, M. S. Kotian, and R. K. Garg (2008). Stature estimation from foot dimensions. *Forensic Science International* 179: 241.e1–241.e5.

Kanchan, T. J., T. S. M. Kumar, G. P. Kumar, and K. Yoganarasimha (2008). Skeletal asymmetry. *Journal of Forensic and Legal Medicine* 15: 177–179.

Kanchan, T., K. Krishan, A. Sharma, and R. G. Menezes (2010). A study of correlation of hand and foot dimensions for personal identification in mass disasters. *Forensic Science International*. 199 (1–3): 112.e1–112.e6.

Kanchan, T., R. G. Menezes, S. W. Lobo, and M. S. Kotian (2010). Forensic anthropology population data: Stature estimation from foot measurements—Comparison of error in sex dependent and independent models. *Forensic Science International* 194(1–3): e29.

Karakas, H. M., O. Celbis, A. Harma, and B. Alicioglu (2010). Total body height estimation using sacrum height in Anatolian Caucasians: Multidetector computed tomography-based virtual anthropometry. *Skeletal Radiology*. DOI: 10.1007/s00256-010-0937-x.

Kieffer, C. L. (2010). Tibia and fibula stature formulae for modern female populations based on digital radiographic measurements. *Journal of Forensic Sciences*. 55(3): 695–700.

Kimmerle, E. H., R. L. Jantz, L. W. Konigsberg, and J. P. Baraybar (2008). Skeletal estimation and identification in American and East European populations. *Journal of Forensic Sciences* 53(3): 524–532.

Klepinger, L. L. (2001). Stature, maturation variation and secular trends in forensic anthropology. *Journal of Forensic Sciences* 46(4): 788–790.

Komar, D. (2003). Lessons from Srebrenica: The contributions and limitations of physical anthropology in identifying victims of war crimes. *Journal of Forensic Sciences* 48(4): 1–4.

Komar, D. A., and C. Grivas (2008). Manufactured populations: What do contemporary reference skeletal collections represent? A comparative study using the Maxwell Museum Documented Collection. *American Journal of Physical Anthropology* 137(2): 224–233.

Konigsberg, L. W., S. M. Hens, L. M. Jantz, and W. L. Jungers (1998). Stature estimation and calibration: Bayesian and maximum likelihood perspectives in physical anthropology. *American Journal of Physical Anthropology* Suppl 27: 65–92.

Koshy, S., S. Vettivel, and K. G. Selvaraj (2002). Estimation of length of calcaneum and talus from their bony markers. *Forensic Science International* 129: 200–204.

Krishan, K. (2008a). Determination of Stature from foot and its segments in a North Indian population. *American Journal of Forensic Medicine and Pathology* 29(4): 297–303.

Krishan, K. (2008b). Estimation of stature from cephalo-facial anthropometry in North Indian population. *Forensic Science International* 181(1–3): 52 e1–6.

Krishan, K. (2008c). Estimation of stature from footprint and foot outline dimensions in Gujjars of North India. *Forensic Science International* 175(2–3): 93–101.

Krishan, K. (2010). Does femur length affect the stride length? Forensic implications. *Journal of Forensic Nursing* 6(1): 51–52.

Krishan, K., T. Kanchan, and J. A. Dimaggio (2010). A study of limb asymmetry and its effect on estimation of stature in forensic case work. *Forensic Science International*. 200 (1–3): 181.e1–181.e5.

Krishan, K., and R. Kumar (2007). Determination of stature from cephalo-facial dimensions in a north Indian population. *Legal Medicine* 9(3): 128–133.

Krishan, K., and A. Sharma (2007). Estimation of stature from dimensions of hands and feet in a north Indian population. *Journal of Forensic and Legal Medicine* 14: 327–332.

Kromeyer-Hauschild, K., and U. Jaeger (2000). Growth studies in Jena, Germany: Changes in sitting height, biacromial and bicristal breadth in the past decenniums. *American Journal of Human Biology* 12: 646–654.

Kurki, H. K., J. K. Ginter, J. T. Stock, and S. Pfeiffer (2010). Body size estimation of small-bodied humans: Applicability of current methods. *American Journal of Physical Anthropology* 141: 169–180.

Larsen, P. K., L. Hansen, E. B. Simonsen, and N. Lynnerup (2008). Variability of bodily measures of normally dressed people using Photomodeler Pro 5. *Journal of Forensic Sciences* 53(6): 1393–1399.

Larsen, P. K., E. B. Simonsen, and N. Lynnerup (2008). Gait analysis in forensic medicine. *Journal of Forensic Sciences* 53(5): 1149–1153.

Lewis, M. E., and G. N. Rutty (2003). The endangered child: The personal identification of children in forensic anthropology. *Science and Justice* 43(4): 201–209.

Li, E., E. Tang, C. Wong, S. Lui, V. Chan, and D. Dai (2000). Predicting stature from knee height in Chinese elderly subjects. *Asia Pacific Journal of Clinical Nutrition* 9(4): 252–255.

Li, L., A. D. Dangour, and C. Power (2007). Early Life Influences on Adult Leg and Trunk Length in the 1958 British Birth Cohort. *American Journal of Human Biology* 19(6): 836–843.

Lynnerup, N. (2001). Cranial thickness in relation to age, sex and general body build in a Danish forensic sample. *Forensic Science International* 117(1–2): 45–51.

Lynnerup, N., and J. Vedel (2005). Person identification by gait analysis and photo-grammetry. *Journal of Forensic Sciences* 50(1): 112–118.

Maat, G. J. R. (2005). Two millennia of male stature development and population health and wealth in the low countries. *International Journal of Osteoarchaeology* 15: 276–290.

Maijanen, H. (2009). Testing anatomical methods for stature estimation on individuals from the W. M. Bass donated skeletal collection. *Journal of Forensic Sciences* 54(4): 746–752.

Maijanen, H., and M. Niskanen (2009) New regression equations for stature estimation for medieval Scandinavians. *International Journal of Osteoarchaeology* doi 10.1002/oa.1071.

Malina, R. M., M. E. Reyes, and B. B. Little (2009). Socioeconomic variation in the growth status of urban school children 6–13 years in Oaxaca, Mexico, in 1972 and 2000. *American Journal of Human Biology* 21(6): 805–816.

Mall, G., M. Hubig, A. Buttner, J. Kuznik, R. Penning, and M. Graw (2001). Sex determination and estimation of stature from the long bones of the arm. *Forensic Science International* 117(1–2): 23–30.

Meadows, L., and R. L. Jantz (1992). Estimation of stature from metacarpal lengths. *Journal of Forensic Science* 37(1): 147–154.

Meadows Jantz, L. M., and R. L. Jantz (1999). Secular change in long bone length and proportion in the United States, 1800–1970. *American Journal of Physical Anthropology* 110(1): 57–67.

Menezes, R. G., T. J. Kanchan, G. P. Kumar, P. P. Jagadish Rao, S. W. Lobo, S. Selma Uysal, K. Krishan, S. G. Kalthur, K. R. Nagesh, and S. Shettigar (2009). Stature estimation from the length of the sternum in south Indian males: A preliminary study. *Journal of Forensic and Legal Medicine* 16: 441–443.

Muñoz, J. I., M. Liñares-Iglesias, J. M. Suárez-Peñaranda, M. Mayo, X. Miguéns, M. S. Rodríguez-Calvo, and L. Concheiro (2001). Stature estimation from radio-graphically determined long bone length in a Spanish population sample. *Journal of Forensic Sciences* 46(2): 363–366.

Musgrave, J. H., and N. K. Harneja (1978). The estimation of adult stature from metacarpal bone length. *American Journal of Physical Anthropology* 48: 113–120.

Nagesh, K. R., and G. P. Kumar (2006). Estimation of stature from vertebral column length in south Indians. *Legal Medicine* 8: 269–272.

Nikolova, G. S., and Y. E. Toshev (2007). Estimation of male and female body segment parameters of the Bulgarian population using a 16-segmental mathematical model. *Journal of Biomechanics* 40(16): 3700–3707.

O'Brien, J. J., J. J. Battista, C. Romagnoli, and R. K. Chhem (2009). CT imaging of human mummies: A critical review of the literature (1979–2005). *International Journal of Osteoarchaeology* 19: 90–98.

Ousley, S. (1995). Should we estimate biological or forensic stature? *Journal of Forensic Sciences* 40(5): 768–773.

Ozaslan, A., M. Y. İşcan, I. Ozaslan, H. Tugcu, and S. Koc (2003). Estimation of stature from body parts. *Forensic Science International* 132(1): 40–45.

Ozden, H., Y. Balci, C. Demiru, A. Turgutd, and M. Ertugrul (2005). Stature and sex estimate using foot and shoe dimensions. *Forensic Science International* 147: 181–184.

Patil, K. R., and R. N. Mody (2005). Determination of sex by discriminant function analysis and stature by regression analysis: A lateral cephalometric study. *Forensic Science International* 147(2–3): 175–180.

Pelin, I. C., and I. Duyar (2003). Estimating stature from tibia length: A comparison of methods. *Journal of Forensic Sciences* 48(4): 708–712.

Pelin, C., I. Duyar, E. M. Kayahan, R. Zagyapan, A. M. Agildere, and A. Erar (2005). Body height estimation based on dimensions of sacral and coccygeal vertebrae. *Journal of Forensic Sciences* 50(2): 294–297.

Pelin, C., R. Zagyapan, C. Yazici, and A. Kurkcuoglu (2010). Body height estimation from head and face dimensions: A different method. *Journal of Forensic Sciences* doi: 10.1111/j.1556–4029.2010.01429.x.

Petersen, H. C. (2005). On the accuracy of estimating living stature from skeletal length in the grave and by linear regression. *International Journal of Osteoarchaeology* 15: 106–114.

Petrovecki, V., D. Mayer, M. Slaus, D. Strinovic, and J. Skavic (2007). Prediction of stature based on radiographic measurements of cadaver long bones: A study of the Croatian population. *Journal of Forensic Sciences* 52(3): 547–552.

Radoinova, D., K. Tenekedjiev, and Y. Yordanov (2002). Stature estimation from long bone lengths in Bulgarians. *Homo* 52/53: 221–232.

Rao, P. P., J. Sowmya, K. Yoganarasimha, R. G. Menezes, T. Kanchan, and R. Aswinidutt (2009). Estimation of stature from cranial sutures in a south Indian male population. *International Journal of Legal Medicine* 123(3): 271–276.

Rastogi, P., T. Kanchan, R. G. Menezes, and K. Yoganarasimha (2009). Middle finger length—A predictor of stature in the Indian population. *Medicine Science and the Law* 49(2): 123–126.

Rastogi, P., K. R. Nagesh, and K. Yoganarasimha (2008). Estimation of stature from hand dimensions of north and south Indians. *Legal Medicine* 10: 185–189.

Raxter, M. H., B. M. Auerbach, and C. B. Ruff (2006). Revision of the Fully technique for estimating statures. *American Journal of Physical Anthropology* 130(3): 374–384.

Raxter, M. H., and C. B. Ruff (2010). The effect of vertebral numerical variation on anatomical stature estimates. *Journal of Forensic Sciences* 55(2): 464–466.

Raxter, M. H., C. B. Ruff and B. M. Auerbach (2007). Technical note: Revised Fully stature estimation technique. *American Journal of Physical Anthropology* 133(2): 817–818.

Raxter, M. H., C. B. Ruff, A. Azab, M. Erfan, M. Soliman, and A. El-Sawaf (2008). Stature estimation in ancient Egyptians: A new technique based on anatomical reconstruction of stature. *American Journal of Physical Anthropology* 136(2): 147–155.

Reed, J. C., and B. F. B. Algee-Hewitt (2010). Comments on "Estimation of stature from cranial sutures in a South Indian male population" by P. P. J. Rao et al. *International Journal of Legal Medicine* doi: 10.1007/s00414–010–0476–y.

Rios, L., J. I. Ovejero, and J. P. Prieto (2010). Identification process in mass graves from the Spanish Civil War I. *Forensic Science International* 199(1–3): e27–e36.

Roberts, C., and S. Mays (2010). Study and restudy of curated skeletal collections in bioarchaeology: A perspective on the UK and the implications for future curation of human remains. *International Journal of Osteoarchaeology* doi: 10.1002/oa.1175.

Robinson, C., R. Eisma, B. Morgan, A. Jeffery, E. A. Graham, S. Black, and G. N. Rutty (2008). Anthropological measurement of lower limb and foot bones using multi-detector computed tomography. *Journal of Forensic Sciences* 53(6): 1289–1295.

Ross, A. H., and L. W. Konigsberg (2002). New formulae for estimating stature in the Balkans. *Journal of Forensic Sciences* 47(1): 165–167.

Ruff, C. (2002). Variation in human body size and shape. *Annual Review of Anthropology* 31: 211–232.

Ruff, C. (2003). Growth in bone strength, body size, and muscle size in a juvenile longitudinal sample. *Bone* 33(3): 317–329.

Ruff, C. (2007). Body size prediction from juvenile skeletal remains. *American Journal of American Anthropology* 133: 698–716.

Ryan, I., and M. A. Bidmos (2007). Skeletal height reconstruction from measurements of the skull in indigenous South Africans. *Forensic Science International* 167(1): 16–21.

Sahni, D., Sanjeev, P. Sharma, Harjeet, G. Kaur, and A. Aggarwal (2010). Estimation of stature from facial measurements in northwest Indians. *Legal Medicine (Tokyo)* 12(1): 23–27.

Sanli, S. G., E. D. Kizilkanat, N. Boyan, E. T. Ozsahin, M. G. Bozkir, R. Soames, H. Erol, and O. Oguz (2005). Stature estimation based on hand length and foot length. *Clinical Anatomy* 18(8): 589–596.

Sciulli, P. W., and S. H. Blatt (2008). Evaluation of juvenile stature and body mass prediction. *American Journal of Physical Anthropology* 136(4): 387–393.

Sen, J., and S. Ghosh (2008). Estimation of stature from foot length and foot breadth among the Rajbanshi: An indigenous population of north Bengal. *Forensic Science International* 181(1–3): 55.e1–55.e6.

Shan, G., and C. Bohn (2003). Anthropometrical data and coefficients of regression related to gender and race. *Applied Ergonomics* 34(4): 327–337.

Sidler, M., C. Jackowski, R. Dirnhofer, P. Vock, and M. Thali (2007). Use of multislice computed tomography in disaster victim identification—Advantages and limitations. *Forensic Science International* 169(2–3): 118–128.

Simmons, T., R. L. Jantz, and W. M. Bass (1990). Stature estimation from fragmentary femora: A revision of the Steele method. *Journal of Forensic Sciences* 35(3): 628–636.

Smith, S. L. (2007). Stature estimation of 3 10-year-old children from long bone lengths. *Journal of Forensic Sciences* 52(2): 538–546.

Smith, S. L., and P. H. Buschang (2004). Variation in longitudinal diaphyseal long bone growth in children three to ten years of age. *American Journal of Human Biology* 16(6): 648–657.

Smith, S. L., and P. H. Buschang (2005). Longitudinal models of long bone growth during adolescence. *American Journal of Human Biology* 17(6): 731–745.

Spradley, M. K., R. L. Jantz, A. Robinson, and F. Peccerelli (2008). Demographic change and forensic identification: Problems in metric identification of Hispanic skeletons. *Journal of Forensic Sciences* 53(1): 21–28.

Steadman, D. W., B. J. Adams, and L. W. Konigsberg (2006). Statistical basis for positive identification in forensic anthropology. *American Journal of Physical Anthropology* 131(1): 15–26.

Steele, D. G., and T. W. Mckern (1969). A method for assessment of maximum long bone length and living stature from fragmentary long bones. *American Journal of Physical Anthropology* 31(2): 215–227.

Steyn, M., and J. R. Smith (2007). Interpretation of ante-mortem stature estimates in South Africans. *Forensic Science International* 171: 91–102.

Stinson, S. (2009). Nutritional, developmental, and genetic influences on relative sitting height at high altitude. *American Journal of Human Biology* 21(5): 606–613.

Sylvester, A. D., P. A. Kramer, and W. L. Jungers (2008). Modern humans are not (quite) isometric. *American Journal of Physical Anthropology* 137(4): 371–383.

Temple, D. H., and H. Matsumura (2010). Do body proportions among Jomon foragers from Hokkaido conform to ecogeographic expectations? Evolutionary implications of body size and shape among northerly hunter-gatherers. *International Journal of Osteoarchaeology* DOI: 10.1002/oa.1129.

Thompson, T. J. (2004). Recent advances in the study of burned bone and their implications for forensic anthropology. *Forensic Science International* 146(Suppl.): S203–S205.

Thompson, T. J. (2005). Heat-induced dimensional changes in bone and their consequences for forensic anthropology. *Journal of Forensic Sciences* 50(5): 1008–1015.

Trotter, M., and G. C. Gleser (1951). The effect of ageing on stature. *American Journal of Physical Anthropology* 9: 311–324.

Trotter, M., and G. C. Gleser (1952). Estimation of stature from long bones of American Whites and Negroes. *American Journal of Physical Anthropology* 16(10): 463–514.

Trotter, M., and G. C. Gleser (1958). A re-evaluation of estimation of stature based on measurements of stature taken during life and of long bones after death. *American Journal of Physical Anthropology* 16: 79–123.

Van Der Lugt, C., N. J. Nagelkerke, and G. J. Maat (2005). Study of the relationship between a person's stature and the height of an ear imprint from the floor. *Medicine Science and the Law* 45(2): 135–141.

Vercellotti, G., A. M. Agnew, H. M. Justus, and P. W. Sciulli (2009). Stature estimation in an early medieval (XI–XII C.) Polish population: Testing the accuracy of regression equations in a bioarcheological sample. *American Journal of Physical Anthropology* 140(1): 135–142.

Verhoff, M. A., F. Ramsthaler, J. Krahahn, U. Deml, R. J. Gille, S. Grabherr, M. J. Thali, and K. Kreutz (2008). Digital forensic osteology—Possibilities in cooperation with the Virtopsy Project. *Forensic Science International* 174(2–3): 152–156.

Wilson, R. J., N. P. Herrmann, and L. M. Janz (2010). Evaluation of stature estimation from the database for forensic anthropology. *Journal of Forensic Sciences* 55(3): 684–689.

Wright, L. E., and M. A. Vasquez (2003). Estimating the length of incomplete long bones: Forensic standards from Guatemala. *American Journal of Physical Anthropology* 120(3): 233–251.

Zeybek, G., I. Ergur, and Z. Demiroglu (2008). Stature and gender estimation using foot measurements. *Forensic Science International* 181: 54.e1–54.e5.

Race and Ancestry

5

EILIDH FERGUSON
NATALIE KERR
DR. CHRISTOPHER RYNN

Contents

Introduction

Throughout its history, the subject of race has been one of the most sensitive and passionately debated topics in the fields of social and biological anthropology. At its heart, the topic is concerned with how anthropologists describe and interpret variation within human populations, specifically whether this variation can be used to classify human population groups. The debate is ongoing and acrimonious and shows no sign of diminishing; often, the mere process of debating the "race" issue in anthropology is seen as implicitly "racist" in itself.

Recently, this has culminated in a special edition of the *American Journal of Physical Anthropology* ("Race Reconciled?" 2009), which reported the findings of a special symposium held in 2007 at the University of New Mexico, the aim of which was to find common ground in the debate among biological anthropologists; this symposium provides a clear case example of why the debate is ongoing and why this discussion is necessary. Participants were asked to address a number of questions, all central to the race debate: What is race? What is the relationship between race and the structure of human biological variation? What specific data methods can be used to investigate this variation, and what are the implications of our understanding of race to research topics such as human evolution, population history, disease expression and management, forensic human identification, and the synthesis of cultural, linguistic, and biological anthropology?

Whether prefixed by "sociocultural" or "biological," the study of "anthropology" (particularly in the United States) focuses on the history of humankind, often in an integrated or synthetic capacity in the Boasian sense. It may be argued that this study is impossible if the differences between human population groups and the individuals who comprise them are denied or ignored, but this has often been the case with much race debate during the last 30 years. It is the interpretation of the meaning and significance of these differences that varies between the social and scientific fields; when sociopolitical, socioeconomic, or social policy elements are added to the debate, this has often led to misunderstanding, to offense, and all too often to cries of "racism."

With these misunderstandings in mind, the *American Journal of Physical Anthropology* special symposium reported some degree of common ground for biological anthropologists (or at least those asked to contribute to the volume), specifically

- There is substantial biological variation among individuals within human populations.
- Some of this biological variation is apportioned between individuals in different populations and among larger population groups.
- Patterns of within- and between-group variation have been shaped by culture, language, environment, and geography.
- Human variation has important social, forensic, and biomedical implications.

The last point is particularly pertinent, with many workers in the biomedical community (e.g., researchers in genetics, epidemiology, psychiatry, pharmacology, etc.) happy to publish research that expressly divides human populations into a priori "racial" or "ethnic" groups (often conflating the two terms) without clear discussion of what those divisions mean. Medically, the reasoning for this is often attributed to the fact that susceptibility to acquired disease, patterns of injury, or psychiatric problems vary between geographical populations; for example, in the United Kingdom, diabetes is five times more common in African Caribbean and South Asian populations than in the general population, sickle cell anemia is predominant in African Americans, and Tay-Sachs disease is common in Ashkenazi Jews. So, race would appear to have not only a genetic component but also a component that plays an important part in the diagnosis and treatment of disease. However, the mapping of the human genome led to the conclusion that "all human beings, regardless of race, are more than 99.9% the same" (Malik 2008:8), which brings the very existence of race into question. Here lies the kernel of the problem: What is "race"? Is it a biological or a cultural classificatory unit or both? What defines the "race": gene frequencies, morphology, or other classificatory factors?

Race and the Human Genome

Human beings are a single species, *Homo sapiens*. Species are the lowest-level of classificatory or basal taxonomic unit for biological organisms, although there is no clear philosophical consensus of exactly *what* a "species" is, despite several comprehensive review volumes in recent years. The unresolved questions include the following: Is a species, in the widest sense, unitary or pluralistic? Is the species a natural unit or artificial construct of the classificatory system? Are all species the same regardless of the organism under consideration? As Gravlee (2009: 54) has pointed out, "race has played a pivotal yet tortured role in the history of anthropology," but we argue that if biologists have significant difficulties defining the basal taxonomic unit, then how can they hope to define a subdivision of that unit, namely, the race?

For decades, the debate regarding the true definition of race and its place in science has been the focus of a great deal of research. Many apportion blame to early physical anthropologists, such as Ales Hrdlicka and Carleton Coon, for initiating a trend for "racist science." Particularly in the wake of World War II, race became a touchy issue in science, with many beginning to denounce its existence. As the *American Association of Physical Anthropologists Statement on Biological Aspects of Race* (American Association of Physical Anthropologists [AAPA] 1996: 569) made clear, the treatment of race in biological characterization was based primarily on "external visible traits, primarily skin color, features of the face, and the shape and size of the head and body, and underlying skeleton," from which biologists and others developed hierarchies of primitive versus advanced "racial" traits that have been used to perpetuate inequalities. In resisting what it sees as racist uses of biology, the AAPA statement goes so far as to state "pure races, in the sense of genetically homogenous populations, do not exist in the human species today, nor is there any evidence that they have ever existed in the past" (AAPA 1996: 569). Thus, as Tattersall pointed out (2004: 24), "to refute or deny the existence of race in the world today, one must deny that there was ever any geographically based differentiation among earlier human populations."

Much of the denial of this differentiation is based on Lewontin's 1972 assertion that human population variation (as determined by genetic traits) is so hypervariable, with so much overlap between populations and individuals within them, that races are rendered meaningless. Lewontin estimated that 85% of genetic variation is found within populations, 8% is found within populations of the same race or regional grouping, and only 6% is found among races or regions. This would suggest that modern human populations are inherently so overlapping in genetic variability that classification or differentiation is impossible. However, Lewontin's assertions have been dismissed by some as misinterpretation and misunderstanding. While Lewontin's conclusions are correct at the single-locus level (meaning that single loci will show significant overlap between groups), the fact that many of these loci are significantly correlated means that they are not independently distributed; analyzing multiple loci will produce less overlap among groups and allow for the investigation of nested hierarchies. Despite low between-population variance, it is still possible to classify individuals into population groups using genotypic analytical methods, often based on nested hierarchies of ancestor-descendant relationships or statistical clustering methods (see DNA section of the bibliography) using single-nucleotide polymorphisms (SNPs), short tandem repeat polymorphisms (STRPs), variable number tandem repeats (VNTRs), and other molecular methods that display geographical patterning in expression.

As attested by any human evolution textbook published in the last 15 years, there are a number of conflicting models and hypotheses regarding how the modern human species (and by extension, modern population distributions) came about. In simplified form, the main two contesting hypotheses are the "multiregional" versus the "replacement" model. The multiregional model is based on the theory that the major geographical groups of modern humans are archaic (Wolpoff et al. 2000), and that each evolved from premodern ancestral forms already existing outside Africa (e.g., *Homo erectus, H. antecessor, H. heidelbergensis, and H. neanderthensis*), such as "Java man," "Peking man," and Neanderthals (Oppenheimer 2004). The model dictates that there are no sharp chronological breaks in the evolutionary lineage, and that regional population characteristics were established during Pleistocene deep time. Thus, the origin of modern humans would have occurred across a broad geographical area from a number of regionally adapted archaic populations in east Asia, Europe, western Asia, and Africa. The key mechanism in this process is continuous gene flow throughout the last 1.8 million years that maintained grade similarities and prevented speciation, with local selection resulting in the persistence of regional features in morphology.

In contrast, replacement models propose that modern humans evolved in a geographically restricted area (sub-Saharan Africa) as a significant evolutionary event and dispersed in the relatively recent past (290–140 Kya [thousand years ago]), completely displacing archaic populations such as the Neanderthals or the archaic successors to *H. erectus* across the Old World during the late Upper Pleistocene. The most high profile of these models is the "out-of-Africa" hypothesis, which postulates that modern, non-African populations are descended from a small group of migrants from sub-Saharan Africa who spread into Eurasia, adapting to changing diet and climate as they slowly spread to cover the globe (Behar et al. 2008; Malik 2008; Oppenheimer 2004; Randolph-Quinney et al. 2009; Richards and Macaulay 2000; Tattersall 2009). Social and physical barriers to gene flow and genetic drift resulting from isolation led to some discontinuity between populations (Edgar 2009; Ousley et al. 2009; Rosenberg et al. 2002; Ross 2004) and hence regional microevolution and differentiation. Recent views suggest that, contrary to the previous "isolation-by-distance" model, global genetic variation has resulted from a history of bottlenecking events and slow, long-distance migrations with local genetic interchange, which may allow taxonomic grouping of human populations (Hunley et al. 2009), particularly if one can differentiate between shared-primitive and shared-derived similarities (Elliot and Collard 2009).

Analysis of nonrecombining Y chromosomes (paternal lineage) and mitochondrial DNA (mtDNA) (maternal lineage), the aptly termed "Adam and Eve" genes, has shed some light on the genealogy of modern populations in terms of the nature of our ancestry and in the estimation of a general timeline and geographical location of where new lines diverged (Behar et al. 2008; Oppenheimer 2004; Richards and Macaulay 2000). Fossil and archaeological records of early modern humans appear to support the hypothesis that humanity shares a common African ancestor (Tattersall 2009). The cumulative results of regional population mapping using sex-specific gene lines have led to the conclusion that a small founder population from sub-Saharan Africa spread first into Asia, possibly somewhere west of the Indian subcontinent, before splitting into the two major haplogroups, termed M and N (from African L3 types), from which the rest of the world is populated (Behar et al. 2008; Oppenheimer 2004; Richards and Macaulay 2000).

The hypothesis that we all share a common African ancestor has been advanced by studies of genetic variation within and between populations and geographical regions (Hunley et al. 2009), indicating that more differences exist between sub-Saharan African populations than between African and non-African populations (Long et al. 2009) due to the prolonged period of diversification within Africa before the exodus of the genetically limited group that was to go on to produce all modern non-Africans (Behar et al. 2008). Interestingly, this suggests that there cannot technically be an African race under the criterion of shared genetic relationship because sub-Saharan African populations are simply too genetically diverse as they "straddle the root of the species-wide population tree" (Hunley et al. 2009: 45). If a race does exist, it is a single non-African race that may be divided further along continental lines.

It has been postulated that anatomically modern humans descended from a single genetic line that evolved around 150,000–190,000 years ago in Africa (Behar et al. 2008; Oppenheimer 2004; Richards and Macaulay 2000). Therefore, all the geographical populations seen today all therefore descend from a limited migration from sub-Saharan Africa less than 100,000 years ago (Behar et al. 2008; Hammer et al. 2005; Oppenheimer 2004; Richards and Macaulay 2000; Tattersall 2009). Earlier migrations are thought by many to have led to the evolution of our *cousins*,* such as Neanderthals, who are generally considered to have been subsequently replaced by modern humans (Hammer et al. 2005; Iltis 2006; Oppenheimer 2004). However, there is recent evidence that these were genetically closer, *sister* groups who may have coexisted with anatomically modern humans for a number of years (Krause et al. 2010). Furthermore, analysis of Neanderthal DNA from archaeological samples from across Eurasia (Green et al. 2010) has led to the conclusion that Neanderthals were genetically closer to modern non-Africans than to modern Africans. This implies a degree of genetic flow, hence interbreeding between Neanderthals in the Middle East and what would become modern humans after their initial migration out of Africa, yet before the divergence of non-African groups: "The data suggest that between 1 and 4% of the genomes of people in Eurasia are derived from Neandertals" (Green et al. 2010). If Neanderthals also originated in Africa and simply migrated earlier, to interbreed with another group of later migrants, does this support the multiregional or single-origin hypothesis? Another possibility is that the shared genes between Neanderthals and modern non-Africans could be traced back to their most recent common ancestor, and they never interbred after this split. Interestingly, Wolpoff (2009) considered Neanderthals to be the only true human race.

Recent DNA research has focused not only on ancestral lineage but also on attempting to distinguish between contemporary population groups by ascertaining phenotypic traits, including skin tone and hair color, from genotypes (Bouakaze et al. 2009). A study (Valenzuela et al. 2010) not only grouped contemporary participants by self-reported ancestry but also measured skin reflectance, scalp hair melanin levels, and eye color to quantify

---

* Studies of mtDNA in Neanderthals have failed to show a genetic lineage that corresponds with the migration of modern humans, suggesting that they are not our direct ancestors but instead diverged from a previous common ancestor long before modern human migration out of Africa (Oppenheimer 2004; Iltis 2006).

these phenotypes more scientifically. Links were discovered between these variables and a number of SNPs, and the researchers believed that these links, with much further investigation, might even be used forensically in the future.

Race: Is It a Problem of Semantics?

Ernst Mayr (2002) suggested that it was the word *race* itself that caused problems and noted that many had chosen to ignore this word in the scientific forum. Goran Štrkalj (2007a) discussed the various opinions of physical and biological anthropologists, concluding that many had dismissed race as a concept altogether. He also noted that opinion correlated with geographical location, or rather socio-political environment, with scientists in the United States much more likely to have concerns about the race concept (Smedley and Smedley 2005), while scientists in China fully supported race as a concept and integrated race into their research, acknowledging that there was still no real consensus with regard to the race debate, particularly as a result of differing regional attitudes toward race (Lieberman et al. 2004; Štrkalj 2007a). As noted in the introduction, the 2009 *American Journal of Physical Anthropology* "Race Reconciled" volume comprised work by experts from several subsets of physical anthropology, including forensic anthropologists (Caspari 2009; Gravlee 2009; Lieberman et al. 2004; Smedley and Smedley 2005; Štrkalj 2007a). In this volume, the problems of semantics and definitional misunderstanding were discussed. In particular, Edgar and Hunley's introduction to the volume outlined the common ground and fundamental disagreements between scientists on the issues. They noted that disagreements seem to exist because scientists in different fields ask different questions; medical and forensic scientists are more concerned with practicality, whereas other scientists debate the evolutionary causes of global phylogenetic variation, continually redefining the concept of race. These disparate groups of scientists may dismiss or not even be aware of the methodological and theoretical contributions of others. Furthermore, Ousley et al. (2009: 68) set out to explain "why forensic anthropologists are good at identifying race" and suggested that the continued use of race within forensic anthropology often faced criticism due to recent developments within physical anthropology that dismiss race as a biological variable. Forensic anthropologists have been criticized as "irresponsible" and guilty of "perpetuating racism" (Smay and Armelagos 2000); however, "despite their more practical focus, forensically-orientated anthropologists continue to provide innovative methods for characterising and interpreting human biological variation and are increasingly applying a more bio-cultural perspective that recognises the consequences of secular changes for forensic estimation of ancestry" (Edgar and Hunley 2009: 2).

Is this heated argument anything more than a semantic debate? It is one thing to demonstrate that there is no biological basis for race and that there is more variation within than between geographical groups, more overlap than difference, and no geographical or genetic boundaries exist, but it is another thing altogether to infer that anyone could mistake a typical Inuit for a typical Somalian. Indistinct or nonexistent boundaries do not mean that apparent differences between geographical populations do not exist: "One cannot always be sure where the city begins and the countryside ends, but it does not follow from this that the city exists only in the imagination" (Dunn and Dobzhansky 1946 as cited in Malik 2008: 18).

Regarding identification of the dead, forensic anthropology is a practically applied science that primarily involves interpretation of skeletal remains to draw conclusions about the identity of the deceased individual. The four primary identifiers of fingerprints, DNA, odontological items, or a unique medical condition may lead directly to identification, but each of these requires a sample of antemortem data from the individual for comparison and matching; hence, some idea of who the deceased might be, provided in the first instance. In the absence of any strongly individuating features or investigative leads, skeletal assessment can at least help to form a biological profile (i.e., indicate the sex, age, stature, and ancestry of the individual) and forensic facial reconstruction, a recognizable approximation of the facial appearance.

The term *identity* in a social context has myriad implications regarding character and preference, but in the context of the scientific practice of forensic human identification, the focus is on biological identity (i.e., physical appearance), and it is rarely if ever appropriate to infer any nonphysical attribute from physical elements. Physical anthropology has, on occasion, been guilty of scientific racism, not only by considering races to be permanent and immutable (Malik 2008) but also by inappropriately linking physical appearance to more cultural and environmentally influenced traits, such as intelligence and sexual behavior, which authors such as John P. Rushton (a psychologist) were doing as recently as 1995.

Semantically speaking, the term *race* appears to pertain to the individual and has largely been succeeded in physical anthropology by the more impersonal term *ancestry*. The distinction between these terms is considered to be important. *Race* may be regarded as a "socially constructed mechanism for self identification and group membership" and so biologically meaningless, whereas *ancestry* is a "scientifically derived descriptor of the biological component of population variation" (Konigsberg et al. 2009: 77–78). So, why do the rather politically sensitive terms *Caucasoid, Mongoloid,* or *Negroid* still appear in published literature (Ousley et al. 2009)?

There are considered to be four basic ancestry groups into which an individual can be placed by physical appearance, not accounting for admixture: the sub-Saharan African group ("Negroid"), the European group ("Caucasoid"), the Central Asian group ("Mongoloid"), and the Australasian group ("Australoid"). The rather outdated names of all but one of these groups were originally derived from geography: The Caucasoid group traversed the Caucasus Mountains as they spread into Europe and eastern Asia. Since the majority of native peoples from the Indian subcontinent, northern and north-eastern Africa and the Near East fall into this group, to say that the group is of "European" ancestry does not really suffice. Plus, the terms *Caucasoid* or *Caucasian* do not have the same oppressive, persecutory connotations as the other terms and so are less likely to cause offense. The American biologist Douglas J. Futuyma believes that features typical to the Mongoloid group arose around Mongolia circa 41,000 YBP (years before present), long after the migration out of Africa (circa 100,000 YBP), but the group subsequently spread to cover central, northern, and eastern Asia, native North and South America, and Eskimo and Inuit populations. Since one of the typical features of this group is the epicanthic fold, a fold in the upper eyelid that crosses the inner canthus of the eye, the term *Mongoloid* was used naively and inappropriately to refer to people with Down syndrome, who do tend to exhibit an epicanthic fold, but for very different anatomical and genetic reasons, and as such it is now a politically incorrect term that causes offense to many for various obvious reasons. The Australoid group applies to the native peoples of Australasia, but the term *Negroid* is derived from the Latin for "black" and as such is the only one of these terms that pertains to perceived physical appearance rather than geographical ancestry. In the early 1960s, Carleton Coon proposed a split into Congoid (southeastern Africa) and Capoid (sub-Saharan Africa), named after the Congo and the Cape of Good Hope, but to identify, for example, a U.K. citizen as being of African ancestry is a different thing altogether than identifying the person as originating from a certain part of sub-Saharan Africa, not least because in the modern developed world, most people are to some extent "mixed race."

Practicality

The purpose of forensic anthropology is to narrow the field of inquiry, facilitating a match between human remains and, for example, a missing persons report (Konigsberg et al. 2009). Law enforcement professionals may request simple answers to the question of the race of the deceased and utilize this information in their search. A forensic anthropologist who denounces the concept of race or attempts to debate its very existence will not be of much practical value to the police officer heading the investigation. The average law enforcement officer or the general public may not appreciate the genetic and biological issues associated with the race debate; their primary concern is to identify an individual as quickly and accurately as possible, and ancestry can assist, if only as an indication of likely physical appearance. Konigsberg (2009: 78) stated that "in order for the forensic anthropologist to assist in identification of unknown remains it is important to function within the same cultural milieu as the medico-legal community and the pool of potential missing individuals." However, when ancestry is used to infer anything other than physical appearance, aside from causing offense, genuine practical problems also inevitably arise. Consider a mass disaster in which disaster victim identification (DVI) teams are deployed to identify and repatriate nationals to their respective countries. The level and speed of human migration and admixture in the modern world means that a citizen of any nation may fall into any ancestral group, or indeed be ancestrally ambiguous, so the use of ancestry to facilitate the sorting of human remains in this context would be not only inappropriate but also obstructive.

Due to the way that past research has been conducted, in some cases ancestry must be assessed to estimate other elements of biological identity. Sauer noted in 1992 that forensic anthropologists were "good at identifying race" due to the level of concordance between American social races and skeletal biology, specifically cranial morphology in Black and White Americans.

Thus, in the case of estimation of stature from the femur, when using regression equations developed by Trotter and Gleser in 1952, ancestry must be described literally in Black or White terms prior to calculating stature to correspond to the way the original American research participants were grouped since different equations were derived for each group. This may cause problems in the case of disrupted remains or ambiguous ancestry. Similarly, Duyar and Pelin (2003) proposed regression equations using tibia length to estimate stature, but grouped subjects into "short" and "tall" groups, which in practicality means that the general *stature* must be known to decide which stature estimation equation to use. The way in which research is conducted will invariably influence how the results can subsequently be put into practice.

Ancestry and Craniometry

Craniofacial morphology appears to show strong geographic patterning (Ousley et al. 2009) and is considered by some to reflect phylogenetic factors, with relatively little influence from natural selection (Harvati and Weaver 2006; Relethford 2002, 2009; Roseman and Weaver 2004). Craniofacial traits undeniably exhibit high heritability (Sparks and Jantz 2002) in that we all tend to resemble our parents, and population differences are observable at a young age (Vidarsdóttir et al. 2002). However, on a much larger time scale, the craniofacial complex has been subject to environmental influence, particularly in adaptive response to diet or extremes of climate (Harvati and Weaver 2006). This process may be ongoing, with the craniofacial complex subject to secular changes (Roseman and Weaver 2004; Ross 2004; Sparks and Jantz 2002), but considering that we are rarely exposed to the elements of nature in the developed world and that modern migration between very different climates takes a matter of hours rather than generations, heredity and admixture undoubtedly play a greater part than environmental variables in the derivation of the face of the modern individual.

Forensic anthropologists still rely, for the most part, on skeletal elements for assessing ancestry. Craniofacial and postcranial regions have been analyzed both morphologically and metrically (Byers 2009; Hefner 2009). The skull is considered to be the best indicator of ancestry (Patriquin et al. 2002; Relethford 2009), with the nasal region said by some to be of most significance (Byers 2009). Recent research on the estimation of nasal morphology from the skull (Rynn et al. 2009) was carried out on clinical CT data of Americans of European, sub-Saharan African, and east Asian ancestry, which was pooled with lateral cephalogram data of British citizens of both European and Indian subcontinental ancestry. Skulls that could be clearly grouped as Caucasoid, Negroid, or Mongoloid using morphological methods were labeled as such, and on analysis of the whole data set, it was apparent that the inclusion of multiple-ancestry groups extended the range of any given bivariate relationship between a bony nasal dimension and a soft tissue nasal dimension, with more overlap occurring between groups than differences. Regression equations were derived that applied across all ancestry groups. This indicates that splitting the participants into groups to derive ancestry group-specific equations is not ideal, even if the individuals clearly represent type examples of a given group. Craniofacial dimensions, as well as genetic material, demonstrate clinical variation between ancestry groups.

The relationship between skull morphology and ancestry is one of propensity, with certain traits more prevalent in one ancestry group than another, but with no clear boundaries between the groups. As a basic overview, the European Caucasoid-type skull tends to exhibit a relatively angular cranium; there are small teeth, leading to a tendency for retrognathism (particularly in more dolichocephalic skulls), leading to a somewhat projecting, narrow nose with a tented nasal bridge (Rynn 2007). The east Asian Mongoloid-type skull tends to exhibit a relatively round, brachycephalic cranium with less incidence of brow ridges; large, projecting zygomatic bones; a distinctive orbital morphology linked to an epicanthic eye fold (Baleuva et al. 2009); a relatively flatter nose; and a wider palate orthognathism to prognathism (particularly in relation to the mandible). The sub-Saharan African Negroid-type skull tends to exhibit a longer, dolichocephalic cranium with a higher incidence of postbregmatic depression; farther apart eyes and more marked prognathism; a "Quonset hut"-shaped nasal aperture with a guttering of the inferior border; and, relatively, the flattest nose. The less geographically pervasive Australoid ancestry group tends to exhibit the largest brow ridges; a higher incidence of a sagittal crest; a "rocker-bottom" mandible; a more distinct occipital torus; relatively large teeth (particularly molars); and orthognathism to prognathism (Wilkinson 2004). All of these tendencies pertain to craniofacial and facial feature morphology. Average tissue depths used in forensic facial reconstruction tend to be grouped by ancestry, age, and sex, but the application of geographically and ancestrally inappropriate tissue depth data has been shown to have negligible effect on recognition of the predicted face (Wilkinson 2004).

Morphological techniques are often perceived as subjective, difficult to reproduce, and reliant on prior experience (Bidmos 2006; Hefner 2009). Hefner (2009) believed this meant that the nonmetric evaluation of ancestry from the skull is an art as much as a science, but it is more appropriate to describe morphological ancestry assignment as an expert's professional opinion, which would naturally become more accurate with experience. Standardization of morphological techniques was first attempted by Hooton in the 1930s; Hooton produced the "Harvard list," but even recently, researchers (Dirkmaat et al. 2008; Hefner 2009) have attempted to describe and illustrate ancestry-related morphological traits to decrease subjectivity and in an attempt to comply with *Daubert* standards and other admissibility criteria, despite the fact that ancestry assignment could only ever really be considered intelligence as opposed to evidence.

Byers (2009) stated that morphological methods remain the most utilized method for ancestry assignment; however, others indicated an ever-increasing reliance on so-called plug-and-play metric systems such as CRANID (Wright 2007) and Fordisc (Ousley and Jantz 2005), particularly in the United States (Dirkmaat et al. 2008; Elliot and Collard 2009). The idea of using discriminant function analysis (DFA) in the assignment of sex and ancestry was demonstrated in the work of Giles and Elliot in the 1960s (Ubelaker et al. 2002). CRANID and Fordisc employ multivariate statistical techniques to assign ancestry and sex based on reference samples taken from Howell's data sets and the Forensic Anthropology Data Bank (FDB) (Ubelaker et al. 2002). Fordisc also utilizes standard postcranial linear measurements, although these have limited utility on their own in ancestry assessment but can supplement assessment from craniometric evaluation.

However, there is debate over the number of craniofacial dimensions to utilize (Konigsberg et al. 2009; Ousley et al. 2009; Ubelaker et al. 2002) and whether "too many" variables could actually reduce reliability. There is also the question regarding which craniofacial dimensions are better at taking ancestral group variation into account since this differs depending on the group, and the large overlap between groups in most dimensions complicates the matter further. Practically and conceptually, there is also a fundamental dichotomy between morphological and metric methods in the characters and states each records; morphological methods recover discrete or codified patterns of shape variation dealing with specific regions of ancestral variation, such as the expression of brow ridge shape, nasal aperture and root form, and so on, whereas metrical methods record size-based chord distances, minima and maxima, and angles. As such, the two approaches may be fundamentally incommensurate in practice.

Fordisc has been the target of concerns due to its inability to classify individuals whose ancestry does not fall within the limited reference populations geographically or chronologically (Belcher et al. 2002; Leathers et al. 2002; Williams et al. 2005), but it has been argued that it is not reasonable to expect Fordisc to be able to correctly classify ancient Nubian skulls (Fried et al. 2005). The developers of Fordisc (Ousley and Jantz 2005) have also expressed that care should be taken when assessing skulls for which there is no corresponding reference sample in the database (Fried et al. 2005), which would be impossible unless the skull in question was already of known provenance, a line of practical reasoning that leads to a logical paradox or Catch 22 situation. Furthermore, even when Howell's own representative sample of 111 Egyptian skulls was used to assess the performance of Fordisc 2.0 (Naar et al. 2006), only approximately half were correctly classified.

Despite the FDB including contemporary forensic samples, Howell's data set consists of a large number of archaeological specimens, and there have been suggestions that this may lead to inaccuracy using Fordisc (Elliot and Collard 2009). It is widely accepted that attempts to attribute modern morphological discriminators to ancient remains can give a skewed result, as was the case with the Kennewick man (Malik 2008), and secular change is beginning to render many skeletal collections, and the techniques derived from them, somewhat obsolete (Dirkmaat et al. 2008). The issue is further compounded, particularly in the United States, by some attempts to differentiate sociological or "ethnic" groups, such as Hispanics/Latinos (Spradley et al. 2008), using skeletal metrical techniques as if they were an ancestry group in and of themselves. In reality, Hispanics/Latinos are a group united simply by a common first language, forming more than 15% of the U.S. population, and comprising ancestrally diverse individuals who could fit into any, all, or none of the classical ancestry groups.

Geometric morphometric (GM) techniques go further than craniometric methods based on linear measurements by allowing the statistical evaluation of shape by repeatable methods of two- (2D) or three-dimensional (3D) shape capture. These use methods of landmark recovery or surface scanning to capture both size-based and shape-based information, which together may be considered as heritable "form" (Franklin et al. 2007). Geometric morphometrics is the statistical analysis of form based on Cartesian landmark coordinates (Mitteroecker and Gunz 2009). While the fundamental underpinnings of the discipline date back to the early 20th century, it is only recently that modern computational and technological advances have allowed for the acquisition, processing, and analysis of shape variables that retain *all* of the geometric information contained within biological data (Free et al. 2001; Slice 2005; Zelditch et al. 2004). GM techniques generally involve the capture of homologous *landmarks*, which can be defined as precise locations on biological specimens that hold some functional, structural, developmental, or evolutionary significance and are directly comparable between specimens. The locations of homologues can be recorded as two- or three-dimensional coordinates, which results in a spatial framework of the relative positions of the chosen landmarks in Euclidean shape space. However, while coordinate data retain the full geometry of the landmarks (and hence shape), they have proved more difficult to compare statistically than conventional linear dimensions, primarily for reasons of registration between configurations. To overcome this, GM analyses allow for the extraction of shape differences between configurations, with residual shape defined as the geometric properties of an object invariant to orientation, location, and scale (Mitteroecker and Gunz 2009).

From a forensic anthropological perspective, if enough data are included, this approach may provide a solution to the problems of subjectivity previously witnessed in nonmetric techniques. However, it has been suggested that forensic anthropologists have been slower than other disciplines in the use of 3D analyses (Franklin et al. 2007), and as such there is limited literature on the utility of GM in ancestry assessment, the majority of which concerns juvenile specimens (Buck and Vidarsdóttir 2004; Franklin et al. 2007; Vidarsdóttir et al. 2002; Weinberg et al. 2005). However, software has been developed (3D-ID; Slice and Ross 2010) that attempts to use 3D coordinate data in a similar way as that utilized by Fordisc in a discriminatory sense; the utility of the program for forensic evaluation and its precision and accuracy of classification have yet to be formally tested in the literature. At its basis, 3D-ID uses fundamentally the same shape information as Fordisc, recording discrete cephalometric landmarks as Cartesian coordinates, not as chord distances; the approach therefore limits the amount of true morphological information that is captured and utilized. Until geometric methods of ancestry assignment use the same data that are used in morphological methods, the two approaches will continue to be incommensurate—a case of apples and oranges rather than an integrated method of statistical ancestry assessment.

Postcranial Skeleton

Fewer studies have been conducted on the postcranial skeleton (Holliday and Falsetti 1999); however, in practicality the skull is often fragmented or absent, so these methods are necessary and employed often (Bidmos 2006; Patriquin et al. 2002). One of the postcranial areas more frequently examined is the highly sexually dimorphic pelvis. In 2002, Patriquin attempted to quantify variation between South African Black and White people using metrical differences in the pelvis. Patriquin examined 400 adult innominate bones (os coxae), grouped into males and females and "Whites" and "Blacks." Thirteen reproducible measurements between repeatable landmarks were used in this study (Patriquin et al. 2002). An effort was also taken to select areas of the pelvis that were more likely to survive inhumation. The results of this study indicated that all measurements taken were significantly larger in the White group than the Black group. Accuracy ranged from 79% to 88% in this study, depending on sex (Patriquin et al. 2002). However, this does not necessarily apply to White and Black people from the United Kingdom, the United States, or anywhere else because they are different populations in different environments, despite sharing ancestry groupings.

Igbigbi and Nanono-Igbibi (2003) undertook another study on the utility of the pelvis in ancestry assessment. This study focused on the subpubic angle of 205 anteroposterior pelvic radiographs of indigenous Ugandans and compared it to previous studies of "Caucasians, Amerindians, and Malawians" grouped by ancestry and sex. Sexual dimorphism was high, and this relationship was consistent across all ancestry groups, with females naturally exhibiting more obtuse pelvic angles. Also demonstrated was an ancestry-related difference between the Caucasian and sub-Saharan African groups measured, even between Ugandans and Malawians, but these regional variations were much smaller than the variation exhibited by sexual dimorphism. Provenance was correctly assigned to only 63% of Ugandans and 71% of Malawians in the data set used in the study (Igbigbi and Nanono-Igbigbi 2003), so it is debatable whether the subpubic angle could be used to assign ancestry to isolated remains of unknown sex.

A study examined the possibility of ancestry assignment using the calcaneus due to its durability and likelihood of recovery (Bidmos 2006). South Africans of European descent (SAEDs) were compared to indigenous South Africans (ISAs), so it should be noted here that the White "Afrikaner" population of over 2.5 million is largely descended from a single source of Dutch immigrants who landed in 1652 (Malik 2008). Nine dimensions were measured on each calcaneus for DFA. Singularly, each variable had low levels of accuracy in differentiating populations; however, stepwise analysis created functions that used five of the measurements in males and four of the measurements in females to improve accuracy. It was observed that in females, accuracy was highest when all nine measurements were employed. Bidmos also attempted to assign ancestry using a nonmetric method of observation, examining the number of articular facets that were present on the calcanei. Three groups of classification were used: Type A had three articular facets (anterior, middle, and posterior), Type B had two articular facets (anterome-dial and posterior), and Type C had one facet, where the anteromedial joins with the posterior facet. Results displayed that SAEDs were more likely to exhibit Type A facets, while ISAs were more likely to exhibit Type B facets. However, Bidmos noted that, as with all indicators of ancestry, it is not a defi-nite feature and should not be used alone but could be used alongside other factors in assigning ancestry (Bidmos 2006).

The femur has also been utilized in several studies regarding assignment of ancestry group. Wescott (2005) analyzed subtrochanteric shape, conclud-ing that White and African Americans tended to exhibit a more eurymeric (round) proximal diaphysis, whereas Native Americans tended to exhibit a more platymeric (oval or flattened) proximal diaphysis. However, it was sug-gested that the differences observed actually reflected environmental plastic-ity more than genetic variance. His results showed that it was a moderately useful trait in distinguishing Native Americans from White and African Americans, with an accuracy of 72–82% (Wescott 2005). A further study tested the method proposed by Gilbert and Gill (in Gill and Rhine 1990) of ancestry assessment using femoral subtrochanteric shape. Platymeric index alone was found to be useful in distinguishing Native Americans from White and African Americans, producing accuracies between 76% and 79% (Wescott and Srikanta 2008). It was noted, however, that this method may not be particularly useful in the broader forensic context as the technique only discriminates Native Americans. Gill (2001) performed a study examining the success of intercondylar notch height in separating White and African Americans. The study noted that Americans of African ancestry tended to exhibit a relatively higher intercondylar notch, which has been attributed to a relatively lower anterior femoral curvature of the diaphysis in the population. Accuracy ranged from 76% to 82% (Gill 2001).

Other studies have utilized bones such as the metacarpals and metatar-sals or teeth, with various success rates (Brook et al. 2009; McFadden and Bracht 2009). Brook and colleagues (2009) found that there were significant ancestry-related differences in tooth size, while McFadden and Bracht (2009) found that the metacarpals of African Americans tended to be larger and more similar in length (within an individual) than metacarpals of Americans of European ancestry.

Conclusion

Geographically related human population groups exist, with differences in the appearance of typical members of each group likely caused by bottle-necking events and environmental adaptation throughout the slow, early migration of humans out of Africa. Modern ancestry groups can be thought of as huge extended families that can be traced back to one or another of these small migrating groups, and this analogy helps us to understand why it is the craniofacial complex that is the most ancestrally diverse part of the body: People tend to resemble their parents. Every nonpathological physical or genetic element in the spectrum of human variation seems to present as a panancestral cline, with no readily definable boundaries.

In the modern world, migration from one climate to another happens on a daily basis, and in modern, multicultural societies, there exist individuals who epitomize type examples of each ancestry group, along with individuals who are ancestrally ambiguous. This is now a global society that contains so much admixture and ambiguity that to divide the human race into more than the four traditional ancestry groups of sub-Saharan African, Caucasoid (Eurasian?), central Asian, and Australasian is probably a mistake. These groupings refer to ancient ancestry and have no bearing on the individual apart from their appearance, whether they represent a type example of a group or are utterly ambiguous between groups. To form new groups based on sociopolitical factors or ethnicity is unnecessarily divisive on the level of physical appearance and is more of a sociological issue. As such, we can view modern "races" as epiphenomena, the consequence of both shared species-level evolutionary history and local patterns of adaptation and familial breeding patterns; the expression of such patterns in the past is different from the expression of such patterns in the present and is thus of limited utility in formal classification. However, the recognition of ancestral markers rather than racial ones is perhaps more useful. In terms of forensic anthropology, ancestry assignment can hugely facilitate identification, provided it is accepted that ancestry merely pertains to a person's appearance and nothing more. Generally, the inference of nonphysical traits from physical traits constitutes a misunderstanding that seems to be at the root of the semantic arguments that surround this topic.

References

American Association of Physical Anthropologists (1996). AAPA statement on biological aspects of race. *American Journal of Physical Anthropology* 101: 569–570.

Baleuva, T., Veselovskaya, E., and Kobyliansky, E. (2009). Craniofacial reconstruction by applying the ultrasound method in live human populations. *International Journal of Anthropology* 24: 87–111.

Behar, D. M., Villems, R., Soodyall, H., Blue-Smith, J., Pereira, L., Metspalu, E., Scozzari, R., Makkan, H., Tzur, S., Comas, D., Bertranpetit, J., Quintana-Murci, L., Tyler-Smith, C., Wells, R. S., Rosset, S., and the Genographic Consortium (2008). The dawn of human matrilineal diversity. *The American Journal of Human Genetics* 82: 1130–1140.

Belcher, R., Williams, F. and Armelagos, G.J. (2002). Misidentification of Meroitic Nubians using Fordisc 2.0. *American Journal of Physical Anthropology* 117: 34, 42.

Bidmos, M. (2006). Metrical and non-metrical assessment of population affinity from the calcaneus. *Forensic Science International* 159: 6–13.

Bouakaze, C., Keyser, C., and Crubézy, E. (2009). Pigment phenotype and bio-geographical ancestry from ancient skeletal remains: Inferences from multi-plexed autosomal SNP analysis. *International Journal of Legal Medicine* 123: 315–325.

Brook, A. H., Griffin, R. C., Townsend, G., Levisianos, Y., Russell, J., and Smith, R. N. (2009). Variability and patterning in permanent tooth size of four human ethnic groups. *Archives of Oral Biology* 54s: s79–s85.

Buck, T. J., and Vidarsdóttir, U. S. (2004). A proposed method for the identification of race in sub-adult skeletons: A geometric morphometric analysis of mandibular morphology. *Journal of Forensic Sciences* 49: 1–6.

Byers, S. N. (2009). *Introduction to forensic anthropology*. Upper Saddle River, NJ: Pearson Education.

Caspari, R. (2009). 1918: three perspectives on race and human variation. *American Journal of Physical Anthropology* 139: 5–15.

Daubert v Merrell Dow Pharmaceuticals (92-102), 509 US 579 (1993). Http://caselaw. lp.findlaw.com/scripts/getcase.pl?court=us&vol=509&invol=579. Last accessed 10.11.2010.

Dirkmaat, D. C., Cabo, L. L., Ousley, S. D., and Symes, S. A. (2008). New perspectives in forensic anthropology. *American Journal of Physical Anthropology* 137: 33–52.

Duyar, I., and Pelin, C. (2003). Body height estimation based on tibia length in different stature groups. *American Journal of Physical Anthropology* 122: 23–27.

Edgar, H. J. H. (2009). Biohistorical approaches to "race" in the United States: Biological distances among African Americans, European Americans, and their ancestors. *American Journal of Physical Anthropology* 139: 58–67.

Edgar, H. J. H., and Hunley, K. L. (2009). Race reconciled? How biological anthropologists view human variation. *American Journal of Physical Anthropology* 139: 1–4.

Elliot, M., and Collard, M. (2009). FORDISC and the determination of ancestry from cranial measurements. *Biology Letters*: 5, 849–852. doi:10.1098/rsbl.2009.0462.

Franklin, D., O'Higgins, P., Oxnard, C. E., and Dadour, I. (2007). Sexual dimorphism and population variation in the adult mandible: forensic applications of geometric morphometrics. *Forensic Science, Medicine and Pathology* 3: 15–22.

Free, S. L., O'Higgins, P., Maudgil, D. D., Dryden, I. L., Lemieux, L., Fish, D. R., and Shorvon, S. D. (2001). Landmark-based morphometrics of the normal adult brain using MRI. *NeuroImage* 13, 801–813.

Fried, D., Spradley, M. K., Jantx, R. L., and Ousley, S. D. (2005). The truth is out there: how NOT to use Fordisc. *American Journal of Physical Anthropology* S40: p103.

Gill, G. W., and Rhine, S. (1990). *Skeletal attribution of race: Methods for forensic anthropology*. Albuquerque, NM: Maxwell Museum of Anthropology.

Gravlee, C. C. (2009). How race becomes biology: Embodiment of social inequality. *American Journal of Physical Anthropology* 139: 47–57.

Green, R. E., Krause, J., Briggs, A. W., Maricic, T., Stenzel, U. et al., (2010). A draft sequence of the Neanderthal genome. *Science*, 328: 710–722.

Hammer, M. F., Garrigan, J. A., Wilder, Z. M., Severson, T., and Kingan, S. B. (2005). Sequence data from the autosomes and X chromosome: Evidence for ancient admixture in the history of *H. sapiens*? *American Journal of Physical Anthropology* S40: 111.

Harvati, K., and Weaver, T. D. (2006). Human cranial anatomy and the differential preservation of population history and climate signatures. *The Anatomical Record Part A* 288A: 1225–1233.

Hefner, J. T. (2009). Cranial nonmetric variation and estimating ancestry. *Journal of Forensic Sciences* 54: 985–995.

Holliday, T. W., and Falsetti, A. B. (1999). A new method for discriminating African-American from European-American skeletons using postcranial osteometrics reflective of body shape. *Journal of Forensic Science* 44: 926–930.

Hunley, K. E., Healy, M. E., and Long, J. C. (2009). The global pattern of gene identity variation reveals a history of long-range migrations, bottlenecks, and local mate exchange: Implications for biological race. *American Journal of Physical Anthropology* 139: 35–46.

Igbigbi, P. S., and Nanono-Igbigbi, A. M. (2003). Determination of sex and race from the subpubic angle in Ugandan subjects. *American Journal of Forensic Medicine and Pathology* 24: 168–172.

Iltis, D. (2006). Revisiting Neanderthal mitochondrial DNA sequence variation. *American Journal of Physical Anthropology* S42: 107.

Konigsberg, L. W., Algee-Hewitt, B. F. B., and Steadman, D. W. (2009). Estimation and evidence in forensic anthropology: Sex and race. *American Journal of Physical Anthropology* 139: 77–90.

Krause, J., Fu, Q., Good, J. M., Viola, B., Shunkov, M. V., Derevianko, A. P., and Pääbo, S. (2010). The complete mitochondrial DNA genome of an unknown hominin from southern Siberia. *Nature* 464: 894–897. DOI:10.1038/nature08976.

Leathers, A., Edwards, J., and Armelagos, G. J. (2002). Assessment of classification of crania using FORDISC 2.0: Nubian X-group test. *American Journal of Physical Anthropology* S34: 99–100.

Lieberman, L., Kaszycka, K. A., Fuentes, A. J. M., Yablonsky, L., Kirk, R. C., Strkalj, G., Wang, Q., and Sun, L. (2004). The race concept in six regions: Variation without consensus. *Collegium Antropologicum* 28: 907–921.

Malik, K. (2008). *Strange fruit: why both sides are wrong in the race debate*. Oxford, UK: Oneworld.

Mayr, E. (2002). The biology of race and the concept of equality. *Daedalus* 131: 89–94.

McFadden, D., and Bracht, M. S. (2009). Sex and race differences in the relative lengths of metacarpals and metatarsals in human skeletons. *Early Human Development* 85: 117–124.

Mitteroecker, P., and Gunz, P. (2009). Advances in geometric morphometrics. *Evolutionary Biology* 36: 235–247.

Oppenheimer, S. (2004). *Out of Eden: The peopling of the world*. London: Robinson.

Ousley, S., and Jantz, R. L. (2002). Social races and human populations: Why foren-
    sic anthropologists are good at identifying races. *American Journal of Physical
    Anthropology* 121–121.
Ousley, S., and Jantz, R. (2005). FORDISC 3.0. Knoxville, TN: Department of
    Anthropology, University of Tennessee.
Ousley, S., Jantz, R., and Freid, D. (2009). Understanding race and human variation:
    Why forensic anthropologists are good at identifying race. *American Journal of
    Physical Anthropology* 139: 68–76.
Patriquin, M. L., Steyn, M., and Loth, S. R. (2002). Metric assessment of race from the
    pelvis in South Africans. *Forensic Science International* 127: 104–113.
Race reconciled? How biological anthropologists view human variation [Special
    issue]. (2009). *American Journal of Physical Anthropology* 139(1).
Randolph-Quinney, P., Mallett, X., and Black, S. M. (2009). Forensic anthropology.
    In A. Jamieson and A. Moenssens (Eds.), *Wiley encyclopedia of forensic science*.
    London: Wiley, pp. 1–27.
Relethford, J. H. (2002). Apportionment of global human genetic diversity based on
    craniometrics and skin color. *American Journal of Physical Anthropology* 118:
    393–398.
Relethford, J. H. (2009). Race and global patterns of phenotypic variation. *American
    Journal of Physical Anthropology* 139: 16–22.
Roseman, C. C., and Weaver, T. D. (2004). Multivariate apportionment of global
    human craniometric diversity. *American Journal of Physical Anthropology* 125:
    257–263.
Rosenberg, N. A., Pritchard, J. K., Weber, J. L., Cann, H. M., Kidd, K. K., Zhivotovsky,
    L. A., and Feldman, M. W. (2002). Genetic structure of human populations.
    Science 298: 2381–2385. doi: 10.1126/science.1078311.
Ross, A. H. (2004). Regional isolation in the Balkan region: An analysis of craniofa-
    cial variation. *American Journal of Physical Anthropology* 124: 73–80.
Ross, A. H., Slice, D. E., and Williams, S. E. (2010). Geometric morphometric tools
    for the classification of human skulls. http://www.ncjrs.gov/pdffiles1/nij/
    grants/231195.pdf Last accessed 10.11.2010.
Rynn, C. (2007). Craniofacial approximation and reconstruction: Tissue depth pat-
    terning and the prediction of the nose. PhD thesis, University of Dundee. P127.
Rynn, C., Wilkinson, C. M., and Peters, H. L. (2009). Prediction of nasal morphology
    from the skull. *Forensic Science, Medicine and Pathology* 6: 20–34.
Sauer, N. J. (1992). Forensic anthropology and the concept of race: If races don't exist,
    why are forensic anthropologists so good at identifying them? *Social Science and
    Medicine* 34: 107–111.
Slice, D. (2005). *Modern morphometrics in physical anthropology*. London: Kluwer
    Academic/Plenum.
Smay, D., and Armelagos, G. (2000). Galileo wept: A critical assessment of the use of
    race in forensic anthropology. *Transforming Anthropology* 9: 19–29.
Smedley, A., and Smedley, B. D. (2005). Race as biology is fiction, racism as a social
    problem is real. *American Psychologist* 60: 16–26.
Sparks, C. S., and Jantz, R. L. (2002). A reassessment of human cranial plasticity: Boas
    revisited. *Proceedings of the National Academy of Sciences of the United States of
    America* 99: 14636–14639.

Spradley, K. M., Jantz, R. L., Robinson, A., and Peccerelli, F. (2008). Demographic change and forensic identification: Problems in metric identification of Hispanic skeletons. *Journal of Forensic Sciences* 53: 21–28.

St. Hoyme, L. E., and İşcan, M. Y. (1989). Determination of sex and race: Accuracy and assumptions. In M. Y. İşcan and K. A. R. Kennedy (Eds.), *Reconstruction of life from the skeleton*. New York: Liss, pp. 53–93.

Štrkalj, G. (2007a). The status of the race concept in contemporary biological anthropology: A review. *Anthropologist* 9: 73–78.

Tattersall, I. (2004). Race: Scientific nonproblem, cultural quagmire. *The Anatomical Record (Part B New Anatomy)* 278: 23–26.

Tattersall, I. (2009). Human origins: Out of Africa. *Proceedings of the National Academy of Science* 106: 16018–16021.

Ubelaker, D. H., Ross, A. H., and Graver, S. M. (2002). Application of forensic discriminant functions to a Spanish cranial sample. *Forensic Science Communications*, 4(3), n/a.

Valenzuela, R. K., Henderson, M. S., Walsh, M. H., Garrison, N. A., Kelch, J. T., Cohen-Barak, O., Erickson, D. T., Meaney, J., Walsh, J. B., Cheng, K. C., Ito, S., Wakamatsu, K., Frudakis, T., Thomas, M., and Brilliant, M. H. (2010). Predicting phenotype from genotype: Normal pigmentation. *Journal of Forensic Sciences* 55: 316–322.

Vidarsdóttir, U. S., O'Higgins, P., and Stringer, C. (2002). A geometric morphometric study of regional differences in the ontogeny of the modern human facial skeleton. *Journal of Anatomy* 201: 211–229.

Weinberg, S. M., Putz, D. A., Mooney, M. P., and Siegel, M. I. (2005). Evaluation of non-metric variation in the crania of black and white perinates. *Forensic Science International* 151: 177–185.

Wescott, D. (2005). Population variation in femur subtrochanteric shape. *Journal of Forensic Science* 50: 1–8.

Wescott, D., and Srikanta, D. (2008). Testing assumptions of the Gilbert and Gill method for assessing ancestry using the femur subtrochanteric shape. *HOMO—Journal of Comparative Human Biology* 59: 347–363.

Wilkinson, C. (2004). *Forensic facial reconstruction*. Cambridge, UK: Cambridge University Press.

Williams, F. L., Belcher, R. L., and Armelagos, G. J. (2005). Forensic misclassification of ancient Nubian crania: Implications for assumptions about human variation. *Current Anthropology* 46: p 684.

Wolpoff, M. H. (2009). How Neandertals inform human variation. *American Journal of Physical Anthropology* 139: 91–102.

Wolpoff, M. H., Hawks, J., and Caspari, R. (2000). Multiregional, not multiple origins. *American Journal of Physical Anthropology* 112: 129–136.

Zelditch, M. L., Swiderski, D. L., David Sheets, H., and Fink, W. L. (2004). *Geometric morphometrics for biologists: A primer*. Oxford, UK: Elsevier.

Bibliography

General References

Albanese, J., and Saunders, S. R. (2006). Is it possible to escape racial typology in forensic identification? In A. Schmitt, E. Cunha, and J. Pinheiro (Eds.), *Forensic anthropology and medicine: Complementary sciences from recovery to cause of death*. Totowa, NJ: Humana Press, pp. 281–316.

Baker, L. D. (2004). A model approach for studying race: Provocative theory, sound science, and very good history. *American Anthropologist* 106: 168–172.

Bauchet, M., and Shriver, M. D. (2006). The use of biogeographical ancestry for forensic, biomedical, and recreational genomics. *American Journal of Physical Anthropology* S42: 62.

Billinger, M. S. (2007). Another look at ethnicity as a biological concept—Moving anthropology beyond the race concept. *Critique of Anthropology* 27: 5–35.

Biondi, G., and Rickards, O. (2002). The scientific fallacy of the human biological concept of race. *Mankind Quarterly* 42: 355–388.

Brace, C. L. (1995). Region does not mean "race"—Reality versus convention in forensic anthropology. *Journal of Forensic Sciences* 40: 171–175.

Brown, K. (2000). Ancient DNA applications in human osteoarchaeology. In M. Cox and S. Mays (Eds.), *Human osteology in archaeology and forensic science*. London: Greenwich Medical Media, pp 455–473.

Brues, A. M. (1992). Forensic diagnosis of race—General race versus specific populations. *Social Science and Medicine* 34: 125–128.

Bulbeck, D., Raghavan, P., and Rayner, D. (2006). Races of *Homo sapiens*: If not in the southwest Pacific, then nowhere. *World Archaeology* 38: 109–132.

Byers, S. N. (2009). *Introduction to forensic anthropology*. Upper Saddle River, NJ: Pearson Education.

Cartmill, M. (1998). The status of the race concept in physical anthropology. *American Anthropologist* 100: 651–660.

Cartmill, M., and Brown, K. (2003). Surveying the race concept: A reply to Lieberman, Kirk, and Littlefield. *American Anthropologist* 105: 114–115.

Caspari, R. (2003). From types to populations: A century of race, physical anthropology, and the American Anthropological Association. *American Anthropologist* 105: 65–76.

Caspari, R. (2009). 1918: Three perspectives on race and human variation. *American Journal of Physical Anthropology* 139: 5–15.

Coon, C. S. (1962). *The origin of races*. New York: Knopf.

Cox, K., Tayles, N. G., and Buckley, H. R. (2006). Forensic identification of "race"—The issues in New Zealand. *Current Anthropology* 47: 869–874.

D'Agostino, P. (2002). Craniums, criminals, and the "cursed race": Italian anthropology in American racial thought, 1861–1924. *Comparative Studies in Society and History* 44: 319–343.

Dirkmaat, D. C., Cabo, L. L., Ousley, S. D., and Symes, S. A. (2008). New perspectives in forensic anthropology. *American Journal of Physical Anthropology* 137: 33–52.

Doyle, J. M. (2001). Discounting the error costs—Cross-racial false alarms in the culture of contemporary criminal justice. *Psychology Public Policy and Law* 7: 253–262.

Dubriwny, T. N., Bates, B. R., and Bevan, J. L. (2004). Lay understandings of race: cultural and genetic definitions. *Community Genetics* 7: 185–195.

Edgar, H. J. H. (2009). Biohistorical approaches to "race" in the United States: Biological distances among African Americans, European Americans, and their ancestors. *American Journal of Physical Anthropology* 139: 58–67.

Edgar, H. J. H., and Hunley, K. L. (2009). Race reconciled? How biological anthropologists view human variation. *American Journal of Physical Anthropology* 139: 1–4.

Editorial (2008). Jame Watson's most inconvenient truth: Race realism and the moralistic fallacy. *Medical Hypotheses* 71: 629–640.

Gannett, L. (2004). The biological reification of race. *British Journal of Philosophy Science* 55: 323–345.

Gill, G. W., and Rhine, S. (1990). *Skeletal attribution of race: Methods for forensic anthropology.* Albuquerque, NM: Maxwell Museum of Anthropology.

Gill-King, H. (2005). Determination of ancestry and skeletal age in forensic anthropology. *The Journal of the Federation of American Societies for Experimental Biology* 19: A226-A226.

Gonzalez-Jose, R., Bortolini, M. C., Santos, F. R., and Bonatto, S. L. (2008). The peopling of America: Craniofacial shape variation on a continental scale and its interpretation from an interdisciplinary view. *American Journal of Physical Anthropology* 137(2): 175–187.

Gould, S. J. (1996). *The mismeasure of man.* England: Clays.

Gravlee, C. C. (2009). How race becomes biology: embodiment of social inequality. *American Journal of Physical Anthropology* 139: 47–57.

Huckenbeck, W., Thiel, W., Krause, D., Lessig, R., and Szibor, R. (2008). Thoughts for the organisation of an early phase response to preserve victim identification information after mass disasters. A contribution to: ISFG: Recommendations regarding the role of forensic genetics for disaster victim identification (DVI by M. Prinz, A. Carracedo, W. R. Mayr, N. Morling, T. J. Parsons, A. Sajantila, R. Scheithauer, H. Schmitter, P. M. Schneider). *Forensic Science International* 177: E39–E42.

İşcan, M. Y. (1990). A comparison of techniques on the determination of race, sex and stature from the Terry and Hamann-Todd collections. In G. W. Gill and S. Rhine (Eds.), *Skeletal attribution of race: Methods for forensic anthropology.* Albuquerque, NM: Maxwell Museum of Anthropology, pp. 73–82.

İşcan, M. Y., Loth, S. R., and Steyn, M. (2000). Determination of racial affinity. In J. Siegel, G. Knupfer, and P. Saukko (Eds.), *Encyclopedia of forensic sciences.* London: Academic Press, pp. 227–235.

Jackson, J. P. (2001). "In ways unacademical": The reception of Carleton S. Coon's *The origin of races. Journal of the History of Biology* 34: 247–285.

Jamieson, J. W. (2002). The reality of race: Contra Biondi and Rickards. *Mankind Quarterly* 42: 389–406.

Kaszycka, K. A., and Strkalj, G. (2002). Anthropologists' attitudes towards the concept of race: The Polish sample. *Current Anthropology* 43: 329–335.

Kaszycka, K. A., and Strzalko, J. (2003a). "Race"—Still an issue for physical anthropology? Results of Polish studies seen in the light of the U.S. findings. *American Anthropologist* 105: 116–124.

Kaszycka, K. A., and Strzalko, J. (2003b). *Race*: Tradition and convenience, or taxonomic reality? More on the race concept in Polish anthropology. *Przeglad Anthropologiczng—Anthropological Review* 66: 23–37.

Kennedy, K. A. R. (1995). But professor, why teach race identification if races don't exist? *Journal of Forensic Sciences* 40: 797–800.

Kenny, M. G. (2006). A question of blood, race, and politics. *Journal of the History of Medicine and Allied Sciences* 61: 456–491.

Komar, D. (2005). Skeletal attributions of race: Methods for forensic anthropology. *Journal of Anthropological Research* 61: 252–253.

Konigsberg, L. W., Algee-Hewitt, B. F. B., and Steadman, D. W. (2009). Estimation and evidence in forensic anthropology: Sex and race. *American Journal of Physical Anthropology* 139: 77–90.

Kornienko, I. V., Vodolazhskii, D. I., Mikhalkovich, L. S., Pavlichenko, G. N., and Ivanov, P. L. (2003). Polymorphism of the gene for subunit 6 of the NADH dehydrogenase complex in ethnic Russians of Russia. *Molecular Biology* 37: 503–507.

Lieberman, L. (2003). Declining fitness of race in the *American Journal of Physical Anthropology*: 1918–1996. *American Journal of Physical Anthropology* 120: 140.

Lieberman, L., Hampton, R. E., Littlefield, A., and Hallead, G. (1992). Race in biology and anthropology—A study of college texts and professors. *Journal of Research in Science Teaching* 29: 301–321.

Lieberman, L., Kaszycka, K. A., Fuentes, A. J. M., Yablonsky, L., Kirk, R. C., Strkalj, G., Wang, Q., and Sun, L. (2004). The race concept in six regions: Variation without consensus. *Collegium Antropologicum* 28: 907–921.

Lieberman, L., and Kirk, R. C. (2002). The 1999 status of the race concept in physical anthropology: Two studies converge. *American Journal of Physical Anthropology* 117: 102.

Lieberman, L., Kirk, R. C., and Littlefield, A. (2003). Perishing paradigm: Race— 1931–99. *American Anthropologist* 105: 110–113.

Littlefield, A., Lieberman, L., and Reynolds, L. (1982). Redefining race: The potential demise of a concept in physical anthropology. *Current Anthropology* 23: 641–655.

Malik, K. (2008). *Strange fruit: Why both sides are wrong in the race debate*. Oxford, UK: Oneworld.

Mayr, E. (2002). The biology of race and the concept of equality. *Daedalus* 131: 89–94.

Mitteroecker, P., and Gunz, P. (2009). Advances in geometric morphometrics. *Evolutionary Biology* 36: 235–247.

Oppenheimer, S. (2004). *Out of Eden: The peopling of the world*. London: Robinson.

Oppenheimer, S., and Richards, M. (2001). Fast trains, slow boats, and the ancestry of the Polynesian islanders. *Science Progress* 84: 157–181.

Ossorio, P., and Duster, T. (2005). Race and genetics—Controversies in biomedical, behavioral, and forensic sciences. *American Psychologist* 60: 115–128.

Ousley, S., and Jantz, R. L. (2002). Social races and human populations: Why forensic anthropologists are good at identifying races. *American Journal of Physical Anthropology* 34: 83–84.

Ousley, S., and Jantz, R. (2005). FORDISC 3.0. Knoxville, TN: Department of Anthropology, University of Tennessee.

Ousley, S., Jantz, R., and Freid, D. (2009). Understanding race and human variation: Why forensic anthropologists are good at identifying race. *American Journal of Physical Anthropology* 139: 68–76.

Parra, E. J., Kittles, R. A., Argyropoulos, G., Pfaff, C. L., Hiester, K., Bonilla, C., Sylvester, N., Parrish-Gause, D., Garvey, W. T., Jin, L., McKeigue, P. M., Kamboh, M. I., Ferrell, R. E., Pollitzer, W. S., and Shriver, M. D. (2001). Ancestral proportions and admixture dynamics in geographically defined African Americans living in South Carolina. *American Journal of Physical Anthropology* 114: 18–29.

Randolph-Quinney, P., Mallett, X., and Black, S. M. (2009). Forensic anthropology. In A. Jamieson and A. Moenssens (Eds.), *Wiley encyclopedia of forensic science*. London: Wiley, pp. 1–27.

Relethford, J. H. (2002). Apportionment of global human genetic diversity based on craniometrics and skin color. *American Journal of Physical Anthropology* 118: 393–398.

Relethford, J. H. (2009). Race and global patterns of phenotypic variation. *American Journal of Physical Anthropology* 139: 16–22.

Roseman, C. C., and Weaver, T. D. (2004). Multivariate apportionment of global human craniometric diversity. *American Journal of Physical Anthropology* 125: 257–263.

Ruffie, J. (1973). Physical anthropology and human races. *Social Science Information Sur Les Sciences Sociales* 12: 7–25.

Sauer, N. J. (1992). Forensic anthropology and the concept of race: If races don't exist, why are forensic anthropologists so good at identifying them? *Social Science and Medicine* 34: 107–111.

Schwartz, J. H. (2006). Race and the odd history of human paleontology. *The Anatomical Record* 289B: 225–240.

Slice, D. (2005). *Modern morphometrics in physical anthropology*. London: Kluwer Academic/Plenum.

Smay, D., and Armelagos, G. (2000). Galileo wept: A critical assessment of the use of race in forensic anthropology. *Transforming Anthropology* 9: 19–29.

Smedley, A., and Smedley, B. D. (2005). Race as biology is fiction, racism as a social problem is real. *American Psychologist* 60: 16–26.

Spradley, K. M., Jantz, R. L., Robinson, A., and Peccerelli, F. (2008). Demographic change and forensic identification: Problems in metric identification of Hispanic skeletons. *Journal of Forensic Sciences* 53: 21–28.

St. Hoyme, L. E., and İşcan, M. Y. (1989). Determination of sex and race: Accuracy and assumptions. In M. Y. İşcan and K. A. R. Kennedy (Eds.), *Reconstruction of life from the skeleton*. New York: Liss, pp. 53–93.

Stephan, C. N. (2003). Race—Is it time for even forensic anthropologists (and other scientists) to let go? *HOMO—Journal of Comparative Human Biology* 54: 78.

Stone, D. (2008). "Not a race but only a people after all": The racial origins of the Jews in fin-de-siecle anthropology. *Patterns of Prejudice* 42: 133–149.

Štrkalj, G. (2007a). The status of the race concept in contemporary biological anthropology: A review. *Anthropologist* 9: 73–78.

Štrkalj, G. 2007. The study of human variation. In V. Bhasin and M. K. Bhasin (Eds.), *Anthropology today: Trends, scope and applications*. New Delhi: Kamla-Raj Enterprises, pp. 161–165.

Tattersall, I. (2004). Race: Scientific nonproblem, cultural quagmire. *The Anatomical Record (Part B New Anatomy)* 278: 23–26.

Tattersall, I. (2009). Human origins: Out of Africa. *Proceedings of the National Academy of Science* 106: 16018–16021.

Thorne, A. G. (1971). The racial affinities and origins of the Australian Aboriginies. In D. J. Mulvaney and J. Golson (Eds.), *Aboriginal man and environment in Australia*. Canberra: Australian National University Press, pp. 316–325.

Tobias, P. V. (1996). Africa-derived skulls and Africa-derived mitochondrial DNA: Towards a reconciliation. In S. Brenner and K. Hanihara (Eds.), *The origin and past of modern humans as viewed from DNA*. Singapore: World Scientific, pp. 189–215.

Trudell, M. B. (1999). Anterior femoral curvature revisited: Race assessment from the femur. *Journal of Forensic Sciences* 44: 700–707.

Valenzuela, R. K., Henderson, M. S., Walsh, M. H., Garrison, N. A., Kelch, J. T., Cohen-Barak, O., Erickson, D. T., Meaney, J., Walsh, J. B., Cheng, K. C., Ito, S., Wakamatsu, K., Frudakis, T., Thomas, M., and Brilliant, M. H. (2010). Predicting phenotype from genotype: Normal pigmentation. *Journal of Forensic Sciences* 55: 316–322.

Wang, Q., Strkalj, G., and Sun, L. (2003). On the concept of race in Chinese biological anthropology: Alive and well. *Current Anthropology* 44: 403–403.

Washburn, S. L. (1962). The study of race. *American Anthropologist* 65: 521–531.

Wilkinson, C. (2004). *Forensic facial reconstruction*. Cambridge, UK: Cambridge University Press.

Winker, M. A. (2004). Measuring race and ethnicity: Why and how? *Journal of the American Medical Association* 292: 1612–1614.

Wolpoff, M. H. (2009). How Neandertals inform human variation. *American Journal of Physical Anthropology* 139: 91–102.

Wright, R. (2008). Detection of likely ancestry using CRANID [online]. In M. Oxenham (Ed.), *Forensic approaches to death, disaster and abuse*. Bowen Hills, Queensland: Australian Academic Press, pp. 111–122.

Yablonsky, L. (2001). Contrasting views of the "Race" concept in the Russian and American physical anthropology. *American Journal of Physical Anthropology* S32: 168–170.

Zelditch, M. L., Swiderski, D. L., David Sheets, H., and Fink, W. L. (2004). *Geometric morphometrics for biologists: A primer*. Oxford, UK: Elsevier.

Race and Ancestry Assessment: Cranial Skeleton (Including Dentition)

Birkby, W. H. (1966). An evaluation of race and sex identification from cranial measurements. *American Journal of Physical Anthropology* 24: 21–27.

Brook, A. H., Griffin, R. C., Townsend, G., Levisianos, Y., Russell, J., and Smith, R. N. (2009). Variability and patterning in permanent tooth size of four human ethnic groups. *Archives of Oral Biology* 54s: s79–s85.

Buck, T. J., and Vidarsdóttir, U. S. (2004). A proposed method for the identification of race in sub-adult skeletons: A geometric morphometric analysis of mandibular morphology. *Journal of Forensic Sciences* 49: 1–6.

Burris, B. G., and Harris, E. F. (1998). Identification of race and sex from palate dimensions. *Journal of Forensic Sciences* 43: 959–963.

Dayal, M. R., Spocter, M. A., and Bidmos, M. A. (2008). An assessment of sex using the skull of Black South Africans by discriminant function analysis. *HOMO—Journal of Comparative Human Biology* 59: 209–221.

Edgar, H. J. H. (2005). Prediction of race using characteristics of dental morphology. *Journal of Forensic Sciences* 50: 1–5.

Edgar, H. J. H. (2006). A test of dental morphological traits used in forensic identification of ancestry. *American Journal of Physical Anthropology* S36: 86.

Elliot, M., and Collard, M. (2009). FORDISC and the determination of ancestry from cranial measurements. *Biology Letters* 5: 849–852. doi: 10.1098/rsbl.2009.0462.

Franklin, D., O'Higgins, P., Oxnard, C. E., and Dadour, I. (2007). Sexual dimorphism and population variation in the adult mandible: Forensic applications of geometric morphometrics. *Forensic Science, Medicine and Pathology* 3: 15–22.

Franklin, D., O'Higgins, P., Oxnard, C. E., and Dadour, I. (2008). Discriminant function sexing of the mandible of Indigenous South Africans. *Forensic Science International* 179: 84.e1–84.e5.

Giles, E., and Elliot, O. (1962). Race identification from cranial measurements. *Journal of Forensic Sciences* 7: 147–157.

Harris, E. F., Hicks, J. D., and Barcroft, B. D. (2001). Tissue contributions to sex and race: Differences in tooth crown size of deciduous molars. *American Journal of Physical Anthropology* 115: 223–237.

Harvati, K., and Weaver, T. D. (2006). Human cranial anatomy and the differential preservation of population history and climate signatures. *The Anatomical Record Part A* 288A: 1225–1233.

Hefner, J. T. (2009). Cranial nonmetric variation and estimating ancestry. *Journal of Forensic Sciences* 54: 985–995.

Hennessy, R. J., and Stringer, C. B. (2002). Geometric morphometric study of the regional variation of modern human craniofacial form. *American Journal of Physical Anthropology* 117: 37–48.

Howells, W. W. (1973). *Cranial variation in man*. Cambridge, MA: Harvard University, Peabody Museum.

Howells, W. W. (1989). *Skull shapes and the map*. Cambridge, MA: Harvard University, Peabody Museum.

Howells, W. W. (1995). *Who's who in skulls*. Cambridge, MA: Harvard University Press.

Howells, W. W. (1996). Howells' craniometric data on the internet. *American Journal of Physical Anthropology* 101: 441–442.

Jantz, R. L., and Owsley, D. W. (2001). Variation among early North American Crania. *American Journal of Physical Anthropology* 114: 146–155.

Kimmerle, E. H., Ross, A., and Slice, D. (2008). Sexual dimorphism in America: Geometric morphometric analysis of the craniofacial region. *Journal of Forensic Sciences* 53: 54–57.

Leathers, A., Edwards, J., and Armelagos, G. J. (2002). Assessment of classification of crania using FORDISC 2.0: Nubian X-group test. *American Journal of Physical Anthropology* S34: 99–100.

Naar, N. A., Hilgenberg, D., and Armelagos, G. J. (2006). FORDISC 2.0 the ultimate test: What is the truth? *American Journal of Physical Anthropology* S42: 136.

Naikmasur, V. G., Shrivastava, R., and Mutalik, S. (2010). Determination of sex in South Indians and immigrant Tibetans from cephalometric analysis and discriminant functions. *Forensic Science International* 197(1–3), 122.e1–122.e6. doi: 10.1016/j.forsciint.2009.12.052.

Perera, P., and Pathmeswaran, A. (2009). A pilot study on assessment of racial affinity of Sri Lankan population using discriminant function statistics and a few established morphological racial traits. *Legal Medicine* 11: s182–s185.

Relethford, J. H. (1994). Craniometric variation among modern human populations. *American Journal of Physical Anthropology* 95: 53–62.

Ross, A. H. (2004). Regional isolation in the Balkan region: An analysis of craniofacial variation. *American Journal of Physical Anthropology* 124: 73–80.

Snow, C. C., Hartman, S. E., Giles, E., and Young, F. A. (1979). Sex and race determination of crania by calipers and computer: A test of the Giles and Elliot discriminant functions in 52 forensic science cases. *Journal of Forensic Sciences* 24: 448–460.

Sparks, C. S., and Jantz, R. L. (2002). A reassessment of human cranial plasticity: Boas revisited. *Proceedings of the National Academy of Sciences of the United States of America* 99: 14636–14639.

Sporer, S. L. (2001). The cross-race effect—Beyond recognition of faces in the laboratory. *Psychology Public Policy and Law* 7: 170–200.

Ubelaker, D. H., Ross, A. H., and Graver, S. M. (2002). Application of forensic discriminant functions to a Spanish cranial sample. *Forensic Science Communications* 4(3), n/a.

Uytterschaut, H. T., and Wilmink, F. W. (1983). On the assumption of equality of variance-covariance matrices in the sex and racial diagnosis of human skulls. *American Journal of Physical Anthropology* 60: 347–357.

Vidarsdóttir, U. S., O'Higgins, P., and Stringer, C. (2002). A geometric morphometric study of regional differences in the ontogeny of the modern human facial skeleton. *Journal of Anatomy* 201: 211–229.

von Cramon-Taubadel, N., and Lycett, S. J. (2008). Brief communication: Human cranial variation fits iterative founder effect model with African origin. *American Journal of Physical Anthropology* 136: 108–113.

Weinberg, S. M., Putz, D. A., Mooney, M. P., and Siegel, M. I. (2005). Evaluation of non-metric variation in the crania of black and white perinates. *Forensic Science International* 151: 177–185.

Race and Ancestry Assessment: Postcranial Skeleton

Bidmos, M. (2006). Metrical and non-metrical assessment of population affinity from the calcaneus. *Forensic Science International* 159: 6–13.

Bidmos, M. A. (2008). Stature reconstruction using fragmentary femora in South Africans of European descent. *Journal of Forensic Sciences* 53: 1044–1048.

Bidmos, M. A., and Asala, S. A. (2003). Discriminant function sexing of the calcaneus of the South African Whites. *Journal of Forensic Sciences* 48: 1–6.

Bidmos, M. A., and Asala, S. A. (2004). Sexual dimorphism of the calcaneus of South African Blacks. *Journal of Forensic Sciences* 49: 1–5.

Craig, E. A. (1995). Intercondylar shelf angle: a new method to determine race from the distal femur. *Journal of Forensic Sciences* 40: 777–782.

Duray, S. M., Morter, H. B., and Smith, F. J. (1999). Morphological variation in cervical spinous processes: Potential applications in the forensic identification of race from the skeleton. *Journal of Forensic Sciences* 44: 937–944.

Feldesman, M. R., and Fountain, R. L. (1996). "Race" specificity and the femur/stature ratio. *American Journal of Physical Anthropology* 100: 207–224.

Gilbert, B. M. (1976). Anterior femoral curvature: Its probable basis and utility as a criterion of racial assessment. *American Journal of Physical Anthropology* 45: 601–604.

Gill, G. W. (2001). Racial variation in the proximal and distal femur: Heritability and forensic utility. *Journal of Forensic Sciences* 46: 791–799.

İşcan, M. Y. (1983). Assessment of race from the pelvis. *American Journal of Physical Anthropology* 62: 205–208.

İşcan, M. Y., and Cotton, T. S. (1990). Osteometric assessment of racial affinity from multiple sites in the postcranial skeleton. In G. W. Gill and S. Rhine (Eds.), *Skeletal attribution of race: Methods for forensic anthropology*. Albuquerque, NM: Maxwell Museum of Anthropology, pp. 83–90.

Lazenby, R. A. (2002). Population variation in second metacarpal sexual size dimorphism. *American Journal of Physical Anthropology* 118: 378–384.

Marino, E. A. (1997). A pilot study using the first cervical vertebra as an indicator of race. *Journal of Forensic Sciences* 42: 1114–1118.

McFadden, D., and Bracht, M. S. (2009). Sex and race differences in the relative lengths of metacarpals and metatarsals in human skeletons. *Early Human Development* 85: 117–124.

Patriquin, M. L., Steyn, M., and Loth, S. R. (2002). Metric assessment of race from the pelvis in South Africans. *Forensic Science International* 127: 104–113.

Shackelford, L. L., and Trinkaus, E. (2002). Late Pleistocene human femoral diaphyseal curvature. *American Journal of Physical Anthropology* 118: 359–370.

Smith, S. L. (1996). Attribution of hand bones to sex and population groups. *Journal of Forensic Science* 41: 469–477.

Stewart, T. D. (1962). Anterior femoral curvature: Its utility for race identification. *Human Biology* 34: 49–62.

Steyn, M. (2009). Osteometric sex determination from the pelvis—Does population specificity matter? *Forensic Science International* 191: 113.e1–113.e5.

Steyn, M., Pretorius, E., and Hutten, L. (2004). Geometric morphometric analysis of the greater sciatic notch in South Africans. *HOMO—Journal of Comparative Human Biology* 54: 197–206.

Wescott, D. (2005). Population variation in femur subtrochanteric shape. *Journal of Forensic Science* 50: 1–8.

Wescott, D., and Srikanta, D. (2008). Testing assumptions of the Gilbert and Gill method for assessing ancestry using the femur subtrochanteric shape. *HOMO—Journal of Comparative Human Biology* 59: 347–363.

Population Genetics and DNA

Acuna, M., Jorquera, H., Armanet, L., and Cifuentes, L. (2000). Gene frequencies for four hypervariable DNA loci in a Chilean population of mixed ancestry. *Journal of Forensic Sciences* 45: 1160–1161.

Aler, M., Salas, A., Sanchez-Diz, P., Murcia, E., Carracedo, A., and Gisbert, M. (2001). Y-chromosome STR haplotypes from a western Mediterranean population sample. *Forensic Science International* 119: 254–257.

Alfonso-Sanchez, M. A., Martinez-Bouzas, C., Castro, A., Pena, J. A., Fernandez-Fernandez, I., Herrera, R. J., and de Pancorbo, M. M. (2006). Sequence polymorphisms of the mtDNA control region in a human isolate: The Georgians from Swanetia. *Journal of Human Genetics* 51: 429–439.

Allard, M. W., Miller, K., Wilson, M., Monson, K., and Budowle, B. (2002). Characterization of the Caucasian haplogroups present in the SWGDAM forensic mtDNA dataset for 1771 human control region sequences. *Journal of Forensic Sciences* 47: 1215–1223.

Allard, M. W., Polanskey, D., Miller, K., Wilson, M. R., Monson, K. L., and Budowle, B. (2005). Characterization of human control region sequences of the African American SWGDAM forensic mtDNA data set. *Forensic Science International* 148: 169–179.

Allard, M. W., Polanskey, D., Wilson, M. R., Monson, K. L., and Budowle, B. (2006). Evaluation of variation in control region sequences for Hispanic individuals in the SWGDAM mtDNA data set. *Journal of Forensic Sciences* 51: 566–573.

Barbosa, A. B. G., da Silva, L. A. F., Azevedo, D. A., Balbino, V. Q., and Mauricio-Da-Silva, L. (2008). Mitochondrial DNA control region polymorphism in the population of Alagoas state, north-eastern Brazil. *Journal of Forensic Sciences* 53: 142–146.

Behar, D. M., Villems, R., Soodyall, H., Blue-Smith, J., Pereira, L., Metspalu, E., Scozzari, R., Makkan, H., Tzur, S., Comas, D., Bertranpetit, J., Quintana-Murci, L., Tyler-Smith, C., Wells, R. S., Rosset, S., and the Genographic Consortium (2008). The dawn of human matrilineal diversity. *The American Journal of Human Genetics* 82: 1130–1140.

Bouakaze, C., Keyser, C., and Crubézy, E. (2009). Pigment phenotype and biogeographical ancestry from ancient skeletal remains: Inferences from multiplexed autosomal SNP analysis. *International Journal of Legal Medicine* 123: 315–325.

Budowle, B., Allard, M. W., Fisher, C. L., Isenberg, A. R., Monson, K. L., Stewart, J. E. B., Wilson, M. R., and Miller, K. W. P. (2002). HVI and HVII mitochondrial DNA data in Apaches and Navajos. *International Journal of Legal Medicine* 116: 212–215.

Budowle, B., and Monson, K. L. (1994). Greater differences in forensic DNA profile frequencies estimated from racial groups than from ethnic subgroups. *Clinica Chimica Acta* 228: 3–18.

Carriquiry, F., Bacallao, K., Acuna, M., and Cifuentes, L. (2003). Gene frequencies for three hypervariable DNA loci in a Chilean population of mixed ancestry. *Journal of Forensic Sciences* 48: 220–220.

Crespillo, M., Luque, J. A., Paredes, M., Fernandez, R., Ramirez, E., and Valverde, J. L. (2000). Mitochondrial DNA sequences for 118 individuals from northeastern Spain. *International Journal of Legal Medicine* 114: 130–132.

Dupuy, B. M., Andreassen, R., Flones, A. G., Tomassen, K., Egeland, T., Brion, M., Carracedo, A., and Olaisen, B. (2001). Y-chromosome variation in a Norwegian population sample. *Forensic Science International* 117: 163–173.

Duster, T. (2006). The molecular reinscription of race: unanticipated issues in biotechnology and forensic science. *Patterns of Prejudice* 40: 427–441.

Excoffier, L., and Schneider, S. (2000). The demography of human populations inferred from patterns of mitochondrial DNA diversity. In C. Renfrew and K. Boyle (Eds.), *Archaeogenetics: DNA and the population prehistory of Europe*. Cambridge, UK: McDonald Institute for Archaeological Research, pp. 101–108.

Figueroa, C. C., Acuna, M., and Cifuentes, L. (2000). Gene frequencies for six STR loci in a Chilean population of mixed ancestry. *Journal of Forensic Sciences* 45: 742–743.

Frudakis, T., Venkateswarlu, K., Thomas, M. J., Gaskin, Z., Ginjupalli, S., Gunturi, S., Ponnuswamy, V., Natarajan, S., and Nachimuthu, P. K. (2003). A classifier for the SNP-based inference of ancestry. *Journal of Forensic Sciences* 48: 771–782.

Gabriel, M. N., Calloway, C. D., Reynolds, R. L., Andelinovic, S., and Primorac, D. (2001). Population variation of human mitochondrial DNA hypervariable regions I and II in 105 Croatian individuals demonstrated by immobilized sequence-specific oligonucleotide probe analysis. *Croatian Medical Journal* 42: 328–335.

Gamero, J. J., Romero, J. L., Gonzalez, J. L., Carvalho, M., Anjos, M. J., Corte-Real, F., Vieira, D. N., and Vide, M. C. (2001). Population-genetic study of the DYS385 haplotypes in two Spanish populations and the African immigrant population in Spain. *Journal of Forensic Sciences* 46: 193. doi: 10.1520/JFS14941J.

Gehrig, C., Hochmeister, M., and Budowle, B. (2000). Swiss allele frequencies and haplotypes of 7 Y-specific STRs. *Journal of Forensic Sciences* 45: 436–439.

Giardina, E., Pietrangeli, I., Martinez-Labarga, C., Martone, C., de Angelis, F., De Stefano, G., Rickards, O., and Novelli, G. (2008). Haplotypes in SLC24A5 gene as ancestry informative markers in different populations. *Current Genomics* 9: 110–114.

Gonzalez-Neira, A., Elmoznino, M., Lareu, M. V., Sanchez-Diz, P., Gusmao, L., Mechthild, P., and Carracedo, A. (2001). Sequence structure of 12 novel Y chromosome microsatellites and PCR amplification strategies. *Forensic Science International* 122: 19–26.

Gonzalez-Oliver, A., Marquez-Morfin, L., Jimenez, J. C., and Torre-Blanco, A. (2001). Founding Amerindian mitochondrial DNA lineages in ancient Maya from Xcaret, Quintana Roo. *American Journal of Physical Anthropology* 116: 230–235.

Graw, M., and Seitz, T. (2000). Y chromosomal short tandem repeat (STR) loci in a representative group of males living in South Wurttemberg: a database for application in forensic medicine. *Forensic Science International* 113: 43–46.

Gusmao, L., Alves, C., and Amorim, A. (2001). Molecular characterisation of four human Y-specific microsatellites (DYS434, DYS437, DYS438, DYS439) for population and forensic studies. *Annals of Human Genetics* 65: 285–291.

Hammer, M. F. (1995). A recent common ancestry for human Y chromosomes. *Nature* 378: 376–378.

Hammer, M. F., Garrigan, J. A., Wilder, Z. M., Severson, T., and Kingan, S. B. (2005). Sequence data from the autosomes and X chromosome: Evidence for ancient admixture in the history of *H. sapiens? American Journal of Physical Anthropology* S40: 111.

Hartmann, J. M., Houlihan, B. T., Keister, R. S., and Buse, E. L. (1997). The effect of ethnic and racial population substructuring on the estimation of multi-locus fixed-bin VNTR RFLP genotype probabilities. *Journal of Forensic Sciences* 42: 232–240.

Hedman, M., Brandstatter, A., Pimenoff, V., Sistonen, P., Palo, J. U., Parson, W., and Sajantila, A. (2007). Finnish mitochondrial DNA HVS-I and HVS-II population data. *Forensic Science International* 172: 171–178.

Hou, Y. P., Zhang, J., Li, Y. B., Wu, J., Zhang, S. Z., and Prinz, M. (2001). Allele sequences of six new Y-STR loci and haplotypes in the Chinese Han population. *Forensic Science International* 118: 147–152.

Hunley, K. E., Healy, M. E., and Long, J. C. (2009). The global pattern of gene identity variation reveals a history of long-range migrations, bottlenecks, and local mate exchange: Implications for biological race. *American Journal of Physical Anthropology* 139: 35–46.

Iltis, D. (2006). Revisiting Neanderthal mitochondrial DNA sequence variation. *American Journal of Physical Anthropology* S42: 107.

Kaestle, F. A., and Smith, D. G. (2001). Ancient mitochondrial DNA evidence for prehistoric population movement: The Numic expansion. *American Journal of Physical Anthropology* 115: 1–12.

Kayser, M., Brauer, S., Schadlich, H., Prinz, M., Batzer, M. A., Zimmerman, P. A., Boatin, B. A., and Stoneking, M. (2003). Y chromosome STR haplotypes and the genetic structure of US populations of African, European, and Hispanic ancestry. *Genome Research* 13: 624–634.

Kim, Y. J., Shin, D. J., Kim, J. M., Jin, H. J., Kwak, K. D., Han, M. S., Choi, S. K., and Kim, W. (2001). Y-chromosome STR haplotype profiling in the Korean population. *Forensic Science International* 115: 231–237.

Krause, J., Fu, Q., Good, J. M., Viola, B., Shunkov, M. V., Derevianko, A. P., and Pääbo, S. (2010). The complete mitochondrial DNA genome of an unknown hominin from southern Siberia. *Nature* 464: 894–897. doi:10.1038/nature08976.

Krings, M., Stone, A., Schmitz, R. W., Krainitzki, H., Stoneking, M., and Paabo, S. (1997). Neandertal DNA sequences and the origin of modern humans. *Cell* 90: 19–30.

Lao, O., van Duijn, K., Kersbergen, P., de Knijff, P., and Kayser, M. (2006). Proportioning whole-genome single-nucleotide-polymorphism diversity for the identification of geographic population structure and genetic ancestry. *American Journal of Human Genetics* 78: 680–690.

Lee, C., and Hong, J. H. (2001). Y chromosomal heterogeneity of six tetrameric microsatellites in a Korean population. *Korean Journal of Genetics* 23: 13–20.

Lessig, R., Edelmann, J., and Krawczak, M. (2001). Population genetics of Y-chromosomal microsatellites in Baltic males. *Forensic Science International* 118: 153–157.

Long, J. C., and Kittles, R. A. (2003). Human genetic diversity and the nonexistence of biological races. *Human Biology* 75: 449–471.

Long, J. C., Li, J., and Healy, M. E. (2009). Human DNA sequences: More variation and less race. *American Journal of Physical Anthropology* 139: 23–34.

Lucotte, G. (1989). Evidence for the paternal ancestry of modern humans: Evidence from a Y-chromosome specific sequence polymorphic DNA probe. In P. Mellars and C. B. Stringer (Eds.), *The human revolution: Behavioural and biological perspectives on the origins of modern humans.* Edinburgh: Edinburgh University Press, pp. 39–46.

Ma, F. C., Deng, Y., Dang, Y., Zhang, B., Mu, H., Yu, X., Li, L., Yan, C., and Chen, T. (2008). Genetic polymorphism of mitochondrial DNA HVS-I and HVS-II of Chinese Tu ethnic minority group. *Journal of Genetic Genomics* 35: 225–232.

Marrero, A. R., Das Neves Leite, F. P., De Almeida Carvalho, B., Peres, L. M., Kommers, T. C., Da Cruz, I. M., Salzano, F. M., Ruiz-Linares, A., Da Silva Junior, W. A., and Bortolini, M. C. (2005). Heterogeneity of the genome ancestry of individuals classified as White in the state of Rio Grande do Sul, Brazil. *American Journal of Human Biology* 17: 496–506.

Melton, T., Holland, C. A., Nelson, K. (2006). Commentary on: Divne A-M, Nilsson M, Calloway C, Reynolds R, Erlich H, Allen M. Forensic casework analysis using the HVI/HVII mtDNA linear array assay. *Journal of Forensic Sciences* 50: 548–554.—Response. *Journal of Forensic Sciences* 51: 937–938.

Nata, M., Brinkmann, B., and Rolf, B. (1999). Y-chromosomal STR haplotypes in a population from north west Germany. *International Journal of Legal Medicine* 112: 406–408.

Ossorio, P. N. (2006). About face: Forensic genetic testing for race and visible traits. *Journal of Law Medicine and Ethics* 34: 277–292. doi: 10.1111/j.1748–720X.2006.00033.x.

Pajnic, I. Z., Balazic, J., and Komel, R. (2004). Sequence polymorphism of the mitochondrial DNA control region in the Slovenian population. *International Journal of Legal Medicine* 118: 1–4.

Parra, F. C., Amado, R. C., Lambertucci, J. R., Rocha, J., Antunes, C. M., and Pena, S. D. (2003). Color and genomic ancestry in Brazilians. *Proceedings of the National Academy of Sciences of the United States of America* 100: 177–182.

Pereira, L., Cunha, C., and Amorim, A. (2004). Predicting sampling saturation of mtDNA haplotypes: An application to an enlarged Portuguese database. *International Journal of Legal Medicine* 118: 132–136.

Pereira, L., Richards, M., Goios, A., Alonso, A., Albarran, C., Garcia, O., Behar, D. M., Golge, M., Hatina, J., Al-Gazali, L., Bradley, D. G., Macaulay, V., and Amorim, A. (2006). Evaluating the forensic informativeness of mtDNA haplogroup H sub-typing on a Eurasian scale. *Forensic Science International* 159: 43–50.

Pfeiffer, H., Forster, P., Ortmann, C., and Brinkmann, B. (2001). The results of an mtDNA study of 1200 inhabitants of a German village in comparison to other Caucasian databases and its relevance for forensic casework. *International Journal of Legal Medicine* 114: 169–172.

Pimenta, J. R., Zuccherato, L. W., Debes, A. A., Maselli, L., Soares, R. P., Moura-Neto, R. S., Rocha, J., Bydlowski, S. P., and Pena, S. D. J. (2006). Color and genomic ancestry in Brazilians: A study with forensic microsatellites. *Human Heredity* 62: 190–195.

Rangel-Villalobos, H., Munoz-Valle, J. F., Gonzalez-Martin, A., Gorostiza, A., Magana, M. T., and Paez-Riberos, L. A. (2008). Genetic admixture, relatedness, and structure patterns among Mexican populations revealed by the Y-chromosome. *American Journal of Physical Anthropology* 135: 448–461.

Richards, M., and Macaulay, V. (2000). Genetic data and the colonization of Europe: geneaologie and founders. In C. Renfrew and K. Boyle (Eds.), *Archaeogenetics: DNA and the population prehistory of Europe.* Cambridge, UK: McDonald Institute Monographs, pp. 139–151.

Rosenberg, N. A., Pritchard, J. K., Weber, J. L., Cann, H. M., Kidd, K. K., Zhivotovsky, L. A., and Feldman, M. W. (2002). Genetic structure of human populations. *Science* 298: 2381–2385. doi: 10.1126/science.1078311.

Salas, A., Bandelt, H. J., Macaulay, V., and Richards, M. B. (2007). Phylogeographic investigations: The role of trees in forensic genetics. *Forensic Science International* 168: 1–13.

Sasaki, M., and Dahiya, R. (2000). The polymorphisms of various short tandem repeats on the Y chromosome in Japanese and German populations. *International Journal of Legal Medicine* 113: 181–188.

Shepard, E. M., and Herrera, R. J. (2006). Genetic encapsulation among Near Eastern populations. *Journal of Human Genetics* 51: 467–476.

Sykes, B., and Irven, C. (2000). Surnames and the Y chromosome. *American Journal of Human Genetics* 66: 1417–1419.

Walsh, B. (2001). Estimating the time to the most recent common ancestor for the Y chromosome or mitochondrial DNA for a pair of individuals. *Genetics* 158: 897–912.

Yang, N., Li, H. Z., Criswell, L. A., Gregersen, P. K., Alarcon-Riquelme, M. E., Kittles, R., Shigeta, R., Silva, G., Patel, P. I., Belmont, J. W., and Seldin, M. F. (2005). Examination of ancestry and ethnic affiliation using highly informative diallelic DNA markers: Application to diverse and admixed populations and implications for clinical epidemiology and forensic medicine. *Human Genetics* 118: 382–392.

Yao, Y. G., Kong, Q. P., Bandelt, H. J., Kivisild, T., and Zhang, Y. P. (2002). Phylogeographic differentiation of mitochondrial DNA in Han Chinese. *American Journal of Human Genetics* 70: 635–651.

Biomedical Aspects of Race

Ahnallen, J. M., Suyemoto, K. L., and Carter, A. S. (2006). Relationship between physical appearance, sense of belonging and exclusion, and racial/ethnic self-identification among multiracial Japanese European Americans. *Cultural Diversity and Ethnic Minority Psychology* 12: 373–386.

Baltrus, P. T., Lynch, J. W., Everson-Rose, S., Raghunathan, T. E., and Kaplan, G. A. (2005). Race/ethnicity, life-course socioeconomic position, and body weight trajectories over 34 years: The Alameda County Study. *American Journal of Public Health* 95: 1595–1601.

Carter, R. T., and Forsyth, J. A. (2007). Examining race and culture in psychology journals: The case of forensic psychology. *Professional Psychology-Research and Practice* 38: 133–142.

Duru, O. K., Li, S., Jurkovitz, C., Bakris, G., Brown, W., Chen, S. C., Collins, A., Klag, M., McCullough, P. A., McGill, J., Narva, A., Pergola, P., Singh, A., and Norris, K. (2008). Race and sex differences in hypertension control in CKD: Results from the Kidney Early Evaluation Program (KEEP). *American Journal of Kidney Disease* 51: 192–198.

Eastham, J. A., Sartor, O., Richey, W., Moparty, B., and Sullivan, J. (2001). Racial variation in prostate specific antigen in a large cohort of men without prostate cancer. *The Journal of the Louisiana State Medical Society* 153(4): 184–189.

Gilsanz, V., Skaggs, D. L., Kovanlikaya, A., Sayre, J., Loro, M., Kaufman, F., and Korenman, S. (1998). Differential effect of race on the axial and appendicular skeletons of children. *Journal of Clinical Endocrinology and Metabolism* 85: 1420–1427.

Golightly, Y. M., and Dominick, K. L. (2005). Racial variations in self-reported osteoarthritis symptom severity among veterans. *Aging Clinical and Experimental Research* 17: 264–269.

Gralnek, I. M., Hays, R. D., Kilbourne, A. M., Chang, L., and Mayer, E. A. (2004). Racial differences in the impact of irritable bowel syndrome on health-related quality of life. *Journal of Clinical Gastroenterology* 38: 782–789.

Gundberg, C. M., Looker, A. C., Nieman, S. D., and Calvo, M. S. (2002). Patterns of osteocalcin and bone specific alkaline phosphatase by age, gender, and race or ethnicity. *Bone* 31: 703–708.

Hicks, J. W. (2004). Ethnicity, race, and forensic psychiatry: Are we color-blind? *Journal of the American Academy of Psychiatry and the Law* 32: 21–33.

Joseph, C. L., Ownby, D. R., Peterson, E. L., and Johnson, C. C. (2000). Racial differences in physiologic parameters related to asthma among middle-class children. *Chest* 117: 1336–1344.

Lavie, C. J., Kuruvanka, T., Milani, R. V., Prasad, A., and Ventura, H. O. (2004). Exercise capacity in adult African-Americans referred for exercise stress testing: Is fitness affected by race? *Chest* 126: 1962–1968.

Mikuls, T. R., Kazi, S., Cipher, D., Hooker, R., Kerr, G. S., Richards, J. S., and Cannon, G. W. (2007). The association of race and ethnicity with disease expression in male U.S. veterans with rheumatoid arthritis. *Journal of Rheumatology* 34: 1480–1484.

Montoya, M. J. (2007). Bioethnic conscription: Genes, race, and Mexicana/o ethnicity in diabetes research. *Cultural Anthropology* 22: 94–128.

Morrison, J. A., Gruppo, R., Glueck, C. J., Stroop, D., Fontaine, R. N., Wang, P., and Smith, K. L. (2004). Population-specific alleles: The polymorphism (K121Q) of the human glycoprotein PC-1 gene is strongly associated with race but not with insulin resistance in Black and White children. *Metabolism—Clinical and Experimental* 53: 465–468.

Ness, R. B., Grisso, J. A., Klapper, J., and Vergona, R. (2000). Racial differences in ovarian cancer risk. *Journal of the National Medical Association* 92: 176–82.

Travison, T. G., Beck, T. J., Esche, G. R., Araujo, A. B., and McKinlay, J. B. (2008). Age trends in proximal femur geometry in men: Variation by race and ethnicity. *Osteoporos International* 19: 277–287.

Dental Identification

6

SALLY CARR
AYMIE MAXWELL
DR. STELLA MCCLURE

Contents

Introduction

> Show me your teeth and I will tell you who you are.
>
> **Georges Cuvier, 1769–1832, as cited in Gysel 1987**

For centuries, scientists have recognized that the human teeth are a special source of personal information. Contained within the morphological complexities of the healthy or the diseased human dentition is the great potential for the existence of one or many features that summate to create a particular "uniqueness" that can be utilized in contrasting one subject's teeth with another's. We can be "identified" as male or female, of a certain age and race, and as an individual by our "dental fingerprints" (Sweet and Pretty 2001a). This premise underlies the science of the specialty of forensic odontology.

There are 32 permanent teeth in the adult dentition, and each is described as comprised of five surfaces. On clinical examination, each of the 160 surfaces has the potential to appear structurally normal or to display abnormal features, whether congenital, acquired, or iatrogenic. Visible abnormalities include enamel hypomineralization, tetracycline staining, hairline fractures, carious lesions, restorations, unusual abrasion, attrition or erosion patterns, or aesthetic, "bling," embellishments. The list is extensive, and the possible permutations even more so, estimated to be greater than 2 billion (Lau et al. 2005).

The teeth exist both as individual units and as integral components of the maxillary and mandibular dental arches. Another source of "abnormality" can therefore be highlighted. Edward Angle's "normal" or "Class I" occlusion, in which the dental arches are essentially "perfect" in terms of completeness, shape, and alignment of the teeth, is almost never encountered in clinical practice, even after successful orthodontic treatment or orthognathic surgery. However, the notion of the normal occlusion is fundamental to recognizing, describing, and measuring malocclusion. Most individuals' dentitions are shades of the abnormal and contain rich pickings for the forensic odontologist: missing, rotated, or malaligned teeth; crowding or spacing; proclined or retroclined incisors; impacted or overerupted teeth. Major Class II and III occlusal abnormalities affecting the anterior teeth may be so distinguishing that they are the basis for the description by a witness of a perpetrator of a crime. Alternatively, some subtle dental rotations are only meaningful to, and therefore noted by, the trained eye. All can potentially be utilized in cases of human identification.

Beneath the crown surfaces and the gingivae, dental imaging techniques reveal many more potential identifiers. Every subgingival crown restoration, root canal filling, post-crown, and unit of bridgework has the potential to display unique features: shape, size, contour, deficiency, and relative degree of radio-opacity. Other anatomical details also emerge from the close inspection of dental radiographs. What is the precise relationship between the roots of the lower wisdom tooth and the inferior alveolar canal? Where is the mental foramen positioned? Are there buried supernumerary teeth or retained roots? Does the height of the alveolar ridge provide evidence of periodontal disease? What is the pattern of the trabecular bone?

Taking all into consideration, it is highly unlikely that any two persons will share exactly the same dental characteristics (Adams 2003). Even monozygotic twins can show similar but different congenital anomalies. Sperger et al. (1994) described an unusual anterior dental fusion and aplasia in both twins of a monozygotic pair that could be used to clearly distinguish one twin from the other.

So, human dentitions can and do demonstrate features described as unique to individuals, but just how unique is unique enough for the courtroom, especially in the most recognizable part of the dentition, the anterior maxillary segment? This chapter considers this question in relation to the still highly controversial area of bite mark analysis and its admissibility as evidence.

In addition to its potential to contain uniquely identifiable features, the dentition is the most likely part of the human form to retain its basic structural integrity on exposure to extreme conditions following death (Avon 2004). Thus, our identities are often best preserved in our teeth, including the possibility of genomic or ribosomal DNA extraction from the dental pulp (Sweet and Pretty 2001a). Current concepts regarding the identification of the victims of fire are presented in the chapter.

The identification of individuals, both living and deceased, is clearly a matter of great concern for both ethical and legal reasons. This creates a real need for reliable and valid methods of determining a person's identity, methods that can hold up in a court of law. Although the teeth are an excellent source of information pertaining to identity, many present-day problems face the profession of forensic odontology in attempting to satisfy this need for stringency.

First, matching the dentition of the deceased individual's remains with that of a known missing person relies on access to reliable antemortem (AM) data. Written or digital records detailing unique features and kept meticulously up to date, clinical photographs, radiographs, and stone models are ideal. As documented in this chapter, however, the availability of recent AM dental information can be severely restricted, especially in mass disaster situations in many parts of the world where dental record keeping is not a legal requirement. Even in the United Kingdom, dental general practitioners are only required (by their Defense Organization) to retain records until 11 years after the date of the patient's last consultation or until a former child patient reaches the age of 25 years.

Poor, albeit improving, standards of dental health and the resultant work of dental practitioners themselves can create problems for the forensic odontologist, none more obvious than the case of the edentulous individual. As discussed in the chapter, denture-labeling systems are currently being investigated and could theoretically revolutionize the approach to identification.

Modern dental materials and patients' aesthetic wishes have led to a situation in which many restorations, particularly of the anterior dentition, are now of tooth-colored composites, compomeres, and ceramics. These are materials that are neither as easy to identify during clinical examination nor as obvious as amalgam or gold radiographically. Research efforts are now focusing on the applicability of computerized tomography (CT) and associated software in the identification of aesthetic restorations. Ideally, a scenario, such as one missed resin restoration resulting in a failure to correctly identify an individual, will be a less likely future occurrence.

Modern aesthetic dentistry, orthodontists, and orthognathic surgeons in combination create another problem for the forensic world by reducing the incidence and the severity of abnormal dental features, certainly within Westernized populations.

Nonetheless, human dentition remains fundamentally important to forensic science as crucial personal details can be retrieved through applying the accredited knowledge and skills of the forensic odontologist to a variety of "missing person" scenarios. As well as matching criminals to evidence of crime, the forensic odontologist can give a name back to a deceased individual, essentially returning the lost loved one to his or her family and friends and providing invaluable peace of mind. Dental matching is accepted as one of the four primary identifiers by Interpol (along with DNA, fingerprints, and a unique medical condition [e.g., a prosthesis with a serial number]).

Identification Problems Associated with Antemortem Dental Records

When human remains are found, a tentative preliminary "identification" can be made from the basic biological profile (age, sex, and ethnicity) in combination with the presence of personal effects at, and the general location of, the scene. These factors can narrow the search for the identity of the individual down to a person likely to hail from a relatively small geographical area (Chen and Jain 2005). Dental practitioners within that area can then be sought and AM data, including radiographs bearing patients' names, obtained for comparative purposes (Chen and Jain 2005). To expedite the identification of discovered remains, when a person is listed as missing Blau et al. (2006) strongly recommend the timely storage of the individual's dental records in a national, or preferably international, dental database. Such a resource, while now available in Canada, Ireland, and certain U.S. states, is not currently available in the United Kingdom. The employment of a forensic odontologist should also be considered routine in all cases of missing persons or found remains to minimize errors in recording or interpreting data pertaining to the teeth (Blau et al. 2006).

A major hindrance to the identification process is encountered when no AM dental records are available to compare with the collated postmortem (PM) data. If AM dental records are available, key to the success of the identification process are the currency and accuracy of these records (Flint et al. 2009; Kirchhoff et al. 2008). Neither can be guaranteed.

People travel far and wide now and may die or be declared missing while abroad and many years after their final visit to their last-known dentist. All dental records, which can only record a momentary point in the lifetime of the dentition, particularly those of children, become gradually less useful with time as the dentition first develops and then ages. Current dental records are not always available.

Regarding the accuracy of dental records, traditionally dentists, or their assistants, have completed handwritten notes after seeing a patient. These have often been error ridden, up to 70% of the time according to Borrman et al.'s 1995 paper (cited in du Chesne et al. 2000). Gross errors such as "wrong side" were noted. In Asian countries in particular, the tsunami of 2004 revealed the routine deficiencies in the recording practices of dentists, with 90% of dental records containing inadequate data. Rather than noting at each visit the condition of the nonoperated teeth, only details of any work undertaken on a single tooth tended to be documented, and essential details such as type of restorative material used and tooth surfaces affected were invariably missing (Petju et al. 2007). In addition, handwritten notes may also be illegible and completed using indecipherable abbreviations unique to the dentist and in a language that requires interpretation. Such records may only be useful when no others exist but might have to be disregarded (Lee et al. 2004). In some countries, such as Estonia, dentists are not legally required to keep records of their patients, and this lack of AM information makes identification challenging (Soomer et al. 2001).

Fortunately, in most developed countries where record keeping is required by law, "written" dental records are now frequently stored digitally, allowing for easier reading and faster global transfer, although errors associated with data input are still to be anticipated.

Such data input errors should not be a feature of human identification using dental radiographs, especially in whole-mouth (panoramic) views in which left and right errors are less frequently encountered than in side-specific intraoral films (Borrman et al. 1995, cited in du Chesne et al. 2000). Dental imaging records do, however, suffer from other problems, such as narrow field, distortions, over- or underexposures, and artifacts, which can limit the value of the usable information they contain. However, AM dental radiographs remain a wonderful source of information in forensic cases.

There are several different types of intra- and extraoral radiographs used in dental practice, with the most common intraoral films being the bite-wing and the periapical (Hosntalab et al. 2010). The bitewing is a small film offering a relatively restricted view of the molar and premolar regions of the maxillary and mandibular arches, usually excluding all root apices (Nassar et al. 2008). Mahoor and Abdel-Mottaleb (2004: 583) presented a "method for robust classification and numbering of molar and premolar teeth in bite-wing images using Bayesian classification" that they hope to develop into an automated dental identification system. This film type was commonly taken as a screening tool for interdental caries in the posterior regions of the arches, although its use has in many ways been superseded in U.K. dental practices by fiber-optic technology. Optical coherence tomography (OCT) (Otis et al. 2000) similarly avoids the need for ionizing radiation exposure. This technology has already been successfully developed for high-precision biometry and tomography of biological tissues, in particular in ophthalmology and, in the forensic sphere, latent fingerprints (Dubey et al. 2008). OCT perhaps offers a developmental opportunity in the field of forensic dentistry given its potential to detect structural changes in the dental and periodontal tissues and within dental materials.

The periapical radiograph usually focuses on a single tooth but includes all of the crown and root and the periapical tissues. It is used to assess the adequacy of root canal fillings and to diagnose and monitor the treatment of periapical abscesses and cysts. It can also provide details regarding apicectomy procedures that could be invaluable to the forensic odontologist as each retrograde amalgam root filling is subtly different in size and shape. Given that "root morphology and alignment were cited most frequently as facilitating matching" in an imaging-based study, this highlights the potential value of the periapical film to the odontologist (Sholl and Moody 2001: 165).

Kogon et al. (2009) did mention that the dental radiographs most often available to the forensic odontologist may omit an important potential identifier because the tooth bearing a unique feature in the dentition of the unidentified human remains was not the subject of any of the AM x-ray investigations performed on that patient. This is particularly likely if the interest is in a distinctive anterior tooth but bitewings are the only radiographs in the records of the missing individual.

Lee et al. (2004) described the diversity of dental patterns that are readily identifiable from orthopantomographic films (dental panoramic tomogram, DPT) and advocated the use of AM and PM panoramic dental images as preferable to the interpretation of dentists' notes during the identification process. In particular, Lee et al. mentioned the identification value of the detail available in the molar regions of the DPT, where there are greater incidences of missing and restored teeth than are generally found in the anterior region.

Radiographs, either plain film or digitized, are the most readily available "snapshots" of pictorial information routinely filed in the average dentist's data records. Particularly when up to date, they are an invaluable asset. Clinical photographs, commonly taken during orthodontic treatment, for example, may also be utilized to provide objective AM data relating to the anterior teeth. One highly interesting development is the potential for recording a biometric "toothprint" of surface enamel Hunter-Schreger banding (HSB) (Ramenzoni and Line 2006) using a simple combination of a fiber-optic light source and digital photography. The authors claimed that this pattern was detectable and recordable by noninvasive means and was accurate and amenable to automated comparison systems. Ramenzoni and Line (2006) also suggested that HSB resists heating to 300°C and mentioned that the pattern has been shown to be retained in fossil teeth. However, HSB could not be detected in 4.5% of the dental sample analyzed.

Identification Problems due to Esthetic Developments in Dentistry

Traditionally, the recording of the presence and the pattern of restorative interventions has been the cornerstone of the forensic odontologist's armamentarium in cases of unidentified human dental remains. However, Sholl and Moody (2001) mentioned that young European and North American individuals are increasingly having fewer restorative works performed, perhaps due to an increasing emphasis on prevention and associated improvements in oral and dental health. Moreover, for many years dental materials science has been providing restorative options that can discreetly merge into the arch. Thus, amalgam restorations are increasingly being replaced by tooth-colored resins (Zondagh and Phillips 2009). Initially, this posed significant problems as odontologists learned to detect these aesthetic restorations visually. Where the margins are extremely well constructed and merge seamlessly with the enamel, recently sited resin restorations can be essentially "invisible." A further problem was that the early resins were also not radio-opaque, although modern constituents usually include elements that can be visualized radiographically (Bush et al. 2006). Various studies have attempted to postulate the most sensitive and specific technique for identifying the presence of aesthetic resin restorations in the teeth to assist the forensic odontologist.

From the clinical perspective, plaque-disclosing solution, dyes, transillumination, and quantitative light-induced fluorescence are all examples of current mortuary practices utilized to optimize the detection of tooth-colored fillings. Disclosing solutions, for example, can detect the plaque that has accumulated premortem in relation to the deficient margin of a resin restoration. Whereas the composite itself may not be visible to the naked eye, the plaque, once stained, highlights the edge of the restoration, bringing it to the attention of the examiner and assisting clinical detection.

From the radiological perspective, Zondagh and Phillips's (2009) work using plain films suggests that these, the cheapest and most readily available imaging modality to date, can be used to detect compound restorations that include features of uniqueness. Zondagh and Phillips (2009) demonstrated, in a small *in vitro* trial using resin restorations in acrylic teeth and bitewing-type plain radiography, that such restorations produced a morphologically distinct and readily recognizable feature, albeit less easily seen than amalgam, but visible to a trained eye nonetheless. Hence, it could still be argued that plain radiographic techniques have a valuable, cost-effective role to play in the identification process in relation to tooth-colored dental materials.

Other authors have pursued the CT route based in part on the premise that three dimensions (3D) will produce a greater "uniqueness" yield than plain two-dimensional (2D) radiography (Hosntalab et al. 2008: 258). Hosntalab's group also mentioned that "CT has become the most frequently used imaging modality to provide clinical datasets for dental pre-operative and intra-operative planning. Recently, the introduction of cone-beam computed tomography (CBCT) has the potential to reduce the size and cost of CT scanners." It is likely therefore that CT scans, both AM and PM, will become more readily available in dental records in the near future. Critically, CT imaging can create a 3D image of delicate structures without disturbing the remains (Jackowski et al. 2006; Thali et al. 2006). Scanning the dentition is a rapid process and produces an instantaneous image without the requirement for darkroom facilities. Furthermore, the user is able to search through the available images to determine which particular slice offers the best comparison with whatever type of AM image is available (Hosntalab et al. 2008; Kirchhoff et al. 2008).

Porcelain (ceramic) restorations are of similar radio-opacity to dentine, rendering CT detection difficult. Jackowski et al. (2008) described an inspection method to overcome this problem, stating that porcelain crowns, inlays, and veneers are held in place with radio-opaque cement, and its detection in CT images will alert the examiner to the probable presence of a restoration. This group drew similar conclusions regarding the discriminative ability of CT in relation to resin restorations. In particular, the ability to distinguish between ceramic and composite restorations was highlighted as an area of real progress in terms of human identification. It should also be noted that poorly fitted ceramic crowns will often demonstrate radiolucent defects or radio-opaque overhangs around their margins that could be useful in identification cases.

However, a current setback in dental CT is the presence of "streak artifacts" due to beam attenuation and scattering by the heavy metals in amalgam restorations. In some instances, these artifacts render the image almost uninterpretable. Hosntalab's group (2010) suggested the employment of a "low-pass Butterworth filter and a morphological erosion" to reduce metal artifacts. Their results seem to represent an improvement on the original CT images. The adaptation of the Hounsefield unit settings for amalgam within the volume-rendered preset could further assist with optimization (Jackowski et al. 2008).

Scanning electron microscopy/energy dispersive x-ray spectroscopy (SEM/EDS) analysis can differentiate, when combined with backscattered electron imaging, between the different elemental compositions of dental resins produced by different manufacturers (Bush et al. 2006). Bush et al. (2008) investigated the utility of the Spectral Library Identification and

Classification Explorer (SLICE) software package in combination with SEM/EDS in an attempt to build up a database of resins in which information such as its manufacturing brand, which can be traced to certain dental practices, is made accessible to forensic teams. The ability to compare spectra of unknown resins to those resins stored in the database would be of great assistance in speeding up the identification process. Emphasis must be placed on the need to update regularly and include the details of every resin that is made or modified so that such a database could remain as useful as possible. In addition, the details of the resins used in all restorations should ideally be recorded in all patients' dental records to optimize the functionality of this database. A major limitation of the application of SEM/EDS is that the equipment is laboratory based at present.

X-ray fluorescence has also been utilized to detect and identify five different resin brands placed in the dentition of six cadavers (Bush et al. 2007). This method proved capable of distinguishing resin brand from tooth, bone, and other substances. Successful identifications were made in 53 of the 70 restorations studied, and the technique enabled positive victim identification (Bush et al. 2007). The equipment in this case has the added advantage of portability and shows some real promise for the future.

Matching Antemortem and Postmortem Records: Problems Making the Identification

Manual dental comparison has generally been held to be the gold standard of choice in cases of human identification (Sholl and Moody 2001). It has been the responsibility of the examining forensic odontologist to make a detailed and accurate clinical examination for comparison with AM dental notes and to take PM images that are technically suitable for comparison with the available AM data.

The problems associated with attempting to compare AM with PM dentists' handwritten notes and charts have been mentioned.

Radiographically speaking, there are no set criteria for the number of "matching points" that must be described to conclude the identification process, in stark contrast with fingerprint identification guidelines. Indeed, one subtle but distinctive dental radiographic feature may be sufficient to prove a match (Flint et al. 2009). Establishing identification therefore relies heavily on the experience of the examining dentist in noting fine detail that may be of major relevance. A study by Pretty et al. (2003) noted that only the most experienced odontologists, with a success rate of 91% in matching AM to PM plain radiographs, might expect to withstand the scrutiny of a courtroom, as emphasized by Flint et al. (2009). Those with little or no experience at attempting to identify a person are more likely to misidentify an individual simply because they have been shown to focus on discrepancies rather than similarities (Soomer et al. 2003). Sholl and Moody (2001) similarly commented that training is no substitute for experience.

Manual matching of AM and PM radiographs is now losing favor somewhat, mainly due to the time required to compare all possible matches and the emergence of promising new automated methodologies (Clement et al. 2006; Nomir and Abdel-Mottaleb 2005). In the last decade in particular, time limitations relating to the identification process have become apparent in the responses to mass casualty situations. Attention has been drawn to the lack of a global, Web-based, automated matching system to optimize efficiency (Fahmy et al. 2004; Clement et al. 2006; Nassar et al. 2008). Furthermore, a robust automation process would theoretically reduce the subjective human error component associated with manual comparisons, especially if less-experienced operators have to be recruited in major disaster victim identification (DVI) situations. As established by Berketa et al. (2010), a greater quantity of detailed information for comparison purposes can also be gleaned by software programs applied to digitized images.

Automated imaging-based methods, a form of "dental biometrics," are supported by databases into which all available AM and PM digitized imaging data are entered. There are various databases currently available or under development, including the Australian "DAVID Web," which is being reexplored post-Asian tsunami in an effort to update counterdisaster measures (Clement et al. 2006).

Subsequent to accessing a suitable database, automated comparisons of imaging material fundamentally involve the three stages of segmentation, feature extraction, and matching. Various approaches to achieving these stages have been developed, each involving complex mathematical equations, but the basic principles remain the same.

First, segmentation involves isolating a tooth from its neighbors, creating the region of interest (ROI), which can be achieved across a spectrum of radiographic investigations from bitewings (Nomir and Abdel-Mottaleb 2005) to volumetric CT scans (Hosntalab et al. 2008). Separation of the tooth is based on grayscale differences at a pixel level (Abdel-Mottaleb et al. 2003). Teeth and their restorations are generally the brightest structures on a radiograph, and this is of value in distinguishing the dental unit from its bony and soft tissue surroundings (Lai and Lin 2008).

Once each tooth has been separated into its own ROI, the next stage is feature extraction. There are different methods, all providing a similar outcome (Hosntalab et al. 2008). Outlining or mapping the external contour of the tooth, which could prove to be unique to the individual, is a popular approach (Chen and Jain 2005). The software selects a number of points along the tooth border to establish an outline (Jain and Chen 2004), and their number is increased along areas of high curvature so that important feature details are not likely to be omitted (Abdel-Mottaleb et al. 2003). If some points are missing along the contour, an average can be taken. However, this may reduce the accuracy of the process. In some methods, the distance from the points is measured against a set point established by the program (Chen and Jain 2005).

The final stage of automation compares AM and PM radiographs to determine if any held in the respective databases match. Sweet and Pretty (2001a) described the possible outcomes of the matching process as a case of positive identification (the match is detailed and contains no discrepancies), a possible identification (consistent features), an outcome of insufficient evidence, or an exclusion (clearly inconsistent).

It must be highlighted that, currently at least, an automation system is not necessarily in itself designed to establish an identification; rather, its function is more to create a short list of possible matches that are then presented to the odontologist for review, often in graphical format (Chomdej et al. 2006).

Automation, in principle, shows great potential, although it is still in its infancy, and further research is clearly required. In particular, the process becomes problematic as available image quality deteriorates. Blurred outlines render segmentation and feature extraction troublesome (Jain and Chen 2004). As of yet, there is no program with the capacity to account for missing and supernumerary teeth, impactions, and retained deciduous teeth, which is a major obstacle to utility (Abdel-Mottaleb et al. 2003; Chen and Jain 2005; Chomdej et al. 2006; Lin et al. 2010). Kirchhoff et al.'s (2008) study illustrated some of these practical problems, with automated matching obtaining a somewhat disappointing and yet equally promising 87% success rate. Another significant problem that has to be considered is file size when working on a Web-based program or database. In practice, pixilation might be sacrificed by operators in favor of increased uploading and downloading speeds. As matching is primarily conducted at the pixel level, this practice should be avoided (Fahmy et al. 2004; Hanaoka et al. 2007; Tsuzuki et al. 2002).

A Special Postmortem Identification Challenge: Features of Burned Dental Remains

Teeth can provide a clinical or radiographic identification resource when no other materials are available (Valenzuela et al. 2000). Dental structures are known to be extremely hard and resilient in comparison with the skeletal and soft tissues of the body (Flint et al. 2009). Teeth resist putrefaction and corrosion and can remain essentially intact in ambient temperatures of up to 1,100°C, although they will disintegrate if exposed to direct heat of that intensity (Fereira et al. 2008).

In burn victims, the location of teeth within the oral cavity also favors their survival as they are relatively protected from an external heat source by the surrounding soft tissues of the face and tongue. However, when buccal and labial musculature burns, the cheek and lip areas contract, leaving anterior teeth exposed. This explains the observation that the greatest damage occurs to the anterior dentition in fires (Delattre 2000). Charred teeth do become dehydrated, leading to shrinkage, which can result in PM avulsion and the loss of restorations (Fereira et al. 2008).

Exposed to heat, a tooth experiences a number of physical alterations, including discolorations, which vary according to how the heat is applied. Short, high-intensity bursts of heat (e.g., in an explosion) will cause the crown to shatter due to rapid expansion of the pulp cavity. If heat is applied slowly over a longer time, as in house fires, a number of stages occur as exposure continues (Fereira et al. 2008; Savio et al. 2006). This knowledge permits the forensic dentist to contribute information toward the determination of the source, temperature, and duration of the fire. After burning, residual tooth structure is chalky and brittle (Bonavilla et al. 2008), and recognizable crown and root morphology may be difficult to preserve for analytical purposes other than imaging.

Amalgam restorations survive heating up to 800°C, while porcelain crowns can withstand 1,000°C, and some base metal alloys used in dentistry resist heat up to 1,500°C (Brandao et al. 2007). Savio et al. (2006) noted radiographically that composite resin fillings maintain their shape until 600°C, and endodontic materials remain recognizable until 1,100°C. Bonavilla et al. (2008) presented the anti-incineration properties of various endodontic fillers in a description of the initial stage of database generation for use as an aid in forensic identification.

An understanding of the effects of burning on dental resins is relevant given that modern dental practices are utilizing adhesive restorations more and more frequently as the materials science, skills of the dentist, and aesthetic concerns of patients increase. In the case of a burned victim in the United Kingdom, there is an increasing probability that a resin restoration will have been present in the mouth AM. A major problem with many previous studies examining the response of these materials to heat is a lack of standardization. Various temperatures have been used and various lengths of heat exposure applied. The results from different experiments have therefore not been directly comparable and have had limited uses (Brandao et al. 2007). However, Bush et al. (2006) subjected 10 resins implanted within extracted teeth to 30 minutes of heat exposure to 900°C within a burnout oven. Color changes were observed that were unique to each resin brand type. Postincineration, it was observed that the elemental composition had altered, which prevented the differentiation of one resin from another. Brandao et al. (2007) presented a novel report of heating-associated color and brightness changes that were characteristic of resin brands. This source of new information has the future potential to link, via the manufacturer, burned resins found in dental remains to a particular dental surgery and hence to an identification.

Mass Casualty Identification Problems: The 2004 Asian Tsunami

Perhaps the greatest challenge to the forensic team is the international mass casualty situation. DVI under such circumstances must involve a highly coordinated, multidisciplinary approach to the retrieval, correct identification, and repatriation of victims. Interpol (1992) described the requirement for national DVI teams, formed from specifically trained individuals, to be deployed immediately following a mass disaster whenever there is a likelihood that citizens from their respective countries may have lost their lives (Lunetta et al. 2003).

Identifications are ascertained by applying the full spectrum of forensic expertise to the entirety of the available human remains. Due to the unique qualities and durability of the dentition previously described, plus the potential for the availability of AM dental records, the victim's teeth provide an invaluable repository of information pertaining to the identification challenge. It is no surprise, therefore, that the DVI process frequently benefits from the contributions of the forensic odontologist.

The Asian tsunami of December 26, 2004, provides an excellent case study demonstrating the application of dental methodology to the successful identification of mass casualties in the face of extreme climactic and organizational difficulties. The tsunami was the result of an Indian Ocean earthquake. This natural disaster left an estimated 230,000 dead in 11 countries (Perrier et al. 2006). The tourist resorts of Thailand were badly affected, specifically the tourist area of Khao-Lak, where approximately half of the 4,225 reported victims were foreign nationals (Petju et al. 2007). Overall, victims were citizens of 58 different countries (De Valck 2006). This created a great need for efficient communication between the victims' home countries, where any AM data would be located, and the DVI teams working at the multiple scenes (Petju et al. 2007).

The Thai Tsunami Victim Identification center was established in Phuket on January 13, 2005, and set up a central mortuary where all of the victims in Thailand were examined (Perrier et al. 2006; Morgan et al. 2006). Once the DVI teams arrived, standard Interpol operating protocols were quickly established (De Valck 2006). Many of the early identifications were unfortunately based on visual recognition by family members (Petju et al. 2007).

In later cases, because of prolonged immersion of the remains, chaotic body recovery, and lack of refrigerated storage facilities, facial and fingerprint identification became extremely problematic (Sweet 2006). Dentistry clearly emerged as the most practically applicable and efficient means of identification under such difficult conditions. The acquisition of AM dental information was therefore a crucial element in the effort (De Valck 2006).

Once an individual had been reported missing in their country of origin, an AM team was dispatched to collect familial DNA and fingerprint samples of the missing person (De Valck 2006). The individual's dentist was also contacted, and AM dental information pertaining to the postulated victim was obtained. Forensic odontologists at the Interpol National Central Bureau carefully transcribed the available AM data into the "Plass data" program for comparison with all incoming PM dental information (De Valck 2006; Lau et al. 2005). In almost all cases for which the head had been retained with the remains PM, the teeth were found to be structurally intact (Petju et al. 2007). Dental examination, performed whenever possible by forensic odontologists, involved visual examination followed by plain radiographic investigations, usually bitewings, to facilitate accurate dental charting. All findings were, ideally, confirmed by a second odontologist. The PM details of victims were then entered into the Plass database. The Plass program did not provide the identification. Rather, it increased the efficacy of the DVI process by compiling a likely short list of AM-PM matches (Lau et al. 2005). The ranked list of possible names and data was then given to a senior odontologist, who offered a determination on the presence or absence of an identity match (Schuller-Gotzburg and Suchanek 2007). To safeguard confidentiality, measures were taken to prevent unauthorized access to the database from outside the network (de Valck 2006).

Approximately 80% of the identifications made on non-Asians involved dental matching. However, regarding Thai nationals, for example, many were not registered with a dentist (Petju et al. 2007), and as previously mentioned, for those who had received treatment, dental record keeping in Thailand is notoriously incomplete. Dental surgeries were also destroyed in the tsunami, along with paper-based notes. Digital data storage is unusual in Thailand. It proved necessary to use other methods to identify Thai nationals, such as fingerprint and DNA analysis. Identity cards incorporating fingerprint data are mandatory in Thailand and provided a comparative source in many cases (Schuller-Gotzburg and Suchanek 2007; Morgan et al. 2006). This represented one valid use for a government-imposed condition of legal citizenship that remains contested in the United Kingdom at present. As an alternative to fingerprint analysis, Perrier et al. (2006) described the approach of the Swiss DVI team to extracting and refrigerating two healthy teeth, usually canines, to be retained as sources of "uncontaminated" DNA for analysis at a later date if required. Of note here is that environmental conditions, including humidity, submersion, and burial, do not impair the capacity to extract DNA from dental pulp (da Silva et al. 2007).

It is generally recognized that dental methods represented a successful means of providing identity for the non-Thai victims of the Asian tsunami. Major problems were still encountered, however. Kieser et al. (2006) highlighted the poor quality of the AM records received by the New Zealand forensic team, stating that 62% were of unacceptable quality. In preparation for an improved international response to a future recurrence on a similarly devastating humanitarian level, regulation by law would effectively enhance AM dental data recording in Asian communities. Furthermore, global standardization of the DVI protocol and the recording, storage, and retrieval of AM records would optimize the efficacy of the identification effort (Petju et al. 2007).

Regarding the acquisition of PM information from the teeth of the deceased in mass casualties, of future benefit could be the handpiece type of intraoral CCD (charge-coupled device) camera (Crystal Cam; GC Corp., Japan). This equipment is mobile and has the capacity to facilitate the examination of the teeth where jaw opening is restricted and lighting conditions are inadequate, as may often be the case in temporary morgues in DVI situations (Tsuzuki et al. 2002). The digital images collected by the camera, although not always ideal in quality, do offer the potential for rapid electronic transference of the PM data to increase the efficiency of coordinating AM-PM comparisons. Jackowski and Persson (2010), in contrast with Kirchhoff et al.'s (2008) conclusions, strongly advocated the institution of PM state-of-the art CT scanning in mass casualty situations. Rutty et al. (2009) have presented a novel national DVI imaging system entitled Fimag (Forensic Identification Imaging System), which may indeed represent the way forward. The advantages of this approach, which incorporates multislice CT technology, include its utility in both contaminated (chemical biological radiological nuclear agents [CBRN]) and noncontaminated mass fatality scenes and that it addresses the "issues of judicial reporting."

Interestingly, once identifications had been made, it was shown that tsunami victims' remains could be "labeled" using radiofrequency identification (RFID) tags inserted into the body (Richmond and Pretty 2009b). This successfully replaced the less-satisfactory traditional labeling methods, such as writing names on or placing labels inside body bags, which proved to be unsatisfactory given the environmental conditions.

Dental Labeling Systems

There is little information referring to the increased difficulties that must have been associated with the identification of the edentulous victims of the tsunami. Deceased edentulous individuals are more challenging to identify as any available AM dental records made after the extraction of the last natural teeth will usually consist only of notes pertaining to the construction and modification of acrylic dentures. Resorption of alveolar bone postextraction can rapidly render any previous radiographic studies of significantly reduced value to the forensic odontologist. In a study by Richmond and Pretty (2007), it was concluded that only 18% of the dental records of edentulous individuals contained information that might reasonably be expected to result in a positive identification. The same authors also mentioned that, in 2005 in the United Kingdom, 300,000 patients were first rendered edentulous, adding to the already large population of full or partial denture-wearing individuals.

The exception to the general rule that edentulous identifications are more difficult is the case of the patient wearing overdentures on dental implants. In such cases, the design, position, and angulations of the osseo-integrated implants provide a wealth of information, both clinically and radiographically. Berketa et al. (2010) concluded that dental implants could be radiologically categorized according to the company of manufacture. In addition, all patients having dental implants inserted should have detailed AM written records and imaging studies within their case notes, which would facilitate the identification process.

If dentures are found with human remains, it may eventually prove possible to use information such as acrylic brand, denture design specifics, or DNA from any saliva remaining on the prosthesis to provide a link to an individual's identity. However, a much more practical solution has been offered: that of a universal denture-labeling system (Richmond and Pretty 2007). The same authors noted that numerous countries other than the United Kingdom currently specify that patients' dentures should be labeled, although there are no data at present on compliance with this practice.

A simple label might include the patient's name and an identifying number implanted clearly into the maxillary and mandibular dentures. Such printed labels can readily be incorporated into denture bases during the manufacturing process (Richmond and Pretty 2007). Tags could theoretically store additional details, such as sex, date of birth, and country of nationality (Thevissen et al. 2006). Rather than use personal data, an Australian denture identification specialist company, Dentident, has established a database that claims to have the potential to identify the manufacturer of the labeled denture, or the dental practitioner, or both (Richmond and Pretty 2009a). Their system relies on an RFID tag (chip). Some authors have further proposed the insertion of RFID tags into living individuals' teeth (Thevissen et al. 2006).

Various denture "marking systems" have been described in the literature, and Richmond and Pretty (2009a) tested the durability of 10 different systems under a variety of extreme physical assaults, simulating potential PM conditions (burial, various immersions, freezing, and heating). The simple stainless steel orthodontic band engraved with identifying details was the only one to perform well under severe thermal challenge. Interestingly, the RFID tag was found to be a close second-best option overall and was the most acceptable with regard to patients' aesthetic desires.

The modified veterinary RFID tags for *in vitro* dental insertion that were investigated by Thevissen et al. (2006) consisted of three components, which measured 8 × 3 × 3 mm and could be inserted into a standard Class I molar cavity within a composite resin restoration. The devices were clearly visualized on periapical images. The point of best readout was located 280 mm from the center of the tag (Thevissen et al. 2006). Richmond and Pretty (2009b) also investigated the scanning range readout ability of RFID tags and found the system to be relatively secure with regard to remote third-party access to personal data. Further trials and clarifications are required.

A major issue with human labeling systems of any description is public acceptability. The potential benefit in mass disaster situations is clear, and the technology is indeed promising. However, additional in-depth consideration is required, including an international agreement on tag and reader specifications (Richmond and Pretty 2009b).

Bite Mark Evidence: The Debate

The human dentition can be utilized as a weapon in both defensive and aggressive situations, and biting is also repeatedly observed in cases of sexual abuse (Sweet and Pretty 2001b). The damage to the victim's skin, the bite mark, not only is a potential source of physical and biological evidence but also is a highly complex wound that requires expert analysis (Sweet and Pretty 2001b). Bite marks on a victim's skin have historically been compared with the suspect's dentition to ascertain whether the accused is probably the biter, possibly the biter, or probably not the biter (Bernitz et al. 2008). Convictions have been based on the expert testimony of the forensic odontologist in matching a bite mark to the dentition of the accused (Davis 2005). However, landmark cases have more recently seen subsequent exonerations in the light of DNA findings, thus demonstrating the fallibilities of the science of bite mark analysis in its current state (Bowers and Pretty 2009; Deitch 2009). In conjunction with the 1993 U.S. Supreme Court *Daubert v. Merrell Dow Pharmaceuticals, Inc. 509 U.S. 579* rulings, the burden of proof has now been firmly placed on the scientific methodology (cited in Deitch 2009):

"If scientific, technical, or other specialized knowledge will assist the trier of fact to understand the evidence or to determine a fact in issue, a witness qualified as an expert by knowledge, skill, experience, training, or education, may testify thereto in the form of an opinion or otherwise. ... Scientific evidence must be both relevant and reliable."

To be "admissible" (cited in Deitch 2009: 1213), (1) the theory or technique must be able to be, and have been, tested; (2) it must have been "subjected to peer review and publication"; (3) the known or possible error rate of the scientific technique must be taken into consideration; (4) the court should take into account the "relevant scientific community" and a determination of the degree to which the theory or technique in question is accepted in that community; and (5) the focus is on the principles and methodology behind the technique, not necessarily on the conclusions generated.

Two major problems have continued to undermine the scientific acceptability of bite mark analysis methodology. First, a necessary assumption must be made that the anterior teeth, the biting part of the dentition, display features of "uniqueness" that might be identifiable within the bite mark (Kieser et al. 2007). In addition, an awareness that the skin behaves unpredictably when bitten is a highly significant problem (Sweet and Pretty 2001b).

Measurement of the "Uniqueness" of the Anterior Human Dentition

Several researchers have attempted to "prove" whether an individual's anterior dentition can be considered "unique." Kouble and Craig (2007) studied the most obvious anterior anomaly, the missing tooth scenario. An audit of missing anterior teeth in 1,010 adult patients was performed. One in five of the sample displayed missing teeth that were either "replaced with a denture (11%), not replaced (6%) or missing with the gap closed (2%)." It was concluded that "unusual" dental features, such as absent teeth, are not therefore as unique a population characteristic as was initially presumed. Bernitz et al. (2006: 19) mentioned that although no epidemiological studies to date have measured the prevalence of rotations of the anterior teeth, it is possible to ascribe quantitative descriptors to such dental anomalies that might provide a measure of uniqueness applicable to the analysis of bite marks.

Perhaps the most compelling evidence to date in favor of the uniqueness hypothesis was provided by Kieser et al. (2007). This study applied a "new family" of 2D geometric morphometric analyses, based on landmark and semi-landmark data, to 50 sets of dental casts, seeking to measure size and shape differences in the occlusal surfaces of the anterior teeth. Details such as interdental spacing and rotations were also fully considered. Specifically, posторthodontic treatment casts displaying unrestored teeth in "normocclusion" were studied to maximally challenge the hypothesis. It was concluded that the anterior dentition can in fact be considered unique, particularly when variations in the depth and width of the maxillary and mandibular arch forms are considered in combination with individual tooth alignments. Further epide-miological data gathering of this nature would no doubt greatly assist with the task of substantiating or refuting the science of bite mark analysis.

Bowers and Pretty (2009) agreed in principle with the notion of unique-ness but criticized Kieser et al.'s (2007) 2D approach to a 3D challenge and raised the question of *degree* of uniqueness, particularly in combination with the second problem encountered in bite mark cases, that of the human skin as a poor medium for bite mark registration.

Do Bite Marks in Human Skin Register and Retain Identifying Details?

Living human skin possesses various biomechanical properties, such as vis-coelasticity, hysteresis, nonlinearity, and anisotropy, plus a variable intrinsic healing capacity, which make it an exceptionally poor material for register-ing and retaining traumatic impressions accurately. These dermal proper-ties, plus the anatomical site of the bite and the victim's age and weight, are known to introduce distortions into the bite mark, which serve to complicate the process of correctly matching the bite mark to the biter's dentition (Bush et al. 2009). Understanding these distortions is a necessary prerequisite to matching a bite mark to a dentition. Sheasby and MacDonald (2001) catego-rized the different types of distortion that are frequently encountered in bite mark incidences as either primary or secondary. Primary distortion involves the stress and strain effects of the biting process (dynamic distortion) and the response of the tissue being bitten (tissue distortion), both being unpre-dictable but related. Secondary distortions include the time since injury and those introduced by suboptimal photographic technique. If distortion is a major feature of a bite mark, but the perpetrator's dentition possesses mini-mally "unique" features, the likelihood of establishing a match must be con-sidered low.

Ethical concerns restrict research in this area with regard to living human skin. Some experiments have, however, involved volunteers willingly biting themselves. In Harvey et al.'s (1975, cited in Dailey 2005) work, quite understandably, none of the bite marks produced resembled the extremes of violent severity habitually witnessed in forensic cases. Various *in vitro* mod-els have been developed using a variety of materials, such as wax, Styrofoam, pig and cadaver skin, none of which adequately resembles the properties of living human skin (Bush et al. 2009). Nonetheless, several studies have used clamp-mounted dental casts to simulate bite marks on cadaver skin, applying pressures within the range of the normal human bite force (Bush et al. 2010; Miller et al. 2009). Bush et al. (2010) acknowledged that their mechanical model failed to apply the bite force as rapidly as the human masticatory sys-tem would and commented on the possible significance of this fact given the time-dependent response of viscoelastic materials, such as skin, to deforming forces. In addition to such technical problems, hollow volume overlay analysis of the resultant bite marks again highlighted the ever-present difficulties with matching bite mark with biter. Distortions of variable and apparently unpredictable dimensions, both increases and decreases in measured dental dimensions, were reported. If different casts used in the study displayed similar dental alignments, ambiguity resulted. Incorrect matches, including false positives, resulted (Miller et al. 2009).

Comparison of the Suspect's Dentition and the Bite Mark

Deitch (2009) stressed that a "match implies that a bite-mark has been made by one individual's dentition to the exclusion of all other individuals' dentitions," and Miller et al.'s (2009: 1209) results lend support to the notion that this is a currently unachievable outcome in this area of forensic science. However, various comparative techniques are in development that will aim to improve on all current practices. Computer-assisted 2D overlay methods, undertaken by a forensic odontologist, either compare a scan of the suspect's dental cast with a photograph of the bite mark or compare the suspect's recorded bite mark with a photograph of the victim's bite mark. These are well-recognized, commonly applied, "accredited" techniques (Al-Talabani et al. 2006), which should now have superseded all hand-tracing methods (Pretty and Sweet 2001). Two-dimensional analysis provides a technique for obtaining quantitative measurements, but both the teeth and the bite mark are 3D entities (Blackwell et al. 2007; Miller et al. 2009). Different 3D approaches have been trialed, with varying results (Blackwell et al. 2007; Thali et al. 2003). Flora et al. (2009) observed that a higher success rate was achieved by the application of an automated matching method when compared to a wholly manual technique.

Martin de las Heras et al. (2007) tested the suitability of the new, fully automated, Dental Print software for bite mark analysis in terms of examiner reliability, sensitivity, specificity, and validity. In a direct comparison with another well-established system, Adobe Photoshop, it was concluded that Dental Print produced better results, but the training and experience of the examiner had a significant impact on the overall accuracy of either analysis. The sensitivity of the methods tested was still relatively poor, resulting in the group concluding that the aim of bite mark analysis at present should be to exclude the definite nonbiter from consideration rather than attempt to establish the identity of the biter. To better focus the applicability of this somewhat "weak" science, Bowers and Pretty (2009) have suggested the use of a "bite mark severity scale." The scale attempts to rationalize case selection at the outset by using markers of bite mark severity as a predictor of the likelihood of achieving a successful comparative analysis

(Pretty 2006). Bite marks demonstrating only mild bruising or, at the other extreme, tissue loss, are less-suitable substrates for analysis and are classified as of "low forensic significance." The scale might lead to a more focused and informed understanding of the limitations of undertaking an analysis in any particular case.

An all-important universal consensus regarding the most suitable analytical method to apply to the physical evidence created by biting has not yet been established.

Problems Relating to the Collection of Bite Mark Evidence

Despite the well-documented problems associated with the analysis of bite mark evidence, instances continue to arise in which the legal system calls on the expertise of the forensic odontologist to interpret an alleged human bite injury. Under such circumstances, and given the lack of a current "gold standard" consensus, the responsibility of the odontologist is to apply up-to-date methodology to the process of the recording, collection, storage, interpretation, and presentation of all information pertaining to the case.

Currently, photographic evidence is the most common initial method for recording the presence and the details of skin bite marks. The American Board of Forensic Odontology (ABFO) advised that a No. 2 (photographic measuring) scale should be included, and multiple shots should be taken, according to a standardized protocol. The last should take into consideration lighting conditions and should also recommend a reconstruction of the likely position of the body at the time of biting to reduce the postural and photographic components of secondary distortion (Pretty 2006). The camera should be oriented at 90° to the center of the wound, also to reduce distortion (Sheasby and MacDonald 2001).

Following photography, an impression will usually be taken of the bite mark to enable the construction of a 3D model in dental stone of any skin indentations associated with the injury. Further sources of secondary distortion relate to the pressure applied to the skin by the operator when taking the impression, the dimensional stability of the impression material, and the accuracy and durability qualities of the dental stone.

Photographs and models of the physical evidence of a bite mark can then be subjected to the comparative analysis methods outlined, bearing in mind the current inadequacies associated with each.

Two promising biomolecular approaches to the collection of biological evidence from bite marks are gaining respect amongst leading researchers. First, a DNA swab can be obtained from the bite mark and subjected to polymerase chain reaction (PCR) analysis. However, DNA is easily degraded or contaminated. DNA cannot therefore be considered the ultimate solution in bite mark cases. In addition, Dorion (2005) stated that any DNA isolated from the skin in the region of a bite mark could belong to an innocent party. Caution is required if relying solely on DNA evidence.

A second, relatively novel, technique relies on the biter transferring oral bacteria onto the victim's skin, producing a bacterial "fingerprint" that can be matched to the perpetrator (Pretty 2006). Tompkins (2005) investigated this method and obtained promising results. The preliminary trial involved eight volunteers biting themselves. The normal oral flora contains up to 2,000 different bacterial species. It was observed that every participant possessed at least one strain of *Streptococcus* that could be isolated from both the participant's dentition and the bite mark. In addition, species genotypes were shown to be unique to every participant involved, and all could be detected 24 hours after a bite mark was inflicted, thus yielding rapid results. A year later, the volunteers were asked to return to the study, which subsequently concluded that the same bacterial genotypes were still present in samples of the participants' saliva. Further research is required to statistically determine the likelihood that two unrelated individuals will possess genotypically identical bacterial strains. This technique has been credited with offering great future potential for identifying bite mark perpetrators (Pretty 2006).

Conclusions

The human dentition is capable of withstanding extreme environmental conditions to become the only remaining, or the most readily accessible, source of information that can identify a deceased individual. The forensic world has historically appreciated the significance of this potential and has actively sought to improve the scientific validity of identification methods dependent on data harvested from the teeth.

Many significant challenges are being encountered by the research community. Globalization has magnified the difficulty of matching remains to the profile of a missing individual who may have originated from the other side of the world. Likewise, international travel has increased the scale of the challenge to the forensic community when repatriating the casualties of mass disasters. Coordinating worldwide efforts to improve the standards of dental record keeping, populate an international dental database, and produce a single automated matching system is a generally desirable next step.

The legal system also awaits a consensus on bite mark analysis: Can forensic science find a way of conclusively validating the evidence it provides? More recent biological approaches seem promising to this end. The jury is out.

Perhaps, though, the most controversial further development in forensic odontology might prove to be a labeling system. The benefits in terms of DVI

are obvious, and many countries already require their citizens to carry identification cards at all times. Given the resilience of the teeth and the potential
to insert an information-carrying chip into a living tooth, might we all be
tagged like our pets in the future?

References

Abdel-Mottaleb, M., Nomir, O., Nassar, D. E., Fahmy, G., and Ammar, H. H. (2003)
Challenges of developing an automated dental identification system. Paper presented
at the 64th IEEE Midwest Symposium on Circuits and Systems, Cairo, Egypt.

Adams, B. J. (2003) The diversity of adult dental patterns in the United States and
the implications for personal identification. *Journal of Forensic Sciences,* 48 (3):
497–503.

Al-Talabani, N., Al-Moussawy, N. D., Baker, F. A., and Mohammed, H. A. (2006)
Digital analysis of experimental human bitemarks: Application of two new
methods. *Journal of Forensic science,* 51 (6): 1327–1375.

Avon, S. L. (2004) Forensic odontology: Roles and responsibilities of the dentist.
Journal of Canadian Dental Association, 70 (7): 453–458.

Berketa, J. W., Hirsch, R. S., Higgins, D. Helen James, H. (2010) Radiographic recognition of dental implants as an aid to identifying the deceased. *Journal of
Forensic Sciences,* 55 (1): 66–70.

Bernitz, H., Owen, J. H., Van Heerden, W. F. P., and Solheim, T. (2008) An integrated
technique for the analysis of skin bite marks. *American Academy of Forensic
Sciences,* 53 (1): 194–198.

Bernitz, H., Van Heerden, W. F. P., Solheim, T., and Owen, J. H. (2006) A technique to
capture, analyze, and quantify anterior teeth rotations for application in court
cases involving tooth marks. *Journal of Forensic Science,* 51 (3): 624–629.

Blackwell, S. A., Taylor, R. V., Gordon, I., Ogleby, C. L., Tanihijiri, T., Yoshino, M.,
Donald, M. R., and Clement, J. G. (2007) 3-D imaging and quantitative com-
parison of human dentitions and simulated bite-marks. *International Journal of
Legal Medicine,* 121 (1): 9–17.

Blau, S., Hill, A., Briggs, C. A., and Cordner, S. M. (2006) Missing persons—Missing
data: The need to collect antemortem dental records of missing persons. *Journal
of Forensic Sciences,* 51 (2): 386–389.

Bonavilla, J. D., Bush, M. A., Bush, P. J., and Pantera, E. A. (2008) Identification of
incinerated root canal filling materials after exposure to high heat incineration.
Journal of Forensic Sciences, 53 (2): 412–418.

Bowers, C. M., and Pretty, I. A. (2009) Expert disagreement in bite-mark casework.
Journal of Forensic Sciences, 54 (7): 915–918.

Brandao, R. B., Martin, C. C. S., Catirse, A. B. C. E. B., De Castro E Silva, M., Evison,
M. P., and Guimar, M. A (2007) Heat induced changes to dental resin composites: A reference in forensic investigations? *Journal of Forensic Sciences,* 52 (4):
913–919.

Bush, M. A., Bush, P. J., and Miller, R. G. (2006) Detection and classification of composite resins in incinerated teeth for forensic purposes. *Journal of Forensic
Sciences,* 51 (3): 636–642.

Bush, M. A., Miller, R. G., Bush, P. J., and Dorion, R. B. J. (2009) Biomechanical factors in human dermal bite-marks in a cadaver model, *Journal of Forensic Sciences*, 54 (1): 167–176.

Bush, M. A., Miller, R. G., Norrlander, A. L., and Bush, P. J. (2008) Analytical survey of restorative resins by SEM/EDS and XRF: databases for forensic purposes. *Journal of Forensic Sciences*, 53 (2): 419–425.

Bush, M. A., Miller, R. G., Prutsman-Pfeiffer, J., and Bush, P. J. (2007) Identification through x-ray fluorescence analysis of dental restorative resin materials: a comprehensive study of non-cremated, cremated, and processed-cremated individuals. *Journal of Forensic Sciences*, 52 (1): 57–165.

Bush, M. A., Thorsrud, K., Miller, R. G., Dorion, R. B. J., and Bush, P. J. (2010) The response of skin to applied stress: Investigation of bitemark distortion in a cadaver model. *Journal of Forensic Sciences*, 55 (1): 71–76.

Chen, H., and Jain, A. K. (2005) Dental biometrics: Alignment and matching of dental radiographs. *IEEE Transactions on Pattern Analysis and Machine Intelligence*, 27 (8): 1319–1326.

Chomdej, T., Pankaowa, W., and Choychumroon, S. (2006) Intelligent dental identification system (IDIS) in forensic medicine. *Forensic Science International*, 158 (1): 27–38.

Clement, J. G., Winship, V., Ceddia, J., Al-Amad, S., Morales, A., and Hill, A. J. (2006) New software for computer-assisted dental-data matching in Disaster Victim Identification and long-term missing persons investigations: "DAVID Web." *Forensic Science International*, 159: 24–29.

Dailey, J. C. (2005) The comparison. In Dorion, R. B. J. (Ed.), *Bitemark evidence*. New York: Dekker, Chap. 20.

Da Silva, R. H., Sales-Peres, A., De Oliveira, R. N., De Oliveira, F. T., and De Carvalho Sales-Peres, S. H. (2007) Use of DNA technology in forensic dentistry. *Journal of Applied Oral Science*, 15 (3): 156–161.

Davis, J. H. (2005) Role of the medical examiner/coroner/pathologist. In Dorion, R. B. J. (Ed.), *Bite-mark evidence*. New York: Dekker, Chap. 3.

Delattre, V. F. (2000) Burned beyond recognition: systematic approach to the dental identification of charred human remains. *Journal of Forensic Sciences*, 45 (3): 589–596.

Deitch, A. (2009) An inconvenient tooth: Forensic odontology is an inadmissible junk science when it is used to "match" teeth to bitemarks in skin. *Wisconsin Law Review*, 5: 1205–1236.

De Valck, E. (2006) Major incident response: Collecting ante-mortem data. *Forensic Science International*, 159: 15–19.

Dorion, R. B. J. (2005) Human bite-marks. In Dorion, R. B. J. (Ed.), *Bite-mark evidence*. New York: Dekker, Chap. 17.

Dubey, S. K., Mehta, D. S., and Anand, A. (2008) Simultaneous topography and tomography of latent fingerprints using full-field swept-source optical coherence tomography. *Journal of Optics A—Pure and Applied Optics*. 10 (1): 015307.

Du Chesne, A., Benthaus, S., Teige, K., and Brinkmann, B. (2000) Post-mortem orthopantomography—An aid in screening for identification purposes. *International Journal of Legal Medicine*, 113 (2): 63–69.

Fahmy, G., Nassar, D. E. M., Haj-Said, E., Chen, H., Nomir, O., Zhou, J., Howell, R., Ammar, H. H., Abdel-Mottaleb, M., and Jain, A. K. (2004) Automated Dental Identification System (ADIS). Available at http://www.dgrc.org/ dgo2004/disc/ presentations/health/fahmy.pdf. Accessed June 22, 2010.

Fereira, J. L., Espina De Fereira, A., and Ortega, A. I. (2008) Methods for the analysis of hard dental tissues exposed to high temperatures. *Forensic Science International,* 178: 119–124.

Flint, D. J., Dove, S. B., Brumit, P. C., White, M., and Senn, D. R. (2009) Computer-aided dental identification: An objective method for assessment of radiographic image similarity. *Journal of Forensic Sciences,* 54 (1): 177–184.

Flora, G., Tuceryan, M., and Blitzer, H. (2009) *Forensic bite mark identification using image processing methods.* New York: ACM.

Gysel, C. (1987) Georges Cuvier (1769–1832). Biology and the teeth. *Revue d'onto-stomatologie,* 16 (6): 385–395.

Hanaoka, Y., Ueno, A., Tsuzuki, T., Kajiwara, M., Minaguchi, K., and Sato, Y. (2007) Proposal for Internet-based digital dental chart for personal dental identification in forensics. *Forensic Science International,* 168: 57–60.

Hosntalab, M., Zoroofi, R. A., Tehrani-Fard, A. A., and Shirani, G. (2008) Segmentation of teeth in CT volumetric dataset by panoramic projection and variational level set. *International Journal of Computer Assisted Radiology and Surgery,* 3 (3): 257–265.

Hosntalab, M., Zoroofi, R. A., Tehrani-Fard, A. A., and Shirani, G. (2010) Classification and numbering of teeth in multi-slice CT images using wavelet-Fourier descriptor. *International Journal of Computer Assisted Radiology and Surgery,* 5 (3): 237–249.

Interpol. (1992) *Manual on disaster victim identification.* Paris: International Criminal Police Organization.

Jackowski, C., Aghayev, E., Sonnenschein, M., Dirnhofer, R., and Thali, M. J. (2006) Maximum intensity projection of cranial computed tomography data for dental identification. *International Journal of Legal Medicine,* 120 (3): 165–167.

Jackowski, C., and Persson, A. (2010) Comments on the paper entitled "Is post-mortem CT of the dentition adequate for correct forensic identification?: comparison of dental computed tomography and visual dental record" by S. Kirchhoff et al. *International Journal of Legal Medicine,* 124: 259.

Jackowski, C., Wyss, M., Persson, A., Classens, M., Thali, M. J., and Lussi, A. (2008) Ultra-high-resolution dual-source CT for forensic dental visualization—Discrimination of ceramic and composite fillings. *International Journal of Legal Medicine,* 122 (4): 301–307.

Jain, A. K., and Chen, H. (2004) Matching of dental X-ray images for human identification. *Pattern Recognition,* 37 (7): 1519–1532.

Kieser, J. A., Bernal, V., Waddell, J. N., and Raju, S. (2007) The uniqueness of the human anterior dentition: A geometric morphometric analysis. *Journal of Forensic Science,* 52 (3): 671–677.

Kieser, J. A., Laing, W., and Herbison, P. (2006) Lessons learned from large-scale comparative dental analysis following the South Asian tsunami of 2004. *Journal of Forensic Sciences,* 51 (1): 109–112.

Kirchhoff, S., Fischer, F., Lindemaier, G., Herzog, P., Kirchhoff, C., Becker, C., Bark, C., Reiser, M. F., and Eisenmenger, W. (2008) Is post-mortem CT of the dentition adequate for correct forensic identification? Comparison of dental computed tomography and visual dental record. *International Journal of Legal Medicine,* 122 (6): 471–479.

Kogon, S., Arnold, J., Wood, R., and Merner, L. (2009) Integrating dental data in missing persons and unidentified remains investigations: The RESOLVE INITIATIVE and DIP3. *Forensic Science International,* 197 (1): 31–35.

Kouble, R. F., and Craig, G. T. (2007) A survey of the incidence of missing anterior teeth: potential value in bite mark analysis. *Science and Justice,* 47 (1): 19–23.

Lai, Y. H., and Lin, P. L. (2008) Effective segmentation for dental X-ray images using texture-based fuzzy inference system. In Blanc-Talon, J., Bourennane, S., and Philips, W. (Eds.), *Advanced concepts for intelligent vision systems: 10th international conference, ACIVS 2008, Juan-Les-Pins, France, October 20–24.*

Lau, G., Tan, W. F., and Tan, P. H. (2005) After the Indian Ocean tsunami: Singapore's contribution to the international disaster victim identification effort in Thailand. *Annals of the Academy of Medicine,* 34 (5): 341–351.

Lee, S. S., Choi, J. H., Yoon, C. Y., Kim, C. Y., and Kyoung-Jin Shin, K. J. (2004) The diversity of dental patterns in the orthopantomography and its significance in human identification. *Journal of Forensic Sciences,* 49 (4): 784–786.

Lin, P. L., Lai, Y. H., and Huang, P. W. (2010) An effective classification and numbering system for dental bitewing radiographs using teeth region and contour information. *Pattern Recognition,* 43 (4): 1380–1392.

Lunetta, P., Ranta, H., Cattaneo, C., Piccinini, A., Niskanen, R., Sajantila, A., and Penttilä, A. (2003) International collaboration in mass disasters involving foreign nationals within the EU: Medico-legal investigation of Finnish victims of the Milan Linate airport SAS SK 686 aircraft accident on 8 October 2001. *International Journal of Legal Medicine,* 117 (4): 204–210.

Mahoor, M. H., and Abdel-Mottaleb, M. (2005). Classification and numbering of teeth in dental bitewing images. *Pattern Recognition,* 38: 577–586.

Martin de las Heras, S., Valenzuela, A., Valverde, A. J., Torres, J. C., and Luna-Del-Castillo, J. D. (2007) Effectiveness of comparison overlays generated with Dental Print software in bite mark analysis. *Journal of Forensic science,* 52 (1): 151–156.

Miller, R. G., Bush, P. J., Dorion, R. B. J., and Bush, M. A. (2009) Uniqueness of the dentition as impressed in human skin: A cadaver model. *Journal of Forensic Sciences,* 54 (4): 909–914.

Morgan, O., Sribanditmongkol, P., Perera, C., Sulasmi, Y., and Van Alphen, D. (2006) Mass fatality management following the South Asian tsunami disaster: Case studies in Thailand, Indonesia, and Sri Lanka. *PLoS Medicine,* 3 (6): 809–815.

Nassar, D. E., Abaza, A., Li, X., and Ammar, H. (2008) Automatic construction of dental charts for postmortem identification. *IEEE Transactions on Information Forensics and Security,* 3 (2): 234–246.

Nomir, O., and Abdel-Mottaleb, M. (2005) A system for human identification from x-ray dental radiographs. *Pattern Recognition,* 38 (8): 577–586.

Otis, L. L., Everett, M. J., and Sathyam, U. S. (2000) Optical coherence tomography: A new imaging technology for dentistry. *Journal of the American Dental Association,* 131 (4): 511–514.

Perrier, M., Bollmann, M., Girod, A., and Mangin, P. (2006) Swiss DVI at the tsunami disaster: Expect the unexpected. *Forensic Science International,* 159: 30–32.

Petju, M., Suteerayongprasertb, A., Thongpudc, R., and Hassirid, K. (2007) Importance of dental records for victim identification following the Indian Ocean tsunami disaster in Thailand. *Public Health,* 121: 251–257.

Pretty, I. A. (2005) *Unresolved Issues in Bitemark Analysis.* In Dorion, R. B. J. (Ed.), *Bitemark evidence.* New York: Dekker, Chap. 28.

Pretty, I. A. (2006) The barriers to achieving an evidence base for bitemark analysis. *Forensic Science international,* 159: 110–120.

Pretty, I. A., and Sweet, D. (2001) The scientific basis for human bite-mark analyses— A critical review. *Science and justice,* 41: 85–92.

Pretty, I. A., Pretty, R. J., Rothwell, B. R., and Sweet, D. (2003) The reliability of digitized radiographs for dental identification: A Web-based study. *Journal of Forensic Sciences,* 48 (6): 1325–1330.

Ramenzoni, L. L., and Line, S. R. P. (2006) Automated biometrics-based personal identification of the Hunter–Schreger bands of dental enamel. *Proceedings of the Royal Society of Biology,* 273: 1155–1158.

Richmond, R., and Pretty, I. A. (2007) Antemortem records of forensic significance among edentulous individuals. *Journal of Forensic Sciences,* 52 (2): 423–427.

Richmond, R., and Pretty, I. A. (2009a) A range of postmortem assault experiments conducted on a variety of denture labels used for the purpose of identification of edentulous individuals. *Journal of Forensic Sciences,* 54 (2): 411–414.

Richmond, R., and Pretty, I. A. (2009b) The use of radio-frequency identification tags for labeling dentures—Scanning properties. *Journal of Forensic Sciences,* 54 (3): 664–668.

Rutty, G. N., Robinson, C., Black, S. M., Adams, C., and Webster, P. (2009) Fimag: The United Kingdom disaster victim/forensic identification imaging system. *Journal of Forensic Sciences,* 54 (6): 1438–1442.

Savio, A., Merlati, G., Danesino, P., Fassina, G., and Menghini, P. (2006) Radiographic evaluation of teeth subjected to high temperatures: Experimental study to aid identification processes. *Forensic Science International,* 158: 108–116.

Schuller-Gotzburg, P., and Suchanek, J. (2007) Forensic odontologists successfully identify tsunami victims in Phuket, Thailand. *Forensic Science International,* 171: 204–207.

Sheasby, D. R., and Macdonald, D. G. (2001) A forensic classification of distortion in human bite marks. *Forensic Science International,* 122: 75–78.

Sholl, S. A., and Moody, G. H. (2001) Evaluation of dental radiographic identification: An experimental study. *Forensic Science International,* 115: 165–169.

Soomer, H., Lincoln, M. J., Ranta, H., Penttilä, A., and Leibur, E. (2003) Dentists' qualifications affect the accuracy of radiographic identification. *Journal of Forensic Sciences,* 48 (5): 1121–1126.

Soomer, H., Ranta, H., and Penttila, A. (2001) Identification of victims from the M/S Estonia. *International Journal of Legal Medicine,* 114: 259–262.

Sperger, G. H., Machin, Ga., and Bamforth, F. J. (1994) Mirror-image dental fusion and discordance in monozygotic twins. *American Journal of Medical Genetics,* 51 (1): 41–45.

Sweet, D. (2006) Solving certain dental records problems with technology—
    The Canadian solution in the Thailand tsunami response. *Forensic Science
    International*, 159: 20–23.
Sweet, D., and Pretty, I. A. (2001a) A look at forensic dentistry—part 1: The role of
    teeth in the determination of human identity. *British Dental Journal*, 190 (7):
    359–366.
Sweet, D., and Pretty, I. A. (2001b) A look at forensic dentistry—part 2: Teeth as
    weapons of violence—identification of bitemark perpetrators. *British Dental
    Journal*, 190 (8): 415–418.
Thali, M. J., Braun, M., Markwalder, T. H., Brueschweiler, W., Zollinger, U., Malik,
    N. J., Yen, K., and Dirnhofer, R. (2003) Bitemark documentation and analysis:
    the forensic 3D/CAD supported photogrammetry approach. *Forensic Science
    International*, 135: 115–121.
Thali, M. J., Markwalder, T., Jackowski, C., Sonnenschein, M., and Dirnhofer, R.
    (2006) Dental CT imaging as a screening tool for dental profiling: Advantages
    and limitations. *Journal of Forensic Sciences*, 51 (1) 113–119.
Thevissen, P. W., Poelman, G., De Cooman, M., Puers, R., and Willems, G. (2006)
    Implantation of an RFID-tag into human molars to reduce hard forensic iden-
    tification labor. Part I: Working principle. *Forensic Science International*, 159:
    33–39.
Tompkins, G. R. (2005) Genotypic comparison of oral bacteria isolated from bite-
    marks and teeth. In Dorion, R. B. J. (Ed.), *Bitemark evidence*. New York: Dekker,
    Chap. 30.
Tsuzuki, T., Ueno A., Kajiwara, M., Hanaoka, Y., Uchiyama, H., Agawa, Y., Takagi, T.,
    and Sato, Y. (2002) Evaluation of intraoral CCD camera for dental examination
    in forensic inspection. *Legal Medicine*, 4 (1), 40–46.
Valenzuela, A., Martin-De Las Heras, S., Marques, T., Exposito, N., and Bohoyo,
    J. M. (2000) The application of dental methods of identification to human
    burn victims in a mass disaster. *International Journal of Legal Medicine*, 113:
    236–239.
Zondagh, H., and Phillips, V. M. (2009) The discrimination potential of radioopaque
    composite restorations for identification: Part 3. *Journal of Forensic
    Odontostomatology*, 27: 27–32.

Skeletal Trauma

7

KYLIE DAVIDSON
CATRIONA DAVIES
DR. PATRICK RANDOLPH-QUINNEY

Contents

Introduction

Trauma is the application of force to the human body sufficient to cause damage, irritation, or inflammation of the soft and hard tissues and can be accidental or nonaccidental in origin. The analysis of trauma is one area of forensic practice that has very much become the purview of the forensic anthropologist over the last two decades, with the growing realization within the medicolegal community of the causal link between the forensic identification of skeletal trauma and criminal prosecutions, human rights advocacy, and humanitarian actions (Tidball-Binz 2008). The reasons for this realization are perhaps not apparent at first glance but may well stem from the epistemological and historical development of the subject; practitioners of forensic anthropology are generally specialists in human skeletal morphology and are trained via human anatomy, physical or biological anthropology, or osteoarchaeology. As such, forensic anthropologists are cognizant of patterns of normal or abnormal skeletal morphology, including the effects of trauma, in a way that many other practitioners, such as medical examiners or forensic pathologists, are not. As a consequence, forensic anthropologists have traditionally been of assistance in documenting and explaining traumatic patterning in relation to violent death through analyses of the effects of applied loading or energy to bone (Black 2005; Berryman and Symes 1998; Galloway 1999a; Kimmerle and Baraybar 2008).

To this end, forensic anthropology has been of particular value in three main areas: (1) investigations resulting from homicide, unexplained natural deaths, accidents, and mass fatalities; (2) noncriminal events resulting in multiple deaths (e.g., arising from natural catastrophes); and (3) war crime investigations and genocide (Randolph-Quinney et al. 2009). Within these areas, anthropologists have looked primarily at the effects of bone fracture and failure caused by extrinsic forces, the interpretation of which can assist the forensic pathologist in analysis of the manner and mechanism of death. Trauma may also be a useful aid to individuation, as evidence of antemortem traumatic events may be left on the skeleton following the decomposition process and can provide the anthropologist with a means of corroborating a presumptive identity, with the proviso that sufficient antemortem clinical documentation exists to allow for comparison (Cunha 2006, Rodríguez-Martín 2006; Cunha and Pinheiro 2009; Randolph-Quinney et al. 2009).

Skeletal trauma is caused by the application of energy to the human body and can be considered as an energy continuum from low to high levels of energy input, which can be arbitrarily divided into three primary manners of application: blunt force (including asphyxia), sharp force, and ballistic trauma. Explosive trauma, however, can be considered separately from these primary forms as it encompasses aspects from all three primary trauma types. Burning trauma is the direct application of thermal energy through heat induction, convection, or radiation, although this may also be concomitant with other primary traumatic types. The quantity of energy applied, and therefore the type of trauma sustained, is dependent on factors that include directionality, velocity, and focus of impact. Skeletal trauma is highly variable, and each case presents its own set of unique characteristics and challenges to the interpretation and reconstruction of the causative events.

The aim of the forensic practitioner in regard to the assessment of trauma is to attempt to answer three primary questions: When did the trauma occur? How was it induced? How much force was applied to cause the observed injury (Komar and Buikstra 2008)? The forensic anthropologist must first isolate evidence of skeletal trauma from natural variations and subsequently determine the nature of the trauma (i.e., blunt, sharp, ballistic, burning, or explosive). Second, determination of the number of insults and the order in which these occurred is required, in conjunction with a determination of the time at which the injuries were sustained (i.e., antemortem, perimortem, or postmortem). As injuries sustained at each of these stages exhibit individual morphological characteristics, the forensic practitioner is able to distinguish between those injuries that occurred prior to, at the time of, or subsequent to death (Komar and Buikstra 2008; Byers 2009; Kimmerle and Baraybar 2008). Trauma is categorized according to its source (Komar and Buikstra 2008); therefore, accurate analysis of trauma may be central to medicolegal casework.

The chapter highlights some of the innovative approaches forensic anthropologists have adopted in an attempt to understand the forensic context of skeletal trauma. The purpose of this chapter is not to provide a guide to skeletal trauma analysis; for such activities, many exceptionally valuable textbooks and core texts are available in the forensic and clinical literature to assist in this purpose (Galloway 1999b; Ortner and Putschar 1981; Kimmerle and Baraybar 2008; Resnick 1995; Aufderheide and Rodríguez-Martin 1998). Instead, this chapter highlights some of the trends we consider prevalent in forensic anthropological research within four primary trauma types: blunt force, sharp force, and ballistic, with burning and explosive traumas considered together.

As we discuss elsewhere in this chapter, many of the early forensic analyses of skeletal trauma were primarily qualitative in nature and relied heavily on the experiential basis of the practitioner. As such, much of the early literature was case based, descriptive, and empirical—the *what*, not the *why*. However, the mid- to late 1990s saw the publication of a number of seminal works that attempted to provide a cogent theoretical *interpretive* framework for skeletal trauma (e.g., Ubelaker and Adams 1995; Berryman and Haun 1996; Rabl et al. 1996; Sacher 1996; Lovell 1997; Quatrehomme and İşcan 1997, 1998, 1999; Berryman and Symes 1998; Brink et al. 1998; Quatrehomme 1998; Di Maio 1999; Fulginiti et al. 1999; Galloway 1999a–1999g; Galloway et al. 1999; Haglund 1999; Herrmann and Bennett 1999; Marks et al. 1999; Nelson and Thornburg 1999; Rockhold and Herrmann 1999; Simmons 1999; Tomczak and Buikstra 1999a; Walsh-Haney 1999; Wienker and Wood 1999), explaining the *why* as well as the *what*.

Many of these related to differential diagnosis of classes of trauma and could as often be considered publications with taphonomic interest, as well as traumatic, being based mainly on well-designed and specifically targeted actualistic studies (e.g., Simmons 1999; Ubelaker and Adams 1995). Others began to apply the mathematical principles of biomechanics to forensic questions (Rabl et al. 1996; Sloan and Talbott 1996; Frost 1997; Shaw and Hsu 1998), although without the explicit modeling approaches afforded by finite element analyses used elsewhere in skeletal biology (Koriath et al. 1992; Krabbel and Appel 1995). It would not be until the mid- to late 2000s that these would begin to be utilized to address issues of relevance to forensic trauma (e.g., Mota et al. 2003; Schoenpflug et al. 2003; Raul et al. 2006, 2007; Raul, Deck, et al. 2008; Raul, Ludes, et al. 2008; Roth et al. 2007).

The 2000s saw the continuation of both case-based and interpretive trauma research trends evidenced in the late 1990s, with the publication of a suite of research articles dealing with aspects of

- Blunt force (e.g., Rybalko and Pauliukevicius 2003; Aghayev, Thali, et al. 2005; Hart 2005; Mays 2006; Moraitis and Spiliopouiou 2006; Ta'ala et al. 2006; Calce and Rogers 2007; Aghayev, Christie, et al. 2008; Dye et al. 2008; Kremer et al. 2008; Jacobsen et al. 2009)
- Sharp force (e.g., Karger et al. 2000; Prahlow et al. 2001; Gill and Catanese 2002; Inoue et al. 2006; Schmidt and Pollak 2006; Hainsworth et al. 2008; Schneider et al. 2009) and hacking trauma (e.g., Alunni-Perret et al. 2005; Tucker et al. 2001)
- Ballistic and gunshot wounds (e.g., Karlsson and Stahling 2000; Hiss et al. 2003; Mastruko and Bijhold 2003; Santucci and Chang 2004; Hart 2005; Dodd and Byrne 2006; Li 2006; Thali, Kneubuehl, et al. 2007; Karger 2008)
- Burning (e.g., de Gruchy and Rogers 2002; Hardman and Manoukian 2002; Mayne-Correia and Beattie 2002; Warren and Schultz 2002; Moisander and Edston 2003; Puskas and Rumney 2003; Bass and Jantz 2004; Pope and O'Brian 2004; Williams 2008; Thompson 2005; Worley 2005; Brooks et al. 2006; Enzo et al. 2007; Zavoi et al. 2007; Bergslien et al. 2008; Ubelaker 2009)
- Blast and explosive trauma (e.g., Kahana and Hiss 2000; Oliver et al. 2002; Brooks and Barker 2003; Born 2005; Garner and Brett 2007; Wolf et al. 2009)

The 2000s also saw the publication of volumes dealing specifically or primarily with the interpretation of skeletal trauma in the specialized context of violent crimes against the person or human rights abuses and genocide (e.g., Schmitt et al. 2006; Ferllini 2007; Kimmerle and Baraybar 2008). The Kimmerle and Baraybar volume *Skeletal Trauma—Identification of Injuries Resulting from Human Rights Abuse and Armed Conflict* is particularly noteworthy as it brings together a variety of researchers and practitioners with extensive experience in trauma analysis in conflict and human rights abuses, presenting both analytical and interpretive protocols in differential diagnosis of trauma together with appropriate case study examples. The volume deals with differential diagnosis and epidemiology of trauma (Snow et al. 2008; Raul, Ludes, et al. 2008); blast injuries (Seneviratne 2008; Pachón 2008; Samarasekera 2008); blunt force trauma (BFT; Finegan 2008; Ta'ala et al. 2008); sharp force trauma (SFT; Chacón et al. 2008); and gunshot wounds (Ross and Suarez 2008; Waters 2008; Cagigao and Lund 2008). The volume is critically important in that it devotes an entire chapter to synthetic research on skeletal manifestations of torture (see Baraybar et al. 2008; Delabarde

2008; Hougen 2008; Maat 2008) the first available in the forensic anthropological literature, and as such should be compulsory reading for students
of trauma (see also Altun and Durmus-Altun 2003; Moisander and Edston
2003; Moreno et al. 2003; Asirdizer et al. 2004; Warren 2004; Keller 2006;
Tournel et al. 2006; Chaudhry et al. 2008; Sanders et al. 2009 for further references relating to acts of torture and abuse).

Elsewhere, we view the adoption of new and innovative methods of noninvasive imaging analysis as one of the most exciting and powerful developments affecting forensic skeletal trauma analysis. Forensic radiology
has traditionally encompassed the use of radiographic images to analyze
traumatic injuries during the process of a forensic postmortem examination (Thali, Yen, Schweitzer, et al. 2003). In the last decade, however, the
use of modern imaging techniques such as multislice computed tomography (MSCT), micro-CT, and magnetic resonance imaging, which enable a
higher-resolution image to be produced, has increased (Schneider et al. 2009;
Stawicki et al. 2008; Thali, Jackowski, et al. 2007). Many of these have focused
on the Virtopsy approach, leading to the establishment of "virtual anthropological" protocols that may be used in conventional autopsy practice, mass
disaster situations, or *in extremis* for chemical, biological, radiological, and
nuclear (CBRN) attacks.

The literature is now replete with guidelines for use and case examples
(e.g., Thali, et al. 2004, 2005, 2006; Thali, Braun, and Dirnhofer 2003; Thali,
Braun, Wirth, et al. 2003; Thali, Jackowski, et al. 2007; Thali, Schweitzer,
et al. 2003; Thali, Yen, et al. 2002; Thali, Yen, Schweitzer, et al. 2003;
Thali, Yen, Vock, Ozdoba, Schroth, et al. 2003; Plattner et al. 2003; Thali
and Dirnhofer 2003; Thali 2003; Aghayev, Christe, et al. 2008; Aghayev,
Jackowski, et al. 2006, 2008; Aghayev, Sonnenschein, et al. 2006; Aghayev,
Thali, Jackowski, Sonnenschein, Dirnhofer, et al. 2008; Aghayev, Thali,
Jackowski, Sonnenschein, Yen, et al. 2004; Aghayev, Thali, Sonnenschein,
Hurlimann, et al. 2005; Aghayev, Thali, Sonnenschein, Jackowski, et al.
2007; Aghayev, Yen, Sonnenschein, Jackowski, et al. 2005; Aghayev, Yen,
Sonnenschein, Ozdoba, et al. 2004; Yen, Sonnenschein, et al. 2005; Yen,
Thali, et al. 2005; Yen, Vock, et al. 2004; Yen, Lövblad, et al. 2007; Jackowski,
Bolliger, et al. 2006; Jackowski, Christe, et al. 2007; Jackowski, Dirnhofer,
et al. 2005; Jackowski, Persson, et al. 2008; Jackowski, Schweitzer, et al.
2005; Jackowski, Sonnenschein, et al. 2005, 2007; Jackowski, Thali, et al.
2005, 2006; Jackowski, Wyss, et al. 2008; Ozdoba et al. 2005; Dirnhofer et
al. 2006; Bolliger et al. 2007, 2008; Buck et al. 2007; Dedouit et al. 2008;
Dedouit, Telmon, Costagliola, et al. 2007; Dedouit, Telmon, Guilbeau-
Frugier, et al. 2007; Hillewig et al. 2007; Levy et al. 2007; Pfaeffli et al. 2007;
Poulsen and Simonsen 2007; Blau et al. 2008; Deml et al. 2008; Pohlenz
et al. 2008; Verhoff, Ramsthaler, et al. 2008; Yartsev and Langlois 2008).
However, studies such as those carried out by Thali, Kneubuehl, Zollinger,

and Dirnhofer (2002c), Schneider and colleagues (2009), and Andematten and colleagues (2008) have examined the efficacy of modern imaging techniques compared to the more traditional radiographic methods in cases of ballistic and SFT. These have determined that the newer methods of imaging enable a more thorough analysis of these trauma types on skeletal tissue.

Although these techniques are of use when examining hard tissues, they have been shown to be less successful when investigating trauma to the soft tissues (Schneider et al. 2009). They are therefore not an adequate replacement for the traditional techniques associated with trauma analysis; however, they can be used effectively to enhance the analysis and render accurate multidimensional images of skeletal trauma (Schneider et al. 2009). As such, they should be considered one of the growing practical and methodological trends of which forensic anthropologists should be cognizant in the coming decade.

Blunt Force Trauma

The skeletal manifestation of trauma is generally seen through the failure of osseous tissue at the macro- or microscopic level in cortical or trabecular bone or both. Such traumatic failure is induced by torsion, shear, or compressive forces, all of which contribute to the general classification of blunt force (Galloway and Mason 2000; Galloway 1999b). In the majority of traumatic cases, the anthropologist is primarily looking at the effects of direct application of force to bone, which often results in dislocations or fractures. From a clinical and pathological perspective, a fracture is an interruption in the structural integrity of the bone and may be variously present from a single crack, fissure, cortical break, dislocation, or bone avulsion to a complete transverse break. Fractures occur through one (at least) of three mechanisms: (1) a single traumatic event with the application of excessive force sufficient to cause mechanical failure of skeletal tissue; (2) repeated stress under either static or dynamic loading; and (3) abnormal weakening of the bone (this may arise through disease processes such as osteoporosis, osteogenesis imperfecta, rickets, or certain types of bone neoplasm). The cause of traumatic lesions can range from the accidental effects of crushes, trips, or falls to the consequence of deliberate action such as beatings, manual asphyxia, torture, suspension, electrocution, or the impact of ballistic projectiles or edged weapons. Traumatic lesions that occur antemortem will show evidence of callus formation and healing; those that take place perimortem or postmortem will show no evidence of cellular recovery. Consequently, it may be extremely difficult to distinguish between the two types of fracture in the perimortem and early postmortem periods.

To understand the fundamental principles of traumatic injuries, an appreciation of bone biomechanics must be established. Bone is a composite structure that exhibits viscoelastic properties and is transversely isotropic (i.e., lines of resistance are aligned in a single plane). In addition to the composition of bone, factors including shape and age influence the pattern of injury (Kimmerle and Baraybar 2008). Bone can only respond to forces in the manner dictated by its biomechanical properties (Fenton et al. 2003). Therefore, the morphology of a traumatic fracture can yield significant information from which a forensic anthropologist can infer the traumatic mechanism from which the skeletal defect arose (Kimmerle and Baraybar 2008). A detailed description of the mechanical properties of bone can be found in the work of Galloway (1999a, 1999c–1999g), but a basic understanding is summarized here.

When a bone is encountered by an object or surface, the applied forces generally do not align with the strengthened areas of the bone adapted for normal weight bearing; consequently, osseous deformations may result due to the inability of the tissue to dissipate the energy. The skeletal response to a loading force is determined by the ability of bone to absorb the applied energy and is described by Young's modulus of elasticity. During the initial phase of loading, elastic deformation, the bone is subject to a degree of force with which the bone is able to cope competently. Once the force is released, the bone returns to its original shape. If, however, the applied force is increased and the yield point is reached, plastic deformation occurs, resulting in a permanent change to the bone structure. Finally, once the applied force exceeds the point of structural competency, the bone will fail, resulting in fracture. When the application of force occurs at an increased velocity, the bone does not progress through these stages and instead immediately fails. This is commonly observed in cases of ballistic or explosive trauma.

There are five main force types that have the potential to cause osseous deformation. These include tension, compression, torsion, bending, and shearing. Fractures occur as a consequence of these abnormal forces, and several types of fracture may result (White and Folkens 2005). A fracture occurs when a discontinuity travels completely through a bone, with an infraction (or greenstick fracture) resulting when the discontinuity is incomplete. Discontinuities or breaks in bone can be classified as two types: displacement and lines. Displacement occurs when two surfaces are no longer in anatomical alignment. An example is a complete fracture, which may be seen in long bones where two broken ends are separated. When an incomplete fracture (i.e., an infraction) occurs, the corresponding surfaces may meet at an abnormal angle. If this is observed, it is termed a *hinge fracture*.

Simple fractures are common as a result of falls; a single discontinuity results, breaking a bone into two segments. Comminuted or complex fractures, however, are more complicated and present as multiple fragments of

bone. The second type of discontinuity commonly observed is the linear fracture, of which radiating and concentric fracture lines are the predominant
forms. These originate at the point of impact and usually intersect preexisting lines of weakness, including sutures or other fracture lines (Byers 2009).
The pattern of intersecting fracture lines can therefore be used to infer the
chronological order of blows if multiple traumatic incidents have occurred.
Radiating lines disperse outward from the focus of the applied force, dissi-
pating the energy. The region of impact can therefore be traced to the common origin from which the lines of fracture radiate. Concentric fractures
form rings around the area of impact and generally are observed in high-
velocity impacts.

Fractures can indicate the timing of the traumatic event in relation to
death due to the effect that collagen composition has on the response to
trauma. Due to the high collagen content of green bone, fractures can be complete or incomplete, depending on the quantity of force applied. In dry bone
(i.e., postmortem cases), infractions are never observed, and complete, transverse fractures will occur due to the lack of collagen in the bone. Fractures
that occur perimortem are most difficult to differentiate as there will still be
collagen present. The distinction is made from antemortem fracturing by the
lack of remodeling to the fracture site.

The BFT injuries are those typically sustained from low-energy impacts
resulting from a broad instrument delivered over a relatively large surface
area (Byers 2009; Kimmerle and Baraybar 2008). This type of trauma can
result from a variety of objects, including hammers, clubs, boards, and
fists; however, most blunt force injuries result from vehicular accidents or
falls (Komar and Buikstra 2008; Byers 2009). BFT low-load injuries can
result from an individual being struck directly with an implement such
as a hammer. High-load injuries, however, are commonly observed as a
result of an explosive blast wind and are included in the group of tertiary
blast injuries, discussed elsewhere in this chapter (Kimmerle and Baraybar
2008). Blunt force soft tissue injuries include contusions, abrasions, and lac-
erations; skeletal manifestations of BFT encompass a wide variety of fracture patterns (Kimmerle and Baraybar 2008; Komar and Buikstra 2008)
that are determined by the intrinsic biomechanical properties of the bone,
including morphology and age. Extrinsic factors, including the nature of
the applied force, and weapon characteristics, including velocity, weight,
and distance, also influence the resulting pattern of fracture (Kimmerle
and Baraybar 2008). The morphology of traumatic fractures can yield significant information from which a forensic anthropologist can infer the
mechanism of trauma that led to the skeletal defects observed (Kimmerle
and Baraybar 2008).

Due to the variety of implements that can produce BFT, however, assessing specific characteristics of a particular implement or weapon is problematic

(Byers 2009). Several external factors associated with the weapon influence the resulting wound morphology. These include the magnitude, duration, direction, and focus of the applied force and the type of load and the rate at which the load was applied. As bone fails first under tension, fracture patterns can indicate the origin and direction of impact as fractures will propagate at the site of tension and radiate toward the site of compression, therefore occurring at the side opposite the area of impact, known as the contracoup (Tuong and Gean 2006). In long bones, the secondary fracture will progress toward the tension side; the breakaway spur will remain on the compression side.

Due to the highly variable nature of BFT, there have been few journal publications in the last 10 years dealing with anything other than anecdotal evidence from case studies. As the manner, cause, and presentation of injuries resulting from this type of trauma are highly variable, these publications are of little use in elucidating the causes of specific injury patterns and have added little to our understanding of mechanistic properties of bone failure. Notable exceptions to this are studies that looked at differential diagnosis of blunt versus ballistic trauma (Moraitis and Spiliopouiou 2006; Puskas and Rumney 2003; Rodríguez-Martín 2006; Torwalt et al. 2002; Langley 2007; Maiden 2009; Mayne-Correia and Beattie 2002; Oliver et al. 2002; Pope and O'Brian 2004) or that utilized engineering-based approaches (e.g., finite element models) to produce predictive and explanative models of bone failure (Hayes et al. 2007; Frost 2001; Liu et al. 2009; Love and Symes 2004; Parkinson and Callaghan 2009; Raul et al. 2007; Ross 2005; Roth et al. 2007; Straus and Porada 2003; Thali, Kneubuehl, and Dirnhofer 2002).

However, an increase in publications regarding BFT with regard to the medical literature has been observed as a consequence of the analysis of biomechanics in road traffic collisions (Jacobsen et al. 2009), often with an aim to develop more effective restraints and safety cells for vehicle occupants or pedestrians struck by moving vehicles (Adams et al. 2003; Schuller et al. 2000). Elsewhere, the forensic literature has focused on the application of preexisting methods of analysis or the modification of existing protocols using new imaging or analytical modalities (Berrizbeitia 2001; Bremer et al. 2003; Fenton et al. 2003; Rybalko and Pauliukevicius 2003; Smith 2003; Thali, Braun, Brueschweiler, et al. 2003; Love and Symes 2004; Atanasijevic et al. 2005; Hart 2005; Nystrom and Buikstra 2005; Mays 2006; Moraitis and Spiliopouiou 2006; Ta'ala et al. 2006; Calce and Rogers 2007; Dye et al. 2008; Kremer et al. 2008; Jacobsen et al. 2009).

Sharp Force Trauma

Sharp force trauma (SFT) is a combination of low- and high-energy forms and refers to an injury sustained by any instrument with a sharp edge or point

(Kimmerle and Baraybar 2008; Byers 2009). The force is applied dynamically over a narrow focus and results in compressive forces (Byers 2009). Injuries caused by SFT are the most easily identifiable of the trauma types on the skeleton (Boylston 2000); however, these may sometimes be confused with postmortem excavation damage or animal activity such as carnivore toothmarks (Byard, James, et al. 2002; Kimmerle and Baraybar 2008). It has long been argued that SFT is the most frequent cause of murder in the United Kingdom (Thompson and Inglis 2009), and as such an ability to determine the wound morphology is imperative and can provide contextual information regarding the circumstances surrounding the traumatic insult.

Criteria such as linearity, a well-defined clean edge, and a flat, smooth, polished cut surface should be observable (Boylston 2000). Instruments are numerous and include sharp knives, machetes, axes, icepicks, and bite marks (Kimmerle and Baraybar 2008; Komar and Buikstra 2008). Saws may also be utilized; however, these are usually applied postmortem in the act of dismemberment (Saville et al. 2007a), although they are occasionally used in an antemortem capacity, including their use as tools for suicide (e.g., Asano et al. 2008; Campman et al. 2000; Gloulou et al. 2009).

There are typically three wound types associated with SFT: punctures, incisions and clefts. If force is applied in a vector perpendicular to the contact area, a penetrating puncture or stab wound is caused that is deeper than it is wide. Conversely, an incised or cut wound results when a sharp-edged object is drawn over the skin with enough pressure to produce an injury that is longer than it is deep (Kimmerle and Baraybar 2008). Cleft or notch formations occur when vertical forces are applied by heavy instruments with long, sharp edges, resulting in a V-shaped notch that may penetrate the interior of the bone structure (Byers 2009). There are several characteristics of SFT that differ depending on the wound type. These include those that are associated with the weapon used (cross-sectional shape, width, depth, length, and striations) and those that occur in the area surrounding the point of impact (fracture lines, hinge fractures, and wastage) (Byers 2009). SFT rarely results in obvious fractures, generally due to the short time frame and narrow focus over which the force is applied. Differences occur due to variations in the weapon characteristics and the energy with which the implement had an impact on the body.

One of the most active areas of forensic anthropological interest in SFT concerns tool mark analysis and weapon-wound matching. Tool marks are the discrete patterns or impressions left by the implement or weapon on contact with the bone or tissue (Komar and Buikstra 2008). When analyzing tool marks, the morphology of the incision or groove created by the implement (known as the *kerf*) (Saville et al. 2007a) and the resulting striae are examined as they may indicate characteristics of the weapon used (Saville et al. 2007a). Other factors, including the direction of force, the number of traumatic events, and the sequence of events, may also be determined (Byers 2009).

The appearance of SFT is best observed microscopically; individual striae and parallel scratch marks on the surface of the bone may be interpreted to infer the class and characteristics of the weapon used (Boylston 2000). Striae are defects or grooves that can be observed on the cut surface and result from the teeth of the sharp edge of the implement cutting the bone. All blades have teeth whether they are manufactured striations or defects resulting from wear (Komar and Buikstra 2008). The striae can determine the blade class (i.e., whether the blade was serrated or nonserrated) (Thompson and Inglis 2009) and can also be used to infer the direction from which the cut was delivered. This may be achieved by studying the angle at which the implement passed through the bone and the resulting kerf morphology (the groove or incision created by the implement). Boylston (2000) described how the opposite side from the polished cut mark side will display roughening and flaking. The exception to this is when the instrument has cut cleanly through the bone. Many injuries resulting from SFT occur on the left-hand side of the body as a result of the greater preponderance of right-handed individuals (Boylston 2000).

Several studies have suggested that the emphasis must be placed on the identification of sharp weapon class as opposed to a particular weapon type (Kimmerle and Baraybar 2008; Reuhl and Bratzke 1999; Walsh-Haney 1999). A study by Bartelink and colleagues (2001) examining three different knife types (a scalpel, a paring knife, and a kitchen knife) revealed that the same instrument can produce different striation marks during different cutting episodes. Furthermore, they demonstrated that implement striation patterns can overlap; thus, caution should be observed when attempting to interpret whether a specific implement caused a specific wound; instead, a weapon class may be better assigned.

Further studies have suggested that weapon class and not specific weapon type should be assigned (Humphrey and Hutchinson 2001; Tucker et al. 2001) based on the conclusion that both macroscopic and microscopic characteristics of SFT wounds resulting from the three different implement classes are fairly distinct, with microscopic analysis providing a more reliable identification of the weapon class. The differences result from variations in weight and blade configuration; consequently, the resultant wound characteristics suggest the class of the weapon used. These studies further established that identification of characteristics within the same class of weapon (i.e., between two different axes) were not sufficiently distinct to link a specific implement to a specific wound.

It is generally agreed that SFT should be analyzed using microscopic analysis as macroscopically, wound morphologies resulting from different implements are on the whole indistinguishable. Alunni-Perret et al. (2005) detailed the characteristic differences of the wound morphology caused by a hatchet and a knife using scanning electron microscopy (SEM) as it allows detailed assessment of the cut marks on bone. This method is preferable to standard light microscopy as a higher magnification is reached, and more of the field is in focus at one time, allowing for a more comprehensive examination (Thompson and Inglis 2009; Komar and Buikstra 2008). With many types of SFT, macroscopic examination of the wound will not reveal sufficient information to determine weapon class, as demonstrated by the cut marks made by the hatchet and knife in the study by Alunni-Perret and colleagues (2005). It was only when the wound was viewed microscopically using SEM that different features were revealed between the instrument types; thus, these could be used to differentiate between the tools.

Much of the literature of the last 10 years comes directly from, or in conjunction with, clinical or pathological specializations and continues to present case-based studies of homicides, suicides (suicide by chainsaw being a particular recurring favorite of some pathologists), unusual weapon types, epidemiological data relating to stabbings or knife attacks, or experimental (neotaphonomic) approaches (Bartelink et al. 2001; Berrizbeitia 2001; Byard, Klitte, et al. 2002; Fedakar et al. 2005; Gill and Catanese 2002; Hainsworth et al. 2008; Hart 2005; Holck 2005; Humphrey and Hutchinson 2001; Inoue et al. 2006; Karger et al. 2000; Kieser et al. 2008; Moisander and Edston 2003; Pope and O'Brian 2004; Prahlow et al. 2001; Schmidt and Pollak 2006; Schneider et al. 2009; Shotar and Jaradat 2007; Tsokos et al. 2003; Wheatley 2008; Zollikofer et al. 2002; Tucker et al. 2001; de Gruchy and Rogers 2002; Alunni-Perret et al. 2005). Recent studies such as those by Humphrey and Hutchinson (2001), Tucker et al. (2001), and Alunni-Perret et al. (2005) are leading the way in making trauma analysis more detailed and thus aiding investigative forces in apprehending perpetrators of knife- or weapon-related crimes (Byers 2008). This literature, however, does not cover many aspects of SFT in any extensive detail; therefore, this paucity of information limits the investigator. Thompson and Inglis (2009) detailed many of the problems relating to the analysis of SFT. This study experimentally established that differences can now be made between serrated and nonserrated blades. Furthermore, the experimental planning of this study controlled for most variables; however, it was limited in that the force and attitude of the blade applied to the bones by each weapon type were not controlled; instead, the blades were applied manually, thus varying the force and attitude of attack and introducing additional covariables in the experiment.

Ballistic Trauma

It is considered by several authors that to understand the pattern of injury sustained due to a gunshot wound, it is first necessary to have a solid grasp of the mechanics of weapons and the factors that affect the projectile prior to impact (Kimmerle and Baraybar 2008; Thali, Kneubuehl, Zollinger, and Dirnhofer 2002b, 2002c). As such, the reader's attention is drawn to standard textbooks of ballistic and gunshot wound mechanics (e.g., Di Maio 1999; Heard 2008). Pre-2000 articles of note dealt with differential diagnosis of trauma types and the effects of projectile types on the human body (Klatt et al. 1989; Randall and Newby 1989; Berryman et al. 1995; Karger 1995; Knudsen et al. 1995; Missliwetz et al. 1995; Oliver et al. 1995; Rabl et al. 1998; Berryman and Haun 1996; Berryman and Symes 1998; Cina et al. 1999; Di Maio 1999; Di Maio and Spitz 1972; Di Maio and Zumwalt 1977; Dixon 1984; Donoghue et al. 1984; Druid 1997; Garavaglia and Talkington 1999; Grey 1993; Jentzen et al. 1995; Prgomet et al. 1998; Quatrehomme 1998; Quatrehomme and İşcan 1997, 1998, 1999; Simmons 1997; Stone et al. 1978; Thogmartin and Start 1998).

To propel a projectile toward a target, there must be a conversion of chemical energy to kinetic energy. This is achieved by activating a controlled explosion of the propellant part of the ammunition, converting the explosive substance from a solid or gel to a gas. As the gas expands within the confined environment of the barrel, the air pressure increases until it is sufficient to fire the projectile from the weapon. The size of the charge used will determine the quantity of gas formation, the pressure generated, and therefore the velocity of the projectile. This is one of the main characteristics thought to determine the severity of damage caused on impact as a higher muzzle velocity equates to a greater amount of kinetic energy and therefore will have an effect on the potential for energy dissipation on contact with body tissues (Brooks and Barker 2003).

The factors that determine the impact of a projectile on human tissue can be divided into those acting on the projectile, so-called extrinsic, and those that influence the response of the body tissue to the projectile, termed the intrinsic variables (Kimmerle and Baraybar 2008; Karger 2008).

Intrinsic factors are those determined by the tissue type that receives the direct impact of the ballistic projectile itself (Kimmerle and Baraybar 2008). The elasticity of a tissue alters the amount of deformation caused by the impact of the projectile and the effect of cavitation (Maiden 2009). Hard and soft tissues have different levels of collagen and therefore exhibit differential levels of elasticity. When a projectile collides with soft tissues, the accompanying shock wave distorts the tissue, forcing it away from the wound track, creating what is known as the temporary cavity. Due to the amount of elastic recoil in the soft tissue, this returns to its natural position, closing the temporary cavity and leaving the permanent cavity. Due to the vacuum created behind the bullet as it enters the body, debris is often pulled into the temporary cavity and is therefore trapped when the cavity collapses. This is one of the main sources of infection-associated complications resulting from gunshot wounds.

Extrinsic factors involved in the determination of the severity of injuries sustained from a gunshot wound are those that are applied to the projectile itself (Kimmerle and Baraybar 2008). If the pattern of injury observed is to be fully understood, it is necessary for these factors to be examined and their contribution to the flight of the projectile recognized:

Projectile Velocity. Previously, it was thought that the velocity of a projectile was the simplest measure of the potential damage it could inflict on the human body (Vogel and Dootz 2007). The velocity of the bullet, however, is dependent on its mass and the size of charge used as the propellant. As the size of the barrel is fixed and the gas produced from the chemical reaction occupies a greater volume than that of the solid substrate, the pressure must increase. When the pressure reaches the critical level, it pushes the projectile, firing it from the barrel. As energy can neither be created nor be destroyed, the velocity of the projectile can be used to predict the energy with which it will have an impact on human tissue and therefore the potential for the projectile to cause damage (Jussila et al. 2005).

Projectile Mass. The mass of a bullet is measured in grains and, coupled with the muzzle velocity, can be used to calculate the momentum and therefore the kinetic energy of the bullet as $E_k = \frac{1}{2}mv^2$ (Brooks and Barker 2003).

Projectile Caliber. The caliber of a projectile is a measure of its diameter and is given as a fraction of an inch (Dodd and Byrne 2006). The caliber of the projectile, and therefore of the weapon, will determine the size of the entrance and exit wounds as well as the size of the internal wound track. It must be noted, however, that although dimensions of the entrance wound may give an indication of the caliber of a projectile, they should only be used as a guide to the minimum dimensions of the bullet as it is possible for a projectile to cause an entrance wound larger than the actual round.

Projectile Composition, Construction, and Design. Ammunition is designed with one purpose in mind: to cause cessation of life. The design of the bullet reflects this. The design and the composition of a projectile are important factors governing the energy transfer between the round and the body and therefore the potential of the bullet to cause injury (Maiden 2009). The type of round used is context dependent; however, ammunition can be broken down into two groups, those designed to fragment on impact and those designed to minimally deform (Brooks and Barker 2003). Frangible bullets such as hollow points or dumdums are designed to distort and fragment on impact with tissue to cause the maximum amount of damage (Martrille et al. 2007; Maiden 2009). These types of ammunition, although used by the U.S. military, were outlawed by Article 23 of the 1907 Hague Convention (Maiden 2009).

Weapon. For an injury pattern sustained from a gunshot wound to be understood, it is first necessary to know what type of weapon fired the round as this will determine the velocity at which the bullet was travelling when it hit the target and possibly the type of round used. Weapons can be divided into two classes by grouping those with short barrels, including pistols and revolvers, and those with long barrels, such as rifles and shotguns (Stuehmer et al. 2009). Traditionally, these groups of weapons were thought of as causing a distinctive injury pattern; however, with new weapon design and technology, there is now overlap between high-powered handguns and low-velocity, long-barreled weapons (Kimmerle and Baraybar 2008).

External Ballistics. *External ballistics* is the term used to explain the behavior of a projectile in flight from the moment it leaves the barrel of the firearm until it comes into contact with its target. Range of fire, gravity, deceleration, and air resistance are the main variables considered in the study of external ballistics (Kimmerle and Baraybar 2008). In their article, considering the effect of gunshot wounds on the viscerocranium, Stuehmer et al. (2009) suggested that the range of fire is one of the most crucial factors in determining the severity of a gunshot wound to the human body.

Intermediate Targets. The damage caused by a projectile is dependent on the ability of the round to dissipate large quantities of energy once it encounters its target. It is this energy transfer that causes the devastation to the body tissues. If, however, a projectile ricochets or passes through a secondary medium prior to hitting its final target, some of this energy is dissipated, and if the round remained on its primary trajectory once passing through the intermediate target, it would cause less damage at its terminus. However, when a projectile hits an intermediate object, it is deviated from its line of flight and will start to yaw and tumble. This causes a greater surface area of the projectile to be in contact with the target and results in a more efficient transfer of energy, therefore resulting in a higher degree of devastation (Thali et al. 2001a). This phenomenon was detailed by Thali et al. (2001a) in their article examining the case of a man who shot a second individual through his own finger. In this incident, the entrance wound on the victim was larger than would have been expected from the weapon used had it not been discovered that an intermediate target was involved.

Characteristics of Gunshot Wounds. Skeletal ballistic trauma can be regarded as a higher-energy BFT, and the injuries caused therefore depend on the region of the skeleton affected. If the cranium is considered, as this is a common site of ballistic insult, the pattern of fractures observed is similar to that of a blunt force attack. The initial entrance wound will exhibit a multitude of radiating and concentric fractures emanating from the site of impact, and internal beveling will be observed due to the bone failing primarily under tension (Kimmerle and Baraybar 2008). This is similar to the fractures observed in BFT; however, the presence of concentric heaving fractures is indicative of a high-energy impact, which is not consistent with a force generated by another human. Similarly, exit wounds will exhibit external beveling due to the same mechanism (Kimmerle and Baraybar 2008). The appearance of the entrance and exit wounds will depend on a number of factors, including the size and type of the projectile, the angle of impact, and whether the defect is due to a single projectile or multiple projectiles (Kimmerle and Baraybar 2008).

Due to the increased incidence of gunshot wounds sustained in both the civilian world and military theater of operations, it is necessary for researchers to obtain a complete understanding of how these events have an impact on the skeleton. However, it should be clear from reading the primary literature relating to ballistics technology and gunshot wounds that there have been few major leaps in weapon or bullet projectile technology in the last 10 years. Indeed many of the most popular and effective ballistic delivery systems (handguns, rifles, shotguns) have altered little in technological capacity over the last 50 years. As such, forensic anthropological analysis of gunshot wounds has not had to keep pace with advances in technological development, with the effect that little new material has been added to our understanding of ballistic wounding mechanics and trauma analysis over the last decade beyond the seminal works of the 1990s (Berryman et al. 1995; Berryman and Symes 1998; Quatrehomme 1998; Quatrehomme and İşcan 1997, 1998, 1999).

Such recent studies as have been carried out have mainly focused on the generalities of gunshot and ballistic trauma (Denton et al. 2006; Dodd and Byrne 2006; Druid and Ward 2000; Karger 2008; Li 2006; Maiden 2009; Mastruko and Bijhold 2003; Oehmichen et al. 2004; Pollak and Rothschild 2004; Rainio et al. 2003; Santucci and Chang 2004; Thali et al. 2001b; Thali, Kneubuehl, Zollinger, and Dirnhofer 2002b, 2002c; Thali, Kneubuehl, et al. 2003); new projectile or bullet types and their effects on the body (de Roux et al. 2001; Hiss et al. 2003; Karlsson and Stahling 2000; Nelson and Winston 2007); patterns of soft tissue damage (Bailey and Mitchell 2007; Baraybar and Gasior 2006; Barbian and Sledzik 2008; Catanese and Gilmore 2002;

Cunliffe and Denton 2008; de la Grandmaison et al. 2001; de Roux et al. 2001; Denton et al. 2006; Dobi-Babic and Katalinic 2001; Dodd and Byrne 2006; Durak et al. 2006; Faller-Marquardt and Pollak 2002; Fenton et al. 2005; Gill et al. 2003; Glattstein et al. 2000; Hardman and Manoukian 2002; Hart 2005; Hiss et al. 2003; Kneubuehl and Thali 2003; Langley 2007; Levy et al. 2006; Lorin et al. 2001; Nelson and Winston 2007; Oehmichen et al. 2003, 2004; Perdekamp and Pollak 2005; Pollak and Rothschild 2004; Puskas and Rumney 2003; Racette and Sauvageau 2008; Rainio et al. 2003; Rainio and Sajantila 2005; Raul et al. 2007; Santucci and Chang 2004; Slaus et al. 2007; Solarino et al. 2007; Spitz and Ouban 2003; Straathof et al. 2000; Thali, Kneubuehl, et al. 2007; Verhoff, Karger, et al. 2008; Vogel and Dootz 2007; Williamson et al. 2003); or the production of finite element predictive models of varying complexity and success (Mota et al. 2003). Elsewhere, studies, such as those carried out by Thali et al. (Thali et al. 2001a; Thali, Kneubuehl, Dirnhofer, and Zollinger 2002a, 2002b, 2002c), have investigated the effects of ballistic trauma on the human body through the use of a "skin-skull-brain" model. Although the majority of studies used ballistic gelatin as a proxy for human tissue, it is imperative that the materials used in investigations mimic human tissue as closely as possible.

Explosive and Burning Trauma

The explosive and burning trauma types are perhaps the least well understood of all forensic trauma categories. Both concern the application of high energies through concussive blast waves, the application of thermal energy, or both. Explosions and fire are some of the most destructive forces encountered in the modern environment. Significant loss of human life can often be encountered in large-scale incidents and require legal identification of any individuals fatally involved in such conflagrations or blasts, or singular loss of life can occur in situations such as house fires or domestic explosions. An understanding of fire and explosive-induced trauma (FET) to skeletal tissue is a necessary prerequisite for the subsequent identification of human remains encountered in fatal fires, explosions, and mass disaster situations, including terrorist attacks. FET has the capability to alter, damage, or destroy evidence that is vital to the identification process. This often entails that fingerprints, DNA, and dental evidence will not survive incineration or deflagration to the degree or quality needed to achieve a positive identification; as such, cases that deal with the accidental or intentional burning or explosive disruption of human remains are among the most difficult for law enforcement and medicolegal investigators to analyze.

At present, both metric and morphological techniques employed to analyze human remains for the purpose of establishing biological and personal identity are generally applied to complete or near-complete skeletal elements; with fragmentation and disruption, the amount of useful biological data such remains yield is reduced. Furthermore, models established for FET have invariably been developed using nonhuman analogues (usually pig or sheep), which present significant structural (morphological and histological) and biochemical differences when compared to human bone. Since bone undergoes extensive alterations when exposed to FET, the accuracy of standard identification methods will therefore be detrimentally affected. Alterations to bone by FET may be substantial and primarily involve cracking, splitting, shrinkage, and fragmentation; subsequently, the accuracy of almost every anthropological technique is affected dramatically. However, FET may also provide valuable evidentiary features as thermal alteration may preserve bone and enamel, albeit in an altered physical state, although these have yet to be adequately quantified in the literature.

Although FET comprises the effects of both explosive blast and fire, most prior research has focused on heat-induced alteration to bone. From this, four stages of heat-induced alteration to osseous tissue have been recorded: degradation, dehydration, decomposition, and inversion/fusion (e.g., Correia 1997; Mayne-Correia and Beattie 2002; Roger and Daniels 2002; Thompson 2004; Walker and Miller 2005; Thompson 2009). Prior works have documented patterns in the accentuation of lamellar structure from carbon deposition, crack propagation in bone matrix, and general loss of microstructure at high temperatures (attributed to inversion and subsequent fusion of hydroxyapatite crystals). During these transitions, the size and shape of bone alters to a statistically significant degree; subsequently, quantification of these stages is of considerable importance to skeletal biologists. In spite of this, there is still a great deal that is not fully understood regarding the transformative processes of bone that heat causes and the most appropriate method for studying this material. This is in part due to the large variation in experimental models used by investigators. Different temperature intervals, recorded measurements, and statistical analyses have led to confusion in the literature regarding the typical mechanism and expression of heat alteration; much of the core science has been of low quality, with poor experimental design and poor control of environmental covariates and invariably was based on small sample sizes of nonhuman analogues (Ubelaker 2009).

Although there is a growing anthology of scientific literature now available to facilitate more accurate interpretation and analyses of burned bone, these studies are largely based on qualitative features and are, at best, misleading. Without quantitative measurements, there is no way to account accurately for the heat- (or blast-) induced alterations that bone experiences or to modify current anthropological techniques. Recording quantitative measurements can therefore help to standardize FET analysis, improve current analytical methods, and in the process, meet the imperative need to develop more accurate identification techniques for FET-affected human remains. Furthermore, although fire scene investigation and recovered debris may provide strong evidence with regard to the cause and development of the fire or blast (electrical, chemically accelerated, accidental, deliberate ignition, incendiary device, improvised explosive device [IED], military-grade munitions, etc.), human skeletal tissues recovered from fatalities have traditionally been ignored with regard to the information they may supply relating to the fire or blast environment, pyrotechnical context, and biochemical markers of life history and habitus. As such, FET-affected remains have the potential to provide information concerning the temperature and the duration of the fire, the weapon yield of the explosive device, the use of ignitable liquids such as accelerants, the pattern and process of any traumas or pathologies, as well as parameters for biological and personal identification, such as DNA, dietary isotope signatures, and evidence of drug use. Understanding the process of trauma as it affects the human body may also allow for the development of more effective clinical treatments of burn and blast victims or the development of protective equipment or clothing that may ameliorate the effects of high-energy or heat transmission.

Explosive and Blast Trauma

For the pattern of injury caused to be understood, it is first necessary to have a thorough comprehension of the underlying processes (Kimmerle and Baraybar 2008). Unlike guns, explosives may not necessarily be designed to kill outright but instead are designed to cause maximum damage to the largest number of targets while creating a sense of fear within a population (Kimmerle and Baraybar 2008). Explosive ordinance devices (EODs) are also used to direct the movement of populations. With the increasing use of IEDs in modern warfare, it is crucial that as much is understood as possible in regard to these munitions to minimize the prolonged effects of these traumatic events on the lives of individuals.

An explosive blast is essentially the result of an exothermic chemical reaction that releases a large amount of energy in an extremely short space of time (Wolf et al. 2009). As with ballistic trauma, explosive trauma requires certain prerequisites if it is to inflict maximum damage; these are an adequate fuel source, oxygen, and some form of frangible material that will fragment on detonation. Factors that affect the strength of the explosion are the size of the charge, the component parts of the explosive, the type of explosive (i.e., whether a high- or low-energy explosive), and finally the medium in which the explosive is detonated (Born 2005). The explosive wave can be broken into three phases, each of which carries with it the potential to inflict different patterns and types of injury.

The first wave of energy following detonation comprises a supersonic shock wave front that travels through the medium almost instantaneously (Trimble et al. 2006; Wolf et al. 2009). This wave propagates in a spherical shape, equally distributing the energy in every direction until it comes into contact with a solid object (Brooks and Barker 2003). It was noted by Mott in 1916 in deaths occurring due to explosive trauma that there were cases for which no outward evidence of insult was obvious (Born 2005). Injuries sustained during this phase of the explosion are classed as first-degree blast injuries (Kimmerle and Baraybar 2008). These types of injury are being increasingly encountered with the use of antipersonnel mines and IEDs.

The second element of an explosion that has the potential to cause severe damage is the blast wave, of which the shock wave mentioned in the previous section is the leading edge (Trimble et al. 2006). The blast wave is also known as the blast wind as it is formed by the area of negative pressure left by the shock wave (Trimble et al. 2006; Wolf et al. 2009). This wind, coupled with the shock front, is known as the blast overpressure wave and is responsible for the majority of blast-associated injuries.

The third element of an explosive wave is the thermal component. Unlike the shock wave and the blast wind, the thermal wind contains the heat energy generated by the exothermic reaction that takes place at detonation. As a consequence, this component has the potential to cause fourth-degree blast injuries (Wolf et al. 2009). Unlike primary, secondary, and tertiary blast injuries, quaternary injuries do not generally involve the skeletal system, other than heat-induced changes to bone. Due to the effects of the other patterns of explosive trauma, however, these effects may not be immediately apparent.

Although most authors consider there to be four classifications of blast-related injury, a quinary pattern has been suggested by Wolf et al. (2009). It is proposed that a separate suite of injuries resulting in hemodynamic instability are caused by the assimilation of toxic substances vaporized during the explosion (Mayo and Kluger 2006). This type of injury therefore is not expected to have any skeletal involvement; however, it is a recent area of research that would benefit from further investigation.

The forensic anthropological literatures relating to explosive and burning trauma are perhaps the least cogently realized areas of current forensic anthropological practice. The analysis of explosive trauma has its roots in the clinical and military milieus, with the effect that little has been published relevant to the forensic anthropological community over the last 20 years. The 1990s saw the publication of a number of articles dealing with the classification of explosive and blast wounds (Eliakis 1977a; Karger et al. 1999; Prgomet et al. 1998), but it was not until the last decade that a more comprehensive literature began to emerge (Bosnar et al. 2006; Botti et al. 2003; Brooks and Barker 2003; Garner and Brett 2007; Kahana and Hiss 2000; Oliver et al. 2002; Shields et al. 2003; Tsokos et al. 2003; Vogel and Dootz 2007; Pachón

2008; Samarasekera 2008; Seneviratne 2008); in the main, these articles deal with the basic mechanics of blast-body interaction or classification of ordnance types in relation to wounding characteristics, particularly from the use of improvised explosive devices (IEDs). Given the greater prevalence of explosive trauma in today's world through armed conflict and terrorist attacks this is a mechanism of trauma that will most likely become more commonplace and widely encountered in forensic anthropological practice; we fully expect to see the available literature expand regarding this subject over the next decade.

Burning Trauma and Thermal Alteration of Bone

Burning trauma, on the other hand, has an extensive literature that can only be generally summarized here. The subject is fully deserving of a single chapter on its own, and this perhaps reflects the complexities and hidden pitfalls of the analysis of this trauma type. Much of the pre-2000 literature regarding burnt skeletal tissue did not originate in the forensic literature, often coming from specialists looking at archaeological cremations or paleoanthropological burnt bone. As such, most early studies relate to attempts to characterize a number of discrete covariables that are encountered as part of the burning process: temperature of burning, duration of burning, the atmosphere (whether oxidative or reducing), whether the tissues were fleshed or defleshed or human or nonhuman, and the presence of artifacts in the burning environment (Bennett and Benedix 1999; Huxley 1994; Kennedy 1996; Murray and Rose 1993; Brain 1993; Cattaneo et al. 1999; Sillen and Hoering 1993; Herrmann and Bennett 1999; Stiner et al. 1995; Owsley 1993; Warren and Maples 1997; Grevin et al. 1998; Huxley and Kosa 1999; Huxley et al. 1999; Warren et al. 1999).

Subsequent research of direct forensic anthropological relevance has focused on the nature of micro- and macrostructural change to osseous tissue following burning but has not expanded the remit of pre-2000 research questions. In a way, much of the research has been fundamentally pedestrian, focusing on the same basic questions of temperature, duration, and context—issues first mooted in the archaeological and cremated bone literature of the 1980s but little resolved in the intervening period. However, some of the work has been of a high experimental quality, investigating issues regarding the effects of burning on human identification, including new imaging modalities (Thompson et al. 2009; Thompson 2004, 2005; Thompson and Chudek 2006); differentiation of burning from other trauma types (de Gruchy and Rogers 2002; Pope and O'Brian 2004); the effects of contamination, commingling, or diagenesis (Bass and Jantz 2004; Bergslien et al. 2008; Brooks et al. 2006; Enzo et al. 2007; Mayne-Correia and Beattie 2002; Warren and Schultz 2002; Worley 2005); or case-based or review studies (Delattre 2000;

Valenzuela et al. 2000; Byard et al. 2001; Phillips 2001; Rothschild et al. 2001b; Thali, Yen, et al. 2002; Bohnert and Rothschild 2003; NicDaeid 2003; Hiller et al. 2003; Koon et al. 2003; Kosanke et al. 2003; Lain et al. 2003; Stauffer 2003; Almirall and Furton 2004; DeHaan et al. 2004; Thompson 2004; Ye et al. 2004; Calacal et al. 2005; Hanson and Cain 2007; Hillier and Bell 2007; Pai et al. 2007; Panaitescu and Rosu 2007; Zavoi et al. 2007; Thompson et al. 2009; Ubelaker 2009).

The 2000s have also seen attempts to synthesize the forensic anthropological study of burnt and thermally altered bone; this has seen the publication of two seminal works that should be required reading for students interested in the subject. The first is the sole-authored *Forensic Cremation: Recovery and Analysis* (Fairgrieve 2008), which synthesized the current literature on fire chemistry, fire scene analysis, and anthropological recovery and placed the whole within a practical and conceptual forensic anthropological framework. The second volume, *The Analysis of Burned Human Remains*, edited by Schmidt and Symes (2008), is more explicitly case based but includes relevant synthetic articles that addressed questions such as those regarding thermal patterning and heat flow, the effects of differing gaseous environments on burning outcomes, quantification of color patterning in burnt bone, and issues of interpretation from archaeological perspectives (Beach et al. 2008; Bontrager and Nawrocki 2008; Curtin 2008; DeHaan 2008; Delvin and Herrmann 2008; McKinley 2008; Schmidt 2008; Schmidt et al. 2008; Schurr et al. 2008; Symes et al. 2008; Wahl 2008; Walker et al. 2008; Weitzel and McKenzie 2008; Williams 2008).

Conclusion

Modern humans are perhaps one of the only animals on earth that habitually seek to injure or kill members of their own species. As a result, the analysis of trauma is an area of forensic anthropology that must continually develop to maintain pace with the novel ways of inflicting devastating traumatic injuries devised by the human species. In reality, however, trauma analysis is an area of forensic anthropology that has remained relatively static over the last 10 years, as despite advances in military and civilian weaponry, the most common types of traumatic injuries are generally inflicted through routine interpersonal violence using implements close to hand, including hammers, fists, and kitchen knives (Fenton et al. 2003; Kimmerle and Baraybar 2008; Komar and Buikstra 2008). Consequently, the recent literature regarding trauma analysis has been flooded by anecdotal case reviews; although these provide an insight into a particular act, they do little to enhance the understanding of what is a highly variable and complex aspect of forensic anthropology. The one exception to this is the work recently carried out to establish the reliability of nonradiographic methods of imaging, including MSCT and CT, and their application in the forensic setting, including their use in virtual postmortem examinations (Andematten et al. 2008; Schneider et al. 2009; ; Thali, Jackowski, et al. 2007; Thali, Schwab, et al. 2003). The resulting data suggest that although these methods should not be thought of as a replacement for the traditional techniques of dissection and x-ray imaging, they can play an important role in locating and analyzing skeletal trauma.

As a result of the modern digital imaging methods that are increasingly being employed by forensic practitioners, it is now possible for three-dimensional models of the traumatized area to be made using the process of volumetric rendering (Thali, Jackowski, et al. 2007). This not only allows better appreciation of the trauma for the forensic practitioner but also is useful during criminal proceedings to illustrate the damage caused and to link it to a class of trauma or weapon, thereby giving the court the opportunity to fully appreciate the complexity of skeletal trauma. Forensic anthropologists have a responsibility as expert witnesses to provide the court with the best information possible for justice to prevail, and the continued advances in the analysis of trauma will play an important role in the future application of forensic anthropology.

References

Adams, J. E., Davis, G. G., Alexander, C. B., and Alonso, J. E. 2003. Pelvic trauma in rapidly fatal motor vehicle accidents. *Journal of Orthopaedic Trauma*, 17, 406–410.

Aghayev, E., Christe, A., Sonnenschein, M., Yen, K., Jackowski, C., Thali, M. J., Dirnhofer, R., and Vock, P. 2008. Postmortem imaging of blunt chest trauma using CT and MRI—Comparison with autopsy. *Journal of Thoracic Imaging*, 23, 20–27.

Aghayev, E., Jackowski, C., Sonnenschein, M., Thali, M., Yen, K., and Dirnhofer, R. 2006. Virtopsy hemorrhage of the posterior cricoarytenoid muscle by blunt force to the neck in postmortem multislice computed tomography and magnetic resonance imaging. *American Journal of Forensic Medicine and Pathology*, 27, 25–29.

Aghayev, E., Jackowski, C., Thali, M. J., Yen, K., Dirnhofer, R., and Sonnenschein, M. 2008. Heart luxation and myocardium rupture in postmortem multislice computed tomography and magnetic resonance imaging. *American Journal of Forensic Medicine and Pathology*, 29, 86–88.

Aghayev, E., Sonnenschein, M., Jackowski, C., Thali, M., Buck, U., Yen, K., Bolliger, S., Dirnhofer, R., and Vock, P. 2006. Postmortem radiology of fatal hemorrhage: Measurements of cross-sectional areas of major blood vessels and volumes of aorta and spleen on MDCT and volumes of heart chambers on MRI. *American Journal of Roentgenology*, 187, 209–215.

Aghayev, E., Thali, M. J., Jackowski, C., Sonnenschein, M., Dirnhofer, R., and Yen, K. 2008. MRI detects hemorrhages in the muscles of the back in hypothermia. *Forensic Science International*, 176, 183–186.

Aghayev, E., Thali, M., Jackowski, C., Sonnenschein, M., Yen, K., Vock, P., and Dirnhofer, R. 2004. Virtopsy—fatal motor vehicle accident with head injury. *Journal of Forensic Sciences*, 49, 809–813.

Aghayev, E., Thali, M. J., Sonnenschein, M., Hurlimann, J., Jackowski, C., Kilchoer, T., and Dirnhofer, R. 2005. Fatal steamer accident; blunt force injuries and drowning in post-mortem MSCT and MRI. *Forensic Science International*, 152, 65–71.

Aghayev, E., Thali, M. J., Sonnenschein, M., Jackowski, C., Dirnhofer, R., and Vock, P. 2007. Post-mortem tissue sampling using computed tomography guidance. *Forensic Science International*, 166, 199–203.

Aghayev, E., Yen, K., Sonnenschein, M., Jackowski, C., Thali, M., Vock, P., and Dirmhofer, R. 2005. Pneumomediastinum and soft tissue emphysema of the neck in postmortem CT and MRI; a new vital sign in hanging? *Forensic Science International*, 153, 181–188.

Aghayev, E., Yen, K., Sonnenschein, M., Ozdoba, C., Thali, M., Jackowski, C., and Dirnhofer, R. 2004. Virtopsy post-mortem multi-slice computed tomograhy (MSCT) and magnetic resonance imaging (MRI) demonstrating descending tonsillar herniation: Comparison to clinical studies. *Neuroradiology*, 46, 559–564.

Almirall, J. R., and Furton, K. G. 2004. Characterization of background and pyrolysis products that may interfere with the forensic analysis of fire debris. *Journal of Analytical and Applied Pyrolysis*, 71, 51–67.

Altun, G., and Durmus-Altun, G. 2003. Confirmation of alleged falanga torture by bone scintigraphy—Case report. *International Journal of Legal Medicine*, 117, 365–366.

Alunni-Perret, V., Muller-Bolla, M., Laugier, J.-P., Lupi-Pégurier, L., Bertrand, M.-F., Staccini, P., Bolla, M., and Quatrehomme, G. 2005. Scanning electron microscopy analysis of experimental bone hacking trauma. *Journal of Forensic Sciences*, 50, 796–801.

Andematten, M. A., Thali, M. J., Kneubuehl, B. P., Oesterhelweg, L., Ross, S., Spendlove, D., and Bolliger, S. A. 2008. Gunshot injuries detected by post-mortem multislice-computed tomography (MSCT): A feasibility study. *Legal Medicine*, 10, 287–292.

Asano, M., Nushida, H., Nagasaki, Y., and Ueno, Y. 2008. Suicide by a circular saw. *Forensic Science International*, 182, E7-E9.

Asirdizer, M., Yavuz, S., Sari, H., Canturk, G., and Yorulmaz, C. 2004. Unusual torture methods and mass murders applied by a terror organization. *American Journal of Forensic Medicine and Pathology*, 25, 314–320.

Atanasijevic, T. C., Savic, S. N., Nikolic, S. D., and Djokic, V. M. 2005. Frequency and severity of injuries in correlation with the height of fall. *Journal of Forensic Sciences*, 50, 608–612.

Aufderheide, A. C., and Rodríguez-Martin, C. 1998. *The Cambridge encyclopedia of human paleopathology*. Cambridge, UK: Cambridge University Press.

Bailey, J., and Mitchell, P. D. 2007. A case for Sherlock Holmes: Forensic investigation of a gunshot wound to the head dating from Victorian London. *International Journal of Osteoarchaeology*, 17, 100–104.

Baraybar, J. P., Cardoza, C. R., and Parodi, V. 2008. Torture and extra-judicial execution in the Peruvian Highlands: Forensic investigation in a military base. In Kimmerle, E. H., and Baraybar, J. P. (Eds.), *Skeletal trauma: Identification of injuries resulting from human rights abuse and armed conflict*. Boca Raton, FL: CRC Press, 255–261.

Baraybar, J. P., and Gasior, M. 2006. Forensic anthropology and the most probable cause of death in cases of violations against International Humanitarian Law: An example from Bosnia and Herzegovina. *Journal of Forensic Sciences*, 51, 103–108.

Barbian, L. T., and Sledzik, P. S. 2008. Healing following cranial trauma. *Journal of Forensic Sciences*, 53, 263–268.

Bartelink, E. J., Wiersema, J. M., and Demaree, R. S. 2001. Quantitative analysis of sharp-force trauma: an application of scanning electron microscopy in forensic anthropology. *Journal of Forensic Science*, 46, 1288–1293.

Bass, W. M., and Jantz, R. L. 2004. Cremation weights in east Tennessee. *Journal of Forensic Sciences*, 49, 901–904.

Beach, J. J., Passalacqua, N. V., and Chapman, E. M. 2008. Heat-related changes in tooth color: temperature versus duration of exposure. In Schmidt, C. W., and Symes, S. A. (Eds.), *The analysis of burned human remains*. London: Academic Press, 137–144.

Bennett, J. L., and Benedix, D. C. 1999. Positive identification of cremains recovered from an automobile based on presence of an internal fixation device. *Journal of Forensic Sciences*, 44, 1296–1298.

Bergslien, E. T., Bush, M., and Bush, P. J. 2008. Identification of cremains using x-ray diffraction spectroscopy and a comparison to trace element analysis. *Forensic Science International*, 175, 218–226.

Berrizbeitia, E. L. 2001. Interpretation of perimortem fractures in a calvarium from Kusia, La Guajira, Zulia State, Venezuela. *Anthropological Science*, 109, 309–314.

Berryman, H. E., and Haun, S. J. 1996. Applying forensic techniques to interpret cranial fracture patterns in an archaeological specimen. *International Journal of Osteoarchaeology*, 6, 2–9.

Berryman, H. E., Smith, O. C., and Symes, S. A. 1995. Diameter of cranial gunshot wounds as a function of bullet caliber. *Journal of Forensic Sciences*, 40, 751–754.

Berryman, H. E., and Symes, S. A. 1998. Recognizing gunshot and blunt cranial trauma through fracture interpretation. In Reichs, K. J. (Ed.), *Forensic osteology: Advances in the identification of human remains*. Springfield, IL: Thomas, 333–352.

Black, S. 2005. Bone pathology and ante-mortem trauma in forensic cases. In Payne-James, J. (Ed.), *Encyclopedia of forensic and legal medicine*. London: Elsevier, 105–113.

Blau, S., Robertson, S., and Johnstone, M. 2008. Disaster victim identification: New applications for postmortem computed tomography. *Journal of Forensic Sciences*, 53, 956–961.

Bohnert, M., and Rothschild, M. A. 2003. Complex suicides by self-incineration. *Forensic Science International*, 131, 197–201.

Bolliger, S. A., Thali, M. J., Aghayev, E., Jackowski, C., Vock, P., Dirnhofer, R., and Christe, A. 2007. Postmortem noninvasive virtual autopsy—Extrapleural hemorrhage after blunt thoracic trauma. *American Journal of Forensic Medicine and Pathology*, 28, 44–47.

Bolliger, S. A., Thali, M. J., Ross, S., Buck, U., Naether, S., and Vock, P. 2008. Virtual autopsy using imaging: bridging radiologic and forensic sciences. A review of the Virtopsy and similar projects. *European Radiology*, 18, 273–282.

Bontrager, A. B., and Nawrocki, S. P. 2008. A taphonomic analysis of human cremains from the Fox Hollow Farm serial homicide site. In Schmidt, C. W., and Symes, S. A. (Eds.), *The analysis of burned human remains*. London: Academic Press, 211–226.

Born, C. T. 2005. Blast trauma: The fourth weapon of mass destruction. *The Scandinavian Journal of Surgery*, 94, 279–285.

Bosnar, A., Stemberga, V., Coklo, M., Grgurevic, E., Zamolo, G., Cucic, T., and Di Nunno, N. 2006. War and suicidal deaths by explosives in southwestern Croatia. *Archives of Medical Research*, 37, 392–394.

Botti, K., Grosleron-Gros, N., Khaldi, N., Oliviera, A., and Gromb, S. 2003. Postmortem findings in 22 victims due to two grain silo explosions in France. *Journal of Forensic Sciences*, 48, 827–831.

Boylston, A. 2000. Evidence for weapon-related trauma in British archaeological samples. In Cox, M., and Mays, S. (Eds.), *Human osteology: In archaeology and forensic science*. Cambridge, UK: Cambridge University Press, 357–380.

Brain, C. K. 1993. The occurrence of burnt bones at Swartkrans and their implications for the control of fire by early hominids. In Brain, C. K. (Ed.), *Swartkrans*. Pretoria, South Africa: Transvaal Museum Monograph 8, 229–242.

Bremer, S., Praxl, N., Schonpflug, M., Schneider, K., and Graw, M. 2003. The human punch—A forensic biomechanical research. *Forensic Science International*, 136, 264–268.

Brink, O., Vesterby, A., and Jensen, J. 1998. Pattern of injuries due to interpersonal violence. *Injury—International Journal of the Care of the Injured*, 29, 705–709.

Brooks, A., and Barker, P. 2003. Missile and explosive wounds. *Surgery*, 21, 190–192.

Brooks, T. R., Bodkin, T. E., Potts, G. E., and Smullen, S. A. 2006. Elemental analysis of human cremains using ICP-OES to classify legitimate and contaminated cremains. *Journal of Forensic Sciences*, 51, 967–973.

Buck, U., Naether, S., Braun, M., Bolliger, S., Friederich, H., Jackowski, C., Aghayev, E., Christe, A., Vock, P., Dirnhofer, R., and Thali, M. J. 2007. Application of 3D documentation and geometric reconstruction methods in traffic accident analysis: With high resolution surface scanning, radiological MSCT/MRI scanning and real data based animation. *Forensic Science International*, 170, 20–28.

Byard, R. W., James, R. A., and Gilbert, J. D. 2002. Diagnostic problems associated with cadaveric trauma from animal activity. *American Journal of Forensic Medicine and Pathology*, 23, 238–244.

Byard, R. W., James, R. A., and Zuccollo, J. 2001. Potential confusion arising from materials presenting as possible human remains. *American Journal of Forensic Medicine and Pathology*, 22, 391–394.

Byard, R. W., Klitte, A., Gilbert, J. D., and James, R. A. 2002. Clinicopathologic features of fatal self-inflicted incised and stab wounds—A 20-year study. *American Journal of Forensic Medicine and Pathology*, 23, 15–18.

Byers, S. N. 2008. *Introduction to forensic anthropology*. Boston: Pearson Education.

Cagigao, E., and Lund, M. 2008. The Pacific War: A Chilean soldier found in Cerro Zig Zag, Peru. In Kimmerle, E. H., and Baraybar, J. P. (Eds.), *Skeletal trauma: Identification of injuries resulting from human rights abuse and armed conflict*. Boca Raton, FL: CRC Press.

Calacal, G. C., Delfin, F. C., Tan, M. M. M., Roewer, L., Magtanong, D. L., Lara, M. C., Fortun, R. D., and De Ungria, M. C. A. 2005. Identification of exhumed remains of fire tragedy victims using conventional methods and autosomal/Y-chromosomal short tandem repeat DNA profiling. *American Journal of Forensic Medicine and Pathology*, 26, 285–291.

Calce, S. E., and Rogers, T. L. 2007. Taphonomic changes to blunt force trauma: A preliminary study. *Journal of Forensic Sciences*, 52, 519–527.

Campman, S. C., Springer, F. A., and Henrikson, D. M. 2000. The chain saw: An uncommon means of committing suicide. *Journal of Forensic Sciences*, 45, 471–473.

Catanese, C. A., and Gilmore, K. 2002. Fetal gunshot wound characteristics. *Journal of Forensic Sciences*, 47, 1067–1069.

Cattaneo, C., Di Martino, S., Scali, S., Craig, O. E., Grandi, M., and Sokol, R. J. 1999. Determining the human origin of burnt bone: A comparative study of histological, immunological and DNA techniques. *Journal of Forensic Sciences* 102, 181–191.

Chacón, S., Peccerelli, F. A., Paiz Diez, L., and Rivera Fernandez, C. 2008. Disappearance, torture, and murder of nine individuals in a community of Nebaj, Guatemala. In Kimmerle, E. H., and Baraybar, J. P. (Eds.), *Skeletal trauma: Identification of injuries resulting from human rights abuse and armed conflict*. Boca Raton, FL: CRC Press, 300–313.

Chaudhry, M. A., Haider, W., Nagi, A. H., Ud-Din, Z., and Parveen, Z. 2008. Pattern of police torture in Punjab, Pakistan. *American Journal of Forensic Medicine and Pathology*, 29, 309–311.

Cina, S. J., Ward, M. E., Hopkins, M. A., and Nichols, C. A. 1999. Multifactorial analysis of firearm wounds to the head with attention to anatomic location. *American Journal of Forensic Medicine and Pathology*, 20, 109–115.

Correia, P. M. M. 1997. Fire modification of bone: A review of the literature. In Haglund, W. D., and Sorg, M. H. (Eds.), *Forensic taphonomy: The postmortem fate of human remains*. Boca Raton, FL: CRC Press, 275–294.

Cunha, E. 2006. Pathology as a factor of personal identity in forensic anthropology. In Schmitt, A., Cunha, E., and Pinheiro, J. (Eds.), *Forensic anthropology and medicine: Complementary sciences from recovery to cause of death*. Totowa, NJ: Humana Press, 333–358.

Cunha, E., and Pinheiro, J. 2009. Antemortem trauma. In Blau, S., and Ubelaker, D. H. (Eds.), *Handbook of forensic anthropology and archaeology*. Walnut Creek, CA: Left Coast Press, 246–262.

Cunliffe, C. H., and Denton, J. S. 2008. An atypical gunshot wound from a home-made zip gun—The value of a thorough scene investigation. *Journal of Forensic Sciences*, 53, 216–218.

Curtin, A. J. 2008. Putting together the pieces: Reconstructing mortuary practices from commingled ossuary cremains. In Schmidt, C. W., and Symes, S. A. (Eds.), *The analysis of burned human remains.* London: Academic Press, 201–209.

Dedouit, F., Loubes-Lacroix, F., Costagliola, R., Guilbeau-Frugier, C., Alengrin, D., Otal, P., Telmon, N., Joffre, F., and Rouge, D. 2008. Post-mortem changes of the middle ear: Multislice computed tomography study. *Forensic Science International,* 175, 149–154.

Dedouit, F., Telmon, N., Costagliola, R., Otal, P., Joffre, F., and Rouge, D. 2007. Virtual anthropology and forensic identification: Report of one case. *Forensic Science International,* 173, 182–187.

Dedouit, F., Telmon, N., Guilbeau-Frugier, C., Gainza, D., Otal, P., Joffre, F., and Rouge, D. 2007. Virtual autopsy and forensic identification—practical application: A report of one case. *Journal of Forensic Sciences,* 52, 960–964.

De Gruchy, S., and Rogers, T. L. 2002. Identifying chop marks on cremated bone: A preliminary study. *Journal of Forensic Sciences,* 47, 933–936.

Dehaan, J. D. 2008. Fire and bodies. In Schmidt, C. W., and Symes, S. A. (Eds.), *The analysis of burned human remains.* London: Academic Press, 1–13.

Dehaan, J. D., Brien, D. J., and Large, R. 2004. Volatile organic compounds from the combustion of human and animal tissue. *Science and Justice,* 44, 223–236.

Delabarde, T. 2008. Multiple healed rib fractures: Timing of injuries with regard to death. In Kimmerle, E. H., and Baraybar, J. P. (Eds.), *Skeletal trauma: Identification of injuries resulting from human rights abuse and armed conflict.* Boca Raton, FL: CRC Press, 236–244.

De La Grandmaison, G. L., Brion, F., and Durigon, M. 2001. Frequency of bone lesions: An inadequate criterion for gunshot wound diagnosis in skeletal remains. *Journal of Forensic Sciences,* 46, 593–595.

Delattre, V. F. 2000. Burned beyond recognition: Systematic approach to the dental identification of charred human remains. *Journal of Forensic Sciences,* 45, 589–596.

Delvin, J. B., and Herrmann, N. P. 2008. Bone color as an interpretive tool of the depositional history of archaeological cremains. In Schmidt, C. W., and Symes, S. A. (Eds.), *The analysis of burned human remains.* London: Academic Press, 109–128.

Deml, U., Verhoff, M. A., Ramsthaler, F., Kra, J., Gille, R. J., Grabherr, S., Thali, M. J., and Kreutz, K. 2008. Digital forensic osteology—Possibilities in cooperation with the Virtopsy 1 project. *Forensic Science International,* 174, 152–156.

Denton, J. S., Segovia, A., and Filkins, J. A. 2006. Practical pathology of gunshot wounds. *Archives of Pathology and Laboratory Medicine,* 130, 1283–1289.

De Roux, S. J., Prendergast, N. C., and Tamburri, R. 2001. Wounding characteristics of Glaser safety ammunition: A report of three cases. *Journal of Forensic Sciences,* 46, 160–164.

Di Maio, V. J. M. 1999. *Gunshot wounds.* Boca Raton, FL: CRC Press.

Di Maio, V. J., and Spitz, W. U. 1972. Variations in wounding due to unusual firearms and recently available ammunition. *Journal of Forensic Sciences,* 17, 377–386.

Di Maio, V. J., and Zumwalt, R. E. 1977. Rifle wounds from high velocity, center-fire hunting ammunition. *Journal of Forensic Sciences,* 22, 132–140.

Dirnhofer, R., Jackowski, C., Vock, P., Potter, K., and Thali, M. J. 2006. Virtopsy: Minimally invasive, imaging-guided virtual autopsy. *Radiographics,* 26, 1305–1333.

Dixon, D. S. 1984. Pattern of intersecting fractures and direction of fire. *Journal of Forensic Sciences*, 29, 651–654.

Dobi-Babic, R., and Katalinic, S. 2001. Death due to accidentally self-inflicted gunshot wound. *Croatian Medical Journal*, 42, 576–578.

Dodd, M. J., and Byrne, K. J. 2006. *Terminal ballistics: A text and atlas of gunshot wounds*. Boca Raton, FL: CRC Press.

Donoghue, E. R., Kalelkar, M. B., Richmond, J. M., and Teas, S. S. 1984. Atypical gunshot wounds of entrance: an empirical study. *Journal of Forensic Sciences*, 29, 379–388.

Druid, H. 1997. Site of entrance wound and direction of bullet path in firearm fatalities as indicators of homicide versus suicide. *Forensic Science International*, 88, 147–162.

Druid, H., and Ward, M. E. 2000. Incomplete shored exit wounds—A report of three cases. *American Journal of Forensic Medicine and Pathology*, 21, 220–224.

Durak, D., Fedakar, R., and Turkmen, N. 2006. A distant-range, suicidal shotgun wound of the back. *Journal of Forensic Sciences*, 51, 131–133.

Dye, D. W., Peretti, F. J., and Kokes, C. P. 2008. Histologic evidence of repetitive blunt force abdominal trauma in four pediatric fatalities. *Journal of Forensic Sciences*, 53, 1430–1433.

Eliakis, E. 1977a. Traumas by explosion—Forensic definition. *Bulletin De Medecine Legale Urgence Medicale Centre Anti-Poisons*, 20, 497–502.

Enzo, S., Bazzoni, M., Mazzarello, V., Piga, G., Bandiera, P., and Melis, P. 2007. A study by thermal treatment and X-ray powder diffraction on burnt fragmented bones from tombs II, IV and IX belonging to the hypogeic necropolis of "Sa Figu" near Ittiri, Sassari (Sardinia, Italy). *Journal of Archaeological Science*, 34, 1731–1737.

Fairgrieve, S. L. 2008. *Forensic cremation: Recovery and analysis*. Boca Raton, FL: CRC Press.

Faller-Marquardt, M., and Pollak, S. 2002. Skin tears away from the entrance wound in gunshots to the head. *International Journal of Legal Medicine*, 116, 262–266.

Fedakar, R., Turkmen, N., Durak, D., and Gundogmus, U. N. 2005. Fatal traumatic heart wounds: Review of 160 autopsy cases. *Israel Medical Association Journal*, 7, 498–501.

Fenton, T. W., Dejong, J. L., and Haut, R. C. 2003. Punched with a fist: The etiology of a fatal depressed cranial fracture. *Journal of Forensic Sciences*, 48, 277–281.

Fenton, T. W., Stefan, V. H., Wood, L. A., and Sauer, N. J. 2005. Symmetrical fracturing of the skull from midline contact gunshot wounds: Reconstruction of individual death histories from skeletonized human remains. *Journal of Forensic Sciences*, 50, 274–285.

Ferllini, R. (Ed.) (2007). *Forensic Archaeology: Human Rights Violations*. Springfield, IL: Charles C Thomas.

Finegan, O. 2008. The interpretation of skeletal trauma resulting from injuries sustained prior to, and as a direct result of, freefall. In Kimmerle, E. H., and Baraybar, J. P. (Eds.), *Skeletal trauma: Identification of injuries resulting from human rights abuse and armed conflict*. Boca Raton, FL: CRC Press, 181–195.

Frost, H. M. 1997. Indirect way to estimate peak joint loads in life and in skeletal remains (insights from a new paradigm). *Anatomical Record*, 248, 475–483.

Frost, H. M. 2001. From Wolff's law to the Utah paradigm: Insights about bone physiology and its clinical applications. *Anatomical Record*, 262, 398–419.

Fulginiti, L., Czuzak, M. H., and Taylor, K. M. 1999. Scatter versus impact during aircraft crashes: implications for forensic anthropologists. In Galloway, A. (Ed.), *Broken bones: Anthropological analysis of blunt force trauma*. Springfield, IL: Thomas, 322–329.

Galloway, A. 1999a. The biomechanics of fracture production. In Galloway, A. (Ed.), Broken bones: Anthropological analysis of blunt force trauma. Springfield, IL: Thomas, 35–62.

Galloway, A. (Ed.). 1999b. *Broken bones: Anthropological analysis of blunt force trauma*. Springfield, IL: Thomas.

Galloway, A. 1999c. The circumstances of blunt force trauma. In Galloway, A. (Ed.), Broken bones: Anthropological analysis of blunt force trauma. Springfield, IL: Thomas, 224–254.

Galloway, A. 1999d. Fracture patterns and skeletal morphology: introduction and the skull. In Galloway, A. (Ed.), *Broken bones: Anthropological analysis of blunt force trauma*. Springfield, IL: Thomas.

Galloway, A. 1999e. Fracture patterns and skeletal morphology: the lower extremity. In Galloway, A. (Ed.), Broken bones: Anthropological analysis of blunt force trauma. Springfield, IL: Thomas, 160–223.

Galloway, A. 1999f. Fracture patterns and skeletal morphology: the upper extremity. In Galloway, A. (Ed.), Broken bones: Anthropological analysis of blunt force trauma. Springfield, IL: Thomas, 113–159.

Galloway, A. 1999g. A traumatic confession. In Galloway, A. (Ed.), Broken bones: Anthropological analysis of blunt force trauma. Springfield, IL: Thomas, 291–296.

Galloway, A., and Mason, R. T. 2000. Forensic impact injuries in skeletal material. *American Journal of Physical Anthropology*, 154–155.

Galloway, A., Symes, S. A., Haglund, W. D., and France, D. L. 1999. The role of the forensic anthropologist in trauma analysis. In Galloway, A. (Ed.), Broken bones: Anthropological analysis of blunt force trauma. Springfield, IL: Thomas, 5–31.

Garavaglia, J. C., and Talkington, B. 1999. Weapon location following suicidal gunshot wounds. *American Journal of Forensic Medicine and Pathology*, 20, 1–5.

Garner, M. J., and Brett, S. J. 2007. Mechanisms of injury by explosive devices. *Anesthesiology Clinics*, 25, 147–160.

Gill, J. R., and Catanese, C. 2002. Sharp injury fatalities in New York City. *Journal of Forensic Sciences*, 47, 554–557.

Gill, J. R., Lenz, K. A., and Amolat, M. J. 2003. Gunshot fatalities in children and adolescents in New York City. *Journal of Forensic Sciences*, 48, 832–835.

Glattstein, B., Zeichner, A., Vinokurov, A., Levin, N., Kugel, C., and Hiss, J. 2000. Improved method for shooting distance estimation. Part III. Bullet holes in cadavers. *Journal of Forensic Sciences*, 45, 1243–1249.

Gloulou, F., Allouche, M., Ben Kheld, M., Bekir, O., Banasr, A., Zhioua, M., and Hamdoun, M. 2009. Unusual suicides with band saws: Two case reports and a literature review. *Forensic Science International*, 183, E7–E10.

Grevin, G., Bailet, P., Quatrehomme, G., and Ollier, A. 1998. Anatomical reconstruction of fragments of burned human bones: A necessary means for forensic identification. *Forensic Science International*, 96, 129–134.

Grey, T. C. 1993. The incredible bouncing bullet—Projectile exit through the entrance wound. *Journal of Forensic Sciences*, 38, 1222–1226.

Haglund, W. 1999. Violent encounters: multiple trauma of differing ages. In Galloway, A. (Ed.), Broken bones: Anthropological analysis of blunt force trauma. Springfield, IL: Thomas, 297–300.

Hainsworth, S. V., Delaney, R. J., and Rutty, G. N. 2008. How sharp is sharp? Towards quantification of the sharpness and penetration ability of kitchen knives used in stabbings. *International Journal of Legal Medicine*, 122, 281–291.

Hanson, M., and Cain, C. R. 2007. Examining histology to identify burned bone. *Journal of Archaeological Science*, 34, 1902–1913.

Hardman, J. M., and Manoukian, A. 2002. Pathology of head trauma. *Neuroimaging Clinics of North America*, 12, 175–187.

Hart, G. O. 2005. Fracture pattern interpretation in the skull: Differentiating blunt force from ballistics trauma using concentric fractures. *Journal of Forensic Sciences*, 50, 1276–1281.

Hayes, W. C., Erickson, M. S., and Power, E. D. 2007. Forensic injury biomechanics. *Annual Review of Biomedical Engineering*, 9, 55–86.

Heard, B. J. 2008. *Handbook of firearms and ballistics: Examining and interpreting forensic evidence*. Chichester, UK: Wiley-Blackwell.

Herrmann, N. P., and Bennett, J. L. 1999. The differentiation of traumatic and heat-related fractures in burned bone. *Journal of Forensic Sciences*, 44, 461–469.

Hiller, J. C., Thompson, T. J. U., Evison, M. P., Chamberlain, A. T., and Wess, T. J. 2003. Bone mineral change during experimental heating: an X-ray scattering investigation. *Biomaterials*, 24, 5091–5097.

Hillewig, E., Aghayev, E., Jackowski, C., Christe, A., Plattner, T., and Thali, M. J. 2007. Gas embolism following intraosseous medication application proven by post-mortem multislice computed tomography and autopsy. *Resuscitation*, 72, 149–153.

Hillier, M. L., and Bell, L. S. 2007. Differentiating human bone from animal bone: A review of histological methods. *Journal of Forensic Sciences*, 52, 249–263.

Hiss, J., Shoshani, E., Zaitsew, K., Giverts, P., and Kahana, T. 2003. Self inflicted gunshot wound caused by a home-made gun—Medico-legal and ballistic examination. *Journal of Clinical Forensic Medicine*, 10, 165–168.

Holck, P. 2005. What can a baby's skull withstand? Testing the skull's resistance on an anatomical preparation. *Forensic Science International*, 151, 187–191.

Hougen, H. P. 2008. Torture sequels to the skeleton. In Kimmerle, E. H., and Baraybar, J. P. (Eds.), *Skeletal trauma: Identification of injuries resulting from human rights abuse and armed conflict*. Boca Raton, FL: CRC Press, 234–235.

Humphrey, J. H., and Hutchinson, D. L. 2001. Macroscopic characteristics of hacking trauma. *Journal of Forensic Sciences*, 46, 228–233.

Huxley, A. K. 1994. Analysis of ceramic substrate found in cremains. *Journal of Forensic Sciences*, 39, 287–288.

Huxley, A. K., and Kosa, F. 1999. Calculation of percent shrinkage in human fetal diaphyseal lengths from fresh bone to carbonized and calcined bone using Petersohn and Kohler's data. *Journal of Forensic Sciences*, 44, 577–583.

Huxley, A. K., and Kósa, F. 1999. Calculation of percent shrinkage in human fetal diaphyseal lengths from fresh bone to carbonized and calcined bone using Petersohn and Köhler's data. *Journal of Forensic Sciences*, 43, 577–583.

Inoue, H., Ikeda, N., Ito, T., Tsuji, A., and Kudo, K. 2006. Homicidal sharp force injuries inflicted by family members or relatives. *Medicine Science and the Law*, 46, 135–140.

Jackowski, C., Bolliger, S., Aghayev, E., Christe, A., Kilchoer, T., Aebi, B., Perinat, T., Dirnhofer, R., and Thali, M. J. 2006. Reduction of postmortem angiography-induced tissue edema by using polyethylene glycol as a contrast agent dissolver. *Journal of Forensic Sciences*, 51, 1134–1137.

Jackowski, C., Christe, A., Sonnenschein, M., Aghayev, E., and Thali, M. J. 2006. Postmortem unenhanced magnetic resonance imaging of myocardial infarction in correlation to histological infarction age characterization. *European Heart Journal*, 27, 2459–2467.

Jackowski, C., Dirnhofer, S., Thali, M., Aghayev, E., Dirnhofer, R., and Sonnenschein, M. 2005. Postmortem diagnostics using MSCT and MRI of a lethal streptococcus group A infection at infancy: A case report. *Forensic Science International*, 151, 157–163.

Jackowski, C., Persson, A., and Thali, M. J. 2008. Whole body postmortem angiography with a high viscosity contrast agent solution using poly ethylene glycol as contrast agent dissolver. *Journal of Forensic Sciences*, 53, 465–468.

Jackowski, C., Schweitzer, W., Thali, M., Yen, K., Aghayev, E., Sonnenschein, M., Vock, P., and Dirnhofer, R. 2005. Virtopsy: Postmortem imaging of the human heart in situ using MSCT and MRI. *Forensic Science International*, 149, 11–23.

Jackowski, C., Sonnenschein, M., Thali, M. J., Aghayev, E., Von Allmen, G., Yen, K., Dirnhofer, R., and Vock, P. 2005. Virtopsy: Postmortem minimally invasive angiography using cross section techniques—Implementation and preliminary results. *Journal of Forensic Sciences*, 50, 1175–1186.

Jackowski, C., Sonnenschein, M., Thali, M. J., Aghayev, E., Yen, K., Dirnhofer, R., and Vock, P. 2007. Intrahepatic gas at postmortem computed tomography: Forensic experience as a potential guide for in vivo trauma imaging. *Journal of Trauma-Injury Infection and Critical Care*, 62, 979–988.

Jackowski, C., Thali, M., Aghayev, E., Yen, K., Sonnenschein, M., Zwygart, K., Dirnhofer, R., and Vock, P. 2006. Postmortem imaging of blood and its characteristics using MSCT and MRI. *International Journal of Legal Medicine*, 120, 233–240.

Jackowski, C., Thali, M., Sonnenschein, M., Aghayev, E., Yen, K., and Dirnhofer, R. 2005. Adipocere in postmortem imaging using multislice computed tomography (MSCT) and magnetic resonance imaging (MRI). *American Journal of Forensic Medicine and Pathology*, 26, 360–364.

Jackowski, C., Wyss, M., Persson, A., Classens, M., Thali, M. J., and Lussi, A. 2008. Ultra-high-resolution dual-source CT for forensic dental visualization—Discrimination of ceramic and composite fillings. *International Journal of Legal Medicine*, 122, 301–307.

Jacobsen, C., Bech, B. H., and Lynnerup, N. 2009. A comparative study of cranial, blunt trauma fractures as seen at medicolegal autopsy and by Computed Tomography. *BMC Medical Imaging*, 9, 18–26.

Jentzen, J. M., Lutz, M., and Templin, R. 1995. Tandem bullet versus multiple gunshot wounds. *Journal of Forensic Sciences*, 40, 893–895.

Jussila, J., Kjellstrom, B. T., and Leppaniemi, A. 2005. Ballistic variables and tissue devitalisation in penetrating injury—Establishing relationship through meta-analysis of a number of pig Tests. *Injury, International Journal of the Care of the Injured*, 36, 282–292.

Kahana, T., and Hiss, J. 2000. Trauma and identification of victims of suicidal terrorism in Israel. *Military Medicine*, 165, 889–893.

Karger, B. 1995. Penetrating gunshots to the head and lack of immediate incapacitation. I. Wound ballistics and mechanisms of incapacitation. *International Journal of Legal Medicine*, 108, 53–61.

Karger, B. 2008. Forensic Ballistics. In Tsokos, M. (Ed.), *Forensic pathology reviews* (Vol. 5). Totowa, NJ: Humana Press, 141–172.

Karger, B., Niemeyer, J., and Brinkmann, B. 2000. Suicides by sharp force: Typical and atypical features. *International Journal of Legal Medicine*, 299, 259–262.

Karger, B., Zweihoff, R. F., and Duchesne, A. 1999. Injuries from hand grenades in civilian settings. *International Journal of Legal Medicine*, 112, 372–375.

Karlsson, T., and Stahling, S. 2000. Experimental blowgun injuries, ballistic aspects of modern blowguns. *Forensic Science International*, 112, 59–64.

Keller, A. S. 2006. Torture in Abu Ghraib. *Perspectives in Biology and Medicine*, 49, 553–569.

Kennedy, K. A. R. 1996. The wrong urn: Commingling of cremains in mortuary practices. *Journal of Forensic Sciences*, 41, 689–692.

Kieser, J., Bernal, V., Gonzalez, P., Birch, W., Turmaine, M., and Ichim, I. 2008. Analysis of experimental cranial skin wounding from screwdriver trauma. *International Journal of Legal Medicine*, 122, 179–187.

Kimmerle, E. H., and Baraybar, J. P. (Eds.). 2008. *Skeletal trauma—Identification of injuries resulting from human rights abuse and armed conflict*. Boca Raton, FL: CRC Press.

Klatt, E. C., Tschirhart, D. L., and Noguchi, T. T. 1989. Wounding characteristics of .38 caliber revolver cartridges. *Journal of Forensic Sciences*, 34, 1387–1394.

Kneubuehl, B. P., and Thali, M. J. 2003. The evaluation of a synthetic long bone structure as a substitute for human tissue in gunshot experiments. *Forensic Science International*, 138, 44–49.

Knudsen, P. J. T., Vigsnaes, J. S., Rasmussen, R., and Nissen, P. S. 1995. Terminal ballistics of 7.62 mm nato bullets—Experiments in ordnance gelatin. *International Journal of Legal Medicine*, 108, 62–67.

Komar, D. A., and Buikstra, J. E. 2008. *Forensic anthropology: Contemporary theory and practice*. New York: Oxford University Press.

Koon, H. E. C., Nicholson, R. A., and Collins, M. J. 2003. A practical approach to the identification of low temperature heated bone using TEM. *Journal of Archaeological Science*, 30, 1393–1399.

Koriath, T. W. P., Romilly, D. P., and Hannam, A. G. 1992. Three-dimensional finite element stress analysis of the dentate human mandible. *American Journal of Physical Anthropology*, 88, 69–96.

Kosanke, K. L., Dujay, R. C., and Kosanke, B. 2003. Characterization of pyrotechnic reaction residue particles by SEM/EDS. *Journal of Forensic Sciences*, 48, 531–537.

Krabbel, G., and Appel, H. 1995. Development of a finite-element model of the human skull. *Journal of Neurotrauma*, 12, 735–742.

Kremer, C., Racette, S., Dionne, C. A., and Sauvageau, A. 2008. Discrimination of falls and blows in blunt head trauma: Systematic study of the hat brim line rule in relation to skull fractures. *Journal of Forensic Sciences*, 53, 716–719.

Lain, R., Griffiths, C., and Hilton, J. M. N. 2003. Forensic dental and medical response to the Bali bombing—A personal perspective. *Medical Journal of Australia*, 179, 362–365.

Langley, N. R. 2007. An anthropological analysis of gunshot wounds to the chest. *Journal of Forensic Sciences*, 52, 532–537.

Levy, A. D., Abbott, R. M., Mallak, C. T., Getz, J. M., Harcke, H. T., Champion, H. R., and Pearse, L. A. 2006. Virtual autopsy: Preliminary experience in high-velocity gunshot wound victims. *Radiology*, 240, 522–528.

Levy, G., Goldstein, L., Blachar, A., Apter, S., Barenboim, E., Bar-Dayan, Y., Shamis, A., and Atar, E. 2007. Postmortem computed tomography in victims of military air mishaps: Radiological-pathological correlation of CT findings. *Israel Medical Association Journal*, 9, 699–702.

Li, D. G. 2006. Ballistics projectile image analysis for firearm identification. *IEEE Transactions on Image Processing*, 15, 2857–2865.

Liu, X. S., Bevill, G., Keaveny, T. M., Sajda, P., and Guo, X. E. 2009. Micromechanical analyses of vertebral trabecular bone based on individual trabeculae segmentation of plates and rods. *Journal of Biomechanics*, 42, 249–256.

Lorin, G., Grandmaison, D., Brion, F., Durigon, M., and D, P. 2001. Frequency of bone lesions: An inadequate criterion for gunshot wound diagnosis in skeletal remains. *Journal of Forensic Sciences*, 46, 593–595.

Love, J. C., and Symes, S. A. 2004. Understanding rib fracture patterns: Incomplete and buckle fractures. *Journal of Forensic Sciences*, 49, 1153–1158.

Lovell, N. C. 1997. Trauma analysis in paleopathology. *Yearbook of Physical Anthropology*, 40, 139–170.

Maat, G. J. R. 2008. Dating of fractures in human dry bone tissue. In Kimmerle, E. H., and Baraybar, J. P. (Eds.), *Skeletal trauma: Identification of injuries resulting from human rights abuse and armed conflict*. Boca Raton, FL: CRC Press, 245–254.

Maiden, N. 2009. Ballistics reviews: Mechanisms of bullet wound trauma. *Forensic Science, Medicine and Pathology*, 5, 204–209.

Marks, M., Hudson, J. W., and Elkins, S. K. 1999. Craniofacial fractures: collaboration spells success. In Galloway, A. (Ed.), Broken bones: Anthropological analysis of blunt force trauma. Springfield, IL: Thomas, 258–286.

Martrille, L., Artuso, A., Cattaneo, C., and Baccino, E. 2007. A Deceptive Case of Gunshot Entry Wounds—Beware of Frangible Bullets. *Journal of Forensic and Legal Medicine*, 14, 161–164.

Mastruko, V., and Bijhold, J. 2003. Forensic 3D: Ballistic computer simulation in homicide cases. *Forensic Science International*, 136, p2.

Mayne-Correia, P., and Beattie, O. 2002. A critical look at methods for recovering, evaluating and interpreting cremated human remains. In Haglund, W. D., and Sorg, M. H. (Eds.), *Advances in forensic taphonomy: Method, theory and archaeological perspectives*. Boca Raton, FL: CRC Press, 435–450.

Mayo, A., and Kluger, Y. 2006. Terrorist bombing. *World Journal of Emergency Surgery*, 1, 33–38.

Mays, S. A. 2006. A possible case of surgical treatment of cranial blunt force injury from medieval England. *International Journal of Osteoarchaeology*, 16, 95–103.

McKinley, J. I. 2008. In the heat of the pyre: Efficiency of oxidation in Romano-British cremations—Did it really matter? In Schmidt, C. W., and Symes, S. A. (Eds.), *The analysis of burned human remains*. London: Academic Press, 163–183.

Missliwetz, J., Denk, W., and Wieser, I. 1995. Study on the wound ballistics of fragmentation protective vests following penetration by handgun and assault rifle bullets. *Journal of Forensic Sciences*, 40, 582–584.

Moisander, P. A., and Edston, E. 2003. Torture and its sequel—A comparison between victims from six countries. *Forensic Science International*, 137, 133–140.

Moraitis, K., and Spiliopouiou, C. 2006. Identification and differential diagnosis of perimortem blunt force trauma in tubular long bones. *Forensic Science, Medicine and Pathology*, 2, 221–229.

Moreno, A., Heisler, M., Keller, A., and Iacopino, V. 2003. Documentation of torture and ill treatment in Mexico: A review of medical forensic investigations, 2000 and 2002. *Journal of General Internal Medicine*, 18, 233–233.

Mota, A., Klug, W. S., Ortiz, M., and Pandolfi, A. 2003. Finite-element simulation of firearm injury to the human cranium. *Computational Mechanics*, 31, 115–121.

Murray, K. A., and Rose, J. C. 1993. The analysis of cremains—A case-study involving the inappropriate disposal of mortuary remains. *Journal of Forensic Sciences*, 38, 98–103.

Nelson, R., and Thornburg, B. 1999. Some examples of survived blunt force head trauma from a nineteenth century medical school comparative collection. In Galloway, A. (Ed.), Broken bones: Anthropological analysis of blunt force trauma. Springfield, IL: Thomas, 304–314.

Nelson, C. L., and Winston, D. C. 2007. A new type of shotgun ammunition produces unique wound characteristics. *Journal of Forensic Sciences*, 52, 195–198.

Nystrom, K. C., and Buikstra, J. E. 2005. Trauma-induced changes in diaphyseal cross-sectional geometry in two elites from Copan, Honduras. *American Journal of Physical Anthropology*, 128, 791–800.

Oehmichen, M., Gehl, H. B., Meissner, C., Petersen, D., Hoche, W., Gerling, I., and Konig, H. G. 2003. Forensic pathological aspects of postmortem imaging of gunshot injury to the head: documentation and biometric data. *Acta Neuropathologica*, 105, 570–580.

Oehmichen, M., Meissner, C., Konig, H. G., and Gehl, H. B. 2004. Gunshot injuries to the head and brain caused by low-velocity handguns and rifles—A review. *Forensic Science International*, 146, 111–120.

Oliver, W. R., Baker, A. M., Powell, J. D., Cotone, C. M., and Meeker, J. 2002. Estimation of body exposure to explosion. *American Journal of Forensic Medicine and Pathology*, 23, 252–256.

Oliver, W. R., Chancellor, A. S., Soltys, M., Symon, J., Cullip, T., Rosenman, J., Hellman, R., Boxwala, A., and Gormley, W. 1995. 3-Dimensional reconstruction of a bullet path—Validation by computed radiography. *Journal of Forensic Sciences*, 40, 321–324.

Ortner, D. J., and Putschar, W. G. J. 1981. *Identification of pathological conditions in human skeletal remains*. Smithsonian contributions to anthropology 28. Washington D. C: Smithsonian Institution Press.

Owsley, D. W. 1993. Identification of the fragmentary, burned remains of 2 U.S. journalists 7 years after their disappearance in Guatemala. *Journal of Forensic Sciences*, 38, 1372–1382.

Ozdoba, C., Weis, J., Plattner, T., Dirnhofer, R., and Yen, K. 2005. Fatal scuba diving incident with massive gas embolism in cerebral and spinal arteries. *Neuroradiology*, 47, 411–416.

Pachón, J. M. 2008. A case of blasting injury from Columbia. In Kimmerle, E. H., and Baraybar, J. P. (Eds.), *Skeletal trauma: Identification of injuries resulting from human rights abuse and armed conflict.* Boca Raton, FL: CRC Press, 124–127.

Pai, C. Y., Jein, M. C., Li, L. H., Cheng, Y. Y., and Yang, C. H. 2007. Application of forensic entomology to postmortem interval determination of a burned human corpse: A homicide case report from Southern Taiwan. *Journal of the Formosan Medical Association*, 106, 792–798.

Panaitescu, V., and Rosu, M. 2007. Problems of forensic anthropological identification of carbonized human remains. *Romanian Journal of Legal Medicine*, 15, 39–44.

Parkinson, R. J., and Callaghan, J. P. 2009. The role of dynamic flexion in spine injury is altered by increasing dynamic load magnitude. *Clinical Biomechanics* 24, 148–154.

Perdekamp, M. G., and Pollak, S. 2005. Elucidation of a strange gunshot injury. *International Journal of Legal Medicine*, 119, 91–93.

Pfaeffli, M., Vock, P., Dirnhofer, R., Braun, M., Bolliger, S. A., and Thali, M. J. 2007. Post-mortem radiological CT identification based on classical ante-mortem X-ray examinations. *Forensic Science International*, 171, 111–117.

Phillips, S. A. 2001. Pyrotechnic residues analysis—Detection and analysis of characteristic particles by scanning electron microscopy/energy dispersive spectroscopy. *Science and Justice*, 41, 73–80.

Plattner, T., Thali, M. J., Yen, K., Sonnenschein, M., Stoupis, C., Vock, P., Zwygart-Brugger, K., Kilchor, T., and Dirnhofer, R. 2003. Virtopsy-postmortem multislice computed tomography (MSCT) and magnetic resonance imaging (MRI) in a fatal scuba diving incident. *Journal of Forensic Sciences*, 48, 1347–1355.

Pohlenz, P., Blessmann, M., Oesterhelweg, L., Habermann, C. R., Begemann, P. G. C., Schmidgunst, C., Blake, F., Schulze, D., Puschel, K., Schmelzle, R., and Heiland, M. 2008. 3D C-arm as an alternative modality to CT in postmortem imaging: Technical feasibility. *Forensic Science International*, 175, 134–139.

Pollak, S., and Rothschild, M. A. 2004. Gunshot injuries as a topic of medicolegal research in the German-speaking countries from the beginning of the 20th century up to the present time. *Forensic Science International*, 144, 201–210.

Pope, E. J., and O'Brian, C. S. 2004. Identification of traumatic injury in burned cranial bone: An experimental approach. *Journal of Forensic Sciences*, 49, 431–440.

Poulsen, K., and Simonsen, J. 2007. Computed tomography as routine in connection with medico-legal autopsies. *Forensic Science International*, 171, 190–197.

Prahlow, J. A., Ross, K. F., Lene, W. J. W., and Kirby, D. B. 2001. Accidental sharp force injury fatalities. *American Journal of Forensic Medicine and Pathology*, 22, 358–366.

Prgomet, D., Danic, D., Milicic, D., Puntaric, D., Soldo-Butkovi, S., Jelic, J., Jakovina, K., and Leovic, D. 1998. Mortality caused by war wounds to the head and neck encountered at the Slavonski Brod Hospital during the 1991–1992 war in Croatia. *Military Medicine*, 163, 482–485.

Puskas, C. M., and Rumney, D. T. 2003. Bilateral fractures of the coronoid processes: Differential diagnosis of intra-oral gunshot trauma and scavenging using a sheep crania model. *Journal of Forensic Sciences*, 48, 1219–1225.

Quatrehomme, G. 1998. Gunshot wounds to the skull: Comparison of entries and exits. *Forensic Science International*, 94, 141–146.

Quatrehomme, G., and İşcan, M. Y. 1997. Bevelling in exit gunshot wounds in bones. *Forensic Science International*, 89, 93–101.

Quatrehomme, G., and İşcan, M. Y. 1998. Analysis of beveling in gunshot entrance wounds. *Forensic Science International*, 93, 45–60.

Quatrehomme, G., and İşcan, M. Y. 1999. Characteristics of gunshot wounds in the skull. *Journal of Forensic Sciences*, 44, 568–576.

Rabl, W., Haid, C., and Krismer, M. 1996. Biomechanical properties of the human tibia: Fracture behavior and morphology. *Forensic Science International*, 83, 39–49.

Rabl, W., Riepert, T., and Steinlechner, M. 1998. Metal pins fired from unmodified blank cartridge guns and very small calibre weapons—Technical and wound ballistic aspects. *International Journal of Legal Medicine*, 111, 219–223.

Racette, S., and Sauvageau, A. 2008. Suicide by drowning after two gunshots to the head: A case report. *Medicine Science and the Law*, 48, 170–172.

Rainio, J., Lalu, K., Ranta, H., and Penttia, A. 2003. Morphology of experimental assault rifle skin wounds. *International Journal of Legal Medicine*, 117, 19–26.

Rainio, J., and Sajantila, A. 2005. Fatal gunshot wounds between 1995 and 2001 in a highly populated region in Finland. *American Journal of Forensic Medicine and Pathology*, 26, 70–77.

Randall, B., and Newby, P. 1989. Comparison of gunshot wounds and field-tipped arrow wounds using morphologic criteria and chemical spot tests. *Journal of Forensic Sciences*, 34, 579–586.

Randolph-Quinney, P., Mallett, X., and Black, S. M. 2009. Forensic Anthropology. In Jamieson, A., and Moenssens, A. (Eds.), *Wiley encyclopedia of forensic science*. London: Wiley, 152–178.

Raul, J. S., Baumgartner, D., Willinger, R., and Ludes, B. 2006. Finite element modelling of human head injuries caused by a fall. *International Journal of Legal Medicine*, 120, 212–218.

Raul, J. S., Deck, C., Meyer, F., Geraut, A., Willinger, R., and Ludes, B. 2007. A finite element model investigation of gunshot injury. *International Journal of Legal Medicine*, 121, 143–146.

Raul, J. S., Deck, C., Willinger, R., and Ludes, B. 2008. Finite-element models of the human head and their applications in forensic practice. *International Journal of Legal Medicine*, 122, 359–366.

Raul, J. S., Ludes, B., and Willinger, R. 2008. Finite element models of the human head in the field of forensic science. In Kimmerle, E. H., and Baraybar, J. P. (Eds.), *Skeletal trauma: Identification of injuries resulting from human rights abuse and armed conflict*. Boca Raton, FL: CRC Press, 87–93.

Resnick, D. 1995. *Diagnosis of bone and joint disorders*. Philadelphia: Saunders.

Reuhl, J., and Bratzke, H. 1999. Death caused by a chain saw-homicide, suicide or accident? A case report with a literature review (with 11 illustrations). *Forensic Science International*, 105, 45–59.

Rockhold, L. A., and Herrmann, N. P. 1999. A case study of a vehicular hit-and-run fatality. In Galloway, A. (Ed.), Broken bones: Anthropological analysis of blunt force trauma. Springfield, IL: Thomas, 287–290.

Rodríguez-Martín, C. 2006. Identification and differential diagnosis of traumatic lesions of the skeleton. In Schmitt, A., Cunha, E., and Pinheiro, J. (Eds.), *Forensic anthropology and medicine: Complementary sciences from recovery to cause of death*. Totowa, NJ: Humana Press, 197–221.

Roger, K. D., and Daniels, P. 2002. An X-ray diffraction study of the effects of heat treatment on bone mineral microstructure. *Biomaterials*, 23, 2577–2585.

Ross, C. F. 2005. Finite element analysis in vertebrate biomechanics. *The Anatomical Record Part A: Discoveries in Molecular, Cellular and Evolutionary Biology*, 238A, 253–258.

Ross, A. H., and Suarez S. L. 2008. Tyranny and torture in the Republic of Panama. In Kimmerle, E. H., and Baraybar, J. P. (Eds.), *Skeletal trauma: Identification of injuries resulting from human rights abuse and armed conflict*. Boca Raton, FL: CRC Press, 438–440.

Roth, S., Raul, J. S., Ludes, B., and Willinger, R. 2007. Finite element analysis of impact and shaking inflicted to a child. *International Journal of Legal Medicine*, 121, 223–228.

Rothschild, M. A., Raatschen, H. J., and Schneider, V. 2001b. Suicide by self-immolation in Berlin from 1990 to 2000. *Forensic Science International*, 124, 163–166.

Rybalko, J., and Pauliukevicius, A. 2003. A correlation between the types of intracranial injury and direction of blunt force to the head. *Forensic Science International*, 136, p236.

Sacher, A. 1996. The application of forensic biomechanics to the resolution of unwitnessed falling accidents. *Journal of Forensic Sciences*, 41, 776–781.

Samarasekera, A. 2008. "Human bomb" and body trauma. In Kimmerle, E. H., and Baraybar, J. P. (Eds.), *Skeletal trauma: Identification of injuries resulting from human rights abuse and armed conflict*. Boca Raton, FL: CRC Press, 128–149.

Sanders, J., Wagner Schuman, M., and Marbella, A. M. 2009. The epidemiology of torture: A case series of 58 survivors of torture. *Forensic Science International*, 189, e1–e7.

Santucci, R. A., and Chang, Y. J. 2004. Ballistics for physicians: Myths about wound ballistics and gunshot injuries. *Journal of Urology*, 171, 1408–1414.

Saville, P. A., Hainsworth, S. V., and Rutty, G. N. 2007a. Cutting crime: The analysis of the "uniqueness" of saw marks on bone. *International Journal of Legal Medicine*, 121, 349–357.

Schmidt, C. W. 2008. The recovery and study of burned human teeth. In Schmidt, C. W., and Symes, S. A. (Eds.), *The analysis of burned human remains*. London: Academic Press, 55–74.

Schmidt, U., and Pollak, S. 2006. Sharp force injuries in clinical forensic medicine—Findings in victims and perpetrators. *Forensic Science International*, 159, 113–118.

Schmidt, C.W., and Sykes, S.A. (Eds.). 2008. The analysis of burned human remains. London: Academic Press.

Schmidt, C. W., Tomak, C., Lockhart, R. A., Greene, T. R., and Reinhardt, G. A. 2008. Fire and bodies. In Schmidt, C. W., and Symes, S. A. (Eds.), *The analysis of burned human remains*. London: Academic Press, 227–237.

Schmitt, A., Cunha, E., Pinheiro, J. (Eds.) 2006. *Forensic anthropology and medicine: Complementary sciences from recovery to cause of death*, Totowa, NJ: Humana Press, 480.

Schneider, J., Thali, M. J., Ross, S., Oesterhelweg, L., Spendlove, D., and Bolliger, S. A. 2009. Injuries due to sharp trauma detected by post-mortem multislice computed tomography (MSCT): A feasibility study. *Legal Medicine*, 11, 4–9.

Schoenpflug, M., Muggenthaler, H., Adamec, J., and Praxl, N. 2003. Numerical simulation in forensic science: Behavior of a numerical human body model in a vehicle-side-impact scenario. *Forensic Science International*, 136, p195.

Schuller, E., Eisenmenger, W., and Beier, G. 2000. Whiplash injury in low speed car accidents: Assessment of biomechanical cervical spine loading and injury prevention in a forensic sample. *Journal of Musculoskeletal Pain*, 8, 55–67.

Schurr, M. R., Hayes, R. G., and Cook, D. C. 2008. Thermally induced changes in the stable carbon and nitrogen isotope ratios of charred bones. In Schmidt, C. W., and Symes, S. A. (Eds.), *The analysis of burned human remains*. London: Academic Press, 95–108.

Seneviratne, A. B. 2008. Skeletal and soft tissue injuries resulting from a grenade. In Kimmerle, E. H., and Baraybar, J. P. (Eds.), *Skeletal trauma: Identification of injuries resulting from human rights abuse and armed conflict*. Boca Raton, FL: CRC Press, 117–123.

Shaw, K. P., and Hsu, S. Y. 1998. Horizontal distance and height determining falling pattern. *Journal of Forensic Sciences*, 43, 765–771.

Shields, L. B. E., Hunsaker, D. M., Hunsaker, J. C., and Humbert, K. A. 2003. Nonterrorist suicidal deaths involving explosives. *American Journal of Forensic Medicine and Pathology*, 24, 107–113.

Shotar, A. M., and Jaradat, S. 2007. A study of wound fatalities in the north of Jordan. *Medicine Science and the Law*, 47, 239–243.

Sillen, A., and Hoering, T. 1993. Chemical characterization of burnt bones from Swartkrans. In Brain, C. K. (Ed.), *Swartkrans*. Pretoria, South Africa: Transvaal Museum Monograph 8, 243–250.

Simmons, G. T. 1997. Findings in gunshot wounds from tandem projectiles. *Journal of Forensic Sciences*, 42, 678–681.

Simmons, T. 1999. Home alone: distinguishing blunt force trauma from possible taphonomic processes. In Galloway, A. (Ed.), Broken bones: Anthropological analysis of blunt force trauma. Springfield, IL: Thomas, 301–303.

Slaus, M., Strinovic, D., Pecina-Slaus, N., Brkic, H., Balicevic, D., Petrovecki, V., and Pecina, T. C. 2007. Identification and analysis of human remains recovered from wells from the 1991 War in Croatia. *Forensic Science International*, 171, 37–43.

Sloan, G. D., and Talbott, A. 1996. Forensic application of computer simulation of falls. *Journal of Forensic Sciences*, 41, 782–785.

Smith, M. O. 2003. Beyond palisades: The nature and frequency of late prehistoric deliberate violent trauma in the Chickamauga reservoir of east Tennessee. *American Journal of Physical Anthropology*, 121, 303–318.

Snow, C. C., Baraybar, J. P., and Spirer, H. 2008. Firefight in Lima: Wounded/killed
ratio analysis of MRTA casualties in the 1997 hostage rescue operation at the
Japanese Embassy. In Kimmerle, E. H., and Baraybar, J. P. (Eds.), *Skeletal trauma:
Identification of injuries resulting from human rights abuse and armed conflict.*
Boca Raton, FL: CRC Press, 14–19.

Solarino, B., Nicoletti, E. M., and Di Vella, G. 2007. Fatal firearm wounds: A retrospective study in Bari (Italy) between 1988 and 2003. *Forensic Science International*,
168, 95–101.

Spitz, D. J., and Ouban, A. 2003. Meningitis following gunshot wound of the neck.
Journal of Forensic Sciences, 48, 1369–1370.

Stauffer, E. 2003. Concept of pyrolysis for fire debris analysts. *Science and Justice*, 43,
29–40.

Stawicki, S. P., Gracias, V. H., Schrag, S. P., Martin, N. D., Dean, A. J., and Hoey, B. A.
2008. The dead continue to teach the living: Examining the role of computed
tomography and magnetic resonance imaging in the setting of postmortem
examinations. *Journal of Surgical Education*, 65, 200–205.

Stiner, M. C., Kuhn, S. L., and Weiner, S. 1995. Differential burning, recrystallization,
and fragmentation of archaeological bone. *Journal of Archaeological Science*, 22,
223–237.

Stone, I. C., Dimaio, V. J., and Petty, C. S. 1978. Gunshot wounds: visual and analytical
procedures. *Journal of Forensic Sciences*, 23, 361–367.

Straathof, D., Bannach, B. G., Wilson, A. J., and Dowling, G. P. 2000. Radiography of
perforating centerfire rifle wounds of the trunk. *Journal of Forensic Sciences*, 45,
597–601.

Straus, J., and Porada, V. 2003. Forensic application of biomechanics. *Forensic Science
International*, 136, 240–241.

Stuehmer, C., Blum, K. S., Kokemueller, H., Tavassol, F., Bormann, K. H., Gellrich,
N.-C., and Rucker, M. 2009. Influence of different types of guns, projectiles,
and propellants on patterns of injury to the viscerocranium. *Journal of Oral and
Maxillofacial Surgery*, 67, 775–781.

Symes, S. A., Rainwater, C. W., Chapman, E. M., Gipson, D. R., and Piper, A. L.
2008. Patterned thermal destruction of human remains in a forensic setting. In
Schmidt, C. W., and Symes, S. A. (Eds.), *The analysis of burned human remains.*
London: Academic Press, 15–54.

Ta'ala, S. C., Berg, G. E., and Haden, K. 2006. Blunt force cranial trauma in the
Cambodian killing fields. *Journal of Forensic Sciences*, 51, 996–1001.

Ta'ala, S. C., Berg, G. E., and Haden, K. 2008. A Khmer Rouge execution method:
Evidence from Choeung Ek. In Kimmerle, E. H., and Baraybar, J. P. (Eds.),
*Skeletal trauma: Identification of injuries resulting from human rights abuse and
armed conflict.* Boca Raton, FL: CRC Press, 196–199.

Thali, M. J. 2003. Virtopsy, a new imaging horizon in forensic pathology: Virtual
autopsy by postmortem multislice computed tomography (MSCT) and magnetic resonance imaging (MRI)—A feasibility study. *Journal of Forensic Sciences*,
48, 922–922.

Thali, M. J., Braun, M., Brueschweiler, W., and Dirnhofer, R. 2003. "Morphological
imprint": Determination of the injury-causing weapon from the wound morphology using forensic 3D/CAD-supported photogrammetry. *Forensic Science
International*, 132, 177–181.

Thali, M. J., Braun, M., Buck, U., Aghayev, E., Jackowski, C., Vock, P., Sonnenschein, M., and Dirnhofer, R. 2005. Virtopsy—Scientific documentation, reconstruction and animation in forensic: Individual and real 3D data based geo-metric approach including optical body/object surface and radiological CT/MRI scanning. *Journal of Forensic Sciences*, 50, 428–442.

Thali, M. J., Braun, M., and Dirnhofer, R. 2003. Optical 3D surface digitizing in forensic medicine: 3D documentation of skin and bone injuries. *Forensic Science International*, 137, 203–208.

Thali, M. J., Braun, M., Wirth, J., Vock, P., and Dirnhofer, R. 2003. 3D surface and body documentation in forensic medicine: 3-D/CAD Photogrammetry merged with 3D radiological scanning. *Journal of Forensic Sciences*, 48, 1356–1365.

Thali, M., and Dirnhofer, R. 2003. Virtopsy—New methods in forensic medicine. *Kriminalistik*, 57, 693–696.

Thali, M. J., Dirnhofer, R., Becker, R., Oliver, W., and Potter, K. 2004. Is "virtual histology" the next step after the "virtual autopsy"? Magnetic resonance microscopy in forensic medicine. *Magnetic Resonance Imaging*, 22, 1131–1138.

Thali, M. J., Jackowski, C., Oesterhelweg, L., Ross, S. G., and Dirnhofer, R. 2007. Virtopsy—The Swiss virtual autopsy approach. *Legal Medicine*, 9, 100–104.

Thali, M. J., Kneubuehl, B. P., Bolliger, S. A., Christe, A., Koenigsdorfer, U., Ozdoba, C., Spielvogel, E., and Dirnhofer, R. 2007. Forensic veterinary radiology: Ballistic-radiological 3D computer tomographic reconstruction of an illegal lynx shooting in Switzerland. *Forensic Science International*, 171, 63–66.

Thali, M. J., Kneubuehl, B. P., and Dirnhofer, R. 2002. A "skin-skull-brain model" for the biomechanical reconstruction of blunt forces to the human head. *Forensic Science International*, 125, 195–200.

Thali, M. J., Kneubuehl, B. P., Dirnhofer, R., and Zollinger, U. 2001a. Body models in forensic ballistics: reconstruction of a gunshot injury to the chest by bullet fragmentation after shooting through a finger. *Forensic Science International*, 123, 54–57.

Thali, M. J., Kneubuehl, B. P., Dirnhofer, R., and Zollinger, U. 2001b. Body models in forensic ballistics: reconstruction of a gunshot injury to the chest by bullet fragmentation after shooting through a finger. *Forensic Science International*, 123, 54–57.

Thali, M. J., Kneubuehl, B. P., Dirnhofer, R., and Zollinger, U. 2002a. The dynamic development of the muzzle imprint by contact gunshot: High-speed documentation utilizing the "skin-skull-brain model." *Forensic Science International*, 127, 168–173.

Thali, M. J., Kneubuehl, B. P., Zollinger, U., and Dirnhofer, R. 2002b. The "skin-skull-brain model": A new instrument for the study of gunshot effects. *Forensic Science International*, 125, 178–189.

Thali, M. J., Kneubuehl, B. P., Zollinger, U., and Dirnhofer, R. 2002c. A study of the morphology of gunshot entrance wounds, in connection with their dynamic creation, utilizing the "skin-skull-brain model." *Forensic Science International*, 125, 190–194.

Thali, M. J., Kneubuehl, B. P., Zollinger, U., and Dirnhofer, R. 2003. A high-speed study of the dynamic bullet-body interactions produced by grazing gunshots with full metal jacketed and lead projectiles. *Forensic Science International*, 132, 93–98.

Thali, M. J., Markwalder, T., Jackowski, C., Sonnenschein, M., and Dirnhofer, R. 2006. Dental CT imaging as a screening tool for dental profiling: Advantages and limitations. *Journal of Forensic Sciences*, 51, 113–119.

Thali, M. J., Schweitzer, W., Yen, K., Vock, P., Ozdoba, C., Spielvogel, E., and Dirnhofer, R. 2003. New horizons in forensic radiology—The 60-second "digital autopsy"—Full-body examination of a gunshot victim by multislice computed tomography. *American Journal of Forensic Medicine and Pathology*, 24, 22–27.

Thali, M. J., Yen, K., Plattner, T., Schweitzer, W., Vock, P., Ozdoba, C., and Dirnhofer, R. 2002. Charred body: Virtual autopsy with multi-slice computed tomography and magnetic resonance imaging. *Journal of Forensic Sciences*, 47, 1326–1331.

Thali, M. J., Yen, K., Schweitzer, W., Vock, P., Ozdoba, C., and Dirnhofer, R. 2003. Into the decomposed body—Forensic digital autopsy using multislice-computed tomography. *Forensic Science International*, 134, 109–114.

Thali, M. J., Yen, K., Vock, P., Ozdoba, C., Kneubuehl, B. P., Sonnenschein, M., and Dirnhofer, R. 2003. Image-guided virtual autopsy findings of gunshot victims performed with multi-slice computed tomography (MSCT) and magnetic resonance imaging (MRI) and subsequent correlation between radiology and autopsy findings. *Forensic Science International*, 138, 8–16.

Thogmartin, J. R., and Start, D. A. 1998. 9 mm ammunition used in a 40 caliber glock pistol: An atypical gunshot wound. *Journal of Forensic Sciences*, 43, 712–714.

Thompson, T. J. U. 2004. Recent advances in the study of burned bone and their implications for forensic anthropology. *Forensic Science International*, 146, S203–S205.

Thompson, T. J. U. 2005. Heat-induced dimensional changes in bone and their consequences for forensic anthropology. *Journal of Forensic Sciences*, 50, 1008–1015.

Thompson, T. 2009. Burned human remains. In Blau, S., and Ubelaker, D. H. (Eds.), *Handbook of forensic anthropology and archaeology*. Walnut Creek, CA: Left Coast Press, 295–303.

Thompson, T. J. U., and Chudek, J. A. 2006. A novel approach to the visualisation of heat-induced structural change in bone. *Science and Justice*, 47, 99–104.

Thompson, T., Gauthier, M., and Islam, M. 2009. The application of a new method of Fourier transform infrared spectroscopy to the analysis of burned bone. *Journal of Archaeological Science*, 36, 910–914.

Thompson, T. J. U., and Inglis, J. 2009. Differentiation of serrated and non-serrated blades from stab marks in bone. *International Journal of Legal Medicine*, 123, 129–135.

Tidball-Binz, M. 2008. Forward. In Kimmerle, E. H., and Baraybar, J. P. (Eds.), *Skeletal trauma: Identification of injuries resulting from human rights abuse and armed conflict*. Boca Raton, FL: CRC Press, xi–xii.

Tomczak, P. D., and Buikstra, J. E. 1999a. Analysis of blunt trauma injuries: Vertical deceleration versus horizontal deceleration injuries. *Journal of Forensic Sciences*, 44, 253–262.

Torwalt, C. R., Balachandra, A. T., Youngson, C., and De Nanassy, J. 2002. Spontaneous fractures in the differential diagnosis of fractures in children. *Journal of Forensic Sciences*, 47, 1340–1344.

Tournel, G., Desurmont, M., Becart, A., Hedouin, V., and Gosset, D. 2006. Child barbarity and torture—A case report. *American Journal of Forensic Medicine and Pathology*, 27, 263–265.

Trimble, K., Adams, S., and Adams, M. 2006. (IV) Anti-personnel mine injuries. *Current Orthopedics*, 20, 354–360.

Tsokos, M., Turk, E. E., Madea, B., Koops, E., Longauer, F., Szabo, M., Huckenbeck, W., Gabriel, P., and Barz, J. 2003. Pathologic features of suicidal deaths caused by explosives. *American Journal of Forensic Medicine and Pathology*, 24, 55–63.

Tucker, B. K., Hutchinson, D. L., Gilland, M. F. G., Charles, T. M., Daniel, H. J., and Wolfe, L. D. 2001. Microscopic and macroscopic characteristics of hacking trauma. *Journal of Forensic Science*, 46, 234–240.

Tuong, H. L., and Gean, A. D. 2006. Imaging of head trauma. *Seminars in Roentgenology*, 41, 177–189.

Ubelaker, D. H. 2009. The forensic evaluation of burned skeletal remains: A synthesis. *Forensic Science International*, 183, 1–5.

Ubelaker, O. A., and Adams, B. J. 1995. Differentiation of perimortem and postmortem trauma using taphonomic indicators. *Journal of Forensic Sciences*, 40, 509–512.

Valenzuela, A., Martin-De Las Heras, S., Marques, T., Exposito, N., and Bohoyo, J. M. 2000. The application of dental methods of identification to human burn victims in a mass disaster. *International Journal of Legal Medicine*, 113, 236–239.

Verhoff, M. A., Karger, B., Ramsthaler, F., and Obert, M. 2008. Investigations on an isolated skull with gunshot wounds using flat-panel CT. *International Journal of Legal Medicine*, 122, 441–445.

Verhoff, M. A., Ramsthaler, F., Krahahn, J., Deml, U., Gille, R. J., Grabherr, S., Thali, M. J., and Kreutz, K. 2008. Digital forensic osteology—Possibilities in cooperation with the Virtopsy (R) project. *Forensic Science International*, 174, 152–156.

Vogel, H., and Dootz, B. 2007. Wounds and weapons. *European Journal of Radiology*, 63, 151–166.

Wahl, J. 2008. Investigations on pre-Roman and Roman cremation remains from southwestern Germany: Results, potentialities and limits. In Schmidt, C. W., and Symes, S. A. (Eds.), *The analysis of burned human remains*. London: Academic Press, 145–161.

Walker, P. L., and Miller, K. P. 2005. Time, temperature, and oxygen availability: An experimental study of the effects of environmental conditions on the color and organic content of cremated bone. *American Journal of Physical Anthropology*, 216–217.

Walker, P. L., Miller, K. W. P., and Richman, R. 2008. Time, temperature, and oxygen availability: An experimental study of the effects of environmental conditions on the color and organic content of cremated bone. In Schmidt, C. W., and Symes, S. A. (Eds.), *The analysis of burned human remains*. London: Academic Press, 129–135.

Walsh-Haney, H. A. 1999. Sharp-force trauma analysis and the forensic anthropologist: Techniques advocated by William R. Maples, Ph.D. *Journal of Forensic Sciences*, 44, 720–723.

Warren, M. W. 2004. A radiologic atlas of abuse, torture, terrorism, and inflicted trauma. *American Journal of Physical Anthropology*, 124, 380–381.

Warren, M. W., Falsetti, A. B., Hamilton, W. F., and Levine, L. J. 1999. Evidence of arteriosclerosis in cremated remains. *American Journal of Forensic Medicine and Pathology*, 20, 277–280.

Warren, M. W., and Maples, W. R. 1997. The anthropometry of contemporary commercial cremation. *Journal of Forensic Sciences*, 42, 417–423.

Warren, M. W., and Schultz, J. J. 2002. Post-cremation taphonomy and artifact preservation. *Journal of Forensic Sciences*, 47, 656–659.

Waters, C. J. 2008. Firearm basics. In Kimmerle, E. H., and Baraybar, J. P. (Eds.), *Skeletal trauma: Identification of injuries resulting from human rights abuse and armed conflict*. Boca Raton, FL: CRC Press, 385–399.

Weitzel, M. A., and Mckenzie, H. G. 2008. Fire as cultural taphonomic agent: Understanding mortuary behavior at Khuzhir-Nuge XIV, Siberia. In Schmidt, C. W., and Symes, S. A. (Eds.), *The analysis of burned human remains*. London: Academic Press, 185–199.

Wheatley, B. P. 2008. Perimortem or postmortem bone fractures? An experimental study of fracture patterns in deer femora. *Journal of Forensic Sciences*, 53, 69–72.

White, T. D., and Folkens, P. A. 2005. *The human bone manual*. New York: Elsevier Academic Press.

Wienker, C. W., and Wood, J. E. 1999. An atypical skull: trauma and asymmetry mimic pathology. In Galloway, A. (Ed.), Broken bones: Anthropological analysis of blunt force trauma. Springfield, IL: Thomas, 315–321.

Williams, H. 2008. Towards an archaeology of cremation. In Schmidt, C. W., and Symes, S. A. (Eds.), *The analysis of burned human remains*. London: Academic Press, 239–269.

Williamson, M. A., Johnston, C. A., Symes, S. A., and Schultz, J. J. 2003. Interpersonal violence between 18th century Native Americans and Europeans in Ohio. *American Journal of Physical Anthropology*, 122, 113–122.

Wolf, S. J., Berbarta, V. S., Bonnett, C. J., Pons, P. T., and Contrill, S. V. 2009. Blast Injuries. *The Lancet*, 374, 405–415.

Worley, F. 2005. Taphonomic influences on cremation burial deposits: Implications for interpretation. In O'Connor, T. P. (Ed.), *Biosphere to lithosphere: New studies in vertebrate taphonomy*. Oxford, UK: Oxbow Books, 64–69.

Yartsev, A., and Langlois, N. E. I. 2008. A comparison of external and internal injuries within an autopsy series. *Medicine Science and the Law*, 48, 51–56.

Ye, J., Ji, A. Q., Parra, E. J., Zheng, X. F., Jiang, C. T., Zhao, X. C., Hu, L., and Tu, Z. 2004. A simple and efficient method for extracting DNA from old and burned bone. *Journal of Forensic Sciences*, 49, 754–759.

Yen, K., Lövblad, K. O., Scheurer, E., Ozdoba, C., Thali, M. J., Aghayev, E., Jackowski, C., Anon, J., Frickey, N., Zwygart, K., Weis, J., and Dirnhofer, R. 2007. Postmortem forensic neuroimaging: Correlation of MSCT and MRI findings with autopsy results. *Forensic Science International*, 173, 21–35.

Yen, K., Sonnenschein, M., Thali, M. J., Ozdoba, C., Weis, J., Zwygart, K., Aghayev, E., Jackowski, C., and Dirnhofer, R. 2005. Postmortem multislice computed tomography and magnetic resonance imaging of odontoid fractures, atlantoaxial distractions and ascending medullary edema. *International Journal of Legal Medicine*, 119, 129–136.

Yen, K., Thali, M. J., Aghayev, E., Jackowski, C., Schweitzer, W., Boesch, C., Vock, P., Dirnhofer, R., and Sonnenschein, M. 2005. Strangulation signs: Initial correlation of MRI, MSCT, and forensic neck findings. *Journal of Magnetic Resonance Imaging*, 22, 501–510.

Yen, K., Vock, P., Tiefenthaler, B., Ranner, G., Scheurer, E., Thali, M. J., Zwygart, K., Sonnenschein, M., Wiltgen, M., and Dirnhofer, R. 2004. Virtopsy: Forensic traumatology of the subcutaneous fatty tissue; multislice computed tomography (MSCT) and magnetic resonance imaging (MRI) as diagnostic tools. *Journal of Forensic Sciences*, 49, 799–806.

Zavoi, R., Marinescu, A., Radu, L., and Albita, C. 2007. Attempt to camouflage an homicide by burning the cadaver. *Romanian Journal of Legal Medicine*, 15, 50–54.

Zollikofer, C. P. E., De Leon, M. S. P., Vandermeersch, B., and Leveque, F. 2002. Evidence for interpersonal violence in the St. Cesaire Neanderthal. *Proceedings of the National Academy of Sciences*, 99, 6444–6448.

Bibliography

Adair, T. W., Delong, L., Dobersen, M. J., Sanamo, S., Young, R., Oliver, B., and Rotter, T. 2003. Suicide by fire in a car trunk: A case with potential pitfalls. *Journal of Forensic Sciences*, 48, 1113–1116.

Adams, D. E., and Cerney, M. 2007. Quantifying biomechanical motion using procrustes motion analysis. *Journal of Biomechanics*, 40, 437—444.

Allaire, M. T., and Manhein, M. H. 2008. Suicide by blasting caps: A case study of rare cranial trauma. *Journal of Forensic Sciences*, 53, 1313–1315.

Atanasijevic, T., Djokic, V., Nikolic, S., Veljkovic, S., and Savic, S. 2003. Fatal falls from height: Epidemiological and medicolegal characteristics. *Forensic Science International*, 136, 263–264.

Ayers, K. M., and Stahl, C. J. 1972. Ballistic characteristics and wounding effects of a tear gas pen gun loaded with ortho-chlorobenzalmalononitrile. *Journal of Forensic Sciences*, 17, 292–297.

Berryman, H. E. 2002. Disarticulation pattern and tooth mark artifacts associated with pig scavenging of remains: A case study. In Haglund, W. D., and Sorg, M. H. (Eds.), *Advances in forensic taphonomy: Method, theory and archeological perspectives*. Boca Raton, FL: CRC Press, 487–495.

Berryman, H. E., and Gunther, W. M. 2000. Keyhole defect production in tubular bone. *Journal of Forensic Sciences*, 45, 483–487.

Berryman, H. E., Kutyla, A. K., and Davis, J. R. 2010. Detection of gunshot primer residue on bone in an experimental setting—An unexpected finding. *Journal of Forensic Sciences*, 55, 488–491.

Besenski, N., Broz, R., Jadrosantel, D., Pavic, D., and Mikulic, D. 1996. The course of the traumatising force in acceleration head injury: CT evidence. *Neuroradiology*, 38, S36-S41.

Blau, S., and Ubelaker, D. H. (Eds.). 2009. *Handbook of forensic anthropology and archaeology*. New York: World Archaeological Congress.

Bleetman, A., Watson, C. H., Horsfall, I., and Champion, S. M. 2003. Wounding patterns and human performance in knife attacks: Optimising the protection provided by knife-resistant body armour. *Journal of Clinical Forensic Medicine*, 10, 243–248.

Brickley, M. 2006. Rib fractures in the archaeological record: A useful source of sociocultural information? *International Journal of Osteoarchaeology*, 16, 61–75.

Brickley, M. 2007. A case of disposal of a body through burning and recent advances in the study of burned human remains. In Brickley, M., and Ferllini, R. (Eds.), *Forensic anthropology: Case studies from Europe.* Springfield, IL: Thomas, 69–85.

Brickley, M., and Ferllini, R. (Eds.). 2007. *Forensic anthropology: Case studies from Europe.* Springfield, IL: Thomas.

Brunel, C., Fermanian, C., Durigon, M., and De La Grandmaison, G. L. 2010. Homicidal and suicidal sharp force fatalities: Autopsy parameters in relation to the manner of death. *Forensic Science International,* 198, 150–154.

Byard, R. W., Gehl, A., and Tsokos, M. 2005. Skin tension and cleavage lines (Langer's lines) causing distortion of ante- and postmortem wound morphology. *International Journal of Legal Medicine,* 119, 226–230.

Byard, R. W., and Gilbert, J. D. 2002. Cervical fracture, decapitation, and vehicle-assisted suicide. *Journal of Forensic Sciences,* 47, 392–394.

Byard, R. W., Langlois, N., and Gilbert, J. D. 2010. Positive "water test"—An external indicator of base of skull hinge-ring fracture. *Journal of Forensic Sciences,* 55, 519–520.

Carson, E. A., Stefan, V. H., and Powell, J. F. 2000. Skeletal manifestations of bear scavenging. *Journal of Forensic Sciences,* 45, 515–526.

Christe, D. B., Bozeman, A. P., Stapleton, T. R., and Ashley, D. W. 2007. Gunshot wound to the femoral neck: A unique case. *Journal of Trauma-Injury Infection and Critical Care,* 62, 785–785.

Clark, E. G. I., and Sperry, K. L. 1992. Distinctive blunt force injuries caused by a crescent wrench. *Journal of Forensic Sciences,* 37, 1172–1178.

Clarot, F., Vaz, E., Papin, F., Clin, B., Vicomte, C., and Proust, B. 2003. Lethal head injury due to tear-gas cartridge gunshots. *Forensic Science International,* 137, 45–51.

Cory, C. Z., Jones, M. D., James, D. S., Leadbeatter, S., and Nokes, L. D. M. 2001. The potential and limitations of utilising head impact injury models to assess the likelihood of significant head injury in infants after a fall. *Forensic Science International,* 123, 89–106.

Cowey, A., Mitchell, P., Gregory, J., Maclennan, I., and Pearson, R. 2004. A review of 187 gunshot wound admissions to a teaching hospital over a 54-month period: training and service implications. *Annals of the Royal College of Surgeons of England,* 86, 104–107.

Croft, A. M., and Ferllini, R. 2007. Macroscopic characteristics of screwdriver trauma. *Journal of Forensic Sciences,* 52, 1243–1251.

Cross, P., and Simmons, T. 2010. The influence of penetrative trauma on the rate of decomposition. *Journal of Forensic Sciences,* 55, 295–301.

Daegling, D. J., Warren, M. W., Hotzman, J. L., and Self, C. J. 2008. Structural analysis of human rib fracture and implications for forensic interpretation. *Journal of Forensic Sciences,* 53, 1301–1307.

Davy, D. T., and Jepsen, K. J. 2001. Bone damage mechanics. In Cowin, S. C. (Ed.), *Bone mechanics handbook.* Boca Raton, FL: CRC Press, 11–16.

De La Grandmaison, G. L., Krimi, S., and Durigon, M. 2006. Frequency of laryngeal and hyoid bone trauma in nonhomicidal cases who died after a fall from a height. *American Journal of Forensic Medicine and Pathology,* 27, 85–86.

Delling, G. 2008. Histopathology of the skeletal system after trauma—Report based on experience from 16 cases. *Rechtsmedizin*, 18, 42–47.

Demirci, S., Dogan, K. H., and Gunaydin, G. 2008. Throat-cutting of accidental origin. *Journal of Forensic Sciences*, 53, 965–967.

Dirkmaat, D. C., Cabo, L. L., Ousley, S. D., and Symes, S. A. 2008. New perspectives in forensic anthropology. *American Journal of Physical Anthropology*, Suppl. 47, 33–52.

Eisele, J. W., Bonnell, H. J., and Reay, D. T. 1983. Boot top fractures in pedestrians—A forensic masquerade. *American Journal of Forensic Medicine and Pathology*, 4, 181–184.

Ejlersen, J. A., Dalstra, M., Uhrenholt, L., and Charles, A. V. 2007. An unusual case of sudden unexpected death: Postmortem investigation and biomechanical analysis of the cervical spine. *Journal of Forensic Sciences*, 52, 462–466.

Eliakis, E. 1977b. Traumatic lesions by simple falls and by precipitation—Forensic approach. *Bulletin De Medecine Legale Urgence Medicale Centre Anti-Poisons*, 20, 197–200.

Esiyok, B., Balci, Y., and Ozbay, M. 2006. Bodies recovered from wells, sewerage systems and pits: What is the cause of death? *Annals Academy of Medicine Singapore*, 35, 547–551.

Evans, F. B. 2005. Trauma, torture, and transformation in the forensic assessor. *Journal of Personality Assessment*, 84, 25–28.

Farmer, N. L., Meier-Augenstein, W., and Kalin, R. M. 2005. Stable isotope analysis of safety matches using isotope ratio mass spectrometry—A forensic case study. *Rapid Communications in Mass Spectrometry*, 19, 3182–3186.

Fayad, L. M., Corl, F., and Fishman, E. K. 2009. Pediatric skeletal trauma: Use of multiplanar reformatted and three-dimensional 64-row multidetector CT in the emergency department. *Radiographics*, 29, 135–150.

Forbes, B. J., Christian, C. W., Judkins, A. R., and Kryston, K. 2004. Inflicted childhood neurotrauma (shaken baby syndrome): Ophthalmic findings. *Journal of Pediatric Ophthalmology and Strabismus*, 41, 80–88.

Fracasso, T., and Karger, B. 2006. Two unusual stab injuries to the neck: Homicide or self-infliction? *International Journal of Legal Medicine*, 120, 369–371.

Frater, C. J., and Haindl, W. 2003. Blunt trauma soft-tissue uptake on skeletal scintigraphy. *Clinical Nuclear Medicine*, 28, 699–700.

Glencross, B. 2000. Childhood trauma in the archaeological record. *International Journal of Osteoarchaeology*, 209, 198—209.

Glencross, B., and Stuart-Macadam, P. 2001. Radiographic clues to fractures of distal humerus in archaeological remains. *International Journal of Osteoarchaeology*, 11, 298–310.

Graw, M., Praxl, N., Schuller, E., Bremer, S., and Schonpflug, M. 2003. The car as a weapon—Biomechanical reconstruction of an atypical homicide. *Forensic Science International*, 136, 190.

Große Perdekamp, M., Kneubuehl, B. P., Ishikawa, T., Nadjem, H., Kromeier, J., Pollak, S., and Thierauf, A. 2010. Secondary skull fractures in head wounds inflicted by captive bolt guns: Autopsy findings and experimental simulation. *International Journal of Legal Medicine*. In print. doi 10.1007/s00414–010–0450–8.

Große Perdekamp, M., Vennemann, B., Mattern, D., Serr, A., and Pollak, S. 2005. Tissue defect at the gunshot entrance wound: What happens to the skin? *International Journal of Legal Medicine*, 119, 217–222.

Guo, X. E. 2001. Mechanical properties of cortical bone and cancellous bone tissue. In Cowin, S. C. (Ed.), *Bone mechanics handbook*. Boca Raton, FL: CRC Press, 510: 11–12.

Gutevska, A., Cakar, Z., Poposka, V., and Duma, A. 2003. Forensic expertise of fractured ribs according the Criminal Law of Republic of Macedonia. *Forensic Science International*, 136, 253–253.

Guyomarc'h, P., Campagna-Vaillancourt, M., Chaltchi, A., and Sauvageau, A. 2009. Skull fracture with brain expulsion in a one-level jumping-fall. *Journal of Forensic Sciences*, 54, 1463–1465.

Guyomarc'h, P., Campagna-Vaillancourt, M., Kremer, C., and Sauvageau, A. 2010. Discrimination of falls and blows in blunt head trauma: A multi-criteria approach. *Journal of Forensic Sciences*, 55, 423–427.

Harper, N. S., and Graff, A. H. 2009. Fractures and skeletal injuries. In Giardino, A. P., Lyn, M. A., and Giardino, E. R. (Eds.), *A practical guide to the evaluation of child physical abuse and neglect*. London: Springer-Verlag, 141–206.

Harruff, R. C. 1995. Comparison of contact shotgun wounds of the head produced by different gauge shotguns. *Journal of Forensic Sciences*, 40 , 801–804.

Hejna, P., and Safr, M. 2010. An unusual zip gun suicide—medicolegal and ballistic examination. *Journal of Forensic Sciences*, 55, 254–257.

Hiss, J., and Kahana, T. 1995. The medicolegal implications of bilateral cranial fractures in infants. *Journal of Trauma-Injury Infection and Critical Care*, 38, 32–34.

Hooper, A. D. 1979. A new approach to upper cervical injuries. *Journal of Forensic Sciences*, 24, 39–45.

Huntington, R. W. 1984. Deaths and wounds due to shrapnel equivalent in civilian forensic practice. *Journal of the Forensic Science Society*, 24, 407.

İşcan, M. Y., and Mccabe, B. Q. 1995. Analysis of human remains recovered from a shark. *Forensic Science International*, 72, 15–23.

Jonsson, H., Bring, G., Rauschning, W., and Sahlstedt, B. 1991. Hidden cervical-spine injuries in traffic accident victims with skull fractures. *Journal of Spinal Disorders*, 4, 251–263.

Jordana, X., Galtés, I., Busquets, F., Isidro, A., and Malgosa, A. 2006. Clay-shoveler's fracture: An uncommon diagnosis in palaeopathology. *International Journal of Osteoarchaeology*, 16, 366–372.

Jurmain, R. 2001. Paleoepidemiological patterns of trauma in a prehistoric population from central California. *American Journal of Physical Anthropology*, 115, 13–23.

Kerley, E. R. 1978. The identification of battered-infant skeletons. *Journal of Forensic Sciences*, 23, 163–168.

Kernback-Wighton, G., Salamat, B., Gotz, W., and Saternus, K. S. 2006. Some medicolegally important aspects of symphyseal injuries due to trauma. *American Journal of Forensic Medicine and Pathology*, 27, 145–150.

Khokhlov, V. D. 1997. Injuries to the hyoid bone and laryngeal cartilages: Effectiveness of different methods of medico-legal investigation. *Forensic Science International*, 88, 173–183.

Kirteke, E., Dokgoz, H., Gokdogan, M. R., and Soysal, Z. 2003. Casual connection between origin of trauma and injuries in pregnancy. Forensic investigation. *Gynakologe*, 36, 260–264.

Kleinman, P. K. 2008. "The roentgen manifestations of unrecognized skeletal trauma in infants"—A commentary. *American Journal of Roentgenology*, 190, 559–560.

Kluger, Y., Peleg, K., Daniel-Aharonson, L., and Mayo, A. 2004. The special injury pattern in terrorist bombings. *Journal of the American College of Surgeons*, 199, 875–879.

Koehler, S. A., Luckasevic, T. M., Rozin, L., Shakir, A., Ladham, S., Omalu, B., Dominick, J., and Wecht, C. H. 2004. Death by chainsaw: Fatal kickback injuries to the neck. *Journal of Forensic Sciences*, 49, 345–350.

Komar, D. A. 2003. Twenty-seven years of forensic anthropology casework in New Mexico. *Journal of Forensic Sciences*, 48, 521–524.

Kosashvili, Y., Hiss, J., Davidovic, N., Lin, G., Kalmovic, B., Melamed, E., Levy, Y., and Blumenfeld, A. 2005. Influence of personal armor on distribution of entry wounds: Lessons learned from urban-setting warfare fatalities. *Journal of Trauma-Injury Infection and Critical Care*, 58, 1236–1240.

Kuker, W., Schoning, M., Krageloh-Mann, I., and Nagele, T. 2006. Shaken baby syndrome. Imaging methods for the recognition of a severe form of infant maltreatment. *Monatsschrift Kinderheilkunde*, 154, 659–668.

Loe, L. 2009. Perimortem trauma. In Blau, S., and Ubelaker, D. H. (Eds.), *Handbook of forensic anthropology and archaeology*. Walnut Creek, CA: Left Coast Press, 263–288.

Love, J. C., and Sanchez, L. A. 2009. Recognition of skeletal fractures in infants: An autopsy technique. *Journal of Forensic Sciences*, 54, 1443–1446.

Lynn, K. S., and Fairgrieve, S. I. 2009. Microscopic indicators of axe and hatchet trauma in fleshed and defleshed mammalian long bones. *Journal of Forensic Sciences*, 54, 793–797.

Macaulay, L. E., Barr, D. G., and Strongman, D. B. 2009. Effects of decomposition on gunshot wound characteristics: Under cold temperatures with no insect activity. *Journal of Forensic Sciences*, 54, 448–451.

Mahoney, P. F., Brooks, A. J., Ryan, J. M., and Schwab, W. C. 2005. *Ballistic trauma: A practical guide*. London: Springer-Verlag.

Mays, S. A. 2006a. A palaeopathological study of Colles' fracture. *International Journal of Osteoarchaeology*, 16, 415–428.

Molina, D. K., Nichols, J. J., and Dimaio, V. J. M. 2007. The sensitivity of computed tomography (CT) scans in detecting trauma: Are CT scans reliable enough for courtroom testimony? *Journal of Trauma-Injury Infection and Critical Care*, 63, 625–629.

Morentin, B., and Biritxinaga, B. 2006. Massive pulmonary embolization by cerebral tissue after head trauma in an adult male. *American Journal of Forensic Medicine and Pathology*, 27, 268–270.

Murphy, M. S., Gaither, C., Goycochea, E., Verano, J. W., and Cock, G. 2010. Violence and weapon-related trauma at Puruchuco-Huaquerones, Peru. *American Journal of Physical Anthropology*, doi 10.1002/ajpa.21291.

Murray, I. P. C. 1993. The role of SPECT in the evaluation of skeletal trauma. *Annals of Nuclear Medicine*, 7, 1–9.

Myers, J. C., Okoye, M. I., Kiple, D., Kimmerle, E. H., and Reinhard, K. J. 1999. Three-dimensional (3-D) imaging in post-mortem examinations: Elucidation and identification of cranial and facial fractures in victims of homicide utilizing 3-D computerized imaging reconstruction techniques. *International Journal of Legal Medicine*, 113, 33–37.

Needham, C., Wilkinson, C. M., and Knusel, C. J. 2003. Reconstructing visual man-ifestations of disease and trauma from archaeological remains. In Collett, L. R. (Ed.), *Graphic archaeology—The Journal of the Association of Archaeological Illustrators and Surveyors*. Exeter, UK: Short Run Press, 15–20.

Nic Daeid, N., Cassidy, M., and Mchugh, S. 2008. An investigation into the corre-lation of knife damage in clothing and the lengths of skin wounds. *Forensic Science International*, 179, 107–110.

Ormstad, K., Karlsson, T., Enkler, L., Law, B., and Rajs, J. 1986. Patterns in sharp force fatalities—A comprehensive forensic medical study. *Journal of Forensic Sciences*, 31, 529–542.

Paper, O. 2008. Characterization of archaeological burnt bones: contribution of a new analytical protocol based on derivative FTIR spectroscopy and curve fit-ting of the v 1 v 3 PO 4 domain. *Analytical and Bioanalytical Chemistry*, 392, 1479–1488.

Pfeiffer, H., Fechner, G., and Brinkmann, B. 2005. Backstabbing—A report of an unusual case. *International Journal of Legal Medicine*, 119, 47–49.

Pickering, T. R., Domínguez-Rodrigo, M., Egeland, C. P., and Brain, C. K. 2005. The contribution of limb bone fracture patterns to reconstructing early hominid behaviour at Swartkrans cave (South Africa): Archaeological application of a new analytical method. *International Journal of Osteoarchaeology*, 15, 247–260.

Plunkett, J. 2006. Resuscitation injuries complicating the interpretation of premor-tem trauma and natural disease in children. *Journal of Forensic Sciences*, 51, 127–130.

Pollanen, M. S., Bulger, B., and Chiasson, D. A. 1995. The location of hyoid fractures in strangulation revealed by xeroradiography. *Journal of Forensic Sciences*, 40, 303–305.

Pollanen, M. S., and Chiasson, D. A. 1996. Fracture of the hyoid bone in strangula-tion: Comparison of fractured and unfractured hyoids from victims of strangu-lation. *Journal of Forensic Sciences*, 41, 110–113.

Powers, N. 2005. Cranial trauma and treatment: A case study from the medieval cem-etery of St. Mary Spital, London. *International Journal of Osteoarchaeology*, 15, 1–14.

Prieto, J. L. 2007. Stab wounds: the contribution of forensic anthropology—a case study. In Brickley, M., and Ferllini, R. (Eds.), *Forensic anthropology: Case studies from Europe*. Springfield, IL: Thomas, 19–37.

Quatrehomme, G. 2007. A strange case of dismemberment. In Brickley, M., and Ferllini, R. (Eds.), *Forensic anthropology: Case studies from Europe*. Springfield, IL: Thomas, 99–119.

Rainio, J., De Paoli, G., Druid, H., Kauppila, R., De Giorgio, F., Bortolotti, F., and Tagliaro, F. 2008. Post-mortem stability and redistribution of carbohydrate-deficient transferrin (CDT). *Forensic Science International*, 174, 161–165.

Ramsay, D. A., and Shkrum, M. J. 1995. Homicidal blunt head trauma, diffuse axonal injury, alcoholic intoxication, and cardiorespiratory arrest—A case-report of a forensic syndrome of acute brain-stem dysfunction. *American Journal of Forensic Medicine and Pathology*, 16, 107–114.

Rao, V. J., and Hart, R. 1983. Tool mark determination in cartilage of stabbing victim. *Journal of Forensic Sciences*, 28, 794–799.

Rautman, A. E., and Fenton, T. W. 2005. A case of historic cannibalism in the American West: Implications for southwestern archaeology. *American Antiquity*, 70, 321–341.

Rawson, R. B., Starich, G. H., and Rawson, R. D. 2000. Scanning electron microscopic analysis of skin resolution as an aid in identifying trauma in forensic investigations. *Journal of Forensic Sciences*, 45, 1023–1027.

Roberts, A., Nokes, L., Leadbeatter, S., and Pike, H. 1994. Impact characteristics of 2 types of police baton. *Forensic Science International*, 67, 49–53.

Rodriguez-Merchan, E. C. 2005. Pediatric skeletal trauma—A review and historical perspective. *Clinical Orthopaedics and Related Research*, 432, 8–13.

Rogers, L. F. 2001a. To see or not to see, that is the question: MR imaging of acute skeletal trauma. *American Journal of Roentgenology*, 176, 1–1.

Rogers, L. F. 2001b. What is the role of MR imaging in acute skeletal trauma? *American Journal of Roentgenology*, 177, 1245–1245.

Rosing, R. W. 2000. Forensic osteology—Anthropology, biomechanics, medicine, archeology. *Homo*, 51, p298.

Rothschild, M. A., Karger, B., and Schneider, V. 2001a. Puncture wounds caused by glass mistaken for with stab wounds with a knife. *Forensic Science International*, 121, 161–165.

Ruff, C. B., and Hayes, W. C. 1983a. Cross-sectional geometry of Pecos Pueblo femora and tibiae—A biomechanical investigation: I. Method and general patterns of variation. *American Journal of Physical Anthropology*, 60, 359–381.

Ruff, C. B., and Hayes, W. C. 1983b. Cross-sectional geometry of Pecos Pueblo femora and tibiae—A biomechanical investigation: II. Sex, age, and side differences. *American Journal of Physical Anthropology*, 60, 383–400.

Saville, P. A., Hainsworth, S. V., and Rutty, G. N. 2007b. Cutting crime: The analysis of the "uniqueness" of saw marks on bone. *International Journal of Legal Medicine*, 121, 349–357.

Schellinger, P. D., Schwab, S., Krieger, D., Fiebach, J. B., Steiner, T., Hund, E. F., Hacke, W., and Meinck, H. M. 2001. Masking of vertebral artery dissection by severe trauma to the cervical spine. *Spine*, 26, 314–319.

Simic, M., Draskovic, D., Stojiljkovic, G., Vukovic, R., and Budimlija, Z. M. 2007. The characteristics of head wounds inflicted by "humane killer" (captive-bolt gun)—A 15-year study. *Journal of Forensic Sciences*, 52, 1182–1185.

Stubblefield, P. R. 1999. Homicide or accident off the coast of Florida: Trauma analysis of mutilated human remains. *Journal of Forensic Sciences*, 44, 716–719.

Thali, M. J., Schwab, C. M., Tairi, K., Dirnhofer, R., and Vock, P. 2002. Forensic radiology with cross-section modalities: Spiral CT evaluation of a knife wound to the aorta. *Journal of Forensic Sciences*, 47, 1041–1045.

Thali, M., Yen, K., Vock, P., Ozdoba, C., Schroth, G., Sonnenschein, M., and Dirnhofer, R. 2003. Virtopsy (virtual autopsy): New horizon in forensic radiology and/or medicine. *Forensic Science International*, 136, 253–254.

Thomsen, H., Klinggraff, C. V., and Rudolph, J. 1998. Forensic aspects in "shaking trauma" of an infant. *Monatsschrift Kinderheilkunde*, 146, 875–878.

Tomczak, P. D., and Buikstra, J. E. 1999a. Analysis of blunt trauma injuries: Vertical deceleration versus horizontal deceleration injuries. *Journal of Forensic Sciences*, 44, 253–262.

Tomczak, P. D., and Buikstra, J. E. 1999b. Commentary on Tomczak PD, Buikstra JE. Analysis of blunt trauma injuries: Vertical deceleration versus horizontal deceleration injuries. Authors' response. *Journal of Forensic Sciences*, 44, 1321–1322.

Treffiletti, T. 2009. Cranial blunt force trauma and the paediatric population. *Homo—Journal of Comparative Human Biology*, 60, 290–290.

Ubelaker, D. H. 1992. Hyoid fracture and strangulation. *Journal of Forensic Sciences*, 37, 1216–1222.

Ubelaker, D. H., Owsley, D. W., Houck, M. M., Craig, E., Grant, W., Woltanski, T., Fram, R., Sandness, K., and Peerwani, N. 1995. The role of forensic anthropology in the recovery and analysis of Branch Davidian Compound victims: Recovery procedures and characteristics of the victims. *Journal of Forensic Sciences*, 40, 341–348.

Vanezis, P. 2000. The wound healing process: Forensic pathological aspects. *Medicine Science and the Law*, 40, 88–89.

Verhoff, M. A., and Karger, B. 2003. Atypical gunshot entrance wound and extensive backspatter. *International Journal of Legal Medicine*, 117, 229–231.

Weilemann, Y., Thali, M. J., Kneubuehl, B. P., and Bolliger, S. A. 2008. Correlation between skeletal trauma and energy in falls from great height detected by post-mortem multislice computed tomography (MSCT). *Forensic Science International*, 180, 81–85.

Wescott, D. J. 2006. Ontogeny of femur subtrochanteric shape in native Americans and American Blacks and Whites. *Journal of Forensic Sciences*, 51, 1240–1245.

Williams, H. 2004. Death warmed up—The agency of bodies and bones in early Anglo-Saxon cremation rites. *Journal of Material Culture*, 9, 263–291.

Wilson, E. F., Davis, J. H., Bloom, J. D., Batten, P. J., and Kamara, S. G. 1998. Homicide or suicide: The killing of suicidal persons by law enforcement officers. *Journal of Forensic Sciences*, 43, 46–52.

Xu, G. C., Ren, F., Hou, X. W., and Yuan, L. B. 2007. Application of the burned bone morphology and DNA technology in human identification. *Fa Yi Xue Za Zhi*, 23, 370–2, 379.

Yanik, A., Karaca, N., Dokgoz, H., and Sozen, S. 2003. Trauma directed to elderly: Forensic medical approach. *Forensic Science International*, 136, 242–243.

Yavuz, M. S., Asirdizer, M., Cetin, G., Balci, Y. G., and Altinkok, M. 2003. The correlation between skull fractures and intracranial lesions due to traffic accidents. *American Journal of Forensic Medicine and Pathology*, 24, 339–345.

Zaba, C., and Przybylski, Z. 2003. Traumatic amputations of body parts in victims of traffic accidents in the case material of Department of Forensic Medicine, University of Medical Sciences in Poznan and of laboratory of traffic accidents in Poznan, Institute of Forensic Expertises. *Forensic Science International*, 136, 188–189.

Zendehrouh, P., Tandon, M., Frankel, H., and Rabinovici, R. 2003. Hyoid bone fracture from a gunshot wound. *Journal of Trauma-Injury Infection and Critical Care*, 55, 1003–1003.

Zhu, B. L., Quan, L., Ishida, K., Taniguchi, M., Oritani, S., Fujita, M. Q., and Maeda, H. 2002. Longitudinal brainstem laceration associated with complex basilar skull fractures due to a fall: An autopsy case. *Forensic Science International*, 126, 40–42.

Bone Pathology

8

NICHOLAS LOCKYER
IAIN ARMSTRONG
PROF. SUE BLACK

Contents

General Introduction

Identification of the deceased from skeletal remains is a dynamic and challenging process, and each case presents with a unique array of information from which the forensic anthropologist must attempt to construct an identity profile or assist the pathologist with the diagnosis of a manner or a cause of death. The four primary biological indicators of identity (sex, age, stature and ancestry) are a reasonable starting point for the process, but the final goal of named-individual identification is significantly more difficult to achieve in the absence of additional confirmatory information (e.g., via DNA, fingerprints, or antemortem dental records). In such circumstances, secondary indicators of identity can prove to be essential and can take many forms, including circumstantial evidence, personal possessions, body modifications, trauma, anomalies, and of course pathology.

This chapter examines some aspects of pathology in relation to identification opportunities; we have chosen to adopt the true definition of the term *pathology*, meaning the "study of disease." Therefore, trauma is not considered in this section. The correct diagnosis of disease-related conditions is particularly important in the identification process, not only as a means of extracting additional information about the deceased but also because of their role as potential proxy indicators of sex, age, or indeed ethnic origin. It is also essential that the impact and alteration resulting from pathology is understood in the light of assigning primary identifiers as it is well recognized that all aspects can be compromised (e.g., the effect of many congenital skeletal conditions on accurate age evaluation).

Bone is extremely limited in the number of ways in which it can respond to changing stimuli: New bone can be added, existing bone can be removed, or a combination of both activities will most likely occur, although one will frequently predominate. As a result of these alterations, the bone will change either in its size or in its shape or appearance; although the patterns may be largely predictable and even definitively diagnostic, there can be considerable ambiguity in presentation. For example, degenerative joint disease results in formation of new bone, extensive bone loss, and alteration to the shape of the bone. Similarly, metastatic carcinomas can result in bone addition, bone loss, and alteration of bone shape, but clearly the pathologies are not equivalent and would not be confused regarding their presentation. Therefore, it is essential that a pathology-specific signature or pattern of manifestation is recognized if possible for each condition to permit a differential diagnosis. To achieve this might require a number of aspects to be examined and recorded, including

- The macroscopic appearance of the bone
- The microscopic appearance of the bone

- The radiographic appearance of the bone
- The proportion of bone loss to bone formation
- The type of bone formed
- Local, regional, or whole-body manifestation of the condition
- Location of the condition within each bone
- Differential responses in different body regions
- Alteration to the size and shape of the bone
- The biological profile of the individual and so on

The diagnosis of the pathology is critical to an accurate evaluation of its significance, relevance, and discriminatory capacity, and this is equally true whether examining material of archaeological or recent provenance. Despite significant common ground, the fields of clinical pathology and paleopathology are distinct in terms of both subjects/patients and practitioners, but they are further segregated through the dichotomous nature of publishing sources (e.g., journals), such that it is not uncommon for the two worlds to overlap by little more than an acknowledged courtesy in passing. However, the work of the forensic anthropologist requires that these two worlds coexist comfortably as the skeletal appearance of pathology may be most clearly illustrated in the historical world, but its relevance to, and prevalence in, the modern world must be clearly understood to facilitate appropriate forensic interpretation. The distinction between the historical deceased and the more recent victim is really little more than a simple matter of time, and the forensic anthropologists must be comfortable to work on both sides of this theoretical and artificial continuous chronological barrier; therefore, they must be equally comfortable to source their information from the research of the clinician and the osteoarchaeologist and thereby occupy their own niche firmly between the two. This chapter aims to combine these somewhat disparate but inextricably related disciplines through the discussion of selected pathologies that are relevant to both fields and therefore common to the forensic anthropologist.

To remain realistic, though, the issue of the "osteological paradox" must be borne in mind. In an archaeological context, it highlights the fact that the skeletal remains found represent a small and likely biased proportion of a wider population. Therefore, calculating the incidence and prevalence of a condition within a past community can be somewhat problematic, so the maxim must hold that "the absence of evidence is not evidence of absence." From a more contemporary perspective, pathologies with a skeletal manifestation represent a minority of the potential clinical conditions encountered in the deceased and convey only a static snapshot of a dynamic event. However, in the archaeological specimen, they may represent the only manifestation of any clinical condition. A persistent challenge to the paleopathologist is that the skeletal material is frequently reduced to its mineral ground substance and is free of much organic component (collagen), cells (osteoblasts, osteoclasts), and associated soft tissues, all of which provide invaluable clues to the clinical pathologist. In addition, many perimortem and taphonomic alterations, such as trauma, animal gnawing, or various physiochemical alterations, can leave misleading traces, which may be difficult to differentiate from those that occurred during life. Further, the early stages of a disease may be more difficult to interpret than the final or chronic stages of its manifestation and may be more likely to be misdiagnosed. Therefore, there are many issues to be taken into consideration by a forensic anthropologist in the differential diagnosis of pathology.

It would be impossible, in a single chapter, to cover every condition reported in the past decade in both the clinical and archaeological literature, so we have selected topics for consideration based on the presence of a well-defined and significant volume of complementary work in both historical and modern sources. It is accepted that many conditions have not been included. Interestingly, both the paleopathology and the clinical pathology literature tend to fall into three types of publication: the descriptive case report; population incidence, epidemiology, and management; and, more recently, bibliometric analyses. As this must also by necessity be a lengthy chapter, we have chosen not to reference within the text but to provide a cross-disciplinary bibliography that is separated into sections at the conclusion of this chapter as it has been considered that this might be a more useful resource for assisting future literature searches.

Developmental, Growth-Related, Congenital, and Genetic Conditions

While at first glance perhaps an odd combination, this categorization of developmental, growth-related, congenital, and genetic conditions represents conditions that fundamentally present from an early age, are not necessarily in themselves fatal in their progression, but leave sufficient markers to witness a less-than-optimal period of development. Infant mortality is of course an issue of major concern in relation to the interpretation of both a cemetery population and within a current community, where intervention might offer an improvement in quality of life and enhance survival. Much of the literature in this category seems to refer to descriptive single-case presentations, whether historical or clinical, and their value is in the photographic or radiographic recording of the condition so that it may be recognized in other instances.

For example, limb deficiencies resulting in amelia, phocomelia, hypoplasias, and the like are important identifiers as they represent a well-defined alteration to the normal body form that is not a common occurrence and is strongly individualistic. As a result, when they arise in the archaeological literature, they tend to receive a high level of attention, but they tend to be buried deeper in the clinical literature, in which they are often consigned to specific and sometimes esoteric publications.

The clinical literature often permits a full history of the patient; therefore, if identification can be achieved in forensic anthropology, there is a significant opportunity to relate the patient presentations to the dry bone appearance. When this occurs, it is strong confirmation of a correct diagnosis in archaeological cases. For example, patients presenting with a primary condition (such as cerebral palsy) that is not bone specific but encompasses a group of disorders that are fundamentally neurological in origin, strengthen a differential diagnosis in the absence of primary skeletal indicators of the condition. This condition has an impact on quality of life and on longevity. As a secondary source skeletal indicator, it is not highly diagnostic; therefore, the likelihood of identifying the condition from skeletal remains alone is unlikely. However, this does not negate the importance of studying the manifestations of the condition as if the missing individual is known to suffer from the condition; then, the anthropologist is heightened to the likely secondary musculoskeletal effects that could be anticipated should skeletal remains be found. An age assessment would also require full cognizance of the likely retardation in epiphyseal fusion, and its known incidence within a current population (approximately 800,000 in the United States) will permit the calculation of likelihood ratios.

A recent case undertaken by Sue Black, one of the chapter's authors, recognized the presence of iliac horns on the gluteal surface of both innominates in a decomposed young male. The clinician was impressed that a forensic anthropologist had heard of onycho-osteodysplasia (nail-patella syndrome), let alone could diagnose it and know that it was an autosomal dominant condition. This, however, typifies the necessary knowledge required to be held by the forensic anthropologist that must be gleaned from both past and present literature and applied for human identification.

As most of the articles relating to this grouping tend to represent either single cases or a summary of a population or cemetery, there is little to be inferred regarding a trend in research as publication is directed by encounter.

Spondylolysis and Spondylolisthesis

Spondylolysis is a defect in the interarticular region of the vertebral hemineural arch, is almost invariably restricted to the lower lumbar region, and is alleged to be unique to the human. The majority of texts view it as an occupation- or activity-related condition and relate it to the onset of upright posture and subsequent habitual activities, which receives considerable attention in relation to athletes. However, there is still an underlying link to a genetic predisposition, so it may not be an exclusively stress- or fatigue-related failure. It is considered that around 5–6% of European individuals show some degree of spondylolytic defect, with a significantly increased incidence in athletes, particularly cricketers, divers, and footballers. While it is a defect that can cause pain and discomfort, it is when this condition is bilateral and results in an anterior slippage of the affected vertebral body (spondylolisthesis) that the most significant damage occurs. Slippage, when it occurs, is not gradual but episodic in nature, and occurrence can be very high in some populations (e.g., the Inuit).

The Wiltse classification system recognizes five different types of spondylolisthesis: dysplastic, isthmic, degenerative, traumatic, and pathologic. Dysplastic spondylolisthesis is rare and a true congenital defect that is most frequently associated with significant neurological complications in the young child. Isthmic spondylolisthesis is probably the most common manifestation and is most frequently detected after the age of 6 years. Many do not become symptomatic other than displaying lower back pain, which becomes more prevalent with increasing age. Degenerative spondylolisthesis is most frequent with advancing age and generally develops in alliance with osteoarthritic change. Traumatic and pathologic spondylolisthesis are rare, but the former has a higher incidence in athletes, and the latter tends to be associated with certain conditions, including metastatic tumors, tuberculosis, and Paget's disease. The principal symptom is low back pain, often with muscle tightness, stiffness, and localized tenderness concomitant with a change in normal gait. Treatment will depend on the presentation and pain scale exhibited by the patient. Laminar fusion is undertaken, as is reduction using pedicular screws; success in pain relief is variable.

The volume of literature relating to this subject is polarized in both the clinical and paleopathological journals. The latter tend to concentrate on single cases or prevalence within a well-defined population group. The clinical literature, on the other hand, naturally displays a high incidence of anatomy-related information, outcomes of spinal surgery, and incidence levels within well-defined groups (e.g., high-level athletes). There is no evidence that the incidence of the condition is in decline, and detection is largely as a result of presentation by the patient. Although physiotherapy techniques are advocated, there seems little alternative for the intensive cases other than surgery; therefore, the presence of pedicle screws or other plating mechanisms is relevant for identification purposes. As most incidences of spondylolysis are asymptomatic, this will have little relevance to the forensic anthropologist unless antemortem radiographs are present for comparison but will provide a likely diagnosis of physical activities during life.

Osteoarthritis, Degenerative Joint Disease, and Osteoporosis

Osteoarthritis (OA), degenerative joint disease (DJD), and osteoporosis all have a strong relationship with advancing age and are therefore conditions that are of similar relevance to both historical and modern populations. Although some authors have identified OA and DJD as being appropriate to be grouped together, many epidemiologists suggest that they should remain separate. Osteoarthritis and DJD result in the most frequent musculoskeletal disorders in contemporary populations, affecting more than 27 million people in the United States alone. It is predicted that by 2030, 25% of the adult U.S. population (67 million) will have physician-diagnosed arthritis at an annual aggregate health expenditure of $186 billion. In the United Kingdom, this disease relates to 8.5 million sufferers and accounts for 25% of all visits to primary care practitioners. With an ever-increasing ageing population, this is a pathological condition that is high on the political agenda due to its cost and the implications for the pharmaceutical industry. Interestingly, there has been a decrease in the number of publications related to this subject in the archaeological literature that bears no resemblance to the importance of this subject to the modern clinician.

Many etiologies have been attributed to OA and DJD and include age, body mass index, activity, genetics, and others, but there is no doubt that it is a multifactorial condition. The rise in genetic information pertaining to the condition has been significant, with many epidemiological investigations centering on familial studies and the ubiquitous twins studies. There is no doubt that there is a genetic link to OA and DJD, but much work still remains to be undertaken as there is evidence that the influence is not evenly dispersed throughout the body, with areas such as the vertebral column and hips having the highest heritability estimates and the hand and knee being significantly lower. Interestingly, these molecular studies seem to suggest that there is little or no heritability regarding presence or absence of the conditions, but genetic predisposition affects the severity of the manifestation. It has also been shown that estrogen has an important effect on the progression of the disease; thus, there is a suggestion of a sex bias in terms of heritability.

Repeated activity (e.g., farming or elite athletics) has frequently been linked to later presentations of OA and DJD, but confirmation of this still remains contentious. What is clear is that when extensive activity is linked to being overweight, then the onset and severity of the conditions are earlier and more severe; that is, heavier people with a greater body mass index have more severe OA than lighter people. A significant amount of work, particularly in relation to molecular investigation of the disease, is emerging from China and the Far East regarding who are most affected by the medical burden (financial and patient) resulting from increased longevity.

Osteoporosis is best defined as an imbalance between excessive bone loss and insufficient bone replacement; as a result, mechanical failure is likely, which presents as fractures, often from limited impact due to the rarefaction of the bone. These fractures are most common in the vertebral column, in the neck of the femur, and at the distal radius. Like OA and DJD, it is a major issue for public health management and affects over 55% of Americans aged 50 and above; of these, approximately 80% are women. It is estimated that worldwide, 1 in 3 women and 1 in 12 men over the age of 50 have clinical osteoporosis; this is set to increase as the population continues to achieve greater longevity. The pathogenesis is well understood, and the contributor factors regarding etiology are also well defined. There is no cure, but treatments such as bisphosphonates and estrogen analogues are clearly defined within the literature as having inhibitory effects. Mimicking the publication pattern for OA and DJD, there is limited literature on this condition from the past decade in the archaeological field, but literature from clinical investigations is extensive.

Within the last decade, understanding of the degenerative pathway of osteoporosis has risen exponentially, paralleling the evolution of high-resolution imaging technology. The ability to quantify architectural parameters accurately has allowed researchers to observe reductions in the thickness of trabeculae as well as a loss of natural trabecular anisotropy. In addition, the platelike trabeculae, which are instrumental in defining the elastic modulus of bone and consequently its compressive strength, have been shown to perforate, adopting a more rodlike structure, consequently reducing bone strength and increasing the risk of fracture.

Geographic patterns in the incidence of osteoporosis were observed. For example, Caucasian populations showed the highest incidence of osteoporotic fractures, Negroid populations showed the lowest incidence, with Asians showing an intermediate incidence. In both sexes, the incidence of osteoporotic fractures increased exponentially with advancing age.

Diffuse Idiopathic Skeletal Hyperostosis and Ankylosing Spondylitis

Diffuse idiopathic skeletal hyperostosis (DISH), also known as Forestier's disease, is a form of degenerative arthritis characterized by flowing calcification across adjacent vertebral bodies, yet the disk spaces remain unaffected. It is most common in the thoracic region of the column; unlike typical degenerative arthritis, it is also associated with inflammation (tendinitis) and calcification of tendons at their attachment points to bone. This can lead to the formation of bone spurs, which is a common nonvertebral symptom of DISH. The condition has an unknown etiology but is clearly most prevalent in the elderly; interestingly, in the archaeological literature it has been associated with individuals of higher social status. The clinical literature suggests a strong link between body mass index, Type II diabetes, and DISH, perhaps due to insulin or insulin-like growth factors, which promote new bone growth.

In 2000, according to the World Health Organization (WHO), at least 171 million people worldwide suffered from diabetes; this equates to 2.8% of the population, and by 2030 it is expected that the incidence will almost double. Type II diabetes is most common in developed countries and reflects urbanization and lifestyle changes, particularly in relation to a Western-type diet. It is estimated that the condition costs the United States over $132 billion per year. The prevalence of diabetes mellitus increases with age, and the number of older persons with diabetes is expected to grow as the elderly population increases in number. Indigenous populations in first-world countries have a higher prevalence than their corresponding nonindigenous populations. In Australia, for example, the age-standardized prevalence of self-reported diabetes in indigenous Australians is almost four times that of nonindigenous Australians.

Therefore, for the forensic anthropologist, the diagnosis of DISH or ankylosing spondylitis may have significant implications for the development of the profile of the deceased.

Sinusitis, Mastoiditis, and Conditions Related to the Ear, Nose, and Throat

The importance of clean air to the modern world in terms of health and mortality is well recognized. Indeed, WHO attributes chronic respiratory disease as one of the most common causes of morbidity and mortality, with over 1.5 million deaths every year caused by respiratory infections arising from environmental pollutants and irritants. A mass fatality event occurred in early December 1952 in London when over 4,000 people died as a result of a 4-day weather situation, and as many as 12,000 would meet a premature death from the Great London Smog of 1952. An anticyclone settled over a windless London on December 4, causing cold air to be trapped. To keep warm, a significant increase in the burning of coal occurred, which served to pollute the already-stagnant air. Most of the victims were young, elderly, or already had respiratory weaknesses, and most deaths occurred due to hypoxia and respiratory infections.

Infections of the respiratory tract, in particular the upper component (ear, nose, and throat [ENT]) have received some attention in osteoarchaeological literature, most frequently as single-case studies. This manifests as communications relating to otitis media, mastoiditis, or sinusitis. In preantibiotic times, these infections could spread directly to endocranial complications, including meningitis, abscesses, or alteration to the venous sinuses. Even today, acute otitis media is recognized as one of the most common clinical conditions, and although largely controlled in the West, frequencies of up to 18% have been reported for countries such as Rwanda.

Tuberculosis (and Leprosy)

Tuberculosis (TB) is a chronic, necrotizing, granulomatous bacterial infection caused by the *Mycobacterium tuberculosis* (MTB) complex: *M. tuberculosis, M. canettii, M. microtia, M. bovis, M. caprae,* and *M. africanum.* Of these, *Mycobacterium tuberculosis* is the most frequent source of infection for humans. It is transmitted by infection from droplets and so is passed from person to person. It is inextricably linked to the complexity of human culture and social change, including agricultural practices, animal husbandry, sedentism, urbanization, and overcrowding and is effectively a disease dependent on population density.

Throughout history, it has been known under many names, including stuma, scrofula, phthisis, consumption, *Lupus vulgaris,* and Pott's disease. Following the 17th century, it rose to epidemic proportions; 20% of all deaths in London in 1667 were due to TB. Following the industrial revolution, there was another peak toward the end of the 18th century and into the beginning of the 19th century.

The bacterial agent was identified in 1882, and the first vaccine for TB was developed at the Pasteur Institute and first used on humans in 1921. The vaccine is prepared from a strain of the attenuated (weakened) live bovine tuberculosis bacillus; TB control programs quickly adopted the BCG (Bacillus Calmette-Guérin) as an effective control mechanism especially for infants. Although mass vaccination did not start until after World War II, according to WHO, this is the most frequently used vaccine worldwide, with 85% of infants in 172 countries immunized in 1993. The protective efficacy of the BCG vaccine is in excess of 80% for children, but this is significantly reduced if it is introduced too late in adolescence or in the adult.

The BCG vaccine was so successful that a well-respected medical historian announced: "Tuberculosis is now a conquered disease in the British Isles and the rest of the industrialized world," (Smith 1998: 266). It was predicted that by the middle to the end of the 20th century it would be eradicated, but that was not to be as it has shown a marked resurgence in recent years, largely due to drug-resistant strains, immune suppression regarding HIV, and lack of resources in the developing world. In 2006, there were 9.2 million new cases reported (7.4 million of these in Asia and sub-Saharan Africa), and 1.7 million deaths occurred globally, mostly in the developing world. London accounts for half of the national burden of TB in the United Kingdom today, and its incidence has doubled in the last 15 years. Around 75% of those with TB were born outside the United Kingdom, and 86% of these individuals are from ethnic minority groups—one-third from Africa and one-third from the Indian subcontinent. Many of the affected are homeless, incarcerated, drug or alcohol dependent, and immune suppressed.

Along with HIV and malaria, WHO recognizes TB as one of the primary diseases of poverty. It is believed that roughly one-third of the population of the world has been infected with *M. tuberculosis*. It is transmitted via respiratory infection, but its symptoms can manifest in any organ of the body, including the skeleton. Once transmitted, the pathogen remains dormant in the host for many days, if not weeks, months, or indeed for life. It takes at least 1 year for an individual who has been exposed to the bacterium to convert from a negative to a positive tuberculin reaction. Clinical symptoms of the infection appear gradually over a period of months or years but generally manifest as a malaise, anorexia, fever, night sweats, and most obviously a mucoid or purulent cough that may contain flecks of blood. In European populations, about 30% of people exposed to the bacilli become infected, but of these only 10% will develop the active disease, and 90% will remain disease free. It is vital therefore that the forensic anthropologist is aware of possible pathogen transmission in the postmortem room.

TB is primarily a respiratory infection, and its skeletal manifestations are almost certainly representative of hematogenous spread of infection. However, these occur in a minority of instances, with only some 5–7% showing bone changes.

An interesting discordance has arisen between the paleopathology and the clinical literature in relation to manifestation of the condition on the visceral rib surfaces. The archaeological literature is dominated by descriptions of destructive lesions and periosteal reaction on the inner surface of the ribs, with reference also made to vertebral and large synovial joint involvement in the limbs. While the clinical literature advises on the skeletal and joint involvement, little attention is paid to any importance of rib lesions. It has been suggested that the imaging modalities used by the clinician are of insufficient resolution to detect these periosteal alterations, which are often surface based, and so perhaps the incidence of TB in the ribs has been markedly underestimated by clinicians. However, the clinicians stated that differential diagnosis in the ribs should be based on lytic changes in agreement with the hematogenous spread of the infection; they therefore would expect little or no reactive bone regeneration. Recent paleopathological research has examined the incidence of rib lesions in juveniles known to have died following TB and compared the incidence with those not recorded as dying of the infection. The results suggested that rib lesions were more common in the known TB sufferers, but with nearly one-third of the population having been infected with TB, this is still insufficient to finally quell the disagreement between the two disciplines, so perhaps care is still required in a diagnosis.

The literature on this infection is still active, and with an infection that is still on the rise, despite an effective vaccine, there is likely to be continued debate, especially as there is still much that is not well understood (e.g., the origin and evolution of the pathogen, its host-pathogen interaction, and its virulence). With an increased involvement in genetic diagnosis of the condition, this may ultimately solve the debate over the origin of rib lesions.

Leprosy is also mentioned here as it also a mycobacterial infection that delineates global poverty. Although generally thought of as a disease of the past, and the paleopathological literature tends to present single-case studies, it is very much a condition of the modern world. It is thought to affect over 2 million people worldwide, with India presenting over 50% of the total global cases. Brazil is listed as the country with the second-highest incidence and Burma as the third. While we may think that a disease has been assigned to the annals of human history, the forensic anthropologist must be conscious that it still exists in the modern world, and although it may be rare to experience a presentation of this condition in a home mortuary, those who work in disaster victim identification (DVI) and mass fatality investigations need to be aware of the epidemiology of conditions worldwide.

Brucellosis

Brucellosis has been included here briefly because of its potential diagnostic confusion with tuberculosis and staphylococcic spondylitis. Brucellosis is caused by infection from a highly contagious epizoonosis belonging to the genus *Brucella*. Until the 19th century, this disease was reported to be endemic only to the Mediterranean basin, but it is highly contagious and therefore open to transmission via both animal and human relocation and displacement. Although there are nine known different species of *Brucella*, infection in the human is largely from the *B. melitensis* strain—gram-negative, non-spore-forming, non-motile facultative anaerobes that act as intracellular parasites. Human infection is primarily caused by ingesting unpasteurized milk or soft cheese or through consumption of meat from an infected animal. However, it is also recognized as a significant occupational farming disease that is contracted through prolonged interaction with infected animals, most frequently goats.

The symptoms of this infection are fever, sweating, weakness, anemia, and musculoskeletal pain. Despite being a chronic infection of the lungs and other body tissues, lesions of the skeleton are frequent via a hematogenous route. Skeletal involvement varies from 2% to 70%, and 20–80% of patients experience osteoarticular symptoms. Osteoarticular localizations are common in this condition, and they are hematogenic in origin, with the lumbar vertebral bodies most commonly involved, where there is erosion of the upper anterior corner. Sacroiliitis is also a common occurrence in this condition with a higher prevalence evident in males. Unlike TB, the pattern of lesions reported in the paleopathological literature mirrors perfectly those referred to in the clinical literature, and there is no mention of the source of rib lesions in either body of literature.

Prevalence is still high in the Mediterranean countries, where it was first encountered, and it is present on all continents, although most new reports originate from North Africa and the Middle East. It is reported to affect half a million new people every year, and although recognized in the historical literature, it receives little attention, although scientific interest has recently been heightened due to its unexpected reaction to blue light deprivation.

Treponemal Diseases

The treponemal diseases are caused by a spirochetal bacterium: *Tremonema pallidum*. It presents in four recognized conditions: syphilis (*T. pallidum pallidum*), yaws (*T. palladium pertenue*), pinta (*T. pallidum carateum*), and bejel (*T. pallidum endemicum*). Although syphilis is perhaps the best studied of these conditions, the others are still extant, with yaws found predominantly in South America, Africa, and Asia; Pinta in Mexico and Central and South America; and Bejel in the eastern Mediterranean and West Africa.

The paleopathological literature tends to report the existence of these conditions as single cases, but syphilis attracts a little more attention not only because of its sexually transmitted etiology but also because of its debate in history with regard to its introduction into the New World. Although syphilis is readily cured through simple antibiotics such as penicillin, it is somewhat surprising to find that its incidence has started to rise recently in the United Kingdom, the United States, Europe, and Australia. The clinical literature and epidemiological studies have related this recent rise to an increase in male-to-male unprotected sexual intercourse, both anal and oral. It is reported that in the last decade, the incidence of male-to-male infection rate has risen by 50%.

Rickets

Rickets (and osteomalacia in the adult) is caused by a lack of vitamin D, either due to malnutrition or malabsorption. It is a disease of infancy and childhood and is characterized by porosity and deformity of inadequately mineralized bone. Although vitamin D can be ingested through food sources, the majority is synthesized by the action of ultraviolet light on the stratum basale of the skin. Indeed, vitamin D is not a vitamin but was misclassified; it is really a prohormone that is essential for the metabolism of calcium. Sufficient vitamin D can be produced in a light-skinned person through 15 minutes of skin exposure to the sun two or three times a week. The darker the skin of the individual, the higher the concentration of melanin in the stratum basale and the more difficult it is for the required intensity of ultraviolet light radiation to be able to produce the required levels of vitamin D in a dark-skinned person, who will require longer exposure to the sun or exposure to a higher level of UV radiation. This forms the basis of the clinical literature pertaining to vitamin D deficiency, rickets, and osteomalacia.

This condition is well documented in the paleopathology literature, and most information is represented by single-case studies. However, there is some evidence of an increasing number of studies that address population levels and have a wider biocultural approach to the disease. In the archaeological literature, the presence of rickets is most frequently identified as a proxy for poor diet and unhealthy living conditions. While the long limb bones are most frequently affected in the child, the effects on the growing female pelvis at puberty can lead to rachitic pelvis, which poses potential obstetric problems in later years. The child commonly presents clinically with bowed legs and rachitic rosary calcifications at the costochondral junctions, which are often visible under the skin. In the Asian, Afro-Caribbean, and Middle Eastern populations, the prevalence of rickets can be as high as 1 in every 100 children. Australian authorities have reported a doubling of cases in 2002/2003 in Sydney, and this is attributed to recent Indian immigrants. This is a major health concern, and there has been a call to screen all immigrant families to detect and manage this potentially debilitating condition.

The incidence is also rising within inner cities in the United Kingdom. In particular, in the Asian communities in the north of England and into Scotland, there is a correlation between the fewer hours of sunlight, the darker skin of the ethnic group, and the tendency to cover more of the skin surface with clothing.

Scurvy

Scurvy was the scourge of historical maritime exploration and the limiting factor for the success of many seafaring adventures. The human cannot synthesize its own vitamin C and must source it from dietary intake, including citrus fruits, green vegetables, and fish. Scurvy is a deficiency in ascorbic acid or vitamin C, and although labeled as "forgotten but not gone" in the developed world, it is not considered to be a condition worthy of current relevance in the developed world. At a biomolecular level, vitamin C acts to convert proline to hydroxyproline, an instrumental amino acid in the production of the major organic component of bone: collagen. Consequently, the impairment of collagen production results in defective osteoid formation as well as weakening of the blood vessels, which leads to the characteristic hemorrhaging associated with scurvy.

It may require several months of vitamin C deprivation for scurvy to become symptomatic in an adult; however, the condition will develop much more rapidly in the child as a result of elevated growth demands and the high rate of connective tissue turnover. Scurvy typically manifests itself in the growth plate of bones, resulting in metaphyseal fractures, which often unite with the epiphysis abnormally. Continued vitamin C deficiency will result in death.

There is a dichotomous attitude toward scurvy; it remains a prevalent threat in both the developing and the developed world, often because of dietary restrictions and prevention awareness. This can be attributed mainly to the rare occurrence of diseases secondary to nutritional deficiencies within the "normal population." In a clinical context, this can have severe consequences as it may result in a delayed diagnosis, despite the patient presenting typical symptoms. However, there appears to be a changing attitude, particularly within the medical literature, with more and more case studies published in the last decade often in relation to the elderly and the institutionalized, and it is often linked to a history of alcoholism or in the young associated with either diminished mental capacity or faddy diets or eating disorders. The last major documented outbreak of scurvy was in Afghanistan in 2002, caused by a combination of severe drought and war.

In an archaeological context, it is suggested that many incidents of scurvy go undiagnosed due to overlapping symptoms with more familiar diseases, such as anemia and infection. For example, scurvy causes bleeding in the roof of the orbits, which results in new bone formation in this area, a symptom that is also characteristic of cribra orbitalis. The diagnosis of scurvy relies heavily on cranial bones, particularly the greater wing of the sphenoid, which may not necessarily be recovered intact. It is suggested that the lack of reported cases of scurvy in past populations may be due to lack of knowledge of its manifestations rather than the paucity of its occurrence. Therefore, knowledge of how scurvy manifests throughout the entire skeleton will aid in future diagnosis of the condition throughout both archaeological and recent remains. This is a recurring theme within the last decade, and with increasing research within this field, a greater understanding of the prevalence of the disease in past populations may develop.

Vascular Conditions and Anemia

Logically, the discussion turns from scurvy, which manifests as hemorrhaging, to a group of conditions that are associated with vascular or hematological pathology. One of the most common symptoms (because it is not a disease) to be reported in the historical literature is the relationship between anemia and porotic hyperostosis and cribra orbitalia. There is much recent discussion that suggests that the two are not necessarily representative of the same condition, or indeed that it is a simple relationship. Some authors suggested that iron-deficient anemia does not provide a reasonable physiological explanation for either porotic hyperostosis or cribra orbitalia. Instead, they argued that they are a result of megaloblastic anemia acquired by nursing infants through the synergistic effects of reduced vitamin B_{12} reserves and linked this to aspects of malnutrition and poor sanitation. Much of the archaeological literature suggests that subperiosteal bleeding, resulting in ossified hematomas, caused by a codeficiency of vitamins C and B_{12} explain the presence of these bone changes. It is true that the level of reporting of these manifestations is high in the paleopathological literature, indicating that it is a highly prevalent condition that is common in the juvenile, but trying to wean osteologists away from the comfortable bond between cribra and iron deficiency anemia takes some persuasion.

Vitamin B_{12} cannot be synthesized by the human, and its absence is often referred to as pernicious anemia. In the developing world, this deficiency is widespread, with a global incidence of between 500 and 600 million people, particularly located in Africa, India, and South and Central America. This has been attributed to low levels of animal protein in the diet, increased bacterial load due to poor sanitation, unprocessed or unsterilized food, and other sources of dietary contamination, which can lead to pathogen-related malabsorption issues. Deficiency of B_{12} is common in the elderly as absorption capability is decreased, and it is also common among vegetarians and vegans who do not take B_{12} supplements.

Anemias fall into two broad categories: acquired and genetic. The latter of these is more rare but is typified by thalassemia and sicklemia, including sickle cell disease (SCD) and sickle cell trait (SCT). Thalassemia is an autosomal recessive blood disease that is most prevalent in individuals from Mediterranean countries and areas with a humid climate in which malaria is endemic. It is alleged that the Maldives has the highest incidence of thalassemia in the world, with a carrier rate of close to 18%.

There are many conditions, some already mentioned, that manifest through transportation and interaction with the vascular system, but common in old age are the symptoms displayed by chronic venous insufficiency (CVI). This often results from incompetent venous valves and can occur after deep vein thrombosis (DVT) and phlebitis. In an ageing population, there are many physiological as well as anatomical factors that a forensic anthropologist must bear in mind when attempting any form of a pathological diagnosis.

Neoplasm

Neoplasm is a term that is used interchangeably with the term *tumor,* which tends to have a greater understanding of meaning with the general public.

A neoplasm is an abnormal cellular proliferation of new tissue that initiates either benign or malignant growth. Benign neoplasms include fibroids, melanocyte nevi, and, for example, button osteoma, around which there is now some controversy. These growths will not develop into a cancer and therefore are viewed as mild and largely nonprogressive or life-threatening conditions. However, malignant neoplasms (cancer) may be life threatening as they invade and destroy surrounding tissues and have the ability to transfer to other locations within the body, usually via the lymphatic or vascular systems, and therefore metastasize.

Due to the diagnostic and prognostic importance of particularly malignant neoplasms, there has been much interest in outlining the history of various conditions throughout archaeological specimens and relating them to modern clinical manifestations. While earlier research might have claimed that malignant neoplasms are more of a symptom due to the modern age, it is now largely realized that the age profile in relation to the manifestation of these conditions may well be a significant factor in their apparent underrepresentation in human history. While some neoplasms are readily identified, the majority cause considerable classification problems for clinicians, histopathologists, and paleoanthropologists alike. Reports from the historical literature tend to be based on single-case histories, and a diagnostic confirmation is rarely verified. This is not a new phenomenon, although as Hooton (1930: 306) noted in the early part of the last century, "We shall never be able to acquire any satisfactory basis for study of palaeopathology until clinical pathologists and anatomists cooperate in the preservation of skeletal material of known clinical history."

Heterotopic Calcifications

No review, however brief, of pathological conditions reported in the past decade would be complete without a section on heterotopic calcification. This represents those calcified features that are an anomaly perhaps as a result of a clinical condition or injury and usually require some element of investigative research to determine their identity. These can range from the rare case of a lithopedion to the more common phleboliths. They tend to be presented as single-case reports and are often considered anecdotal publications or the unusual and absurd. Therefore, rather than try to make sense of a topic that is often rather random, we simply offer a sample of the articles that may be consulted on this topic.

Conclusion

There are a number of trends in various areas relating to skeletal pathology that have either emerged or have continued to be explored over the last decade. It is an important area of biological identity and can provide an insight into the life history of an individual. The uncertainty surrounding the interpretation of skeletal pathologies and the lack of significant populational studies has led to the exclusion of skeletal pathology from many recent texts. However, its use in forensic anthropology has been vindicated on a number of occasions, with a key example a case report published in the *American Journal of Forensic Medicine and Pathology* relating to the identification of a Croatian war victim from an untreated shoulder dislocation (Petrovecki et al. 2008: 253).

With the advent of more accurate noninvasive imaging methods, skeletal pathologies present in modern populations can be documented far more easily than before. This in turn contributes to the move away from individual case studies and toward a more population-based field of study. It is also important that efforts continue to enforce the collaboration between areas of medicolegal and osteoarchaeological research.

Disease patterns are constantly changing as different drug-resistant strains develop or as population immunity diminishes. It is important that these trends are monitored as they can give an indication regarding the geographical or temporal origins of an individual. The diseases discussed each show a trend toward an increased incidence, although in different demographics. However, the general trend is toward a decreased incidence of severe skeletal manifestations of such diseases due to better health care. This is why it is important that both imaging techniques and dry bone studies are used to detect the more subtle skeletal lesions associated with disease processes. Further, in the modern world where human migration, legal and trafficked, is on the increase, there is a heavy burden of pathology awareness placed on the shoulders of the forensic anthropologist.

Bibliography

General

Adler, C. P. (2000). *Bone diseases. Macroscopic, histological and radiological diagnosis of structural changes in the skeleton.* Springer, Heidelberg.

Armelagos, G. J., and van Gerven, D. P. (2003). A century of skeletal biology and palaeopathology: contrasts, contradictions and conflicts. *American Anthropologist* 105: 53–64.

Black, S. M. (2005). Bone pathology and antemortem trauma in forensic cases. In *Encyclopedia of forensic and legal medicine* (Ed. Payne-James, J.). Elsevier, London.

Black, S. M., Walker, G., Hackman, S., and Books, C. (2010). *Disaster victim identification: The practitioner's guide.* Dundee University Press, Dundee, Scotland.

Blau, S., and Ubelaker, D. H. (2009). *Handbook of forensic anthropology and archaeology.* World Archaeological Congress Series, New York.

Cunha, E. (2006). Pathology as a factor of personal identity in forensic anthropology. In *Forensic anthropology and medicine: Complementary sciences from recovery to cause of death* (Eds. Schmitt, A., Cunha, E., and Pinhero, J.). Humana Press, Totowa, NJ.

Greenblatt, C., and Spigelman, M. (2003). *Emerging pathogens: Archaeology, ecology and evolution of infectious diseases.* Oxford University Press, Oxford, UK.

Hens, S. M., and Godde, K. (2008). Skeletal biology past and present: Are we moving in the right direction? *American Journal of Physical Anthropology* 137: 234–239.

Katzenberg, A., and Saunders, S. (2001). *Biological anthropology of the human skeleton.* Wiley-Liss, New York.

Mays, S. (2010). Human osteoarchaeology in the UK 2001–2007: A bibliometric perspective. *International Journal of Osteoarchaeology* 20: 192–204.

Mays, S., and Pinhasi, R. (2008). *Advances in human palaeopathology.* Wiley, Chichester, UK.

Ortner, D. (2003). *Identification of pathological conditions in human skeletal remains* (2nd ed.). Academic Press, New York.

Park, V. M., Roberts, C. A., and Jakob, T. (2009). Palaeopathology in Britain: A critical analysis of publications with the aim of exploring recent trends (1997–2006). *International Journal of Osteoarchaeology* doi: 10.1002/oa.1068.

Petrovecki, V., Salopek, D., Topic, I., and Marusic, A. (2008). Chronic unreduced anterior shoulder dislocation: application of anatomy to forensic identification. *American Journal of Forensic Medicine & Pathology* 29: 89–91.

Resnick, D. (2002). *Diagnosis of bone and joint disorders* (4th ed.). Saunders, Philadelphia.

Roberts, C. A., and Cox, M. (2003). *Health and disease in Britain.* Sutton, Stroud, UK.

Roberts, C., and Manchester, K. (2005). *The archaeology of disease* (3rd ed.). Sutton, Gloucester, UK.

Stojanowski, C. M., and Buikstra, J. E. (2005). Research trends in human osteology: A content analysis of papers published in the *American Journal of Physical Anthropology* 128: 98–109.

Wood, J. W., Milner, G. R., Harpending, H. C., and Weiss, K. M. (1992). The osteological paradox. *Current Anthropology* 33: 343–370.

Developmental, Growth-Related, Congenital, and Genetic Conditions

Arora, A. S., and Chung, K. C. (2006). Otto W. Madelung and the recognition of Madelung's deformity. *Journal of Hand Surgery* 31A: 177–182.

Bourbou, C. (2001). Infant mortality: The complexity of it all! *Eulimene* 2: 187–203.

Brooks, T. J. (2001). Madelung deformity in a collegiate gymnast: A case report. *Journal of Athletic Training* 36: 170–173.

Canci, A., Marini, E., Mulliri, G., Usai, E., Vacca, L., Floris, G., and Borgognini Tarli, S. M. (2002). A case of Madelung's deformity in a skeleton from Nuragic Sardinia. *International Journal of Osteoarchaeology* 12: 173–177.

Case, D. T., Hill, R. J., Merbs, C. F., and Fong, M. (2006). Polydactyly in the prehistoric American southwest. *International Journal of Osteoarchaeology* 16: 221–235.

Cormier-Daire, V., Chauvet, M. L., Lyonnet, S., Briard, M. L., Munnich, A., and Le Merrer, M. (2000). Genitopatellar syndrome: A new condition comprising absent patellae, scrotal hypoplasia, renal anomalies, facial dysmorphism and mental retardation. *Journal of Medical Genetics* 37: 520–524.

Cummings, C., and Rega, E. (2008). A case of dyschondrosteosis in an Anglo-Saxon skeleton. *International Journal of Osteoarchaeology* 18: 431–437.

Dostalova, S., Sonka, K., Smahel, Z., Weiss, V., and Marek, J. (2003). Cephalometric assessment of cranial abnormalities in patients with acromegaly. *Journal of Cranio-Maxillofacial Surgery* 31: 80–87.

Drapkin, R. I., Genest, D. R., Holmes, L. B., Huang, T., and Vargas, S. O. (2003). Unilateral transverse arm defect with subterminal digital nubbins. *Pediatric and Developmental Pathology* 6: 348–354.

Gilbert, S. R., Gilbert, A. C., and Henderson, R. C. (2004). Skeletal maturation in children with quadriplegic cerebral palsy. *Journal of Pediatric Orthopedics* 24: 292–297.

Gladykowska-Rzeczycka, J. J., and Mazurek, T. (2009). A rare case of forearm hypoplasia from 18th century Gdansk, Poland. *International Journal of Osteoarchaeology* 19: 726–734.

Goshen, E., Schwartz, A., Zilka, L. R., and Zwas, S. T. (2000). Bilateral accessory horns: pathognomonic findings in Nail-patella syndrome. Scintigraphic evidence on bone scan. *Clinical Nuclear Medicine* 25: 476–477.

Henderson, R. C., Gilbert, S. R., Clement, M. E., Abbas, A., Worley, G., and Stevenston, R. D. (2005). Altered skeletal maturation in moderate to severe cerebral palsy. *Developmental Medicine and Child Neurology* 47: 229–236.

Ihkkan, D. Y., and Yalcin, E. (2001). Changes in skeletal maturation and mineralization in children with cerebral palsy and evaluation of related factors. *Journal of Child Neurology* 16: 425–430.

Jain, S., and Lakhtakia, P. K. (2002). Profile of congenital transverse deficiencies among cases of congenital orthopaedic anomalies. *Journal of Orthopaedic Surgery* 10: 45–52.

Kjellstrom, A. (2004). A case of os cuneiforme mediale bipartum from Sigtuna, Sweden. *International Journal of Osteoarchaeology* 14: 475–480.

Kummer, A. (2001). *Cleft palate and craniofacial anomalies: Effects on speech and resonance.* Singular, San Diego, CA.

Marfat, B., Kefi, R., and Beraud-Colomb, E. (2007). Palaeopathological and palaeogenetic study of 13 cases of developmental dysplasia of the hip with dislocation in a historical population from southern France. *International Journal of Osteoarchaeology* 17: 26–38.

McEwan, J. M., Mays, S., and Blake, G. M. (2005). The relationship of bone mineral density and other growth parameters to stress indicators in a Medieval juvenile population. *International Journal of Osteoarchaeology* 15: 155–163.

McGurick, C. K., Westgate, M. N., and Holmes, L. B. (2001). Limb deficiencies in newborn infants. *Pediatrics* 108(4): e64.

Megyesi, M. S., Tubbs, R. M., and Sauer, N. J. (2009). An analysis of human skeletal remains with cerebral palsy: Associated skeletal age delay and dental pathologies. *Journal of Forensic Sciences* 54(2): 270–274.

Merbs, C. F. (2004). Sagittal clefting of the body and other vertebral developmental errors in Canadian Inuit skeletons. *American Journal of Physical Anthropology* 123: 236–249.

Mirad, T. (2002). Incidence and pattern of developmental dysplasia in Aseer region of Saudi Arabia. *West African Journal of Medicine* 21: 218–222.

Mitchell, P. D., and Redfern, R. C. (2008). Diagnostic criteria for developmental dislocation of the hip in human skeletal remains. *International Journal of Osteoarchaeology* 18: 61–71.

Mooney, M. P., and Siegel, M. I. (2002). *Understanding craniofacial anomalies: The etiopathogenesis of craniosynostoses and facial clefting*. Wiley-Liss, New York.

Mulhern, D. M. (2005). A probable case of gigantism in a fifth dynasty skeleton from the western cemetery at Giza, Egypt. *International Journal of Osteoarchaeology* 15: 261–275.

Neville, B., and Goodman, R. (2000). *Congenital hemiplegia*. Cambridge University Press, Cambridge, UK.

Pany, D., and Teschler-Nicola, M. (2007). Klippel-Feil syndrome in an early Hungarian period juvenile skeleton form Austria. *International Journal of Osteoarchaeology* 17: 403–415.

Patrick, P., and Waldron, T. (2003). Congenital absence of the patella in an Anglo-Saxon skeleton. *International Journal of Osteoarchaeology* 13: 147–149.

Phillips, S. M., and Silvilich, M. (2006). Cleft palate: A case study of disability and survival in prehistoric North America. *International Journal of Osteoarchaeology* 16: 528–535.

Roberts, C. A., Knusel, C. J., and Race, L. (2004). A foot deformity from a Romano-British cemetery at Gloucester, England and the current evidence for Talipes in palaeopathology. *International Journal of Osteoarchaeology* 14: 389–403.

Sables, A. (2010). Rare example of an early medieval dwarf infant from Brownslade, Wales. *International Journal of Osteoarchaeology* 20: 47–53.

Sarry El Din, M. A., and El Banna, A. R. (2006). Congenital anomalies of the vertebral column: A case study on ancient and modern Egypt. *International Journal of Osteoarchaeology* 16: 200–207.

Schmidt-Rohlfing, B., Schwobel, S., Pauschert, R., and Neithard, F. U. (2001). Madelung deformity: Clinical features, therapy and results. *Journal of Pediatric Orthopaedics* 10: 344–348.

Shapiro, F. (2001). *Pediatric orthopaedic deformities: Basic science, diagnosis and treatment*. Academic Press, San Diego, CA.

Sonel, B., Yalcin, P., Ozturk, E. A., and Bokesoy, I. (2001). Butterfly vertebra: A case report. *Clinical Imaging* 25: 206–208.

Tillier, A-M., Arensburg, B., Duday, H., and Vandermeersch, B. (2001). An early case of hydrocephalus: The middle Paleolithic Qafzeh 12 child (Israel). *American Journal of Physical Anthropology* 114: 166–170.

Usher, B. M., and Norregaard Christensen, M. (2000). A sequential developmental field defect of the vertebrae, ribs and sternum in a young woman of the 12th century AD. *American Journal of Physical Anthropology* 111: 355–367.

Wyszynski, D. (2002). *Cleft lip and palate: From origin to treatment*. Oxford University Press, Oxford, UK.

Spondylolysis and Spondylolisthesis

Aihara, T., Takahashi, K., Yamagata, M., Moriya, H., and Shimada, Y. (2000). Does the ilio-lumbar ligament prevent anterior displacement of the fifth lumbar vertebra with defects of the pars? *Journal of Bone and Joint Surgery (Br)* 82: 846–850.

Axelsson, P., Johnsson, R., and Stromqvist, B. (2000). Is there increased intervertebral mobility in isthmic adult spondylolisthesis? *Spine* 25: 1701–1703.

Beutler, W. J., Fredrickson, B. E., Murtland, A., Sweeney, C. A., Grant, W. D., and Baker, D. (2003). The natural history of spondylolysis and spondylolisthesis. *Spine* 28: 1027–1035.

Chosa, E., Totoribe, K., and Tajima, N. (2004). A biomechanical study of lumbar spondylolysis based on a three-dimensional finite element method. *Journal of Orthopedic Research* 22: 158–163.

Fibiger, L., and Knusel, C. J. (2005). Prevalence rates of spondylolysis in British skeletal populations. *International Journal of Osteoarchaeology* 15: 164–174.

Ganju, A. (2002). Isthmic spondylolisthesis. *Neurosurgical Focus* 13: 1–6.

Gerszten, P. C., Gerszten, E., and Allisio, M. J. (2001). Diseases of the spine in South American mummies. *Neurosurgery* 48(1): 208–213.

Hammerberg, K. W. (2005). New concepts on the pathogenesis and classification of spondylolisthesis. *Spine* 30: S4–S11.

Hanson, D. S., Bridwell, K. H., Rhee, J. M., and Lenke, L. G. (2002). Correlation of pelvic incidence with low- and high-grade isthmic spondylolisthesis. *Spine* 27: 2026–2029.

Inoue, H., Ohmori, K., and Miyasaka, K. (2002). Radiographic classification of spondylolisthesis as adolescent or adult vertebral slip. *Spine* 27: 831–838.

Iwamoto, J., Abe, H., Tsukimura, Y., and Wakano, K. (2005). Relationship between radiographic abnormalities of lumbar spine and incidence of low back pain in high school rugby players: A prospective study. *Scandinavian Journal of Medicine and Science in Sports* 15: 163–168.

Jackson, R. P., Phipps, T., Hales, C., and Surber, J. (2003). Pelvic lordosis and alignment in spondylolisthesis. *Spine* 28: 151–160.

Jimenez-Brobeil, S. A., Oumaoui, I. Al., and du Souich, Ph. (2010). Some types of vertebral pathologies in the Argar culture (Bronze Age, SE Spain). *International Journal of Osteoarchaeology* 20: 36–46.

Kahl, K., and Ostendorf, M. (2000). The pattern of spondylolysis deformans in prehistoric samples from west-central New Mexico. *International Journal of Osteoarchaeology* 10: 432–446.

Labelle, H., Roussouly, P., Berthonnaud, E., Transfeldt, E., O'Brien, M., Chopin, D., Hresko, T., and Dimnet, J. (2004). Spondylolisthesis, pelvic incidence and sinopelvic balance. *Spine* 29: 2049–2054.

Ludin, D. A., Wiseman, D. B., and Shaffrey, C. I. (2002). Spondylolysis and spondylolisthesis in the athlete. *Clinical Neurosurgery* 49: 528–547.

MacThiong, J-M., Berthonnaud, E., Dimar, J. R., Betz, R. R., and Labelle, H. (2004). Sagittal alignment of the spine and pelvis during growth. *Spine* 29: 1642–1647.

Masnicov, S., and Benus, R. (2003). Developmental anomalies in skeletal remains from the Great Moravia and Middle Ages cemeteries at Devin (Slovakia). *International Journal of Osteoarchaeology* 13: 266–274.

Mays, S. (2006). Spondylolysis, spondylolisthesis and lumbo-sacral morphology in a Medieval English skeletal population. *American Journal of Physical Anthropology* 131: 352–362.

Mays, S. (2007a). Spondylolysis in the lower thoracic-upper lumbar spine in a British medieval population. *International Journal of Osteoarchaeology* 17: 608–618.

Mays, S. (2007b). Spondylolysis in non-adult skeletons excavated from a medieval rural archaeological site in England. *International Journal of Osteoarchaeology* 17: 504–513.

Merbs, C. F. (2001). Degenerative spondylolisthesis in ancient and historic skeletons from New Mexico Pueblo sites. *American Journal of Physical Anthropology* 116: 285–295.

Merbs, C. F. (2002a). Asymmetrical spondylolysis. *American Journal of Physical Anthropology* 119: 156–174.

Merbs, C. F. (2002b). Spondylolysis in Inuit skeletons from Arctic Canada. *International Journal of Osteoarchaeology* 12: 279–290.

Nyska, M., Constantini, N., Cale-Benzoor, M., Back, A., Kahn, G., and Mann, G. (2000). Spondylolysis as a cause of low back pain in swimmers. *International Journal of Sports Medicine* 21: 375–379.

Rassi, G. E., Takemitsu, M., Woratanarat, P., and Shah, S. A. (2005). Lumbar spondylolysis in pediatric and adolescent soccer players. *American Journal of Sports Medicine* 33: 1688–1693.

Reiter, L., Frater, C. J., Qurashi, S., and Loneragan, R. (2006). Degenerative spondylolysis: A concise report of scintigraphic observations. *Rheumatology* 45: 209–211.

Ruiz-Cotorro, A., Balius-Matas, R., Estruch-Massana, A., and Vilara, A. J. (2006). Spondylolysis in young tennis players. *British Journal of Sports Medicine* 40: 441–446.

Sairyo, K., Katoh, S., Ikata, T., Fujii, K., Kajiura, K., and Goel, V. K. (2001). Development of spondylolytic olisthesis in adults. *Spine Journal* 1: 171–175.

Shrier, I. (2001). Spondylolysis incidence in various sports. *Physical Sports Medicine* 29: 5.

Soler, T., and Calderon, C. (2000). The prevalence of spondylolysis in the elite Spanish athlete. *American Journal of Sports Medicine* 28: 57–62.

Standaert, C. J., and Herring, S. J. (2000). Spondylolysis: A critical review. *British Journal of Sports Medicine* 34: 415–422.

Stretch, R., Botha, T., Chandler, S., and Pretorius, P. (2003). Back injuries in young fast bowlers—Radiological investigation of the healing of spondylolysis and pedicle sclerosis. *South African Medical Journal* 93: 611–616.

Ward, C., and Latimer, B. (2005). Human evolution and the development of spondylolysis. *Spine* 30: 1808–1814.

Ward, C. V., Mays, S. A., Child, S., and Latimer, B. (2010). Lumbar vertebral morphology and isthmic spondylolysis in a British medieval population. *American Journal of Physical Anthropology* 141: 273–280.

Weiss, E. (2009). Spondylolysis in a pre-contact San Francisco Bay population: Behavioural and anatomical sex differences. *International Journal of Osteoarchaeology* 19: 375–385.

Whiteside, T. E., Horton, W. C., and Hodges, L. (2005). Spondylolytic spondylolisthe-
    sis: a study of pelvic and lumbosacral parameters of possible etiologic effect in
    two genetically and geographically distinct groups with high occurrence. *Spine*
    30: S12–S21.
Young, K. J., and Koning, W. (2003). Spondylolysis of L2 in identical twins. *Journal of
    Manipulative and Physiological Therapeutics* 26: 196–201.

Osteoarthritis, Degenerative Joint Disease, and Osteoporosis

Adams, M. A., Pollintine, P., Tobias, J. H., Wakley, G. K., and Dolan, P. (2006).
    Itervertebral disc degeneration can predispose to anterior vertebral fractures in
    the thoracolumbar spine. *Journal of Bone and Mineral Research* 21: 1409–1416.
Berginik, A. P., van Meurs, J. B., Loughlin, J., Arp, P. P., Fang, Y., Hofman, A., van
    Leeuwen, J., van Duijn, C. M., Uitterlinden, A. G., and Pol, H. A. P. (2003).
    Estrogen receptor α gene haplotype is associated with radiographic osteoar-
    thritis of the knee in elderly men and women. *Arthritis and Rheumatism* 48:
    1913–1922.
Brickley, M. (2002). An investigation of historical and archaeological evidence for age-
    related bone loss and osteoporosis. *International Journal of Osteoarchaeology* 12:
    364–371.
Conaghan, P. G. (2002). Update on osteoarthritis part 1: Current concepts and the
    relation to exercise. *British Journal of Sports Medicine* 36: 330–333.
Dumond, H., Presle, N., Terlain, B., Mainard, D., Loeuille, D., Netter, P., and Pottie,
    P. (2003). Evidence for a key role of leptin in osteoarthritis. *Arthritis and
    Rheumatism* 48: 3118–3129.
Felson, D. T., Nevitt, M. C., Zhang, Y., Aliabadi, P., Baumer, B., Gale, D., Li, W.,
    Yu, W., and Xu, L. (2002). High prevalence of lateral knee osteoarthritis in
    Beijing Chinese compared with Framingham Caucasian subjects. *Arthritis and
    Rheumatism* 46: 1217–1222.
Gelse, K., Soder, S., Eger, W., Diemtar, T., and Aigner, T. (2003). Osteophyte develop-
    ment—Molecular characterization of differentiation stages. *Osteoarthritis and
    Cartilage* 11: 141–148.
Gries, N. C., Berlemann, U., Moore, R. J., and Vernon-Roberts, B. (2000). Early his-
    tological changes in lower lumbar discs and facet joints and their correlation.
    European Spine Journal 9: 23–29.
Heaney, R. P. (2009). Calcium in the prevention and treatment of osteoporosis. *Journal
    of Internal Medicine* 231: 169–180.
Holmberg, S., Thelin, A., and Thelin, N. (2004). Is there an increased risk of
    knee osteoarthritis among farmers? A population-based case-controlled
    study. *International Archives of Occupational and Environmental Health* 77:
    345–350.
Hunter, D. J., Niu, J., Zhang, Y., Nevitt, M. C., Xu, L., Lui, L. Y., Yu, W., Aliabadi,
    P., Buchanan, T. S., and Felson, D. T. (2005). Knee height, knee pain and knee
    osteoarthritis. *Arthritis and Rheumatism* 52: 1418–1423.

Hussien, F. J., Sarry El-Din, A. M., Sami Kandeel, W. A., and El Banna, R. A. E-S. (2009). Spinal pathological findings in ancient Egyptians of the Greco-Roman period living in Bahriyah Oasis. *International Journal of Osteoarchaeology* 19: 613–627.

Ingvarsson, T., Steffansson, S. E., Hallgrimdottir, I. B., Frigge, M. L., Jonsson, J., and Gulcher, J. (2000). The inheritance of hip osteoarthritis in Iceland. *Arthritis and Rheumatism* 43: 2785–2792.

Jensen, L. K., Millelsen, S., Loft, I. P., Eenberg, W., Bergmann, I., and Logager, V. (2000). Radiographic knee osteoarthritis in floorlayers and carpenters. *Scandinavian Journal of Work and Environmental Health* 26: 257–262.

Jones, G., Cooley, H. M., and Stankovich, J. M. (2002). A cross sectional study of the association between sex, smoking and other lifestyle factors and osteoarthritis of the hand. *Journal of Rheumatology* 29: 1719–1724.

Jonsson, H., Manolescu, I., Stefansson, S. E., Ingvarsson, T., Jonsson, H. H., Manolescu, A., Gulcher, J., and Stefansson, K. (2003). The inheritance of hand osteoarthritis in Iceland. *Arthritis and Rheumatism* 48: 391–395.

Korpelainen, R., Korpelainen, J., Heikkinen, J., Vaananen, K., and Keinanen-Kiukaanniemi, S. (2003). Lifestyle factors are associated with osteoporosis in lean women but not in normal and overweight women: A population-based cohort study of 1222 women. *Osteoporosis International* 14: 34–43.

Laib, A., Barou, O., Vico, L., Lafage-Proust, M., Alexandre, C., and Rugsegger, P. (2000). 3D micro-computed tomography of trabecular and cortical bone architecture with application to a rat model of immobilization osteoporosis. *Medical and Biological Engineering and Computing* 38: 326–332.

Lanyon, P., Muir, K., Doherty, S., and Doherty, M. (2000). Assessment of a genetic contribution to osteoarthritis of the hip: Sibling study. *British Medical Journal* 321: 1179–1183.

Lau, E. M. C. (2001). Epidemiology of osteoporosis. *Best Practice and Research Clinical Rhematology* 15: 335–344.

Law, A. (2005). A simple method for calculating the prevalence of disease in a past human population. *International Journal of Osteoarchaeology* 15: 146–147.

Liu, X. S., Bevill, G., Keaveny, T. M., Sajda, P., and Guo, X. E. (2009). Micromechanical analyses of vertebral trabecular bone based on individual trabeculae segmentation of plates and rods. *Journal of Biomechanics* 42: 249–256.

Lopez, A. D., Mathers, C. D., Ezzati, M., Jamison, D. T., and Murray, C. J. L. (2006). Global and regional burden of disease and risk factors 2001: Systematic analysis of population health data. *The Lancet* 367: 1747–1757.

Manek, N. J., Hart, D., Spector, T. D., and MacGregor, A. J. (2003). The association of body mass index and osteoarthritis of the knee joint. *Arthritis and Rheumatism* 48: 1024–1029.

Manninen, P., Heliovaara, M., Riihimaki, H., and Suomalainen, O. (2002). Physical workload and the risk of severe knee osteoarthritis. *Scandinavian Journal of Work and Environmental Health*. 28: 25–32.

Martin, R. B. (2000). Toward a unifying theory of bone remodeling. *Bone* 26: 1–6.

Mays, S. (2000). Age-dependent cortical bone loss in women from 18th and 19th century London. *American Journal of Physical Anthropology* 112: 349–362.

Min, J. L., Meulenbelt, I., Riyazi, N., Kloppenburg, M., Houwing-Duistermaat, J. J., Seymour, A. B., Pols, H. A., van Duijn, C. M., and Slagboom, P. E. (2005). Association of the frizzled-related protein gene with symptomatic osteoarthritis at multiple sites. *Arthritis and Rheumatism* 52: 1077–1080.

Papageorgopoulou, C., Kuhn, G., Ziegler, U., and Rhuli, F. J. (2009). Diagnostic morphometric applicability of confocal laser scanning microscopy in osteoarchaeology. *International Journal of Osteoarchaeology* doi: 10.1002/oa.1078.

Pollintine, P., Przbyla, A. S., Dolan, P., and Adams, M. A. (2004). Neural arch load-bearing in old and degenerated spines. *Journal of Biomechanics* 37: 197–204.

Punzi, L., Oliviero, F., and Plebani, M. (2005). New biochemical insights into the pathogenesis of osteoarthritis and the role of laboratory investigations in clinical assessment. *Clinical Laboratory Sciences* 42: 279–309.

Reijman, M., Hazes, J. M. W., Pols, H. A. P., Koes, B. W., and Bierma-Zeinstra, S. M. A. (2005). Acetabular dysplasia predicts incident osteoarthritis of the hip. *Arthritis and Rheumatism* 52: 787–793.

Robson Brown, K., Pollintine, P., and Adams, M. A. (2008). Biomechanical implications of degenerative joint disease in the apophyseal joints of human thoracic and lumbar vertebrae. *American Journal of Physical Anthropology* 136: 318–326.

Rojas-Sepulveda, C., Ardagna, Y., and Dutour, O. (2008). Paleoepidemiology of vertebral degenerative disease in a Pre-Columbian Muisca series from Colombia. *American Journal of Physical Anthropology* 135: 416–430.

Rossignol, M. (2004). Osteoarthritis and occupation in the Quebec national health and social survey. *Occupational and Environmental Medicine* 61: 729–735.

Sandmark, H., Jogstedt, C., and Vingard, E. (2000). Primary osteoarthrosis of the knee in men and women as a result of lifelong physical load from work. *Scandinavian Journal of Work and Environmental Health* 26: 20–25.

Sarry El Din, M. A. (2002). Degenerative spinal arthritis in ancient Egyptians from the old kingdom. *Egyptian Journal of Anatomy* 25: 179–193.

Schmitt, H., Brocai, D. R., and Lukoschek, M. (2004). High prevalence of hip arthrosis in former elite javelin throwers and high jumpers: 41 athletes examined more than 10 years after retirement from competitive sports. *Acta Orthopaedica Scandinavia* 75: 34–39.

Schoffl, V., Hochholzer, T., and Imhoff, A. (2004). Radiographic changes in the hands and fingers of young high-level climbers. *American Journal of Sports Medicine* 32: 1688–1694.

Seki, S., Yikawaguchi, K., Chiba, K., Mikami, Y., Kizawa, H., Oya, T., Mio, F., Mori, M., Miyamoto, Y., Masuda, I., Tsunoda, T., Kamata, M., Kubo, T., Toyama, Y., Kimura, T., and Nakamura, Y. (2005). A functional SNP in *CILP*, encoding cartilage intermediate layer protein is associated with susceptibility to lumbar disk disease. *Nature Genetics* 37: 607–612.

Shaeo, Z., Rompe, G., and Schiltenwolf, M. (2002). Radiographic changes in the lumbar vertebral discs and lumbar vertebrae with age. *Spine* 27: 263–268.

Shepard, G. J., Banks, A. J., and Ryan, W. G. (2003). Ex-professional association footballers have an increased prevalence of osteoarthritis of the hip compared with age matched controls despite not having sustained notable hip injuries. *British Journal of Sports Medicine* 37: 80–81.

Solano, M. (2002). Activity related pathology in the Albany county almshouse cemetery, Albany, NY. *American Journal of Physical Anthropology* 34S: 145.

Spector, T. D., and MacGregor, A. J. (2004). Risk factors for osteoarthritis: genetics. *Osteoarthritis and Cartilage* 12: S39–S44.

Steckel, R. H., and Rose, J. C. (2002). *The backbone of history, health and nutrition in the Western Hemisphere.* Cambridge University Press, Cambridge, UK.

Sutton, A. J., Muir, K. R., Mockett, S., and Fentem, P. (2001). A case-controlled study to investigate between low and moderate levels of physical activity and osteoarthritis of the knee using data collected as part of the Allied Dunbar National Fitness Survey. *Annals of the Rheumatic Diseases* 60: 756–764.

Teitz, C. C., O'Kane, J. W., and Lind, B. K. (2003). Back pain in former intercollegiate rowers. *American Journal of Sports Medicine* 31: 590–595.

Thelin, A., Vingard, E., and Holmberg, S. (2004). Osteoarthritis of the hip joint and farm work. *American Journal of Industrial Medicine.* 45: 202–209.

Tischer, T., Aktas, T., Milz, S., and Putz, R. V. (2006). Detailed pathological changes of human lumbar facet joints L1–L5 in elderly individuals. *European Spine Journal* 15: 308–315.

Uitterlinden, A. G., Burger, H., van Duijn, C. M., Huang, Q., Hofman, A., and Birkenhager, J. C. (2000). Adjacent genes, for COL2A1 and vitamin D receptor, are associated with separate features of radiographic osteoarthritis of the knee. *Arthritis and Rheumatism* 43: 1456–1464.

Van der Merwe, A. E., İşcan, M. Y., and L'Abbe, E. N. (2006). The pattern of vertebral osteophyte development in a South African population. *International Journal of Osteoarchaeology* 16: 459–464.

Weber, J., Czarnetzki, A., and Spring, A. (2003). Paleopathological features of the cervical spine in the early Middle Ages: Natural history of degenerative disease. *Neurosurgery* 53: 1418–1424.

Weiss, E. (2005). Understanding osteoarthritis patterns: an examination of aggregate osteoarthritis. *Journal of Palaeopathology* 16: 88–98.

Weiss, E., and Jurmain, R. (2007). In and out of joint: Osteoarthritis revisited. *International Journal of Osteoarchaeology* 17:437–450.

Zhang, Y., Hunter, D. J., Nevitt, M. C., Zu, L., Niu, J., Ly, L., Yu, W., Aliabadi, P., and Felson, D. T. (2004). Association of squatting with increased prevalence of radiographic tibiofemoral knee osteoarthritis: The Beijing Osteoarthritis Study. *Arthritis and Rheumatism* 50: 1187–1192.

Diffuse Idiopathic Skeletal Hyperostosis and Ankylosing Spondylitis

Canci, A., Marchi, D., Caramella, D., Fornaciari, G., and Borgognini Tarli, S. M. (2005). Coexistence of melorheostosis and DISH in a female skeleton from Magna Graecia (sixth century BC). *American Journal of Physical Anthropology* 126: 305–310.

Coaccioli, S., Fatai, G., Di Cato, L., Marioloi, D., Patucchi, E., Pizzurti, C., Ponteggia, M., and Puxeddu, A. (2000). Diffuse idiopathic skeletal hyperostosis in diabetes mellitus, impaired glucose tolerance and obesity. *Panminerva Medica* 42(4): 247–251.

Di Franco, M., Mauceri, M. T., Sili-Scavalli, A., Iagnocco, A., and Ciocci, A. (2000). Study of peripheral bone mineral density in patients with diffuse idiopathic skeletal hyperostosis. *Clinical Rheumatology* 19: 188–192.

Feldtkeller, E., Vosse, D., Geusens, P., and van der Linden, S. (2006). Prevalence and annual incidence of vertebral fractures in patients with ankylosing spondylitits. *Rheumatology International* 26: 234–239.

Hukuda, S., Inoue, K., Nakai, M., and Katayama, K. (2000). Did ossification of the posterior longitudinal ligament of the spine evolve in the modern period? A paleopathological study of ancient human skeletons in Japan. *Journal of Rheumatology* 27: 2647–2657.

Hukuda, S., Inoue, K., Ushiyama, T., Saruhashi, Y., Iwasaki, A., Huang, J., Mayeda, A., Nakai, M., Fang, X. O., and Zhao, Q. Y. (2000). Spinal degenerative lesions and spinal ligamentous ossifications in ancient Chinese populations of the Yellow river civilization. *International Journal of Osteoarchaeology* 10: 108–124.

Jacobs, W. B., and Fehlings, M. G. (2008). Ankylosing spondylitis and spinal cord injury: Origin, incidence, management and avoidance. *Neurosurgery Focus* 24: E12.

Jankauskas, R. (2003). The incidence of diffuse idiopathic skeletal hyperostosis and social correlations in Lithuanian skeletal materials. *International Journal of Osteoarchaeology* 13: 289–293.

Kiss, C., Szilagyi, M., Paksy, A., and Poor, G. (2002). Risk factors for diffuse idiopathic skeletal hyperostosis: A case control study. *Rheumatology* 41: 27–30.

Mader, R. (2003). Diffuse idiopathic skeletal hyperostosis: A distinct clinical entity. *Israel Medical Association Journal* 5: 506–508.

Oxenham, M. F., Matsumura, H., and Nishimoto, T. (2006). Diffuse idiopathic skeletal hyperostosis in late Jomon Hokkaido, Japan. *International Journal of Osteoarchaeology* 16: 34–46.

Rogers, J., and Waldron, T. (2001). DISH and the monastic way of life. *International Journal of Osteoarchaeology* 11: 357–365.

Sencan, D., Elden, H., Nacitarhan, V., Sencan, M., and Kaptanoglu, E. (2005). The prevalence of diffuse idiopathic skeletal hyperostosis in patients with diabetes mellitus. *Rheumatology International* 25: 518–521.

Thomsen, A. H., Jurik, A. G., Uhrenholt, L., and Vesterby, A. (2010). Traumatic death in ankylosing spondylitis. *Journal of Forensic Sciences* doi: 10.1111/j.1556–4029.2010.01376.x.

Vidal, P. (2000). A paleoepidemiologic study of diffuse idiopathic skeletal hyperostosis. *Joint Bone Spine* 67: 210–214.

Sinusitis, Mastoiditis, and Conditions Related to the Ear, Nose, and Throat

Bell, M. L., Davis, D. L., and Fletcher, T. (2004). A retrospective assessment of mortality from the London smog episode of 1952: The role of influenza and pollution. *Environmental Health Perspectives* 112: 6–8.

El-Bitar, M. A., and Choi, S. S. (2002). Bilateral occurrence of congenital middle ear cholesteatoma. *Otolaryngology Head and Neck Surgery* 127: 480–482.

Flohr, S., Kierdorf, U., and Schultz, M. (2009). Differential diagnosis of mastoid hypo-
    cellularity in human skeletal remains. *American Journal of Physical Anthropology*
    140: 442–453.
Flohr, S., and Scultz, M. (2009a). Mastoiditis—Paleopathological evidence of a rarely
    reported disease. *American Journal of Physical Anthropology* 138: 266–273.
Flohr, S., and Schultz, M. (2009b). Osseous changes due to mastoiditis in human skel-
    etal remains. *International Journal of Osteoarchaeology* 19: 99–106.
Helibrun, M. E., Salzman, K. L., Glastonbury, C. M., Harnsberger, H. R., Kennedy, R.
    J., and Shelton, C. (2003). External auditory canal cholesteatoma: Clinical and
    imaging spectrum. *American Journal of Neuroradiology* 24: 751–756.
Homoe, P. (2001). Otitis media in Greenland. Studies on historical epidemio-
    logical, microbiological and immunological aspects. *International Journal of
    Circumpolar Health* 60: 1–54.
Jung, J. Y., and Chole, R. A. (2002). Bone resorption in chronic otitis media: the role
    of the osteoclast. *ORL Journal of Otorhinolaryngology and Related Specialties* 64:
    95–107.
Koltai, P. J., Nelson, M., Castellon, R. J., Garabedian, E-N., Triglia, J-M., Roman, S.,
    and Roger, G. (2002). The natural history of congenital cholesteatoma. *Archives
    of Otolaryngology Head and Neck Surgery* 128: 804–809.
Leskinen, K., and Jero, J. (2005). Acute complications of otitis media in adults. *Clinical
    Otolaryngology* 30: 511–516.
Lubianca Neto, J. F., Hemb, L., and Silva, D. B. (2006). Systematic literature review of
    modifiable risk factors for recurrent acute otitis media in childhood. *Journal of
    Pediatrics* 82: 87–96.
Mays, S., and Holst, M. (2006). Paleo-otology of cholesteatoma. *International Journal
    of Osteoarchaeology* 16: 1–15.
Merrett, D. C., and Pfeiffer, S. (2000). Maxillary sinusitis as an indicator of respira-
    tory health in past populations. *American Journal of Physical Anthropology* 111:
    301–318.
Mey, K. H., Sorensen, M. S., and Homoe, P. (2006). Histomorphometric estima-
    tion of air cell development in experimental otitis media. *Laryngoscope* 116:
    1820–1823.
Olszewska, E., Wagner, M., Bernal-Sprekelsen, M., Ebmeyer, J., Dazert, S., Hildman,
    H., and Sudhoff, H. (2004). Etiopathogenesis of cholesteatoma. *European
    Archives of Otorhinolaryngology* 261: 6–24.
Paparella, M. M., Schachern, P. A., and Cureoglu, S. (2002). Chronic silent otitis
    media. *ORL Journal of Otorhinolaryngology and Related Specialties* 64: 65–72.
Qvist, M., and Grontved, A. M. (2001). Chronic otitis media sequelae in skeletal
    material from medieval Denmark. *Laryngoscope* 111: 114–118.
Roberts, C. A. (2007). A bioarchaeological study of maxillary sinusitis. *American
    Journal of Physical Anthropology* 133: 792–807.
Sade, J., Russo, E., Fuchs, C., and Ar, A. (2006). Acute otitis media and mastoid
    growth. *Acta Otolaryngologica* 126: 1036–1039.
Sanchez Fernandez, J. M., Anta Escuredo, J. A., Sanchez Del Rey, A., and Sanaolalla
    Montoya, F. (2000). Morphometric study of the paranasal sinuses in normal and
    pathological conditions. *Acta Otolaryngologica* 120: 273–278.

Slavin, R. G., Sheldon, L., and Bernstein, I.. L. (2005). The diagnosis and management of sinusitis: A practice parameter update. *Journal of Allergy and Clinical Immunology* 116: S13–S47.

Soldati, D., and Mudry, A. (2001). Knowledge about cholesteatoma from the first description to modern histopathology. *Otology and Neurotology* 22: 723–730.

Stankiewicz, J. A., and Chow, J. M. (2002). A diagnostic dilemma for chronic rhinosinusitis: Definition, accuracy and validity. *American Journal of Rhinology* 16: 199–202.

Vicente, J., Trinidad, A., Ramirez-Camacho, R., Garcia-Berrocal, J. R., Gonzalez-Garcia, J. A., Ibanez, A., and Pinilla, M. T. (2007). Evolution of middle ear changes after permanent Eustachian tube blockage. *Archives of Otolaryngology and Head and Neck Surgery* 133: 587–592.

Tuberculosis (and Leprosy)

Anderson, T. (2001). A case of skeletal tuberculosis from Roman Towcester. *International Journal of Osteoarchaeology* 11: 444–446.

Belcastro, M. G., Mariotti,V., Facchini, F., and Dutour, O. (2005). Leprosy in a skeleton from the 7th century Necropolis of Vicenne-Campochario (Molise, Italy). *International Journal of Osteoarchaeology* 15: 431–448.

Blau, S., and Yagodin, V. (2005). Osteoarchaeological evidence for leprosy from western Central Asia. *American Journal of Physical Anthropology* 126:150–158.

Boldsen, J. L. (2001). Epidemiological approach to the palaeopathological diagnosis of leprosy. *American Journal of Physical Anthropology* 115: 380–387.

Brosch, R., Gordon, S. V., Marmiesse, M., Brodin, P., Buchrieser, C., Eiglmeier, K., Garnier, T., Guiterrez, C., Hewison, G., Kremer, K., Parsons, L. M., Pym, A. S., Samper, S., van Soolinger, D., and Cole, S. T. (2002). A new evolutionary scenario for the *Mycobacterium tuberculosis* complex. *Proceedings of the National Academy of Sciences of the United States of America* 99: 3684–3689.

Canci, A., Nencioni, S., Minozzi, P., Catalano, D., and Fornaciari, G. (2005). A case of healing spinal infection from classical Rome. *International Journal of Osteoarchaeology* 15: 77–83.

Cule, J. (2002). The stigma of leprosy: Its historical origins and consequences with particular reference to the laws of Wales. In *The past and present of leprosy. Archaeological, palaeopathological and clinical approaches* (Eds. Roberts, C. A., Lewis, M. E., and Manchester, K.). *BAR International Series* 1054: 149–154.

Dabernat, H., and Crubezy, E. (2009). Multiple bone tuberculosis in a child from predynastic Upper Egypt (3200 BC). *International Journal of Osteoarchaeology* doi: 10.1002/oa.1082.

De Vuyst, D., Vanhoenacker, F., Gielen, J., Bernaerts, A., and De Schepper, A. M. (2003). Imaging features of musculoskeletal tuberculosis. *European Radiology* 13: 1809–1819.

Donoghue, H. D., Spigelman, M., Greenblatt, C. L., LevMaor, G., Kahila Bar-Gal, G., Matheson, C., Vernon, K., Nerlich, A. G., and Zink, A. R. (2004). Tuberculosis: From prehistory to Robert Koch as revealed by ancient DNA. *Lancet Infectious Diseases* 4: 584–592.

Flavin, R., Gibbons, N., and O'Briain, D. S. (2007). *Mycobacterium tuberculosis* at autopsy—Exposure and protection: An old adversary revisited. *Journal of Clinical Pathology* 60: 487–491.

Fletcher, H. A., Donoghue, H. D., Taylor, G. M., van der Zanden, A. G. M., and Spigelman, M. (2003). Molecular analysis of *Mycobacterium tuberculosis* DNA from a family of 18th century Hungarians. *Microbiology* 149: 143–151.

Hurtado, A. M., Hill, K. R., Rosenblatt, W., Bender, J., and Scharmen, T. (2003). Longitudinal study of tuberculosis outcomes among immunologically naïve Ache natives of Paraguay. *American Journal of Physical Anthropology* 121: 134–150.

Kochi, A. (2001). The global tuberculosis situation and the new control strategy of the World Health Organization. *Bulletin of the World Health Organization* 79: 71–75.

Konomi, N., Lebwohl, E., Mowbray, K., Tattersall, I., and Zhang, D. (2002). Detection of mycobacterial DNA in Andean mummies. *Journal of Clinical Microbiology* 40: 4738–4740.

Lambert, P. M. (2002). Rib lesions in a prehistoric Puebloan sample from southwestern Colorado. *American Journal of Physical Anthropology* 117: 281–292.

Lefort, M., and Bennike, P. (2007). A case study of possible differential diagnoses of a Medieval skeleton from Denmark: Leprosy, ergotism, treponematosis, sarcoidosis or smallpox? *International Journal of Osteoarchaeology* 17: 337–349.

Manchester, K. (2002). Infective bone changes in leprosy. *BAR International Series* 1054: 69–72.

Marais, B. J., Gie, R. P., Schaaf, H. S., Hesseling, A. C., Obihara, C. C., Nelson, L. J., Enarson, D. A., Donald, P. R., and Beyers, N. (2004). The clinical epidemiology of childhood pulmonary tuberculosis: A critical review of literature from the pre-chemotherapy era. *The International Journal of Tuberculosis and Lung Disease* 8: 278–285.

Mariotti, V., Dutour, O., Belcastro, M. G., Facchini, F., and Brasili, P. (2005). Probable early presence of leprosy in Europe in a Celtic skeleton of the 4th–3rd century BC (Casalecchio de Reno, Bologna, Italy). *International Journal of Osteoarchaeology* 15: 311–325.

Matos, V., and Santos, A. L. (2006). On the trail of pulmonary tuberculosis based on rib lesions: Results from the Human Identified Skeletal Collection from the Museu Bocage (Lisbon, Portugal). *American Journal of Physical Anthropology* 130: 190–200.

Mays, S., Fysh, E., and Taylor, G. M. (2002). Investigation of the link between visceral surface rib lesions and tuberculosis in a medieval skeletal series from England using ancient DNA. *American Journal of Physical Anthropology* 119: 27–36.

Mays, S., and Taylor, G. M. (2003). A first prehistoric case of tuberculosis from Britain. *International Journal of Osteoarchaeology* 13: 189–196.

Mays, S., Taylor, G. M., Legge, A. J., Young, D. B., and Turner-Walker, G. (2001). Palaeopathological and biomolecular study of tuberculosis in a Mediaeval skeletal collection from England. *American Journal of Physical Anthropology* 114: 298–311.

Molnar, E., Maczel, M., Marcsik, A., Gyorgy, P., Nerlich, A. G., and Zink, A. (2005). Molecular biological investigation of skeletal tuberculosis in a medieval cemetery of Hungary. *Folia Anthropologica* 3: 41–51.

Molto, J. E. (2002). Leprosy in Roman period skeletons from Kellis 2, Dakhleh, Egypt. *BAR International Series* 1054: 179–192.

Morris, B. S., Varma, R., Garg, A., Awasthi, M., and Maheshwari, M. (2002). Multifocal musculoskeletal tuberculosis in children: Appearances on computed tomography. *Skeletal Radiology* 31: 1–8.

Murphy, E. M., and Manchester, K. (2002). Evidence for leprosy in Medieval Ireland. *BAR International Series* 1054: 193–199.

Ozsoy, S., Demirel, B., Albay, A., Kisa, O., Dinc, A. H., and Safali, M. (2010). Tuberculosis prevalence in forensic autopsies. *American Journal of Medical Pathology* 31: 55–57.

Roberts, C. A. (2002). The antiquity of leprosy in Britain: The skeletal evidence. *BAR International Series* 1054: 213–221.

Roberts, C. A., and Buikstra, J. E. (2003). *The bioarchaeology of tuberculosis: A global view on a re-emerging disease*. University Press of Florida, Gainesville.

Ruhli, F. J., Hodler, J., and Boni, T. (2002). CT-guided biopsy: A new diagnostic method for paleopathological research. *American Journal of Physical Anthropology* 117: 272–275.

Santos, A. L., and Roberts, C. A. (2001). A picture of tuberculosis in young Portuguese people in the early 20th century: A multidisciplinary study of the skeletal and historical evidence. *American Journal of Physical Anthropology* 115: 38–49.

Santos, A. L., and Roberts, C. A. (2006). Anatomy of a serial killer: Differential diagnosis of tuberculosis based on rib lesions of adult individuals from the Coimbra Identified Skeletal Collection, Portugal. *American Journal of Physical Anthropology* 130: 38–49.

Smith, F. B. (1988). *The retreat of tuberculosis 1850–1950*. London: Croom Helm.

Stone, A. C., Wilbur, A. K., Buikstra, J. E., and Roberts, C. A. (2009). Tuberculosis and leprosy in perspective. *Yearbook of Physical Anthropology* 52: 66–94.

Suzuki, T., and Inoue, T. (2007). Earliest evidence of spinal tuberculosis from the Aneolithic Yayoi period in Japan. *International Journal of Osteoarchaeology* 17: 392–402.

Tayles, N., and Buckley, H. R. (2004). Leprosy and tuberculosis in iron age southeast Asia. *American Journal of Physical Anthropology* 125: 239–256.

Taylor, G. M., Young, D. B., and Mays, S. A. (2005). Genotypic analysis of the earliest known prehistoric case of tuberculosis in Britain. *Journal of Clinical Microbiology* 43: 2236–2240.

Turgut, M. (2001). Spinal tuberculosis (Pott's disease) its clinical presentation, surgical management and outcome—A survey study on 694 patients. *Neurosurgery Review* 24: 8–13.

Walls, T., and Shingadia, D. (2004). Global epidemiology of paediatric tuberculosis. *Journal of Infection* 48: 13–22.

Wilkinson, R. J., Llewelyn, M., Toossi, Z., Patel, P., Pasvol, G., Lalvani, A., Wright, D., Latif, M., and Davidson, R. N. (2000). Influence of vitamin D deficiency and vitamin D receptor polymorphisms on tuberculosis among Gujarati Asians in West London: A case-control study. *The Lancet* 355: 618–621.

Zink, A. R., Grabner, W., and Nerlich, A. G. (2005). Molecular identification of human tuberculosis in recent and historic bone tissue samples. A study on the role of molecular techniques for the study of historic tuberculosis. *American Journal of Physical Anthropology* 126: 32–47.

Zink, A. R., Molnar, E., Notamedi, N., Palfy, G., Marcsik, A., and Nerlich, A. G. (2007). Molecular history of tuberculosis from ancient mummies and skeletons. *International Journal of Osteoarchaeology* 17: 380–391.

Brucellosis

Anderson, T. (2003). The first evidence of brucellosis from British skeletal material. *Journal of Paleopathology* 15: 153–158.

Aubin, M. (2004). Brucellosis in ancient Nubia: Identification, differential diagnosis and implications for morbidity. *Supplement to Paleopathology Newsletter* 126: 9–10.

Bosilkovski, M., Krteva, L., Caparoska, S., and Dimzova, M. (2004). Osteoarticular involvement in brucellosis: Study of 196 cases in the Republic of Macedonia. *Croatian Medical Journal* 45: 727–733.

Christos, H., Popa, M., Afsar, O., Vasileios, D., and Pirounaki, M. (2000). Surveillance of communicable diseases in the Balkans. *The Lancet* 355: 1–3.

Curate, F. (2006). Two possible cases of brucellosis from a clarist monastery in Alcacer do Sal, Southern Portugal. *International Journal of Osteoarchaeology* 16: 453–458.

D'Anastasio, R., Staniscia, T., Milia, M. L., Manzoli, L., and Capasso, L. (2010). Origin, evolution and paleoepidemiology of brucellosis. *Epidemiology and Infection* doi: 10.1017/S095026881000097X.

Geyik, M., Gur, A., Nas, K., Cevik, R., Sarac, J., Dikici, B., and Ayaz, C. (2002). Musculoskeletal involvement in brucellosis in different age groups: A study of 195 cases. *Swiss Medical Weekly* 132: 98–105.

Gokhale, Y. A., Ambardekar, A. G., Bhasin, A., Patil, M., Tillu, A., and Kamath, J. (2003). Brucella spondylitis and sacroiliitis in the general population of Mumbai. *Journal of the Association of Physicians of India* 51: 659–666.

Mays, S. (2007). Lysis at the anterior vertebral body margin: Evidence for brucellar spondylitis. *International Journal of Osteoarchaeology* 17: 107–118.

Nicoletti, P. (2002). A short history of Brucellosis. *Veterinary Microbiology* 90: 5–9.

Ozaksoy, D., Yucesoy, K., Yucesoy, M., Kovanlikaya, I., Yuce, A., and Naderi, S. (2001). Brucellar spondylisis: MRI findings. *European Spine Journal* 10: 529–533.

Ozgocmen, S., Ardicoglu, A., Kocakoc, E., Kiris, A., and Ardicoglu, O. (2001). Paravertebral abscess formation due to brucellosis in a patient with ankylosing spondylitis. *Joint Bone Spine* 68: 521–524.

Pappas, G., Papadimitriou, P., Akritidis, N., Christou, L., and Tsianos, E. (2006). The new global map of human brucellosis. *Lancet Infectious Diseases* 6: 91–99.

Sauret, J., and Vilissova, N. (2002). Human brucellosis. *Journal of the American Board of Family Practice* 15: 401–406.

Swartz, T. E., Tseng, T-S., Frederickson, M. A., Paris, G., Comerci, D. J., Rajashekara,
    G., Kim, J-G., Mudgett, M. B., Splitter, G. A., Ugalde, R. A., Goldbaum, F. W.,
    Briggs, W. R., and Bogomolni, R. A. (2007). Blue-light-activated histidine
    kinases: Two-component sensors in bacteria. *Science* 317: 1090–1093.

Treponemal Diseases

Antal, G. M., Lukehart, S. A., and Meheus A. Z. (2002). The endemic treponematoses.
    Microbes and Infection. 4: 83–94.
Buckley, H. R., and Dias, G. J. (2002). The distribution of skeletal lesions in trepone-
    mal disease: Is the lymphatic system responsible? *International Journal of
    Osteoarchaeology* 12: 178–188.
Erdal, Y. S. (2006). A pre-Columbian case of congenital syphilis from Anatolia (Nicaea,
    13th century AD). *International Journal of Osteoarchaeology* 16: 16–33.
Fairley, C. K., Hocking, J. S., and Medland, N. (2005). Syphilis: Back on the rise but
    not unstoppable. *Medical Journal of Australia* 183: 172–173.
Fenton, K. A., Nicoll, A., and Kinghorn, G. (2001). Resurgence of syphilis in England:
    Time for more radical and nationally coordinated approaches. *Sexually
    Transmitted Infections* 77: 309–310.
Jochelson, K. (2001). *The colour of diseases: Syphilis and racism in South Africa 1880–
    1950.* Palgrave, New York.
Mays, S., Crane-Kramer, G., and Bayliss, A. (2003). Two probable cases of trepone-
    mal diseases of medieval date from England. *American Journal of Physical
    Anthropology* 120: 133–143.
Meyer, C., Jung, C., Kohn, T., Poenicke, A., Poppe, A., and Alt, K. W. (2002). Syphilis
    2001—A paleopathological reappraisal. *Homo* 53: 39–58.
Mitchell, P. D. (2003). Pre-Columbian treponemal disease from 14th century AD
    Safed, and implications for the medieval eastern Mediterranean. *American
    Journal of Physical Anthropology* 121: 117–124.
Primary and secondary syphilis—United States, 2003–2004. (2006). *Morbidity and
    Mortality Weekly Report* 55(10): 269–273.
Rothschild, B. M., Calderon, F. L., Coppa, A., and Rothschild, C. (2000). First European
    exposure to syphilis: The Dominican Republic at the time of Columbian con-
    tact. *Clinical Infectious Diseases* 31: 936–941.
Von Hunnius, T. E., Roberts, C. A., Boylston, A., and Saunders, S. R. (2006).
    Histological identification of syphilis in pre-Columbian England. *American
    Journal of Physical Anthropology* 129: 559–566.
Wicher, V., and Wicher, K. (2001). Pathogenesis of maternal-fetal syphilis revisited.
    Clinical Infectious Diseases 33: 354–363.

Rickets

Al-Jurayyan, N. A., El-Desouki, M. E., Al_Herbish, A. S., Al-Mazyad, A. S., and
    Al-Qhtani, M. M. (2002). Nutritional rickets and osteomalacia in school chil-
    dren and adolescents. *Saudi Medical Journal* 23: 182–185.
Berry, J., Davies, M., and Mee, A. (2002). Vitamin D metabolism, rickets and
    osteomalacia. *Seminars in Musculoskeletal Radiology* 6(3): 173–181.

Blondiaux, G., Blondiaux, J., Secousse, F., Cotton, A., Danze, P-M., and Flipo, R-M. (2002). Rickets and child abuse: The case of a two year old girl from the 4th century in Lisieux (Normandy). *International Journal of Osteoarchaeology* 12: 209–215.

Brickley, M., Mays, S., and Ives, R. (2005). Skeletal manifestations of vitamin D deficiency osteomalacia in documented historical collections. *International Journal of Osteoarchaeology* 15: 389–403.

Brickley, M., Mays, S., and Ives, R. (2007). An investigation of skeletal indicators of vitamin D deficiency in adults: Effective markers for interpreting past living conditions and pollution levels in 18th and 19th century Birmingham, England. *American Journal of Physical Anthropology* 132: 67–79.

Brickley, M., Mays, S., and Ives, R. (2010). Evaluation and interpretation of residual rickets deformities in adults. *International Journal of Osteoarchaeology* 20: 54–66.

Callaghan, A. L., Moy, R. J. D., Booth, I. W., Debelle, G., and Shaw, N. J. (2006). Incidence of symptomatic vitamin D deficiency. *Archives of Disease in Childhood* 91: 606–607.

Cheema, J. I., Grissom, L. E., and Harcke, H. T. (2003). Radiographic characteristics of lower-extremity bowing in children. *Radiographics* 23: 871–880.

Davids, J. R., Blackhurst, D. W., and Allen, B. L. (2000). Clinical evaluation of bowed legs in children. *Journal of Pediatric Othropedics* 9: 278–284.

Ericksen, E. F., and Glerup, H. (2002). Vitamin D deficiency and aging: Implications for general health and osteoporosis. *Biogerontology* 3: 73–77.

Gartner, L. M., and Greer, F. R. (2003). Prevention of rickets and vitamin D deficiency: New guidelines for vitamin D intake. *Pediatrics* 111: 908–910.

Haduch, E., Szczepanek, A., Skrzat, J., Srodek, R., and Brzegowy, P. (2009). Residual rickets or osteomalacia: A case dating from the 16th–18th centuries from Krosno Odrzanskie, Poland. *International Journal of Osteoarchaeology* 19: 593–612.

Herm, F. B., Killguss, H., and Stewart, A. G. (2005). Osteomalacia in Hazara district, Pakistan. *Tropical Doctor* 35: 8–10.

Hockberg, Z. (2003). *Vitamin D and Rickets.* Karger, Basel.

Holick, M. F. (2003). Vitamin D: A millennium perspective. *Journal of Cellular Biochemistry* 88: 296–307.

Holick, M. F. (2005). The vitamin D epidemic and its health consequences. *Journal of Nutrition* 135: 2739S–2784S.

Holick, M. F. (2006). Resurrection of vitamin D deficiency and rickets. *Journal of Clinical Investigation* 116: 2062–2072.

Ives, R. (2005). Vitamin D deficiency osteomalacia in a historic urban collection. An investigation of age, sex and lifestyle related variables. *Palaeopathology Newsletter* 130: 6–15.

Mays, S., Brickley, M., and Ives, R. (2006). Skeletal manifestations of rickets in infants and young children in an historic population from England. *American Journal of Physical Anthropology* 129: 362–374.

Mays, S., Brickley, M., and Ives, R. (2007). Skeletal evidence for hyperparathyroidism in a 19th century child with rickets. *International Journal of Osteoarchaeology* 17: 73–81.

Mays, S., Rogers, J., and Watt, I. (2001). A possible case of hyperparathyroidism in a burial of 15th–17th century AD date from Wharram Percy, England. *International Journal of Osteoarchaeology* 11: 329–335.

Pearce, S. H. S., and Cheetham, T. D. (2010). Diagnosis and management of vitamin D deficiency. *British Medical Journal* 340: b5664.

Pinhasi, R. (2006). Morbidity, rickets and long bone growth in post-medieval Britain—A cross-population analysis. *Annals of Human Biology* 33: 372–389.

Reginato, A. J., and Coquia, J. A. (2003). Musculoskeletal manifestations of osteomalacia and rickets. *Best Practice and Research Clinical Rheumatology* 17: 1063–1080.

Robinson, P. D., Hogler, W., Craig, M. E., Verge, C. F., Walker, J. L., Piper, A. C., Woodhead, H. J., Cowell, C. T., and Ambler, G. R. (2006). The re-emerging burden of rickets: A decade of experience from Sydney. *Archives of Disease in Childhood* 91: 564–568.

Sachan, A., Gupta, R., Das, V., Agarwal, A., Awasthi, P. K., and Bhatia, V. (2005). High prevalence of vitamin D deficiency among pregnant women and their newborns in northern India. *American Journal of Clinical Nutrition* 81: 1060–1064.

Schmall, D., Teschler-Nicola, M., Kainberger, F., Tangl, S. T., Brandstatter, F., Patzak, B., Muhsil, J., and Plenk, H. (2003). Changes in trabecular bone structure in rickets and osteomalacia: The potential of a medico-historical collection. *International Journal of Osteoarchaeology* 13: 283–288.

Zink, A., Panzer, S., Fesq-Martin, M., Burger-Heinrich, W., Wahl, J., and Nerlich, A. G. (2005). Evidence for a 7,000 year-old case of primary hyperparathyroidism. *Journal of the American Medical Association* 293: 40–42.

Scurvy

Akikusa, J. D., Garrick, D., and Nash, M. C. (2003). Scurvy: Forgotten but not gone. *Journal of Paediatric Child Health* 39: 75–77.

Brickley, M., and Ives, R. (2006). Skeletal manifestations of infantile scurvy. *American Journal of Physical Anthropology* 129: 163–172.

Brown, S. R. (2004). *Scurvy: How a surgeon, a mariner and a gentleman discovered the greatest medical mystery of the age of sail.* Summersdale, Chichester, UK.

Clemetson, C. A. B. (2003). Child abuse or Barlow's disease? *Pediatrics International* 45: p758.

de Luna, R. H., Colley, B. J., Smith, K., Divers, S. G., Rinehart, J., and Marques, M. B. (2003). Scurvy: An often forgotten cause of bleeding. *American Journal of Hematology* 73: 85–87.

Fain, O. (2005). Musculoskeletal manifestations of scurvy. *Joint Bone Spine* 72: 124–128.

Hampl, J. S., Taylor, C. A., and Johnston, C. S. (2004). Vitamin C deficiency and depletion in the United States: The third National Health and Nutrition Examination Survey, 1988 to 1994. *American Journal of Public Health* 94: 870–875.

Maat, G. J. R. (2002). History and pathology of a disregarded disease. *Histopathology* 41: 460–462.

Maat, G. J. R. (2004). Scurvy in adults and youngsters: The Dutch experience. A review of the history and pathology of a disregarded disease. *International Journal of Osteoarchaeology* 14: 77–81.

Martini, E. (2003). How did Vasco de Gama sail for 16 weeks without developing scurvy? *Lancet* 361: p1480.

Mays, S. (2008). A likely case of scurvy from early bronze age Britain. (2008). *International Journal of Osteoarchaeology* 18: 178–187.

Melikian, M., and Waldron, T. (2003). An examination of skulls from two British sites for possible evidence of scurvy. *International Journal of Osteoarchaeology* 13: 207–212.

Milne, I., and Chalmers, I. (2004). Documenting the evidence: The case of scurvy. *Bulletin of the World Health Organisation* 82: 791–796.

Narchi, H., and Thomas, M. (2000). A painful limp. *Journal of Paediatric Child Health* 36: 277–278.

Ortner, D. J., Butler, W., Cafarella, J., and Miligan, L. (2001). Evidence of probably scurvy in subadults from archaeological sites in North America. *American Journal of Physical Anthropology* 114: 343–351.

Pangan, A. L., and Robinson, D. (2001). Hemarthrosis as initial presentation of scurvy. *Journal of Rheumatology* 23: 1923–1925.

Pimentel, L. (2003). Scurvy: Historical review and current diagnostic approach. *American Journal of Emergency Medicine* 21: 328–332.

Schneider, J. B., and Norman, R. A. (2004). Cutaneous manifestations of endocrine metabolic disease and nutritional deficiency in the elderly. *Dermatological Clinics* 22: 23–31.

Van der Merwe, A. E., Steyn, M., and Maat, G. J. R. (2009). Adult scurvy in skeletal remains of late 19th century mineworkers in Kimberley, South Africa. *International Journal of Osteoarchaeology* 20: 307–316.

Velandia, B., Centor, R. M., McConnell, V., and Shah, M. (2007). Scurvy is still present in developed countries. *Journal of General Internal Medicine* 23(8): 1281–1284.

Weinstein, M., Babyn, P., and Zlotkin, S. (2001). An orange a day keeps the doctor away: Scurvy in the year 2000. *Pediatrics* 108(3): e55.

Vascular Conditions and Anemia

Almeida, A., and Roberts, I. (2005). Bone involvement in sickle cell disease. *British Journal of Haematology* 29(4): 482–490.

Aroojis, A. J., and Johari, A. N. (2000). Epiphyseal separations after neonatal osteomyelitis and septic arthritis. *Journal of Pediatric Orthopedics* 20(4): 544–549.

Blom, D. E., Buikstra, J. E., Keng, L., Tomczak, P., Shoreman, E., and Stevens-Tuttle, D. (2005). Anemia and childhood mortality: Latitudinal patterning along the coast of pre-Columbian Peru. *American Journal of Physical Anthropology* 127: 152–169.

Brickley, M., and Ives, R. (2006). Skeletal manifestations of infantile scurvy. *American Journal of Physical Anthropology* 129: 163–172.

Brugnara, C. (2003). Iron deficiency and erythropoiesis: New diagnostic approaches. *Clinical Chemistry* 49: 1573–1578.

Casella, E. B., Valente, M., de Navarro, J. M., and Kok, F. (2005). Vitamin B_{12} deficiency in infancy as a cause of developmental regression. *Brain Development* 27: 592–594.

Cetinkaya, F., Yildirmak, Y., Kutluk, G., and Erdem, E. (2007). Nutritional vitamin B_{12} deficiency in hospitalized young children. *Pediatric Hematology and Oncology* 24: 15–21.

Faerman, M., Nebel, A., Filon, D., Thomas, M. G., Bradman, N., Ragsdale, B. D., Schultz, M., and Oppenheim, A. (2000). From a dry bone to a genetic portrait: A case of sickle cell anemia. *American Journal of Physical Anthropology* 111: 153–163.

Fairgrieve, S. I., and Molto, J. E. (2000). Cribra orbitalia in two temporally distinct population samples from the Dakhleh Oasis, Egypt. *American Journal of Physical Anthropology* 111: 319–331.

Halvorsen, S., and Bechensteen, A. G. (2002). Physiology of erythropoietin during mammalian development. *Acta Paediatrica Supplement* 91: 17–26.

Keenleyside, A., and Panayotova, K. (2006). Cribra orbitalia and porotic hyperostosis in a Greek colonial population (5th to 3rd centuries BC) from the Black Sea. *International Journal of Osteoarchaeology* 16: 373–384.

Kepron, C., Somers, G. R., and Pollanen, M. S. (2009). Sickle cell trait mimicking multiple inflicted injuries in a 5 year old boy. *Journal of Forensic Sciences* 54(5): 1141–1145.

Lagia, A., Eliopoulos, C., and Manolis, S. (2007). Thalassemia: Macroscopic and radiological study of a case. *International Journal of Osteoarchaeology* 17: 269–285.

Lerner, V., and Kanevsky, M. (2002). Acute dementia with delirium due to vitamin B_{12} deficiency: a case report. *International Journal of Psychiatry Medicine* 32: 215–220.

Marchant, T., Armstrong Schellenber, J. R., Edgar, T., Ronsmans, C., Nathan, R., Abdulla, S., and Mukasa, O. (2002). Anaemia during pregnancy in southern Tanzania. *Annals of Tropical Medicine and Parasitology* 96: 477–487.

McEwan, J. M., Mays, S., and Blake, G. M. (2005). The relationship of bone mineral density and other growth parameters to stress indicators in a medieval juvenile population. *International Journal of Osteoarchaeology* 15: 155–163.

Mendis, K., Sina, B., Marchesini, P., and Carter, R. (2001). The neglected burden of *Plasmodium vivax* malaria. *American Journal of Tropical and Medical Hygiene* 64: 97–106.

Pinheiro, J., Cunha, E., Cordeiro, C., and Vieira, D. N. (2004). Bridging the gap between forensic anthropology and osteoarchaeology—A case of vascular pathology. *International Journal of Osteoarchaeology* 14: 137–144.

Sabet, S. J., Tarbet, K. J., Lemke, B. N., Smith, M. E., and Albert, D. M. (2001). Subperiosteal hematoma of the orbit with osteoneogenesis. *Archives of Ophthalmology* 119: 301–303.

Salvadei, L., Ricci, F., and Manzi, G. (2001). Porotic hyperostosis as a marker of health and nutritional conditions during childhood: Studies at the transition between Imperial Rome and early middle ages. *American Journal of Human Biology* 13: 709–717.

Schultz, M. (2001). Paleohistopathology of bone: A new approach to the study of ancient diseases. *Yearbook of Physical Anthropology* 44: 106–147.

Segal, L. S., and Wallach, D. M. (2004). Slipped capital femoral epiphysis in a child with sickle cell disease. *Clinical Orthopedics and Related Research* 419(2): 198–201.

Stabler, S. P., and Allen, R. H. (2004). Vitamin B$_{12}$ deficiency as a worldwide problem. *Annual Review of Nutrition* 24: 299–326.

Sullivan, A. (2005). Prevalence and etiology of acquired anemia in medieval York, England. *American Journal of Physical Anthropology* 128: 252–272.

Thein, S. L. (2004). Genetic insights into the clinical severity of beta thalassemia. *British Journal of Haematology* 124: 264–274.

Van der Merwe, A. E., Maat, G. J. R., and Steyn, M. (2010). Ossified haematomas and infectious bone changes on the anterior tibia: Histomorphological features as an aid for accurate diagnosis. *International Journal of Osteoarchaeology* 20: 227–239.

Walker, P. L., Bathurst, R. R., Richman, R., Gjerdrum, T., and Andrushko, V. A. (2009). The causes of porotic hyperostosis and cribra orbitalia: A reappraisal of the iron-deficiency-anaemia hypothesis. *American Journal of Physical Anthropology* 139: 109–125.

Wapler, U., Crubezy, E., and Schultz, M. (2004). Is cribra orbitalia synonymous with anemia? Analysis and interpretation of cranial pathology in Sudan. *American Journal of Physical Anthropology* 123: 333–339.

Weiss, R., Fogelman, Y., and Bennett, M. (2004). Severe vitamin B$_{12}$ deficiency in an infant associated with a maternal deficiency and a strict vegetarian diet. *Journal of Pediatric Hematology and Oncology* 26: 270–271.

Neoplasm

Alt, K. W., Adler, C. P., Buitrago-Tellez, C. H., and Lohrke, B. (2002). Infant osteosarcoma. *International Journal of Osteoarchaeology* 12: 442–448.

Barberi, A., Cappabianca, S., and Collela, G. (2003). Bilateral cemento-ossifying fibroma of the maxillary sinus. *British Journal of Radiology* 76: 279–280.

Buzon, M. R. (2005). Two cases of pelvic osteochondroma in New Kingdom Nubia. *International Journal of Osteoarchaeology* 15: 377–382.

Capasso, L. (2005). Antiquity of cancer. *International Journal of Cancer* 113: 2–13.

Civelek, B., Oktem, F., Karamursel, S., and Celebioglu, S. (2005). A rare entity: Cemento-ossifying fibroma. *Plastic and Reconstructive Surgery* 116: 2049–2050.

Collard, T., Gabart, N., and Blondiaux, J. (2008). A palaeopathological case of a right maxilla's cemento-ossifying fibroma. *International Journal of Osteoarchaeology* 18: 195–201.

Czametzki, A., and Pusch, C. M. (2000). Identification of sarcomas in two burials of the 9th century in western Germany. *Journal of Palaeopathology* 12: 47–62.

Eshed, V., Latimer, B., Greenwald, C. M., Jellema, L. M., Rothschild, B. M., Wish-Baratz, S., and Hershkovitz, I. (2002). Button osteoma: Its etiology and pathophysiology. *American Journal of Physical Anthropology* 118: 217–230.

Hamilton, M. D., and Marks, M. K. (2004). Metastatic carcinoma: Skeletal pattern and diagnosis. *American Journal of Physical Anthropology* 38: 107.

Hildesheim, A., Dosemeci, M., Chan, C.-C., Chen, C.-J., Chen, Y.-J., Hsu, M.-M., Chen, I.-H., Mittle, B. F., Sun, B., Levine, P. H., Chen, J.-Y., Brinton, L. A., and Yang, C.-S. (2001). Occupational exposure to wood, formaldehyde, solvents and risk of nasopharyngeal carcinoma. *Cancer Epidemiology, Biomarkers and Prevention* 10: 1145–1153.

Hooton, E. (1930). *The Indians of Pecos Pueblo: A study of their skeletal remains*. Yale University Press, New Haven, CT.

Hoshimoto, K., Mitsuya, K., and Ohkura, T. (2000). Osteochondroma of the pubis symphysis associated with sexual disturbance. *Gynecologic and Obstetric Investigation* 50: 70–72.

Luna, L. H., Aranda, C. M., Bosio, L. A., and Beron, M. A. (2008). A case of multiple metastasis in late Holocene hunter-gatherers from the Argentine Pampean region. *International Journal of Osteoarchaeology* 18: 492–506.

MacDonald-Jankowski, D. S. (2004). Fibro-osseous lesions of the face and jaws. *Clinical Radiology* 59: 11–25.

Mark, S. (2007). Nasopharyngeal carcinoma: A review of its causes and its diagnosis in skeletal material. *International Journal of Osteoarchaeology* 17: 547–562.

Marks, M. K., and Hamilton, M. D. (2007). Metastatic carcinoma: Palaeopathology and differential diagnosis. *International Journal of Osteoarchaeology* 17: 217–234.

Melikian, M. (2006). A case of metastatic carcinoma from 18th century London. *International Journal of Osteoarchaeology* 16: 138–144.

Ostendorf Smith, M. (2002). A probable case of metastatic carcinoma from the late prehistoric eastern Tennessee River Valley. *International Journal of Osteoarchaeology* 12: 235–247.

Phillips, S. S., and Verano, J. W. (2010). Differential diagnosis of an unusual tibial pathology from Peru. *International Journal of Osteoarchaeology* doi: 10.1002/oa.1165.

Robbin, M. R., and Murphey, M. D. (2000). Benign chondroid neoplasms of bone. *Seminars in Musculoskeletal Radiology* 4: 45–58.

Rothschild, B. M., Ruhli, F., and Rotschild, C. (2002). Skeletal clues apparently distinguishing Waldenstroms macroglobulinemia from multiple myeloma and leukemia. *American Journal of Physical Anthropology* 14: 532–537.

Schajowicz, F., and McGuire, M. H. (1989). Diagnostic difficulties in skeletal pathology. *Clinical Orthopedics and Related Research* 240: 281–310.

Sefcakova, A., Strouhal, E., Nemeckova, A., Thurzo, M., and Stassikova-Stukovska, D. (2001). Case of metastatic carcinoma from end of the 8th to early 9th century Slovakia. *American Journal of Physical Anthropology* 116: 216–229.

Slaus, M., Dubravko, O., and Peaeina, M. (2000). Osteochondroma in a skeleton from an 11th century Croatian cemetery. *Croatian Medical Journal* 41: 336–340.

Smith, M. O. (2002). A probable case of metastatic carcinoma from the late prehistoric eastern Tennessee River Valley. *International Journal of Osteoarchaeology* 4: 235–247.

Strouhal, E., and Nemeckova, A. (2004). A paleopathological find of a sacral neurilemmoma from ancient Egypt. *American Journal of Physical Anthropology* 125: 320–328.

Takano, A., Takasaki, K., Kumagami, H., Higami, Y., and Kobayashi, T. (2001). A case of bilateral middle-ear squamous cell carcinoma. *Journal of Laryngology and Otology* 11: 815–818.

Vrabec, J. T., Lambert, P. R., and Chaljub, G. (2000). Osteoma of the internal auditory canal. *Archives Otolaryngology Head and Neck Surgery* 126: 895–898.

Warren, M. W., and Schultz, J. J. (2004). Lytic lesions of the cranial vault: Differential diagnosis in dry bone. *American Journal of Physical Anthropology* 38: 203.

Weber, J., and Czarnetzki, A. (2002). Primary intraosseous meningioma in a skull of the medieval period of southwestern Germany. *International Journal of Osteoarchaeology* 12: 385–392.

Williams, H. K., Mangham, C., and Speight, P. M. (2000). Juvenile ossifying fibroma. An analysis of eight cases and a comparison with other fibro-osseous lesions. *Journal of Oral Pathology and Medicine* 29: 13–18.

Zupi, A., Ruggiero, A. M., Insabato, L., Senghore, N., and Califano, L. (2000). Aggressive cemento-ossifying fibroma of the jaws. *Oral Oncology* 36: 129–133.

Miscellaneous and Heterotopic Calcification

Alkadhi, H., and Garzoli, E. (2005). Calcified filariasis of the breasts. *New England Journal of Medicine* 352: e2.

Anderson, R. (2003). A medieval bladder stone from Norwich, Norfolk. *International Journal of Osteoarchaeology* 13: 165–167.

Bach, A., Hann, L., Hadar, O., Shi, W., Yoo, H-H., Giess, C., Sheinfeld, J., and Thaler, H. (2001). Testicular microlithiasis: What is its association with testicular cancer? *Radiology* 220: 70–75.

Bastarrika, G., Pina, L., Vivas, I., Elorz, M., San Julian, M., and Alberro, J. (2001). Calcified filariasis of the breast: Report of four cases. *European Radiology* 11: 1195–1197.

Bennett, H. F., Middleton, W. D., Bullock, A. D., and Teefey, S. A. (2001). Testicular microlithiasis: U.S. follow-up. *Radiology* 218: 359–363.

Borman, P., Bodur, H., and Ciliz, D. (2002). Ochronotic arthropathy. *Rheumatology International* 21: 205–209.

Bovo, G., Romano, F., Perego, E., Franciosi, C., Buffa, R., and Uggeri, F. (2004). Heterotopic mesenteric ossification (intra-abdominal myositis ossificans): A case report. *International Journal of Surgery and Pathology* 12(4): 407–409.

Chanchairujira, K., Chung, C. B., Kim, J. Y., Papakonstantinou, O., Lee, M. H., Clopton, P., and Resnick, D. (2004). Intervertebral disk calcification of the spine in an elderly population: Radiographic prevalence, location and distribution and correlation with spinal degeneration. *Radiology* 230: 499–503.

Feydy, A., Liote, F., Carlier, R., Chevrot, A., and Drape, J-L. (2006). Cervical spine and crystal-associated diseases: Imaging findings. *European Radiology* 16: 459–468.

Gear, A. J. L., Buckley, C., Kaplan, F., and Vaneek, A. (2004). Multifactorial refractory heterotopic ossification. *Annals of Plastic Surgery* 52(3): 319–324.

Goff, A. K., and Reichard, R. (2006). A soft tissue calcification: Differential diagnosis and pathogenesis. *Journal of Forensic Sciences* 51(3): 493–497.

Hakim, M., and McCarthy, E. F. (2001). Heterotopic mesenteric ossification. *American Journal of Roentgenology* 176: 260–261.

Kanava, H., Saito, U., Gama, N., Konno, W., Hirabayashi, H., and Haruna, S.-I. (2008). Intramuscular hemangioma of masseter muscle with prominent formation of phleboliths: A case report. *International Journal of ORL and HNS* 35: 587–591.

Kishimoto, K. M., Watanabe, Y., Nakamura, H., and Kokubun, S. (2002). Ectopic bone formation by electroporatic transfer of bone morphogenetic protein-4 gene. *Bone* 31: 340–347.

Komar, D., and Buikstra, J. E. (2003). Differential diagnosis of a prehistoric biological object from the Koster (Illinois) site. *International Journal of Osteoarchaeology* 13: 157–164.

Lai, C-T., Chuang, F-P., and Chuang, T-H. (2004). Heterotopic ossification in testicular microlithiasis. *Urology* 64: 585–586.

Lee, R. S., Kayser, M. V., and Ali, S. Y. (2006). Calcium phosphate microcrystal deposition in the human intervertebral disc. *Journal of Anatomy* 208: 13–19.

Leis, V. M., and Cotlar, A. M. (2003). Fractured heterotopic bone in a midline abdominal wound. *Current Surgery* 60(2): 193–195.

Massinde, A. N., Rumanyika, R., and Im, H. B. (2009). Coexistent lithopedion and live abdominal ectopic pregnancy. *Obstetrics and Gynecology* 114: 458–460.

Mays, S., and Dungworth, D. (2009). Intervertebral chondrocalcinosis: An exercise in differential diagnosis in palaeopathology. *International Journal of Osteoarchaeology* 19: 36–49.

Mooney, E., Vaidya, K., Tavassoli, F. (2000). Ossifying well-differentiated Sertoli-Leydig cell tumor of the ovary. *Annals of Diagnostic Pathology* 4: 34–38.

Perry, M., Newnam, J., and Gilliland, M. (2008). Differential diagnosis of a calcified object from a 4th–5th century AD burial in Aqaba, Jordan. *International Journal of Osteoarchaeology* 18: 507–522.

Qayyum, A., Cowling, M., and Adam, I. (2000). Small bowel volvulus related to a calcified mesenteric lymph node. *Clinical Radiology* 55: 483–485.

Quintelier, K. (2009). Calcified uterine leimyomata from a post-medieval nunnery in Brussels, Belgium. *International Journal of Osteoarchaeology* 19: 436–442.

Shehab, D., Elgazzar, A. H., and Collier, B. D. (2002). Heterotopic ossification. *Journal of Nuclear Medicine* 43(3): 346–353.

Wang, D., Shurafa, M. S., Acharya, R., Strand, V. F., and Linden, M. D. (2004). Chronic abdominal pain caused by heterotopic ossification with functioning bone marrow. *Archives of Pathology and Laboratory Medicine* 128: 321–323.

Taphonomy

9

JOANNE BRISTOW
ZOE SIMMS
DR. PATRICK RANDOLPH-QUINNEY

Contents

Introduction

The term *taphonomy* was first introduced by the Russian geologist Efremov (1940: 85) to encompass studies in what he referred to as the "transition of animal remains from the biosphere into the lithosphere," the word being derived from the Greek *taphos*, meaning "burial," and *nomos*, meaning "law." In 1962, Olson introduced the word into Western usage in his consideration of late Permian terrestrial vertebrates of the United States and the former Soviet Union. Since then, the term has been variously applied to a wide range of studies in paleontology, paleoanthropology, paleoecology, and archaeology and lately has been adopted by the forensic anthropological community under the umbrella term *forensic taphonomy*. However, the wider application of taphonomic principles has seen a watering down of the strict definition of the "laws of burial," which have been modified, adapted, and altered as nonpaleontological disciplines coopt the principles of taphonomy for their own use; in particular, the term has become associated with the study of site formation and cultural processes (*n* and *c* transforms) in archaeology and has been adopted by the forensic anthropological community for a variety

279

of studies addressing the fate of human remains. No longer being strictly confined to biological remains, taphonomy has ceased to be purely associated with the biosphere in practice; it may be argued that it is now synonymous with all aspects of the burial or postmortem process and indeed may be applied to ante- and perimortem issues as well (see the next section for a critical evaluation of this statement).

The cooption of taphonomy into the forensic sphere was described by Dirkmaat and colleagues (2008: 34) as "the most significant development [to] alter the field of forensic anthropology" in the last 20 years; given this statement, the unfamiliar reader may well hold high expectations of the forensic taphonomic literature available. Further purported by the authors as no less than a genuine Khunian paradigm shift, "provid[ing] a more solid scientific underpinning to the discipline, from both a methodological and theoretical point of view," advances in forensic anthropology would appear indebted to the invaluable introduction of taphonomic approaches to the field through the application of uniformitarian methodologies and assumptions in order to understand pattern, process, and mechanism in the recent (i.e., forensic) past. Forensic taphonomy is perhaps unique in that the subject area marks a decadian shift in the temporal nature of taphonomic studies, away from longitudinal studies of complex time-averaged assemblages accumulated over millennia to shorter postmortem time frames spanning days to years, with the acknowledgment of humans as taphonomic agents and the emergence of the cadaver or carcass as a key unit of analysis. As such, this chapter discusses some of the prevalent trends in the forensic application of taphonomic principles and what sets these apart from conventional classical taphonomic approaches; given the space limitations imposed by this volume, a particular emphasis on decompositional studies and the assessment of postmortem interval is adopted, although other related research areas are highlighted.

The Theoretical and Epistemological Bases of Forensic Taphonomy

The pattern of research into the taphonomic processes affecting vertebrate skeletal assemblages (from which forensic taphonomy developed) can be seen to have followed a broadly uniformitarian approach utilizing the study of modern analogues as a means of interpreting observed past phenomena. Much of the impetus for this work came out of the procedures set up to test the validity of R. A. Dart's 1949 *Osteodontokeratic* cultural hypothesis for the behavior of early hominids recovered from the cave deposits at Makapansgat, South Africa (Quinney 2000). Early taphonomic studies centered on the search for principles governing the transformations and transitory pathways involved in the progression of biosphere entities and organismal remains into the lithosphere and were often established to answer or address research problems related to early hominid behaviors, such as the controlled use of fire or hunting versus scavenging economies. This early work represents a vast corpus of literature relating to aspects of necrology, biostratinomy, burial, and diagenesis (Grupe 2007), and the reader is directed to the work of Allison and Briggs (1991), Behrensmyer and Hill (1980), Binford (1981, 1983), Bonnichsen and Sorg (1989), and Lyman (1994) for relevant taphonomic overviews that underpin much of the subsequent work in the forensic sphere. Given the nature of the early work in taphonomy, in-depth discussion of founding concepts falls largely outside the discussion in this chapter; however, several important concepts are worthy of note in relation to both the methodological approaches and the key principles directing their actualization.

In attempting to understand the burial and postmortem process, taphonomists can be seen to have adopted two complementary lines of approach (Quinney 2000): (1) neotaphonomy or actualistic taphonomy, which concentrates on the modern environment and applies its results to the past by analogy, and (2) paleotaphonomy, which examines the context and content of depositional sites in great detail using temporospatial patterning, skeletal part representation, and the pattern of skeletal damage as a means of interpreting formation processes. The former analogous approach can be seen as primarily hypothetico-deductive in nature, while the latter can be inductive, deductive, or a combination of both. Forensic taphonomic research or reporting can fall into either category; in the main, experimental approaches can be considered neotaphonomic, while much of the case-based single-study reports can be considered paleotaphonomic in nature. However, the scientific validity of what was (and indeed still is) a largely anecdotal, case-based literature, suffers from limitations in application above and beyond the site-specific conditions of the original study. One of the reasons for this may be that while other branches of the historical sciences have attempted to produce middle- or high-level taphonomic models that aim to construct overarching laws of burial, forensic taphonomic research has primarily been empirical in nature, with the production of low-level rather than high-level theoretical output. The distinction is important and has profound implications for the applicability of much of the forensic taphonomic literature.

Low-level theories can be described as empirical research with generalizations. Such generalizations are often based on regularities that are repeatedly observed and that can be refuted by the observations of contrary cases; in taphonomy, these observations can be neotaphonomic or paleotaphonomic in nature and provide the basal data set of the discipline, often published on a case-by-case or single-incidence basis; the forensic taphonomic literature is replete with examples spanning a wide range of areas, including the taphonomy of trauma on an individual basis, unusual cases of preservation or decomposition, or case examples that highlight the nature of commingling, transport, or dispersal of body parts on an individual basis. Middle-level theories can be defined as generalizations that attempt to account for the regularities that occur between two or more sets of variables in multiple instances. Middle-level theory thus provides a conceptual bridge between low-level data collection and high-level encompassing theory (i.e., Efremov's laws of burial).

Reliant on objective evaluation and extreme empiricism, neotaphonomic research utilizing actualistic approaches (often equated to methodological uniformitarianism and the idea of "argument by analogy") fluoresced throughout the late 1980s and into the 1990s. With a heavy focus on vertebrate taphonomy and developing a greater understanding of material transport and bone weathering processes, the 1970s witnessed some of the first truly anthropological taphonomic publications outside the paleontological literature (Dirkmaat et al. 2008). These publications were primarily interested in the stepwise *loss* of information at each dynamic stage of assemblage or site formation and were termed *megabiases*; it was not until the mid-1980s that the untapped potential for information *gain* cemented the positive contributions of taphonomic research within the anthropological arena (Behrensmeyer et al. 2000; Lyman 2010). It was only a matter of time before forensic anthropologists (many of them trained in bioarchaeology, field archaeology, and paleoanthropology) began to realize the important role that the analysis of taphonomic traces could bring to forensic investigation.

The landmark 1997 edited volume of Haglund and Sorg (and its successor; Haglund and Sorg 2002a) remain the most comprehensive monographs on the subject of forensic taphonomy to date. In collating the previously disparate literature, standardizing terminology, and highlighting the major outcomes of taphonomic analyses for the forensic anthropologist in mass disaster and victim identification, these texts represent an invaluable introduction to the world of forensic taphonomy for both anthropology students and taphonomic practitioners alike. The first volume (Haglund and Sorg 1997) is primarily decomposition process-driven, and highlights major areas of research in hard and soft tissue decomposition (including hairs and fibers), the effects of scavenging, weathering and transport, the burial environment, burning, and bodies in water. Having established a need for the forensic application of taphonomy, the second volume (Haglund and Sorg 2002a) considers taphonomic principles in a more applied manner through case studies and, in particular, the application of taphonomic principles in mass grave anthropology (Anderson and Cervenka 2002; Berryman 2002; Brothwell and Gill-Robinson 2002; Darwent and Lyman 2002; Dirkmaat 2002; Ebbesmeyer and Haglund 2002; Graver et al. 2002; Haglund 2002; Haglund et al. 2002; Haglund and Sorg 2002b; Harvey and King 2002; Hochrein 2002; Janaway 2002; Mayne-Correia and Beattie 2002; Morton and Lord 2002; Nordby 2002; Roksandic

2002; Saul and Saul 2002; Schmitt 2002; Simmons 2002; Skinner et al. 2002; Sledzik and Rodriguez 2002; Sorg and Haglund 2002; Symes et al. 2002; Ubelaker 2002). These seminal volumes are essential background reading and provide a yardstick by which to measure the development and evolution of forensic taphonomy over the last decade.

Above and beyond early studies investigating postmortem alterations to bone such as color changes, surface texture modifications, weathering and scavenging effects, forensic taphonomy represents "the analysis of the spatial distribution of remains at their location of discovery, a careful consideration of the environmental setting after death, analysis of the soft tissue remaining, insect and animal interaction with the body and a thorough analysis of bone modification from staining to trauma" (Dirkmaat et al. 2008: 46). Closely related to zooarchaeological taphonomic approaches (e.g., Bartosiewicz 2008), the medicolegal responsibility implied by the forensic definition of this applied taphonomic field necessitated a significant change in emphasis from the previously qualitative assessments of experienced practitioners and logical inferences and estimates from early case studies (Tibbett and Carter 2009) to the systematic and quantitative collation of data using rigorous scientific methodologies.

However, the widespread adoption of taphonomic principles by other disciplines has come into criticism by Lyman (2010: 2), who lamented that the term has been adopted (particularly by archaeologists) without a clear understanding of what the term was originally intended to mean and as such is now applied to a different set of phenomena than originally intended. Forensic anthropology, it may be argued, may now find itself in a similar situation, with research undertaken that, although using uniformitarian and actualistic approaches, may be stretching the boundaries of what may be comfortably considered taphonomy. Thus, within the catchall term *forensic anthropology* a wide range of research has been undertaken that has been both diverse and innovative but may not be considered truly taphonomic using a classical definition (Lyman 2010). This has included research areas that may overlap in terms of subject matter with other practical subdivisions within the forensic sciences (i.e., entomology, forensic pathology, trauma analysis, etc.) but may still fall under the wider remit of forensic taphonomic actualistic studies. These include

- Issues of commingling in assemblages (Adams and Byrd 2008; Adams and Konigsberg 2008; Byrd 2008; Egana et al. 2008; Herrmann and Devlin 2008; L'Abbé 2005; Schaefer and Black 2007; Skinner et al. 2003; Tuller et al. 2008; Warren 2008; Warren and Schultz 2002)
- Analyses of differential trauma types (Adams and Hall 2003; Alunni-Perret et al. 2005; Bartelink et al. 2001; Carson et al. 2000; Cross and Simmons 2010; Kanz and Grossschmidt 2006; Moraitis and Spiliopouiou 2006; Wheatley 2008)

- The taphonomy of bodies in water (Bassett and Manhein 2002; Ebbesmeyer and Haglund 2002; Fernández-Jalvo and Andrews 2003; Gruspier and Pollanen 2000; Haglund and Sorg 2002b; Heaton et al. 2010)
- The formation of adipocere (Carter et al. 2007; Fielder and Graw 2003; Forbes et al. 2005a, 2005b; Forbes, Stuart, Dent, and Fenwick-Mulcahy 2005; Notter et al. 2008; O'Brien and Kuehner 2007; Widya 2009; Wilson et al. 2007; Yan et al. 2001)
- The pattern and rate of decomposition in varying environments (Adlam and Simmons 2007; Archer 2004; Benninger et al. 2008; Carter and Tibbett 2008; Carter et al. 2007, 2008a; Davis and Goff 2000; Goff 2009; Haslam and Tibbett 2009; Janjua and Rogers 2008; Pakosh and Rogers 2009; Prieto et al. 2004; Shalaby et al. 2000; Vass 2001; Vass et al. 2002; Weitzel 2005; Wilson et al. 2007)
- The effects of burning and cremation (Mayne-Correia and Beattie 2002; Warren 2008; Warren and Schultz 2002)

Notwithstanding the incontrovertible impact that forensic taphonomy has had in moving forensic anthropology from the lab into the field, importantly highlighting the need for anthropologists to understand the taphonomic context of remains under examination (Duhig 2003), it has not been until recently that the dearth of forensic taphonomic literature accumulated over the last 20 years has come under scientific scrutiny (e.g., Simmons et al. 2010a) and, as these authors would attest, for good reason. In the United States, the landmark cases of *Daubert vs. Merrel Dow Pharmaceuticals* and *Kumho Tire vs. Carmichael* (Grivas and Komar 2008) hold significant ramifications for the field of forensic taphonomy. Particularly in relation to the *Daubert* standard, the necessity for reproducible methods, acceptable error rates, and methodological peer review has proved a heavy burden on taphonomic research. As a science fraught with inherent difficulties in both controlling multivariate experimental environments and reconstructing the complex events surrounding death, body disposal, and recovery commonly represented at a forensic crime scene, forensic taphonomy stands somewhat apart from the standards required of it to garner a solid future in the courtroom (Tibbett and Carter 2009). In particular, the article by Dirkmaat and colleagues (2008) makes for uncomfortable or, at the least, unsatisfactory reading. Flying in the face of logical empiricism and falsificationism sensu stricto Popper, the omnipotent portrayal of forensic taphonomy by these authors belies a literature littered with studies founded on at best questionable scientific method and at worst bad science.

Acutely aware of the cautionary words of Lyman (1994: 38) insomuch that "it is one thing to criticize a method and entirely another to offer an equal or better alternative," this chapter is not intended as a direct criticism of the years of study by researchers in the field of forensic taphonomy but an introduction to the forensic anthropology student of the difficulties and limitations of such approaches. As such, students should be aware of the highly theoretical basis of much of the literature available, based on small sample sizes insufficient to stand as forensic *evidence*, the general principles presented through case studies, anecdotal descriptions, and animal surrogates (e.g., Archer 2004; Abraham et al. 2008) stand alone as a consequence of their unstandardized protocols (Adlam and Simmons 2007). At their polar opposite stands the gold standard of experimentation—the truly isotaphonomic study, in which equality of both the general and the specific depositional environments and the processes of accumulation between samples allow direct comparison of equivalent taphonomic modes through time (Behrensmeyer et al. 2000).

Debatable in terms of achievable practicality, only a handful of attempts at controlled, reproducible, and falsifiable experimental methods are identifiable in the literature (e.g., Heaton et al. 2010; Simmons, Adlam, and Moffatt 2010; Simmons, Cross, et al. 2010). Based around two general themes, the use of accumulated degree days as a means of standardization across seasons and geographic areas (Adlam and Simmons 2007) versus reductionist approaches utilizing simple substrates as a preliminary understanding of more complex processes (Tibbett et al. 2004) represents conscientious attempts toward the isotaphonomic ideal. Notwithstanding the ethical implications and difficulties in acquiring human cadavers for experimental use and the necessity to currently use human analogues (Tibbett et al. 2004), the employment of such approaches provides acceptable models toward understanding the extensive array of extraneous factors and compounding variables expressed in the cycling of various forms of energy within the cadaveric ecosystem and surrounding environment. As such, these studies formally realize the issues of equifinality as a central concept in taphonomic inference, a realization that is singularly lacking in many other studies. The term was defined by von Bertalanffy in 1949 as "reaching the same final state from different initial states" in an open system, one capable of "exchanging materials with its environment." As such, taphonomists have typically defined equifinality as reaching the same final state from different initial conditions and in different ways, without consideration of whether a system was open or closed. Lyman (2004) highlighted the issues that equifinality raises and whether the fact that two alternate taphonomic hypotheses can be distinguished is due to equifinality or a problem of statistical indistinguishability. This is one of the great problems with taphonomic interpretation in that while there is only one physical past, there may be multicasuative agents that produce that past and as such can affect our reconstruction of an event or a taphonomic trace. The problem resonates in Behrensmeyer's notion of *isotaphonomic contexts*, and the issue of equifinality is perhaps one of the major concepts within taphonomy that forensic taphonomists have yet to address with any gusto.

The Application of Forensic Taphonomy: Postmortem Interval Estimation

In recognition of the need to establish scientifically grounded estimates of postmortem interval (PMI) and postburial interval (PBI), recent studies have endeavored to provide a better understanding of cadaver decomposition processes (e.g., Vass et al. 2002), forensically important entomological evidence (e.g., Benecke 2001; Amendt et al. 2007; Gallagher et al. 2010), cadaver-environment exchange processes (e.g., Carter and Tibbett 2006, 2008; Haslam and Tibbett 2009), and trauma-related taphonomic changes (e.g., Mayne-Correia and Beattie 2002; Saul and Saul 2002; Cross and Simmons 2010). In particular, the plethora of studies relating to decompositional aspects of human cadavers represents an ideal body of literature for discourse on the methodological inadequacies and limitations of earlier studies. To this end, the next section highlights both the requirements of a good taphonomic experiment and the currently limited nature of our knowledge in relation to the influences of environmental and edaphic parameters on decomposition processes (Denys 2002; Carter et al. 2008a).

Continuing this theme, we look at recent advances in the area of soil analysis and the increased recognition of the soil-cadaver interface. Marking a shift from traditional studies of the body itself and the aboveground activity of insects and scavengers (Berryman 2002; Devault et al. 2003, 2004; Tibbett and Carter 2008) to the grave soils immediately surrounding it. Research on soil analysis in a taphonomic context has gained significant momentum in the last 10 years. Often utilizing novel, multivariate techniques and controlled microcosmal methods (e.g., Stokes et al. 2009), discourse on this rapidly expanding field provides some excellent ideas in terms of methodological approaches for other taphonomic studies in the forensic sciences.

Although by no means exhaustive given the broad-ranging research areas that fall within the remit of forensic taphonomy and the somewhat restricted word limits of this discussion, it is important to note the continuing research in the more classical areas of taphonomic study. Largely focused on the role of humans as taphonomic agents and the removal of all other natural processes affecting the presentation of remains at a crime scene (Dirkmaat et al. 2008), publications on context- and species-specific scavenging effects on bone frequently present within the literature (e.g., DeVault et al. 2003; Brown et al. 2006; Morton and Lord 2006; Pokines and Peterhans 2007; Kjorlien et al. 2009; Fernández-Jalvo et al. 2010). Interestingly, in relation to bone-weathering processes, only a single study by Janjua and Rogers (2008) represents the taphonomic literature since the now-seminal studies of Behrensmeyer and Kidwell in the 1980s at the Amboseli National Park in Kenya. Despite several other studies for which weathering effects are discussed, but do not present as the main focus for study (e.g., Littleton 2000; Tersigni 2007; Huculak and Rogers 2009), the qualitative nature of their conclusions and the inherently complex, climate-specific covariance of weathering pattern expressions in distinct areas on the same bone have ultimately resulted in no discernible progression beyond the original stages defined by Behrensemeyer and Kidwell in the 1970s.

Breaking Down Decomposition

Decomposition can be described as the process by which the body breaks down and decays, finally resulting in skeletonization. It is a continuous process that is often difficult to divide into discrete defining categories, even though much of the literature attempts to pinpoint such divisions accurately. Understanding human decomposition is critical for its use in determining time since death, which may have a significant impact on forensic investigations. An adequate understanding of all of the processes that influence decomposition and the stages through which a body passes as it decomposes can be used to estimate time since death. This cannot be accurately or precisely determined and will only ever be an estimate of PMI, usually constructed around the presence of entomological evidence (Goff 2009).

Decompositional changes to a body that occur immediately after death are often much more rapid than those occurring later in the process, making it difficult to establish an exact time interval. Decomposition can be retarded by several processes, including physical and chemical barriers and climatic factors (Goff 2009). The factors that affect the rate at which postmortem changes occur were suggested by Prieto et al. (2004) as being classified into two groups: those dependent on the cadaver or intrinsic factors and those dependent on the postmortem environment of the cadaver or extrinsic factors such as temperature, humidity, insect activity, and scavenging. Methods of estimating PMI are often subjective and limited in use to early stages of decomposition (Swann et al. 2010). The time it takes for human remains to reach skeletonization is highly variable and dependent on the burial or depositional environment as well as other factors relating to the remains themselves, such as body mass and whether the individual was attired, for example. Indeed, Fielder and Graw (2003) stated that it may take between 3 and 12 years for an interred body to fully decompose under favorable conditions.

Early Decompositional Changes: Livor to Rigor

Livor mortis is the first change in external appearance of the cadaver and is also named lividity, postmortem hypostasis, or vibices (Goff 2009). A cessation of heart function prevents the circulation of blood around the body, and blood begins to "pool" under the influences of gravity in the regions of the body that are in closest proximity to the lowest point, causing the area to become reddish/pink in color (Goff 2009). Hypostasis can appear like a newly formed bruise under the surface of the skin. Pressing on the skin surface at this time will result in blanching of the area, and lividity will return on removal of the pressure (Goff 2009). This occurs as the blood is still quite viscous and lividity is not yet fixed. Turning the body onto the opposite side during this time will express a change in lividity onto the opposing area (Henssge and Madea 2007). After approximately 9–12 hours, a change in position of the body will not change the position of hypostasis, and livor is described as fixed (Goff 2009).

As the body begins to cool subsequent to cessation of life, its temperature will reach equilibrium with the surrounding ambient temperature. This process is called *algor mortis* and may take between 18 and 20 hours (Vass et al. 2002). Goff (2009) discussed a "rule-of-thumb equation" for estimating the PMI using body temperature: PMI(h) = [98.6-body temperature (°F)]/1.5. The author advised that this method should only be used during early stages of decomposition and used with caution. Al-Alousi (2002) and Al-Alousi and colleagues (2002) provided arguably the most comprehensive investigation of the postmortem cooling curve in humans—highlighting the compound nature of the curve and deviations from the sigmoidal shape often cited in the literature. Studying 117 forensic cases, recording rectal, liver, and brain temperatures up to 60 hours after death, the authors' findings are interestingly not cited once in the forensic taphonomic literature on decomposition processes.

Rigor mortis results in a stiffness of the joints of the cadaver due to a change in the myofibrils of the muscle tissues. Onset of rigor mortis can be observed within the first 2–6 hours following death and develops fully over the first 12 hours. The process is governed by two primary factors: temperature and the metabolic state of the cadaver (Goff 2009). Reduced ambient temperatures were suggested by Goff (2009) to accelerate and prolong rigor mortis, whereas warmer temperatures tend to decrease rigor onset and reduce its duration. Onset of rigor initiates in the muscles of the face and continues to spread to the rest of the muscles of the body over subsequent hours. The conversion of adenosine triphosphate (ATP) to adenosine diphosphate (ADP) leads to an increased production of lactic acid, which increases cellular pH and prevents the actin and myosin fibers moving over one another, resulting in rigor. Rigor mortis is not a permanent process and tends to become absent from the body within 24 to 84 hours depending on the environment (Goff 2009).

Cadaveric Breakdown

A depletion of internal oxygen levels occurs subsequent to the cessation of life and allows for enzymatic digestion (autolysis) and initiates widespread cell degradation via anaerobic microorganisms (Carter et al. 2007), specifically those situated within the gastrointestinal tract and the respiratory system, such as bacteria, fungi, and protozoa (Vass et al. 2002). This is suggested to begin approximately 4 minutes after death has occurred (Vass et al. 2002). This process leads to an increased permeability of cell membranes throughout the body and a sanguineous-aqueous saturation of body tissues (hemolysis) (Fielder and Graw 2003). Microorganisms metabolize lipids and proteins into organic acids and gases, such as propionic acid, lactic acid, methane, and hydrogen sulfide, and ammonia. Production of quantities of by-products results in a color change of the integumentary system and bloating of the cadaver, signaling the primary bloat stage of putrefaction (Carter et al. 2007) (Table 9.1).

A continued internal buildup of decompositional gases eventually leads to purging through body orifices, such as the mouth, nose, and anus. Pressure buildup of decomposition by-products eventually leads to complete purging and rupturing of the soft tissues (secondary bloat stage; Table 9.1) (Carter et al. 2007). Insect activity will also have an important influence on this process. Rupturing allows for a larger surface area for insect activity as well as increased oxygen content for anaerobic microorganism involvement and initiates the active decay process (Carter et al. 2007). The active decay process is most often associated with a decrease in body mass and is suggested to be used

Table 9.1 Decomposition Stages and the Physical Appearance of Remains at Each Stage

Decomposition Stage	Descriptions of Body Stages
Fresh stage	Begins at death; includes rigor mortis; postmortem hypostasis and cooling; continues until bloating of the carcass is visible.
Primary bloat stage	Accumulation of gases within the body; no disarticulation; hair and epidermis loose; soil-skin interface gray; strong odor.
Secondary bloat stage	Body still bloated; disarticulation of limbs; purging; soil-skin interface black; strong odor.
Active decay stage	Deflation of the carcass; disarticulation of the limbs and head; flesh and skin still present; carcass very wet; strong odor.
Advanced decay stage	Collapse of abdomen/rib cage; most of the flesh liquefied/gone; skin, bone, fat, and cartilage may remain; carcass very wet; adipocere formation.
Skeletonization	Flesh, skin. Fat and cartilage disappear; some adipocere and ligaments may remain

Source: Modified from Wilson, A. S., Janaway, R. C., Holland, A. D., Dodson, H. I., Baran, E., Pollard, A. M., and Tobin, D. J. *Forensic Science International*, 169, 6–18, 2007.

to assess decomposition staging (Adlam and Simmons 2007). Putrefaction processes, such as the formation of hydrocarbons, ammonia compounds, and biogenic amines, function under anaerobic conditions. Further decay by bacteria and fungi is purely anaerobic and leads to full skeletonization of the corpse (Fielder and Graw 2003).

Most of the scientific literature regarding the observations of decompositional processes of remains refers to those that have been deposited on the surface of the ground. Different depositional and burial environments will lead to a difference in observed or expected results since neither environment is static (Wilson et al. 2007). In burial environments, there is a restriction of access to the remains from scavengers and insects who pose a major role in decomposition (Simmons, Adlam, and Moffatt 2010; Simmons, Cross, et al. 2010).

Decomposition processes are influenced by many different variables, including humidity, insect activity, sunlight, rainfall, scavenging, and burial environment, among others. However, the most influential of these factors is temperature. Ironically, none of the previous research has attempted to correlate the overall physical changes in appearance of decompositional stages with temperature. Methodology and analysis, however, have changed within much of the recent literature after the seminal article written by Megyesi et al. (2005). Their research suggested that decomposition rate is more accurately dependent on accumulated temperature than on time, and they attempted to quantify a more appropriate method for estimating PMI from decomposing remains. As such, the development of total body scoring (TBS) methods and the use of accumulated degree days (ADD) has revolutionized the experimental recording and analysis of much of the recent decomposition literature, creating a standardized method for measuring temperature over a particular number of days (Simmons, Adlam, and Moffatt 2010; Simmons, Cross, et al. 2010). The use of ADD has proven beneficial, particularly in relation to its use alongside TBS as developed by Megyesi et al. (2005). The use of both of these methods together allows for a comparison of results with other studies. However, a study by Dabbs (2010) highlighted the need for refinement in application and warned that utilization of National Weather Service data from the closest weather station may not represent the most accurate model of average daily temperatures for the calculation of ADD.

The principal difficulties with previous research concerning decomposition processes has been the inability for direct comparisons between results and observations, making it extremely difficult to draw clear conclusions (Simmons, Cross, et al. 2010b). Much of the literature presents case studies, which provide "snapshots" in time of single incidences and do not provide data in a standardized manner. The results are anecdotal and neither scientifically testable nor repeatable, making their use in forensic contexts limited. Dirkmaat et al. (2008) reported that degradation of bone, decomposition of soft tissues, and subsequent estimates of PMI or TSD depend wholly on environmental factors that often cannot be referred to a practical context.

Some of the results published by Simmons, Adlam, and Moffatt (2010) reported fairly low correlations with relatively low R^2 values. It could be considered that using more appropriate statistical analysis may confer a more accurate representation of results. However, the research methodology produced by Simmons and colleagues is more reproducible and scientifically robust than previous research by other authors, particularly their use of controls. Simmons, Adlam, and Moffatt (2010) stated that continued taphonomic research concerning body decomposition must continue to do so in a scientific manner, using controls and appropriate sample sizes to ensure that the experimental procedure is repeatable and tested.

Insects are suggested to be the primary factor aside from temperature that have a highly significant effect on the rate of decomposition of remains (Simmons, Adlam, and Moffatt 2010; Simmons et al. 2010). With the decomposition rate of remains in the presence of insects shown to be dependent on carcass size, with smaller carcasses decomposing at a faster rate than larger carcasses. In the absence of any insect activity, carcass size is reported to have no influence on the rate of the decomposition process (Simmons, Adlam, and Moffatt 2010). With a wealth of published forensic entomological literature, there exists a significant overlap in the utility of insects within many taphonomic processes, particularly decomposition. As such, although one must remain aware of their importance in many areas of taphonomic study and as an important taphonomic agent in their own right, the literature regarding forensic entomology is not discussed here. For further information on this topic, the work by the following authors has been published since 2000, and the reader is advised to consult these texts as part of the progress in decomposition studies over the last 10 years: Amendt et al. (2004, 2007), Anderson and Hobischak (2004), Benecke (2001), Harvey et al. (2008), Huntington et al. (2007), and Mazzanti et al. (2009).

Adipocere

Often, decompositional processes can be slowed and the body preserved under the appropriate conditions (O'Brien and Kuehner 2007). These processes include mummification; peat or bogland burials, which have a reduced oxygen supply; and the formation of adipocere by a process known as saponification (Fielder and Graw 2003). In a forensic context, the formation and presence of adipocere can yield important information about the environmental context in which the body was deposited (Notter et al. 2008). Burial environment conditions such as soil type, pH, temperature, oxygen, and moisture content all have a significant effect on the production of adipocere, but it most commonly occurs in wet, anaerobic conditions, such as submersion in water or flooded burial environments (Forbes et al. 2005a,b,c; O'Brien and

Kuehner 2007; Goff 2009). Preservation of internal organs is dependent on the stage of decomposition at which adipocere formation begins. The reduced water solubility of fatty acid compounds maintains the integrity and shape of the cadaver (Fielder and Graw 2003).

Appearing as a grayish-white solid material with a waxlike consistency, adipocere forms during late postmortem changes as a product of adipose tissue in cadaveric material and should not be confused with normal soft tissue decay or decomposition (Forbes et al. 2005a, 2005b; O'Brien and Kuehner 2007; Notter et al. 2008). The formation of adipocere is often expressed in many cases and is formed by the hydrolysis of triglycerides into glycerine and free fatty acids (Forbes et al. 2005c). Neutral fats liquefy and penetrate into the surrounding tissues, such as the muscles, where they solidify (Fielder and Graw 2003; Forbes et al. 2005a; Notter et al. 2008). Salts of fatty acids and hydroxyl and oxo fatty acids have also been discovered as constituents of adipocere (Forbes et al. 2005c). The resulting mixture of mainly saturated fatty acids is termed *adipocere*, of which the main constituents are thought to be myristic, palmitic, and stearic acids, with palmitic the most abundant (Forbes et al. 2005c; Notter et al. 2008). Palmitoleic, oleic, and linoleic acids (unsaturated fatty acids) are also suggested to be composites of adipocere (Forbes et al. 2005a; Forbes 2005c; Notter et al. 2008). O'Brien and Kuehner (2007) described how the process of adipocere formation requires a "Goldilocks phenomenon" in which the environmental requirements of ambient conditions are "just right."

As with much of the taphonomic literature, the discussion and analysis of adipocere is largely in reference to case studies. Since the formation of adipocere is influenced by many differing factors, all variables must be tested if it is to be used to predict a time for PMI effectively (O'Brien and Kuehner 2007). Adipocere is not an end product and is capable of degrading and decomposing over a long period of time; however, it does help reduce the rate at which normal decomposition occurs in an unchanging environment (Fielder and Graw 2003).

Delving into the Detritusphere: The Cadaveric Human Island

Utilized in the location of clandestine graves (Carter and Tibbett 2006) and as a form of associative evidence in the estimation of PMI and PBI (Vass 2001; Carter and Tibbett 2006; Tibbett et al. 2004), soil analysis in a taphonomic context is now recognized as essential for understanding biodegradation phenomena and decomposition processes occurring at and around the cadaver. With particular soil types known to have specific decomposition dynamics and time frames (Haslam and Tibbett 2009), further research linking above- and below-ground taphonomic processes is now understood to be of vital importance.

The formation and ecology of grave soil represent a dynamic medium of complex microspheres with the capability to rapidly respond to ground disturbances resulting from the input of a carbon- and nutrient-rich habitat with a heavy, indigenous microbial flora: the cadaver (Carter et al. 2007; Parkinson et al. 2009). At the earliest stages, grave soil formation is known to be dependent on the competitive interactions of insects (Amendt et al. 2004) and scavengers (DeVault et al. 2004) and intrinsic properties of the cadaver itself, such as mass (Carter and Tibbett 2008). With small cadavers, such as fetuses or neonates, likely to be carried away and consumed *ex situ*, the amount of cadaveric material entering the primary grave soil is often minimal. Contra to this, the consumption of larger adult cadavers and carcasses is observed to occur largely *in situ* (Towne 2000), allowing significant amounts of decomposition fluids and materials to enter the surrounding soil matrix. However, with the possibility of whole cadaver movement due to insect activity (Ururahy-Rodrigues et al. 2008), the extent of the grave soil in association with the cadaver may well be highly variable and represent more than one localized area of formation.

Providing a localized pulse of water, carbon, and nutrients, the entrance of compounds and materials produced throughout the various stages of decomposition produces a concentrated island of fertility surrounding the corpse, the cadaver decomposition island (CDI) (Carter et al. 2007). Although understood to change over time in terms of its biophysicochemical characteristics (Towne 2000), the dynamic alterations in biochemistry (Towne 2000; Forbes 2008), insect succession (Chin et al. 2008; Voss et al. 2009; Matuszewski et al. 2010), and plant (Towne 2000) and fungal flora (Tibbett and Carter 2003; Sagara et al. 2008; Menezes et al. 2008, 2009; Sidrim et al. 2010) of the CDI still remain poorly understood (Carter and Tibbett 2008). Most likely related to the decompositional stage of the cadaver and factors relating to both soil texture and cadaver mass (Carter and Tibbett 2008), changes in the vertical and lateral extent of the CDI are also known to correlate with time (Towne 2000). As such, given the clearly limited nature of current knowledge on cadaver decomposition, the considerable overlap between aboveground and belowground studies of these processes has a direct impact on the ability of soil researchers to draw numerical and statistical conclusions from what are essentially general observations. In light of this, research into the correlation of CDI formation with subjective decomposition stages (e.g., Megyesi et al. 2005), knowledge of the factors affecting decomposition and thus CDI formation, and indeed duration are limited.

With most grave soil research conducted on material within the later stages of decomposition (i.e., advanced decay to fully skeletonized remains), the utility of soil analysis in the estimation of extended PMI, when insect and scavenger activity is largely quiescent, is often cited (Carter and Tibbett 2008). However, as a potentially enduring component of the death scene, to understand the finality of the CDI requires an appreciation of the factors and process shaping its ultimate presentation. To this end, currently it is known that the relative aboveground effects of temperature (Megyesi et al. 2005) and humidity as well as the belowground effects of soil temperature (Carter and Tibbett 2006; Carter et al. 2008a), moisture content, soil texture and type (Fielder and Graw 2003; Tibbett et al. 2004), and to a lesser extent soil pH (Haslam and Tibbett 2009; Prangnell and McGowan 2009) as well as decomposer adaptation (Carter and Tibbett 2008), all play an important role in the formation of a CDI. Furthermore, those ecologically well-understood factors governing the decomposition of organic and plant matter within terrestrial ecosystems are now beginning to be investigated in terms of the biochemical residues (and their chemical stability) and the microbial load and activity of soil organisms in relation to forensic remains (Hopkins 2008). Of particular note, the microbiology and mycology (largely untouched for the last 30 years) of grave soil, somewhat in the shadow of the surge in popularity of forensic entomology over the last decade, remain largely untouched as legitimate research areas in their own right (Hopkins et al. 2000; Carter and Tibbett 2006; Sagara et al. 2008).

Of those studies investigating the two-way exchange processes occurring at the soil cadaver interface, a methodological theme within the recent literature is readily identifiable. The use of soil microcosms (e.g., Stokes et al. 2009) and cubes of animal musculoskeletal tissue as human tissue analogues (e.g., Tibbett et al. 2004; Stokes et al. 2009; Haslam and Tibbett 2009) represent the latest attempts at controlling the extraordinary number of variables confronting researchers designing such experiments. Not intended to "replicate the decomposition of a whole cadaver with its enteric flora," Haslam and Tibbett (2009: 900) justified the use of such an approach as "an enquiry into how edaphic differences can affect the decomposition of an important cadaveric substrate ... provid[ing] a framework for more predictive, 'real-world' experiments with cadavers in the field." In this vein, Tibbett et al. (2004) demonstrated a worthy attempt at addressing the robusticity of previous scientific methods. In their incubation study of skeletal muscle tissue decomposition and temperature variation, the authors highlighted the need to standardize the water-holding capacity and soil moisture content of all samples used. As such, although not without flaw, presenting a method that attempts to address any confounding covariables is a sure step in the right direction toward admissibility in the courtroom.

Several interesting trends in the analysis of grave soil are also apparent. The increasing number of studies focused on characterizing the proteolytic, lypolytic, and glycolytic products of protein, fats, and carbohydrates purged into the soil from the cadaver (Carter et al. 2008a, 2008b; Forbes 2008) hints at a move toward the identification of more robust techniques that may survive the unprecedented scrutiny of the courts. In particular, preliminary analyses of the timely release of nitrogen compounds from the liquefying cadaver into the surrounding grave soil and their color-specific reaction with ninhydrin reagent hold promise for the detection of clandestine graves and the estimation of PMI (Van Belle et al. 2009).

Interestingly, an apparent schism exists between the traditional above-ground research on decomposition discussed and those studies of lesser antiquity focused on soil-cadaver relationships in forensic investigation. Undoubtedly by no means mutually exclusive, a single study currently in press represents the first tentative steps toward traversing this gap. Measuring decomposition fluid conductivities in conjunction with the ADD technique of Megyesi et al. (2005), Pringle et al. (2010) offer a tentative glance into the potential power of soil water analyses in the calculation of PBIs. Given the importance of temperature effects, it is envisaged that the application of ADD to taphonomic soil analyses will be an emerging trend in the near future. Furthermore, coupled with novel methods such as that of Prangnell and McGowan (2009), whose application of an equation more frequently utilized in civil engineering permitted the calculation of soil temperatures from ambient values at a known cemetery site, one moves slowly, yet ever so surely, closer to a more scientifically grounded understanding of the factors contributing to the condition in which human remains frequently present to the forensic anthropologist.

Conclusions

Forensic taphonomy has a lot to offer the forensic anthropologist. Widening the perspective of anthropological investigation above and beyond the four commonly cited pillars of osteological protocol (age, sex, ancestry, and stature), taphonomic considerations in a forensic context have proved valuable intelligence in relation to both the estimation of time since death or deposition interval and the discernment of postmortem artifacts resulting from natural processes as distinct from those of medicolegal significance.

Currently, however, too little of the taphonomic information available within the primary source literature is grounded in sound scientific, empirical methodology. Certainly, as students of physical anthropology (J. B. and Z. S.) at the very start of our professional careers, confronting the complexities of taphonomic processes that may present at a potential crime scene without the knowledge of case studies and the experience of seasoned professionals would seem a daunting task. The question is, on what do we base our work?

Fortunately, the last few years has seen a metamorphosis in methodological approaches within this research area, moving from the qualitative to the quantitative. Acknowledging the need for reproducible methods, more data, larger sample sizes, and the use of robust statistical techniques, these studies do not stand in opposition to the wealth of information previously published within the field but represent a timely reminder that without scientific progress, an area that holds great potential may well end up consigned to the margins of credibility.

From one student to another, if one was to offer a single piece of advice for attempting to navigate through the labyrinthine field of forensic taphonomy, it would be this: Read the literature, talk about it with your fellow peers and learned teachers, do not be afraid to question it, and if in questioning you find it to be wanting, test it. In the words of Pigliucci and Kaplan (2000): "These are not reasons to despair, just inspiration for more work to come … simply saying that the true answer lies in the proverbial middle is not really saying much—unless one is prepared to roll up one's sleeves and thoroughly investigate that middle ground for decades to come."

References

Abraham, E., Cox, M., and Quincey, D. 2008. Pig-mentation: Postmortem iris color change in the eyes of *Sus scrofa*. *Journal of Forensic Sciences*, 53, 626–631.

Adams, B. J., and Byrd, J. E. 2008. *Recovery, analysis, and identification of commingled human remains*. New York: Humana Press.

Adams, B. J., and Konigsberg, L. W. 2008. How many people? Determining the number of individuals represented by commingled human remains. In: Adams, B. J., and Byrd, J. E. (Eds.), *Recovery, analysis, and identification of commingled human remains*. New York: Humana Press, 241–256.

Adams, Z. J. O., and Hall, M. J. R. 2003. Methods used for the killing and preservation of blowfly larvae, and their effect on post-mortem larval length. *Forensic Science International*, 138, 50–61.

Adlam, R. E., and Simmons, T. 2007. The effect of repeated physical disturbance on soft tissue decomposition—Are taphonomic studies an accurate reflection of decomposition? *Journal of Forensic Sciences*, 52, 1007–1013.

Al-Alousi, L. M. 2002. A study of the shape of the post-mortem cooling curve in 117 forensic cases. *Forensic Science International*, 125, 237–244.

Al-Alousi, L. M., Anderson, R. A., Worster, D. M., and Land, D. V. 2002. Factors influencing the precision of estimating the postmortem interval using the triple-exponential formulae (TEF) Part I. A study of the effect of body variables and covering of the torso on the postmortem brain, liver and rectal cooling rates in 117 forensic cases. *Forensic Science International*, 125, 223–230.

Allison, P. A., and Briggs, D. E. G. (Eds.). 1991. *Taphonomy: Releasing the data locked in the fossil record*. New York: Plenum Press.

Alunni-Perret, V., Muller-Bolla, M., Laugier, J. P., Lupi-Pegurier, L., Bertrand, M. F., Staccini, P., Bolla, M., and Quatrehomme, G. R. 2005. Scanning electron microscopy analysis of experimental bone hacking trauma. *Journal of Forensic Sciences*, 50, 796–801.

Amendt, J., Campobasso, C. P., Gaudry, E., Reiter, C., Leblanc, H. N., and Hall, M. J. R. 2007. Best practice in forensic entomology—Standards and guidelines. *International Journal of Legal Medicine*, 121, 90–104.

Amendt, J., Krettek, R., and Zehner, R. 2004. Forensic entomology. *Naturwissenschaften*, 91, 51–65.

Anderson, G. S., and Cervenka, V. J. 2002. Insects associated with the body: their use and analysis. In Sorg, M. H., and Haglund, W. D. (Eds.), *Advances in forensic taphonomy: Method, theory, and archaeological perspectives*. Boca Raton, FL: CRC Press, 173–200.

Anderson, G. S., and Hobischak, N. R. 2004. Decomposition of carrion in the marine environment in British Columbia, Canada. *International Journal of Legal Medicine*, 118, 206–209.

Archer, M. S. 2004. Rainfall and temperature effects on the decomposition rate of exposed neonatal remains. *Science and Justice*, 44, 35–41.

Bartelink, E. J., Wiersema, J. M., and Demaree, R. S. 2001. Quantitative analysis of sharp-force trauma: An application of scanning electron microscopy in forensic anthropology. *Journal of Forensic Sciences*, 46, 1288–1293.

Bartosiewicz, L. 2008. Taphonomy and palaeopathology in archaeozoology. *Geobios*, 41, 69–77.

Bassett, H. E., and Manhein, M. H. 2002. Fluvial transport of human remains in the lower Mississippi River. *Journal of Forensic Sciences*, 47, 719–724.

Behrensmeyer, A. K., and Hill, A. P. (Eds.). 1980. *Fossils in the making*. Chicago: Chicago University Press.

Behrensmeyer, A. K., Kidwell, S. M., and Gastaldo, R. A. 2000. Taphonomy and paleobiology. *Palaeobiology*, 26, 103–147.

Benecke, M. 2001. A brief history of forensic entomology. *Forensic Science International*, 120, 2–14.

Benninger, L. A., Carter, D. O., and Forbes, S. L. 2008. The biochemical alteration of soil beneath a decomposing carcass. *Forensic Science International*, 180, 70–75.

Berryman, H. E. 2002. Disarticulation pattern and tooth mark artifacts associated with pig scavenging of remains: A case study. In Haglund, W. D., and Sorg, M. H. (Eds.), *Advances in forensic taphonomy: Method, theory and archeological perspectives*. Boca Raton, FL: CRC Press, 487–495.

Binford, L. R. 1981. *Bones: Ancient men and modern myths*. New York: Academic Press.

Binford, L. R. 1983. *In pursuit of the past: Decoding the archaeological record*. London: Thames and Hudson.

Bonnichsen, R., and Sorg, M. H. 1989. *Bone modification*, Orono, ME: University of Maine.

Brothwell, D., and Gill-Robinson, H. 2002. Taphonomic and forensic aspects of bog bodies. In Haglund, W. D., and Sorg, M. H. (Eds.), *Advances in forensic taphonomy: Method, theory, and archaeological perspectives*. Boca Raton, FL: CRC Press, 119–133.

Brown, O. J. F., Field, J., and Letnic, M. 2006. Variation in the taphonomic effect of scavengers in semi-arid Australia linked to rainfall and the El Nino southern oscillation. *International Journal of Osteoarchaeology*, 16, 165–176.

Byrd, J. E. 2008. Models and methods for osteometric sorting In Adams, B. J., and Byrd, J. E. (Eds.), *Recovery, analysis, and identification of commingled human remains*. New York: Humana Press, 199–220.

Carson, E. A., Stefan, V. H., and Powell, J. F. 2000. Skeletal manifestations of bear scavenging. *Journal of Forensic Sciences*, 45, 515–526.

Carter, D. O., and Tibbett, M. 2003. Taphonomic mycota: Fungi with forensic potential. *Journal of Forensic Sciences*, 48, 168–171.

Carter, D. O., and Tibbett, M. 2006. Microbial decomposition of skeletal muscle tissue (*Ovis aries*) in a sandy loam at different temperatures. *Soil Biology and Biochemistry*, 38, 1139–1145.

Carter, D. O., and Tibbett, M. 2008. Cadaver decomposition and soil: processes. In Tibbett, M., and Carter, D. O. (Eds.), *Soil analysis in forensic taphonomy: Chemical and biological effects of buried human remains*. Boca Raton, FL: CRC Press.

Carter, D. O., Yellowlees, D., and Tibbett, M. 2007. Cadaver decomposition in terrestrial ecosystems. *Naturwissenschaften*, 94, 12–24.

Carter, D. O., Yellowless, D., and Tibbett, M. 2008a. Temperature affects microbial decomposition of cadavers (*Rattus rattus*) in contrasting soils. *Applied Soil Ecology*, 40, 129–137.

Carter, D. O., Yellowlees, D., and Tibbett, M. 2008b. Using ninhydrin to detect gravesoil. *Journal of Forensic Sciences*, 53, 397–400.

Chin, H. C., Marwi, M. A., Salleh, A. F. M., Jeffery, J., Kurahashi, H., and Omar, B. 2008. Study of insect succession and rate of decomposition on a partially burned pig carcass in an oil palm plantation in Malaysia. *Tropical Medicine*, 25, 202–208.

Cross, P., and Simmons, T. 2010. The influence of penetrative trauma on the rate of decomposition. *Journal of Forensic Sciences*, 55, 295–301.

Dabbs, G. R. 2010. Caution! All data not created equal: The hazards of using national weather service data for calculating accumulated degree days. *Forensic Science International*, in press. doi: 10.1016/j.forsciint.2010.02.024.

Darwent, C. M., and Lyman, R. L. 2002. Detecting the postburial fragmentation of carpals, tarsals and phalanges. In Sorg, M. H., and Haglund, W. D. (Eds.), *Advances in forensic taphonomy: Method, theory and archeological perspectives*. Boca Raton, FL: CRC Press, 355–378.

Davis, J. B., and Goff, M. L. 2000. Decomposition patterns in terrestrial and intertidal habitats on Oahu Island and Coconut Island, Hawaii. *Journal of Forensic Sciences*, 45, 836–842.

Denys, C. 2002. Taphonomy and experimentation. *Archaeometry*, 44, 469–484.

Devault, T. L., Brisbin, I. L., Jr., and Rhodes, O. E. 2004. Factors influencing the acquisition of rodent carrion by vertebrate scavengers and decomposers. *Canadian Journal of Zoology*, 82, 502–509.

Devault, T. L., Rhodes, O. E., and Shivik, J. A. 2003. Scavenging by vertebrates: Behavioural, ecological and evolutionary perspectives on an important energy pathway in terrestrial ecosystems. *Oikos*, 102, 225–234.

Dirkmaat, D. C. 2002. Recovery and interpretation of the fatal fire victim: the role of the forensic anthropologist. In Sorg, M. H., and Haglund, W. D. (Eds.), *Advances in forensic taphonomy: Method, theory and archeological perspectives*. Boca Raton, FL: CRC Press, 451–472.

Dirkmaat, D. C., Cabo, L. L., Ousley, S. D., and Symes, S. A. 2008. New perspectives in forensic anthropology. *Yearbook of Physical Anthropology*, 51, 33–52.

Duhig, C. 2003. Non-forensic remains: The use of forensic archaeology, anthropology and burial taphonomy. *Science and Justice*, 43, 211–214.

Ebbesmeyer, C. C., and Haglund, W. D. 2002. Floating remains on Pacific Northwest waters. In Haglund, W. D., and Sorg, M. H. (Eds.), *Advances in forensic taphonomy: Method, theory, and archaeological perspectives*. Boca Raton, FL: CRC Press, 220–240.

Efremov, I. A. 1940. Taphonomy: A new branch of paleontology, *Pan-Am. Geol.* 74: 81–93.

Egana, S., Turner, S., Doretti, M., Bernardi, P., and Ginarte, A. 2008. Commingled remains and human rights investigations. In Adams, B. J., and Byrd, J. E. (Eds.), *Recovery, analysis, and identification of commingled human remains*. New York: Humana Press, 57–80.

Fernández-Jalvo, Y., Andrew, P., Pesquero, D., Smith, C., Marin-Monfort, D., Sanchez, B., Geigl, E. M., and Alonso, A. 2010. Early bone diagenesis in temperate environments: Part I: Surface features and histology. *Palaeogeography, Palaeoclimatology, Palaeoecology*, 288, 62–81.

Fernández-Jalvo, Y., and Andrews, P. 2003. Experimental effects of water abrasion on bone. *Journal of Taphonomy*, 1, 147–163.

Fielder, S. R., and Graw, M. 2003. Decomposition of buried corpses, with special reference to the formation of adipocere. *Naturwissenschaften*, 90, 291–300.

Forbes, S. L. 2008. Potential determinants of post-mortem and postburial interval of buried remains. In Tibbett, M., and Carter, D. O. (Eds.), *Soil analysis in forensic taphonomy*. Boca Raton, FL: CRC Press, 225–246.

Forbes, S. L., Stuart, B. H., and Dent, B. B. 2005a. The effect of the burial environment on adipocere formation. *Forensic Science International*, 154, 24–34.

Forbes, S. L., Stuart, B. H., and Dent, B. D. 2005b. The effect of the method of burial on adipocere formation. *Forensic Science International*, 154, 44–52.

Forbes, S. L., Stuart, B. H., Dent, B. B., and Fenwick-Mulcahy, S. 2005c. Characterization of adipocere formation in animal species. *Journal of Forensic Sciences*, 50, 633–640.

Gallagher, M. B., Sandhu, S., and Kimsey, R. 2010. Variation in development time for geographically distinct populations of the common green bottle fly, *Lucilia sericata* (Meigen). *Journal of Forensic Sciences*, 55, 438–442.

Goff, M. L. 2009. Early post-mortem changes and stages of decomposition in exposed cadavers. *Experimental and Applied Acarology*, 49, 21–36.

Graver, S., Sobolik, K. D., and Whittaker, J. 2002. Cannibalism or violent death alone? Human remains at a small Anasazi site. In Sorg, M. H., and Haglund, W. D. (Eds.), *Advances in forensic taphonomy: Method, theory and archeological perspectives*. Boca Raton, FL: CRC Press, 309–320.

Grivas, C. R., and Komar, D. A. 2008. Kumho, Daubert, and the nature of scientific inquiry: Implications for forensic anthropology. *Journal of Forensic Sciences*, 53, 771–776.

Grupe, G. 2007. Taphonomic and diagenetic processes. In Henke, W., and Tattershall, I. (Eds.), *Handbook of paleoanthropology.* Berlin: Springer, 242–259.

Gruspier, K. L., and Pollanen, M. S. 2000. Limbs found in water: Investigation using anthropological analysis and the diatom test. *Forensic Science International,* 112, 1–9.

Haglund, W. D. 2002. Recent mass graves: An introduction. In Sorg, M. H., and Haglund, W. D. (Eds.), *Advances in forensic taphonomy: Method, theory, and archaeological perspectives.* Boca Raton, FL: CRC Press, 243–262.

Haglund, W. D., Connor, M., and Scott, D. D. 2002. The effect of cultivation on buried human remains. In Sorg, M. H., and Haglund, W. D. (Eds.), *Advances in forensic taphonomy: Method, theory and archeological perspectives.* Boca Raton, FL: CRC Press, 133–150.

Haglund, W. D., and Sorg, M. H. (Eds.). 1997a. *Forensic taphonomy: The postmortem fate of human remains.* London: CRC Press.

Haglund, W. D., and Sorg, M. H. 1997b. Introduction to forensic taphonomy. In Haglund, W. D., and Sorg, M. H. (Eds.), *Forensic taphonomy: The postmortem fate of human remains.* London: CRC Press.

Haglund, W. D., and Sorg, M. H. (Eds.). 2002a. *Advances in forensic taphonomy: Method, theory, and archaeological perspectives.* Boca Raton, FL: CRC Press, 1–13.

Haglund, W. D., and Sorg, M. H. 2002b. Human remains in water environments. In Haglund, W. D., and Sorg, M. H. (Eds.), *Advances in forensic taphonomy: Method, theory, and archaeological perspectives.* Boca Raton, FL: CRC Press, 202–218.

Harvey, M. L., Gaudieri, S., Villet, M. H., and Dadour, I. R. 2008. A global study of forensically significant calliphorids: Implications for identification. *Forensic Science International,* 177, 66–76.

Harvey, M., and King, M.-C. 2002. The use of DNA in the identification of postmortem remains. In Sorg, M. H., and Haglund, W. D. (Eds.), *Advances in forensic taphonomy: Method, theory and archeological perspectives.* Boca Raton, FL: CRC Press, 473–486.

Haslam, T. C. F., and Tibbett, M. 2009. Soils of contrasting ph affect the decomposition of buried mammalian (*Ovis aries*) skeletal muscle tissue. *Journal of Forensic Sciences,* 54, 900–904.

Haskell, N. H., Hall, R. D., Cervenka, V. J., and Clark, M. A. 1997. On the body: Insects' life stage presence and their postmortem artifacts. In Haglund, W. D., and Sorg, M. H. (Eds.), *Forensic taphonomy: The postmortem fate of human remains.* London: CRC Press, 415–448.

Heaton, V., Lagden, A., Moffatt, C., and Simmons, T. 2010. Predicting the post-mortem submersion interval for human remains recovered from U.K. waterways. *Journal of Forensic Sciences,* 55, 302–307.

Henssge, C., and Madea, B. 2007. Estimation of time since death. *Forensic Science International,* 165, 182–184.

Herrmann, N. P., and Devlin, J. B. 2008. Assessment of commingled human remains using a GIS-based approach. In Byrd, J. E., and Adams, B. J. (Eds.), *Recovery, analysis, and identification of commingled human remains.* New York: Humana Press, 257–270.

Hochrein, M. J. 2002. A autopsy of the grave: Recognizing, collecting, and preserving forensic geotaphonomic evidence. In Haglund, W. D., and Sorg, M. H. (Eds.), *Advances in forensic taphonomy: Method, theory, and archaeological perspectives.* Boca Raton, FL: CRC Press, 45–70.

Hopkins, D. W. 2008. The role of soil organisms in terrestrial decomposition. In Tibbett, M., and Carter, D. O. (Eds.), *Soil analysis in forensic taphonomy: chemical and biological effect of buried human remains.* Boca Raton, FL: CRC Press, 53–66.

Hopkins, D. W., Wiltshire, P. E. J., and Turner, B. D. 2000. Microbial characteristics of soils from graves: An investigation at the interface of soil microbiology and forensic science. *Applied Soil Ecology,* 14, 283–288.

Huculak, M. A., and Rogers, T. L. 2009. Reconstructing the sequence of events surrounding body disposition based on color staining of bone. *Journal of Forensic Sciences,* 54, 979–984.

Huntington, T. E., Hugley, L. G., and Baxendale, F. P. 2007. Maggot development during morgue storage and its effect on estimating the post-mortem interval. *Journal of Forensic Sciences,* 52, 453–458.

Janaway, R. C. 2002. Degradation of clothing and other dress materials associated with buried bodies of both archaeological and forensic interest. In Sorg, M. H., and Haglund, W. D. (Eds.), *Advances in forensic taphonomy: Method, theory and archeological perspectives.* Boca Raton, FL: CRC Press, 379–402.

Janjua, M. A., and Rogers, T. L. 2008. Bone weathering patterns of metatarsal versus femur and the postmortem interval in southern Ontario. *Forensic Science International,* 178, 16–23.

Kanz, F., and Grossschmidt, K. 2006. Head injuries of Roman gladiators. *Forensic Science International,* 160, 207–216.

Kjorlien, Y. P., Beattie, O. B., and Peterson, A. E. 2009. Scavenging activity can produce predictable patterns in surface skeletal remains scattering: Observations and comments from two experiments. *Forensic Science International,* 188, 103–106.

L'Abbé, E. N. 2005. A case of commingled remains from rural South Africa. *Forensic Science International,* 151, 201–206.

Littleton, J. 2000. Taphonomic effects of erosion on deliberately buried bodies. *Journal of Archaeological Science,* 27, 5–18.

Lyman, R. L. 1994. *Vertebrate taphonomy.* Cambridge, UK: Cambridge University Press.

Lyman, R. L. 2004. The concept of equifinality in taphonomy. *Journal of Taphonomy,* 2, 15–26.

Lyman, R. L. 2010. What taphonomy is, what it isn't, and why taphonomists should care about the difference. *Journal of Taphonomy,* 8, 1–16.

Matuszewski, S., Bajerlein, D., Konwerski, S., and Szpila, K. 2010. Insect succession and carrion decomposition in selected forests of Central Europe. Part 1: Pattern and rate of decomposition. *Forensic Science International,* 194, 85–93.

Mayne-Correia, P., and Beattie, O. 2002. A critical look at methods for recovering, evaluating and interpreting cremated human remains. In Haglund, W. D., and Sorg, M. H. (Eds.), *Advances in forensic taphonomy: Method, theory and archeological perspectives.* Boca Raton, FL: CRC Press, 435–450.

Mazzanti, M., Alessandrini, F., Tagliabracci, A., Wells, J. D., and Campobasso, C. P. 2009. DNA degradation and genetic analysis of empty puparia: Genetic identification limits in forensic entomology. *Forensic Science International*, 195, 99–102.

Megyesi, M. S., Nawrocki, S. P., and Haskell, N. H. 2005. Using accumulated degree-days to estimate the postmortem interval from decomposed human remains. *Journal of Forensic Sciences*, 50, 618–626.

Menezes, R. G., Kanchan, T., Bhat, N. B., Lobo, S. W., Jain, A., and Rai, N. G. 2009. Cadaveric fungi: Not as yet an established forensic tool—Author's response. *Journal of Forensic and Legal Medicine*, 16, 361–365.

Menezes, R. G., Kanchan, T., Lobo, S. W., Jain, A., Bhat, N. B., and Rao, N. G. 2008. Cadaveric fungi: Not yet an established forensic tool. *Journal of Forensic and Legal Medicine*, 15, 124–125.

Moraitis, K., and Spiliopouiou, C. 2006. Identification and differential diagnosis of perimortem blunt force trauma in tubular long bones. *Forensic Science, Medicine, and Pathology*, 2, 221–229.

Morton, R. J., and Lord, W. D. 2002. Detection and recovery of abducted and murdered children: Behavioral and taphonomic influences. In Sorg, M. H., and Haglund, W. D. (Eds.), *Advances in forensic taphonomy: Method, theory and archeological perspectives*. Boca Raton, FL: CRC Press.

Morton, R. J., and Lord, W. D. 2006. Taphonomy of child-sized remains: A study of scattering and scavenging in Virginia, USA. *Journal of Forensic Sciences*, 51, 475–479.

Nordby, J. J. 2002. Is forensic taphonomy scientific? In Haglund, W. D., and Sorg, M. H. (Eds.), *Advances in forensic taphonomy: Method, theory, and archaeological perspectives*. Boca Raton, FL: CRC Press.

Notter, S. J., Stuart, B. H., Dent, B. B., and Keegan, J. 2008. Solid-phase extraction in combination with GC/MS for the quantification of free fatty acids in adipocere. *European Journal of Lipid Science and Technology*, 110, 73–80.

O'Brien, T. G., and Kuehner, A. C. 2007. Waxing grave about adipocere: Soft tissue change in an aquatic context. *Journal of Forensic Sciences*, 52, 294–301.

Pakosh, C. M., and Rogers, T. L. 2009. Soft tissue decomposition of submerged, dismembered pig limbs enclosed in plastic bags. *Journal of Forensic Sciences*, 54, 1223–1228.

Parkinson, R. A., Dias, K.-R., Horswell, J., Greenwood, P., Banning, N., Tibbett, M., and Vass, A. A. 2009. Microbial community analysis of human decomposition on soil. In Ritz, K., Dawson, L., and Miller, D. (Eds.), *Criminal and environmental soil forensics*. AK Houten, Netherlands: Springer.

Pigliucci, M., and Kaplan, J. 2000. The fall and rise of Dr Pangloss: adaptationism and the Spandrels paper 20 years later. *Tree*, 15, 66–70.

Pobiner, B. L., and Braun, D. R. 2005. Applying actualism: considerations for future research. *Journal of Taphonomy*, 3, 57–65.

Pokines, J. T., and Peterhans, J. C. K. 2007. Spotted hyena (*Crocuta crocuta*) den use and taphonomy in the Masai Mara National Reserve, Kenya. *Journal of Archaeological Science*, 34, 1914–1931.

Prangnell, J., and Mcgowan, G. 2009. Soil temperature calculation for burial site analysis. *Forensic Science International*, 191, 104–109.

Prieto, J. L., Magana, C., and Ubelaker, D. H. 2004. Interpretation of postmortem change in cadavers in Spain. *Journal of Forensic Sciences*, 49, 918–923.

Pringle, J. K., Cassella, J. P., and Jervis, J. R. 2010. Preliminary soilwater conductivity analysis to date clandestine burials of homicide victims. *Forensic Science International*, in press. doi: 10.1016/j.forsciint.2010.02.005.

Quinney, P. S. 2000. Paradigms lost: changing interpretations of hominid behavioural patterns since ODK. In Rowley-Conwy, P. (Ed.), *Animal bones, human societies.* Oxford, UK: Oxbow Press, 12–19.

Roksandic, M. 2002. Position of skeletal remains as a key to understanding mortuary behavior. In Haglund, W. D., and Sorg, M. H. (Eds.), *Advances in forensic taphonomy: Method, theory, and archaeological perspectives.* Boca Raton, FL: CRC Press, 99–118.

Sagara, N., Yamanaka, T., and Tibbett, M. 2008. Soil fungi associated with graves and latrines: towards a forensic mycology. In Tibbett, M., and Carter, D. O. (Eds.), *Soil analysis in forensic taphonomy: Chemical and biological effects of buried human remains.* Boca Raton, FL: CRC Press, 67–108.

Saul, J. M., and Saul, F. P. 2002. Forensics, archaeology, and taphonomy: the symbiotic relationship. In Haglund, W. D., and Sorg, M. H. (Eds.), *Advances in forensic taphonomy: Method, theory, and archaeological perspectives.* Boca Raton, FL: CRC Press, 71–98.

Schaefer, M., and Black, S. 2007. Epiphyseal union sequencing: Aiding in the recognition and sorting of commingled remains. *Journal of Forensic Science*, 52, 277–285.

Schmitt, S. 2002. Mass graves and the collection of forensic evidence: Genocide, war crimes, and crimes against humanity. In Haglund, W. D., and Sorg, M. H. (Eds.), *Advances in forensic taphonomy: Method, theory, and archaeological perspectives.* Boca Raton, FL: CRC Press, 277–292.

Shalaby, O. A., Decarvalho, L. M. L., and Goff, M. L. 2000. Comparison of patterns of decomposition in a hanging carcass and a carcass in contact with soil in a xerophytic habitat on the Island of Oahu, Hawaii. *Journal of Forensic Sciences*, 45, 1267–1273.

Sidrim, J. J. C., Filho, R. E. M., Cordeiro, R. A. G., Rocha, M. F. G., Caetano, E. P., Monteiro, A. J., and Brilhante, R. S. N. 2010. Fungal microbiotic dynamics as a postmortem investigation tool: Focus on *Aspergillus, Penicillium* and *Candida* species. *Journal of Applied Microbiology*, in press. doi: 10.1111/j.1365–2672.2009.04573.x.

Simmons, T. 2002. Taphonomy of a karstic cave execution site at Hrgar, Bosnia-Herzegovina. In Sorg, M. H., and Haglund, W. D. (Eds.), *Advances in forensic taphonomy: Method, theory and archeological perspectives.* Boca Raton, FL: CRC Press, 263–276.

Simmons, T., Adlam, R. E., and Moffatt, C. 2010. Debugging decomposition data— Comparative taphonomic studies and the influences of insects and carcass size on decomposition rate. *Journal of Forensic Sciences*, 55, 8–13.

Simmons, T., Cross, P., Adlam, R. E., and Moffatt, C. 2010. The influence of insects on decomposition rate in buried and surface remains. *Journal of Forensic Sciences*, 55, 889–892.

Skinner, M., Alempijevic, D., and Djuric-Srejic, M. 2003. Guidelines for international forensic bio-archaeology monitors of mass grave exhumations. *Forensic Science International*, 134, 81–92.

Skinner, M., York, H. P., and Connor, M. A. 2002. Postburial disturbance of graves in Bosnia-Herzegovina. In Sorg, M. H., and Haglund, W. D. (Eds.), *Advances in forensic taphonomy: Method, theory and archeological perspectives.* Boca Raton, FL: CRC Press, 293–308.

Sledzik, P. S., and Micozzi, M. S. 1997. Autopsied, embalmed, and preserved human remains: Distinguishing features in forensic and historic contexts. In Haglund, W. D., and Sorg, M. H. (Eds.), *Forensic taphonomy: The postmortem fate of human remains.* London: CRC Press, 483–496.

Sorg, M. H., and Haglund, W. D. 2002. Advancing forensic taphonomy: Purpose, theory, and process. In Sorg, M. H., and Haglund, W. D. (Eds.), *Advances in forensic taphonomy: Method, theory and archeological perspectives.* Boca Raton, FL: CRC Press, 4–29.

Stokes, K. L., Forbes, S. L., and Tibbett, M. 2009. Freezing skeletal muscle tissue does not affect its decomposition in soil: Evidence from temporal changes in tissue mass, microbial activity and soil chemistry based on excised samples. *Forensic Science International*, 183, 6–13.

Symes, S. A., Williams, J. A., Murray, E. A., Hoffman, M. J., Holland, T. D., Saul, J. M., Saul, F. P., and Pope, E. J. 2002. Taphonomic context of sharp-force trauma in suspected cases of human mutilation and dismemberment. In Sorg, M. H., and Haglund, W. D. (Eds.), *Advances in forensic taphonomy: Method, theory and archeological perspectives.* Boca Raton, FL: CRC Press, 403–434.

Swann, L., Chidlow, G. E., Forbes, S., and Lewis, S. W. 2010. Preliminary studies into the characterisation of chemical markers of decomposition for geoforensics. *Journal of Forensic Sciences*, 55, 308–314.

Tersigni, M. A. 2007. Frozen human bone: A microscopic investigation. *Journal of Forensic Sciences*, 52, 16–20.

Tibbett, M., and Carter, D. O. 2008. *Soil analysis in forensic taphonomy: Chemical and biological effects of buried human remains.* Boca Raton, FL: CRC Press.

Tibbett, M., and Carter, D. O. 2009. Research in forensic taphonomy: A soil based perspective. In Ritz, K., Dawson, L., and Miller, D. (Eds.), *Criminal and environmental soil forensics.* AK Houten, Netherlands: Springer, 317–331.

Tibbett, M., Carter, D. O., Haslam, T., Major, R., and Haslam, R. 2004. A laboratory incubation method for determining the rate of microbiological degradation of skeletal muscle tissue in soil. *Journal of Forensic Sciences*, 49, 560–565.

Towne, E. G. 2000. Prairie vegetation and soil nutrient responses to ungulate carcasses. *Oecologica*, 122, 232–239.

Tuller, H., Hofmeister, U., and Daley, S. 2008. Spatial analysis of mass grave mapping data to assist in the reassociation of disarticulated and commingled human remains. In Adams, B. J., and Byrd, J. E. (Eds.), *Recovery, analysis, and identification of commingled human remains.* New York: Humana Press, 7–29.

Ubelaker, D. H. 2002. Approaches to the study of commingling in human skeletal biology. In Sorg, M. H., and Haglund, W. D. (Eds.), *Advances in forensic taphonomy: Method, theory and archeological perspectives.* Boca Raton, FL: CRC Press, 331–351.

Ururahy-Rodrigues, A., Rafael, J. A., Wanderley, R. F., Marques, E., and Pujol-Luz, J. R. 2008. Coprophanaeus lancifer (Linnaeus, 1767) (Coleoptera, Scarabaeidae) activity moves a man-size pig carcass: Relevant data for forensic taphonomy. *Forensic Science International*, 182, 19–22.

Van Belle, V. E., Carter, D. O., and Forbes, S. L. 2009. Measurement of ninhydrin reactive nitrogen influx into grave soil during aboveground and belowground carcass (*Sus domesticus*) decomposition. *Forensic Science International*, 193, 37–41.

Vass, A. A. 2001. Beyond the grave—Understanding human decomposition. *Microbiology Today*, 28, 190–192.

Vass, A. A., Barshick, S. A., Sega, G., Caton, J., Skeen, J. T., and Love, J. C. 2002. Decomposition chemistry of human remains: A new methodology for determining the postmortem interval. *Journal of Forensic Sciences*, 47, 542–553.

Voss, S. C., Spafford, H., and Dadour, I. R. 2009. Annual and seasonal patterns of insect succession on decomposing remains at two locations in Western Australia. *Forensic Science International*, 193, 26–36.

Warren, M. 2008. Detection of commingling in cremated human remains In Adams, B. J., and Byrd, J. E. (Eds.), *Recovery, analysis, and identification of commingled human remains*. New York: Humana Press, 185–198.

Warren, M. W., and Schultz, J. J. 2002. Post-cremation taphonomy and artefact preservation. *Journal of Forensic Sciences*, 47, 656–659.

Weitzel, M. A. 2005. A report of decomposition rates of a special burial type in Edmonton, Alberta from an experimental field study. *Journal of Forensic Sciences*, 50, 641–647.

Wheatley, B. P. 2008. Perimortem or postmortem bone fractures? An experimental study of fracture patterns in deer femora. *Journal of Forensic Sciences*, 53, 69–72.

Widya, M. 2009. The formation of early stage adipocere in submerged remains. MSc thesis, Preston, UK: University of Central Lancashire.

Wilson, A. S., Janaway, R. C., Holland, A. D., Dodson, H. I., Baran, E., Pollard, A. M., and Tobin, D. J. 2007. Modelling the buried human body environment in upland climes using three contrasting field sites. *Forensic Science International*, 169, 6–18.

Yan, F., Mcnally, R., Kontanis, E. J., and Sadik, O. A. 2001. Preliminary quantitative investigation of postmortem adipocere formation. *Journal of Forensic Sciences*, 46, 609–614.

Bibliography

Al-Alousi, L. M., Anderson, R. A., Worster, D. M., and Land, D. V. 2001. Multiple-probe thermography for estimating the postmortem interval: I. Continuous monitoring and data analysis of brain, liver, rectal and environmental temperatures in 117 forensic cases. *Journal of Forensic Sciences*, 46, 317–322.

Al-Talabani, N., Al-Moussawy, N. D., Baker, F. A., and Mohammed, H. A. 2006. Digital analysis of experimental human bitemarks: Application of two new methods. *Journal of Forensic Sciences*, 51, 1372–1375.

Amendt, J., Zehner, R., and Reckel, F. 2008. The nocturnal oviposition behaviour of blowflies (Diptera: Calliphoridae) in central Europe and its forensic implications. *Forensic Science International*, 175, 61–64.

Ames, C., and Turner, B. 2003. Low temperature episodes in development of blowflies: Implications for postmortem interval estimation. *Medical and Veterinary Entomology*, 17, 178–186.

Ames, C., Turner, B., and Daniel, B. 2006. The use of mitochondrial cytochrome oxidase I gene (COI) to differentiate two UK blowfly species—*Calliphora vicina* and *Calliphora vomitoria*. *Forensic Science International*, 164, 179–182.

Andrushko, V. A., Schwitalla, A. W., and Walker, P. L. 2010. Trophy-taking and dismemberment as warfare strategies in prehistoric central California. *American Journal of Physical Anthropology*, 141, 83–96.

Archer, M. S., and Elgar, M. A. 2003. Yearly activity patterns in southern Victoria (Australia) of seasonally active carrion insects. *Forensic Science International*, 132, 173–176.

Atici, A. L. 2006. Middle-Range Theory in paleolithic archaeology: The past and the present. *Journal of Taphonomy*, 4, 29–45.

Barba, R., and Domínguez-Rodrigo, M. 2005. The taphonomic relevance of the analysis of bovid long limb bone shaft features and their application to element identification: Study of bone thickness and morphology of the medullary cavity. *Journal of Taphonomy*, 3, 29–42.

Bar-Oz, G., and Munro, N. D. 2004. Beyond cautionary tales: A multivariate taphonomic approach for resolving equifinality in zooarchaeological studies. *Journal of Taphonomy*, 2, 201–220.

Barus, J. I. M., Suarez-Penaranda, J. M. S., Otero, X. L., Rodriguez-Calvo, M. S., Costas, E., Miguens, X., and Concheiro, L. 2002. Improved estimation of postmortem interval based on differential behaviour of vitreous potassium and hypoxantine in death by hanging. *Forensic Science International*, 125, 67–74.

Bendroth, P., Kronstrand, R., Helander, A., Greby, J., Stephanson, N., and Krantz, P. 2008. Comparison of ethyl glucuronide in hair with phosphatidylethanol in whole blood as post-mortem markers of alcohol abuse. *Forensic Science International*, 176, 76–81.

Benecke, M. 2005. Insect infestation of the corpse as a source of knowledge in forensic medicine. *Zeitschrift Fur Semiotik*, 27, 389–406.

Bleetman, A., Watson, C. H., Horsfall, I., and Champion, S. M. 2003. Wounding patterns and human performance in knife attacks: Optimising the protection provided by knife-resistant body armour. *Journal of Clinical Forensic Medicine*, 10, 243–248.

Bocaz-Beneventi, G., Tagliaro, F., Bortolotti, F., Manetto, G., and Havel, J. 2002. Capillary zone electrophoresis and artificial neural networks for estimation of the post-mortem interval (PMI) using electrolytes measurements in human vitreous humour. *International Journal of Legal Medicine*, 116, 5–11.

Bohnert, M., and Pollak, S. 2003. Heat mediated changes to the hands and feet mimicking washerwoman's skin. *International Journal of Legal Medicine*, 117, 102–105.

Boniolo, G., Libero, M., and Aprile, A. 2005. Causality and methodology. Notes on thanatochronological estimations. *History and Philosophy of the Life Sciences*, 27, 381–393.

Bourel, B., Callet, B., Hedouin, V., and Gosset, D. 2003. Flies' eggs: A new method for the estimation of short-term post-mortem interval? *Forensic Science International*, 135, 27–34.

Bull, P. A., Morgan, R. M., Sagovsky, A., and Hughes, G. J. A. 2006. The transfer and persistence of trace particulates: Experimental studies using clothing fabrics. *Science and Justice*, 46, 185–195.

Buynevich, I. V. 2009. Taphonomic applications of georadar. *Journal of Taphonomy*, 7, 47–52.

Byrd, J. H., and Allen, J. C. 2001. The development of the black blow fly, Phormia *regina* (Meigen). *Forensic Science International*, 120, 79–88.

Campobasso, C. P., Di Vella, G., and Introna, F. 2001. Factors affecting decomposition and Diptera colonization. *Forensic Science International*, 120, 18–27.

Campobasso, C. P., and Introna, F. 2001. The forensic entomologist in the context of the forensic pathologist's role. *Forensic Science International*, 120, 132–139.

Cardoso, H. F. V., Santos, A., Dias, R., Garcia, C., Pinto, M., Sérgio, C., and Magalhães, T. 2009. Establishing a minimum postmortem interval of human remains in an advanced state of skeletonization using the growth rate of bryophytes and plant roots. *International Journal of Legal Medicine*. doi: 10.1007/s00414-009-0372-5.

Carvalho, L. M. L., Thyssen, P. J., Linhares, A. X., and Palhares, F. A. B. 2000. A checklist of arthropods associated with pig carrion and human corpses in southeastern Brazil. *Memorias Do Instituto Oswaldo Cruz*, 95, 135–138.

Charlier, P., Georges, P., Bouchet, F., Huynh-Charlier, I., Carlier, R., Mazel, V., Richardin, P., Brun, L., Blondiaux, J., and Lorin De La Grandmaison, G. 2008. The microscopic (optical and SEM) examination of putrefaction fluid deposits (PFD). Potential interests in forensic anthropology. *Virchows Archiv*, 453, 377–386.

Chen, W. Y., Hung, T. H., and Shiao, S. F. 2004. Molecular identification of forensically important blow fly species (Diptera: Calliphoridae) in Taiwan. *Journal of Medical Entomology*, 41, 47–57.

Clark, M. A., Worrell, M. B., and Pless, J. E. 1997. Postmortem changes in soft tissues. In Haglund, W. D., and Sorg, M. H. (Eds.), *Forensic taphonomy: The postmortem fate of human remains*. Boca Raton, FL: CRC Press, 151–164.

Collins, M. J., Nielsen-Marsh, C. M., Hiller, J., Smith, C. I., Roberts, J. P., Prigodich, R. V., Wess, T. J., Csapo, J., Millard, A. R., and Turner-Walker, G. 2002. The survival of organic matter in bone: A review. *Archaeometry*, 44, 383–394.

Congram, D. R. 2008. A clandestine burial in Costa Rica: Prospection and excavation. *Journal of Forensic Sciences*, 53, 793–796.

Costamagno, S., Théry-Parisot, I., Brugal, J.-P., and Guibert, R. 2005. Taphonomic consequences of the use of bones as fuel: Experimental data and archaeological implications. In O'Connor, T. (Ed.), *Biosphere to lithosphere: New studies in vertebrate taphonomy*. Oxford, UK: Oxbow Books, 52–63.

Courtin, G. M., and Fairgrieve, S. L. 2004. Estimation of postmortem interval (PMI) as revealed through the analysis of annual growth in woody tissue. *Journal of Forensic Sciences*, 49, 781–783.

Cox, M., Flavel, A., Hanson, I., Laver, J., and Wessling, R. 2008. *The scientific investigation of mass graves*. Cambridge, UK: Cambridge University Press.

Day, D. M., and Wallman, J. F. 2006. Influence of substrate tissue type on larval growth in *Calliphora augur* and *Lucilia cuprina* (Diptera : Calliphoridae). *Journal of Forensic Sciences*, 51, 657–663.

Day, D. M., and Wallman, J. F. 2008. Effect of preservative solutions on preservation of *Calliphora augur* and *Lucilia cuprina* larvae (Diptera: Calliphoridae) with implications for post-mortem interval estimates. *Forensic Science International*, 179, 1–10.

Day, F., Clegg, S., McPhillips, M., and Mok, J. 2006. A retrospective case series of skeletal surveys in children with suspected non-accidental injury. *Journal of Clinical Forensic Medicine*, 13, 55–59.

Dedouit, F., Loubes-Lacroix, F., Costagliola, R., Guilbeau-Frugier, C., Alengrin, D., Otal, P., Telmon, N., Joffre, F., and Rouge, D. 2008. Post-mortem changes of the middle ear: Multislice computed tomography study. *Forensic Science International*, 175, 149–154.

Dokgoz, H., Arican, N., Elmas, I., and Fincanci, S. K. 2001. Comparison of morphological changes in white blood cells after death and in vitro storage of blood for the estimation of postmortem interval. *Forensic Science International*, 124, 25–31.

Doukas, A. G., Bamberg, M., Gillies, R., Evans, R., and Kollias, N. 2000. Spectroscopic determination of skin viability. A predictor of postmortem interval. *Journal of Forensic Sciences*, 45, 36–41.

Dumser, T. K., and Türkay, M. 2008a. Crack propagation in teeth: A comparison of perimortem and postmortem behavior of dental materials and cracks. *Journal of Forensic Sciences*, 53, 1049–1052.

Dumser, T. K., and Turkay, M. 2008b. Postmortem changes to human bodies on the bathyal sea floor—Two cases of aircraft accidents above the open sea. *Journal of Forensic Sciences*, 53, 1049–1052.

Eberhardt, T. L., and Elliot, D. A. 2008. A preliminary investigation of insect colonisation and succession on remains in New Zealand. *Forensic Science International*, 176, 217–223.

Elmas, I., Baslo, B., Ertas, M., and Kaya, M. 2001. Analysis of gastrocnemius compound muscle action potential in rat after death: Significance for the estimation of early postmortem interval. *Forensic Science International*, 116, 125–132.

Fernández-Lopez, S. R. 2006. Taphonomic alteration and evolutionary taphonomy. *Journal of Taphonomy*, 4, 111–142.

Fujita, M. Q., Zhu, B. L., Ishida, K., Quan, L., Oritani, S., and Maeda, H. 2002. Serum C-reactive protein levels in postmortem blood—An analysis with special reference to the cause of death and survival time. *Forensic Science International*, 130, 160–166.

Galloway, A. 1997. The process of decomposition: A model from the Arizona-Sonoran Desert. In Haglund, W. D., and Sorg, M. H. (Eds.), *Forensic taphonomy: The postmortem fate of human remains*. London: CRC Press, 139–150.

Gill-King, H. 1997. Chemical and ultrastructural aspects of decomposition. In Haglund, W. D., and Sorg, M. H. (Eds.), *Forensic taphonomy: The postmortem fate of human remains*. Boca Raton, FL: CRC Press, 93–108.

Girela, E., Villanueva, E., Irigoyen, P., Girela, V., Hernandez-Cueto, C., and Peinado, J. M. 2008. Free amino acid concentrations in vitreous humor and cerebrospinal fluid in relation to the cause of death and postmortem interval. *Journal of Forensic Sciences*, 53, 730–733.

Gomes, L., Gomes, G., Oliveira, H. G., Morlin, J. J., Desuo, I. C., Quelroz, M. M. C., Giannotti, E., and Von Zuben, C. J. 2007. Occurrence of Hymenoptera on *Sus scrofa* carcasses during summer and winter seasons in southeastern Brazil. *Revista Brasileira De Entomologia*, 51, 394–396.

Gomes, L., and Von Zuben, C. J. 2006. Forensic entomology and main challenges in Brazil. *Neotropical Entomology*, 35, 1–11.

Grassberger, M., and Frank, C. 2004. Initial study of arthropod succession on pig carrion in a central European urban habitat. *Journal of Medical Entomology*, 41, 511–523.

Große Perdekamp, M., Pollak, S., Thierauf, A., Straßburger, E., Hunzinger, M., and Vennemann, B. 2009. Experimental simulation of reentry shots using a skin-gelatine composite model. *International Journal of Legal Medicine*, 123, 419–425.

Große Perdekamp, M., Vennemann, B., Kneubuehl, B. P., Uhl, M., Treier, M., Braunwarth, R., and Pollak, S. 2008. Effect of shortening the barrel in contact shots from rifles and shotguns. *International Journal of Legal Medicine*, 122, 81–85.

Gruner, S. V., Slone, D. H., and Capinera, J. L. 2007. Forensically important Calliphoridae (Diptera) associated with pig carrion in rural north-central Florida. *Journal of Medical Entomology*, 44, 509–515.

Harvey, M. L., Dadour, I. R., and Gaudieri, S. 2003. Mitochondrial DNA cytochrome oxidase I gene: Potential for distinction between immature stages of some forensically important fly species (Diptera) in western Australia. *Forensic Science International*, 131, 134–139.

Harvey, M., Dadour, R. I., Gaudieri, S., Mansell, M. W., and Villet, M. H. 2003. MtDNA-based identification of blowflies in forensic entomology: More accurate postmortem interval estimation and beyond. *Forensic Science International*, 136, 389–398.

Harvey, M. L., Mansell, M. W., Villet, M. H., and Dadour, I. R. 2003. Molecular identification of some forensically important blowflies of southern Africa and Australia. *Medical and Veterinary Entomology*, 17, 363–369.

Hejna, P. 2010. Multiple suicidal injuries with shotgun slugs. *International Journal of Legal Medicine*, 124, 79–82.

Henderson, J. P., Morgan, S. E., Patel, F., and Tiplady, M. E. 2005. Patterns of non-firearm homicide. *Journal of Clinical Forensic Medicine*, 12, 128–132.

Hiller, J. C., Thompson, T. J. U., Evison, M. P., Chamberlain, A. T., and Wess, T. J. 2003. Bone mineral change during experimental heating: An X-ray scattering investigation. *Biomaterials*, 24, 5091–5097.

Hiller, J., and Wess, T. 2006. The use of small-angle X-ray scattering to study archaeological and experimentally altered bone. *Journal of Archaeological Science*, 33, 560–572.

Hiss, J., Shoshani, E., Zaitsew, K., Giverts, P., and Kahana, T. 2003. Self inflicted gunshot wound caused by a home-made gun—Medico-legal and ballistic examination. *Journal of Clinical Forensic Medicine*, 10, 165–168.

Høiseth, G., Karinen, R., Johnsen, L., Normann, P. T., Christophersen, A. S., and Mørland, J. 2008. Disappearance of ethyl glucuronide during heavy putrefaction. *Forensic Science International*, 176, 147–151.

Honda, J. Y., Brundage, A., Happy, C., Kelly, S. C., and Melinek, J. 2008. New records of carrion feeding insects collected on human remains. *Pan-Pacific Entomologist*, 84, 29–32.

Huang, P., Ke, Y., Lu, Q. Y., Xin, B., Fan, S. L., Yang, G. D., and Wang, Z. Y. 2008. Analysis of postmortem metabolic changes in rat kidney cortex using Fourier transform infrared spectroscopy. *Spectroscopy-an International Journal*, 22, 21–31.

Hughes, C. E., and White, A. 2009. Crack propagation in teeth: a comparison of perimortem and postmortem behavior of dental materials and cracks. *Journal of Forensic Sciences*, 5, 263–266.

Introna, F., Campobasso, C. P., and Goff, M. L. 2001. Entomotoxicology. *Forensic Science International*, 120, 42–47.

Ith, M., Bigler, P., Scheurer, E., Kreis, R., Hofmann, L., Dirnhofer, R., and Boesch, C. 2002. Observation and identification of metabolites emerging during postmortem decomposition of brain tissue by means of in situ H-1-magnetic resonance spectroscopy. *Magnetic Resonance in Medicine*, 48, 915–920.

Jadhav, S. P., and Swischuk, L. E. 2008. Commonly missed subtle skeletal injuries in children: A pictorial review. *Emergency Radiology*, 15, 391–398.

Johnson, L. A., and Ferris, J. A. J. 2002. Analysis of postmortem DNA degradation by single-cell gel electrophoresis. *Forensic Science International*, 126, 43–47.

Joy, J. E., Liette, N. L., and Harrah, H. L. 2006. Carrion fly (Diptera : Calliphoridae) larval colonization of sunlit and shaded pig carcasses in West Virginia, USA. *Forensic Science International*, 164, 183–192.

Kaiser, C., Bachmeier, B., Conrad, C., Nerlich, A., Bratzke, H., Eisenmenger, W., and Peschel, O. 2008. Molecular study of time dependent changes in DNA stability in soil buried skeletal residues. *Forensic Science International*, 177, 32–36.

Karger, B., Bratzke, H., Graß, H., Lasczkowski, G., Lessig, R., Monticelli, F., Wiese, J., and Zweihoff, R. F. 2004. Crossbow homicides. *International Journal of Legal Medicine*, 118, 332–336.

Karlsson, T., and Stahling, S. 2000. Experimental blowgun injuries, ballistic aspects of modern blowguns. *Forensic Science International*, 112, 59–64.

Kharbouche, H., Augsburger, M., Cherix, D., Sporkert, F., Giroud, C., Wyss, C., Champod, C., and Mangin, P. 2008. Codeine accumulation and elimination in larvae, pupae, and imago of the blowfly *Lucilia sericata* and effects on its development. *International Journal of Legal Medicine*, 122, 205–211.

Klippel, W. E., and Synstelien, J. A. 2007. Rodents as taphonomic agents: Bone gnawing by brown rats and gray squirrels. *Journal of Forensic Sciences*, 52, 765–773.

Klotzbach, H., Krettek, R., Bratzke, H., Puschel, K., Zehner, R., and Amendt, J. 2004. The history of forensic entomology in German-speaking countries. *Forensic Science International*, 144, 259–263.

Koon, H. E. C., Nicholson, R. A., and Collins, M. J. 2003. A practical approach to the identification of low temperature heated bone using TEM. *Journal of Archaeological Science*, 30, 1393–1399.

Kovarik, C., Stewart, D., and Cockerell, C. 2005. Gross and histologic postmortem changes of the skin. *American Journal of Forensic Medicine and Pathology*, 26, 305–308.

Kringsholm, B., Jakoben, J., Sejrsen, B., and Gregersen, M. 2001. Unidentified bodies/skulls found in Danish waters in the period of 1992–1996. *Forensic Science International*, 123, 150–158.

Kulshrestha, P., and Satpathy, D. K. 2001. Use of beetles in forensic entomology. *Forensic Science International*, 120, 15–17.

Lam, Y. M., and Pearson, O. M. 2004. The fallibility of bone density values and their use in archaeological analyses. *Journal of Taphonomy*, 2, 99–115.

Lasczkowski, G. E., Aigner, T., Gamerdinger, U., Weiler, G., and Bratzke, H. 2002. Visualization of postmortem chondrocyte damage by vital staining and confocal laser scanning 3D microscopy. *Journal of Forensic Sciences*, 47, 663–666.

Liu, L. J., Shu, X. J., Ren, L., Zhou, H. Y., Li, Y., Liu, W., Zhu, C., and Liu, L. 2007. Determination of the early time of death by computerized image analysis of DNA degradation: Which is the best quantitative indicator of DNA degradation? *Journal of Huazhong University of Science and Technology-Medical Sciences*, 27, 362–366.

Liu, Q., Cai, X., Liu, Y., Zhou, L., Yi, S., and Liu, L. 2008. Spectrophotometric determination of trimethylamine-nitrogen in cadaver tissues for the estimation of late postmortem interval: A pilot study. *Journal of Huazhong University of Science and Technology-Medical Sciences*, 28, 630–633.

Lucy, D., Aykroyd, R., and Pollard, M. 2001. Commentary on Munoz JI, Suarez-Penaranda JM, Otero XL, Rodriguez-Calvo MS, Costas E, Miguens X, Concheiro L. A new perspective in the estimation of postmortem interval (PMI) based on vitreous [K+]. *Journal of Forensic Sciences*, 46, 209–214.

Madea, B. 2005. Is there recent progress in the estimation of the postmortem interval by means of thanatochemistry. *Forensic Science International*, 151, 139–149.

Manhein, M. H., Listi, G. A., and Leitner, M. 2006. The application of geographic information systems and spatial analysis to assess dumped and subsequently scattered human remains. *Journal of Forensic Sciences*, 51, 469–474.

Manlove, J. D., and Disney, R. H. L. 2008. The use of *Megaselia abdita* (Diptera: Phoridae) in forensic entomology. *Forensic Science International*, 175, 83–84.

Marean, C. W., Abe, Y., Frey, C. J., and Randall, R. C. 2000. Zooarchaeological and taphonomic analysis of the Die Kelders Cave 1 layers 10 and 11 Middle Stone Age larger mammal fauna. *Journal of Human Evolution*, 38, 197–233.

Marean, C. W., Domínguez-Rodrigo, M., and Pickering, T. R. 2004. Skeletal element equifinality in zooarchaeology begins with method: The evolution and status of the "shaft critique". *Journal of Taphonomy*, 2, 69–98.

Martinez, E., Duque, P., and Wolff, M. 2007. Succession pattern of carrion-feeding insects in Paramo, Colombia. *Forensic Science International*, 166, 182–189.

Mazza, A., Merlati, G., Savio, C., Fassina, G., Menghini, P., and Danesino, P. 2005. Observations on dental structures when placed in contact with acids: Experimental studies to aid identification processes. *Journal of Forensic Sciences*, 50, 406–410.

Mendonca, P. M., Dos Santos-Mallet, J. R., De Mello, R. P., Gomes, L., and De Carvalho Queiroz, M. M. 2008. Identification of fly eggs using scanning electron microscopy for forensic investigations. *Micron*, 39, 802–807.

Micozzi, M. S. 1997. Frozen Environments and Soft Tissue Preservation. In Haglund, W. D., and Sorg, M. H. (Eds.), *Forensic taphonomy: The postmortem fate of human remains*. London: CRC Press, 171–179.

Moretti, T. D. C., and Ribeiro, O. B. 2006. *Cephalotes clypeatus* Fabricius (Hymenoptera: Formicidae): Nesting habits and occurrence in animal carcass. *Neotropical Entomology*, 35, 412–415.

Moriya, F., and Hashimoto, Y. 2005. Site-dependent production of gamma-hydroxybutyric acid in the early postmortem period. *Forensic Science International*, 148, 139–142.

Morton, R. J., and Lord, W. D. 2006. Taphonomy of child-sized remains: A study of scattering and scavenging in Virginia, USA. *Journal of Forensic Sciences*, 51, 475–479.

Mulla, A., Massey, K. L., and Kalra, J. 2005. Vitreous humor biochemical constituents—Evaluation of between-eye differences. *American Journal of Forensic Medicine and Pathology*, 26, 146–149.

Mundorff, A. Z., Bartelink, E. J., and Mar-Cash, E. 2009. DNA preservation in skeletal elements from the World Trade Center disaster: Recommendations for mass fatality management. *Journal of Forensic Sciences*, 54, 739–745.

Munoz, J. I., Suarez-Penaranda, J. M., Otero, X. L., Rodriguez-Calvo, M. S., Costas, E., Miguens, X., and Concheiro, L. 2001. A new perspective in the estimation of postmortem interval (PMI) based on vitreous [K+]. *Journal of Forensic Sciences*, 46, 209–214.

Munoz, J. I., Suarez-Penaranda, J. M., Rodriguez-Calvo, M. S., Otero, X. L., and Concheiro, L. 2001. Commentary on Munoz JI, Suarez-Penaranda JM, Otero XL, Rodriguez-Calvo MS, Costas E, Miguens X, Concheiro L. A new perspective in the estimation of postmortem interval (PMI) based on vitreous [K+]. *Journal of Forensic Sciences*, 46, 1527–1528.

Munro, N. D., and Bar-Oz, G. 2004. Debating issues of equifinality in ungulate skeletal part studies. *Journal of Taphonomy*, 2, 1–13.

Myskowiak, J. B., and Doums, C. 2002. Effects of refrigeration on the biometry and development of *Protophormia terraenovae* (Robineau-Desvoidy) (Diptera: Calliphoridae) and its consequences in estimating post-mortem interval in forensic investigations. *Forensic Science International*, 125, 254–261.

Nawrocki, S. P., Pless, J. E., Hawley, D. A., and Wagner, S. A. 1997. Fluvial transport of human crania. In Haglund, W. D., and Sorg, M. H. (Eds.), *Forensic taphonomy: The postmortem fate of human remains*. London: CRC Press, 529–552.

Nelson, E. L. 2000. Estimation of short-term postmortem interval utilizing core body temperature: A new algorithm. *Forensic Science International*, 109, 31–38.

Nordby, J. J. 2002. Is forensic taphonomy scientific? In Haglund, W. D., and Sorg, M. H. (Eds.), *Advances in forensic taphonomy: Method, theory, and archaeological perspectives*. London: CRC Press, 31–45.

Oakley, K. 2005. Forensic archaeology and anthropology. *Forensic Science, Medicine, and Pathology*, 1, 169–172.

O'Brien, T. G. 1997. Movement of bodies in Lake Ontario. In Haglund, W. D., and Sorg, M. H. (Eds.), *Forensic taphonomy: The postmortem fate of human remains*. London: CRC Press, 559–566.

O'Brien, R. C., Forbes, S. L., Meyer, J., and Dadour, I. 2010. Forensically significant scavenging guilds in the southwest of Western Australia. *Forensic Science International*, 198, 85–91.

O'Brien, R. C., Forbes, S. L., Meyer, J., and Dadour, I. R. 2007. A preliminary investigation into the scavenging activity on pig carcasses in Western Australia. *Forensic Science, Medicine, and Pathology*, 3, 194–199.

Oesterhelweg, L., Krober, S., Rottmann, K., Willhoft, J., Braun, C., Thies, N., Puchel, K., Silkenath, J., and Gehl, A. 2008. Cadaver dogs—A study on detection of contaminated carpet squares. *Forensic Science International*, 174, 35–39.

Ordonez, A., Garcia, M. D., and Fagua, G. 2008. Evaluation of efficiency of Schoenly trap for collecting adult sarcosaprophagous dipterans. *Journal of Medical Entomology*, 45, 522–532.

Outram, A. K. 2004. Applied models and indices vs. high-resolution, observed data: Detailed fracture and fragmentation analyses for the investigation of skeletal part abundance patterns. *Journal of Taphonomy*, 2, 167–184.

Outram, A. K., Knusel, C. J., Knight, S., and Harding, A. F. 2005. Understanding complex fragmented assemblages of human and animal remains: A fully integrated approach. *Journal of Archaeological Science*, 32, 1699–1710.

Pampin, J. B., and Rodriguez, B. A. L.-A. 2001. Surprising drifting of bodies along the coast of Portugal and Spain. *Legal Medicine*, 3, 177–182.

Perera, C., and Briggs, C. 2008. Guidelines for the effective conduct of mass burials following mass disasters: Post-Asian Tsunami disaster experience in retrospect. *Forensic Science, Medicine, and Pathology*, 4, 1–8.

Phengon, P., Wongwiggarn, S., and Panvisavas, N. 2008. Analysis of DNA from degraded tissue. *Forensic Science International, Genetics Supplement Series*, 1, 439–441.

Pickering, T. R. 2001. Carnivore voiding: A taphonomic process with the potential for the deposition of forensic evidence. *Journal of Forensic Sciences*, 46, 406–411.

Pickering, T. R., and Carlson, K. J. 2004. Baboon taphonomy and its relevance to the investigation of large felid involvement in human forensic cases. *Forensic Science International*, 144, 37–44.

Pickering, T. R., Domínguez-Rodrigo, M., Egeland, C. P., and Brain, C. K. 2005. The contribution of limb bone fracture patterns to reconstructing early hominid behaviour at Swartkrans cave (South Africa): Archaeological application of a new analytical method. *International Journal of Osteoarchaeology*, 15, 247–260.

Pickering, T. R., Egeland, C. P., Schnell, A. G., Osborne, D. L., and Enk, J. 2006. Success in identification of experimentally fragmented limb bone shafts: Implications for estimates of skeletal element abundance in archaeofaunas. *Journal of Taphonomy*, 4, 97–108.

Pickering, T. R., and Hensley-Marschand, B. 2008. Cutmarks and hominid handedness. *Journal of Archaeological Science*, 35, 310–315.

Pigliucci, M., and Kaplan, J. 2000. The fall and rise of Dr. Pangloss: Adaptationism and the Spandrels paper 20 years later. *Tree*, 15, 66–70.

Pobiner, B. L., and Braun, D. R. 2005. Applying actualism: Considerations for future research. *Journal of Taphonomy*, 3, 57–65.

Potter, S. L. 2005. The physics of cutmarks. *Journal of Taphonomy*, 3, 91–106.

Prieto-Castello, M. J., Del Rincon, J. P. H., Perez-Sirvent, C., Alvarez-Jimenez, P., Perez-Carceles, M. D., Osuna, E., and Luna, A. 2007. Application of biochemical and X-ray diffraction analyses to establish the postmortem interval. *Forensic Science International*, 172, 112–118.

Proctor, H. C. 2009. Can freshwater mites act as forensic tools? *Experimental and Applied Acarology*, 49, 161–165.

Pujol-Luz, J. R., Francez, P. A. D. C., Ururahy-Rodrigues, A., and Constantino, R. 2008. The black soldier-fly, *Hermetia illucens* (Diptera, Stratiomyidae), used to estimate the postmortem interval in a case in Amapa State, Brazil. *Journal of Forensic Sciences*, 53, 476–478.

Pye, K., and Croft, D. 2007. Forensic analysis of soil and sediment traces by scanning electron microscopy and energy-dispersive X-ray analysis: An experimental investigation. *Forensic Science International*, 165, 52–63.

Rainio, J., De Paoli, G., Druid, H., Kauppila, R., De Giorgio, F., Bortolotti, F., and Tagliaro, F. 2008. Post-mortem stability and redistribution of carbohydrate-deficient transferrin (CDT). *Forensic Science International*, 174, 161–165.

Rainio, J., Lalu, K., Ranta, H., and Penttia, A. 2003. Morphology of experimental assault rifle skin wounds. *International Journal of Legal Medicine*, 117, 19–26.

Raul, J.-S., Deck, C., Meyer, F., Geraut, A., Willinger, R., and Ludes, B. 2007. A finite element model investigation of gunshot injury. *International Journal of Legal Medicine*, 121, 143–146.

Raul, J.-S., Deck, C., Willinger, R., and Ludes, B. 2008. Finite-element models of the human head and their applications in forensic practice. *International Journal of Legal Medicine*, 122, 359–366.

Reeves, N. M. 2009. Taphonomic effects of vulture scavenging. *Journal of Forensic Sciences*, 54, 523–528.

Richards, C. S., Paterson, I. D., and Villet, M. H. 2008. Estimating the age of immature *Chrysomya albiceps* (Diptera: Calliphoridae), correcting for temperature and geographical latitude. *International Journal of Legal Medicine*, 122, 271–279.

Ruffell, A. 2010. Forensic pedology, forensic geology, forensic geoscience, geoforensics and soil forensics. *Forensic Science International*, in Press. doi:10.1016/j.forsciint.2010.03.044.

Rühli, F. J., Kuhn, G., Evison, R., Müller, R., and Schultz, M. 2007. Diagnostic value of micro-CT in comparison with histology in the qualitative assessment of historical human skull bone pathologies. *American Journal of Physical Anthropology*, 133, 1099–1111.

Rutty, G. 2005. The estimation of the time since death using temperatures recorded from the external auditory canal. Forensic Science, Medicine, and Pathology, 1, 41–51.

Sabucedo, A. J., and Furton, K. G. 2003. Estimation of postmortem interval using the protein marker cardiac troponin I. *Forensic Science International*, 134, 11–16.

Sajdok, J., Pilin, A., Auinger, F., and Pudil, F. 2007. Determination of post-mortem age from human tissues in forensic medicine. *Journal of Biotechnology*, 131, S56–S57.

Sanders, J., Wagner Schuman, M., and Marbella, A. M. 2009. The epidemiology of torture: A case series of 58 survivors of torture. *Forensic Science International*, 189, e1–e7.

Savio, C., Merlati, G., Danesino, P., Fassina, G., and Menghini, P. 2006. Radiographic evaluation of teeth subjected to high temperatures: Experimental study to aid identification processes. *Forensic Science International*, 158, 108–116.

Scheurer, E., Ith, M., Dietrich, D., Kreis, R., Husler, J., Dirnhofer, R., and Boesch, C. 2005. Statistical evaluation of time-dependent metabolite concentrations: estimation of post-mortem intervals based on in situ H-1-MRS the brain. *NMR in Biomedicine*, 18, 163–172.

Schoenly, K. G., Haskell, N. H., Hall, R. D., and Gbur, J. R. 2007. Comparative performance and complementarity of four sampling methods and arthropod preference tests from human and porcine remains at the forensic anthropology center in Knoxville, Tennessee. *Journal of Medical Entomology*, 44, 881–894.

Schoenly, K. G., Shahid, S. A., Haskell, N. H., and Hall, R. D. 2005. Does carcass enrichment alter community structure of predaceous and parasitic arthropods? A second test of the arthropod saturation hypothesis at the anthropology research facility in Knoxville, Tennessee. *Journal of Forensic Sciences*, 50, 134–142.

Sledzik, P. S., and Rodriguez, W. C. 2002. *Damnum fatale*: the taphonomic fate of human remains in mass disasters. In Sorg, M. H., and Haglund, W. D. (Eds.), *Advances in forensic taphonomy: Method, theory and archeological perspectives*. Boca Raton, FL: CRC Press, 321–330.

Slone, D. H., and Gruner, S. V. 2007. Thermoregulation in larval aggregations of carrion-feeding blow flies (Diptera: Calliphoridae). *Journal of Medical Entomology*, 44, 516–523.

Solsona, M., and Wagensberg, J. 2002. Taphonomy, a discovery for museology. *Contributions to Science*, 2, 277–279.

Stiner, M. C. 2004. A comparison of photon densitometry and computed tomography parameters of bone density in ungulate body part profiles. *Journal of Taphonomy*, 2, 117–145.

Stojanowski, C. M., Seidemann, R. M., and Doran, G. H. 2002. Differential skeletal preservation at Windover Pond: Causes and consequences. *American Journal of Physical Anthropology*, 119, 15–26.

Suby, J. A., Guichón, R. A., Cointry, G., and Ferretti, J. L. 2009. Volumetric BMD values of archaeological human bone remains with pQCT and DEXA. *Journal of Taphonomy*, 7, 29–45.

Sukontason, K., Narongchai, P., Kanchai, C., Vichairat, K., Sribanditmongkol, P., Bhoopat, T., Kurahashi, H., Chockjamsai, M., Piangjai, S., Bunchu, N., Vongvivach, S., Samai, W., Chaiwong, T., Methanitikorn, R., Ngern-Klun, R., Sripakdee, D., Boonsriwong, W., Siriwattanarungsee, S., Srimuangwong, C., Hanterdsith, B., Chaiwan, K., Srisuwan, C., Upakut, S., Moopayak, K., Vogtsberger, R. C., Olson, J. K., and Sukontason, K. L. 2007. Forensic entomology cases in Thailand: A review of cases from 2000 to 2006. *Parasitology Research*, 101, 1417–1423.

Sukontason, K. L., Ngern-Klun, R., Sripakdee, D., and Sukontason, K. 2007. Identifying fly puparia by clearing technique: Application to forensic entomology. *Parasitology Research*, 101, 1407–1416.

Tabor, K. L., Brewster, C. C., and Fell, R. D. 2004. Analysis of the successional patterns of insects on carrion in southwest Virginia. *Journal of Medical Entomology*, 41, 785–795.

Tabor, K. L., Fell, R. D., and Brewster, C. C. 2005. Insect fauna visiting carrion in southwest Virginia. *Forensic Science International*, 150, 73–80.

Tagliaro, F., Bortolotti, F., Manetto, G., Cittadini, F., Pascali, V. L., and Marigo, M. 2001. Potassium concentration differences in the vitreous humour from the two eyes revisited by microanalysis with capillary electrophoresis. *Journal of Chromatography A*, 924, 493–498.

Tarone, A. M., Jennings, K. C., and Foran, D. R. 2007. Aging blow fly eggs using gene expression: A feasibility study. *Journal of Forensic Sciences*, 52, 1350–1354.

Thaik-Oo, M., Tanaka, E., Tsuchiya, T., Kominato, Y., Honda, K., Yamazaki, K., and Misawa, S. 2002. Estimation of postmortem interval from hypoxic inducible levels of vascular endothelial growth factor. *Journal of Forensic Sciences*, 47, 186–189.

Thompson, J. C., and Lee-Gorishti, Y. 2007. Carnivore bone portion choice and surface modification on modern experimental boiled bone assemblages. *Journal of Taphonomy*, 5, 121–135.

Thompson, T. J. U., and Chudek, J. A. 2006. A novel approach to the visualisation of heat-induced structural change in bone. *Science and Justice*, 47, 99–104.

Thyssen, P. J., Lessinger, A. C., Azeredo-Espin, A. M. L., and Linhares, A. X. 2005. The value of PCR-RFLP molecular markers for the differentiation of immature stages of two necrophagous flies (Diptera: Calliphoridae) of potential forensic importance. *Neotropical Entomology*, 34, 777–783.

Thyssen, P. J., and Linhares, A. X. 2007. First description of the immature stages of *Hemilucilia segmentaria* (Diptera: Calliphoridae). *Biological Research*, 40, 271–280.

Tibbett, M., and Carter, D. O. 2003. Mushrooms and taphonomy: The fungi that mark woodland graves. *Mycologist*, 11, 20–24.

Toms, C., Rogers, C. B., and Sathyavagiswaran, L. 2008. Investigation of homicides interred in concrete—The Los Angeles experience. *Journal of Forensic Sciences*, 53, 203–207.

Törő, K., Hubay, M., Sótonyi, P., and Keller, E. 2005. Fatal traffic injuries among pedestrians, bicyclists and motor vehicle occupants. *Forensic Science International*, 151, 151–156.

Trotter, M., and Hixon, B. 2005. Sequential changes in weight, density, and percentage ash weight of human skeletons from an early fetal period through old age. *The Anatomical Record*, 179, 1–18.

Vass, A. A. 2010. The elusive universal post-mortem interval formula. *Forensic Science International*, in press. doi: 10.1016/j.forsciint.2010.04.052.

Verhoff, M. A., Karger, B., Ramsthaler, F., and Obert, M. 2008. Investigations on an isolated skull with gunshot wounds using flat-panel CT. *International Journal of Legal Medicine*, 122, 441–445.

Vincent, S., Vian, J. M., and Carlotti, M. P. 2000. Partial sequencing of the cytochrome oxydase b subunit gene I: A tool for the identification of European species of blow flies for postmortem interval estimation. *Journal of Forensic Sciences*, 45, 820–823.

Wang, J., Li, Z., Chen, Y., Chen, Q., and Yin, X. 2008. The succession and development of insects on pig carcasses and their significances in estimating PMI in south China. *Forensic Science International*, 179, 11–8.

Watson, E. J., and Carlton, C. E. 2003. Spring succession of necrophilous insects on wildlife carcasses in Louisiana. *Journal of Medical Entomology*, 40, 338–347.

Wedel, V. L. 2007. Determination of season at death using dental cementum increment analysis. *Journal of Forensic Sciences*, 52, 1334–1337.

Weitzel, M. A. 2005. A report of decomposition rates of a special burial type in Edmonton, Alberta from an experimental field study. *Journal of Forensic Sciences*, 50, 641–647.

Wells, J. D., and Stevens, J. R. 2008. Application of DNA-based methods in forensic entomology. *Annual Review of Entomology*, 53, 103–120.

Wells, J. D., and Williams, D. W. 2007. Validation of a DNA-based method for identifying Chrysomyinae (Diptera: Calliphoridae) used in a death investigation. *International Journal of Legal Medicine*, 121, 1–8.

Wilson, A. S., Dodson, H. I., Janaway, R. C., Pollard, A. M., and Tobin, D. J. 2007. Selective biodegradation in hair shafts derived from archaeological, forensic and experimental contexts. *British Journal of Dermatology*, 157, 450–457.

Wiltshire, P. E. J. 2006. Consideration of some taphonomic variables of relevance to forensic palynological investigation in the United Kingdom. *Forensic Science International*, 163, 173–182.

Worley, F. 2005. Taphonomic influences on cremation burial deposits: implications for interpretation. In: O'Connor, T. P. (Ed.), *Biosphere to lithosphere: New studies in vertebrate taphonomy*. Oxford, UK: Oxbow Books, 64–69.

Yang, T. T., Li, Z. W., Liu, L., and Zhen, N. 2008. Estimation of postmortem interval with single-voxel proton 1H-MR spectroscopy at different temperature. *Fa Yi Xue Za Zhi*, 24, 85–89.

Ying, B. W., Liu, T. T., Fan, H., Wei, D., Wen, F. Q., Bai, P., Huang, J., and Hou, Y. P. 2007. The application of mitochondrial DNA cytochrome oxidase II gene for the identification of forensically important blowflies in western China. *American Journal of Forensic Medicine and Pathology*, 28, 308–313.

Zhou, B., Zhang, L., Zhang, G. Q., Zhang, X. S., and Jiang, X. P. 2007. The determination of potassium concentration in vitreous humor by low pressure ion chromatography and its application in the estimation of postmortem interval. *Journal of Chromatography B-Analytical Technologies in the Biomedical and Life Sciences*, 852, 278–281.

Zhu, G. H., Xu, X. H., Yu, X. J., Zhang, Y., and Wang, J. R. 2007. Puparial case hydrocarbons of *Chrysomya megacephala* as an indicator of the postmortem interval. *Forensic Science International*, 169, 1–5.

Comparative Osteology

10

RACHEL GILCHRIST
SARAH VOOGHT
PROF. ROGER SOAMES

Contents

Introduction

Skeletal material is frequently encountered in both forensic and archaeological scenarios. Forensic anthropologists are frequently asked "Are these remains human or nonhuman?" To determine the origin of skeletal material and therefore answer this question, a number of approaches and techniques can be used. Each approach or technique has both benefits and limitations depending on the condition of the bone and the circumstances under which it is found. In addition, the individual undertaking the analysis should be trained to an appropriate standard and be familiar with the relevant techniques and the taxonomic groups likely to be encountered in the geographical area where they are operating.

The skeletal assemblage may include material from more than one species and may consist of complete or incomplete individuals. It is imperative that any human remains are distinguished from nonhuman material as the discovery of human bone may ultimately merit a full forensic investigation. The condition of the remains will determine which techniques can be applied. When the material is represented by a complete bone in relatively good condition, gross morphology may be all that is necessary to determine its origin. Geographical location may also play an important role as this may help to determine which animal species are most commonly encountered there. The ability to distinguish between different species may also be necessary; to do so may require reference to known samples or an appropriate textbook or atlas of comparative osteology. Large and small nonhuman mammalian material commonly found in the United Kingdom include horse (*Equus caballus*); cow (*Bos Taurus*); sheep (*Ovis aries*); pig (*Sus scrofa domesticus*); chicken (*Gallus gallus domesticus*); dog (*Canis familiaris*); cat (*Felis catus*); rabbit (*Oryctolagus cuniculus*); deer (*cervus sp.*); and fox (*Vulpes vulpes*).

Gross Morphology

The overall morphology and specific structural features present on skeletal remains can be used to determine if they are human or nonhuman in origin. This method of anthropological species differentiation has been explored in previous literature (Byers 2008). Although human skeletal remains can be distinguished from other animals by comparison, due to anatomical variation the precise determination of whether a bone is human or nonhuman is a more difficult process (Byers 2008). This is largely attributed to potential confusion between skeletal material in terms of size and shape (Oxenham and Barwick 2008), particularly when the skull is not available for analysis (Byers 2008).

Morphological differences in structure between human and animal bones arise due to the differing functional requirements of the species. In humans, for example, the femur has developed in response to bipedal weight bearing and locomotion. Although weight bearing and mode of locomotion will also determine the morphological appearance of bony features in quadrupeds, the bones are more specifically adapted to support body weight through all four limbs. Depending on muscle mass, the long bones of the limb will show differences in the regions that have major muscles or muscle groups attached to them. According to Saulsman et al. (2010), noninvasive morphometric analysis of long bones can be used to distinguish human from animal bones. In addition, differences in gait patterns between species can also be used as a basis for the identification of human from nonhuman remains, although it should be noted that not all quadrupeds and bipeds will share an identical morphological appearance even though some similarities may be observed (Croker et al. 2009).

The analysis of intact bones enables accurate species identification and differentiation. Consequently, having a complete bone available presents a larger range of morphological features for examination, increasing the certainty of identifying human from nonhuman remains. Furthermore, comparison of the gross morphology of human and nonhuman bones may be aided by the presence of epiphyses in relation to the size and shape of the bone (Byers 2008; Oxenham and Barwick 2008).

A number of atlases have been published that compare the gross morphology of similar bones from a range of different animal species that could be encountered within a forensic setting, although they are often country specific (Adams and Crabtree 2008; Oxenham and Barwick 2008; France 2009). Although these reference atlases may initially be used to determine whether the remains are human or nonhuman, if the latter is suspected, then the ability to determine the species may still not be achieved, although this is often not the object of an initial examination.

Atlases such as those referenced are of most use when intact bones are available for analysis. Where there has been trauma to the bones, resulting in fragmentation or damage to their morphological features, a different approach must be utilized to determine if the material is human or nonhuman (Cattaneo et al. 1999; Croker et al. 2009; Dawnay et al. 2007).

Fragmented Remains

If the remains presented are fragmented, this can be due to a number of reasons, including fire, mass disasters, and domestic crimes. In these situations, it is less likely that the bony elements will retain species-specific morphology; thus, additional methods must be employed. One such technique is histological analysis, involving the examination of sections of cortical bone to assess its appearance and the subsequent identification of its histological structure (Hillier and Bell 2007).

Histological Methods

In a review of the literature, Hillier and Bell (2007) confirmed that it is possible in many cases to differentiate between human and nonhuman cortical bone on the basis of histological appearance (Martinakova et al., 2006). In such analyses, it is Haversian system diameter and Haversian canal diameter that are the most optimal measurements to use.

Histological techniques have been used in an archaeological context, with Walter et al. (2004) documenting a new approach in the examination of bone-tempered pottery utilizing histological methods. The application of their technique has the potential to shed light on the animals used for bone tempering and may therefore be helpful in species differentiation and identification.

Cuijpers (2006) used histological assessment techniques on archaeological bone and observed that there was a general difference in the primary bone types between humans and large mammals (horses and cattle). Cuijpers (2006) also stated that human bone was of a lamellar type, whereas horses and cattle showed fibrous bone; a difference in the secondary bone structure was also observed.

Mammalian compact and trabecular bone both display two different types of bone tissue when viewed under a microscope: woven and lamellar bone. On closer examination, the internal structure of compact bone may differ between animals of the same species and between different bones of the same animal. Furthermore, variations may also be seen in cross sections of the same bone. This difference may be due to factors such as the age and sex of the animal or as a result of mechanical stresses acting on the bone (Hillier and Bell 2007). When studying the histology of bone the potential for these differences should be taken into account as it may lead to misidentification of the material.

When looking at differences between human and animal bone, the general microstructure of the Haversian bone and measurements of the histological structures should be considered. On microscopic analysis of the bone fragments from an assemblage, one type of bone that may be present is plexiform bone. This consists of stacks of lamellae separated by vascular spaces containing capillary network sheets (Locke 2004), which give the bone a "bricklike" appearance, making it easy to identify. Similar to woven bone, plexiform bone is also formed more rapidly than lamellar bone; however, in contrast, plexiform bone cannot be formed de novo as is the case with woven bone. The presence of plexiform bone may be used as an indicator of nonhuman bone as it is rarely seen in humans.

However, if plexiform bone is not present or cannot be seen, osteon banding patterns may be useful in distinguishing human from nonhuman bone. Mulhern and Ubelaker (2001) have compared patterns of osteon organization in human and nonhuman bone to determine whether the patterns are distinctive. They concluded that banding patterns, if present, may be useful for identification purposes as the distribution of osteons observed are different in human and nonhuman bones. Furthermore, secondary osteons may also be used to distinguish human from nonhuman bone. However, as the human pattern can be shared with some other vertebrate species, the presence of plexiform bone or osteon banding is suggestive but not conclusive, and their absence is not indicative either way.

Similarities do exist between species, with Byers (2008) highlighting the similarities between the metacarpals and metatarsals of humans and bears.

DNA Analysis

Due to the advantages associated with DNA analysis as a method of species differentiation, many investigations have focused on the development of this technique. Although the analysis of DNA structure is already used within forensic investigations as a method of differentiating between individuals (Hiroshige et al. 2009; Karlsson and Holmlund 2007), its use to determine the origin of skeletal tissue has until recently not been explored.

A mixture of trace samples representing both human and nonhuman remains may be presented within forensic investigations (Tobe and Linacre 2008). DNA analysis can be employed when analysis of the gross morphology of skeletal elements is unavailable due to damage or degradation associated with the samples (Dawnay et al. 2007). Although histological methods of analysis may also be employed in similar situations, in comparison to DNA analysis, this approach is more time and labor consuming (Croker et al. 2009). Traditionally, however, immunological analysis was employed in such circumstances (Bellis et al. 2003; Parson et al. 2000). This method of analysis has a number of limitations, including a limited number of species available for comparison; it is not sufficiently unique to differentiate precisely between species; it may be affected if the sample is degraded; and importantly, it requires destruction of the evidence in the analysis (Bataille et al. 1999; Parson et al. 2000). Due to the limitations of immunological analysis, examination of DNA has therefore been favored in the recent literature. Nevertheless, Ubelaker et al. (2004) and Lowenstein et al. (2005) reported that animal species can be identified by protein radioimmunoassy of small bone fragments. DNA is unique between species (Balitzki-Korte et al. 2005) and as such can be used to differentiate, with accuracy, human from nonhuman skeletal remains (Karlsson and Holmlund 2007; Parson et al. 2000; Pun et al. 2009). It also has the advantage of being a relatively easy procedure to perform (Pun et al. 2009), and simultaneously is cost efficient (Pun et al. 2009; Tobe and Linacre 2008). Furthermore, research utilizing DNA analysis has also succeeded in reducing the time associated with this method (Pun et al. 2009).

DNA samples may be extracted from many tissues, including blood and bone samples. Mitochondrial DNA, genomic DNA, and ribosomal RNA (Melton and Holland 2007) are most commonly employed for identification purposes (Bellis et al. 2003). Of these, mitochondrial DNA is perhaps the most widely used (Tobe and Linacre 2008) as it is found more abundantly within cells (Bataille et al. 1999; Pun et al. 2009). The frequency with which genetic material has been found in collected samples, and therefore can be used for identification, is often not sufficient for later analysis. Consequently, the available genetic material must be amplified to increase its concentration sufficiently to enable analysis to be undertaken. Amplification of genetic material is achieved by polymerase chain reaction (PCR), a process involving the denaturing of the DNA material to unwind the double-helix structure of the DNA. A number of primers are then used to initiate replication of the exposed DNA strands; each complete DNA replication that is achieved is referred to as a *cycle*. On the completion of each cycle, the number of DNA sequences is doubled. This process is continued until a sufficient quantity of genetic material is available for analysis (Hartl and Jones 1999; Weaver and Hedrick 1997).

The DNA analysis of bone to determine the species from which it is derived relies on genetic differences between species. It is the fragmentation of DNA sequences at unique genetic points by primers that enables a determination of species to be made as each genetic sample yields a different number of fragment lengths corresponding to the different locations of the genes between species. Recent literature has therefore focused on using different primers associated with genes at varying locations between different species, resulting in differing fragmentation lengths (Kitano et al. 2007; Nakamura et al. 2009; Nicklas and Buel 2006). However, other investigators have aimed to differentiate between human and nonhuman material by choosing genes that are unique to humans. Hiroshige et al. (2009), for example, concentrated on investigating the gene related to language development in humans. The determination of whether the genetic material is human or nonhuman is based on comparison of a sample of unknown species with a control sample from a known species (Dawnay et al. 2007). A number of investigators have also tried to quantify the occurrence of human material within a mixed sample of both human and nonhuman tissue (Tobe and Linacre 2008).

Although DNA analysis of skeletal remains is of use in forensic investigations, there are still a number of limitations associated with the technique, including the equipment needed and preparation of the skeletal material (Rennick et al., 2005), in addition to a sterile environment (Tobe and Linacre 2008). Comparison of an unknown species sample against a control sample may be limited in terms of defining the species if insufficient sample data exist (Dawnay et al. 2007; Pun et al. 2009). DNA may also be subject to degradation in some environments, having an impact on the certainty of identifying human remains (Balitzki-Korte et al. 2005). Further investigation into the effect of degradation on genetic samples would be beneficial for this technique (Bellis et al. 2003), as would the establishment of a more substantial collection of reference control samples.

Other Methods of Identification: Cortical Bone Thickness

Although analysis of the gross morphology, histology, and DNA associated with skeletal elements may be used to differentiate between human and nonhuman material, other techniques for species differentiation have become the focus of recent research. Cross-sectional cortical bone thickness is such a technique. Although previous studies have suggested that this may be useful for species determination (Croker et al. 2009), only recently has it been more fully developed. This was investigated initially by Urbanova and Novotny (2005) in combination with histological analysis and more recently by Croker et al. (2009).

The technique is based on the fact that cortical bone thickness increases partially as a result of increasing body mass. Thus, larger animals with a greater body mass would be expected to possess a greater amount of cortical bone than smaller animals. This technique may not be able to differentiate between bones of large animals or humans as these may be readily separated on the basis of general observation of the bones themselves. Significant differences in the size and diameter of human and large-animal bones will enable the nonhuman elements to be readily identified without the need to analyze cortical bone thickness. This method may therefore be of greater use in differentiating between nonhuman and human bones that are of the same general shape and size (Croker et al. 2009).

Consequently, previous investigations have focused on the comparison of cortical bone thickness between humans and other animal species with a similar body mass. Croker et al. (2009) analyzed bones from humans, sheep, and kangaroos to determine whether (a) human skeletal material could be separated from nonhuman material and (b) if bones from a quadruped could be identified when associated with bipedal remains. It was thought that the different patterns of weight distribution may be observed on analysis of the cortical bone content of species with different modes of locomotion. Differences in transverse cortical bone samples were quantified by the production of a cortical thickness index using the following equation:

$$\text{Cortical Thickness Index} = [1 - (\text{Medullary Diameter/Shaft Diameter})] \times 100\%$$

In contrast, Urbanova and Novotny (2005) only studied human and pig skeletal material and noted certain similarities in cortical bone thicknesses between the two sets of samples, although little other information relating to this comparison was provided.

Although both of these investigations demonstrated the ability of this technique to differentiate between human and nonhuman bone samples based on cortical bone thickness, further investigation is still required. Despite the comparison of kangaroo, sheep, and pig bones with human material, none of the animal samples used were of similar body mass to humans (Croker et al. 2009; Urbanova and Novotny 2005). As differences in cortical bone thicknesses are suggested to be partly attributed to the difference in body mass (Croker et al. 2009), it is essential that this method is used if species of similar mass are available for analysis. Therefore, further investigation using skeletal material from humans and animals of similar mass, such as larger pigs or cows (Urbanova and Novotny 2005), is required. Variation in cortical bone thickness as a result of age must also be analyzed to determine if this technique can be used on bones from older human individuals (Croker et al. 2009). One drawback of both studies is that only femora were analyzed

(Croker et al. 2009; Urbanova and Novotny 2005); further investigations using other bones are therefore required.

Conclusion

The ability to distinguish between human and nonhuman skeletal remains is dependent on a number of factors. A high level of training as well as appropriate experience and access to relevant comparative material are essential. The skill of determining the origin of skeletal material accurately can take many years to perfect and must include fieldwork and not rely solely on information gained from books. If the presented material is fragmentary, gross determination by the forensic anthropologist may not be possible. In such cases, techniques such as histological assessment or DNA profiling can be used to aid in the assessment of human and nonhuman material. In some cases, the origin of the bone may never be determined; the fragment may be too small or so badly damaged that an estimation of the species simply cannot be determined.

References

Adams, B. J., and Crabtree, P. J. (2008). *Comparative skeletal anatomy: A photographic atlas for medical examiners, coroners, forensic anthropologists, and archaeologists.* Totowa, NJ: Humana Press.

Balitzki-Korte, B., Anslinger, K., Bartsch, C., and Rolf, B. (2005). Species identification by means of pyrosequencing the mitochondrial 12S rRNA gene. *International Journal of Legal Medicine* 119: 291–294.

Bataille, M., Crainic, K., Leterreux, M., Durigon, M., and de Mazancourta, P. (1999). Multiplex amplification of mitochondrial DNA for human and species identification in forensic evaluation. *Forensic Science International* 99: 165–170.

Bellis, C., Ashton, K. J., Freney, L., Blairb, B., and Griffiths, L. R. (2003). A molecular genetic approach for forensic animal species identification. *Forensic Science International* 134: 99–108.

Byers, S. N. (2008). *Introduction to forensic anthropology: International edition* (3rd ed.). Boston: Pearson Education.

Cattaneo, C., DiMartino, S., Scali, S., Craig, O. E., Grandi, M., and Sokol, R. J. (1999). Determining the human origin of fragments of burnt bone: A comparative study of histological, immunological and DNA techniques. *Forensic Science International* 102: 181–191.

Croker, S. L., Clement, J. G., and Donlon, D. (2009). A comparison of cortical bone thickness in the femoral midshaft of humans and two non-human mammals. *HOMO—Journal of Comparative Human Biology* 60: 551–565.

Cuijpers, A. G. F. M. (2006). Histological identification of bone fragments in archaeology: telling humans apart from horses and cattle. *International Journal of Osteoarchaeology* 16: 465–480.

Dawnay, N., Ogden, R., McEwing, R., Carvalho, G. R., and Thorpe, R. S. (2007). Validation of the barcoding gene COI for use in forensic genetic species identification. *Forensic Science International* 173: 1–6.

France, D. L. (2009). *Human and nonhuman bone identification: A color atlas.* Boca Raton, FL: CRC Press.

Hartl, D. L., and Jones, E. W. (1999). *Essential genetics* (2nd ed.). New York: Jones and Bartlett.

Hillier, M. L., and Bell, L. S. (2007). Differentiating human bone from animal bone: A review of histological methods. *Journal of Forensic Sciences* 52: 249–263.

Hiroshige, K., Soejima, M., Nishioka, T., Kamimura, S., and Koda, Y. (2009). Simple and sensitive method for identification of human DNA by allele-specific polymerase chain reaction of FOXP2. *Journal of Forensic Sciences* 54: 857–861.

Karlsson, A. O., and Holmlund, G. (2007). Identification of mammal species using species-specific DNA pyrosequencing. *Forensic Science International* 173: 16–20.

Kitano, T., Umetsu, K., Tain, W., and Osawa, M. (2007). Two universal primer sets for species identification among vertebrates. *International Journal of Legal Medicine* 121: 423–427.

Locke, M. (2004). Structure of long bones in mammals. *Journal of Morphology* 265: 546–565.

Lowenstein, J. M., Reuther, J., Hood, D., Scheuenstuhl, G., Gerlach, S., and Ubelaker, D. H. (2005). Identification of animal species by protein radioimmunoassay of bone fragments and bloodstained stone tools. *Forensic Science International* 159: 182–188.

Martinakova, M., Grosskopf, B., Omelka, R., Vondrakova, M., and Bauerova, M. (2006). Differences among species in compact bone tissue microstructure of mammalian skeleton: Use of a discriminant function analysis for species identification. *Journal of Forensic Sciences* 51: 1235–1239.

Melton, T., and Holland, C. (2007). Routine forensic use of the mitochondrial 12S ribosomal RNA gene for species identification. *Journal of Forensic Sciences* 52: 1305–1307.

Mulhern, D. M., and Ubelaker, D. H. (2001). Differences in osteon banding between human and nonhuman bone. *Journal of Forensic Sciences* 46: 220–222.

Nakamura, H., Muro, T., Imamura, S., and Yuasa, I. (2009). Forensic species identification based on size variation of mitochondrial DNA hypervariable regions. *International Journal of Legal Medicine* 123: 177–184.

Nicklas, J. A., and Buel, E. (2006). Simultaneous determination of total human and male DNA using a duplex real-time PCR assay. *Journal of Forensic Sciences* 51: 1005–1015.

Oxenham, M., and Barwick, R. (2008). Human, sheep or kangaroo: A practical guide to identifying human skeletal remains in Australia. In Oxenham, M. (Ed.), *Forensic approaches to death, disaster and abuse.* Bowen Hills, Qld, Australia: Australian Academic Press.

Parson, W., Pegoraro, K., Niederstätter, H., Föger, M., and Steinlechner, M. (2000). Species identification by means of the cytochrome b gene. *International Journal of Legal Medicine* 11: 23–28.

Pun, K-M., Albrecht, C., Castella, V., and Fumagalli, L. (2009). Species identification in mammals from mixed biological samples based on mitochondrial DNA control region length polymorphism. *Electrophoresis* 30: 1008–1014.

Rennick, S. L., Fenton, T. M., and Foran, D. R. (2005). The effects of skeletal preparation techniques on DNA from human and non-human bone. *Journal of Forensic Sciences* 50: 1016–1019.

Saulsman, B., Oxnard, C. E., and Franklin, D. (2010). Long bone morphometrics for human from non-human identification. *Forensic Science International* 202(1–3): 110.e1-5.

Tobe, S. S., and Linacre, M. T. (2008). A technique for the quantification of human and non-human mammalian mitochondrial DNA copy number in forensic and other mixtures. *Forensic Science International Genetics* 2: 249–256.

Ubelaker, D. H., Lowenstein, J. M., and Hood, D. G. (2004). Use of solid-phase double antibody radioimmunoassay to identify species from small skeletal fragments. *Journal of Forensic Sciences* 49: 1–6.

Urbanova, P., and Novotny, V. (2005). Distinguishing between human and non-human bones: Histometric method for forensic anthropology. *Anthropologie* 43: 77–85.

Walter, T. L., Paine, R. R., and Horni, H. (2004). Histological examination of bone-tempered pottery from mission Espiritu Santo (41VT11), Victoria County, Texas *Journal of Archeological Science* 31: 393–398.

Weaver, R. F., and Hedrick, P. W. (1997). *Genetics* (3rd ed.). Dubuque, IA: Brown.

Identification from Soft Tissues

11

NEAL ARCHIBALD
LOUISE CULLEN
DR. JAN BIKKER

Contents

Introduction to Soft Tissue Identification and Biometrics

A forensic anthropologist will frequently be presented with the task of identifying deceased remains; however, expertise pertaining to this field is increasingly called on to investigate situations involving living individuals (Isçan 2001). Scenarios such as these may present themselves in the form of criminal proceedings for identification of a suspect or victim. When faced with such judicial investigations, the use of forensic evidence is focused toward the indisputable link of a perpetrator to a crime. Regularly, markers of this nature present as forms of trace evidence unintentionally left at a scene. Historically, these include fingerprints, hair strands, or other remnants from which DNA can be extracted, such as saliva, semen, skin cells, and others (Allen et al. 1998; Jobling and Gill 2004). Since many of the aforementioned samples do not necessitate the presence of that individual at a given location (Turvey 2008), efforts have been made to use impressions and prints of alternate soft tissues for the recovery and comparison of trace evidence. Various forms of alternative prints, such as those of the hand, lips, and ears, as well as the use of biometrics from CCTV (closed-circuit television) footage may be used as viable tools in the process of identification.

Medically, *soft tissues* are referred to as any tissues other than bone or tooth that connect, support, or envelop other structures and viscera of the body. Identification based on soft tissues can be accomplished in a number of ways: examination of the anatomical structure itself; examination of prints and impressions; analysis of photos, videos, or other pictorial evidence; and analysis of chemical, genetic, or biological properties of the tissue. Matching decisions are usually achieved by manual or automated (computerized) comparison, the latter referred to as *biometrics*. Biometrics can be defined as the identification of individuals from the measurement of biological and behavioral features (Wei and Li 2005; *Biometric Technology Today* 2003). Biometric software has been referred to as pattern recognition systems (Ratha et al. 2001). It is therefore not unexpected that the majority of the published work on biometrics can be found in the computational literature. Arguably, the role of anatomical sciences in the development of biometric systems should not be ignored.

Over the past decade, a trend emerged that much time and resources have been forwarded to furthering the development and publication of new and revised techniques in biometric identification, primarily for the purpose of quick and easy identification of the living (De Luis-Garcia et al. 2003). According to Ratha et al. (2001), the most commonly used biometric systems are fingerprints, face, voice, hand geometry, signature, and iris. In this review, we focus on physiological metrics of the soft tissues; behavioral characteristics such as voice biometrics and signatures, although naturally dependent on anatomical features (Ratha et al. 2001), are not discussed.

Biometric systems are primarily used to resolve two complexities in establishing identity: verification (authentication) and recognition, also referred to as identification (Lammi 2003). It has been argued that the terms *verification, identification*, and *recognition* should be considered separately since each term has a different meaning (National Science and Technology Council 2006). This chapter is mainly concerned with the issue of recognition and forensic identification of both the living and the dead and focuses more directly on both emerging and matured areas of soft tissue identification not commonly discussed in the forensic anthropological literature as well as some rapidly developing aspects of biometric analysis. Many of these new techniques transcend the barrier not only between investigations of the deceased to those involving the living but also between the "traditional" forensic anthropological examination of hard tissues to those of the soft tissues when questions regarding an individual's identity arise.

For a comprehensive review of various methods of soft tissue identification, refer to the relevant chapters in the work of Thompson and Black (2007).

Since it would be impossible to cite every publication related to soft tissue identification between the years 2000 and 2010, only major developments in soft tissue identification in the last 10 years are referred to in this chapter. Refer to references published in the articles mentioned in this review for additional publications on the subject. It is our intention to provide an overview of emerging and maturing trends in soft tissue identification that may be useful for the forensic anthropologist and will provide ideas for further research. Indeed, many of the articles published on biometric identification involving the soft tissues are primarily addressed to software engineers and are therefore not necessarily directly relevant to the field of forensic anthropology.

Personal Identification Using the Hand

The earliest use and knowledge of the formations scientifically categorized as friction ridges is still very much the subject of scientific and historical debate, with one study reporting fingerprint impressions in clay tablets believed to be from the Babylonians, dated as early as 2000 BC (Burghardt 2009, citing Cummins 1941). For millennia, humankind has had an awareness, to some degree, of the discrete patterns present on fingers, palms, and feet; however, it has been only relatively recently that their distinctive nature has been calculated and investigated to such an extent that they can be used to distinguish individuals with some accuracy, even monozygotic twins (Jain et al. 2002). The use of friction ridges and the impressions caused by those ridges (hereafter referred to as *prints*) has been widely accepted by the scientific and judicial communities.

It was decided that for the purpose of this review, the most commonly used and scientifically scrutinized of these prints would be focused on less attentively, thus allowing greater and more in-depth discussions of more recently developed soft tissue identifiers. Auspiciously, it is observed that numerous texts have given greatly critical and comprehensive reviews of the literature regarding the use of unique forms of identification such as finger-, palm, and footprints (Lee and Gaensslen 2001; Maltino et al. 2003; Champod et al. 2004). Only major developments and seminal articles regarding friction ridges are therefore considered, followed by a review of other major developments in human identification using the hand.

Studies in 2000–2010

Prints and Impressions

This decennium saw the introduction of electronic finger- and palm print systems (Rutty et al. 2008; Breitmeier et al. 2008; Garrett 2006; Kahana et al. 2001) as an alternative to traditional finger- and palm print extraction techniques. Michael et al. (2008) offered a novel approach to palm print recognition systems by pioneering a "touchless" system in which the individual's hand image is captured using video and therefore does not need to be placed directly onto a surface (for the sake of hygiene). The outcome of the tests proved hopeful, with the system performing admirably in both static and dynamic environments and under varying levels of illumination (Michael et al. 2008).

In the same year, Breitmeier et al. (2008) investigated the suitability of a mobile one-finger scanner (Cross Match MV5) for capturing fingerprints in 12 corpses aged 5 weeks to 76 years and 28 living persons aged 6 weeks to 87 years. "Qualitatively good prints" were obtained in the living study objects, while discoloration, soot blackening, and postmortem rigidity resulted in partial prints in the corpses (Breitmeier et al. 2008). The authors recommended that mobile fingerprint scanners would be suitable for fresh corpses.

Also in 2008, Rutty and coworkers examined the use of an electronic fingerprint system for the identification of deceased individuals. The authors used both a handheld, mobile wireless unit in conjunction with a personal digital assistant (PDA) device and a handheld, single-digit fingerprint scanner that utilized a USB laptop connection. Rutty et al. (2008) concluded that fingerprints can be obtained from bodies with both devices if ridge detail is visible to the naked eye but prints were not acquired from bodies affected by fire or showing advanced changes of decomposition.

Jasuja et al. (2009) investigated a previously unconsidered area of latent fingerprint acquisition: the effects of pressure and perspiration on the quality of the lift attainable. It was found that even after 120 seconds of induced sweating, the grade of the print was severely reduced (Jasuja et al. 2009).

A large number of studies in the last 10 years have been published presenting alternative techniques for the detection and extraction of latent fingerprints. An elaborated review of these techniques is beyond the scope of this chapter; therefore, those interested should refer to the published work of Chen et al. (2009), Bicknell and Ramotowski (2008), Sapse and Petraco (2007), and Tahtouh et al. (2007), among others.

In 2007, Egli et al. discussed the effects of "within-finger variability" and proposed methods that can be utilized to circumvent any major differences present. Their results showed that the effects of within-finger variability are susceptible to the method of visualization used and the number and configuration of the minutiae (Egli et al. 2007). Another area of research emerging in the past decade is focused toward the probabilistic quantification of fingerprint evidence (Neumann et al. 2006, 2007; Stoney 2001). Traditionally, identity is confirmed by matching a specific number of minutiae between antemortem and postmortem fingerprints or between a crime scene print and those obtained from a suspect. This numerical threshold varies between different countries since a minimum number of minutiae to establish identity has not been internationally agreed (Gutiérrez et al. 2007). Unlike DNA, for which the evidence is presented as a probability, taking into account the uniqueness of a set of markers or alleles within a population, research into the distribution and probabilistic quantification of a set of fingerprint minutiae within and between populations is still in its infancy, although a few studies have been published sporadically since the 1950s (for a review, see Gutiérrez et al. 2007) and since then revitalized in the second half of this decennium. Indeed, as Gutiérrez et al. (2007) noted, further research into frequency distributions of the various types of minutiae within human populations as well as their relation to gender, finger, pattern type, and the area of the finger, may aid the development of probabilistic models to assess fingerprint evidence.

Before a probabilistic or mathematical model can be defined, research into one of the most pertinent issues in fingerprint analysis, agreement within the scientific community must be conducted on a commonly accepted mechanism by which fingerprint patterns form. Research has been undertaken in recent years. Kücken (2007) concluded that the pattern arises as the result of a buckling (folding) process in a cell layer of the epidermis and is therefore related to the geometry of the fingertip of the embryo. For a detailed review of the various theories of fingerprint formation, see the work of Kücken (2007). Around the same time, Neumann et al. (2006, 2007) proposed a probabilistic model to evaluate forensic fingerprint evidence. In 2006, Neumann et al. presented a likelihood ratio method for the quantification of any configuration of three minutiae. The same authors later refined this method to take into account the configuration of any number of fingerprint minutiae (Neumann et al. 2007).

Another interesting area of research emerging recently is the study of fingerprint classification and gender differences in various populations, including a sample of the Indian (Nayak et al. 2010b; Nithin et al. 2009), Chinese and Malaysian (Nayak et al. 2010a), and Spanish populations (Gutiérrez-Redomero et al. 2008). The inference of gender from fingerprints is not a new concept and was first suggested in the 1940s (Cummins 1941). It has been proposed that one aspect of the epidermal ridge detail, the number of ridges that are visible in a given space (also referred to as ridge density), may give a clue regarding the gender of the subject who left the fingerprint. Due to small sample sizes in previous studies, statistically significant observations in gender differences had not been demonstrated (Acree 1999) until a study in 1999 showed that gender may be inferred from the ridge density using Bayesian likelihood ratios regardless of whether the subject is of Caucasian or African American descent (Acree 1999). The author found that women tended to have a statistically significant greater ridge density ("fine" epidermal ridge detail) than men ("coarse" epidermal ridge detail), with those with a density of 12 ridges/25 mm^2 or greater likely to belong to a female and a density of 11 ridges/25 mm^2 or less likely to belong to a male subject.

Since then, studies into gender differences in ridge density have been published for a number of other populations, most notably the studies of Nayak et al. (2010a, 2010b) and Nithin et al. (2009). These studies agreed with the findings of Acree (1999) that statistically significant gender differences in ridge density can be observed in various populations, although Gutiérrez-Redomero et al. (2008), based on a sample of the Spanish Caucasian population, found that this may not necessarily hold true depending on whether the proximal or distal region of a print is examined, as noted a year earlier by Gutiérrez et al. (2007).

Although fingerprint evidence is widely accepted in court as a means of human identification, some studies in the second half of this decennium have scrutinized the examination of such prints following the misidentification of an individual suspected of being involved in the 2004 Madrid bombing (Stacey 2004) and perhaps the case in 1997 of police officer Shirley McKie in Scotland. Since then, attention has increasingly focused on the etiology of individualization errors. Those extraneous factors studied include behavioral (Dror and Cole 2010), emotional (Charlton et al. 2010; Saks 2009; Hall and Player 2008), and contextual influences (Langenburg et al. 2009; Dror and Rosenthal 2008; Schiffer and Champod 2007; Dror and Charlton 2006; Dror et al. 2005, 2006).

Vascular Pattern Identification and Other Features of the Hand

The hand has received much attention in the anthropological literature, possibly because there is widespread belief among anthropologists that the human race, from an evolutionary prospective, survived and evolved due to its relatively large brains and opposable thumbs, the latter allowing us to grasp, throw, and produce tools (Zunkel 1999). Not only is the hand essential for our existence, but also the human hand contains a wide variety of features that can be used for both manual identification and automated biometric systems (Mamode Khan et al. 2009). Black et al. (2009) demonstrated that several features pertaining to the hand can be used successfully for the forensic comparison of images of a suspect's hand and photos retrieved from the suspect's digital camera. These features may include general shape and size of the finger and hand, nail bed morphology, skin color/pigmentation, variations in knuckle and skin creases, scars, birthmarks, freckle patterns, moles, and any other characteristics that may demonstrate that the offender and suspect are the same or can exclude this possibility if incompatible differences are observed (Black et al. 2009).

Earlier, in 2005, George researched the potential of fingernail plate shape and size for personal identification. The author used a southwestern Nigerian population sample of 496 individuals, four family units, and four sets of monozygotic twins to determine the variation in the shapes and sizes of the fingernail plate and their distribution in different fingers. He demonstrated that no two members of the family groups had identical fingernail plates in the pair of hands, while further showing that no difference in the shapes and sizes of the fingernails on each finger of monozygotic twins were observed (George 2005). Seven gross fingernail plate shapes were identified in the population sample. George did not take any other potentially distinguishing anatomical features of the fingernails into account, such as the lunule. He concluded that the fingernail plate can be used for human identification purposes as a low-cost technique, including for disaster victim identification (DVI; George 2005).

Other applications of the nail for human identification proposed in the last decennium include, but are not limited to, stable isotope analysis (Fraser and Meier-Augenstein 2007; Fraser et al. 2006), DNA extraction (Allouche et al. 2008; Oz and Zamir 2000), and gender classification using Raman spectroscopy of fingernail clippings (Widjaja et al. 2008). As a small note, it is also interesting to mention that nail polish may be used for human identification purposes (e.g., by comparing the chemical signature of the nail polish found on the suspect with flakes or chips found at a crime scene). Methods proposed for the analysis of fingernail polish include laser desorption mass spectrometry (O'Neill et al. 2009), thin-layer chromatography (Gupta et al. 2006), and static secondary ion mass spectrometry (Gresham et al. 2000). Refer to the aforementioned articles for more detail on the uses of the nail in human identification.

A relatively new area of research emerging in the last 10 years is vascular pattern recognition in the hand. Originally introduced as a means for medical imaging (Haxthausen 1933), the use of subcutaneous vein patterns as a means of (biometric) identification gained recognition in 2000 following an article by Im et al. (2000). Research has since progressed in this field, and this may be explained by several advantages of the vascular system compared to other (biometric) methods of soft tissue identification. In this section, we only focus on the vascular system of the hand. Since arteries are located deeper in the tissues of the hand and are therefore more difficult to discern and visualize, veins are often used for comparison (Watanabe 2008). The pattern of the veins in the hand is difficult to duplicate since veins are internal to the human body (Watanabe et al. 2005). Furthermore, they are permanent unless affected by disease or injury (Watanabe 2008; López and González 2003), considered unique between individuals (Badawi 2006; López and González 2003) and monozygotic twins (Watanabe 2008), and unique between the left and right hand (Badawi 2006). Mamode Khan et al. (2009) noted, however, that as humans grow, the size of veins grows as well, and thus only the shape ("skeleton") of the vein can be used for comparison. Factors such as age, humidity, ambient temperature, amount of subcutaneous fat, physical activity, and hand position may affect the visibility of the vein pattern (Badawi 2006; Tanaka and Kubo 2004). Various anatomical regions of the hand have been used for vein pattern recognition systems, including the back of the hand (Badawi 2006), palm of the hand (Bhattacharyya et al. 2009; Watanabe et al. 2005), and the dorsal and palmar surfaces of the finger (Wu and Ye 2009; Miura et al. 2004; Kono et al. 2002).

It has been claimed that the vascular pattern of the palm is more complex and broader and is therefore favorable compared to the finger and back of the hand (Watanabe et al. 2005). In addition, the palm of the hand is hairless and is less susceptible to skin color changes compared to the dorsal aspect of the hand (Mamode Khan et al. 2009; Watanabe et al. 2005; Ding et al. 2005). The most commonly used techniques for the visualization of hand vein patterns are thermographic imaging (Watanabe et al. 2005) and infrared imaging (Wang et al. 2008; Wang and Leedham 2006; Badawi 2006). Infrared imaging is particularly useful since veins absorb the spectrum of light rays better than other tissues (Tanaka and Kubo 2004) and appear darker than the rest of the hand (López and González 2003). High recognition rates have been obtained in the matching of hand vein patterns, even up to 100% (López and González 2003). Hybrid systems combining several features have been proposed, including a system that uses vein triangulation and knuckle shape (Kumar and Prathyusha 2009) as well as hand shape and texture (Kumar and Zhang 2006).

The forensic utilization of hand vein patterns is still in its infancy; however, research in this area is continuing. One potential application includes the comparison of vein patterns in suspect-offender images in pedophile cases (undocumented U.K. court case). On a different note, although related and relevant to vein pattern analysis, is a recent pedophile court case in the United States (*United States v. Donatos Sarras*, Case No. 6:07-cr-92-Orl-22DAB). In this case, the penis shown in the images of the offender sexually abusing a child were compared to the flaccid and erect penis of the suspect. Dr. Ferdon, who visually examined the suspect, testified that "the position and lengths of the visible dorsal vein and other superficial veins on the shaft of Mr. Sarras' penis are different from those of the penis in the photographs." A mole seen on the offender's penis was also not observed. More interesting is the court's judgment that "this is not a subject necessitating expertise; no specialized knowledge is required here. The doctor's observations are simply a visual comparison between the characteristics of the penises. The same visual comparison can be made just as easily by a nonexpert, including the jurors themselves (from photographs)." It was ruled that Dr. Ferdon's testimony "would not assist the trier of fact in any meaningful fashion, and is therefore inadmissible pursuant to Daubert" (Order of the United States District Court, Middle District of Florida, Orlando Division 2007).

Two other areas emerging in the anthropological and biometrics literature are knuckle pattern identification and hand geometry. As far as we are aware, knuckle pattern and hand geometry have been used solely for authentication purposes so far, such as in access control systems. Black et al. (2009) noted that knuckle skin crease patterns, since they reflect responses to intrauterine development and individual growth, are a useful indicator for personal identification. Studies of knuckle coding include those of Kumar and Zhou (2009) and Kumar and Ravikanth (2009).

Hand geometry is a technique in which the hand is scanned and measurements are taken from a number of anatomical points of the hand. Several limitations of hand geometry have been reported, and those particularly relate to hand changes with advancing age and injuries (Zunkel 1999). Although both hands are symmetrical at birth, they continually change due to environmental factors and advancing age. The dominant hand may grow slightly larger than the other hand. Age changes and pathological processes, such as arthritis, may alter the shape of the hand, along with surgical and medical procedures, including amputation. Since only the hand outline is often extracted from the scans, other identifying features, such as scars, moles, and skin pigmentation, are ignored. A detailed summary and overview of published work in this area can be found in the work of Kumar et al. (2006), Duta (2009), and Adán et al. (2008).

Personal Identification Using the Lips

Despite universal recognition of more commonly used prints, such as those of the fingertips and palms, there are alternative regions of the body utilized for determination of identity that have begun to emerge over the last 40 years. One such example of this is the study of impressions of lines and ridges within the soft tissue of the lips, also referred to as cheiloscopy (Saraswathi et al. 2009; Sivapathasundharam et al. 2001). Recognition of this biological parameter for use in human identification was first initiated by Fischer in 1902 (Saraswathi et al. 2009) and further investigated by Edmond Locard, a French criminologist, in 1932. The applicability of cheiloscopy to crime scene analysis and personal identification was further developed in the 1970s by the prominent work of Suzuki and Tsuchihashi (1970a, 1970b, 1975).

Research in this particular field progresses to the present day, exploring the applicability of latent prints to judicial environments and situations necessitating personal identification in both the living and unidentified remains. For a comprehensive review of the history of cheiloscopy, anatomical aspects of the lip, lip print classification systems, and examination principles, refer to the work of Caldas et al. (2007).

Studies in 2000–2010

In the area of crime scene identification, Seguí et al. (2000) examined the use of lip prints as a result of lipstick markings deposited at crime scenes as "hidden evidence." Prints were created by applying lipstick to subjects before utilizing a variety of impression supports—ceramics, glass, fabric, and paper—to deposit the print. These prints were then developed with intervals ranging from 2 hours to 30 days following collection of the sample (Seguí et al. 2000). Results of this study were positive, with viable prints still in collection at 30 days for use in identification. This result was dependent on the impression surface as well as the method utilized to develop the print (Seguí et al. 2000). Substances such as cotton fabric produced no identifiable print even after only 2 hours, whereas prints developed from ceramics and glass were still viable after 30 days (Seguí et al. 2000).

In 2004, Kim et al. utilized lip prints as a potential unique identifier for personal recognition in security systems. Although this is not linked inherently to forensic anthropology, results generated from such a study reinforce the utilization of prints as a reliable personal identifier. The system uses multiresolution architecture to convert lip print patterns to digital data, which can then be compared for verification of identity (Kim et al. 2004). Recognition rates ranged from 85% to 95.3% depending on resolution of the image utilized, and reliability rates ranged between 92% and 98.2% depending on the same parameter (Kim et al. 2004). This illustrates a highly reliable and accurate method of personal identification associated with the soft tissue of the lips.

Also in 2004, a trend emerged in which the examination of lips for use in identification focused not only on latent prints but also on the DNA traces that may be obtained from such prints (Castelló et al. 2004). A study conducted by Castelló et al. (2004) utilized knowledge of the polymerase chain reaction to amplify particularly small DNA samples such as those obtained from latent prints. Five subjects were required to apply a layer of lipstick before creating a lip impression on paper napkins. After a minimum of 24 hours, these prints were developed to determine the amount of DNA available for analysis. Results of this study were positive, with conclusions stating that adequate amounts of DNA, even from the smallest of samples, could be utilized in a positive identification (Castelló et al. 2004). This work was also explored by Barbaro and coworkers (2009), examining DNA typing from lipstick impressions left on the skin. This study reported results to be highly dependent on the number of cells present within the DNA sample, although it was determined possible to obtain a reliable lip print from skin contact. These results were particularly variable, with some individuals depositing more DNA than others (Barbaro et al. 2009).

Following in 2005, Castelló et al. conducted a study examining modes for detecting prints at a scene and the different methods of developing such prints. Results were promising, with viable impressions capable of producing a positive identification emerging even when analyzing prints over 1 year old (Castelló et al. 2005). Utsuno et al. (2005) examined the use of lip prints for postmortem identification as a preliminary study. Twenty cadavers of known biological parameters were utilized to examine postmortem alternation of lip prints (Utsuno et al. 2005). This was conducted to determine how comparable such patterns are between living and deceased individuals. Samples taken to represent "antemortem" records were collected 24 hours following death, while those obtained to represent "postmortem" records were collected 48 hours after death (Utsuno et al. 2005). Lip prints were then split into quadrants for comparison, with the matching of patterns in at least one area constituting a positive identification. The matching accuracy reported in this study was low, with an identification rate of only 30% (Utsuno et al. 2005). Accuracies of such a low value may have been witnessed in this study due to a small sample size and the fact that cadavers were embalmed utilizing 10% formalin solution, which may have altered lip morphology.

A relatively large study of 100 individuals was conducted by Kaur and Garg (2007) to verify the use of lip prints in a judicial environment. Confirmation of individuality was achieved during the study, with no two prints exhibiting similar characteristics, which assists in demonstrating this parameter as a unique identifier (Kaur and Garg 2007). In another study in 2007, Choraś conducted work to create a computer recognition system capable of identifying individuals on the basis of lip patterns and color from facial images. Results illustrated a positive correlation with rates of 76% identification for database images, but unfortunately, satisfactory rates were not achieved for use with surveillance camera imaging (Choraś 2007b). A higher recognition rate of 96.9% was achieved by Gomez et al. (2002), who developed a biometric identification system based on lip shapes and outlines using a multilayer neural network and Cartesian coordinates for the comparison of lip prints. It should be noted that a relatively small sample of 50 subjects was included in the database. By comparison, this may suggest that lip outline features are more discriminatory than lip groove patterns.

Future Trends in Lip Print Analysis

Research over the last 10 years appears to have expanded on what was previously a slightly sparse topic despite knowledge of the existence of such a parameter and its possible use in forensic situations, and this initial hesitation may be due to the belief that lip prints have little discriminative power (Gomez et al. 2002). Since then, research has progressed and lip prints have been further verified as a unique parameter, with no two yet found to be the same (El Domiaty et al. 2010; Bindal et al. 2009; Caldas et al. 2007; Castelló et al. 2005; Sivapathasundharam et al. 2001; Vahanwahal and Parekh 2000; Tsuchihashi 1974). Furthermore, they are stable over time (El Domiaty et al. 2010; Bindal et al. 2009; Coward 2007) and remodel to their original lip pattern configuration after healing of an injury to the lip (Tsuchihashi 1974).

Although based on a relatively small sample of a Saudi Arabian population, El Domiaty et al. (2010) observed nonidentical lip print patterns between twins and family members; however, they found some similarities in lip groove patterns, possibly as a result of hereditary factors, which supports earlier theories based on studies in the 1970s on uniovular twins (Suzuki and Tsuchihashi 1970b) and families (Hirth et al. 1975). In addition, statistically significant differences have been observed in gender distribution of certain lip print patterns and therefore may aid in sex estimation (Gondivkar et al. 2009; Sharma et al. 2009a, 2009b; Sonal et al. 2005; Vahanwahal and Parekh 2000). A positive correlation between lip thickness and height of the teeth was reported by Wilkinson et al. (2003). The application of such a parameter is evident for use in personal identification as well as verification of identity in criminal situations. The rather low accuracy rates witnessed in postmortem studies, however, warrants extreme caution in the use of this method in cases of unidentified human remains.

As there are relatively few conducted studies on this topic, in comparison with several other areas of forensic anthropology, there are many issues that still must be considered before lip prints can be regarded as highly as alternative forms of prints (Ball 2002).

However, lip print evidence has already been applied successfully in judicial situations. Several examples of casework utilizing this biological parameter include the conviction of a "peeping tom" in 1998 due to the deposition of a lip print on a glass window, from which a unique pattern was analyzed to identify the individual (*The Washington Post*, "Lip Print Leads" 1998). Following in 2007, at the 18th International Symposium on Human Identification, Tony Tambasco presented the case of an armed robbery; on fleeing the scene, the perpetrator ran into a glass door, leaving behind a lip print from which DNA was later extracted to make a conviction (Sundquist 2009).

Personal Identification Using the Ear

An additional parameter for use in forensic identification is that of the human ear. Although knowledge of ear prints has existed since the 18th century (Champod et al. 2001), literature pertaining to this trait in a modern forensic environment is relatively sparse, even though the specialized knowledge required to study the ear and its relation to forensic applications have been referred to as one of the "ologies": "earology" or "otomorphology" (Feenstra and van der Lugt 2000). The use of ear morphology and the prints created by its anatomical form are implemented principally for identification of perpetrators at scenes of crime (Meijerman, Thean, and Maat 2005). This can be achieved utilizing CCTV imaging (Hoogstrate et al. 2001) or ear prints, which can be deposited on doors or windows before criminal acts such as burglary (Meijerman et al. 2007). There have been claims in recent years that the external ear may be utilized for personal identification of both living and deceased individuals (Abbas and Rutty 2005; Swift and Rutty 2003).

More commonly, the anatomical structure of the external ear is utilized for personal identification of living subjects in relation to criminal activity. This is possible through a number of mechanisms, all of which appear to be tertiary indicators. This refers to traits pertaining to the subject that are not completely unique and would therefore reinforce rather than establish identity. Features pertaining to the human ear that may be used for identification include piercings, localized tattoos, pathologies or abnormalities, trauma, and surgery (Abbas and Rutty 2005). Meijerman et al. (2004) added that final individualization may further depend on characteristic ear minutiae, such as the position, size, or pattern of creases, papules, moles, scars, dimples, hillocks, and features along the inner rim of the helix. Utilization of this parameter pertains to the belief that individual ears are entirely unique; however, like most biological traits, this is based mainly on the principle that no two have as yet been found to be identical (Meijerman et al. 2004). Second, ears have a more uniform distribution of color, are less affected by facial expressions, and have reduced spatial dimensions compared to the face (Lammi 2003). A comprehensive, critical review conducted by Champod and colleagues (2001) should be consulted for discussion of work pre-dating the year 2000.

Studies in 2000–2010

Included in the elusive measurements of Bertillon (1890), the "father" of anthropometrics, the ear has long been considered a prospective area of study for the verification of personal identity (Arbab-Zavar et al. 2007). In 1989, Iannarelli proposed work that he had been undertaking since 1949 on the use of ears for personal identification (Jeges and Máté 2007). Auspiciously, the abilities of anthropometrics have progressed far since these founding techniques, based on simple linear relationships between points of soft tissue forming the external ear, allowing much greater differentiations to be made and removing the upper limit of the number of diverse combinations available, stated as being roughly 16.7 million (Jeges and Máté 2007).

Hoogstrate et al. (2001) conducted a study to establish how unique ear patterns are and if sufficient information presents in CCTV images to identify individuals utilizing these patterns. Results of this study were relatively positive, with accuracy rates of 65% (Hoogstrate et al. 2001). Although this method produces inaccuracies 35% of the time, it should be noted that both experienced and nonexperienced individuals examining good and bad quality footage were utilized, creating a realistic environment (Hoogstrate et al. 2001). Studies of this nature are more useful than those producing extremely high rates of accuracy based on unrealistic techniques which do not simulate real-world situations.

Perhaps the most prevalent area of human identification utilizing the external ear is the analysis of print evidence recovered from scenes of crime. Employing ear prints as a technique for criminal identification began to emerge in the 1960s (Meijerman, Thean, and Maat 2005), with research principally driven by those working in the field of forensic science or investigating officers associated with cases of this nature (Abbas and Rutty 2003). As a result, much of the evidence presented for utility and efficacy of this parameter is based on cases in which prints have been available to confirm a matching identity. There are a vast number of cases that present this type of evidence as well as several that have obtained a conviction dependent on analysis of the trait (Meijerman, Thean, and Maat 2005).

Recent work pertains mainly to the development, quantification, and validation of this parameter for utilization in a judicial environment now that it has been illustrated as a viable technique for identification. Much of the literature (Champod et al. 2001; Meijerman, Thean, and Maat 2005) highlights key issues that researchers are now trying to address to fully establish ear prints as reliable scientific evidence. The most common of these issues is with regard to "uniqueness" of ears on an intra- and interpersonal scale as the individuality of this trait is yet to be established (Broeders 2006). Meijerman, Thean, and Maat (2005) stressed the importance of such an issue as unique ears do not equate to unique prints, even when created by the same individual. Following in 2006, Meijerman analyzed the differences in prints between six pairs of monozygotic twins, finding little intraindividual variation while still detecting interpersonal differences (Meijerman, Thean, van der Lugt, et al. 2006). This assists in the reinforcement of such a trait as individualistic; however, debates with regard to this issue are ongoing (Chattopadhyay and Bhatia 2009).

The question of individuation is also prevalent within the field addressing the link between a print and the subject who created it (Purkait and Singh 2008). When listening to a surface a balance must be maintained between adequate hearing and comfort of the ear and cheek (Meijerman et al. 2007); thus, formation of the resultant print will reflect these parameters. Placement of the ear to a surface will create deformation of the structural components and distortion of the print, which are in turn related to the pressure on application, structure of the soft tissues, and composition of the external surface (Meijerman, Nagelkerke, Brand, et al. 2005).

Over the past few years, investigation of these parameters has primarily been conducted by Meijerman and his team as well as the development of the Forensic Ear Identification (FEARID) research project. This system was developed between 2002 and 2005 to strengthen the use of ear print evidence in court by standardizing methods of print acquisition and creating a comparative database of prints from 1,229 individuals (Alberink and Ruifrok 2007).

The final central aspect that has been recognized in terms of advancement is the application of extraneous variables that may have an effect on the structure of ear prints when compared to the actual morphology of the ear. These variables include moisture within the ear at the time of deposition (Meijerman, Nagelkerke, Basten, et al. 2006), the effect of movement of the ear against a surface (Kieckhoefer et al. 2006), factors that may affect the force with which the ear is applied and how these can be interpreted (Meijerman, Nagelkerke, Basten, et al. 2006), any modifications to the external structure (Abbas and Rutty 2005), and the effect of biological parameters such as age and sex (Sforza et al. 2009) as well as stature (van der Lugt et al. 2005). Furthermore, Abbas and Rutty (2005) discovered that modification in the form of piercing could alter the presentation of an ear print only when jewelry was worn, by elevating the tissue from the external surface as a possible reason for discovery of partial prints. Work is being conducted to address several of the aforementioned issues.

Another important development is that of biometric ear identification systems. Purportedly, the first biometric systems utilizing the ear were developed by Burge and Burger (1997, 1999, 2000), and their work paved the way for much that followed. Chang, Bowyer, Sarkar, et al. (2003) proposed a technique that could utilize multimodal recognition systems based on a combination of two-dimensional (2D) images of the face and ear. It was stated that the ear is more accurate, and the initial stage of Chang et al.'s work proves this, although not irrefutably; when combining both face and ear, a statistically significant difference is noticed, and accuracies of up to 90.9% are achieved (Chang, Bowyer, Sarkar, et al. 2003). The system proposed by Chang, Bowyer, Sarkar, et al. (2003) used a principal component algorithm (PCA), referred to by the authors as "Eigenface" and "Eigenears." Pun and Moon (2004) suggested that the commonality of these algorithms in ear biometrics at this time is likely due to its established use in facial biometrics; however, as Yan and Bowyer (2005) pointed out, PCA is only usable when both illumination and registration of the individual are controlled. Pun and Moon (2004) offered a review, "Recent Advances in Ear Biometrics," and covered techniques including PCA, force field transformations, local surface patch comparisons, Voronoi diagrams, neural network analysis (NNA), and genetic local search algorithms. Table 11.1 summarizes the techniques reviewed until 2004 by Pun and Moon (2004).

Table 11.1   Summary of Techniques Discussed by Pun and Moon

Approach	Data Source	Dataset size	Recognition Rate	References
Principal component analysis	2D	197 (training) 88 (registrant)	71.60%	Victor et al. 2002; Chang, Bowyer, Sarkar, et al. 2003; Iwano et al. 2003
Force field transformation	2D	n/a	n/a	Hurley et al. 2000a, 2000b, 2002
Local surface patch	3D	10 (training) 10 (registrant)	100%	Bhanu and Chen 2003
AGM (Voronoi)	2D	n/a	n/a	Burge and Burger 1997, 1999, 2000
Neural networks	2D	84 (training) 28 (validation) 56 (registrant) 20 (unregistrant)	93%	Careira-Perpinan 1995
Genetic local search	2D	300 (registrant) 180 (unregistrant) 180 (unknown)	100%	Yuizono et al. 2002

Source: Modified from Pun, K., and Moon, Y. 2004. Recent advances in ear biometrics. In: *Proceedings of the 6th IEEE International Conference on Automatic Face and Gesture Recognition,* Seoul, South Korea: May 17–19, 2004. 164–169. IEEE Computer Society Press: Los Alamitos, California.

Since Pun and Moon's review in 2004, several other ear recognition studies have been published, all reporting high accuracy levels of over 90%. Yan and Bowyer (2005: 41) published "results of the largest experimental investigation of ear biometrics to date." Utilizing both PCA and ICP (iterative closest point)-based matching and considering 2D and three-dimensional (3D) image recognition, the techniques covered in this article are extremely thorough and gained high accuracies using ICP (98.7%). Also, the article considers, apparently for the first time, the effects of asymmetry of subjects' ears, finding that 90% of the sample used had symmetrical ears.

A short article published by Saleh et al. (2006) presented the results of a series of tests using varying image-based classifiers and feature extraction methods. The article opened by stating that little work has been carried out in this area, yet by 2006, several reviews of the literature had already been published (Saleh et al. 2006). The outcome of the various tests led to a maximum accuracy of 94.12% achieved using a 2D discrete cosine transformed image, classified by an artificial neural network. A novel approach was proposed by Sana and Gupta (2006) in which an image (monochromatic) was dismantled into a series of coefficients based on Haar wavelet transformation. It was claimed that the technique is simple, effective, and highly accurate (based on a large sample size), claiming accuracies of greater than 96%.

Nanni and Lumini (2007) described a 2D approach for the extraction of local features from several overlapping "subwindows" of the whole image using Gabor filters and Laplacian eigenmaps. Using a database of 464 ears, the authors obtained an accuracy of 80% positive identification, while 93% of the ears were identified correctly among the top five matches. Interestingly, Nanni and Lumini concluded that considering only a few small areas or subwindows of the ear may be more discriminatory than matching features of the whole ear, such as in a PCA-based approach. It is understandable why the idea of 3D shape analysis was never likely to become a common trend among biometrics.

In reality, there is little practical use for a volunteer-based image acquisition technique that is more expensive and more computationally difficult. Therefore, the method proposed by Islam et al. (2009) appears well suited; the proposed method is capable of accepting 2D or 3D inputs, crops the ear region by way of a pretrained classifier, and extracts the analogous 3D ear data for interpretation. The 3D mesh produced is reduced by a quadratic error factor of 10 (Islam et al. 2009). Based on a data set of 200 profile images (of a standard size 640 × 480 pixels) accuracies were 93%, 94%, and 95% (rank 1, 2, and 7, respectively). The technique was said to be robust even when faced with partial occlusion due to hair or earrings. The system also does not rely on having the ear concha to analyze the image to a high accuracy as was seen in previous recognition systems.

Future Trends in Ear Research and Ear Print Analysis

The application of ear prints to a judicial environment, and for use in personal identification of the living and deceased, is an evolving research area with much emphasis now placed on development of preexisting knowledge for application as a viable scientific method. However, ear print identification is still recognized as an emerging technique, with further work required before it can be fully established. The literature on ear identification supersedes those of other emerging areas of soft tissue identification, such as the lips. This is surprising since, as Lammi noted (2003), variation in ear growth over time, ageing, and injury make this parameter only averagely stable. Another important consideration is that ear mark evidence has been scrutinized in recent years due to the subjective nature with which data are analyzed (Alberink and Ruifrok 2008; Champod et al. 2001). Usually, determination of identity will be conducted by an "expert" in the field on visualization of comparative prints for common points. Even the use of partially automated systems (Alberink and Ruifrok 2007; Rutty et al. 2005) has come under fire after several miscarriages of justice in relation to the field, as the final conclusion of identity is still conducted by a relevant expert.

While the majority of published work primarily focused on ear print identification of the living, research has recently been extended to the potential application of ear prints in DVI (Bronselaer et al. 2007; De Winne and Purkait 2004). It was previously reported in a case study that characteristics of the pinna can be used successfully in the identification of disaster victims (Saul and Saul 2003). Veerappan, a wood smuggler killed by special task forces in India in 2004 was also reportedly identified by several morphological features of his ear, including "a flat tragus being contiguous with the curved portion of the helix and an enlarged and squarish lobule" (Purkait 2007: 218). The value of ears is also recognized in the Interpol DVI protocol, and both antemortem and postmortem details pertaining to the ear can be recorded on the existing Interpol DVI forms. Although the legal application of ear prints appears to occur in several countries, such as Holland, Sweden, and Germany (Abbas and Rutty 2003; Champod et al. 2001), trends tending toward scientific analysis, development of preexisting knowledge, and quantification of data suggest that this could be incorporated into more regulated judicial systems such as those of the United States (Champod et al. 2001). Further research in the quantification and frequencies of occurrence of various ear features in human populations are ongoing, for example, the studies of Indian (Singh and Purkait 2009), American (Iannarelli 1989), and Dutch populations (van der Lugt 2001).

From articles published and those cited by others, there appears to have been a slight decrease in work regarding ear biometrics in the latter half of the present decade. Islam et al. (2009) cited only four pieces of work published after 2006. The trend seen in the study of ear biometrics appears to be a tendency toward making more robust, less-dependable systems, capable of "learning" quickly and efficiently to constantly improve accuracies. To date, there appears to be no preferred method or criteria universally implemented for this task; therefore, it can be insinuated that the "perfect system" is yet to be seen. Additional research is needed to overcome varying imaging and illumination conditions affecting the extraction of ear features from images as well as partial occlusion of the ear by hair (Burge and Burger 1999). Thermal imaging may be a solution for the latter (Hurley et al. 2007; Lammi 2003). However, much of the work carried out in this decade has carried the idea of ear recognition from the dreams of men such as Bertillon (1890) and Iannarelli (1989) into a powerful and highly studied scientific reality.

Other Methods of Human Identification from the Soft Tissues

It should be noted that the biometrics discussed in this section are limited to soft tissue; however, not every area has been considered in the review. Biometrics are not in this way limited and are utilized for purposes as diverse as identification by body odor (Korotkaya 2003; Kwak et al. 2008), electro-cardiogram (ECG) biometrics (Plataniotis et al. 2006), gait analysis (Grant 2007; Gafurov et al. 2006), finger surface biometrics (Woodard and Flynn 2005), biometric identification from knee x-rays (Shamir et al. 2009), and nose recognition (Drira et al. 2009a, 2009b). Hybrid systems based on mul-timodal recognition methods such as those of the face and hand combined (Tsalakanidou et al. 2007) have been proposed. The use of integrating mul-tiple types of data for recognition is not a recent phenomenon; however, it has become more prevalent in the past decade and more commonly uses 3D data (Chang et al. 2003b). Chang, Bowyer, and Flynn (2003) briefly discussed previous works utilizing such integrated systems before introducing their own work. The authors concluded from their results that "the path to higher accuracies and robustness in biometrics involves use of multiple biometrics'" (p. 187) after achieving significantly greater results from multi-modal tests.

Common problems encountered when attempting to utilize the face for automated identification include the innate nature of humans to express emotions facially, positional variation, and illumination (Yang et al. 2002). This problem has been approached from multiple directions. That of Chang et al. (2006) made use of the nose as a (generally) stable structure during facial expression. This method was tested on a "baseline" sample primarily to quantify variation and power of the system, then the system was run using an algorithm to locate and extract the "nose area" for the construction of the gallery. The results were promising but noted a 10% drop from baseline accuracy to "expression" accuracy (Chang et al. 2006). The method adopted by Kakadiaris et al. (2007) was to create a deformable framework capable of "shifting" to fit an expression from a common gallery by transforming 3D data into a 2D grid, thus making it computationally less demanding. Another aspect of the work presented in this article was the construction of a "fully automatic" facial biometric system (Kakadiaris et al. 2007). There was little difference observed between neutral expressions and nonneutral expressions in this study, with both achieving above 95% accuracy.

As methods for facial recognition tend heavily toward the use of 3D forms over a 2D model (Bowyer et al. 2006), it has become apparent in the literature that as well as research focusing on the implications of 3D techniques, studies have been carried out on refining these 3D imaging techniques in the second half of the last decade. Samir et al. (2009) reported on methods to improve readouts from 3D images and retain structures during cropping of regions of interest. These techniques are based on using Riemannian structures placed on the nose and measuring "work done" between varying shapes of alter-nating structures. This method is similar to that of Drira et al. (2009b), in which Riemannian analysis was used for 3D analysis of the nose as a biomet-ric independent of the surrounding structures of the face. Use of isocurves removes all weight previously placed on position, rotation, and mirroring (translation). Although mathematically demanding, such analysis can be calculated at low cost using modern computers. The output from such a system is reached by way of a hierarchical gallery in which nodes of differentiation are used to reduce the computational demands for any given analysis. Since aforementioned methods have as yet been used primarily for authentication or verification purposes rather than for forensic identification, those research areas are not discussed in detail in this review. The references cited may be used by those interested as a resource for further study, and further discussion of the face is considered in Chapter 12.

Conclusion

Traditionally, forensic anthropologists have dealt primarily with the hard tissues in cases of unidentified remains; however, there is an increasing shift toward soft tissue identification of the living in judicial cases. A detailed and accurate description of external identifying features of a body forms an important aspect in medicolegal autopsies (Burton 2007). An appreciation of these anatomical characteristics is beneficial in the identification process when the anthropologist is confronted with decomposed remains or dismembered body parts. Equally important to consider is the role of the soft tissues in the identification of remains in underdeveloped countries, some of which may lack the resources for a detailed forensic examination of the deceased. This is also recognized in the Interpol DVI protocol; a large section of the antemortem (yellow) and postmortem (pink) forms allow the recording of individuating soft tissue features. For further reading on the "traditional" examination and comparison of soft tissues for human identification, refer to the forensic pathological literature or for short reviews to Hill (2007), Milroy (2007), Clarkson and Schaefer (2007), and Burton (2007).

During the process of human identification, it is important to utilize all possible available parameters to obtain an accurate, reliable estimation to ultimately assign an identity to the unknown. As the process of decomposition begins, several parameters will be lost or disfigured, rendering them inadequate as a means of identification (Byers 2008). Also, as criminals become more aware of utilized parameters, methods are being implemented to evade capture, such as the use of gloves to mask finger and palm prints (Smith et al. 2007).

Advancements in the utility and efficacy of latent print examination have broadened beyond the use of friction ridge markings, such as those of the fingers and palm, to incorporate alternative biological features. These now include unique traits pertaining to the soft tissue of the head, namely, ears and lips, expanding the avenues available for use in personal identification rather than solely depending on characteristics that may not be applicable to all scenarios. It is therefore necessary to explore all available methods for identification to obtain maximum information, regardless of the situation. Investigation of possible variables and scrutiny of scientific techniques allow the positive development of data and quantification of parameters through the application of statistics for advancement of identification methods. It can be predicted that, in the future, further work with regard to these biological parameters could form the basis for application in forensic investigations and as evidence in court, and admissibility may therefore be dependent on stringent *Daubert* standards. The application of lip and ear prints, although not fully established at present, appears to be following trends similar to those traversed by data obtained from fingerprint analysis (German 2010). Future research in the computational comparison of prints, including those of the ear, lip, finger, and palm, is likely to be focused on four matching problems (O'Gorman 1999): matching of minutiae in different locations in two images (*translational freedom*), matching of minutiae with different orientations (*rotational freedom*), alignment issues due to skin elasticity (*nonlinear warping*), and resolution of noise in images, such as caused by both image and print quality. Indeed, the majority of the published articles in the last 10 years have focused on those four problems, and it is expected that the issues in print comparison mentioned will continue to be addressed in the next decennium.

It appears that most published work on soft tissue identification is focused toward the face and hand, possibly because those anatomical features are frequently visible on CCTV or video recordings. Although not fully established in the judicial system, much work is being done to attain levels of accuracy and reliability expected for implementation in such an environment. Ideally, the anatomical biometric is individualistic to each person, and the characteristics are not shared by two individuals (*unique*), are found on each human being (*universal*), are easy to collect or obtain (*collectable*), and most importantly are *permanent* and do not change over time (Jain et al. 2000). These principles equally apply when a forensic anthropologist is asked to give an opinion regarding whether two anatomical features (e.g., those discernible on images of the suspect and offender) are sufficiently individualistic to support the hypothesis that an offender and a suspect are one and the same. Indeed, as Fields et al. (1960) noted, an effective and conclusive identification system must inherently possess a "high degree of individuality," "unbroken continuity," and an "unquestioned immutability."

One way in which these anatomical regions are being utilized is through the application of automated systems to provide computerized data analysis to alleviate the subjective interpretation associated with manual methods. Trends appear to be moving toward the more common use of biometric technologies, for identification, to achieve the levels of accuracy necessary for irrefutable application as evidence in a medicolegal context. Strengths of these systems lie mainly in their consistency between operators and their unbiased interpretation of data. Over the past 10 years, several areas of biometric analysis have been studied extensively, with countless novel approaches presented in all faculties of this diverse recognition system. With the implementation of biometric passports in the last decade (*Biometric Technology Today* 2005a, 2005b; Schouten and Jacobs 2009), there has been a lot of focus directed toward improving many of these methods. Over the past several years, there have been numerous reviews published that discuss in great detail the fundamentals of biometric technologies and the principles behind many of the scientific methods utilized (Bolle et al. 2002; Choraś 2007a; De Luis-Garcia et al. 2003; Jain et al. 2004, 2006; Ratha et al. 2001). For a greater understanding of the science behind these systems, refer to the review articles mentioned as well as the relevant citations within the appropriate biometric articles. It has become apparent that biometric technologies are set to replace traditional modes of identification as they supersede these methods in many respects, such as convenience, automation, reliability, hygiene, and practical application (Mordini and Ottolini 2007). Although biometric systems have many advantages, mismanagement of storage and access to those data may leave society open to identity fraud. Feng and Jain (2009), Ross et al. (2007), and Cappelli et al. (2007), for example, demonstrated that it would be possible to reconstruct fingerprints from minutiae templates stored in biometric fingerprint systems. A minutiae template is a coded compact data representation of a fingerprint, and it was earlier thought that it would be impossible to re-create a fingerprint image from those data (Feng and Jain 2009). Another fascinating development proposed in recent years is a liveness detection approach for fingerprint scanners to establish if the image received by the scanner is coming from a living source (DeCann et al. 2009). The authors claimed a success rate of 95.5% using a data set of 1,526 live and 1,588 faked fingerprints.

Trends in personal identification are developing rapidly, and it would be impossible to cover all the areas of emerging and maturing soft tissue methods in one review chapter. Rather, we have focused on potentially useful methods of soft tissue identification for the forensic examination of both the living and unidentified human remains. Indeed, forensic anthropologists are increasingly being asked to assist in the forensic investigation of issues relating to living individuals, such as offender-suspect image analysis and the provision of age estimates when the chronological age of an individual is disputed. Interestingly, as observed from the literature on biometric identification (or recognition) systems in the past decade, the vast majority of the scientific articles on biometric soft tissue recognition systems were published in the computer or engineering literature and authored by computer and software engineers. From a forensic point of view, questions may therefore arise if the anatomical basis of soft tissue development, maturation, and degeneration and its inherent biological, environmental, and genetic variability have been taken into account fully in those systems. The involvement of anatomically trained forensic anthropologists in the development of forensic biometric recognition and authentication systems may therefore be beneficial.

It is increasingly recognized that the identification of unidentified remains not only relies on the estimation of biological parameters obtained from the examination of the hard tissues but also on any individuating anatomical features of the soft tissues. In underdeveloped countries, lacking resources for the scientific identification of unidentified remains, the deceased are frequently identified based on external soft tissue characteristics, such as seen in recent disasters. The modern forensic anthropologist should therefore be aware of the anatomy, developmental progression, and their relationship to the skeletal system of those anatomical soft tissue structures useful for forensic human identification, along with an understanding of the postmortem decompositional changes related to those structures after death. As Black et al. (2009) pointed out, individualization is best achieved when features are taken into account that are environmentally dependent, individualistic, genetically inherited, or strongly genetically controlled and influenced by intrauterine development and growth. Knowledge of soft tissue structures and its uses in human identification may not only aid the identification of unidentified remains but also may be beneficial to investigation of judicial issues involving the identification of the living.

References

Abbas, A., and Rutty, G. N. 2003. Forensic web watch. *Journal of Clinical Forensic Medicine* 10: 129–131.

Abbas, A., and Rutty, G. N. 2005. Ear piercing affects earprints: the role of ear piercing in human identification. *Journal of Forensic Sciences* 50(2): 386–392.

Acree, M. A. 1999. Is there a gender difference in fingerprint ridge density? *Forensic Science International* 102 (1): 35–44.

Adán, M. Adán, A., Vázquez, A. S., et al. 2008. Biometric verification/identification based on hand's natural layout. *Image and Vision Computing* 26(4): 451–465.

Alberink, I., and Ruifrok, A. 2007. Performance of the FearID earprint identification system. *Forensic Science International* 166: 145–154.

Alberink, I., and Ruifrok, A. 2008. Repeatability and reproducibility of earprint acquisition. *Journal of Forensic Sciences* 53(2): 325–330.

Allen, M., Engström, A. S., Meyers, S., et al. 1998. Mitochondrial DNA sequencing of shed hairs and saliva on robbery caps: Sensitivity and matching probabilities. *Journal of Forensic Sciences* 43(3): 453–464.

Allouche, M., Hamdoum, M., Mangin, P., et al. 2008. Genetic identification of decomposed cadavers using nails as DNA source. *Forensic Science International: Genetics* 3 (1): 46–49.

Arbab-Zavar, B., Nixon, M. S., and Hurley, D. J. 2007. On model-based analysis of ear biometrics. In *First IEEE International Conference on Biometrics: Theory, Applications, and Systems*, Washington, DC, Sept. 27–29. 1–5.

Badawi, A. M.. 2006. Hand vein biometric verification prototype: A testing performance and patterns similarity. In *Proceedings of the 2006 International Conference on Image Processing, Computer Vision, and Pattern Recognition (IPCV'06)*, June 26–29, Las Vegas, NV.

Ball, J. 2002. The current status of lip prints. *Forensic Odonto-Stomatology* 20(2): 43–46.

Barbaro, A., Cormaci, P., and Barbaro, A. 2009. DNA typing from lipstick prints left on the skin. *Forensic Science International* 2: 125–126.

Bertillon, A. 1890. *La photographie judiciaire, avec un appendice sur la classification et l'identification anthropométriques*. Paris: Gauthier-Villars.

Bhanu, B., and Chen, H. 2003. Human ear recognition in 3D. *Proceedings of the Workshop on Multimodal User Authentication, Santa Barbara, California, USA*, pp. 91–98.

Bhattacharyya, D., Das, P., Kim, T. H., et al. 2009. Vascular pattern analysis towards pervasive palm vein authentication. *Journal of Universal Computer Science* 15(5): 1081–1089.

Bicknell, D. E., and Ramotowski, R. S. 2008. Use of an optimized 1,2-indanedione process for the development of latent prints. *Journal of Forensic Sciences* 53(5): 1108–1016.

Bindal, U., Jethani, S. L., Mehrotra, N., et al. 2009. Lip prints as a method of identification in human being. *Journal of the Anatomical Society of India* 58(2): 152–155.

Biometric Technology Today. 2003. Recognition versus identity—The role of biometrics. *Biometric Technology Today* 11(6): 7–8.

Biometric Technology Today. 2005a. Biometric passports planned by 40 nations. *Biometric Technology Today* 13(9): 5.

Biometric Technology Today. 2005b. EU passport will contain two biometrics. *Biometric Technology Today* 13(1): 12.

Black, S., Mallett, X., Rynn, C., et al. 2009. Forensic hand image comparison as an aid for paedophile investigations. *Police Professional* 184: 21–24.

Bolle, R. M., Connell, J. H., and Ratha, N. K. 2002. Biometric perils and patches. *Pattern Recognition* 35: 2727–2738.

Bowyer, K., Chang, K., and Flynn, P. 2006. A survey of approaches and challenges in 3D and multi-modal 3D + 2D face recognition. *Computer Vision and Image Understanding* 101(1): 1–15.

Breitmeier, D., Landmesser, B., Schulz, Y., and Albrecht, K. 2008. Practicability of the mobile one-finger scanner Cross Match MV5 in fingerprinting of corpses: Are mobile fingerprinting scanners suitable for use in mass disasters? [In German.] *Archiv für Kriminologie* 221(5–6): 138–148.

Broeders, A. P. A. 2006. Of earprints, fingerprints, scent dogs, cot deaths, and cognitive contamination—A brief look at the present state of play in the forensic arena. *Forensic Science International* 159: 148–157.

Bronselaer, A., De Winne, J., and De Tré, G. 2007. Flexible matching of ear biometrics. In *Proceedings of the First International VLDB Workshop on Management of Uncertain Data (MUD)*, pp. 5–17.

Buddharaju, P., Pavlidis, I., and Kakadiaris, I. 2004. Face recognition in the thermal infrared spectrum. In *Proceedings of the IEEE Conference on Computer Vision and Pattern Recognition, 2004 (CVPRW '04)*, p. 133.

Burge, M., and Burger W. 1997. Ear biometrics for computer vision. In *Proceedings of the 21st Workshop of the Austrian Association for Pattern Recognition, Hallstatt, May 1997*, pp. 275–282.

Burge, M., and Burger W. 1999. Ear biometrics. In *Biometrics—Personal identification in a networked society* (Eds. Jain, A., Bolle, R., and Pankanti, S.). Dordrecht, the Netherlands: Kluwer Academic, pp. 273–286.

Burge, M., and Burger, W. 2000. Ear biometrics in computer vision. *Proceedings of the International Conference on Pattern Recognition* 2: 822–826.

Burghardt, T. 2009. A brief review of biometric identification. http://www.cs.bris.ac.uk/~burghard/pdf/2009-02-07_review_of_biometric_identification_by_tilo_burghardt.pdf (accessed June 4, 2010).

Burton, J. L. 2007. The external examination: An often-neglected autopsy component. *Current Diagnostic Pathology* 13: 357–365.

Byers, S. N. 2008. *Introduction to forensic anthropology* (3rd ed.). New York: Pearson.

Caldas, I. M., Magalhães, T., and Afonso, A. 2007. Establishing identity using cheiloscopy and palatoscopy. *Forensic Science International* 165 (1): 1–9.

Cappelli, R., Lumini, A., Maio, D., et al. 2007. Fingerprint image reconstruction from standard templates. *IEEE Transactions on Pattern Analysis and Machine Intelligence* 29(9): 1489–1503.

Carreira-Perpiñán, M. Á. 1995. Compression neural networks and feature extraction: Application to human recognition from ear images. MSc thesis, Technical University of Madrid, Spain.

Castelló, A., Alvarez, M., and Verdú, F. 2004. Just lip prints? No: There could be something else. *The Federation of American Societies for Experimental Biology* 18: 615–616.

Castelló, A., Seguí, M. A., and Verdú, F. 2005. Luminous lip prints as criminal evidence. *Forensic Science International* 155: 185–187.

Champod, C., Evett, I. W., and Kuchler, B. 2001. Earmarks as evidence: A critical review. *Journal of Forensic Sciences* 46(6): 1275–1284.

Champod, C., Lennard, C., Margot, P., et al. 2004. *Fingerprints and other ridge skin impressions*. Boca Raton, FL: CRC Press.

Chang, K., Bowyer, K. W., Sarkar, S., et al. 2003. Comparison and combination of ear and face images in appearance-based biometrics. *IEEE Transactions on Pattern Analysis and Machine Intelligence* 25(9): 1160–1165.

Chang, K. I., Bowyer, K., and Flynn, P. 2003. Multi-modal 2D and 3D biometrics for face recognition. In *Proceedings of the IEEE International Workshop on Analysis and Modelling of Faces and Gestures*, p. 187.

Chang, K. I., Bowyer, K., and Flynn, P. 2006. Multiple nose region matching for 3D face recognition under varying facial expression. *IEEE Transactions on Pattern Analysis and Machine Intelligence* 28(10): 1695–1700.

Charlton, D., Fraser-Mackenzie, P., and Dror, I. E. 2010. Emotional experiences and motivating factors associated with fingerprint analysis. *Journal of Forensic Sciences* 55: 385–393.

Chattopadhyay, P. K., and Bhatia, S. 2009. Morphological examination of ear: A study of an Indian population. *Legal Medicine* 11: S190–S193.

Chen, Q., Kerk, W. T., Soutar, A. M., et al. 2009. Application of dye intercalated bentonite for developing latent fingerprints. *Applied Clay Science* 44: 156–160.

Choraś, M. 2007a. Emerging methods of biometrics human identification. In *Proceedings of the Second International Conference on Innovative Computing, Information and Control,* pp. 365–380.

Choraś, M. 2007b. Human lips recognition. In *Computer recognition systems. Vol. 2: Advances in soft computing* (Eds. Kurzyski, M., et al.) Berlin: Springer-Verlag, pp. 838–843.

Clarkson, J., and Schaefer, M. 2007. Surgical intervention. In *Forensic human identification: An introduction* (Eds. Thompson, T. J. U., and Black, S.). London: CRC Press/Taylor and Francis Group, pp. 127–146.

Coward, R. C. 2007. The stability of lip pattern characteristics over time. *Journal of Forensic Odontostomatology* 25(2): 40–56.

Cummins, H. 1941. Ancient finger prints in clay. *Journal of Criminal Law and Criminology* 34(4): 468–481.

DeCann, B., Tan, B., and Schuckers, S. 2009. A novel region based liveness detection approach for fingerprint scanners. In *Advances in Biometrics* (Eds. Tistarelli, M., and Nixon, M. S.). Berlin: Springer-Verlag, pp. 627–636.

De Luis-Garcia, R., Alberola Lopez, C., Aghzout, O., et al. 2003. Biometric identification systems. *Signal Processing* 83(12): 2539–2557.

De Winne, J., and Purkait, R. 2004. Ear Biometrics: Its possibility as an aid to establishing identity. Paper presented at XXV Annual Conference of Indian Academy of Forensic Medicine, Goa, February 7–9.

Ding, Y., Zhuang, D., and Wang, K. 2005. The study of hand vein recognition method. *Proceedings of the IEEE International Conference on Mechatronics and Automation* July: 2106–2110.

Drira, H., Ben Amor, B., Daoudi, M., et al. 2009a. Nasal region contribution in 3D face biometrics using shape analysis framework. In *Proceedings of the 3rd IAPR/IEEE International Conference on Biometrics,* June 2–5, University of Sassari, Italy.

Drira, H., Ben Amor, B., Srivastava, A., et al. 2009b. A Riemannian analysis of 3D nose shapes for partial human biometrics. In proceedings of the twelfth International Conference on Computer Vision, Kyoto, Japan.

Dror, I. E., and Charlton, D. 2006. Why experts make errors. *Journal of Forensic Identification* 56(4): 600–616.

Dror, I. E., Charlton, D., and Peron, A. 2006. Contextual information renders experts vulnerable to making erroneous identifications. *Forensic Science International* 156: 74–78.

Dror, I. E., and Cole, S. 2010. The vision in "blind" justice: Expert perception, judgment and visual cognition in forensic pattern recognition. *Psychonomic Bulletin and Review* 17(2):161–167.

Dror, I. E., Peron, A., Hind, S. L., et al. 2005. When emotions get the better of us: The effect of contextual top-down processing on matching fingerprints. *Applied Cognitive Psychology* 19(6): 799–809.

Dror, I. E., and Rosenthal, R. 2008. Meta-analytically quantifying the reliability and biasability of forensic experts. *Journal of Forensic Sciences* 53(4): 900–903.

Duta, N. 2009. A survey of biometric technology based on hand shape. *Pattern Recognition* 42 (11): 2797–2806.

Egli, N. M., Champod, C., and Margot, P. 2007. Evidence evaluation in fingerprint comparison and automated fingerprint identification systems—modelling within finger variability. *Forensic Science International* 167: 189–195.

El Domiaty, M. A., Al-Gaidi, S. A., Elayat, A. A., et al. 2010. Morphological patterns of lip prints in Saudi Arabia at Almadinah Almonawarah province. *Forensic Science International*, http://dx.doi.org/10.1016/j.forsciint.2010.03.042.

Feenstra, L., and van der Lugt, C. 2000. Ear witness. *Journal of Laryngology and Otology* 114(7): 497–500.

Feng, J., and Jain, A. K. 2009. FM model based fingerprint reconstruction from minutiae template. *Advances in Biometrics: ICB 2009 (5558)*: 544–553.

Fields, C., Falls, H. C., Warren C. P., et al. 1960. The ear of the newborn as an identification constant. *Obstetrics and Gynecology* 16(1): 98–102.

Fraser, I., and Meier-Augenstein, W. 2007. Stable 2H isotope analysis of modern-day human hair and nails can aid forensic human identification. *Rapid Communications in Mass Spectrometry* 21 (20): 3279–3285.

Fraser, I., Meier-Augenstein, W., and Kalin, R. M. 2006. The role of stable isotopes in human identification: A longitudinal study into the variability of isotopic signals in human hair and nails. *Rapid Communications in Mass Spectrometry* 20 (7): 1109–1116.

Gafurov, D., Helkala, K., and Søndrol, T. 2006. Biometric gait authentication. *Journal of Computers* 1(7): 51–59.

Garrett, R. 2006. Printing decomps. Livescan and digital fingerprint systems streamline identifying the deceased. *Law Enforcement Technology* 33(6): 22–33. Available at http://www.officer.com/article/article.jsp?siteSection=20&id=31702 (accessed June 12, 2010).

George, A. O. 2005. Finger nail plate shape and size for personal identification—a possible low technology method for the developing world—preliminary report. *African Journal of Health Sciences* 12(1–2): 13–20.

German, E. 2010. *The history of fingerprints* [Online]. Available at http://www.Onin.Com/Fp/Fphistory.Html (accessed March 10, 2010).

Gomez, E., Travieso, C. M., Briceno, J. C., et al. 2002. Biometric identification system by lip shape. In *Proceedings of the 36th Annual 2002 International Carnahan Conference on Security Technology*, pp. 39–42.

Gondivkar, S. M., Indurkar, A., Degwekar, S., and Bhowate, R. 2009. Cheiloscopy for sex determination. *Journal of Forensic Dental Sciences* 1(2): 56–60.

Grant, M. G. 2007. Gait. In *Forensic human identification: An introduction* (Eds. Thompson, T. J. U., and Black, S.). Boca Raton, FL: CRC Press, pp. 343–362.

Gresham, G. L., Groenewold, G. S., Bauer, W. F., et al. 2000. Secondary ion mass spectrometric characterization of nail polishes and paint surfaces. *Journal of Forensic Sciences* 45 (2): 310–323.

Gupta, N., Saroa, J. S., and Sharma, R. M. 2006. Thin-layer chromatography of nail enamels. *Journal of Forensic Identification* 56 (2): 198–209.

Gutiérrez, E., Galera, V., Martínez, J. M., et al. 2007. Biological variability of the minutiae in the fingerprints of a sample of the Spanish population. *Forensic Science International* 172(2–3): 98–105.

Gutiérrez-Redomero, E., Alonso, C., Romero, E., et al. 2008. Variability of fingerprint ridge density in a sample of Spanish Caucasians and its application to sex determination. *Forensic Science International* 180 (1): 17–22.

Hall, L. J., and Player, E. 2008. Will the introduction of an emotional context affect fingerprint analysis and decision-making? *Forensic Science International* 181: 36–39.

Haxthausen, H. 1933. Infrared photography of subcutaneous veins. *British Journal of Dermatology* 45: 506–511.

Hill, I. 2007. Physical appearance. In *Forensic human identification: An introduction* (Eds. Thompson, T. J. U., and Black, S.). London: CRC Press/Taylor and Francis Group, pp. 87–98.

Hirth, L., Gottsche, H., and Goedde, H. W. 1975. Lip prints—Variability and genetics. *Humangenetik.* 30(1): 47–62.

Hoogstrate, A., Heuvel, H. V. D., and Huyben, E. 2001. Ear identification based on surveillance camera images. *Science and Justice* 41: 167–172.

Hurley D. J., Nixon, M. S., and Carter J. N. 2000a. Automatic ear recognition by force field transformations. *Proceedings of IEE Colloquium on Visual Biometrics* (00/018): 8/1–8/5.

Hurley, D. J., Nixon, M. S., and Carter, J. N. 2000b. A new force field transform for ear and face recognition. In *Proceedings of the IEEE International Conference on Image Processing (ICIP 2000).* pp. 25–28.

Hurley, D. J., Arbab-Zavar, B., and Nixon, M. S. 2007. The ear as a biometric. In *Handbook of biometrics* (Eds. Jain, A., Flynn, P., and Ross, A.). New York, Springer Science, pp. 131–150.

Hurley, D. J., Nixon, M. S., and Carter, J. N. 2002. Force field energy functionals for image feature extraction. *Image Vision Computer Journal* 20(5–6): 311–317.

Iannarelli, A. 1989. *Ear Identification* (Forensic Identification Series). California: Paramont.

Im, S. K., Park, H. M., and Kim, S. W., et al. 2000. Improved vein pattern extracting algorithm and its implementation. *Digest of Technical Papers—IEEE International Conference on Consumer Electronics,* pp. 2–3.

İşcan, M. Y. 2001. Global forensic anthropology in the 21st century. *Forensic Science International* 117(1–2): 1–6.

Islam, S. M. S., Bennamoun, M., Mian, A. S., et al. 2009. Fully automatic approach for human recognition from profile images using 2D and 3D ear data. In *Proceedings of the 4th International Symposium of 3D Data Processing, Visualization and Transmission,* pp. 131–135.

Iwano, K., Hirose, T., Kamibayashi, E., et al. 2003. Multi-modal person authentication using speech and ear images. In *Proceedings of the Workshop on Multimodal User Authentication,* Santa Barbara, CA, December 11–12, pp. 85–90.

Jain, A. K., Hong, L., and Pankanti, S. 2000. Biometrics identification. *Communications of the ACM* 43(2): 91–98.

Jain, A. K., Pankanti, S., Prabhakar, S., et al. 2004. Biometrics: A grand challenge. In *Proceedings of the 17th International Conference on Pattern Recognition, Cambridge,* pp. 935–942.

Jain, A. K., Prabhakar, S., and Pankanti, S. 2002. On the similarity of identical twin fingerprints. *Pattern Recognition* 35(11): 2653–2663.

Jain, A. K., Ross, A., and Pankanti, S. 2006. Biometrics: A tool for information security. *IEEE Transactions on Information Forensics and Security* 1(2): 125–143.

Jasuja, O. P., Toofany, M. A., Singh, G., et al. 2009. Dynamics of latent fingerprints: the effect of physical factors on quality of ninhydrin developed prints—A preliminary study. *Science and Justice* 49: 8–11.

Jeges, E., and Máté, L. 2007. Model-based human ear localization and feature extraction. *International Journal of Intelligent Computing in Medical Sciences and Image Processing* 1(2): 101–112.

Jobling, M. A., and Gill, P. 2004. Encoded evidence: DNA in forensic analysis. *Nature Reviews Genetics* 5(10): 739–751.

Kahana, T., Grande, A., Tancredi, D. M., et al. 2001. Fingerprinting the deceased: traditional and new techniques. *Journal of Forensic Sciences* 46(4): 908–912.

Kakadiaris, I., Passalis, G., Toderici, G., et al. 2007. Three-dimensional face recognition in the presence of facial expressions: an annotated deformable model approach. *IEEE Transaction on Pattern Analysis and Machine Intelligence* 29(4): 640–649.

Kaur, R., and Garg, R. K. 2007. Personal identification from lip prints. *Forensic Science International* 169(Suppl.): S47–S49.

Kieckhoefer, H., Ingleby, M., and Lucas, G. 2006. Monitoring the physical formation of earprints: optical and pressure mapping evidence. *Measurement* 39 (10): 918–935.

Kim, J. O., Lee, W., Hwang, J., Baik, K. S., et al. 2004. Lip print recognition for security systems by multi-resolution architecture. *Future Generation Computer Systems* 20: 295–301.

Kono, M., Ueki, H., and Umemura, S. 2002. Near-infrared finger vein patterns for personal identification, *Applied Optics* 41(35): 7429–7436.

Korotkaya, Z. 2003. *Biometric person authentication: Odor* [Online]. Available at http://www.It.Lut.Fi/Kurssit/03–04/010970000/Seminars/Korotkaya.Pdf (accessed March 16, 2010).

Kücken, M. 2007. Models for fingerprint pattern formation. *Forensic Science International* 171(2–3): 85–96.

Kumar, A., and Prathyusha, K. V. 2009. Personal authentication using hand vein triangulation and knuckle shape. *IEEE Trans Image Process* 18(9): 2127–36.

Kumar, A., and Ravikanth, C. H. 2009. Personal authentication using finger knuckle surface. *IEEE Transactions on Information Forensics and Security* 4(1): 98–110.

Kumar, A., Wong, D. C. M., Shen, H., et al. 2006. Personal authentication using hand images. *Pattern Recognition Letters* 27(13): 1478–1486.

Kumar, A., and Zhang, D. 2006. Personal recognition using hand shape and texture. *IEEE Transactions on Image Processing* 15(8): 2454–2461.

Kumar, A., and Zhou, Y. 2009. Human identification using knucklecodes. In *Proceedings of the IEEE 3rd International Conference on biometrics: theory, applications, and systems.* Washington, pp. 1–6.

Kwak, J., Willse, A., Matsumura, K., et al. 2008. Genetically-based olfactory signatures persist despite dietary variation. *PLoS ONE* 3(10): e3591.

Lammi, H. K. 2003. *Ear biometrics.* Technical report, Lappeenranta University of Technology, Department of Information Technology, Laboratory of Information Processing. Available at http://www2.it.lut.fi/kurssit/03–04/010970000/seminars/Lammi.pdf.

Langenburg, G., Champod, C., and Wertheim, P. 2009. Testing for potential contextual bias effects during the verification stage of the ACE-V methodology when conducting fingerprint comparisons. *Journal of Forensic Sciences* 54: 571–582.

Lee, H. C., and Gaensslen, R. E. 2001. *Advances in fingerprint technology*. Boca Raton, FL: CRC Press.

Locard, E. 1932. Les preuves de l'identite. Lyon. Desvignes et fils.

Lip print leads to peeping Tom conviction. 1998. Washington Post, Feb. 15. http://www.highbeam.com/doc/1P2-641120.html Last accessed 12.10.2010.

López, S., and González, A. 2003. Hand vein segmentation and matching under adverse conditions. *Proceedings of SPIE* 5119: 166–177.

Maltino, D., Maio, D., Jain, A. K., et al. 2003. *Handbook of fingerprint recognition*: New York: Springer Science and Business Media.

Mamode Khan, M. H., Subramanian, R. K., and Mamode Khan, N. A. 2009. Low dimensional representation of dorsal hand vein features using principle component analysis (PCA). *World Academy of Science, Engineering and Technology* 49: 1001–1007.

Meijerman, L., Nagelkerke, N. J. D., Basten, R. V., et al. 2006. Inter- and intra-individual variation in applied force when listening at a surface, and resulting variation in earprints. *Medicine, Science and The Law* 46(2): 141–151.

Meijerman, L., Nagelkerke, N., Brand, R., et al. 2005. Exploring the effect of the occurrence of sound on force applied by the ear when listening at a surface. *Forensic Science, Medicine and Pathology* 1(3): 187–191.

Meijerman, L., Sholl, S., De Conti, F., et al. 2004. Exploratory study on classification and individualisation of earprints. *Forensic Science International* 140: 91–99.

Meijerman, L., Thean, A., and Maat, G. J. R. 2005. Earprints in forensic investigations. *Forensic Science, Medicine and Pathology* 1(4): 247–256.

Meijerman, L., Thean, A., van der Lugt, C., et al. 2006. Individualization of earprints variation in prints of monozygotic twins. *Forensic Science, Medicine and Pathology* 2(1): 39–49.

Meijerman, L., Thean, A., van der Lugt, C., et al. 2007. Earprints. In *Forensic human identification: An introduction*. (Eds. Thompson, T. J. U., and Black, S.). London: CRC Press/Taylor and Francis Group, pp. 73–84.

Michael, G. K. O., Connie, T., and Teoh, A. B. J. 2008. Touch-less palm print biometrics: novel design and implementation. *Image and Vision Computing* 26: 1551–1560.

Milroy, C. 2007. Soft tissue pathology. In *Forensic human identification: An introduction*. (Eds. Thompson, T. J. U., and Black, S.). London: CRC Press/Taylor and Francis Group, pp. 99–112.

Miura, N., Nagasaka, A., and Miyatake, T. 2004. Feature extraction of finger-vein patterns based on repeated line tracking and its application to personal identification. *Machine Vision and Applications* 15(4): 194–203.

Mordini, E., and Ottolini, C. 2007. Body identification, biometrics and medicine: ethical and social considerations. *Annali Dell'istituto Superiore Di Sanità* 43(1): 51–60.

Nanni, L., and Lumini, A. 2007. A multi-matcher for ear authentication. *Pattern Recognition Letters* 28(16): 2219–2226.

National Science and Technology Council (NSTC). 2006. Biometric testing and statistics. Available at http://www.biometrics.gov/Documents/BioTestingAndStats.pdf (accessed June 4, 2010).

Nayak, V. C., Rastogi, P., Kanchan, T., et al. 2010a. Sex differences from finger-print ridge density in Chinese and Malaysian population. *Forensic Science International* 197(1–3): 67–69.

Nayak, V. C., Rastogi, P., Kanchan, T., et al. 2010b. Sex differences from fingerprint ridge density in the Indian population. *Journal of Forensic and Legal Medicine* 17(2): 84–86.

Neumann, C., Champod, C., Puch-Solis, R., et al. 2006. Computation of likelihood ratios in fingerprint identification for configurations of three minutiae. *Journal of Forensic Sciences* 51(6): 1255–1266.

Neumann, C., Champod, C., Puch-Solis, R., et al. 2007. Computation of likelihood ratios in fingerprint identification for configurations of any number of minu-tiae. *Journal of Forensic Sciences* 52(1): 54–64.

Nithin, M. D., Balaraj, B. M., Manjunatha, B., et al. 2009. Study of fingerprint classifi-cation and their gender distribution among South Indian population. *Journal of Forensic and Legal Medicine* 16(8): 460–463.

O'Gorman, L. 1999. Fingerprint verification. In *Biometrics—Personal identification in a networked society* (Eds. Jain, A., Bolle, R., and Pankanti, S.). Dordrecht, the Netherlands: Kluwer Academic, pp. 43–63.

O'Neill, E., Harrington, D., and Allison, J. 2009. Interpretation of laser desorption mass spectra of unexpected inorganic species found in a cosmetic sample of forensic inter-est: fingernail polish. *Analytical and Bioanalytical Chemistry* 394(8): 2029–2038.

Order of the United States District Court, Middle District of Florida, Orlando Division (US v. Donatos Sarras). 2007. Available at http://www.websupp.org/data/MDFL/794995-MDFL.pdf (accessed June 14, 2010).

Oz, C., and Zamir, A. 2000. An evaluation of the relevance of routine DNA typing of fingernail clippings for forensic casework. *Journal of Forensic Sciences* 45(1): 158–160.

Plataniotis, K. N., Hatzinakos, D., and Lee, J. K. M. 2006. ECG biometric recognition without fiducial detection. In *Proceedings of Biometrics Symposiums (Bsym'06)*, Baltimore, MD, Sept. 19–21, 2006.

Pun, K., and Moon, Y. 2004. Recent advances in ear biometrics. In *Proceedings of the 6th IEEE International Conference on Automatic Face and Gesture Recognition*, Seoul, South Korea, pp. 164–169.

Purkait, R. 2007. Ear biometric: An aid to personal identification. *Anthropologist Special Volume* 3: 215–218.

Purkait, R., and Singh, P. 2008. A test of individuality of human external ear pat-tern: Its application in the field of personal identification. *Forensic Science International* 178: 112–118.

Ratha, N., Senior, A., and Bolle, R. 2001. Automated biometrics. In Singh, S., Murshed, N., and Kropatsch,W. (Eds.). *International Conference on Advances in Pattern Recognition (ICAPR)*, 445–454.

Ross, A., Shah, J., and Jain, A. K. 2007. From template to image: Reconstructing fingerprints from minutiae points. *IEEE Transactions on Pattern Analysis and Machine Intelligence* 29(4): 544–560.

Rutty, C. N., Abbas, A., and Crossling, D. 2005. Could earprint identification be com-puterized? An illustrated proof of concept paper. *International Journal of Legal Medicine* 119: 335–343.

Rutty, G. N., Stringer, K., and Turk, E. E. 2008. Electronic fingerprinting of the dead. *International Journal of Legal Medicine* 122(1): 77–80.

Saks, M. J. 2009. Concerning L. J. Hall, E. Player, "Will the introduction of an emotional context affect fingerprint analysis and decision-making?" [*Forensic Sci. Int.* 181 (2008) 36–39]. *Forensic Science International* 191(1–3): e19; author reply e21.

Saleh, M., Fadel, S., and Abbott, L. 2006. Using ears as a biometric for human recognition. In: *Proceedings of the International Conference on Computer Theory and Applications*, Alexandria, pp. 311–314.

Samir, C., Srivastava, A., Daoudi, M., et al. 2009. On analyzing symmetry of objects using elastic deformations. In VISSAP: *Proceedings of the international Conference on Computer Vision Theory and Applications*, February 5–8, Lisbon, Portugal, pp. 194–200.

Sana, A., and Gupta, P. 2006. Ear biometrics: A new approach. In *Advances in pattern recognition* (Ed. Pal, P.). Singapore: World Scientific Publishing.

Sapse, D., and Petraco, N. D. 2007. A step on the path in the discovery of new latent fingerprint development reagents: substituted Ruhemann's purples and implications for the law. *Journal of Molecular Modeling* 13(8): 943–948.

Saraswathi, T. R., Mishra, G., and Ranganathan, K. 2009. Study of lip prints. *Journal of Forensic Dental Sciences* 1(1): 28–31.

Saul, F. P., and Saul, J. M. 2003. Planes, trains, and fireworks. In *Hard evidence: Case Studies in Forensic Anthropology* (Ed. Steadman, D. W.). Englewood Cliffs, NJ: Prentice Hall, pp. 266–277.

Schiffer, B., and Champod, C. 2007. The potential (negative) influence of observational biases at the analysis stage of fingermark individualization. *Forensic Science International* 167:116–120.

Schouten, B., and Jacobs, B. 2009. Biometrics and their use in e-passports. *Image and Vision Computing* 27: 305–312.

Seguí, M. A., Feucht, M. M., Ponce, A. C., et al. 2000. Persistent lipsticks and their lip prints: new hidden evidence at the crime scene. *Forensic Science International* 112(1): 41–47.

Sforza, C., Grandi, G., Binelli, M., et al. 2009. Age and sex related changes in the normal human ear. *Forensic Science International* 187: 110.E1–110.E7.

Shamir, L., Ling, S., Rahimi, S., et al. 2009. Biometric identification using knee X-rays. *International Journal of Biometrics* 1(3): 365–370.

Sharma, P., Saxena, S., and Rathod, V. 2009a. Cheiloscopy: the study of lip prints in sex identification. *Journal of Forensic Dental Sciences* 1(1): 24–27.

Sharma, P., Saxena, S., and Rathod, V. 2009b. Comparative reliability of cheiloscopy and palatoscopy in human identification. *Indian Journal of Dental Research* 20(4): 453–457.

Singh, P., and Purkait, R. 2009. Observations of external ear—An Indian study. *Homo* 60 (5): 461–472.

Sivapathasundharam, B., Prakash, P. A., and Sivakumar, G. 2001. Lip prints (cheiloscopy). *Indian Journal of Dental Research* 12(4): 234–237.

Smith, S. M., Patry, M. W., and Stinson, V. 2007. But what is the CSI effect? How crime dramas influence people's beliefs about forensic evidence. *The Canadian Journal of Police and Security Services* 5: 187–195.

Sonal, V., Nayak, C. D., and Pagare, S. S. 2005. Study of lip-prints as aid for sex deter-
    mination. *Medico-Legal Update* 5(3): 93–98.
Stacey, R. B. 2004. Report on the erroneous fingerprint individualization bombing
    case. *Journal of Forensic Identification* 54: 706–718.
Stoney, D. A. 2001. Measurement of fingerprint individuality. In: *Advances in finger-
    print technology* (2nd ed.) (Eds. Lee, H. C., and Gaensslen, R. E.). New York:
    CRC Press, pp. 327–387.
Sundquist, T. 2009. DNA evidence from lip prints and used cups: interesting cases
    from the international symposium on human identification. Part I [Online].
    Available at http://Promega.Wordpress.Com/2009/10/13/Interesting-Cases-
    From-The-International-Symposium-On-Human-Identification-Part-I/
    (accessed March 3, 2010).
Suzuki, K., and Tsuchihashi, Y. 1970a. A new attempt of personal identification by
    means of lip print. *Journal of the Indian Dental Association* 42: 8–9.
Suzuki, K., and Tsuchihashi, Y. 1970b. Personal identification by means of lip print.
    Journal of Forensic Medicine 17: 52–57.
Suzuki, K., and Tsuchihashi, Y. 1975. Two criminal cases of lip print. *ACTA
    Criminologica Japan* 41: 61–64.
Swift, B., and Rutty, G. N. 2003. The human ear: Its role in forensic practice. *Journal
    of Forensic Sciences* 48(1): 153–160.
Tahtouh, M., Despland, P., Shimmon, R., et al. 2007. The application of infrared
    chemical imaging to the detection and enhancement of latent fingerprints:
    Method optimization and further findings. *Journal of Forensic Sciences* 52(5):
    1089–1096.
Tanaka, T., and Kubo, N. 2004. Biometric authentication by hand vein patterns. *SICE
    Annual Conference*, Sapporo, Japan, August 4–6, pp. 249–253.
Thompson, T. J. U., and Black, S. 2007. *Forensic human identification: An introduction.*
    London: CRC Press/Taylor and Francis Group.
Tsalakanidou, F., Malassiotis, S., and Strintzis, M. G. 2007. A 3D face and hand bio-
    metric system for robust user-friendly authentication. *Pattern Recognition
    Letters* 28(16): 2238–2249.
Tsuchihashi, Y. 1974. Studies on personal identification by means of lip prints. *Forensic
    Science* 3(3): 233–248.
Turvey, B. E. 2008. *Criminal profiling: An introduction to behavioral evidence analysis.*
    London: Elsevier.
Utsuno, H., Kanoh, T., Tadokoro, O., et al. 2005. Preliminary study of post mortem
    identification using lip prints. *Forensic Science International* 149: 129–132.
Vahanwahal, S. P., and Parekh, D. K. 2000. Study of lip prints as an aid to forensic
    methodology. *Journal of Indian Dental Association* 71: 269–271.
Van der Lugt, C. 2001. *Ear identification.* Amsterdam: Elsevier, Bedrijfsinformatie's
    Gravenhage.
Van der Lugt, C., Nagelkerke, N., and Maat, G. J. R. 2005. Study of the relationship
    between a person's stature and height of an ear print from the floor. *Medicine,
    Science and the Law* 45(2): 135–141.
Victor, B., Bowyer, K. W., and Sarkar, S. 2002. An evaluation of face and ear biomet-
    rics. In *Proceedings of International Conference on Pattern Recognition, 16th I,*
    Quebec, Canada, Aug. 11–15. pp. 429–432.

Wang, L., Leedham, G., and Siu-Yeung Cho, D. 2008. Minutiae feature analysis for infrared hand vein pattern biometrics. *Pattern Recognition* 41(3): 920–929.

Wang, L., and Leedham, G. 2006. Near- and far-infrared imaging for vein pattern biometrics. In *Proceedings of the Syndey, Australia, IEEE International Conference on Video and Signal Based Surveillance*, Nov. 22–24. p. 52.

Watanabe, M. 2008. Palm vein authentication. In *Advances in biometrics, sensors, algorithms and systems* (Eds. Ratha, N. K., and Govindaraju, V.). London: Springer, pp. 75–88.

Watanabe, M., Endoh, T., Shiohara, M., et al. 2005. Palm vein authentication technology and its applications. In *Proceedings of the Biometric Consortium Conference*, September 19–21, Arlington, VA.

Wei, G., and Li, D. 2005. Biometrics: applications, challenges and the future. In *Privacy and technologies of identity—A cross-disciplinary conversation* (Eds. Strandburg, K. J., and Raicu, D. S.). New York: Springer, pp. 135–149.

Widjaja, E., Lim, G. H., and An, A. 2008. A novel method for human gender classification using Raman spectroscopy of fingernail clippings. *Analyst* 133(4): 493–498.

Wilkinson, C. M., Motwani, M., and Chiang, E. 2003. The relationship between the soft tissues and the skeletal detail of the mouth. *Journal of Forensic Sciences* 48 (4): 1–5.

Woodard, D. J., and Flynn, P. J. 2005. Finger surface as a biometric identifier, *Computer Vision and Image Understanding* 100(3): 357–384.

Wu, J. D., and Ye, S. H. 2009. Driver identification using finger-vein patterns with Radon transform and neural network. *Expert Systems with Applications* 36(3): 5793–5799.

Yan, P., and Bowyer, K. W. 2005. Empirical evaluation of advanced ear biometrics. In *4th IEEE Workshop on Empirical Evaluation Methods in Computer Vision (EEMCV, 2005)*, San Diego, June, 41.

Yang, M. H., Kriegman, D. J., and Ahuja, N. 2002. Detecting faces in images: A survey. *IEEE Transactions on Pattern Analysis and Machine Intelligence* 24: 34–58.

Yuizono, T., Wang, Y., Satoh, K., et al. 2002. Study on individual recognition for ear images by using genetic local search. In *Proceedings of the 2002 Congress on Evolutionary Computation*, Honolulu, May 12–17. pp. 237–242.

Zunkel, R. L. 1999. Hand geometry based verification. In *Biometrics—Personal identification in a networked society* (Eds. Jain, A., Bolle, R., and Pankanti, S.). Dordrecht, the Netherlands: Kluwer Academic, pp. 87–101.

Facial Identification of the Dead $\quad$ 12

WON-JOON LEE
STENTON MACKENZIE
DR. CAROLINE WILKINSON

Contents

Introduction

At the turn of the last century, a pioneering researcher in forensic facial identification predicted that anthropologists in the new millennium would spend "considerably more time [trying] to understand the human face, how expressions are made and how the face changes" (İşcan 2001: 4). Commenting on the then 60-year contribution anthropology had made to forensic research and medicolegal processes, İşcan anticipated that diet, physical environment, disease, genetics, and ageing were prime sources for information on transformative human facial morphology. In the first decade of the 21st century, other practitioners evoked this shared perception of forensic anthropology as increasingly multidisciplinary (Cattaneo 2007), anticipating further ingress of improvements already achieved in "computer science and ... medical imaging technologies," which would continue to have "significant repercussions" in the field (De Greef and Willems 2005: 12).

This chapter explains how these expectations have in part been real-ized. Research on forensic facial reconstruction (FFR) techniques incor-porate new information on estimating the facial appearance in manual and computerized applications: New soft tissue depth data sets obtained with computed tomographic (CT) scanning, magnetic resonance imag-ing (MRI), and ultrasound provide a wider range of information for those reconstructions; continued development of computer-mediated image pro-duction and manipulation predominate in FFR; at the same time, these technical expansions contribute to new studies on postmortem depiction and influence the execution of facial superimposition. Debate on the nature and position of FFR in science, as opposed to art, recur unabated, as does argument about its accuracy.

The aim of FFR is to re-create the facial appearance of a deceased and unidentified individual, so that it is sufficient in resemblance to facilitate recognition (Wilkinson and Whittaker 2002). Facial reconstruction is often a last resort when other means of identification have failed and must be corroborated by radiographic, dental, or DNA evidence to stand as a positive identification (De Greef and Willems 2005). Two basic techniques are utilized: two-dimensional (2D) and three-dimensional (3D) recon-struction. Each technique is further divided into manual and computer-generated methods (Wilkinson 2007a). The 3D manual methods include the anatomical (Russian), anthropometrical (American), and combination (Manchester) methods (Taylor 2001; Wilkinson 2004). The differences in nomenclature have arisen from variation in disciplinary approaches and diverse regional origins. The anatomical method relies on the primary influ-ence of muscles (as informed by skull morphology) in constructing facial form and features; the anthropometrical method, in contrast, emphasizes average facial tissue depths in facial depiction rather than the anatomical relation between skull and facial structure. The combination method is a fusion of the two in which average soft tissue contours, although impor-tant, serve as confirmation of structural details provided by muscle and bone morphology (Verzé 2009).

Manual 3D Facial Reconstruction

Other than research relating to the relationship between the hard and soft tissues of the face and accuracy studies (discussed further in this chap-ter), 3D manual FFR publications have been mainly limited to case studies, reviews, and some focal texts. Two reviews (Vanezis and Vanezis 2000; Verzé 2009) summarized the history and current practice of facial reconstruc-tion in forensic identification: both describe the origins, aims, advantages, limitations, and essential methods. Both reviews referenced research documenting the critical relationship between the uniqueness of skull structures and the individuality of human faces, thus directing students of FFR to familiarize themselves with foundational material underwriting the theory of facial reconstruction (Krogman and İşcan 1986; Fedosyutkin and Nainys 1993; İşcan and Helmer 1993). In addition, Verzé (2009) describes progress in the field, including Neolithic skull overmodeling, death mask techniques, the Anatomica Plastica movement of the 18th century Europe, a number of early forensic U.K. cases, and the powerful computing systems that contribute to current developments.

Forensic Facial Reconstruction (Wilkinson 2004), a comprehensive text, examines our fascination with the human face and gives an account of the history, methods, and accuracy of facial reconstruction (Ubelaker 2005). Published soft tissue data available at the time were collated, and a chapter on the complex and difficult task of juvenile facial reconstruction was included. Wilkinson reiterated the primary scientific concerns expressed by researchers reviewing forensic facial identification, namely, that the limitations of craniofacial reconstruction itself may best be addressed by improving the reliability of facial reconstructions and determining more select or skillful assessments of that reliability. Vanezis and Vanezis (2000) and Verzé (2009), like Wilkinson, emphasized the benefit that increased incorporation of cognitive approaches to understanding facial recognition may yield.

Many publications have described archaeological facial reconstruction, including the depiction of Egyptian mummies (Wilkinson 2003a, 2008; Cesarani et al. 2004; Gill-Robinson et al. 2006); bog bodies (Wilkinson 2007b; Lynnerup 2009); a 19th century Hungarian priest (Kustár 2004); a Danish 17th century nobleman (Gregersen et al. 2006); J. S. Bach (Wilkinson and Aitken 2009); Dante Alighieri (Benazzi, Fantini, et al. 2009); a Korean Medieval child mummy (Lee et al. 2007); and an Italian Renaissance nobleman (Benazzi et al. 2010). Historical depictions of facial disease and trauma include the South American case of leontiasis ossea (Gaytán et al. 2009), a healed wound from the Battle of Towton (Wilkinson and Neave 2003), and meningioma hyperostosis (Wilkinson 2008).

Some research has evaluated manual and computer-based skull reassembly and missing fragment remodeling, for which the effects of misalignment and errors in remodeling were assessed in relation to any resulting facial reconstruction. A pilot study (Wilkinson and Neave 2001) using manual reassembly and remodeling as applied to a forensic case suggested good levels of reliability; later studies of computer-based reassembly and remodeling (Mackenzie 2007; Ismail 2008) confirmed this conclusion, with the exception of the mandible, for which large errors in remodeling will have a negative effect on any reconstruction accuracy.

Computer Mediation and Virtual Reality Tools

As computer-generated image production and manipulation techniques evolve, a new discourse and lexicon associated with what can be accomplished with virtual reality is employed in research literature (Sherman and Craig 2003). For the student with a background in, or an affinity with, computer technology, particularly as it concerns image creation and adaptation, many of these concepts are familiar. For those requiring additional orientation, certain texts may prove useful; among them are guides specific to the computerized method of facial reconstruction (Clement and Marks 2005) and a primer in computer-assisted facial reconstruction from a paleontological and biomedical point of view (Zollikofer and Ponce de Leon 2005).

The contents of *Understanding Virtual Reality* (Sherman and Craig 2003) are now slightly dated but nonetheless offer an introduction to many of the hardware/software combinations and much of the terminology encountered by those working in facial anthropology labs. It defined and positioned virtual reality as the emergent communication platform of computer capability and made computer systems integration generally comprehensible. Of interest is an orientation to the "usability" of haptic force feedback (employed in computer skull and facial reconstruction and superimposition tasks utilizing 3D craniofacial models).

As reflected in the title, *Virtual Reconstruction: A Primer in Computer-Assisted Palaeontology and Biomedicine*, Zollikofer and Ponce de Leon (2005) wrote in depth about practices that implement computer-based concepts and tools to, on one hand, create the facial image of a Neanderthal child from a fragile, fragmented, and distorted fossil cranium and on the other hand model reparative maxillofacial surgery for motor vehicle accident victims. The relation between the theory and method for such projects and that used for forensic craniofacial identification is strong—the same procedures, incorporating identical strategies for reconstitution of the facial image, are reliant on accurate collection and interpretation of morphometric data and the subsequent processing, graphical representation, and interactive manipulation of anatomical information. The juxtaposition and interpolation of image development and representation—from physical to virtual reality and back again to physical—are shared processes.

The text aimed to "bridge the gap between theory and practice" (Zollikofer and Ponce de Leon 2005: 3) with substantial use of metaphor to enable intuitive understanding and so is especially suited to the student. It stresses an inductive approach, posing bioscientific questions to promote practical computer-based solutions rather than the less-manageable tactic of deducing computer resolutions to questions from computational theory. The following are introduced and explored:

- concepts and practicalities of virtual reality
- relations between the types of medical imaging capture techniques, including surface, volume, and vertex data and formats for storage of these data
- means of 2D and 3D data acquisition, including CT and surface scanners
- processing of 2D/3D images in virtual reality
- rendering multidimensional images visually accessible: lighting and shading of object materials; object manipulation; volume rendering
- reconstruction of virtual fossil crania
- procedures of rapid prototyping: reverse engineering
- primary characteristics of geometric morphometric data
- appendices include formal, algebra-based alternatives to comprehending computer graphics and biomedical imaging

A constantly updated companion Web site to the book (http://www.wiley.com/go/virtualreconstruction) encourages practice at "interactive visualization."

Computer-Graphic Facial Reconstruction edited by Clement and Marks (2005), is oriented toward advancing semi- and fully automated computer prototype methods for analysis and modeling of skulls and faces—the aims of which include prediction (change in a face, differences between faces, relations between one facial feature set and another) and comparison between faces (for offender and missing persons identification, verification or invalidation of identity, and explication of the correlation between craniofacial hard and soft tissues). A principal concern expressed by advocates of the superiority of computer-mediated methods is that traditional, manual methods are dependent on "presumptive means" in the translation of facial soft tissue morphology from bone, and that computer-based approaches attenuate the "subjectivity" inherent in the manual method. Clement and Marks acknowledged this controversy, noting evidence of practitioner rivalry in the literature. What is potentially problematic in this text, and may appear to the student as contradictory, are arguments over which technique, computer or manual, is most desirable or reliable and what the terms *approximation* and *reconstruction* really mean—real or imagined.

Average facial soft tissue data sets are integral to facial depiction methods (De Greef and Willems 2005). Citing the recent augmentation of soft tissue records with updated data for specific anatomic sites of the face from CT and MRI scans; Clement and Marks admitted (2005) that these new data have not improved the success rates of facial approximations. This is of importance in light of the fact that reliance on averages is greater in those manual and computer-based methods using "averaged" data (hence the term *approximation*) rather than when a reconstruction is determined more by individual skull morphology as it relates specifically to soft tissue structures (the "reconstruction" method). There is confusion about how the terms *approximation* and *reconstruction* are used, particularly in relation to critiques of reconstructions in which average soft tissue depth data *do not* dominate. Stephan, Penton-Voak, Clement, et al. (2005) said that the process of averaged faces is useful for facial approximation (here, they described approximation as it is practiced in the American technique); they continued that averaging methods are used in *all* facial reconstitutions irrespective of skull morphology (İşcan and Helmer 1993) and then added that such approximations, since they are all based on averaged faces that are stretched to fit an individual skull, should look alike—but do not. This is described as the result of "facial-approximation" practitioners (when what is actually meant is facial *reconstruction*) using "subjective interpretation" to interpolate facial features that cannot be determined from the skull.

Approximation and reconstruction have been consistently acknowledged as correlated with the anthropometrical and anatomical/morphological methods, respectively, and differentiated from one another regarding method in relation to manual and computer facial rebuilding from a skull (or skull model) by a significant number of authors writing on this subject over the last 10 years (Vanezis and Vanezis 2000; De Greef and Willems 2005; Wilkinson 2005; Verzé 2009). Aspects of soft facial anatomy for which no reference from any aspect of the skull can be found include skin color, surface textures (horizontal forehead creases, skin thickness, pore size, or blemishes), the amount and dispersal of fat in the face, eye color, facial and head hair density and distribution, and aspects of lip thickness, vermillion outline, and ear shape. For all other features, established guides for facial reconstruction exist (İşcan and Helmer 1993; Wilkinson 2004, 2010). The inability of Stephan and colleagues (Stephan, Penton-Voak, Clement, et al. 2005) to use the term *reconstruction* with respect to these specific guides (skull morphology over average tissue data) in the morphological method leads to a contentious estimation about the level of "objectivity and repeatability" attached to approximation approaches (computer or manual).

To add further confusion, the combined authors of *Computer-Graphic Facial Reconstruction* (Clement and Marks 2005) discussed their reluctance to morph template or donor faces onto an unknown skull because the face of the decedent tends to end up looking more like a composite of donor faces rather than the premortem individual's face (Davy et al. 2005: 9); they claimed that it is better instead to use "the skull to dictate facial appearance"—to base "reconstructions upon a meticulous anthropological and anatomical analysis of the particular skeletal remains in order to record any information that is unique or individualizing"—rather than on facial templates (Clement and Marks 2005: 194). They stated that landmarks are better placed manually than computationally to "ensure that the nuances of the skull are taken into account," (p.194) and that facial reconstructions are still best achieved via the use of the human hand—placing splines individually (which interpolate, connecting continuously at tissue depth markers) because human intervention (in conference with computerized action) produces a better face build (Davy et al. 2005).

This discussion converges in an itemizing of accuracy rates for various practitioners in facial approximation or reconstruction. Researchers' claims are presented to contradict and conflate each other without adequate clarification of the confusing information (Stephan, Penton-Voak, Clement, et al. 2005). Clement and Marks (2005) asserted that they were not advocating redundancy of approaches *other* than computational or computer-graphics processes. Key words like *improvement* and *collaboration* express their attitude toward the apparent rivalry between schools of technique, with *their* goal being one in which the artistic community, in a mutual exchange of knowledge, will serve the needs of "the software development stage" as artists offer shape, form, color, texture—and believability—to computational technique.

Automated 3D Facial Reconstruction

In part as a response to criticism of manual 3D facial reconstruction as subjective, time consuming, and overly invested with intuitive artistic expertise, forensic scientists have strived to employ computer imaging technology in the domain of facial reconstruction. Initially, the principles of computer-generated 3D FFR were derived from a system for the simultaneous visualization of soft and hard tissues to study changes in facial form in maxillofacial surgery. Vanezis and colleagues (2000) applied the developing 3D computer visualizing systems to FFR, modifying and upgrading the method utilizing a low-power laser scanner and video camera interfaced with a computer to produce more accurate facial reconstructions.

A computer-generated (semi-/fully automated) 3D FFR is commonly obtained by fitting one or more face templates to the skull to be reconstructed. Tilotta and colleagues (2009) suggested that there are two main approaches to the computer-generated 3D FFR: a "sparse approach," which is based on a set of anatomical landmarks placed on the face template, and a "dense approach" based on a complete template of both the face and the skull. The sparse approach is processed first via a set of landmarks on the face template that correspond to equivalent landmarks of the unidentified skull. Disagreement may exist between the face template and skull landmarks. Second, the correspondence of the two landmark sets is extended to connect between the landmark points, utilizing interpolation, which compensates for disagreements between landmarks on either object. Instead of utilizing the sparse (pointed) landmarks, the dense approaches employ dense (volumetric surface) placement of soft tissue. In these methods, the reference skull is mapped on the questioned skull by use of a registration technique—a deformable transform or "warping." The warping process converts the shape of the known reference skull to the same shape of the questioned skull. This means that each point on the questioned skull is matched to a corresponding point on the known skull. The deformation acquired from the skull registration is subsequently applied to the reference face, leading to an estimation of the questioned skull face. Turner and colleagues (2005: 150) said that "these methods are analogous to taking a rubber mask of the soft tissue and stretching it over the questioned skull."

The sparse approach technique has been developed by Vanezis and colleagues (1989): The target skull is scanned with a laser scanner and viewed by a video camera. The image from the camera is digitalized. During 3D skull imaging, craniofacial landmarks are placed, and the ancestry, sex, and age of the skull are assessed. A face that matches as closely as possible to that of the target skull is selected from a databank of previously scanned faces. The corresponding landmarks of the face relative to the skull are indicated with tissue depth markers. Now in the form of a mask, the facial image is superimposed onto the skull with respect to orientation, position, and scale. The tissue depth markers and corresponding skull landmarks are checked during the alignment process to avoid minor position shifts. The skin thickness and surface contour of the face are then altered using a 3D transformation program (warp), with consideration of determined facial soft tissue depth data that are "morphed" to the underlying target skull. Features such as open eyes, hairstyle, and facial hair can be added.

Following further development of the sparse method (Vanezis et al. 2000), employing an updated system constructed using a scripting language (TCL/Tk), the computer image could be exported as a solid model in stereolithography (STL) format. TCL stands for Tool Command Language, which is a scripting language commonly used for rapid prototyping. Tk is an open-source, cross-platform widget tool kit comprising a library of basic elements for building a graphic user interface (GUI). The research team reported a successful identification of a forensic case (confirmed by DNA profiling) making use of this method. Kähler and colleagues (2003) introduced a geometry-based muscle-modeling method integrating the facial deformation technique with 3D animation software to better facilitate creation of variable facial expressions in facial models. More recently, Claes and colleagues (2006) proposed a flexible statistical model to reduce the facial template-related bias and unrealistic facial appearance in the reconstructions.

The dense approach (Quatrehomme et al. 1997) involves collecting scans of two skulls (and facial soft tissue depths) with a CT scanner. Once the geometric 3D models of both skulls/faces are created, one set of skull and facial data is used as reference, while the other set is considered "unknown" (for the purpose of method validation). A global parametric transformation, implemented by generating a deformable transform (warping), is applied to change the shape of the reference skull into the skull to be reconstructed. The implemented algorithm in this research (Quatrehomme et al. 1997) is based on skull "crest lines." In other words, correspondences guiding the warping are automatically discerned by benefit of matching crest lines between the reference and questioned skulls. The algorithm calculated from the relationship between the two skulls is subsequently applied to the reference face to obtain the reconstructed face. This algorithmic method has been modified and improved by other researchers through manipulating a dense placement of soft tissue depths (Turner et al. 2005; Pei et al. 2008). A statistical shape model of both the skull and the face, instead of a single extrapolation of the deformation field (Berar et al. 2006), results in a reference database of densely sampled distances between skull and face (Vandermeulen et al. 2006).

Semi-/fully automated 3D FFR overcomes some of the shortcomings of the manual methods with increased efficiency, greater facial variation, and reduction in practitioner subjectivity. It does, however, have some drawbacks: Reconstructed faces are biased toward appearing like the template (generated) faces as the templates are usually derived from a limited database. In addition, in an attempt to eliminate subject-specific bias, the reconstructed face tends to look smooth and generic (Wilkinson 2005; Vandermeulen et al. 2006; Claes et al. 2006). To minimize these difficulties, De Greef and colleagues (2005, 2006) collected broadly based data from a specific ethnic group representing different ages and body builds and both sexes. Other researchers have also developed statistical average models by acquiring analysis from large and diverse databases (Claes et al. 2006). Significantly, few studies provided a report on the accuracy and reliability of the FFRs generated from computerized 3D methods. Claes and colleagues (2006) investigated the degree of the resemblance between computer-generated FFRs and target-scanned faces using "leave-one-out cross-validation tests," but it is doubtful that results can account for the criticism that no computerized facial approximation system has yet produced more reliable results than comparable manual methods (Wilkinson et al. 2006). Nevertheless, semi-/fully automated 3D FFR has progressed rapidly in the last few decades, and expectations are high for promising results in the future.

Computer-Generated 3D Modeling

Another approach to computer-generated FFR designed by Wilkinson (2003b) elaborated a "virtual sculpture" method utilizing a 3D computer modeling system (FreeForm Modelling Plus™ SensAble Technologies) with haptic feedback (Phantom Desktop™). Haptic devices are used in forensic investigations, engaging our tactile senses to shape and manipulate digitized 3D models in a noninvasive manner (Buck et al. 2008).

The modeling system in this FFR virtual technique mimics traditional 3D manual methods. The skull to be reconstructed is imported into FreeForm Plus as an STL file or as Digital Imaging and Communication in Medicine (DICOM) data. Once the skull is imported, operators are able to "feel" the surface of the skull in detail to determine the physical profile (ancestry, sex, and age) or to predict facial features from analysis of skull patterns or landmarks. The advantage of haptic feedback is that muscles, layer by layer, and skin can be visualized as separate units, with the "see-through" tool—a process not available in the manual method. The strengths of the computerized modeling method are reproducibility, time conservation, and little or no damage to the original specimen. The additions of skin texture, eyelid position, and hairstyle, as well as altering degrees of facial tissue depth, are quicker and easier to integrate with animation or other computerized programs.

As in the traditional 3D manual method, there are some disadvantages: Practitioners need training and experience to operate the systems skillfully, and artistic skills are essential to finish the facial reconstruction. Demands for computerized modeling have increased, especially in historical or archaeological facial reconstructions, for which realistic facial depictions are required. Using a laser scan image of a bronze head from the Bachhaus Museum, Wilkinson and Aitken (2009) reconstructed the face of J. S. Bach using the modeling method discussed. Benazzi and colleagues (Benazzi, Fantini, et al. 2009; Benazzi, Stansfield, et al. 2009) have employed these computerized modeling methods and integrated them with the technology of geometric morphometry in archaeological research. In the reconstruction of faces belonging to Dante Alighieri and Angelo Poliziano, missing portions of the fragmented cranium were reconstructed in virtual 3D.

Accuracy of Forensic Facial Reconstruction

From the time facial reconstruction was scientifically introduced to the world in the late 19th century by anatomist Wilhelm His (Wilkinson 2004), there has been a great deal of research into the reliability and accuracy of the techniques. On one hand, scientists argue that the techniques are too subjective and rely significantly on individual artistic skill, resulting in reconstructions that are inaccurate. On the other hand, some researchers insist that FFR demonstrates good levels of likeness—sufficient to be employed in forensic identification and justified if there are no other tools available to identify human remains. These conflicting points of view were reviewed by Wilkinson (2010).

Wilkinson and Whittaker (2002) reported optimistic results on the reliability of facial reconstruction. They employed five forensic cases from the West serial murder investigation in Gloucester, United Kingdom. The 3D facial reconstructions using the combination manual method were produced from five juvenile female skulls and then compared to a face pool by 50 assessors. The volunteers were asked to select a face from the face pool that most resembled each reconstruction. The mean hit rate was 44% (where the rate by chance was 10%), demonstrating that facial reconstruction can produce a good resemblance to an individual.

In contrast, Stephan and Henneberg (2001) investigated the accuracy and reliability of facial reconstruction of 16 reconstructed faces employing four skulls and four different 2D and 3D facial reconstruction methods. The facial reconstructions were then assessed by 37 volunteers with facial photographs in a face pool. Only one facial reconstruction showed true positive identification at above chance rate, and 403 incorrect identifications were made in 592 identification scenarios. The researchers maintained that facial approximation/reconstruction should be considered highly inaccurate and unreliable as a forensic identification technique.

Further accuracy studies on computer-generated facial reconstructions have been performed; Wilkinson and colleagues (2006) produced facial reconstructions from two CT-scanned skulls with a computer-generated 3D modeling system. Two reconstructed faces, a White male and female, were tested for accuracy employing face pool comparison methods. Assessors were asked to match the facial reconstruction to the face from a face pool of five CT-scanned faces (including the target face) that best resembled the target face. Results demonstrated that combined hit rates for both facial reconstructions were 50% above the level recorded by chance (20%). Researchers (Wilkinson et al. 2006) subsequently completed a morphometric comparison using 3D surface software (Rapidform™) to assess the quantitative accuracy of facial reconstructions. Results showed that 67% of the facial reconstruction surfaces had less than 2 mm error compared to the scanned target face, suggesting high validity for computerized facial reconstruction.

More recently, Quatrehomme and colleagues (2007) carried out an accuracy study using 25 3D facial reconstructions produced by a manual method. The subjects were divided into three groups. Two scientists took part in this study; one with no experience in the field reconstructed the faces of the first group (A) without the benefit of any information on methods of reconstruction. The other scientist trained in FFR produced the faces of the second group (B) with detailed anthropological analysis of the skull and facial tissue depth data. For the third group (C), the trained scientist assigned to Group B reconstructed the faces with the results of anthropological assessment and facial tissue depth data as in Group B but also utilized profile cephalometric radiographic images. Every reconstructed face was matched to a postmortem photograph of the target to evaluate accuracy by an independent scientist applying a graduated scale (three degrees of resemblance ranging from good to poor). Results demonstrated different performance rates across groups: 0% for Group A, 27% for Group B, and 75% for Group C. The researchers suggested that resemblance rate is improved in proportion to the experience of practitioners and the amount of information available to the reconstruction from skull analysis.

Claes and colleagues (2006) attempted to evaluate the accuracy and identification success rate from facial reconstructions issuing from automated computerized systems employing combined statistical models. Results demonstrated an average of 1.14 mm difference between the scanned target and the computer-generated face. The identification rate was 100% (based on Euclidean distance matrix [EDM] signatures of the facial surfaces in the database of 118 individuals). Identification success rate was 81.2% when employing a face pool comparison with 28 participants. However, this study must be viewed with caution as the researchers employed leave-one-out cross validation, which involved "predicting" the skull models from the 53 landmark soft tissue measurements only. In this way, the study did not include an actual test skull; it only tested the method against the same reverse-engineered technique and did not accurately reflect a forensic scenario.

Reviewing the studies on the accuracy of FFRs, it appears that there are disagreements between researchers over the levels of accuracy and their reliability. Claes and colleagues (2006) and Wilkinson (2010) pointed out that facial reconstruction is not a method of identification; the final goal is not complete accuracy in reconstruction but rather success in recognition. In assessing the limitations involved in assessing the accuracy of facial reconstructions, we are reminded that most successful facial reconstructions are recognized or identified by those familiar with the person in question, whereas current empirical accuracy tests are based on unfamiliar face recognition due to practical and ethical difficulties (Wilkinson 2010). It is established that people are much better at recognizing familiar faces than unfamiliar faces (Hancock et al. 2000). It is therefore suggested that the reliability of FFRs should be considered in light of the problems encountered in "measuring" success with accuracy tests. Nevertheless, recent research demonstrated an acceptable accuracy level for identification in both manual and computerized methods. Forensic cases have proved that the technique of facial reconstruction can be used to assist in the identification of individuals from unknown skulls, particularly when other forensic tools are unavailable (Van den Eerenbeemt 2001; South Wales Police Museum 2005; Algemeen 2009).

Assessment Methods for Accuracy Evaluation

There are a number of methods in use to evaluate the accuracy of FFR, and they may be divided into qualitative and quantitative assessments. Face pool and one-to-one matching comparisons are representative of the qualitative approach, in which participants are asked to identify a target individual from a range of faces in a pool or a single photograph of a face. Quantitative methods utilize numerical grading systems or specific computer software to measure the accuracy of facial reconstruction. The resemblance rating method directly compares the reconstructed face to the corresponding target face; assessors are asked to determine the degree of resemblance. The superimposition method overlays a facial reconstruction and a photograph of a target face (with computer software), comparing facial morphology and proportions. Wilkinson and colleagues (2006) employed a surface comparison method in FFR reliability research to assess the accuracy between facial reconstructions and CT or laser-scanned target heads. In this technique, the reconstructed face was overlaid with the scanned (target) face, and computer software compared 3D morphology to identify differences in surface contours between the two models. Claes and colleagues (2006) have also applied the 3D surface comparison method to evaluate the accuracy of computer-generated facial reconstructions.

The suitability of these methods for evaluating the accuracy of facial reconstruction is hotly debated. Stephan and Arthur (2006) and Stephan and Cicolini (2008) maintained that a resemblance rating assessment is an insensitive method as resemblance scores are not particularly discriminatory. They performed two experiments to establish the applicability of two accuracy tests: the resemblance rating and the face pool comparison. In the first experiment, both accuracy methods were engaged for the same facial reconstruction; results showed a poor true-positive recognition accuracy rate (21%) for the face pool comparison in relation to a resemblance rating (scored at three of five on a five-point scale test). The second experiment utilizing a resemblance rating method using three distractor faces from the same face array used in the first experiment revealed that there was no statistically significant difference in the resemblance scores between each side-by-side comparison of distractor faces to the target face and the facial reconstruction to the target face. The authors insisted that resemblance ratings generated from a five-point scale yield little value information in regard to accuracy tests of FFRs, and that the current scale for resemblance rating needs to be replaced with one that is more discriminating. They suggested that the face pool assessment method is a more appropriate tool for investigating facial reconstruction accuracy. On the other hand, Wilkinson and Whittaker (2002) stated that the usefulness of a resemblance rating assessment must not be underestimated, and that a best assessment can be produced using *both* face pool and resemblance rating systems. As mentioned by Wilkinson (2010), the extent to which facial reconstructions are directly responsible for recognition (and therefore identification) is somewhat obscured. Perhaps the issue of which methods are most useful in assessing the accuracy of FFRs should be considered based on the perceptual processing of human faces in cognitive psychology and different levels of artistic interpretation in practitioners.

Measurement of Facial Soft Tissue Thickness

In FFR, average facial soft tissue depth data sets indicate the thickness of soft tissue on any given area of a facial surface. All methods currently employed in facial reconstructions incorporate average tissue depth to estimate facial surface contours. Therefore, whichever FFR techniques are applied, average facial soft tissue depths are regarded as an important factor in accuracy. Taylor (2001) and Wilkinson (2004) illustrated in detail the early attempts at facial tissue depth research, such as needle puncture methods. In a needle puncture practice on cadavers, the most serious drawback is the loss of muscle tone and shrinkage after death, which may cause changes to the tissues and distortion of the skin surface (Manhein et al. 2000; Wilkinson 2002). Despite these recognized problems, cadaver studies are still employed in soft tissue depth research since measurements can be taken directly using a simple instrument at low cost, and researchers can measure at sites anywhere on the head (Simpson and Henneberg 2002; Domaracki and Stephan 2006; Galdames et al. 2007; Tedeschi-Oliveira et al. 2009; Codinha 2009). Two studies have compared fresh and embalmed soft tissue data (Simpson and Henneberg 2002, Galdames et al. 2008). Both studies found that embalming caused significant initial increases in tissue depth.

Taking advantage of rapid development in 3D medical diagnostic technologies, scientists have attempted noninvasive measuring of soft tissue depths in vivo. Lateral cephalometric radiographs have been used to measure soft tissue depths in the facial median plane since the 1980s. Although limited to collecting depths at midline landmarks, there is abundant data collected for orthodontic purposes. In addition, the measurements obtained at midline craniofacial landmarks are relatively accurate (Utsuno et al. 2005, 2007, 2010).

CT scanning (Kim et al. 2005; Vandermeulen et al. 2006; Tilotta et al. 2009) and MRI methods (Sahni et al. 2002, 2008) have also been employed to investigate average facial soft tissue depths. Beyond the potentially prohibitive cost of this technology, there are other problems associated with this method: A prone body position equates with distortion of tissue depth measurement due to gravity (especially at the cheek), and radiation exposure is a health risk for the subject during scanning. In contrast, ultrasonic equipment allows for an upright, seated scanning position and no health risk (Manhein et al. 2000; Wilkinson 2002; Smith and Throckmorton 2004). A number of studies on average facial soft tissue depth for various ethnic groups, age, and sex have been completed using the ultrasonic method (Manhein et al. 2000; El-Mehallawi and Soliman 2001; Wilkinson 2002; Smith and Throckmorton 2004; De Greef et al. 2006, 2009).

While it is true that an ultrasound-based system is an effective tool for the measurement of soft tissue depths, it also has drawbacks. As the underlying bony surface is not seen directly by the operator, an intended landmark point can be verified only by the transducer's orientation to the bone, which may cause measurement error. It is also difficult to reproduce the same measurement from a specific point on the skull. When manipulating the ultrasound pen, care is required not to indent tissue at the point of collection. Some researchers are exploring new approaches with recently developed cone-beam CT (CBCT) scanner and holographic topometry; combined with low-dose CT, images can be obtained with the subject in an upright position with a lower radiation dose than a typical multislice CT system (Prieels et al. 2009; Fourie et al. 2010). Further development of either of these two methods could mean the collection of more precise data for automated 3D FFR.

There is a dilemma in the placement of landmarks on hard and soft tissue because landmarks on specific points of the skull do not necessarily correspond to landmarks on the soft tissue. Brown and her colleagues (2004), in their review of previous publications, highlighted the need for the standardization of landmarks and definitions.

The majority of average facial soft tissue depth studies have examined White Europeans or Black Africans in European countries, Australia, or North America (Manhein et al. 2000; Simpson and Henneberg 2002; Wilkinson 2002; De Greef et al. 2006; Domaracki and Stephan 2006; Galdames et al. 2007; Tilotta et al. 2009). This is because FFRs are performed mostly in Europe and North America. Other groups in which there has been some research using ultrasound, cephaloradiography, MRI, and cadaver studies include Egyptian adults (El-Mehallawi and Soliman 2001), Japanese children (Utsuno et al. 2005, 2007), Northwest Indian adults (Sahni et al. 2008), and Brazilian adults (Tedeschi-Oliveira et al. 2009). Further research is required to provide more up-to-date facial soft tissue profiles across diverse groups.

It is usual for tissue depth data to be split by sex, ethnic group, and sometimes age. However, Stephan and Simpson (2008a, 2008b) reviewed existing data sets to establish the usefulness of subcategorization and the possibility of data combination. They found only minor differences between adult sexes and ethnic groups and recommended the use of pooled adult data (Stephan and Simpson 2008a). De Greef and colleagues (2009) evaluated the influence of sex on facial soft tissue depths but suggested caution when pooling male

with female data as sex differences in mouth and cheek tissues are significant. Stephan and Simpson (2008b) also reviewed juvenile data and found
that only two subdivisions relating to age were appropriate (0–11 years and
12–18 years); De Greef and his colleagues (2009) evaluated the influence of
BMI (body mass index) on facial soft tissue depths and found a strong correlation between the two parameters.

Several researchers have considered how overall craniofacial pattern
is related to the soft tissues. Simpson and Henneberg (2002) studied tissue
depths in relation to craniometry and found that skulls with larger craniometric dimensions had thicker soft tissues. Şatıroğlu and colleagues (2005)
studied the thickness of several muscles using ultrasound in relation to vertical facial pattern and found that individuals with thick masseter muscles had
short, wide faces, but that muscles of facial expression were not correlated to
vertical facial pattern.

Two studies have been carried out exploring the importance of tissue
depth data for craniofacial reconstruction (Wilkinson et al. 2002; Starbuck
and Ward 2007). The first study (Wilkinson et al. 2002) employed one
Caucasoid skull, three practitioners, and data sets from six different ethnic groups (White European, Black American, Native American, Korean,
Japanese, and mixed-race African). There were 247 volunteers who answered
questionnaires rating the resemblance of the reconstructions to the target
individual and to each other. The volunteers rated the White European and
mixed-race heads as most like the target, and 60% rated all the reconstructions as similar to each other. Structurally, the White European and mixed-
race heads were closest to the target individual (who was White European in
origin). The authors suggested that data from the correct ethnic group will
produce the most accurate reconstruction, but that data from a different ethnic group will not affect the face to the extent that it cannot be recognized.
The second study (Starbuck and Ward 2007) explored the importance of ema-
ciated, normal, and obese tissue depths to craniofacial reconstruction using
one Caucasoid skull and one practitioner. Results implied that observers frequently perceived the reconstructions as representing different individuals,
and that differences in facial fatness may blind observers to similarities in
facial form. The conclusion was that multiple reconstructions representing a
range of facial fatness might lead to more success in forensic investigations.

Prediction of Facial Features

Determination of the location, size, and morphology of facial features—
eyes, nose, mouth, and ears—are critical for accurate facial reconstruction. The greater part of feature prediction is based on an analysis of the
relation between skull structures and soft tissue components; the aim is to

establish reliable standards for individual feature prediction. Taylor (2001) and Wilkinson (2004) provided guidelines in skull analysis to estimate facial morphology and features.

Placement of eyeballs within orbits is one of the first procedures in facial rebuilding. Stephan (2002) explored whether the (then) existing eyeball protrusion guideline was acceptable using Caucasoid-type skulls and secondary data from related literature. Results from 28 measured adult skulls demonstrated that the average distance from the left lateral orbital rim to the tangent connecting the superior and inferior midsagittal orbital margins was 12.5 ± 1.5 mm. This value was less than the average globe projection (from the deepest point on the lateral orbital rim to the most anterior point of the cornea), at 16.2 ± 2.3 mm, as reported by 11 prior studies. This means that the traditional rule for the determination of eyeball protrusion, in which eyeballs project from the orbits so that the apex of the cornea touches a tangent from midsupraorbital to midinfraorbital margins, was *under*estimated by 4 mm (on average).

Research by Wilkinson and Mautner (2003) confirmed these conclusions with primary in vivo data. MRI scans of eyes from 78 White European adults were studied, and results demonstrated a significant correlation between eyeball protrusion and orbital depth. Eyeball position was shown to be as much as 3.9 mm too deep in the orbit; the exact relationship was calculated by the following formula: Eyeball Protrusion = 18.3 − (0.4 × Orbital Depth). They concluded that the eyeball is best positioned in the orbit so that a tangent taken from the superior to the inferior orbital margins touches the iris rather than the cornea.

In subsequent research using cadaver studies (Stephan and Davidson 2008; Stephan et al. 2009), the average globe projection was 15.9 mm (very close to the previous 11 studies at 16.2 ± 2.3 mm). It was determined that eyeballs are better positioned closer to the orbital roof and lateral orbital wall by approximately 1–2 mm on average, rather than in a central position within the orbits. Although the research by the Stephan group demonstrated an inherent limitation as a result of using cadavers rather than living subjects in data collection, it does suggest that the accepted rules for eyeball placement in facial reconstruction are less than ideal.

Nose shape, angle, and length have been much debated, remaining until recently a facial feature with low levels of reconstruction accuracy. It has been thought that the soft tissue of the nose is anatomically predictable, and researchers have attempted to estimate the shape of the nose from the analysis of the nasal bony aperture. Stephan and colleagues (2003) compared four guidelines for nose prediction using cephalograms of 59 White European Australians, concluding that two methods showed better performance than others. Results generated regression equations for calculating nose projection. Rynn and Wilkinson (2006) used 122 lateral head cephalograms of

Caucasoid subjects in an analysis of six methods (employed in previous studies), including four examined by Stephan and colleagues (2003). It was demonstrated that the most reliable and useful method of nasal tip prediction was the two-tangent method, as suggested by Gerasimov in 1955, in which the soft nose end is estimated from the point where a tangent line at the last part of the nasal bones intersects a line extending from the nasal spine.

In a subsequent study (Rynn et al. 2009), the accuracy of the two-tangent method was confirmed. CT head scans of 79 adult North Americans and blind tests using a sample of six skulls demonstrated that the nasal tip profile is related to the nasal aperture profile shape, and the maximum width of the nasal aperture is approximately three-fifths the maximum width of the soft nose. As asserted by Gerasimov (1955), the morphology of the nasal aperture is reflected in the soft nose form.

The mouth is key to the appearance of the face. Research on predicting mouth morphology from the skull has so far determined that mouth width relates to either interpupillary distance, the medial borders of the iris, or the lateral aspects of canine width. Wilkinson and colleagues (2003) reviewed previous studies on mouth prediction and tested traditional guidelines employing 191 volunteers. Subject faces with neutral facial expressions were collected with digital cameras and facial reference points measured with digital calipers. Results showed the interlimbus distance (between the medial borders of the iris) is the most reliable and accurate guideline in comparison to the interpupillary distance. Wilkinson and her colleagues (2003) suggested lip thickness is positively related to teeth height, generating formulae for thickness prediction in White European and Indian subcontinent subjects. Stephan and Henneberg (2003) employed photogrammetry of living subjects to study mouth width prediction, demonstrating that intercanine width is equivalent to 75.8% of mouth width. In a further study, Stephan and Murphy (2008) suggested a standard for edentulous skulls; the infraorbital foramen predicts the cheilion points. However, this study was carried out using cadavers, and it is uncertain whether embalmed subjects are wholly representative of the living, particularly as postmortem changes in the mouth and eyes are well documented.

It is not possible to predict with complete accuracy these facial components from a morphological skull assessment; some researchers maintained that practitioner experience and intuition influence the accuracy of facial reconstructions as much as the methods of prediction. There is therefore the tendency to believe certain "schools" of facial reconstruction operate beyond the bounds of science. As described, the prediction of facial features in the process of FFR is based on methods derived from scientific research that analyzed the relationship between the shape of individual soft tissue components and corresponding skull morphology. Wilkinson (2010) asserted that the majority of facial features can be determined from skull morphology with up to 67% accuracy.

Craniofacial Superimposition

Superimposition is a comparison between the antemortem photograph of an individual and an unidentified skull, although it may also be a method of facial comparison in the living (Oxlee 2007). Craniofacial superimposition has been used as a legally accepted method for identification since the Buck Ruxton case in 1937 (Glaister and Brash 1937) and is frequently used to confirm identity in difficult forensic investigations (Ross 2004; Fenton et al. 2008). Currently, craniofacial comparisons may be completed entirely within a video or computer software environment (Glassman 2001; Taylor 2001). However, there are few published accuracy studies for new craniofacial superimposition techniques. Stephan (2009) stated: "Presently, it is not possible to draw firm statements concerning the overarching performance of superimposition methods because formal published studies on the accuracy and reliability of the methods have been infrequent, have used small samples and have often not been replicated."

A recent review of craniofacial superimposition techniques was published (Damas et al. 2010) with an emphasis on automated systems. It described computer-based craniofacial superimposition processes and craniometric and cephalometric landmarks and made recommendations for future research. The authors described the process in three stages:

1. Acquisition of digital 3D model of the skull and enhancement of the face image. The face image/photograph will be acquired under fixed, unknown conditions, whereas the skull will be available as a physical object, and a 3D model will be acquired by the practitioner. Recent developments in imaging technology have allowed forensic experts to employ CT, laser scan, or holographic data (Ikeuchi and Sato 2001; Nakasima et al. 2005; Biwasaka et al. 2005; Fantini et al. 2008; Singare et al. 2009). Damas and colleagues (2010) explained the principles of laser scanning and the processing of the scans to construct the 3D model through cleaning, smoothing, filling, stitching, and registration (Ghosh and Sinha 2001; Ricci et al. 2006; Gonzalez and Woods 2008). Galantucci and colleagues (2006) described a comparison study between CT and laser scanning acquisition techniques and found that both methods delivered good levels of accuracy, but the CT data produced a cleaner model with shorter processing time and additional internal structure imaging. Damas and colleagues (2010) described the different methods of registration, including evolutionary

algorithms (Santamaría et al. 2007, 2009), point cloud merging (Benazzi, Stansfield, et al. 2009), and digital editing (Ballerini et al. 2007). While 3D skull images produced by scans offer the advantage of full-range-of-motion positioning during superimposition, some distortion in the reconstructed image is unavoidable. Difficulties the scanner experiences collecting data on images that are black, shiny, or especially convoluted in morphology contribute to inaccuracy, as do small variances in operator movement (as the wand is swept over the object) if scans are collected using handheld rather than automated devices (Park et al. 2006). Biwasaka and colleagues (2005) investigated and tested holographic production of 3D images for use in forensic superimposition, and this may well prove to be a superior system.

2. Manual or automatic skull-face overlay by matching correspond-ing landmarks. The orientation of the skull to match the position of the face in the image is key to the success of identification and is a challenging and time-consuming process. Damas and colleagues (2010) described the pre-2000 manual methods relying on cranio-facial landmark alignment and estimation of face size and orienta-tion through a mathematical procedure using dual projection, video overlay, or negative photographic prints. More recent methods using algorithms (Ricci et al. 2006) and photo-editing software (Bilge et al. 2003; Al-Amad et al. 2006) are also discussed, along with automated overlay methods such as artificial neural networks (Ghosh and Sinha 2001, 2008), genetic algorithms (Ballerini et al. 2007), real-coded evolutionary algorithms (Ibáñez et al. 2009), and fuzzy logic/land-marks (Santamaría et al. 2009). Facial and cranial anthropometric landmarks from the facial photograph and the skull image, respec-tively, are correlated with one another (Ibáñez et al. 2009). Overall "best fit" is guided, depending on whether the photograph is of the face in lateral or frontal view, by alignment of general shape, inferior and oblique mandible borders, interorbital breadth, orbital contours, nasal root width and depth, projection of nasal bones, nasal aper-ture width, total facial width and length, midface ratio in relation to upper and lower face length, vault and forehead height, teeth and dental sockets, and any discernible skull anomalies (adapted from Glassman 2001). In addition, when soft tissue depth markers are used, the relationship between the markers and the fleshy contours of the face are taken into consideration (Taylor 2001). As the facial position in the photograph cannot be changed, the skull position must change to align with the face in the photograph. Very small differences in the skull position relative to that of the face or head in the photograph dramatically affect the operator's ability to deter-mine match or exclusion (Glassman 2001). If 1:1 proportions for the

comparisons are part of the method, one image may be scaled to the other (which is representative of life-size scale); if 3D laser scanning of the skull is employed, the photograph may be scaled to the skull model as the laser produces a 1:1 proportioned image.

3. Identification decision. This may be by expert alone or with automatic decision support. Differences between the face and skull landmarks are calculated using Fourier harmonic analysis and polynomial functions (Damas et al. 2010) to support the interpretation of the expert. Despite the research focused on supporting the expert in the decision-making stage (Scully and Nambiar 2002; Ricci et al. 2006), there is alternative research (Jayaprakash et al. 2001) suggesting that visual assessment is more effective than metrical studies. When automated quantification and comparison of landmarks and facial features are possible, the degree of congruity between facial contours and soft tissue depths in relation to skull morphology remain, to some degree or another, a qualitative visual assessment. As a result, even when the probability of one skull having the same craniometric profile as another is one in many billions (Helmer et al. 1989), the analysis is still qualitative, and judgment is therefore ranked rather than absolute. Glassman (2001) used grades of 1 to 4 to define parameters for match analysis:
   - Grade 1 is a close match with strong concordance of all anatomical features; no areas dictate exclusion.
   - Grade 2 is a reasonable match with strong concordance in most anatomical features; no areas dictate exclusion.
   - Grade 3 is a comparison that cannot exclude a match, but it exhibits poor concordance and is unlikely to be a match.
   - Grade 4 is a definite exclusion.

Ibáñez and colleagues (2009) described these categories in the following alternate way: positive, likely positive, likely negative, negative identification.

The goal of image registration is to define a mapping process that can place a skull in the identical position in which a missing or unidentified person's face or head appears in an available photograph. The really difficult part of the superimposition—accurate alignment of facial image and skull image—is frustrated by a number of what the authors called "unknown transformation parameters" (as many as 12) originating from two different sources: camera configuration and the skull model. Those related to the collection of the camera configuration in antemortem photograph acquisition could include factors such as lighting, object distance, aperture, lens type, and general perspective. The skull model possesses unique specifications: 3D spatial position, resolution, and size.

Three previous identification cases solved via computer-assisted manual superimposition of 2D photograph and 3D skull model by forensic practitioners were attempted as trials, using two variants of algorithmic program genetic algorithms and a "state-of-the-art" (Ibáñez et al. 2009) adaptation evolution algorithm. Results were positive; the evolutionary method was better than the genetic algorithm method. In terms of the time required for the task, the fully automated evolutionary-based superimpositions were each done in less than 18 seconds, whereas the time taken to do the same alignment by manual-computer-assisted method is estimated at 24 hours. Visual comparison of the three examples of superimposition revealed that for the automated evolutionary alignment, one was better than the assisted, one was not as good, and the third was very similar. The researchers said superimposition quality achieved by the automated evolutionary method was "outstanding," although also still in need of improvement. They clearly saw that the time will come when the process will work exactly as they have promoted it—automatically, but subject to secondary checking and tweaking, faster than any manual or computer-assisted manual technique can ever manage and with equal, if not greater, accuracy.

Postmortem Depiction

The dearth of literature, theoretical or practical, on postmortem facial depiction in forensic science is a puzzle. Techniques for reconstituting the physiognomy of individuals, when decomposition or environmental exposure has rendered faces unrecognizable after death, remains an area of research largely unexamined. Decomposition is the destruction of tissues (Hill 2006); it is enacted by internal (chemical autolysis) or external factors (insects, carnivores, environmental) and is known collectively as *taphonomic processes* (Scheuer and Black 2007).

Postmortem facial depiction is most frequently employed by forensic artists, who utilize artistic ability, their knowledge of hard and soft tissue facial anatomy, and an understanding of the processes of body decomposition and taphonomic effects. A hand-drawn sketch or a computer-assisted resemblance of the individual face is produced in the hope that a public presentation results in recognition (Taylor 2001). When artifacts in association with the body are available (e.g., clothing, jewelry, evidence of hair type or style, or notable features of the head or face that may still be partially discernible), the artist is able to incorporate such information into the depiction. The forensic artist may work from photographs of grossly bloated, discolored, and distorted faces, often with missing facial features. If crime scene image collection is inadequate, further photographs should be taken at the mortuary or following exhumation (Taylor 2001).

Postmortem depiction is utilized for deaths that are natural, suicidal, or homicidal. In homicide fatalities, blunt or sharp trauma and gunshot wounds to the face are frequent. Extensive damage to the face also occurs as a result of accidents involving traffic, drowning, and fire (DiMaio and DiMaio 2001; Saukko and Knight 2004). A number of reliable descriptions of changes wrought by decomposition, including the effects of variant environments on that decomposition, have been documented over the last three decades; they inform and guide facial image depiction as the forensic artist attempts the closest approximation of an in vivo appearance of the deceased as possible.

Knowledge about a relatively rare product of body decay—adipocere—is limited. First identified in 1658, and subsequently studied from the latter part of the 18th century (Kumar et al. 2009), it was the focus of a study at the Anthropological Research Facility in Knoxville, Tennessee (O'Brien and Kuehner 2007). More recently, Kumar and colleagues (2009), in a combined case report and review of literature on adipocere formation on human remains, cited what they believed to be the earliest documented development of adipocere. The relevance to postmortem facial prediction is that facial features are preserved with little alteration to appearance, a condition favorable to reconstituting a desirable, publishable, sketched or computer-assisted facial depiction (O'Brien and Kuehner 2007).

Photographs of the deceased may, with the addition of skills in image manipulation and alteration utilizing photo-editing tools in software programs like Adobe Photoshop, allow the forensic artist to create a facial appearance acceptable for publication. The removal of mortuary or crime scene backgrounds from photographs, the editing of wounds, blood, and other substances from the face—in combination with a reduction of bloating and discoloration, which are then replaced with neutral tones, normalized contours, open eyes, and relaxed facial expression—can transform the most graphically damaged visage to one that may spark recognition. Databases of facial features amassed and classified by age, sex, and ethnicity can be pasted and blended as layers when insufficient clarity of detail in the damaged face promotes extrapolation of normalized appearance. It must be said, however, that the more distorted the postmortem image, the greater the need for experience and expertise with regard to decomposition—and the greater the demand for estimation and interpretation.

Data comparing differences in decomposition patterns that reflect sex, ethnicity, age, variant craniofacial shapes, and facial features are necessary. This reality is strikingly apparent when one considers the range in origins and ages of victims in mass disasters like the Bali bombing in 2002, the 2004 tsunami, and Hurricane Katrina in 2005. The psychological barriers encountered by friends and family who suffer through identifying loved ones in the aftermath of disasters (Hill 2006) are compounded by the complications that decomposition in hot climates imposes (Lessig et al. 2006), as evidenced by the 50% false visual recognition rate of victims by families in the Bali bombing (Lain et al. 2003).

Conclusion

In the effort to establish effective evaluations of facial reconstruction accuracy and the most reliable methods for predictive feature models, the need for a cooperative balance between art and science must be acknowledged. By embracing the increasingly multidisciplinary nature of FFR, which demands rigor in science *and* the experienced interpretations of practitioners, the ultimate goals of FFR—providing legal and medical identification of unknown individuals—will best be served.

As researchers cited here agreed, a lot of work remains to be done: The effects of ageing, genetics, environment, hormones, and diet on the face must be further explored; identifying and incorporating human cognitive recognition pattern responses may yield better-informed presentations of facial depictions to the public. Increased diversity in the availability of population tissue depth data sets will add to the reconstruction practitioner's tool set, and the sophistication of semi- and fully automated computer techniques will benefit from applications creating greater realism of surface textures and facial features.

References

Al-Amad, S., McCullough, M., Graham, J., Clement, J., and Hill, A. (2006). Craniofacial identification by computer-mediated superimposition. *Journal of Forensic Odonto-Stomatology*, 24 (2): 47–52.

Algemeen. (2009). *Vader Maasmeisje overleden in gevangenis.* Available at http://www.nu.nl/algemeen/1962980/vader-maasmeisje-overleden-in-gevangenis.html. Accessed June 28, 2010.

Ballerini, L., Cordon, O., Santamaría, J., Damas, S., Aleman, I., and Botella, M. (2007). Craniofacial superimposition in forensic identification using genetic algorithms. *Proceedings—IAS 2007 Third International Symposium on Information Assurance and Security*, art. no. 4299811: 429–434.

Benazzi, S., Bertelli, P., Lippi, B., Bedini, E., Caudana, R., Gruppioni, G., and Mallegni, F. (2010). Virtual anthropology and forensic arts: The facial reconstruction of Ferrante Gonzaga. *Journal of Archaeological Science*, 37 (7): 1572–1578.

Benazzi, S., Fantini, M., De Crescenzio, F., Mallegni, G., Mallegni, F., Persiani, F., and Gruppioni, G. (2009). The face of the poet Dante Alighieri reconstructed by virtual modelling and forensic anthropology techniques. *Journal of Archaeological Science*, 36 (2): 278–283.

Benazzi, S., Stansfield, E., Milani, C., and Gruppioni, G. (2009). Geometric morphometric methods for three-dimensional virtual reconstruction of a fragmented cranium: The case of Angelo Poliziano. *International Journal of Legal Medicine*, 123 (4): 333–344.

Berar, M., Desvignes, M., Bailly, G., and Payan, Y. (2006). 3D semi-landmarks-based statistical face reconstruction. *Journal of Computing and Information Technology*, 14 (1): 31–43.

Bilge, Y., Kedici, P. S., Alakoç, Y. D., Ülküer, K. Ü., and Ilkyaz, Y. Y. (2003). The identification of a dismembered human body: A multidisciplinary approach. *Forensic Science International*, 137 (2–3): 141–146.

Biwasaka, H., Saigusa, K., and Aoki, Y. (2005). The applicability of holography in forensic application: A fusion of the traditional optical technique and digital technique. *Journal of Forensic Science*, 50 (2): 1–7.

Brown, R. E., Kelliher, T. P., Tu, P. H., Turner, W. D., Taister, M. A., and Miller, K. W. P. (2004). A survey of tissue-depth landmarks for facial approximation. *Forensic Science Communication*, 6 (1). Available at http://www2.fbi.gov/hq/lab/fsc/backissu/jan2004/research/2004_01_research02.htm. Accessed June 28, 2010.

Buck, U., Naether, S., Braun, M., and Thali, M. (2008). Haptics in forensics: The possibilities and advantages in using the haptic device for reconstruction approaches in forensic science. *Forensic Science International*, 180 (2–3): 86–92.

Cattaneo, C. (2007). Forensic anthropology: Developments of a classical discipline in the new millennium. *Forensic Science International*, 165 (2–3): 185–193.

Cesarani, F., Martina, M. C., Grilletto, R., Boano, R., Roveri, A. M. D., Capussotto, V., Giuliano, A., Celia, M., and Gandini, G. (2004). Facial reconstruction of a wrapped Egyptian mummy using MDCT. *American Journal of Roentgenology*, 183 (3): 755–758.

Claes, P., Vandermeulen, D., De Greef, S., Willems, G., and Suetens, P. (2006). Craniofacial reconstruction using a combined statistical model of face shape and soft tissue depths: Methodology and validation. *Forensic Science International*, 159 (Suppl.): S147–S158.

Clement, J. G., and Marks, M. K. (Eds.). (2005) *Computer-graphic facial reconstruction*. Amsterdam: Elsevier.

Codinha, S. (2009). Facial soft tissue thicknesses for the Portuguese adult population. *Forensic Science International*, 184 (1–3): 80.e1–80.e7.

Damas, S., Cordon, O., Ibanez, O., Santamar J., Aleman, I., Botella, M., and Navarro, F. (2010). *Forensic identification by computer-aided craniofacial superimposition: A survey*. Technical report, European Centre for Soft Computing, Mieres, Spain. Available at http://www.uhu.es/estylf2010/trabajos/SS08–04.pdf. Accessed June 28, 2010.

Davy, S. L., Gilbert, T., Schofield, D., and Evison, M. P. (2005). Forensic facial reconstruction using computer modeling software. In Clement, J. C., and Marks, M. K. (Eds.), *Computer-graphic facial reconstruction*, Burlington, MA: Elsevier. pp. 183–196.

De Greef, S., Claes, P., Mollemans, W., Loubele, M., Vandermeulen, D., Suetens, P., and Willems, G. (2005). Semi-automated ultrasound facial soft tissue depth registration: Method and validation. *Journal of Forensic Sciences*, 50 (6): 1282–1288.

De Greef, S., Claes, P., Vandermeulen, D., Mollemans, W., Suetens, P., and Willems, G. (2006). Large-scale in-vivo Caucasian facial soft tissue thickness database for craniofacial reconstruction. *Forensic Science International*, 159 (1): S126–S146.

De Greef, S., Vandermeulen, D., Claes, P., Suetens, P., and Willems, G. (2009). The influence of sex, age and body mass index on facial soft tissue depths. *Forensic Science, Medicine and Pathology*, 5 (2): 60–65.

De Greef, S., and Willems, G. (2005). Three-dimensional cranio-facial reconstruction in forensic identification: Latest progress and new tendencies in the 21st century. *Journal of Forensic Science*, 50 (1): 12–17.

DiMaio, V. J., and DiMaio, D. (2001). *Forensic pathology* (2nd ed.). Boca Raton, FL: CRC Press.

Domaracki, M., and Stephan, C. N. (2006). Facial soft tissue thicknesses in Australian adult cadavers. *Journal of Forensic Sciences*, 51 (1): 5–10.

El-Mehallawi, I. H., and Soliman, E. M. (2001). Ultrasonic assessment of facial soft tissue thicknesses in adult Egyptians. *Forensic Science International*, 117 (1–2): 99–107.

Fantini, M., De Crescenzio, F., Persiani, F., Benazzi, S., and Gruppioni, G. (2008). 3D restitution, restoration and prototyping of a medieval damaged skull. *Rapid Prototyping Journal*, 14 (5): 318–324.

Fedosyutkin, B. A., and Nainys, J. V. (1993). The relationship of skull morphology to facial features. In İşcan, M. Y., and Helmer, R. P. (Eds.), *Forensic analysis of the skull: Craniofacial analysis, reconstruction and identification*. New York: Wiley-Liss, pp. 199–213.

Fenton, T. W., Heard, A. N., and Sauer, N. J. (2008). Skull-photo superimposition and border deaths: Identification through exclusion and the failure to exclude. *Journal of Forensic Sciences*, 53 (1): 34–40.

Fourie, Z., Damstra, J., Gerrits, P. O., and Ren, Y. (2010). Accuracy and reliability of facial soft tissue depth measurements using cone beam computer tomography. *Forensic Science International*, 199 (1–3): 9–14.

Galantucci, L. M., Percoco, G., Angelelli, G., Lopez, C., Introna, F., Liuzzi, C., and De Donno, A. (2006). Reverse engineering techniques applied to a human skull, for CAD 3D reconstruction and physical replication by rapid prototyping. *Journal of Medical Engineering and Technology*, 30 (2): 102–111.

Galdames, I. C. S., López, M. C., Matamala, D. A. Z., Rojas, F. J. P., and Muñoz, S. R. T. (2008). Comparisons in soft-tissue thicknesses on the human face in fresh and embalmed corpses using needle puncture method. *International Journal of Morphology*, 26 (1): 165–169.

Galdames, I. C. S., Rojas, F. J. P., and Muñoz, S. R. T. (2007). Tissue thickness in Spanish corpses and their applications on the medicolegal identification. *International Journal of Morphology*, 25 (1): 109–116.

Gaytán, E., Mansilla-Lory, J., Leboreiro, I., and Pineda, S. C. (2009). Facial reconstruction of a pathological case. *Forensic Science, Medicine and Pathology*, 5 (2): 95–99.

Gerasimov, M. M. (1955). *The reconstruction of the face from the basic structure of the skull* (Tshernezky, W, Trans.). Russia: Publisher unknown.

Ghosh, A. K., and Sinha, P. (2001). An economised craniofacial identification system. *Forensic Science International*, 117 (1–2): 109–119.

Ghosh, A. K., and Sinha, P. (2008). An unusual case of cranial image recognition. *Forensic Science International*, 148 (2–3): 93–100.

Gill-Robinson, H., Elias, J., Bender, F., Allard, T. T., and Hoppa, R. D. (2006). Using image analysis software to create a physical skull model for the facial reconstruction of a wrapped Akhmimic mummy. *Journal of Computing Information Technology*, 14 (1): 45–51.

Glaister, J., and Brash, J. C. (1937) *Medicolegal aspects of Ruxton case*. Edinburgh: E & S Livingstone.

Glassman, D. M. (2001). Methods of superimposition. In Taylor, K. T. (Ed.), *Forensic art and Illustration*. Boca Raton, FL: CRC Press, pp. 477–498.

Gonzalez, R. C., and Woods, R. E. (2008). *Digital image processing* (3rd ed.). Upper Saddle River, NJ: Prentice Hall.

Gregersen, M., Boldsen, J., Björn, H., Boel, L. W., and Fromholt, P. (2006). Examination and identification of a Danish 17th-century nobleman, Laurids Ebbesen: A multidisciplinary study. *Forensic Science, Medicine, and Pathology*, 2 (1): 51–58.

Hancock, P. J., Bruce, V. V., and Burton, A. M. (2000). Recognition of unfamiliar faces. *Trends in Cognitive Sciences*, 4 (9): 330–337.

Helmer, R. P., Schimmler, J. B., and Rieger, J. (1989). On the conclusiveness of skull identification via the video superimposition technique. *Canadian Society of Forensic Science*, 22 (2): 177–194.

Hill, I. (2006) Physical Appearance. Chapter 5, In Thompson, T., and Black, S. (Eds.), *Forensic human identification: An introduction*. Boca Raton, FL: CRC Press, pp. 365–378.

Ibáñez, O., Ballerini, L., Cordón, O., Damas, S., and Santamaría, J. (2009). An experimental study on the applicability of evolutionary algorithms to craniofacial superimposition in forensic identification. *Information Sciences*, 179: 3998–4028.

Ikeuchi, K., and Sato, Y. (2001). *Modeling from reality*. Norwell, MA: Kluwer Academic.

İşcan, M. Y. (2001). Global forensic anthropology in the 21st century. *Forensic Science International*, 117: 1–6.

İşcan, M. Y., and Helmer, R. P. (1993). *Forensic analysis of the skull: Craniofacial analysis, reconstruction and identification*, eds. New York: Wiley-Liss.

Ismail, N. A. (2008). Computerised 3D craniofacial remodelling of incomplete skulls: The effect on facial reconstruction. Unpublished MSc human identification dissertation, University of Dundee, Scotland.

Jayaprakash, P. T., Srinivasan, G. J., and Amravaneswaran, M. G. (2001). Craniofacial morphanalysis: A new method for enhancing reliability while identifying skulls by photo superimposition. *Forensic Science International*, 117 (1–2): 121–143.

Kähler, K., Haber, J., and Seidel, H.-P. (2003). Reanimating the dead: Reconstruction of expressive faces from skull data. *ACM Transactions on Graphics*, 22 (3): 554–561.

Kim, K. D., Ruprecht, A., Wang, G., Lee, J. B., Dawson, D. V., and Vannier, M. W. (2005). Accuracy of facial soft tissue thickness measurements in personal computer-based multiplanar reconstructed computed tomographic images. *Forensic Science International*, 155 (1): 28–34.

Krogman, W. M., and İşcan, M. Y. (1986). *The human skeleton in forensic medicine* (2nd ed.). Springfield, IL: Thomas.

Kumar, T. S. M., Monteiro, F. N. P., Bhagavath, P., and Bakkannavar, S. M. (2009). Early adipocere formation: A case report and review of literature. *Journal of Forensic and Legal Medicine*, 16: 475–477.

Kustár, À. (2004). The facial restoration of Antal Simon, a Hungarian priest-teacher of the 19th century. *Homo*, 55 (1–2): 77–90.

Lain, R., Griffiths, C., and Hilton, J. M. N. (2003). Forensic dental and medical response to the Bali Bombing: A personal perspective. *Medical Journal of Australia*, 179 (7): 362–365.

Lee, I. S., Kim, M. J., Yoo, D. S., Lee, Y. S., Park, S. S., Bok, G. D., Han, S. H., Chung, Y. H., Chang, B. S., Yi, Y. S., Oh, C. S., and Shin, D. H. (2007). Three-dimensional reconstruction of a medieval child mummy in Yangje Korea, using multi-detector computed tomography. *Annals of Anatomy*, 189 (6): 558–568.

Lessig, R., Grundmann, C., Dahlmann, F., Rötzscher, K., Edelmann, J., and Schneider, P. M. (2006). Tsunami 2004: A review of one year of continuous forensic medical work for victim identification. *Journal of Experimental and Clinical Sciences, International Online Journal for Advances in Sciences*, 5: 128–139.

Lynnerup, N. (2009). Medical imaging of mummies and bog bodies. *Gerontology*, December 11, doi: 10.1159/000266031.

Mackenzie, S. (2007). An evaluation of computer assisted skull re-assembly using hand held and automated laser scanners. Unpublished MSc human identification dissertation, University of Dundee, Scotland.

Manhein, M. H., Listi, G. A., Barsley, R. E., Musselman, R., Barrow, N. E., and Ubelaker, D. H. (2000). In vivo facial tissue depth measurements for children and adults. *Journal of Forensic Sciences*, 45 (1): 48–60.

Nakasima, A., Terajima, M., Mori, N., Hoshino, Y., Tokumori, K., Aoki, Y., and Hashimoto, S. (2005). Three-dimensional computer-generated head model reconstructed from cephalograms, facial photographs, and dental cast models. *American Journal of Orthodontics and Dentofacial Orthopedics*, 127 (3): 282–292.

O'Brien, T. G., and Kuehner, A. C. (2007). Waxing grave about adipocere: Soft tissue change in an aquatic context. *Journal of Forensic Science*, 52 (2): 294–301.

Oxlee, G. (2007). Facial recognition and imagery analysis. In Thompson, T., and Black, S. (Eds.), *Forensic human identification: An introduction*. Boca Raton, FL: CRC Press, pp. 257–270.

Park, H. K., Chung, J. W., and Kho, H. S. (2006). Use of hand-held laser scanning in the assessment of craniometry. *Forensic Science International*, 160: 200–206.

Pei, Y., Zha, H., and Yuan, Z. (2008). The craniofacial reconstruction from the local structural diversity of skulls. *Computer Graphics Forum*, 27 (7): 1711–1718.

Prieels, F., Hirsch, S., and Hering, P. (2009). Holographic topometry for a dense visualization of soft tissue for facial reconstruction. *Forensic Science, Medicine and Pathology*, 5 (1): 11–16.

Quatrehomme, G., Balaguer, T., Staccini, P., and Alunni-Perret, V. (2007). Assessment of the accuracy of three-dimensional manual craniofacial reconstruction: A series of 25 controlled cases. *International Journal of Legal Medicine*, 121 (6): 469–475.

Quatrehomme, G., Cotin, S., Subsol, G., Delingette, H., Garidel, Y., Grévin, G., Fidrich, M., Bailet, P., and Ollier, A. (1997). A fully three-dimensional method for facial reconstruction based on deformable models. *Journal of Forensic Sciences,* 42 (4): 649–652.

Ricci, A., Marella, G. L., and Apostol, M. A. (2006). A new experimental approach to computer-aided face/skull identification in forensic anthropology. *American Journal of Forensic Medicine and Pathology,* 27 (1): 46–49.

Ross, A. H. (2004). Use of digital imaging in the identification of fragmentary human skeletal remains: A case from the Republic of Panama. *Forensic Science Communications,* 6 (4). Available at http://www.fbi.gov/hq/lab/fsc/backissu/oct2004/case/2004_10_case01.htm. Accessed June 28, 2010.

Rynn, C., and Wilkinson, C. M. (2006). Appraisal of traditional and recently proposed relationships between the hard and soft dimensions of the nose in profile. *American Journal of Physical Anthropology,* 130 (3): 364–373.

Rynn, C., Wilkinson, C. M., and Peters, H. L. (2009). Prediction of nasal morphology from the skull. *Forensic Science, Medicine, and Pathology,* 6 (1): 20–34.

Sahni, D., Jit, I., Gupta, M., Singh, P., Suri, S., Sanjeev, and Kaur, H. (2002). Preliminary study on facial soft tissue thickness by magnetic resonance imaging in northwest Indians. *Forensic Science Communication,* 4: 1–7.

Sahni, D., Sanjeev, Singh, G., Jit, I., and Singh, P. (2008). Facial soft tissue thickness in northwest Indian adults. *Forensic Science International,* 176 (2–3): 137–146.

Santamaría, J., Cordón, O., and Damas, S. (2007). Evolutionary approaches for automatic 3D modeling of skulls in forensic identification. *Lecture Notes in Computer Science (including subseries Lecture Notes in Artificial Intelligence and Lecture Notes in Bioinformatics),* 4448 LNCS: 415–422.

Santamaría, J., Cordon, O., Damas, S., and Ibanez, O. (2009). Tackling the coplanarity problem in 3D camera calibration by means of fuzzy landmarks: A performance study in forensic craniofacial superimposition. In *Proceedings of the 12th International Conference on Computer Vision, IEEE International Workshop on 3-D Digital Imaging and Modeling,* Kyoto, Japan, 1686–1693.

Şatıroğlu, F., Arun, T., and Işık, F. (2005). Comparative data on facial morphology and muscle thickness using ultrasonography. *European Journal of Orthodontics,* 27 (6): 562–567.

Saukko, P., and Knight, B. (2004) *Knight's forensic pathology* (3rd ed.). London: Arnold.

Scheuer, L., and Black, S. (2007). Osteology. In Thompson, T., and Black, S. (Eds.), *Forensic human identification: An introduction.* Boca Raton, FL: CRC Press, pp. 199–219.

Scully, B., and Nambiar, P. (2002). Determining the validity of Furue's method of craniofacial superimposition for identification. *Malaysian Journal of Computer Science,* 9 (1): 17–22.

Sherman, W. R., and Craig, A. B. (2003). *Understanding virtual reality interface, application, and design.* San Francisco: Morgan Kaufmann.

Simpson, E., and Henneberg, M. (2002). Variation in soft-tissue thicknesses on the human face and their relation to craniometric dimensions. *American Journal of Physical Anthropology,* 118 (2): 121–133.

Singare, S., Lian, Q., Wang, W. P., Wang, J., Liu, Y., Li, D., and Lu, B. (2009). Rapid prototyping assisted surgery planning and custom implant design. *Rapid Prototyping Journal,* 15 (1): 19–23.

Smith, S. L., and Throckmorton, G. S. (2004). A new technique for three-dimensional ultrasound scanning of facial tissues. *Journal of Forensic Sciences*, 49 (3): 451–457.

South Wales Police Museum (2005). *A chronology of 50 years of policing Cardiff's Capital.* Available at http://www.southwalespolicemuseum.org.uk/en/content/cms/visit_the_archives/50_years of_policing/50_years_of_policing.aspx. Accessed June 28, 2010.

Starbuck, J. M., and Ward, R. E. (2007). The affect of tissue depth variation on craniofacial reconstructions. *Forensic Science International*, 172 (2–3): 130–136.

Stephan, C. N. (2002). Facial approximation: Globe projection guideline falsified by exophthalmometry literature. *Journal of Forensic Sciences*, 47 (4): 730–735.

Stephan, C. N. (2009). Craniofacial identification: Method, background and overview. Available at http//www.craniofacialidentification.com. Accessed June 28, 2010.

Stephan, C. N., and Arthur, R. (2006). Assessing facial approximation accuracy: How do resemblance ratings of disparate faces compare to recognition tests? *Forensic Science International*, 159 (Suppl. 1): 159–163.

Stephan, C. N., and Cicolini, J. (2008). Measuring the accuracy of facial approximations: A comparative study of resemblance rating and face array methods. *Journal of Forensic Sciences*, 53 (1): 58–64.

Stephan, C. N., and Davidson, P. L. (2008). The placement of the human eyeball and canthi in craniofacial identification. *Journal of Forensic Sciences*, 53 (3): 612–619.

Stephan, C. N., and Henneberg, M. (2001). Building faces from dry skulls: Are they recognized above chance rates? *Journal of Forensic Sciences*, 46 (3): 432–440.

Stephan, C. N., and Henneberg, M. (2003). Predicting mouth width from inter-canine width—A 75% rule. *Journal of Forensic Sciences*, 48 (4): 725–727.

Stephan, C. N., and Murphy, S. J. (2008). Mouth width prediction in craniofacial identification: Cadaver tests of four recent methods, including two techniques for edentulous skulls. *Journal of Forensic Odonto-Stomatology*, 26 (1): 2–7.

Stephan, C. N., Henneberg, M., and Sampson, W. (2003). Predicting nose projection and pronasale position in facial approximation: A test of published methods and proposal of new guidelines. *American Journal of Physical Anthropology,* 122 (3): 240–250.

Stephan, C. N., Penton-Voak, I. S., Clement, J. G., and Henneberg, M. (2005). Ceiling recognition limits of two-dimensional facial approximations constructed using averages. In Clement, J. G., and Marks, M. K. (Eds.), *Computer-graphic facial reconstruction*, Burlington, MA: Elsevier. pp. 199–219.

Stephan, C. N, Penton-Voak, I. S., Perrett, D. I., Tiddeman, B. P., Clement, J. G., and Henneberg, M. (2005). Two-dimensional computer-generated average human face morphology and facial approximation. In Clement, J. G., and Marks, M. K. (Eds.), *Computer-graphic facial reconstruction*, pp. 105–127.

Stephan, C. N., and Simpson, E. K. (2008a). Facial soft tissue depths in craniofacial identification (Part I): An analytical review of the published adult data. *Journal of Forensic Sciences*, 53 (6): 1257–1272.

Stephan, C. N., and Simpson, E. K. (2008b). Facial soft tissue depths in craniofacial identification (Part II): An analytical review of the published sub-adult data. *Journal of Forensic Sciences*, 53 (6): 1273–1279.

Stephan, C. N., Huang, A. J. R., and Davidson, P. L. (2009). Further evidence on the anatomical placement of the human eyeball for facial approximation and craniofacial superimposition. *Journal of Forensic Sciences*, 54 (2): 267–269.

Taylor, K. T. (2001). *Forensic art and illustration*. Boca Raton, FL: CRC Press.

Tedeschi-Oliveira, S. V., Melani, R. F. H., de Almeida, N. H., and de Paiva, L. A. S. (2009). Facial soft tissue thickness of Brazilian adults. *Forensic Science International*, 193 (1–3): 127.e1–127.e7.

Tilotta, F., Richard, F., Glaunès, J., Berar, M., Gey, S., Verdeille, S., Rozenholc, Y., and Gaudy, J. F. (2009). Construction and analysis of a head CT-scan database for craniofacial reconstruction. *Forensic Science International*, 191 (1–3): 112.e1–112.e12.

Turner, W. D., Brown, R. E. B., Kelliher, T. P., Tu, P. H., Taister, M. A., and Miller, K. W. P. (2005). A novel method of automated skull registration for forensic facial approximation. *Forensic Science International*, 154 (2–3): 149–158.

Ubelaker, D. H. (2005). Review of: *Forensic Facial Reconstruction*. *Journal of Forensic Science*, 50 (1): 1.

Utsuno, H., Kageyama, T., Deguchi, T., Umemura, Y., Yoshino, M., Nakamura, H., Miyazawa, H., and Inoue, K. (2007). Facial soft tissue thickness in skeletal type I Japanese children. *Forensic Science International*, 172 (2–3): 137–143.

Utsuno, H., Kageyama, T., Deguchi, T., Yoshino, M., Miyazawa, H., and Inoue, K. (2005). Facial soft tissue thickness in Japanese female children. *Forensic Science International*, 152 (2–3): 101–107.

Utsuno, H., Kageyama, T., Uchida, K., Yoshino, M., Oohigashi, S., Miyazawa, H., and Inoue, K. (2010). Pilot study of facial soft tissue thickness differences among three skeletal classes in Japanese females. *Forensic Science International*, 195 (1–3): 165.e1–165.e5.

Van den Eerenbeemt, M. (2001). "Van Nulde" krijgt gezicht. De Volkskrant. October 16, 2001, updated January 20, 2009. Available at http://www.volkskrant.nl/archief_gratis/article907549.ece/Meisje_van_Nulde_krijgt_gezicht. Accessed June 28, 2010.

Vandermeulen, D., Claes, P., Loeckx, D., De Greef, S., Willems, G., and Suetens, P. (2006). Computerized craniofacial reconstruction using CT-derived implicit surface representations. *Forensic Science International*, 159 (1): S164–S174.

Vanezis, P., Blowes, R. W., Linney, A. D., Tan, A. C., Richards, R., and Neave, R. (1989). Application of 3-D computer graphics for facial reconstruction and comparison with sculpting techniques. *Forensic Science International*, 42 (1–2): 69–84.

Vanezis, M., and Vanezis, P. (2000). Cranio-facial reconstruction in forensic identification: Historical development and a review of current practice. *Medicine, Science and the Law*, 40 (3): 197–205.

Vanezis, P., Vanezis, M., McCombe, G., and Niblett, T. (2000). Facial reconstruction using 3-D computer graphics. *Forensic Science International*, 108 (2): 81–95.

Verzé, L. (2009). History of facial reconstruction. *Acta Biomedica*, 80: 5–12.

Wilkinson, C. M. (2002). In vivo facial tissue depth measurements for white British children. *Journal of Forensic Sciences*, 47 (3): 459–465.

Wilkinson, C. M. (2003a). The facial reconstruction of the Marina El-Alamein Mummy. *Polish Archaeology in the Mediterranean XIV Reports 2002*, Warsaw University, 66–71.

Wilkinson, C. M. (2003b). Virtual sculpture as a method of computerized facial reconstruction. *Proceedings of the First International Conference on Reconstruction of Soft Facial Parts,* Potsdam, Germany, 59–63.

Wilkinson, C. M. (2004). *Forensic Facial Reconstruction,* UK, Cambridge University Press.

Wilkinson, C. M. (2005). Computerized forensic facial reconstruction: A review of current systems. *Forensic Science, Medicine and Pathology,* 1 (3): 173–177.

Wilkinson, C. M. (2007a). Facial anthropology and reconstruction. In Thompson, T., and Black, S. (Eds.), *Forensic human identification: An introduction.* Boca Raton, FL: CRC Press, pp. 231–256.

Wilkinson, C. M. (2007b). Facial reconstruction of Grauballe man. In Asingh, P., and Lynnerup, N. (Eds.), *Grauballe man—An Iron Age bog body revisited.* Jutland Archaeological Society, Moesgaard, Denmark, pp. 260–273.

Wilkinson, C. M. (2008). The facial reconstruction of ancient Egyptians. In David, R. (Ed.), *Egyptian mummies and modern science.* Cambridge, UK: Cambridge University Press, pp. 162–180.

Wilkinson, C. M. (2010). Facial reconstruction—Anatomical art or artistic anatomy? *Journal of Anatomy,* 216(2): 235–250.

Wilkinson, C. M., and Aitken, J. (2009). The face of Bach. Abstracts from IACI 2008 conference. *Journal of Forensic Science, Medicine, and Pathology,* 5: 47–55.

Wilkinson, C. M., and Mautner, S. A. (2003). Measurement of eyeball protrusion and its application in facial reconstruction. *Journal of Forensic Sciences,* 48 (1): 12–16.

Wilkinson, C. M., Motwani, M., and Chiang, E. (2003). The relationship between the soft tissues and the skeletal detail of the mouth. *Journal of Forensic Sciences,* 48 (4): 728–732.

Wilkinson, C. M., and Neave, R. A. H. (2001). Skull re-assembly and the implications for forensic facial reconstruction. *Science and Justice,* 41 (3): 5–6.

Wilkinson, C. M., and Neave, R. A. H. (2003). The reconstruction of a face showing a healed wound. *Journal of Archaeological Science,* 30 (10): 1343–1348.

Wilkinson, C. M., Neave, R. A. H., and Smith, D. S. (2002). How important to facial reconstruction are the correct ethnic group tissue depths? *Proceedings of the 10th Conference of the International Association of Craniofacial Identification (IACI),* September 11–14, Bari, Italy, 111–121.

Wilkinson, C. M., Rynn, C., Peters, H., Taister, M., Kau, C. H., and Richmond, S. (2006). A blind accuracy assessment of computer-modeled forensic facial reconstruction using computed tomography data from live subjects. *Forensic Science, Medicine, and Pathology,* 2 (3): 179–188.

Wilkinson, C. M., and Whittaker, D. K. (2002). Juvenile forensic facial reconstruction: a detailed accuracy study. *Proceedings of the 10th Conference of the International Association of Craniofacial Identification (IACI),* September 11–14, Bari, Italy, 98–110.

Zollikofer, C. P. E., and Ponce de Leon, M. S. (2005). *Virtual reconstruction: A primer in computer-assisted palaeontology and biomedicine.* New York: Wiley.

Index